LESSON
21

LESSON
22

LESSON
23

LESSON
24

REVIEW
LESSON
25

Grade 5 • Theme 5

At a Glance

ISBN 10 0-15-372147-2
ISBN 13 978-0-15-372147-2

3 4 5 6 7 8 9 10   468   17 16 15 14 13 12 11 10 09

Program Authors

SENIOR AUTHORS

Isabel L. Beck
Professor of Education and Senior Scientist at the Learning Research and Development Center, *University of Pittsburgh*

RESEARCH CONTRIBUTIONS:
Reading Comprehension, Vocabulary, Beginning Reading, Phonics

Roger C. Farr
Chancellor's Professor Emeritus of Education and Former Director for the Center for Innovation in Assessment, *Indiana University, Bloomington*

RESEARCH CONTRIBUTIONS:
Instructional Assessment, Reading Strategies, Reading in the Content Areas

Dorothy S. Strickland
Samuel DeWitt Proctor Professor of Education and The State of New Jersey Professor of Reading, *Rutgers University, The State University of New Jersey*

RESEARCH CONTRIBUTIONS:
Early Literacy, Elementary Reading/ Language Arts, Writing, Intervention

AUTHORS

Alma Flor Ada
Professor Emerita, *University of San Francisco*

RESEARCH CONTRIBUTIONS:
Literacy, Biliteracy, Multicultural Children's Literature, Home-School Interaction, First and Second Language Acquisition

Roxanne F. Hudson
Assistant Professor, Area of Special Education *University of Washington*

RESEARCH CONTRIBUTIONS:
Reading Fluency, Learning Disabilities, Interventions

Margaret G. McKeown
Senior Scientist at the Learning Research and Development Center, *University of Pittsburgh*

RESEARCH CONTRIBUTIONS:
Vocabulary, Reading Comprehension

Robin C. Scarcella
Professor, Director of Academic English and ESL, *University of California, Irvine*

RESEARCH CONTRIBUTIONS:
English as a Second Language

Julie A. Washington
Professor, College of Letters and Sciences, *University of Wisconsin*

RESEARCH CONTRIBUTIONS:
Understanding of Cultural Dialect with an emphasis on Language Assessment, Specific Language Impairment and Academic Performance; Early Childhood Language and Early Literacy of African American Children

CONSULTANTS

F. Isabel Campoy
President, Transformative Educational Services

RESEARCH CONTRIBUTIONS:
English as a Second Language, Applied Linguistics, Writing in the Curriculum, Family Involvement

Tyrone C. Howard
Associate Professor Urban Schooling, *University of California, Los Angeles*

RESEARCH CONTRIBUTIONS:
Multicultural Education, The Social and Political Context of Schools, Urban Education

David A. Monti
Professor Emeritus Department of Reading and Language Arts, *Central Connecticut State University*

RESEARCH CONTRIBUTIONS:
Reading Comprehension, Alternative Assessments, Flexible Grouping

Theme 5: Making a Difference

Lesson 21
T16

SCIENCE

Interrupted Journey: Saving Endangered Sea Turtles T38
by Kathryn Lasky • photographed by Christopher G. Knight •
EXPOSITORY NONFICTION

Paired Selections

Kids in Action T52
by Elizabeth Schleichert • from Ranger Rick • MAGAZINE ARTICLE

Theme Writing   **Reading-Writing Connection** T76

Student Writing Model: Persuasive Composition

Lesson 22
T92

MATH

The Power of W.O.W.! T114
by Crystal Hubbard • illustrated by Eric Velasquez • PLAY

Paired Selections

Got a Problem? Get a Plan! T128
by Karen Bledsoe • illustrated by Eric Sturdevant • from Appleseeds •
MAGAZINE ARTICLE

Reference Materials

Small-Group Instruction

Assessment

Additional Resources

Data-Driven Instruction

① ASSESS

Use assessments to track student progress.

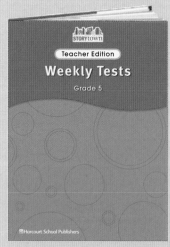

▲ **Weekly Lesson Tests**

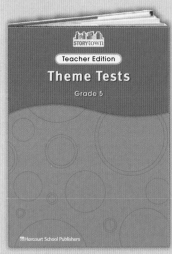

▲ **Theme Tests**

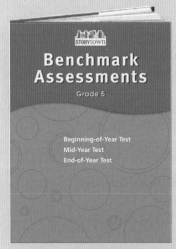

▲ **Benchmark Assessments**
- Beginning-of-Year
- Mid-Year
- End-of-Year

  *StoryTown* Online Assessment

② TEACH

Provide instruction in key areas of reading.

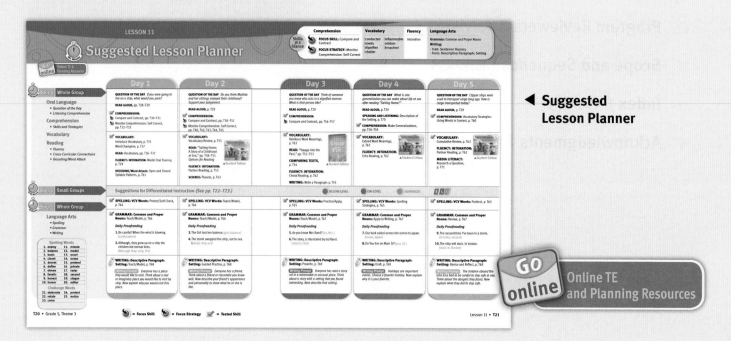

◀ **Suggested Lesson Planner**

3 DIFFERENTIATE INSTRUCTION

Use daily Monitor Progress notes to inform instruction.

▲ Suggested Small-Group Planner

MONITOR PROGRESS

Partner Reading

IF students need more support in fluency-building and in using appropriate pace,	THEN have them echo-read with you, paying close attention to punctuation marks to direct their pace.

Small-Group Instruction, p. S7:

● BELOW-LEVEL: Reteach

● ON-LEVEL: Reinforce

● ADVANCED: Extend

4 ASSESS, REMEDIATE, AND EXTEND

Use assessment results to remediate instruction.

▲ Strategic Intervention Resource Kit

▲ Challenge Resource Kit

INTERVENTION STATION, Intermediate

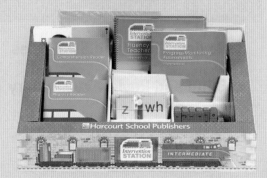

- Phonics
- Comprehension
- Vocabulary
- Fluency

Overview of a Theme

x

FIRST FOUR LESSONS

- **Explicit Systematic Instruction**

- **Spiral Review of Key Skills**

- **Abundant Practice and Application**

- **Point-of-Use Progress-Monitoring**

- **Support for *Leveled Readers***

- **Digital Support for Teachers and Students**

FIFTH LESSON THEME REVIEW

- **Review Skills and Strategies**

- **Build and Review Vocabulary**

- **Celebrate with Readers' Theater**

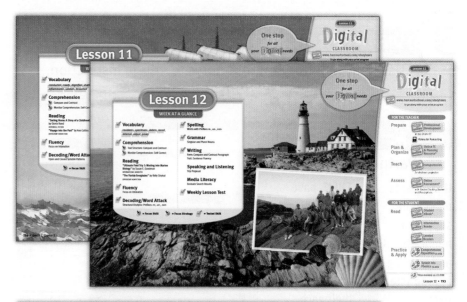

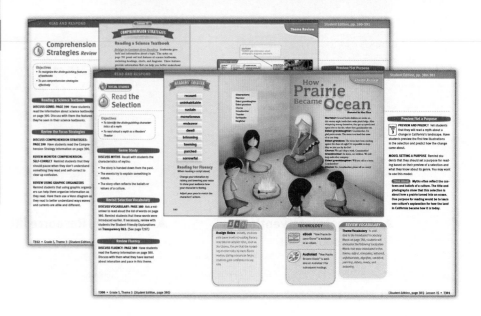

READING-WRITING CONNECTION

- **Reading-Writing Connection in *Student Edition***

- **Instruction in *Teacher Edition***

- **Focus on the Six Traits of Good Writing:**
  - Organization
  - Ideas
  - Sentence Fluency
  - Word Choice
  - Voice
  - Conventions

- **Develop a Variety of Writing Strategies**

- **Develop One Major Form Through the Writing Process:**
  - Personal Narrative
  - Response to Literature
  - Explanatory Essay
  - Persuasive Essay
  - Story
  - Research Report

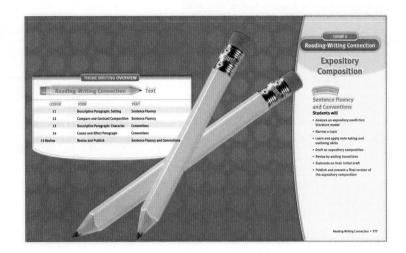

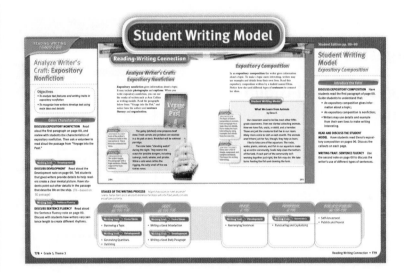

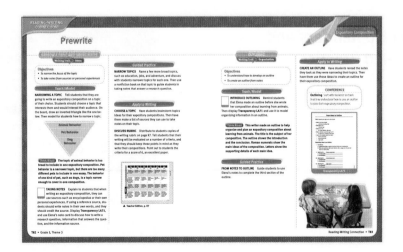

Overview of a Lesson

PLANNING THE LESSON

- **Lesson Resources**

- **Suggested Lesson Planner**

- **Suggested Small-Group Planner**

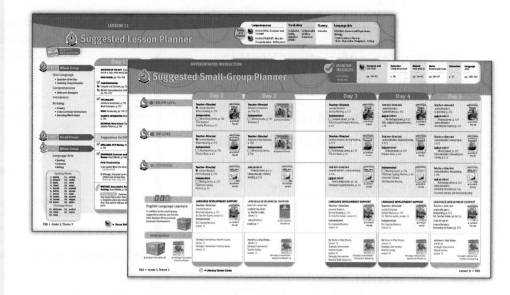

- **Leveled Readers and Leveled Practice**

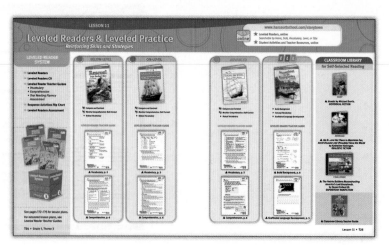

Listening Comprehension

- Read-Aloud
- Model Oral Fluency

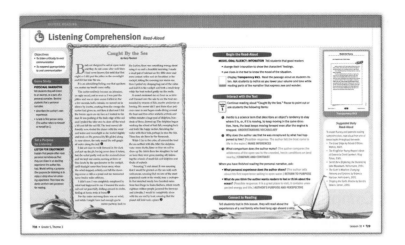

Focus Skill

Focus Strategy

Build Background

Build Robust Vocabulary

- Tier Two Words
- Student-Friendly Explanations

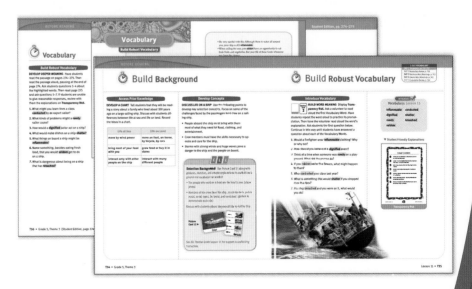

Overview of a Lesson (continued)

READ AND RESPOND

- ### Read the Selection

- ### Apply the Focus Skill and Focus Strategy
  - Develop Higher-Order Thinking Skills

- ### Think Critically

- ### Check Comprehension
  - Retell and Summarize

- -

- ### Paired Selection

- ### Connections
  - Comparing Texts
  - Vocabulary Review
  - Fluency Practice
  - Writing

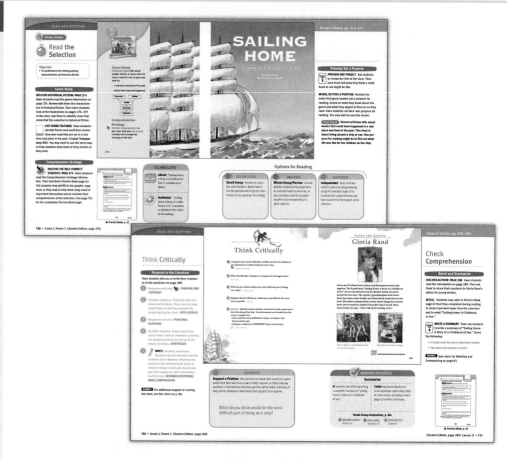

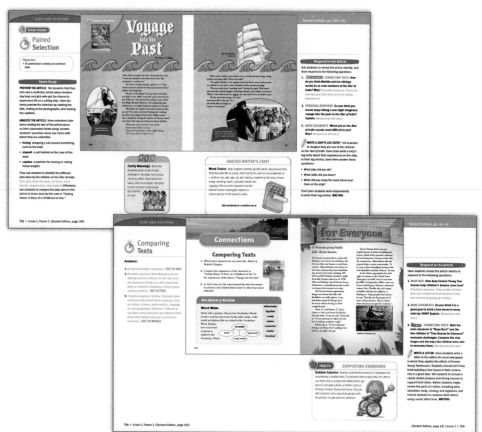

Reinforcing Skills

- Focus Skills
- Comprehension
- Vocabulary Strategies
- Literary Analysis
- Research/Study Skills

Fluency

Enriching Robust Vocabulary

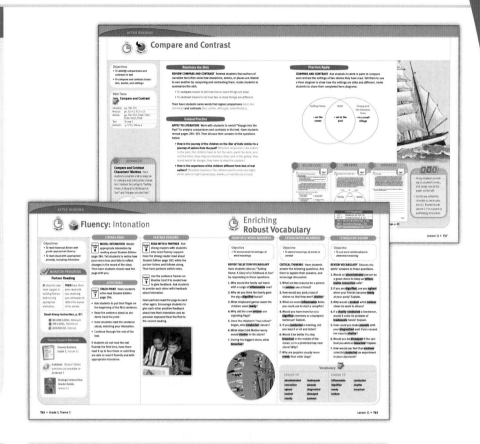

Spelling, Grammar, and Writing

Speaking and Listening

Media Literacy

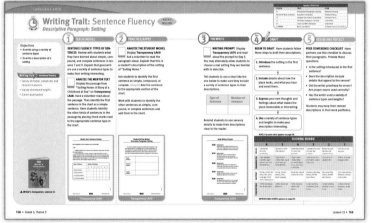

Reinforce Skills and Strategies

Review Vocabulary

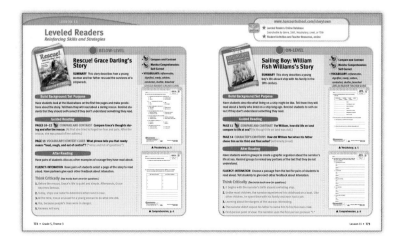

Introducing the Book

Discuss the Book's Organization

Have students turn to each of the following features in the *Student Edition*. Briefly discuss how each part helps readers use the book and understand the literature.

- **Contents** Shows titles, authors, and page numbers.

- **Comprehension Strategies** Describes tools readers can use to read well.

- **Theme Overview** Lists literature, skills, and strategies in that theme.

- **Lesson Overview** Lists literature, focus skill, and focus strategy in that lesson.

- **Focus Skill** Provides instruction in skills related to the literature.

- **Vocabulary** Builds robust vocabulary words from the selection.

- **Genre Study** Describes the characteristics of the selection's genre.

- **Focus Strategy** Tells how to use strategies during reading.

- **Paired Selection** Presents literature connected to the main selection.

- **Connections** Provides questions and activities related to both selections.

- **Reading-Writing Connection** Connects the literature to a good model of student writing.

- **Glossary** Provides student-friendly explanations for robust vocabulary words from each selection.

- **Index of Titles and Authors** Shows titles and authors of literature in alphabetical order.

Introduce Comprehension Strategies

Read with students pages 16–17. Tell them that these pages introduce the strategies they will use as they read the *Student Edition*.

Monitor Comprehension

PERSONAL READING PORTFOLIO Have each student begin a personal reading portfolio. Students can use the My Reading Log page on *Teacher Resource Book* page 34 to record how they self-select books, the strategies they use before, during, and after reading, and how long they read outside of class each day.

STRATEGY BOOKMARK Have students make a bookmark from a sheet of heavy paper and write the strategies on it. Tell students that as they read, they should use the bookmark to remind them of the strategies they can use.

RESPONSE NOTEBOOK Ask students to keep a notebook to record their responses to selections and to monitor their progress as readers.

- They may use a spiral-bound notebook or sheets of paper stapled together.

- They should create sections to write about which strategies work best for them and to develop their own plans for reading different kinds of selections.

- They should also set aside a section of the notebook for a vocabulary journal, where they will list new or interesting words they come across in their reading.

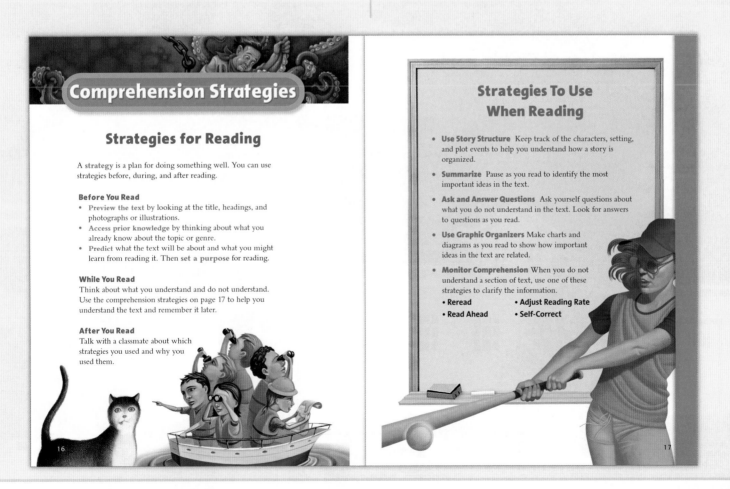

Comprehension Strategies

Strategies for Reading

A strategy is a plan for doing something well. You can use strategies before, during, and after reading.

Before You Read
- Preview the text by looking at the title, headings, and photographs or illustrations.
- Access prior knowledge by thinking about what you already know about the topic or genre.
- Predict what the text will be about and what you might learn from reading it. Then set a purpose for reading.

While You Read
Think about what you understand and do not understand. Use the comprehension strategies on page 17 to help you understand the text and remember it later.

After You Read
Talk with a classmate about which strategies you used and why you used them.

16

Strategies To Use When Reading

- **Use Story Structure** Keep track of the characters, setting, and plot events to help you understand how a story is organized.
- **Summarize** Pause as you read to identify the most important ideas in the text.
- **Ask and Answer Questions** Ask yourself questions about what you do not understand in the text. Look for answers to questions as you read.
- **Use Graphic Organizers** Make charts and diagrams as you read to show how important ideas in the text are related.
- **Monitor Comprehension** When you do not understand a section of text, use one of these strategies to clarify the information.
  - Reread
  - Read Ahead
  - Adjust Reading Rate
  - Self-Correct

17

THEME 5

Making a Difference

Theme Resources

GO online • eBook STUDENT EDITION

STUDENT EDITION LITERATURE

Lesson 21

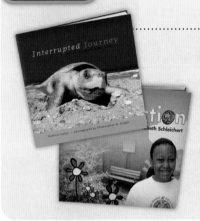

PAIRED SELECTIONS

"Interrupted Journey: Saving Endangered Sea Turtles,"
pages 542–555
EXPOSITORY NONFICTION

"Kids in Action,"
pages 556–557
MAGAZINE ARTICLE

Lesson 24

PAIRED SELECTIONS

"Chester Cricket's Pigeon Ride,"
pages 618–631
FANTASY

"Central Park,"
pages 632–635
POETRY

Lesson 22

PAIRED SELECTIONS

"The Power of W.O.W.!,"
pages 570–583
PLAY

"Got a Problem? Get a Plan!,"
pages 584–585
MAGAZINE ARTICLE

Lesson 25 Theme Review

READERS' THEATER

"The Compassion Campaign,"
pages 640–649
NEWS REPORT

Lesson 23

PAIRED SELECTIONS

"Any Small Goodness: A Novel of the Barrio,"
pages 594–607
REALISTIC FICTION

"The Ant and the Dove; The Lion and the Mouse,"
pages 608–609
FABLE

COMPREHENSION STRATEGIES

"How Beaver Stole Fire,"
pages 650–655
FOLKTALE

 Literature selections are available on Audiotext Grade 5, CD 7 and CD 8.

THEME 5 CLASSROOM LIBRARY

For Self-Selected Reading

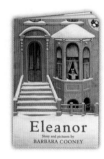

▲ **Eleanor**
by Barbara Cooney

Eleanor Roosevelt grew up in a discouraging household as a child, but later blossomed into an intelligent woman who would work to change America.

▲ **Doña Flor**
by Pat Mora

Doña Flor is different. She is a giant who can talk to the animals and helps out others any way she can.

▲ **Classroom Library Books Teacher Guide**

ADDITIONAL RESOURCES

▲ **Writer's Companion**

▲ **Grammar Practice Book**

▲ **Spelling Practice Book**

▲ **Literacy Center Kit**

▲ **Reading Transparencies**

▲ **Language Arts Transparencies**

▲ **Fluency Builders**

▲ **Picture Card Collection**

PROFESSIONAL DEVELOPMENT

- **Professional Development Book**
- **Videos for Podcasting**

Leveled Resources

BELOW-LEVEL

- **Focus Skills**
- **Focus Strategies**
- **Robust Vocabulary**

ON-LEVEL

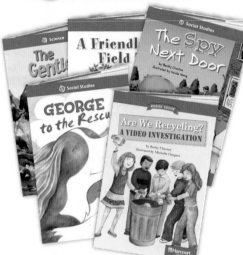

- **Focus Skills**
- **Focus Strategies**
- **Robust Vocabulary**

ADVANCED

- **Focus Skills**
- **Focus Strategies**
- **Robust Vocabulary**

E L L

- **Build Background**
- **Concept Vocabulary**
- **Scaffolded Language Development**

Leveled Readers System

- **Leveled Readers**

- **Leveled Readers CD**

- **Leveled Readers Teacher Guides**
  - Vocabulary
  - Comprehension
  - Oral Reading Fluency Assessment

- **Response Activities**

- **Leveled Readers Assessment**

TECHNOLOGY

 www.harcourtschool.com/storytown

- ✓ **Leveled Readers Online Database**
  Searchable by Genre, Skill, Vocabulary, Level, or Title

- ✓ **Student Activities and Teacher Resources, *online***

Teaching suggestions for the Leveled Readers can be found on pp. T72–T75, T148–T151, T208–T211, T268–T271, T320–T323.

Strategic Intervention Resource Kit,
Lessons 21–25

Strategic Intervention Interactive Reader:
Catch a Wave

- "Can You Hear the Frogs?"
- "Elm Street Speaks!"
- "The Quiet Neighbor"
- "Carmine's Backyard"
- "Kid Power!"

Also available:

- Strategic Intervention Teacher Guide
- Strategic Intervention Practice Book
- Skill Cards
- Audiotext CD

Strategic Intervention Interactive Reader eBook

 ## ELL Extra Support Kit,
Lessons 21–25

- ELL Teacher Guide
- ELL Student Handbook
- ELL Copying Master
- ELL Proficiency Assessment

Challenge Resource Kit,
Theme 5

- Challenge Book Pack
- Challenge Student Activities
- Challenge Teacher Guide

Leveled Practice

 BELOW-LEVEL
Extra Support Copying Masters

 ON-LEVEL
Practice Book

 ADVANCED
Challenge Copying Masters

INTERVENTION STATION, Intermediate

GRADES 4–6 Sets of intervention material providing targeted instruction in:

- Phonics
- Comprehension
- Vocabulary
- Fluency

Digital Classroom

to go along with your Print Program www.harcourtschool.com/storytown

---

FOR THE TEACHER

Prepare

GO online Professional Development

in the Online TE

📱 Videos for Podcasting

PROFESSIONAL DEVELOPMENT

Plan & Organize

GO online Online TE and Planning Resources*

Teach

GO online Transparencies

access from the Online TE

Assess

GO online Online Assessment*

with Student Tracking System and Prescriptions

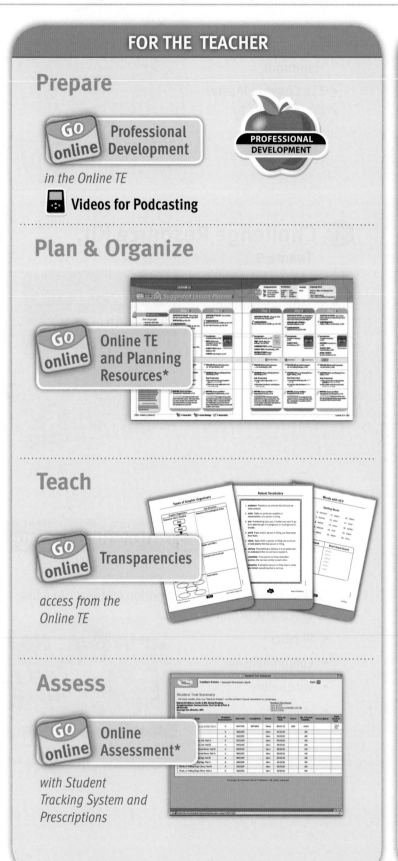

FOR THE STUDENT

Read

GO online Student eBook*

GO online Strategic Intervention Interactive Reader

GO online Leveled Readers

● BELOW-LEVEL
● ON-LEVEL
● ADVANCED

E L L

Practice & Apply

💿 Comprehension Expedition CD-ROM

---

 * Also available on CD-ROM

Monitor Progress
to inform instruction for Theme 5

MONITOR PROGRESS

Looking Back to Theme 4

IF performance was	THEN, in addition to core instruction, use these resources:
BELOW-LEVEL: Reteach	• Below-Level Leveled Readers • Leveled Readers System • Extra Support Copying Masters • Strategic Intervention Resource Kit • Intervention Station, Intermediate
ON-LEVEL: Reinforce	• On-Level Leveled Readers • Leveled Readers System • Practice Book
ADVANCED: Extend	• Advanced Leveled Readers • Leveled Readers System • Challenge Copying Masters • Challenge Resource Kit

GO online ONLINE ASSESSMENT

✔ Prescriptions for Reteaching

✔ Weekly Lesson Tests

✔ Theme Test

✔ Student Profile System to track student growth

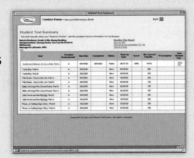

 www.harcourtschool.com/storytown

Tested THEME 5 TESTED SKILLS

Domain	Skills
COMPREHENSION	• Comprehension of Grade-level Text • Author's Purpose and Perspective • Literary Devices • Draw Conclusions • Literary Patterns and Symbols
VOCABULARY	• Robust Vocabulary
WRITING FORM	• Persuasive Composition
WRITING TRAITS	• Sentence Fluency • Organization
GRAMMAR	• Action and Linking Verbs • Present Tense; Subject-Verb Agreement • Past and Future Tenses • Perfect Tenses
SPELLING	• Words with Word Parts *in-, out-, down-, up-* • Words with Word Parts *-ation, -ition, -sion, -ion* • Words with Silent Letters • Words with Unusual Plurals
FLUENCY	• Oral Reading Fluency • Videos for Podcasting

Theme at a Glance

LESSON 21
....
pp. T16–T75

LESSON 22
....
pp. T92–T151

- **Oral Language**

- **Comprehension**

- **Reading**

- **Fluency**

READ ALOUD INFORMATIONAL NARRATIVE
SPEAKING AND LISTENING

✔ **COMPREHENSION**
- Author's Purpose and Perspective
- Summarize

✔ **VOCABULARY**
basking, sleek, vital, damage, analyzing, detect

PAIRED SELECTIONS
"Interrupted Journey: Saving Endangered Sea Turtles"
EXPOSITORY NONFICTION
"Kids in Action"
MAGAZINE ARTICLE

✔ **FLUENCY: EXPRESSION**

READ ALOUD NARRATIVE NONFICTION
SPEAKING AND LISTENING

✔ **COMPREHENSION**
- Author's Purpose and Perspective
- Summarize

✔ **VOCABULARY**
somberly, stammers, monopolize, deflated, enraptured, enterprising, cumbersome

PAIRED SELECTIONS
"The Power of W.O.W.!"
PLAY
"Got a Problem? Get a Plan!"
MAGAZINE ARTICLE

✔ **FLUENCY: EXPRESSION**

| **Theme Writing** | **Reading-Writing Connection** | ▶ Persuasive Composition, pp. T76–T91 |

- **Spelling**

- **Writing**

- **Grammar**

✔ **SPELLING:** Words with Word Parts
in-, out-, down-, up-

✎ **WRITING FORM:** Persuasive Letter

✎ **WRITING TRAIT:** Sentence Fluency

✔ **GRAMMAR:** Action and Linking Verbs

✔ **SPELLING:** Words with Word Parts
-ation, -ition, -sion, -ion

✎ **WRITING FORM:** Persuasive Paragraph

✎ **WRITING TRAIT:** Sentence Fluency

✔ **GRAMMAR:** Present Tense; Subject-Verb Agreement

THEME 5

**Theme Project:
What Our Community Needs**

 = Focus Skill   = Focus Strategy    = Tested Skill

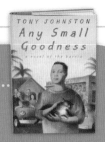

LESSON 23
pp. T152–T211

LESSON 24
pp. T212–T271

Theme Review

LESSON 25
pp. T272–T323

READ ALOUD EXPOSITORY NONFICTION

SPEAKING AND LISTENING

 COMPREHENSION
 Literary Devices
 Answer Questions

 VOCABULARY
gouges, desolate, bustles, fervor, immaculate, assuage

PAIRED SELECTIONS
"Any Small Goodness: A Novel of the Barrio"
REALISTIC FICTION
"The Ant and the Dove;
The Lion and the Mouse" FABLE

 FLUENCY: PACE

READ ALOUD REALISTIC FICTION

SPEAKING AND LISTENING

 COMPREHENSION
 Literary Devices
 Answer Questions

 **VOCABULARY**
excursions, giddy, pinnacle, gleeful, panic, turbulent, precious

PAIRED SELECTIONS
"Chester Cricket's Pigeon Ride"
FANTASY
"Central Park"
POETRY

 FLUENCY: PACE

READERS' THEATER

"The Compassion Campaign"

- Build Fluency

- Review and Build Vocabulary

COMPREHENSION STRATEGIES

"How Beaver Stole Fire"

REVIEW FOCUS STRATEGIES
 Summarize

 Answer Questions

Writing Traits Sentence Fluency, Organization

 SPELLING: Words with Silent Letters

 WRITING FORM: Poem

 WRITING TRAIT: Organization

 GRAMMAR: Past and Future Tenses

 SPELLING: Words with Unusual Plurals

 WRITING FORM: Narrative

 WRITING TRAIT: Organization

 GRAMMAR: Perfect Tenses

ADDITIONAL REVIEW
 Focus Skills

- Author's Purpose and Perspective

- Literary Devices

Decoding/Word Attack

Spelling

 Writing: Revise and Publish

Grammar

Making a Difference • **T9**

Planning for Reading Success

✓ Tested Skill	Teach/Model	✓ Monitor Progress	Additional Support
COMPREHENSION 🌀 Author's Purpose and Perspective	Lesson 21, pp. T30–T31	Lesson 21, p. T31	Small-Group Instruction, pp. S2–S3, S10–S11
🌀 Literary Devices	Lesson 23, pp. T166–T167	Lesson 23, p. T167	Small-Group Instruction, pp. S20–S21, S28–S29
PERSUASIVE TECHNIQUES	Lesson 21, pp. T58–T59		
DRAW CONCLUSIONS	Lesson 22, pp. T134–T135	Lesson 22, p. T135	Small-Group Instruction, pp. S16–S17
LITERARY PATTERNS AND SYMBOLS			
ROBUST VOCABULARY	Lessons 21–25, Build Robust Vocabulary, pp. T35–T37, T111–T113, T171–T173, T231–T233, T287–T288 Lessons 21–25, Extend Word Meanings, pp. T63, T139, T199, T259, T301	Lessons 21–24, pp. T55, T131, T191, T253	Small-Group Instruction, pp. S4–S5, S12–S13, S22–S23, S30–S31
WRITING	Lesson 21, pp. T68–T69 Reading-Writing Connection, pp. T76–T91 Lesson 22, pp. T144–T145 Lesson 23, pp. T204–T205 Lesson 24, pp. T264–T265	Scoring Rubric, p. T69 Scoring Rubric, p. T82 Scoring Rubric, p. T145 Scoring Rubric, p. T205 Scoring Rubric, p. T265	Small-Group Instruction, pp. S8–S9, S18–S19, S26–S27, S34–S35
WRITING—CONVENTIONS Grammar	Lessons 21–24, pp. T66–T67, T142–T143, T202–T203, T262–T263	Lessons 21–24, pp. T66, T142, T202, T262	Small-Group Instruction, pp. S8–S9, S18–S19, S26–S27, S34–S35
Spelling	Lessons 21–24, pp. T64, T140, T200, T260	Lessons 21–24, **Spelling Practice Book,** pp. 83–86, 87–90, 91–94, 95–98	Lessons 21–24, pp. T65, T141, T201, T261 Lessons 21–24, **Challenge Words,** pp. T64, T140, T201, T260

🌀 = Focus Skill

Review	Assess
Lesson 21, pp. T56–T57 Lesson 22, pp. T106–T107, T132–T133 Lesson 25, p. T308	Weekly Lesson Tests 21, 22 Theme 5 Test
Lesson 23, pp. T192–T193 Lesson 24, pp. T226–T227, T254–T255 Lesson 25, p. T309	Weekly Lesson Tests 23, 24 Theme 5 Test
Lesson 23, p. T195	
Lesson 24, p. T256 Lesson 25, p. T311	Weekly Lesson Tests 22, 24 Theme 5 Test
Lesson 23, p. T194 Lesson 25, p. T310	Weekly Lesson Test 23
Lessons 21–25 Cumulative Review, pp. T63, T139, T199, T259, T301	Weekly Lesson Tests 21–25 Theme 5 Test
Lesson 25, pp. T318–T319	Weekly Lesson Test 23
Lesson 25, pp. T316–T317	Weekly Lesson Tests 21–24 Theme 5 Test
Lesson 25, pp. T314–T315 **Spelling Practice Book**, pp. 99-102	Theme 5 Test

INTEGRATED TEST PREP

In the *Teacher Edition*

- 4-Point Rubric, p. R8
- Daily Writing Prompts, Transparencies LA134, LA146, LA152, LA158
- Writing on Demand, pp. T90–T91
- Short Response, pp. T50, T126, T186
- Extended Response, p. T246

TEST PREP

- Practice Workbook: Reading and Writing

TEST PREP MINUTES

For early finishers, beginning of class, or anytime:

- **LITERARY DEVICES Think about a cold winter day.** Use imagery to describe the day, making sure to use all five senses.

- **DRAW CONCLUSIONS Imagine you saw a water hose next to a large metal tub in someone's front yard.** What conclusions could you draw?

- **VOCABULARY Describe a cumbersome chair.** Is it a chair you would like in your room?

- **WRITING What excursions do you enjoy?** Write a paragraph telling about the excursions, and why you enjoy them.

Theme Project
What Our Community Needs

Objectives

- *To use a problem-solving process to identify and address a community problem or issue*
- *To create and implement a plan for community service demonstrating an understanding of civic responsibility*

Materials

- pencils
- notebook paper
- several recent issues of local newspapers
- Internet resources about local community service projects
- computer with Internet access (optional) See *Teacher Resource Book* page 35 for Contract for Internet Safety.

See **Project Ideas from The Bag Ladies,** pp. 10–11

A Community Service Project

Share the background information below with students. Then display the following research question in a visible place in the classroom: What can we do to address a problem or need within our community?

Build Background

Citizens of a democratic society must be active participants. In order for society to function properly, citizens can perform community services and political activities, such as voting and campaigning. In these ways, citizens help make their communities better.

Good citizens address important issues. Steps citizens can take to help work on a community issue include identifying problems and needs, gathering information about and considering possible solutions, and then choosing and implementing one of those solutions.

Follow Project Steps

1. **Identify Community Issues** Engage students in a discussion about some of the problems or issues that face your local community. You might choose to define the community as your class, the school, your neighborhood, or your city. To generate ideas, review with students the city section of a local newspaper. Record the ideas on the board. Have students form small groups based on the topic in which they are interested.

   - Reducing the amount of waste the community generates
   - Providing food for the hungry
   - Providing books to people who don't have them
   - Raising funds for a worthy project

② Gather Information Tell small groups to gather more information about their topics and take notes on what they find, recording bibliographic information. Suggest that they answer questions such as
- *What is the scope of the problem? How many people are affected?*
- *Who is working to address the problem? What are they doing?*

③ Consider Options Have group members brainstorm ways they could get involved in trying to solve the problem. Ask them to discuss the advantages and disadvantages of each solution. Have them work together to choose the solution that seems the most effective.

④ Develop a Plan Instruct students to compile their research in a report that includes an explanation of the problem as well as their plan for working towards a solution.

⑤ Present Allow group members to present their plans. Encourage them to try to convince their classmates to implement their community service project. Additional suggestions for presentations are provided at the end of the theme on page T325.

SUGGESTIONS FOR INQUIRY

The theme "Making a Difference" can be a springboard for inquiry into a variety of topics and ideas. Students may wish to design their own theme projects based on topics that interest them.

- Have students brainstorm topics for inquiry, and organize their responses in a web.

- Once students have selected a topic to research, ask them to write a research question and then list the steps necessary to complete the project.

- Review students' plans before they begin. Students may use some of the resources shown here to help them begin.

SUGGESTED RESOURCES

- *It's Our World Too!: Stories of Young People Who Are Making a Difference* by Phillip Hoose. Little, Brown and Company, 1993.

- *The Kid's Guide to Social Action* by Barbara A. Lewis. Free Spirit Publishing, 1991.

- *Acting for Nature: What Young People Around the World Are Doing to Protect the Environment* by Sneed B. Collard. Heyday Books, 2000.

- *The Kid's Guide to Service Projects* by Barbara A. Lewis. Free Spirit Publishing, 1995.

Making a Difference

Introduce the Theme

DISCUSS THEME CONCEPTS Have students look at the painting by Jane Wooster Scott on pages 534–535. Point out to students that the name of the painting is *Good Neighbors*. Ask students to tell how the people in the painting are acting like good neighbors. Then share with them the following theme information:

> Each person can make a difference in his or her community. In this theme, you will take a closer look at how individuals have worked to make a difference in the lives of others.

Access Prior Knowledge

PREVIEW THE THEME Invite volunteers to share the names of people who have made a difference in their lives. Then have students tell about community projects in which they have participated. Ask them to page through the selections in this theme and tell which selections might be about people who make a difference by

- helping animals.
- supporting a special program.
- helping a neighbor.
- helping a friend.

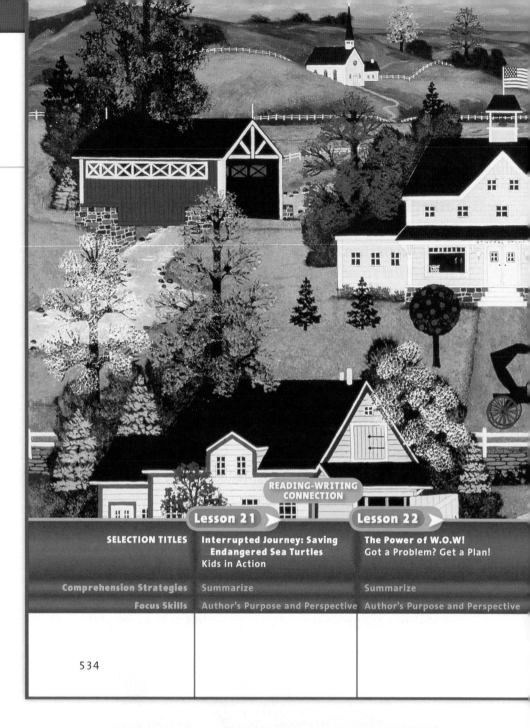

READING-WRITING CONNECTION

SELECTION TITLES	Lesson 21	Lesson 22
	Interrupted Journey: Saving Endangered Sea Turtles / Kids in Action	The Power of W.O.W! / Got a Problem? Get a Plan!
Comprehension Strategies	Summarize	Summarize
Focus Skills	Author's Purpose and Perspective	Author's Purpose and Perspective

534

BELOW-LEVEL

Cause and Effect Tell students that a character's decision to make a difference is often caused by a problem. As students read each selection, guide them to identify the cause of the main character's actions by having them ask themselves *What causes the main character to make a difference?* Tell them to identify the effect by asking *What happens as a result of the main character's actions?*

Cause		Effect
Max finds a distressed turtle.		Max rescues the turtle, and the turtle's life is saved.

Theme 5 Making a Difference

Good Neighbors, Jane Wooster Scott

<table>
<tr><td>Lesson 23 ▶</td><td>Lesson 24 ▶</td><td>Lesson 25 Review</td></tr>
<tr><td>Any Small Goodness:
A Novel of the Barrio
The Ant and the Dove,
The Lion and the Mouse
Answer Questions

Literary Devices</td><td>Chester Cricket's Pigeon Ride
Central Park

Answer Questions

Literary Devices</td><td>The Compassion Campaign
How Beaver Stole Fire

Review Skills and Strategies</td></tr>
</table>

535

Develop Theme Concepts

DEVELOP A WEB Have students draw a web like the one below and think of ways that people can make a difference in their communities. Begin by asking them to list things people can do to make a difference. As they read the Theme 5 selections, ask them to add new information to their webs.

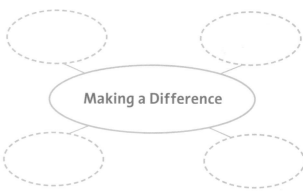

Making a Difference

FINE ART CONNECTION

Americana Tell students that Americana is a folk art that shows the traditions and celebrations of American culture. Jane Wooster Scott is well known for her oil paintings depicting life in America. She is one of the most reproduced American artists, and her work can be seen on products such as greeting cards and calendars. Invite students to share reasons for the popularity of her work.

▲ *Good Neighbors* by Jane Wooster Scott

 **SOCIAL STUDIES**

CONTENT-AREA VOCABULARY

Word Bank: Social Studies Tell students that in this theme they will encounter many words that describe ways people make a difference in their community. Ask them to keep a running list in their vocabulary journal of these words along with the meaning of each word. At the end of each week, have students share their words and explain how the words relate to the theme of Making a Difference.

Lesson 21

WEEK AT A GLANCE

✓ Vocabulary
basking, sleek, vital, damage, analyzing, detect

✓ Comprehension
 Author's Purpose and Perspective

 Summarize

Reading
"Interrupted Journey: Saving Endangered Sea Turtles" by Kathryn Lasky
EXPOSITORY NONFICTION

"Kids in Action" by Elizabeth Schleichert
MAGAZINE ARTICLE

✓ Fluency
Focus on Expression

Decoding/Word Attack
Structural Analysis: Word Parts *in-*, *out-*, *down-*, *up-*

✓ Spelling
Words with Word Parts *in-*, *out-*, *down-*, *up-*

✓ Writing
Form: Persuasive Letter
Trait: Sentence Fluency

✓ Grammar
Action and Linking Verbs

Speaking and Listening
Persuasive Speech

Media Literacy
Survey of Personal Communication

Weekly Lesson Test

= Focus Skill   = Focus Strategy   ✓ = Tested Skill

One stop

for all
your **Digital** *needs*

Digital
CLASSROOM

 www.harcourtschool.com/storytown
To go along with your print program

FOR THE TEACHER

Prepare Professional Development

in the Online TE

 Videos for Podcasting

Plan & Organize Online TE & Planning Resources*

Teach  Transparencies

access from the Online TE

Assess Online Assessment*

with Student Tracking System and Prescriptions

FOR THE STUDENT

Read Student eBook*

 Strategic Intervention Interactive Reader

 Leveled Readers

Practice & Apply Comprehension Expedition CD-ROM

 *Also available on CD-ROM

Literature Resources

STUDENT EDITION

 eBook STUDENT EDITION

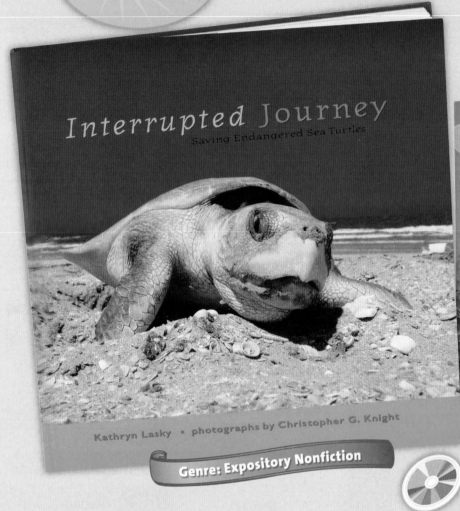

Interrupted Journey
Saving Endangered Sea Turtles

Kathryn Lasky • photographs by Christopher G. Knight

Genre: Expository Nonfiction

Genre: Magazine Article

◄ **Audiotext** *Student Edition selections are available on Audiotext Grade 5, CD7.*

Accelerated Reader™   ◄ *Practice Quizzes for the Selection*

THEME CONNECTION: MAKING A DIFFERENCE
Comparing Expository Nonfiction and Magazine Article

Paired Selections

 **SCIENCE** **Interrupted Journey: Saving Endangered Sea Turtles, pp. 542–555**

SUMMARY Author Kathryn Lasky tells about the rescue, recovery, and release of an endangered Kemp's ridley sea turtle.

SOCIAL STUDIES **Kids in Action, pp. 556–557**

SUMMARY Author Elizabeth Schleichert profiles three children whose good deeds help the environment.

Support for Differentiated Instruction

 LEVELED READERS

 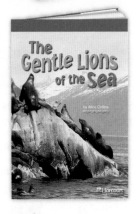 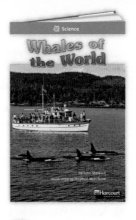 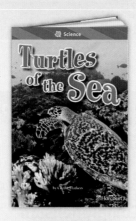

● BELOW-LEVEL　　**● ON-LEVEL**　　**● ADVANCED**　　**ELL**

LEVELED PRACTICE

◀ **Strategic Intervention Resource Kit, Lesson 21**

◀ **Strategic Intervention Interactive Reader, Lesson 21**
Strategic Intervention Interactive Reader Online

◀ **ELL Extra Support Kit, Lesson 21**

◀ **Challenge Resource Kit, Lesson 21**

● BELOW-LEVEL
Extra Support Copying Masters, pp. 123, 125–126

● ON-LEVEL
Practice Book, pp. 123–128

● ADVANCED
Challenge Copying Masters, pp. 123, 125–126

ADDITIONAL RESOURCES

◀ **Picture Card Collection**
◀ **Fluency Builders**
◀ **Literacy Center Kit, Lesson 21**
- Test Prep System
- Writer's Companion, Lesson 21
- Grammar Practice Book, pp. 73–76
- Spelling Practice Book, pp. 83–86
- Reading Transparencies R87–R91
- Language Arts Transparencies LA129–LA134

✓ ASSESSMENT

✓ **Monitor Progress**

✓ **Weekly Lesson Tests, Lesson 21**
- Comprehension
- Focus Skill
- Robust Vocabulary
- Grammar
- Fluency

✓ **Rubrics, pp. R3–R8**

 www.harcourtschool.com/storytown
- Online Assessment
Also available on CD-ROM—ExamView®

Suggested Lesson Planner

Online TE & Planning Resources

Step 1 Whole Group

Oral Language
- *Question of the Day*
- *Listening Comprehension*

Comprehension
- *Skills and Strategies*

Vocabulary

Reading
- *Fluency*
- *Cross-Curricular Connections*
- *Decoding/Word Attack*

Step 2 Small Groups

Step 3 Whole Group

Language Arts
- *Spelling*
- *Writing*
- *Grammar*

Spelling Words
1. incompetent	11. outpatient
2. uphold	12. outspoken
3. inconsiderate	13. outwit
4. indecisive	14. downbeat
5. outrank	15. downgrade
6. inhumane	16. downplay
7. inorganic	17. downtown
8. income	18. uplift
9. invertebrate	19. upstage
10. outgoing	20. uptight

Challenge Words
21. insensitive	24. downstage
22. outcry	25. insecure
23. upkeep	

Day 1

QUESTION OF THE DAY *What types of animals do you know that take a journey each year?*

READ ALOUD, pp. T28–T29

COMPREHENSION:
Author's Purpose and Perspective, pp. T30–T31
Summarize, pp. T32–T33

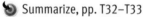
VOCABULARY:
Introduce Vocabulary, p. T35
Word Champion, p. T37

READ: Vocabulary, pp. T36–T37

FLUENCY: EXPRESSION: Model Oral Fluency, p. T29

DECODING/WORD ATTACK: Structural Analysis: Word Parts: *in-, out-, down-, up-,* p. T61

Day 2

QUESTION OF THE DAY *Why is it important to rescue sea turtles caught in cold waters?*

READ ALOUD, p. T29

COMPREHENSION:
Author's Purpose and Perspective, pp. T38–T50
Summarize, pp. T43, T45, T47

VOCABULARY:
Vocabulary Review, p. T55

READ: "Interrupted Journey: Saving Endangered Sea Turtles," pp. T38–T51
Options for Reading

▲Student Edition

FLUENCY: EXPRESSION: Recorded Reading, p. T55

SCIENCE: Body Temperature, p. T41

Suggestions for Differentiated Instruction *(See pp. T22–T23.)*

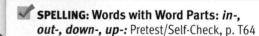
SPELLING: Words with Word Parts: *in-, out-, down-, up-:* Pretest/Self-Check, p. T64

WRITING: Persuasive Letter: Teach/Model, p. T66

Writing Prompt There are many interesting ocean animals. Choose one that interests you. Write a paragraph that tells about this animal.

GRAMMAR: Action and Linking Verbs: Teach/Model, p. T68

Daily Proofreading

1. Has you ever seen a Sea Turtle? (Have; sea turtle?)

2. He is an friendly, out going person. (a friendly; outgoing)

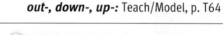
SPELLING: Words with Word Parts: *in-, out-, down-, up-:* Teach/Model, p. T64

WRITING: Persuasive Letter: Practice/Apply, p. T66

Writing Prompt "Inturrupted Journey" begins with Max Nolan and his mother rescuing Yellow-Blue. Think about what they may have said to each other after finding the turtle. Now write a short dialogue that might have occurred between them.

GRAMMAR: Action and Linking Verbs: Teach/Model, p. T68

Daily Proofreading

3. We'ell work for an hour and, then eat lunch. (We'll; and then)

4. This organization has two office down-town. (offices; downtown)

 = **Focus Skill**  = **Focus Strategy**   = **Tested Skill**

Comprehension	Vocabulary	Fluency	Language Arts
FOCUS SKILL: Author's Purpose and Perspective **FOCUS STRATEGY:** Summarize	basking sleek vital damage analyzing detect	Expression	**Writing:** - Trait: Sentence Fluency - Form: Persuasive Letter **Grammar:** Action and Linking Verbs

Skills at a Glance

Day 3

QUESTION OF THE DAY *Think of a time when someone persuaded you to do something. How did the person persuade you? Why was the person's method effective?*

READ ALOUD, p. T29

COMPREHENSION:
 Author's Purpose and Perspective, pp. T56–T57

VOCABULARY: Reinforce Word Meanings, p. T63

READ: "Kids in Action," pp. T52–T53

COMPARING TEXTS, p. T54

FLUENCY: EXPRESSION: Choral-Read, p. T62

WRITING: Write about an Endangered Species, p. T55

▲Student Edition

Day 4

QUESTION OF THE DAY *What is a cause that you consider vital? Why?*

READ ALOUD, p. T29

SPEAKING AND LISTENING: Persuasive Speech, p. T70

VOCABULARY: Extend Word Meanings, p. T63

FLUENCY: EXPRESSION: Echo-Read, p. T62

▲Student Edition

Day 5

QUESTION OF THE DAY *What are some ways students in your area can help endangered animals?*

READ ALOUD, p. T29

COMPREHENSION: Make Inferences, p. T60

VOCABULARY: Cumulative Vocabulary, p. T63

FLUENCY: EXPRESSION: Partner Reading, p. T62

MEDIA LITERACY: Survey of Personal Communication, p. T71

▲Student Edition

 BELOW-LEVEL   ON-LEVEL   ADVANCED   E L L

SPELLING: Words with Word Parts: *in-, out-, down-, up-:* Practice/Apply, p. T65

WRITING: Persuasive Letter: Prewrite, p. T67

Writing Prompt *Most communities have volunteer projects that help the environment. Learn about one such project that you think is important. Write a letter to a friend describing the project and explaining why you think it is important.*

GRAMMAR: Action and Linking Verbs: Teach/Model, p. T69

Daily Proofreading

5. She are being undecisive. (She is; indecisive.)

6. Snakes is unvertebrates. (Snakes are invertebrates.)

SPELLING: Words with Word Parts: *in-, out-, down-, up-:* Spelling Strategies, p. T65

WRITING: Persuasive Letter: Draft, p. T67

Writing Prompt *"Inturrupted Journey" is told from a third-person point of view. Think about how the story would be different if it were told from the turtle's point of view. Write a paragraph describing one event from the story from the turtle's perspective.*

GRAMMAR: Action and Linking Verbs: Apply to Writing, p. T69

Daily Proofreading

7. Marco being patient with unconsiderate woman. (was being; an inconsiderate)

8. We have talking about the interestingest animals. (have been; most interesting)

SPELLING: Words with Word Parts: *in-, out-, down-, up-:* Posttest, p. T65

WRITING: Persuasive Letter: Revise and Reflect, p. T67

Writing Prompt *Most communities have a landmark or natural area that should be preserved or protected. Think of such a place in your community. Now write a letter to the editor of a local newspaper calling for it to be protected.*

GRAMMAR: Action and Linking Verbs: Review, p. T69

Daily Proofreading

9. Wow that is an up lifting story! (Wow!; uplifting)

10. We is spreading the word about these unhumane practices. (We are; inhumane)

Suggested Small-Group Planner

45–60+ Minutes

	Day 1	**Day 2**

BELOW-LEVEL *15–20+ Minutes*	**Teacher–Directed**
	 Leveled Readers:
	 Before Reading, p. T72
	
	 Independent
	 Word Study Center, p. T26
	 Extra Support
	 Copying Masters, p. 123
	  ▲ Leveled Reader
		Teacher–Directed
		 Reread the Selection,
		 pp. T38–T51
		
		 Independent
		 Writing Center, p. T27
		 Audiotext Grade 5, CD7
		  ▲ Student Edition

 **ON-LEVEL** *15–20+ Minutes*	**Teacher–Directed**
	 Leveled Readers:
	 Before Reading, p. T73
	
	 Independent
	 Reading Center, p. T26
	 Practice Book, p. 123
	  ▲ Leveled Reader
		Teacher–Directed
		 Respond to the Literature,
		 p. T50
		
		 Independent
		 Word Study Center,
		 p. T26
		  ▲ Student Edition

ADVANCED *15–20+ Minutes*	**Teacher–Directed**
	 Leveled Readers:
	 Before Reading, p. T74
	
	 Independent
	 Writing Center, p. T27
	 Challenge Copying
	 Masters, p. 123
	  ▲ Leveled Reader
		Independent
		 Fluency Center, p. T27
		 Leveled Readers:
		 Partner Reading, p. T74
		  ▲ Leveled Reader

 E L L

English-Language Learners

In addition to the small-group suggestions above, use the ELL Extra Support Kit to promote language development.

LANGUAGE DEVELOPMENT SUPPORT	**LANGUAGE DEVELOPMENT SUPPORT**
Teacher–Directed Leveled Readers: Build Background, p. T75 ELL Teacher Guide, Lesson 21 **Independent** ELL Copying Masters, Lesson 21 ▲ Leveled Reader	**Teacher–Directed** Scaffold Core Skills ELL Teacher Guide, Lesson 21 **Independent** *Audiotext Grade 5,* CD7  ▲ ELL Student Handbook

Intervention

| Strategic Intervention Teacher Guide,
 Lesson 21
 Strategic Intervention Practice Book,
 Lesson 21 | Catch a Wave,
 Lesson 21
 Strategic Intervention
 Teacher Guide,
 Lesson 21
  Strategic Intervention Interactive Reader ▲ |

▲ Strategic Intervention Resource Kit

▲ Strategic Intervention Interactive Reader

 = **Literacy Center Cards**

MONITOR PROGRESS

Small-Group Instruction

	Author's Purpose and Perspective	Selection Comprehension	Robust Vocabulary	Expression	Language Arts
	pp. S2–S3	p. S6	pp. S4–S5	p. S7	pp. S8–S9

Day 3

Teacher–Directed
Leveled Readers:
During Reading, p. T72

Independent
⭐ Reading Center, p. T26
Extra Support Copying Masters, p. 121

▲ Leveled Reader

Teacher–Directed
Leveled Readers:
During Reading, p. T73

Independent
⭐ Technology Center, p. T27
Practice Book, p. 121

▲ Leveled Reader

Teacher–Directed
Leveled Readers:
During Reading, p. T74

Independent
⭐ Word Study Center, p. T26
Challenge Copying Masters, p. 121

▲ Leveled Reader

LANGUAGE DEVELOPMENT SUPPORT

Teacher–Directed
Leveled Readers:
During Reading, p. T75
ELL Teacher Guide, Lesson 21

Independent
ELL Copying Masters, Lesson 21

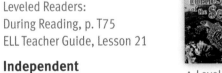
▲ Leveled Reader

Catch a Wave,
Lesson 21
Strategic Intervention
Teacher Guide,
Lesson 21
Strategic Intervention
Practice Book, Lesson 21

Strategic Intervention
Interactive Reader ▲

Day 4

Teacher–Directed
Leveled Readers:
Guided Fluency, p. T72

Independent
⭐ Technology Center, p. T27
Extra Support Copying Masters, p. 126

▲ Leveled Reader

Teacher–Directed
Leveled Readers:
Guided Fluency, p. T73

Independent
⭐ Fluency Center, p. T27
Practice Book, p. 126

▲ Leveled Reader

Independent
⭐ Reading Center, p. T26
Challenge Copying Masters, p. 126
Classroom Library: Self-Selected Reading

▲ Leveled Reader

LANGUAGE DEVELOPMENT SUPPORT

Teacher–Directed
Leveled Readers:
Guided Fluency, p. T75
ELL Teacher Guide, Lesson 21

Independent
ELL Copying Masters, Lesson 21

▲ Leveled Reader

Catch a Wave,
Lesson 21
Strategic Intervention
Teacher Guide,
Lesson 21

Strategic Intervention
Interactive Reader ▲

Day 5

Teacher–Directed
Leveled Readers:
Responding, p. T72

Independent
⭐ Fluency Center, p. T27
Leveled Readers:
Rereading for Fluency, p. T72

▲ Leveled Reader

Teacher–Directed
Leveled Readers:
Responding, p. T73

Independent
⭐ Writing Center, p. T27
Leveled Readers: Rereading for Fluency, p. T73

▲ Leveled Reader

Teacher–Directed
Leveled Readers:
Responding, p. T74

Independent
⭐ Technology Center, p. T27
Leveled Readers:
Rereading for Fluency, p. T74
Classroom Library: Self-Selected Reading

▲ Leveled Reader

LANGUAGE DEVELOPMENT SUPPORT

Teacher–Directed
Leveled Readers:
Responding, p. T75
ELL Teacher Guide, Lesson 21

Independent
Leveled Readers:
Rereading for Fluency, p. T75

▲ Leveled Reader

Catch a Wave,
Lesson 21
Strategic Intervention
Teacher Guide,
Lesson 21

Strategic Intervention
Interactive Reader ▲

Leveled Readers & Leveled Practice
Reinforcing Skills and Strategies

LEVELED READERS SYSTEM

- **Leveled Readers**
- **Leveled Readers CD**
- **Leveled Reader Teacher Guides**
  - *Vocabulary*
  - *Comprehension*
  - *Oral Reading Fluency Assessment*
- **Response Activities**
- **Leveled Readers Assessment**

See pages T72–T75 for lesson plans.

For extended lesson plans, see *Leveled Reader Teacher Guides.*

BELOW-LEVEL

MARVELOUS MARINE MAMMALS
by John Stewart

- **Author's Purpose and Perspective**
- **Summarize**
- **Robust Vocabulary**

LEVELED READER TEACHER GUIDE

▲ Vocabulary, p. 5

▲ Comprehension, p. 6

ON-LEVEL

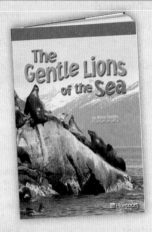

The Gentle Lions of the Sea

- **Author's Purpose and Perspective**
- **Summarize**
- **Robust Vocabulary**

LEVELED READER TEACHER GUIDE

▲ Vocabulary, p. 5

▲ Comprehension, p. 6

ADVANCED

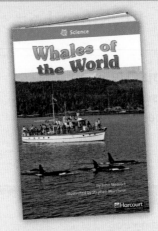

Science
Whales of the World
by John Stewart
Illustrated by Stephen Marchesi

🔵 **Author's Purpose and Perspective**

🔵 **Summarize**

• **Robust Vocabulary**

LEVELED READER TEACHER GUIDE

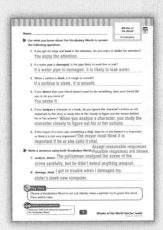

▲ Vocabulary, p. 5

▲ Comprehension, p. 6

ELL

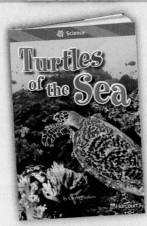

Science
Turtles of the Sea
by Cecilia Fathers

• **Build Background**

• **Concept Vocabulary**

• **Scaffolded Language Development**

LEVELED READER TEACHER GUIDE

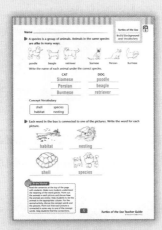

▲ Build Background, p. 5

▲ Scaffolded Language Development, p. 6

CLASSROOM LIBRARY

for Self-Selected Reading

EASY

▲ *Doña Flor* by Pat Mora.
TALL TALE

Eleanor
Story and pictures by
BARBARA COONEY

AVERAGE

▲ *Eleanor* by Barbara Cooney.
BIOGRAPHY

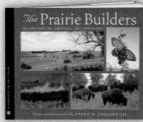

The Prairie Builders
RECONSTRUCTING AMERICA'S LOST GRASSLANDS
by SNEED B. COLLARD III

CHALLENGE

▲ *The Prairie Builders: Reconstructing America's Lost Grasslands* by Sneed B. Collard III.
EXPOSITORY NONFICTION

Classroom
Library Books
Teacher Guide
Grade 5

▲ Classroom Library Books
Teacher Guide

Literacy Centers

15+ Min. each

Management Support

While you provide direct instruction to individuals or small groups, other students can work on these activities.

▲ Literacy Centers Pocket Chart

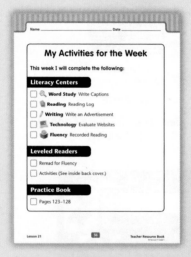

Name _____ **Date** _____

My Activities for the Week

This week I will complete the following:

Literacy Centers
- ☐ Word Study Write Captions
- ☐ Reading Reading Log
- ☑ Writing Write an Advertisement
- ☐ Technology Evaluate Websites
- ☐ Fluency Recorded Reading

Leveled Readers
- ☐ Reread for Fluency
- ☐ Activities (See inside back cover.)

Practice Book
- ☐ Pages 123–128

▲ Teacher Resource Book, p. 56

Homework for the Week

Teacher Resource Book, page 24

The *Homework Copying Master* provides activities to complete for each day of the week.

GO online www.harcourtschool.com/storytown

WORD STUDY

Write Captions

Objective
To write captions to extend understanding of word meanings

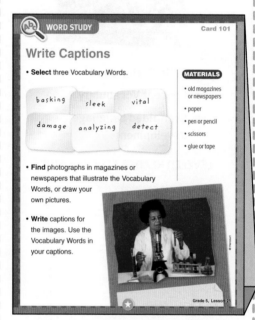

WORD STUDY Card 101

Write Captions

- **Select** three Vocabulary Words.

  basking · sleek · vital · damage · analyzing · detect

- **Find** photographs in magazines or newspapers that illustrate the Vocabulary Words, or draw your own pictures.

- **Write** captions for the images. Use the Vocabulary Words in your captions.

MATERIALS
- old magazines or newspapers
- paper
- pen or pencil
- scissors
- glue or tape

Grade 5, Lesson 21

⭐ **Literacy Center Kit,** Card 101

The scientist is analyzing the sample taken from the patient.

READING

Reading Log

Objective
To select and read books independently

READING Card 102

Reading Log

- **Look for** these books about people making their communities better.
- **Choose one** that you find interesting.
- **Use your Reading Log** to keep track of what you read.

MATERIALS
- library book
- My Reading Log
- pen or pencil

Doña Flor by Pat Mora. TALL TALE

Eleanor by Barbara Cooney. BIOGRAPHY

The Prairie Builders: Reconstructing America's Lost Grasslands by Sneed B. Collard III. EXPOSITORY NONFICTION

Grade 5, Lesson 21

⭐ **Literacy Center Kit,** Card 102

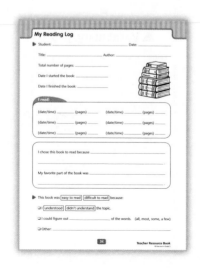

My Reading Log

▶ Student: _____ Date: _____

Title: _____ Author: _____

Total number of pages: _____

Date I started the book: _____

Date I finished the book: _____

I read:

(date/time) _____ (pages) _____ (date/time) _____ (pages) _____
(date/time) _____ (pages) _____ (date/time) _____ (pages) _____
(date/time) _____ (pages) _____ (date/time) _____ (pages) _____

I chose this book to read because _____

My favorite part of the book was _____

▶ This book was ☐ easy to read ☐ difficult to read because:
- ☐ I understood ☐ didn't understand the topic.
- ☐ I could figure out _____ of the words. (all, most, some, a few)
- ☐ Other: _____

34 Teacher Resource Book

www.harcourtschool.com/storytown

★ Additional Literacy Center Activities
★ Resources for Parents and Teachers

● BELOW-LEVEL   ● ADVANCED   ● ON-LEVEL

Differentiated
for Your Needs

WRITING

Write an Advertisement

Objective
To write to persuade and inform

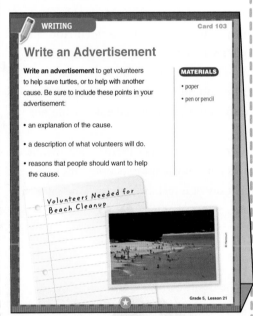

WRITING   Card 103

Write an Advertisement

Write an advertisement to get volunteers to help save turtles, or to help with another cause. Be sure to include these points in your advertisement:

• an explanation of the cause.

• a description of what volunteers will do.

• reasons that people should want to help the cause.

MATERIALS
• paper
• pen or pencil

Volunteers Needed for Beach Cleanup

Grade 5, Lesson 21

 Literacy Center Kit, Card 103

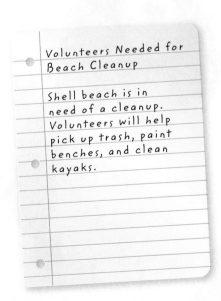

Volunteers Needed for Beach Cleanup

Shell beach is in need of a cleanup. Volunteers will help pick up trash, paint benches, and clean kayaks.

TECHNOLOGY

Evaluate Websites

Objective
To evaluate websites for relevant information

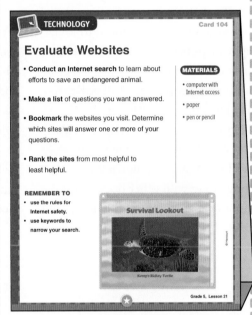

TECHNOLOGY   Card 104

Evaluate Websites

• **Conduct an Internet search** to learn about efforts to save an endangered animal.

• **Make a list** of questions you want answered.

• **Bookmark** the websites you visit. Determine which sites will answer one or more of your questions.

• **Rank the sites** from most helpful to least helpful.

REMEMBER TO
• use the rules for Internet safety.
• use keywords to narrow your search.

MATERIALS
• computer with Internet access
• paper
• pen or pencil

Survival Lookout

Kemp's Ridley Turtle

Grade 5, Lesson 21

 Literacy Center Kit, Card 104

Most Helpful Websites

1. Sea Island University—Department of Zoology website

2. Survival Lookout Web site

FLUENCY

Recorded Reading

Objective
To read aloud with appropriate expression

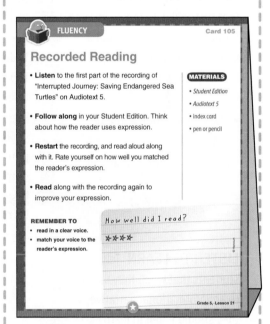

Recorded Reading

• **Listen** to the first part of the recording of "Interrupted Journey: Saving Endangered Sea Turtles" on Audiotext 5.

• **Follow along** in your Student Edition. Think about how the reader uses expression.

• **Restart** the recording, and read aloud along with it. Rate yourself on how well you matched the reader's expression.

• **Read** along with the recording again to improve your expression.

REMEMBER TO
• read in a clear voice.
• match your voice to the reader's expression.

MATERIALS
• *Student Edition*
• *Audiotext 5*
• index card
• pen or pencil

How well did I read?
☆☆☆☆

Grade 5, Lesson 21

Literacy Center Kit, Card 105

How well did I read?
☆☆☆☆
☆☆☆☆☆

Listening Comprehension *Read-Aloud*

Objectives

- *To listen critically to oral communication*
- *To respond appropriately to oral communication*

Genre Study

INFORMATIONAL NARRATIVE Tell students that they will listen to an informational narrative about a volunteer program. Point out that an informational narrative

- gives information about a topic.
- is told in an interesting way.

Set a Purpose for Listening

LISTEN TO LEARN Tell students that when they listen to an informational narrative, they should listen to learn about the topic. Model setting a purpose for listening: *One purpose for listening is to learn about who participates in the volunteer program.* Then have students set their own purposes for listening.

Lending a Paw

by Andrea Ptak

Kristy, 11, and her springer spaniel, Buffy, 10, know what it means to lend a hand—or a paw. They're part of a volunteer program called Pet Partners. Pet Partners sets up visits from animal–human teams to patients in nursing homes and hospitals. Kristy first heard about the program from her grandmother. Later, when she read about how much Pet Partners teams cheer up the people they visit, she was convinced to join. Being happy helps people feel better—and Kristy knew her gregarious dog had a special talent for making people happy. Plus, Kristy says, "Buffy loves people petting her!"

To take part in the program, the Florida pair had to attend classes to review basic dog commands like sit, stay, and down. Buffy practiced getting along with other dogs and she learned not to eat anything off the floor. After seven weeks of class, Buffy took a test to make sure she would be comfortable visiting patients in hospitals. "Buffy stayed calm no matter what," Kristy says proudly. "We passed!" ❶

Buffy and Kristy started visiting nursing homes right away. "I love listening to peoples' stories," Kristy says, "and seeing how they love Buffy." One special friend they've made is a resident at the nursing home and she always enjoys spending time with Kristy and her dog. And Buffy's quite fond of the resident, too. She runs to her whenever she sees her. The resident, a lifelong dog lover, knows how to make Buffy happy. She bought her dog friend a special water dish so she can have a drink during her visits.

Kristy recommends Pet Partners for anyone who loves pets—or helping people. "It's indescribable how you feel after a visit," she says. "It just makes you so happy!" ❷ ❸

Begin the Read-Aloud

MODEL ORAL FLUENCY: EXPRESSION Tell students that good readers

- read aloud with appropriate expression.
- adjust the volume and intonation of their voice to express meaning.

 Display **Transparency R87**. Demonstrate reading aloud with appropriate expression as students follow along. Have them pay attention to the rise and fall of your voice and to the words you emphasize as you read.

Interact with the Text

Routine Card 1 Continue reading aloud "Lending a Paw." Pause to point out or ask students the following items:

❶ Why do you think it's important for the dogs in Pet Partners to remain calm? (Possible response: because the dogs may be around ill people, or people who can't move around easily) **MAKE INFERENCES**

❷ The word *indescribable* means "something that cannot be described." **UNDERSTANDING VOCABULARY**

❸ Would you like to volunteer in a program like Pet Partners? Why or why not? (Responses will vary.) **PERSONAL RESPONSE**

When you have finished reading the selection, ask:

- **Why do you think the author wrote this informational narrative?** (Possible response: to inspire other people to volunteer) **RETURN TO PURPOSE**
- **What techniques did the author use to make the information more interesting?** (Responses will vary.) **AUTHOR'S CRAFT**

Connect to Reading

Tell students that in this lesson they will read about a group of volunteers that work to help save an endangered species.

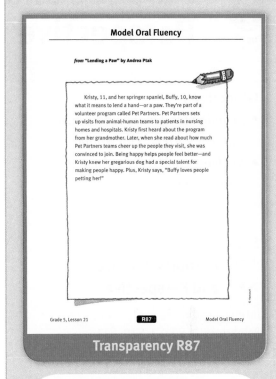

Transparency R87

Suggested Daily Read-Aloud

To model fluency and promote listening comprehension, read aloud from one of these books throughout the week:

- *Sea Turtles* by Lorraine A. Jay. NorthWord, 2000.
- *The Kid's Volunteering Book* by Arlene Erlbach. Lerner, 1998.
- *Neighborhood Odes* by Gary Soto. Harcourt, 2005.
- *Chester Cricket's New Home* by George Selden. Random House, 1984.
- *My Backyard Garden* by Carol Lerner. Morrow, 1998.

Author's Purpose and Perspective

Objectives

- *To understand that authors have different purposes for writing*
- *To identify and discuss an author's perspective*

Skill Trace

Tested **Author's Purpose and Perspective**

Introduce	pp. T30–T31
Reteach	p. S2–S3, S10–S11
Review	pp. T56–T57, T106–T107, T132–T133, T308
Test	Theme 5
Maintain	p. T274, Theme 6

Teach/Model

INTRODUCE AUTHOR'S PURPOSE AND PERSPECTIVE Read page 538 with students. Then use the information below to summarize:

- The **author's purpose**, or reason, for writing may be to entertain, to inform, or to persuade.

- Readers can use the genre of a selection to determine the author's purpose. Nonfiction is often used to inform or persuade; fiction is often used to entertain.

- The **author's perspective** is the author's viewpoint, or feelings, about the subject.

Explain to the students that as they read, they should ask themselves whether the author includes facts, reasons, or entertaining details.

Focus Skill

Author's Purpose and Perspective

The reason an author writes is called the **author's purpose.** Authors of nonfiction write to **inform** or **persuade** readers. Authors of fiction usually write to **entertain** readers. An author's opinion about a subject is called the **author's perspective,** or viewpoint. Look for evidence, such as the author's choice of words and details, to help you determine the author's purpose and perspective.

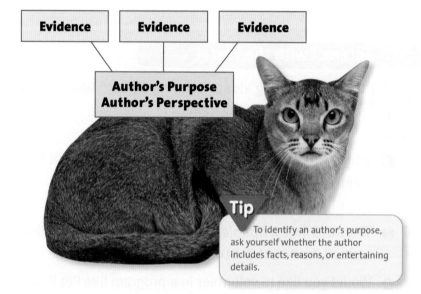

| Evidence | Evidence | Evidence |

Author's Purpose Author's Perspective

Tip
To identify an author's purpose, ask yourself whether the author includes facts, reasons, or entertaining details.

538

BELOW-LEVEL

Explain Author's Purpose Help students understand each purpose by giving a definition and an example:

- To **entertain** means "to enable others to enjoy something." Example: a funny story about a dog

- To **persuade** means "to try to get others to do something." Example: an article to get people to recycle glass bottles

- To **inform** means "to provide others with facts about a topic." Example: an article about the history of a city

Answer questions students have about each purpose.

Read the paragraph below. Then look at the graphic organizer. It shows evidence from the paragraph that helps you identify the author's purpose and perspective.

When Hurricane Katrina struck the Gulf Coast of the United States in 2005, many people had to leave their pets behind. After the disaster, animal rescue organizations made a mighty effort to save the many cats and dogs stranded by the storm. When local shelters ran out of space, shelters in other areas stepped in. Charter flights flew animals to shelters as far away as California.

Evidence	**Evidence**	**Evidence**
gives information about pet rescues after a disaster	organizations worked to save stranded pets	shelters in various areas helped

Author's Purpose

to inform

Author's Perspective

People work together in times of need.

 Try This!

Look back at the paragraph. How does the author feel about the subject? What words and details help you identify the author's perspective?

 www.harcourtschool.com/storytown

539

(TEACH/MODEL CONTINUED) Ask a volunteer to read aloud the passage on page 539. Then model identifying the author's purpose.

Think Aloud This passage is nonfiction. Nonfiction is often used to inform or persuade. The author gives facts about the efforts of rescuers to save pets after a hurricane. The author probably wrote to inform readers about those efforts.

Guided Practice

IDENTIFY EVIDENCE Guide students to identify a fourth piece of evidence that supports the author's purpose and perspective. (Charter flights flew animals to other shelters.)

Practice/Apply

Try This! Have students discuss how the author's perspective influences the text. Have them locate and share words and phrases in the passage that support their view.

DURING AND AFTER READING
- Practice the Skill • Apply to Text, pp. T40, T42, T48
- Reinforce the Skill • Practice/Apply, pp. T56–T57

 **MONITOR PROGRESS**

Author's Purpose and Perspective

IF students have difficulty identifying the author's perspective about the rescuers' efforts,

THEN point out the phrases *made a mighty effort*, *shelters in other areas stepped in*, and *to shelters as far away as California*. Show that the author admires the effort made to rescue the pets.

Small-Group Instruction, pp. S2–S3:

● **BELOW-LEVEL:** Reteach   ● **ON-LEVEL:** Reinforce   ● **ADVANCED:** Extend

Comprehension Strategy
Summarize

Objectives

- *To use strategies appropriate to the reading situation*
- *To monitor comprehension by summarizing*

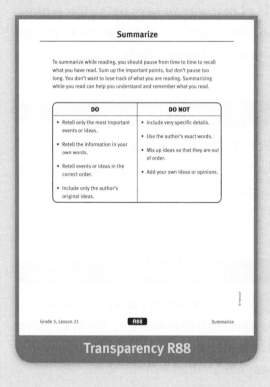

Summarize

To summarize while reading, you should pause from time to time to recall what you have read. Sum up the important points, but don't pause too long. You don't want to lose track of what you are reading. Summarizing while you read can help you understand and remember what you read.

DO	DO NOT
• Retell only the most important events or ideas.	• Include very specific details.
• Retell the information in your own words.	• Use the author's exact words.
• Retell events or ideas in the correct order.	• Mix up ideas so that they are out of order.
• Include only the author's original ideas.	• Add your own ideas or opinions.

Grade 5, Lesson 21   R88   Summarize

Transparency R88

Teach/Model

REVIEW SUMMARIZING Tell students that one way to better understand what they read is to pause periodically to **summarize**.

Display **Transparency R88**. Refer to information on the transparency as you explain that

- when you summarize a selection, you **retell the most important events or ideas.**
- a **summary** does not include minor details.
- a summary should **present ideas in the same order** as the selection.
- a summary should be told **in the reader's own words** but should not change any of the author's ideas.

Tell students that when reading a nonfiction text, they should pause after each section of text to summarize what they read. Point out that many nonfiction texts have headings that can help the reader quickly and easily identify the most important idea in a section of text.

Display **Transparency R89**. Read aloud the first paragraph. Then demonstrate for students how to summarize. Fill in the chart on the transparency as you model summarizing.

Think Aloud **To summarize this passage, first identify who or what it is about and then retell the most important ideas. This first paragraph explains that the world's coastal regions are important ecosystems. It says that animals, birds, and plants as well as people depend on these regions. It also says that finding a delicate balance between competing needs benefits all. These are the main points of the paragraph, so they should be included in the summary.**

Guided Practice

SUMMARIZE TEXT Remind students that they should pause regularly to summarize. Explain that this may mean stopping after every paragraph, at the end of each page, or at the end of a section of text, depending on how difficult the text is. Display **Transparency R89** again. Have volunteers continue reading the passage aloud. Work with students to note ideas that should be included in a summary of the second paragraph. Then ask a volunteer to summarize the entire passage.

Practice/Apply

PRACTICE SUMMARIZING Have partners select a passage from an expository nonfiction book. Tell them to take turns reading it and summarizing it for each other.

DURING READING
- Apply the Focus Strategy, pp. T43, T47
- Review Comprehension Strategies, p. T41

Summarize

Every continent is surrounded by oceans. Where land and ocean meet, there are unique and vibrant ecosystems. The coastal regions of the world share certain qualities. They support many different animals, birds, and plants. These regions also provide people with places to live and work. In fact, many coastal cities are hubs for transportation and trade. Maintaining a balance between the competing needs of wildlife and people is important to all.

Protecting coastal lands is one way people try to make sure that both people's needs and the needs of other living things are met. The governments of states and countries have created many coastal wildlife refuges and sanctuaries. These special areas are off limits to most human activities. Many of these areas provide critical habitat for certain endangered species of birds, plants, and animals. By protecting wildlife refuges, people show their concern for other living things.

Important Ideas to Include	Details Not to Include
• Where land and ocean meet, there are unique and vibrant ecosystems.	• Every continent is surrounded by oceans.
• The coastal regions provide homes for many types of animals, birds, and plants.	• The coastal regions of the world share certain qualities.
• These regions also provide people with places to live and work.	• Many coastal cities are hubs for transportation and trade.
• Maintaining a balance between the competing needs of wildlife and people is important to all.	

Grade 5, Lesson 21   R89   Summarize

Transparency R89

○ **BELOW-LEVEL**

Make the Strategy Visual
Duplicate and distribute a nonfiction passage from a science or social studies textbook. Give each student a colored pencil or highlighter. Read the passage aloud once with students. Discuss each sentence and help students decide if the information belongs in a summary. Have students highlight or underline those sentences that belong in a summary.

 Build Background

Access Prior Knowledge

DEVELOP A LIST Ask students to share what they know about the things or conditions that wild animals need in order to survive and thrive in the wild. Record their ideas in a list.

What Animals Need to Survive

- safe places to live
- adequate food and water
- a way to protect themselves from danger

Then ask students: **What can threaten the survival of wild animals?** (Possible responses: destruction of the places they live and the foods they eat; loss of water supply; too much hunting by other animals or people; diseases)

Develop Concepts

DISCUSS ENDANGERED SPECIES Use the information in the list to begin a discussion about endangered species. Include the following information:

- A species is a unique type of animal or plant, such as a grizzly bear or a coastal redwood tree.

- Some species are considered endangered because so few of them are left that they are in danger of dying out altogether.

- People protect endangered animals by working to save habitats and limiting other threats to their survival.

Selection Background Use *Picture Card 2* along with gestures and pantomime to scaffold background and vocabulary as needed:

- A **turtle** is a type of animal called a **reptile**. Different kinds of turtles range in size from 3 inches to 8 feet long. (show photos)

- Sea turtles have a **shell** (gesture to your back) and **flippers** that they use to swim. (pantomime swimming)

Have students list words that describe turtles.

Picture Card 2 ▶

See *ELL Teacher Guide* Lesson 21 for support in scaffolding instruction.

Build Robust Vocabulary

5-DAY VOCABULARY
DAY 1 Vocabulary, pp. T35–T37
DAY 2 Vocabulary Review, p. T55
DAY 3 Reinforce Word Meanings, p. T63
DAY 4 Extend Word Meanings, p. T63
DAY 5 Cumulative Review, p. T63

Introduce Vocabulary

BUILD WORD MEANING Display **Transparency R90**. Have a volunteer read aloud the first Vocabulary Word, and have the class repeat the word aloud to practice its pronunciation. Then have the volunteer read the explanation for the word. Ask students the first question below. Continue in this way until students have answered a question about each Vocabulary Word.

1. Are you most likely to find a seal **basking** on a rock at noon or at midnight?

2. Which is **sleek**—a silk shirt or a piece of sandpaper? Why?

3. Are cake and presents a **vital** part of a birthday celebration? Why or why not?

4. Which of these actions can help you prevent **damage** to your head—combing your hair or wearing a bicycle helmet? Why?

5. Why is **analyzing** the results an important part of an experiment?

6. Which of your senses can you use to **detect** dinner cooking in the kitchen?

▼The sleek panther rests in the shade.

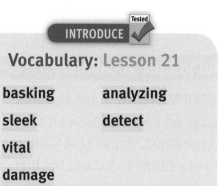

INTRODUCE Tested ✓

Vocabulary: Lesson 21

basking	analyzing
sleek	detect
vital	
damage	

▼ **Student-Friendly Explanations**

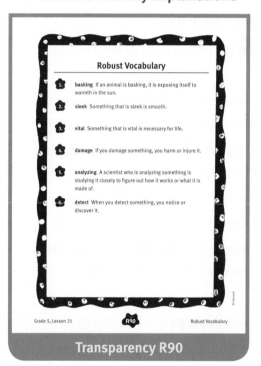

Robust Vocabulary

1. **basking** If an animal is basking, it is exposing itself to warmth in the sun.

2. **sleek** Something that is sleek is smooth.

3. **vital** Something that is vital is necessary for life.

4. **damage** If you damage something, you harm or injure it.

5. **analyzing** A scientist who is analyzing something is studying it closely to figure out how it works or what it is made of.

6. **detect** When you detect something, you notice or discover it.

Grade 5, Lesson 21 · R90 · Robust Vocabulary

Transparency R90

Vocabulary

Build Robust Vocabulary

DEVELOP DEEPER MEANING Have students read the passage on pages 540–541. Then read the passage aloud. Pause at the end of page 540. Ask questions 1–3 about the high-lighted words. Discuss students' answers. Then read aloud page 541 and discuss questions 4–6. If students are unable to give reasonable responses, refer them to the explanations on **Transparency R90**.

1. What is **vital** to the survival of the Florida panther?

2. What characteristics make the Florida panther a **sleek** creature?

3. Why might a Florida panther be **basking** in the early morning sunlight?

4. How do you think researchers went about **analyzing** the panthers' blood and tissue?

5. What did researchers **detect** as a possible cause for the decline of the Florida panthers?

6. What else can **damage** the healthy growth of panthers?

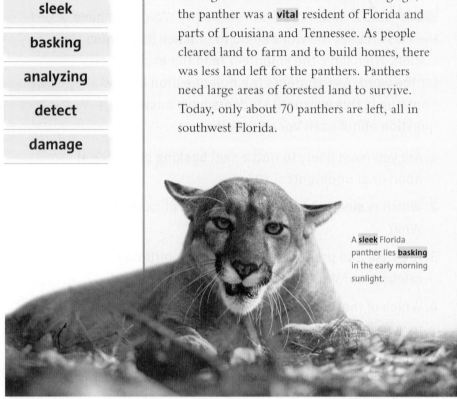

Vocabulary

Build Robust Vocabulary

vital

sleek

basking

analyzing

detect

damage

Panther Protection

The Florida panther is one of the most endangered animals in the world. Long ago, the panther was a **vital** resident of Florida and parts of Louisiana and Tennessee. As people cleared land to farm and to build homes, there was less land left for the panthers. Panthers need large areas of forested land to survive. Today, only about 70 panthers are left, all in southwest Florida.

A **sleek** Florida panther lies **basking** in the early morning sunlight.

540

E L L

Pictures for Words Have students list the Vocabulary Words on separate sheets of paper. Next to each word, have them draw a sketch to remind them of the meaning of the word. For example, next to the word *damage*, they might draw a tree with a broken branch and write the sentence "Strong wind can **damage** a tree."

Strong wind can damage a tree. ▶

See *ELL Teacher Guide* Lesson 21 for support in scaffolding instruction.

Loss of land isn't the panthers' only problem. By **analyzing** blood and tissue, researchers were able to **detect** that some Florida panthers were dying from metal poisoning. Air pollution from the mining of metals can **damage** the healthy growth of panthers.

However, the news is not all bad. People are working to extend the panthers' habitat and to make the air cleaner. With effort, we can help the Florida panther population grow so that these beautiful animals will be around for the future.

Male panthers need room to roam. An average male needs about 250 square miles of territory in order to thrive.

 www.harcourtschool.com/storytown

Word Champion

Your challenge this week is to use Vocabulary Words outside your classroom. Keep the list of words in a place at home where you can see it. Use as many of the words as you can. For example, you might ask a family member what can damage a plant's growth. At the end of each day, write in your vocabulary journal the ways in which you used the words.

541

Word Champion

Use Words in Everyday Speech Ask students to use two words from the list each day in their everyday conversations. Help students use the words correctly by guiding them to sort the words into action words and describing words. At the end of the week, call on volunteers to share the sentences containing the Vocabulary Words that they used. **HOMEWORK/ INDEPENDENT PRACTICE**

"RESEARCH SAYS"

"The meta-analysis shows a significant positive effect for instruction in the skill of deriving word meaning in context."

—Fukkink & de Glopper (1998)

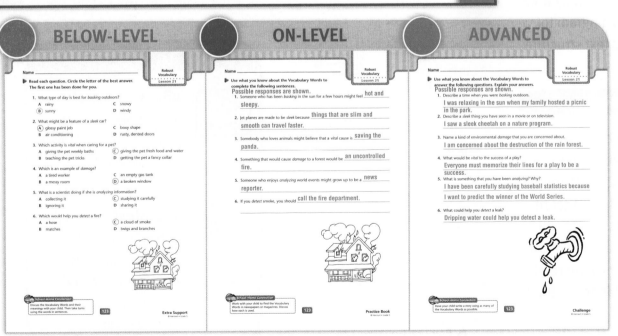

▲ Extra Support, p. 123   ▲ Practice Book, p. 123   ▲ Challenge, p. 123

E L L

- Group students according to academic levels, and assign one of the pages on the left.

- Clarify any unfamiliar concepts as necessary. See *ELL Teacher Guide* Lesson 21 for support in scaffolding instruction.

SCIENCE

Read **the Selection**

Objective
- *To understand the distinguishing characteristics of expository nonfiction*

Genre Study

DISCUSS EXPOSITORY NONFICTION: PAGE 542 Have students read the genre information on page 542. Review with students the relationship between headings and text structure. Then point out and read aloud the headings for the first two sections in "Interrupted Journey: Saving Endangered Sea Turtles." Have students suggest what the topic of each section might be.

LIST GENRE FEATURES Have students preview "Interrupted Journey: Saving Endangered Sea Turtles" and list and compare the text features to the features in other works of expository nonfiction they have read. Display **Transparency GO5.** You may want to use the main-idea-and-details diagram to review the main-idea-and-details text structure.

Comprehension Strategy

SUMMARIZE: PAGE 542 Have students read the Comprehension Strategy information on page 542. Distribute *Practice Book* page 124. Tell students that filling in the main-idea-and-details charts will help them monitor their understanding of the selection and summarize what they are reading. See page T51 for completed Practice Book page.

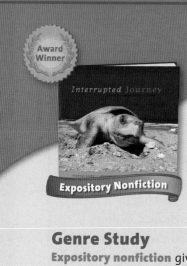

Genre Study

Expository nonfiction gives you facts and information about a topic. As you read, look for

- headings that begin sections of related information.

- the way the author organized ideas and information.

Detail	Detail	Detail

Main Idea

Comprehension Strategy
Summarize sections of text as you read to help you keep track of information.

542

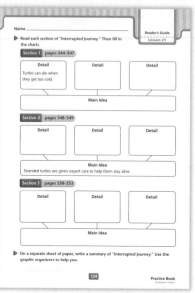

▲ Practice Book, p. 124

TECHNOLOGY

GO online **eBook** "Interrupted Journey: Saving Endangered Sea Turtles" is available in an eBook.

Audiotext "Interrupted Journey: Saving Endangered Sea Turtles" is available on *Audiotext Grade 5,* CD7 for subsequent readings.

INTERRUPTED *Journey*
Saving Endangered Sea Turtles

by Kathryn Lasky
photographs by Christopher G. Knight

Preview/Set a Purpose

Routine Card 3

PREVIEW Have a volunteer read the title aloud. Next, page through the selection with students, read aloud the headings of the first few sections, and discuss the photographs. Then ask students what they think they will learn about sea turtles.

MODEL SETTING A PURPOSE Remind students that they can use the title, headings, and photographs or drawings in expository nonfiction to help them set a purpose for reading. Use this model:

Think Aloud The title indicates that this selection is about sea turtles that take a journey, which has been interrupted for some reason. The photos show children and adults with the turtles. One purpose for reading would be to find out what interrupts the turtles' journeys and how the people work to help them complete the journeys.

Options for Reading

 BELOW-LEVEL

Small Group Preview the selection with students. Model how to use the preview and the genre information to set a purpose for reading.

 ON-LEVEL

Whole Group/Partner Use the Monitor Comprehension questions as students read the selection, or have partners read the selection together and complete *Practice Book* page 124.

 ADVANCED

Independent Have students read the selection independently, using *Practice Book* page 124 to monitor their comprehension and keep track of the information in the selection.

Monitor Comprehension

1 **CAUSE AND EFFECT**

What causes the turtles to become confused and have difficulty swimming?
(The water temperature has dropped too low for the turtle.)

2 **AUTHOR'S PURPOSE AND PERSPECTIVE**

What is the author's perspective about the work Max and his mother do? How do you know? (Possible response: She thinks it is important. She describes the work as "vital.")

3 **MAKE PREDICTIONS**

Will Max and his mother play a role in helping the young turtle that has been stunned by the cold? (Responses will vary.)

See *Questioning the Author Comprehension Guide,* Lesson 21, as an alternate questioning strategy to guide student interaction with the text.

Questioning the Author Comprehension Guide, Lesson 21 ▶

STRANDED

The young turtle has been swimming for three months now in the same warm shallow bay, grazing on small crabs and plankton, basking in an endless dream of calm water and plentiful food. But as the days begin to shorten and the light drains out of the sky earlier and earlier, the water grows colder. It drops to fifty degrees Fahrenheit. The turtle is confused. Swimming is harder. Its heartbeat slows—and almost stops. **1**

544

Clarify Vocabulary Use simple definitions and a diagram to help students understand the following terms:

- **high-water mark**—line on the beach marking the highest point that the waves reach as they roll onto shore
- **tide line**—line on the beach left by waves as they roll onto the shore at a given moment; moves in and out with the rise and fall of the tide

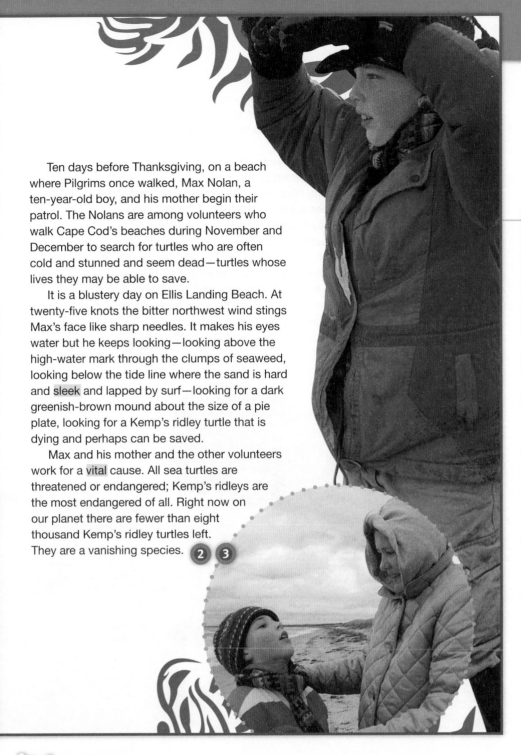

Ten days before Thanksgiving, on a beach where Pilgrims once walked, Max Nolan, a ten-year-old boy, and his mother begin their patrol. The Nolans are among volunteers who walk Cape Cod's beaches during November and December to search for turtles who are often cold and stunned and seem dead—turtles whose lives they may be able to save.

It is a blustery day on Ellis Landing Beach. At twenty-five knots the bitter northwest wind stings Max's face like sharp needles. It makes his eyes water but he keeps looking—looking above the high-water mark through the clumps of seaweed, looking below the tide line where the sand is hard and sleek and lapped by surf—looking for a dark greenish-brown mound about the size of a pie plate, looking for a Kemp's ridley turtle that is dying and perhaps can be saved.

Max and his mother and the other volunteers work for a vital cause. All sea turtles are threatened or endangered; Kemp's ridleys are the most endangered of all. Right now on our planet there are fewer than eight thousand Kemp's ridley turtles left. They are a vanishing species. **②** **③**

Apply Comprehension Strategies

Monitor Comprehension: Adjust Reading Rate

ANALYZE TEXT Remind students that good readers pay attention to the amount of information contained in the text they are reading. If they notice that a section contains many facts, they read more slowly.

Use the second paragraph on page 545 to model adjusting reading rate.

Think Aloud This paragraph contains a lot of information about looking for sea turtles on the beach. Reading more slowly can help you accurately picture what is being described: The wind blows strong and cold at the beach. The surf breaks on hard, smooth sand dotted by piles of seaweed. The volunteers search for a pie-plate-sized mound in the sand.

Remind students that when they come to unfamiliar ideas or text that gives a lot of information, they should slow their reading rate. Have volunteers model reading aloud the paragraph at an appropriate reading rate.

 **SCIENCE** SUPPORTING STANDARDS

Body Temperature Guide students to understand that mammals and birds—which are warm-blooded animals—have the ability to regulate their body temperature. However, the body temperature of animals such as turtles and other reptiles—which are cold-blooded animals—changes according to their surroundings. Discuss how blood flows through the body, and how temperature may affect animal behavior.

Monitor Comprehension

4 **MAKE INFERENCES**

How do you know that Max has received special training about what to do after discovering a stranded turtle? (Possible response: The author says that Max remembers the instructions given to all rescuers. Then she describes how he follows the various steps.)

5 **CAUSE AND EFFECT**

Why must the turtle be brought out of its cold, stunned condition? (Possible response: because otherwise it will be unable to eat or move and will probably die)

6 **AUTHOR'S PURPOSE AND PERSPECTIVE**

Why doesn't the author immediately tell the reader whether the turtle has survived? (Possible response: to build suspense and keep the reader interested in the turtle's fate)

On Ellis Landing Beach, snow squalls begin to whirl down. The waves are building, and as they begin to break, the white froth whips across their steep faces. So far there is no sign of a turtle.

Max is far ahead of his mother when he sees the hump in the sand being washed by the surf. He runs up to it and shouts to his mom, "Got one!" The turtle is cold. Its flippers are floppy. Its eyes are open, but the turtle is not moving at all. It might be dead, but then again, it might not.

Max remembers the instructions given to all rescuers. He picks up the turtle, which weighs about five pounds, and moves it above the high-tide mark to keep it from washing out to sea. Then he runs to find seaweed to protect it from the wind. He finds a stick to mark the spot, and next, he and his mother go to the nearest telephone and call the sea-turtle rescue line of the Massachusetts Audubon Society. **4**

546

BELOW-LEVEL

Clarify Content To help students grasp content-rich portions of this selection, restate complex sentences as a series of shorter sentences and read them aloud.

He picks up the turtle, which weighs about five pounds, and moves it above the high-tide mark to keep it from washing out to sea.	• Max picks up the turtle. • The turtle weighs about five pounds. • Max moves the turtle above the high-tide mark. • This keeps the turtle from washing out to sea.

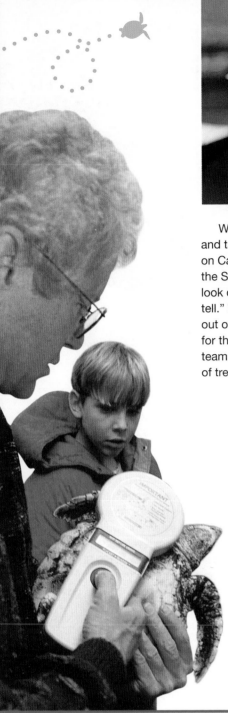

Within an hour the turtle has been picked up and taken to the Wellfleet Bay Wildlife Sanctuary on Cape Cod. Robert Prescott, the director of the Sanctuary, examines the turtle. "It sure does look dead," he says softly. "But you never can tell." If the turtle is really alive, it must be brought out of its cold, stunned condition. That is a task for the New England Aquarium with its medical team who, over the years, have made a specialty of treating turtles. **5**

Robert puts the new turtle in a plastic wading pool with another turtle that is quite lively. Max crouches by the edge and watches his turtle. It is as still as a stone. He gently touches a flipper. Nothing moves. Then after about twenty minutes, he thinks he might see a flicker in the turtle's left eyelid. He leans closer. "Hey, it's moving!" It wasn't just the eyelid. He saw the right rear flipper move a fraction of an inch. Over the next five minutes, he sees the turtle make three or four microscopically small motions with its right rear flipper. Soon, the rescue team from the New England Aquarium arrives. **6**

547

Apply Comprehension Strategies

Summarize

RETELL IMPORTANT INFORMATION Remind students that restating main ideas and important details as they read can help them remember the most important information. Ask volunteers to summarize how Max rescues the turtle. If students have difficulty, model the strategy.

Think Aloud To summarize the steps Max follows, restate his actions in simple language. First he moves the turtle. Then he covers it and marks the spot. Finally he calls the Audubon Society.

Remind students to pause to summarize after reading each section of the text.

SCIENCE   CONTENT-AREA VOCABULARY

Word Bank: Science Reread the first sentence on page 547. Write on the board the term *wildlife sanctuary*. Ask students to share what they know about wildlife sanctuaries. Then tell students that some places where wildlife is protected are called by different names, such as *nature reserve*, *nature preserve*, and *wildlife refuge*. Write these terms on the board. Then discuss wildlife refuges in your area.

(Student Edition, page 547) Lesson 21 • **T43**

Monitor Comprehension

7 CAUSE AND EFFECT

Why is body temperature and a low heart rate less of a problem for the turtle than for some other animals? (Possible response: Turtles have less complicated brains and can survive without damage in these conditions, unlike animals with more complex brains.)

8 AUTHOR'S CRAFT

How does the author add humor to the selection? Why do you think she does this? (She includes details about Howard Crum holding the turtle against his ear like a seashell to try to find its heartbeat. She may do this to change the mood of the story and show that the turtle has a chance to survive.)

9 TEXT STRUCTURE

What text structure does the author use to organize her information? How does this structure affect the text? (Possible response: sequence; It makes the events easier to follow and remember since they are told in the order in which they happened.)

EMERGENCY

Beth Chittick is a vet at the New England Aquarium. When the turtles arrive she is ready for them. The turtles are taken immediately into the examination room. Beth is joined by head veterinarian, Howard Crum. The temperature of the turtle Max found is fifty degrees Fahrenheit. Normal temperature for a turtle is usually about seventy-five degrees. Howard next tries to find a heartbeat. He listens intently. "I think I can hear a faint sound . . ." He holds the stiff turtle against his ear as one might hold a seashell. "Why, gee whiz, I can hear the ocean," he jokes. **7** **8**

Howard tries to find a heartbeat.

548

Howard is still not convinced that the turtle is dead. "With turtles," Howard says, "death is a relative term." Turtles can operate, can survive, even when their hearts slow down for periods of time. Events that might damage the larger, more complicated brains of other animals will not always prove fatal to turtles.

In fact, a turtle's heartbeat naturally slows down at times to just one or two beats per minute in order to conserve oxygen and keep vital organs like the brain working. So Howard won't give up on this turtle yet. The turtle does not seem dehydrated. The skin on its limbs is not wrinkled—a good sign.

ADVANCED

Use Structural Analysis Have students work in pairs to examine the structure of the following words: *conserve, dehydrated, intravenous.* Ask students to tell what word parts they see and how they used them to determine the meanings of the words.

Word	Meaning	Prefix (meaning)	Word Root (meaning)	Suffix (meaning)
intravenous	characterized by being within a vein	*intra-* (within)	*ven-* (vein)	*ous-* (characterized by)

An assistant swabs down an area on the turtle's neck, from which a blood sample will be taken. By analyzing the blood, Howard and Beth will be able to see how the turtle's kidneys and other organs are functioning.

Next the turtle is cleaned. The algae are washed and wiped from its shell. The doctors detect movement in its tail and then see some of the same movements that Max saw in its flippers. They are the motions a turtle makes when it swims. They do not necessarily mean that it is alive, though.

Nonetheless, the vets hook up the turtle to an intravenous needle through which fluids will be pumped very slowly at a temperature slightly higher than the turtle's body. Beth and Howard have learned much about the condition of this turtle but they are still not sure if it is really alive or dead.

Finally the turtle is tagged with a yellow-blue band. It will be known as Yellow-Blue. It is put in the Intensive Care Unit, a large temperature-controlled stainless steel box with a glass window. Inside, the turtle is placed on a soft pile of towels so its shell is supported and it will not have to rest on its ventrum, or bottom shell. **9**

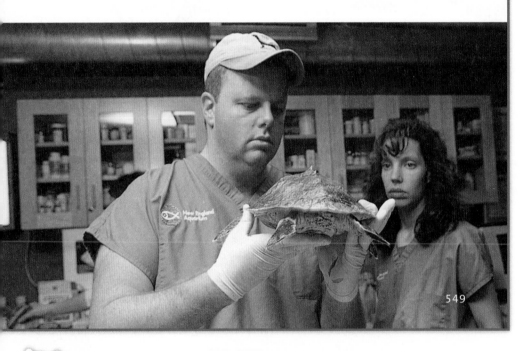

549

SCIENCE   **SUPPORTING STANDARDS**

Circulatory System Engage students in a discussion about the circulatory system. Work with them to identify the different organs that make it up, and discuss how those parts work together. Ask students to explain why the circulatory system is essential to the survival of many organisms.

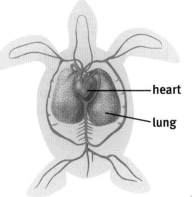

—heart

—lung

Monitor Comprehension

10 **INTERPRET GRAPHIC AIDS**
About how far is Yellow-Blue's jet flight from Boston, Massachusetts, to Marathon, Florida? (1,300 miles) **How do you know?** (by measuring the distance on the map and then comparing it to the map scale)

11 **USE TEXT FEATURES**
What will this section of text be about? How do you know? (It will be about Yellow-Blue's release; the heading of the section is *Release*.)

12 **PERSONAL RESPONSE**
Would you enjoy staying at the Hidden Harbor Motel? Why or why not?
(Responses will vary.)

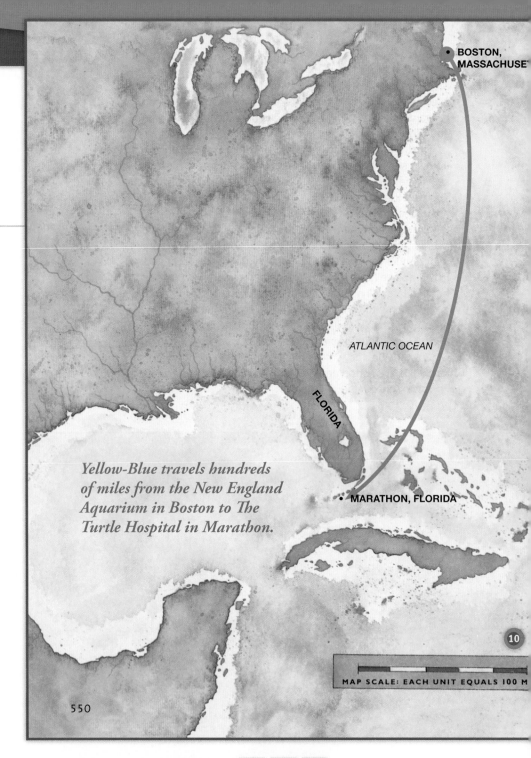

BOSTON, MASSACHUSE...

ATLANTIC OCEAN

FLORIDA

Yellow-Blue travels hundreds of miles from the New England Aquarium in Boston to The Turtle Hospital in Marathon.

MARATHON, FLORIDA

10

MAP SCALE: EACH UNIT EQUALS 100 M...

550

E L L

Multiple-Meaning Words Remind students that some words have more than one meaning. Write the following multiple-meaning words from the selection and guide students to use context to determine the meaning the author intended.

leg	a body part	a part of a journey
run	to move quickly	to own, operate, or manage
calling	yelling out	a job/task a person feels he or she is supposed to do

RELEASE

On a windy spring morning in April, five months after it was found, Yellow-Blue is taken from its small tank in the New England Aquarium and put into a plastic box with wet towels. Yellow-Blue has recovered from its ordeal. But for the first leg of its journey it will not swim—Yellow-Blue will fly. A small cargo jet will take the turtle to The Turtle Hospital in Marathon, in the Florida Keys.

Richie Moretti is the owner, director, and founder of the hospital. He is not a veterinarian. He is not a marine biologist. He is a man who loves turtles, and his calling in life is to help injured animals. In order to do this, Richie runs Hidden Harbor, a motel. With the money he makes from the motel, he runs the hospital.

The people who come to the motel can no longer swim in the motel pool. It is filled with injured sea turtles—loggerheads, green turtles, Kemp's ridleys, and hawksbills. Guests cannot even sunbathe or sit around the pool, for there are smaller tanks for baby and juvenile turtles not big enough, or too sick, to swim in the big pool. Veterinarians and volunteers come to the hospital to work with the turtles. 12

551

Apply Comprehension Strategies

Summarize

Focus Strategy

MONITOR COMPREHENSION Ask students to summarize the journey that Yellow-Blue has taken so far. If necessary, suggest they revisit earlier parts of the selection to refresh their memory. Record students' responses in a sequence chart.

> **First, Yellow-Blue is found cold and stunned by Max Nolan on Ellis Landing Beach on Cape Cod, Massachusetts.**

> **Next, Yellow-Blue is taken to Wellfleet Bay Wildlife Sanctuary on Cape Cod, Massachusetts.**

> **Then, Yellow-Blue is taken to New England Aquarium in Boston, Massachusetts, where it stays for five months.**

> **Finally, Yellow-Blue is flown by cargo jet to The Turtle Hospital in Marathon, Florida, in the Florida Keys.**

Monitor Comprehension

13 **AUTHOR'S PURPOSE AND PERSPECTIVE**

How can you tell that the author is in favor of Yellow-Blue's release? (Possible responses: She uses the word *exciting* to describe it; she describes the release in a very positive way.)

14 **MAKE INFERENCES**

What threats might Yellow-Blue face while swimming to the Sargasso Sea? (Possible responses: Yellow-Blue might get hit by a boat, chopped by a propeller, or tangled in fishermen's nets or lines.)

15 **NOTE DETAILS**

Why is the cove off Content Key "the perfect place to release Yellow-Blue"? (Possible responses: The waters are shallow and calm; there are no people fishing in the area.)

16 **SPECULATE**

Do you think Yellow-Blue will be successful in continuing his interrupted journey? Why or why not? (Responses will vary.)

On the day of the release, Richie and his assistant remove Yellow-Blue from the tank and attach a permanent metal tag to its flipper so that the turtle can be tracked throughout its sea voyage. The turtle is feisty and flaps its flippers, perhaps sensing that something exciting is about to happen. Richie and his crew load Yellow-Blue and several larger turtles into his high-speed, shallow-bottomed boat. Before departing from the pier, Richie checks the charts of the waters around the southern keys. He wants to take Yellow-Blue to the quietest, calmest, and safest waters he knows—a place where there are no tourists racing around in speedboats or fishing boats or shrimp trawlers. He wants this turtle to have a fair chance of swimming out to the Sargasso Sea without getting hit by a boat, chopped by a propeller, or tangled in the deadly nets and lines of fishermen. They put Yellow-Blue in a box, cover its shell with wet towels, and then roar out into Florida Bay. **13** **14**

552

Clarify Understanding Help students understand the following expressions by using simple definitions and pantomime:

- **roar out into Florida Bay**—move fast with a roaring engine into the bay
- **cut the boat's engine**—turn off the boat's engine
- **poles in to**—uses a pole to move a boat over shallow water
- **streaks through the water**—moves very quickly through the water

The boat goes fast, close to sixty miles an hour. Soon they are forty miles to the south and west. They are on the very most outlying keys of the Gulf side. The waters are shallow and calm. They cut the boat's engine and now the water is so shallow that Richie raises the outboard motor and poles in to what he considers the perfect place to release Yellow-Blue. It is in the still waters of a cove off a key named Content. Susan, a volunteer, lifts Yellow-Blue from its box and holds it half-in, half-out of the water. "Oh, you want to go! You want to go! Hang on, fella! Let's get used to things!" **15**

Then she lowers Yellow-Blue so it is completely underwater. The flippers beat, and finally Susan's hands let go! Yellow-Blue streaks through the turquoise water, leaving a curling wake of bubbles. "So long, buddy," Richie calls. **16**

553

Additional Related Reading

Students interested in this topic may want to locate these titles.

- *Sea Turtles* by Jason Glaser. Bridgestone, 2006.
  EASY
- *Esio Trot* by Roald Dahl. Puffin, 1999.
  AVERAGE
- *Sea Turtles* by Lorraine A. Jay. North-Word, 2000.
  CHALLENGE

ANALYZE AUTHOR'S PURPOSE

Author's Purpose Remind students that authors have a purpose, or reason, for writing. After students have finished reading "Interrupted Journey: Saving Endangered Sea Turtles" ask them:

Why did the author write this selection?

- **to tell a humorous story about a turtle rescue**
- **to convince readers to volunteer to save turtles**
- to inform readers about efforts to save endangered turtles
- **to teach a lesson about not harming wild animals**

Think **Critically**

Respond to the Literature

Have students discuss or write their responses to the questions on page 554.

1 Possible response: It is a refuge for injured sea turtles. **NOTE DETAILS**

2 He knows that turtles can survive even with a very low heart rate. **MAIN IDEA**

3 Possible response: Yes; she seems to feel that people should protect endangered species and so has written a story that explains and praises the efforts of people who do so. **AUTHOR'S PURPOSE AND PERSPECTIVE**

4 Responses will vary. **EXPRESS PERSONAL OPINIONS**

5 **WRITE** Possible response: First, make sure the turtle is protected from the waves and the wind. Then, mark the location and call people who rescue turtles. Next, wait for those people to arrive. Finally, help the rescuers any way you can. **SHORT RESPONSE**

RUBRIC For additional support in scoring this item, see the rubric on p. R6.

THINK *Critically*

1 What is special about the Hidden Harbor motel? NOTE DETAILS

2 Why does Howard Crum refuse to give up on Yellow-Blue even though he has difficulty locating his heartbeat? MAIN IDEA

3 Do you think the author's feelings about endangered species affected the way she wrote the selection? Explain. AUTHOR'S PURPOSE AND PERSPECTIVE

4 Why do you think it is important to help endangered animals? EXPRESS PERSONAL OPINIONS

5 **WRITE** Imagine that you have found a cold, stunned turtle that has washed up onto a beach. Explain what you would do to help the turtle. Use information and details from the selection in your answer. SHORT RESPONSE

554

BELOW-LEVEL

Reread and Summarize If students have difficulty answering question 5, point out that they are being asked to summarize the steps in rescuing a turtle. Have them reread the steps Max Nolan and his mother follow at the beginning of the selection to help them answer the question.

About the Author
Kathryn Lasky

As a child, Kathryn Lasky often made up stories. One day, her mother told her that with her love of words, she should become a writer. For the first time, she gave the idea serious thought. Kathryn Lasky is equally comfortable writing fiction and nonfiction. She is married to Christopher Knight, a photographer who takes the pictures for many of her books, including this book.

About the Photographer
Christopher G. Knight

When they were in college, Christopher Knight and his brother paddled a kayak from Alaska to Seattle, Washington. Christopher Knight photographed the entire voyage. Later, he photographed a canoe trip through seven European countries. These journeys marked the beginning of his career as a professional photographer. He and his wife, Kathryn Lasky, have traveled the world together, working on books. They have written and taken photographs for stories about the monarch butterfly, the birth of a new volcanic island near Iceland, and a fossil dig.

For *Interrupted Journey*, they traveled to the cold waters of Cape Cod, the warm waters of the Florida Keys, and the Kemp's ridley nesting site at Rancho Nuevo, Mexico.

 www.harcourtschool.com/storytown

555

MONITOR PROGRESS

Summarize

IF students have difficulty summarizing the selection,

THEN review with them the information they recorded on *Practice Book* page 124, and help them use it to write a summary.

Small-Group Instruction, p. S6:

- 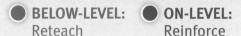 **BELOW-LEVEL:** Reteach
- **ON-LEVEL:** Reinforce
-  **ADVANCED:** Extend

---

Check Comprehension

Summarize

DISCUSS AUTHOR AND PHOTOGRAPHER: PAGE 555 Have students read the author and photographer information independently. Ask them how the topic of this selection fits with the topics of other books the couple has created.

Routine Card 4 **WRITE A SUMMARY** Ask students to write a summary of the selection. Share the following tips:

- Begin with the selection title and genre.
- Describe the important events in the order in which they happened.
- Review the headings to confirm that you have included important information from each section.

Students may want to refer to *Practice Book* page 124, which they completed during reading, to help them summarize.

RUBRIC See rubric for Summarizing on page R4.

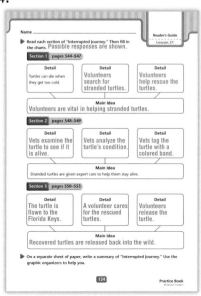

▲ Practice Book, p. 124

SOCIAL STUDIES

Paired Selection

Objectives

- *To read and understand a variety of non-fiction texts*
- *To use text features to gain information*

Genre Study

DISCUSS MAGAZINE ARTICLES Remind students that magazine articles often give facts about a topic. Headings and photographs help inform readers about the topic. Have students preview the article by reading the headings and looking at the photographs. Then ask them what they think the article will be about. (Possible response: children who are working to help wildlife and the environment)

ANALYZE THE ARTICLE Have students read the article. Work with them to develop a problem-solution chart for each section in the article.

Social Studies

Magazine Article

Kids

These kids are pitching in to help nature, and so can you! If you're like lots of other kids, you care about nature. And you want to do something to help wildlife and the environment. Check out what these kids have been up to.

Sea Savers

Some kids in the coastal town of Davenport, California, were worried. They noticed lots of trash piling up on the local beaches. They decided to find out where the trash was coming from—and to learn more about other problems facing the world's oceans.

They were shocked to learn that many people were dumping trash into the seas and all along the coasts too. Also, in places, fishermen have been catching too many fish. As a result, some kinds of fish have been nearly wiped out.

So, the students got busy! They grabbed some trash bags and headed out to clean up the nearby beaches. They talked to beachgoers too. The kids reminded them not to litter and to please carry their trash out. And they handed out guides to the best kinds of fish to buy—the kinds that aren't dying out. People agreed to do what the kids asked. So it was a great start toward helping the oceans!

556

E L L

Clarify Meanings Use simple explanations to help students understand the following expressions:

- **pitching in**—People who are pitching in are becoming part of an effort to do something.

- **headed out to**—If you headed out to a beach, you traveled to it.

- **nearly wiped out**—If a kind of fish has been nearly wiped out, it has been fished until very few are left.

- **speaking up for**—If you are speaking up for a cause, you are speaking in public in support of it.

in Action

by Elizabeth Schleichert

Flower Girl

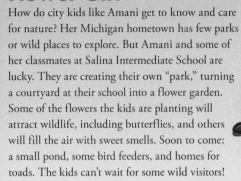

How do city kids like Amani get to know and care for nature? Her Michigan hometown has few parks or wild places to explore. But Amani and some of her classmates at Salina Intermediate School are lucky. They are creating their own "park," turning a courtyard at their school into a flower garden. Some of the flowers the kids are planting will attract wildlife, including butterflies, and others will fill the air with sweet smells. Soon to come: a small pond, some bird feeders, and homes for toads. The kids can't wait for some wild visitors!

Super Star

At age 12, Illai wanted to do something special. Many kids she knew in her hometown in Georgia were having breathing problems because of the polluted air. Illai saw how people living in the poorer parts of the city suffered from the effects of pollution. And so she helped start Georgia Kids Against Pollution. KAP, as it's called, encourages people to work for clean air and water. Four years later, Illai is still speaking up for her cause.

Not long ago, Illai won a Brower Youth Award. It's given to a few outstanding young environmental heroes. Illai's proud mom was at the award ceremony—to give her daughter an even better award: a big hug!

557

Respond to the Article

Ask students to reread the magazine article silently, paying careful attention to the information about each volunteer effort. Then ask:

1. **COMPARE AND CONTRAST Think about the efforts of kids described in each section. In what ways are they similar?** (Possible response: All three sections tell about kids working to preserve the natural world. The kids in California and Michigan work directly to improve the environment, while the kids in California and the girl in Georgia inform others about how to help the environment.)

2. **PERSONAL RESPONSE Which of these efforts would you most want to be a part of? Why?** (Responses will vary.)

3. **SOCIAL STUDIES CONNECTING TEXTS Would Max Nolan, the turtle rescue volunteer in "Interrupted Journey: Saving Endangered Turtles," appreciate the efforts of the Sea Savers? Why do you think that?** (Possible response: Yes, because he cares about turtles and probably would also care about other sea creatures.)

WRITE AN ARTICLE Ask students to find out about a volunteer effort in your community related to the environment and write a brief article describing it. Remind students that their description should state the problem that is being addressed as well as its solution. Point out the leads the author used in each section of "Kids in Action." Tell students to include an interesting lead in their article, such as an interesting fact, a dramatic scene, or a question. **WRITING**

(*Student Edition*, page 557) Lesson 21 • **T53**

ANALYZE MENTOR TEXT

Persuasive Techniques Point out to students the persuasive techniques the author uses in the introductory paragraph to get readers to act or think in a particular way. Then have students explain what kind of persuasive technique the author is using.

- "These kids are pitching in to help nature, and so can you!" (Possible response: This is an emotional appeal that focuses on people's love for nature.)

- "If you're like lots of other kids, you care about nature. And you want to do something to help wildlife and the environment." (Possible response: This technique is an example of peer pressure. It tries to sway readers to join "everyone else" to act or think in a particular way.)

Comparing Texts

Answers:

1. Reponses will vary. **TEXT TO SELF**

2. In both, the authors inform readers about kids working in volunteer roles to protect their environment. **TEXT TO TEXT**

3. Possible response: People can keep the community clean and work to protect the places where animals live. **TEXT TO WORLD**

Connections

Comparing Texts

1. Max Nolan likes to make a difference by helping turtles. What would you enjoy doing to make a difference?

2. How is the author's purpose for writing "Interrupted Journey" similar to the author's purpose for writing "Kids in Action"?

3. What are some ways your community can become a safer place for the people and animals that live there?

Vocabulary Review

Word Webs

Work with a partner. Choose three Vocabulary Words. Create a word web for each. In the outer circles of the web, write related words and phrases. Share your work with your classmates, explaining how the words in the webs are related.

basking

sleek

vital

damage

analyzing

detect

558

T54 • Grade 5, Theme 5 (*Student Edition*, page 558)

Fluency Practice

Recorded Reading

Listen to "Interrupted Journey: Saving Endangered Sea Turtles" on *Audiotext 5*. Start at the beginning and follow along through page 546, where Max discovers the turtle. Listen carefully to the reader's expression. Replay the recording, and read aloud to match the reader's expression. Practice reading the section aloud until you are satisfied with your expression.

Writing

Write About an Endangered Species

Choose an endangered animal that lives in your state. Then write a paragraph describing the problems facing the animal and what you think should be done to keep the animal safe in the future.

My Writing Checklist

Writing Trait ➤ Sentence Fluency

✓ I used complete sentences to describe the problem and solution.

✓ I used a graphic organizer to plan my writing.

✓ I included specific reasons and details to support my perspective.

Evidence	Evidence	Evidence

Author's Purpose
Author's Perspective

559

 VOCABULARY REVIEW

Word Webs Have students work in pairs to complete the activity. Suggest that they use a thesaurus and discuss their webs with their partners before sharing them with the class.

 FLUENCY PRACTICE

Recorded Reading: Expression Have students practice reading along with the tape recording of the passage several times. Then ask them to read the passage to a partner, who can give feedback about the reader's use of expression. **For additional fluency practice, see p. T62.**

For additional fluency practice, see p. T62.

 WRITING

 Write About an Endangered Species Help students search for information about your state's endangered species. Then encourage them to take notes. Remind them to clearly describe the problem and the solution. Have them use the checklist to evaluate their writing.

📁 **PORTFOLIO OPPORTUNITY** Students may choose to place their paragraphs in their portfolios.

 MONITOR PROGRESS

Vocabulary Review

IF students have difficulty creating webs of related words,

THEN show them an example for *basking*.

resting — lying
basking
napping — sunbathing

Small-Group Instruction, pp. S4–S5:

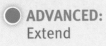

● **BELOW-LEVEL:** Reteach ● **ON-LEVEL:** Reinforce ● **ADVANCED:** Extend

Author's Purpose and Perspective

Objectives

- *To understand that authors have different purposes for writing*
- *To identify and discuss an author's perspective*

Skill Trace

 Tested **Author's Purpose and Perspective**

Introduce	pp. T30–T31
Reteach	p S2–S3, S10–S11
Review	pp. T56–T57, T106–T107, T132–T133, T308
Test	Theme 5
Maintain	p. T274, Theme 6

BELOW-LEVEL

Review Genre Characteristics
Remind students that the first step in determining the author's purpose is identifying the genre. Review with students the characteristics of different types of fiction and nonfiction texts, and discuss the purposes of each.

Reinforce the Skill

REVIEW AUTHOR'S PURPOSE AND PERSPECTIVE Remind students that authors have different reasons for writing. Have students recall that an author may also have a perspective, or an opinion, about a topic, which she or he reveals in the text. Review these points:

- Nonfiction is often written to inform or to persuade; fiction is often written to entertain.

- An author may have more than one purpose. For example, a writer's main purpose for writing about a science topic may be to inform, but the author may also include humorous facts or examples to entertain readers as they learn.

- Readers can use clues and details in the text, such as the author's word choice or characters' feelings and actions, to determine the author's purpose and perspective.

Guided Practice

APPLY TO LITERATURE Work with students to revisit "Interrupted Journey: Saving Endangered Sea Turtles" and find clues that indicate the author's purpose and perspective. Have students reread the sections listed below and answer the questions.

- **Page 545** How does the author feel about her topic—the efforts to protect Kemp's ridley turtles? (Possible response: She thinks the efforts are important.) **What details reveal her perspective?** (Possible responses: She says the volunteers are working for a vital cause; the turtles are a vanishing species; and she focuses on efforts to save them.)

- **Page 548, second paragraph:** What might the author want to teach readers with this paragraph? (Possible response: that sea turtles can survive with very low heart rates)

- **Page 552, first paragraph:** What is the author's perspective about speedboats and fishing nets? How do you know? (Possible response: She doesn't like them because they are dangerous for turtles. She uses words like *chopped* and *deadly* to describe what could happen to the turtles.)

Practice/Apply

IDENTIFY AUTHOR'S PURPOSE Have students work in pairs. Distribute two types of reading material to each pair; for example, a fiction story and a science article. Ask partners to survey each by reading the title, scanning any headings, illustrations, or captions, and reading the first few lines of text. Then have partners complete a sheet like the one below for each text they evaluated. Allow time for students to share their results.

1. Title: _____

2. Genre: _____

3. Author's name: _____

4. Author's purpose or purposes: _____

5. Clues to the author's perspective: _____

6. How the author's perspective influences the text: _____

BELOW-LEVEL

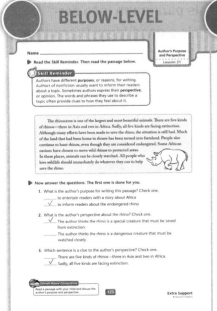

▲ Extra Support, p. 125

ON-LEVEL

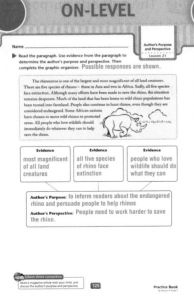

▲ Practice Book, p. 125

ADVANCED

▲ Challenge, p. 125

ELL

- Group students according to academic levels, and assign one of the pages on the left.

- Clarify any unfamiliar concepts as necessary. See *ELL Teacher Guide* Lesson 21 for support in scaffolding instruction.

Persuasive Techniques

Objectives

- *To understand the characteristics of persuasive writing*
- *To identify techniques of persuasion*

Skill Trace
Persuasive Techniques

Introduce	pp. T58-59
Review	p. T195

Persuasive Techniques

- To **persuade** means to convince someone to act or think in a particular way.
- Writers can use a variety of methods to try to persuade readers.

Though the peaceful manatee has no natural predators, it is protected under the Federal Endangered Species Act. This is because, sadly, people have put manatee populations at risk in several ways. Human development has resulted in a loss of habitat. Some manatees have died after becoming tangled in fishing gear. Perhaps most troublesome, manatees have been injured in senseless, avoidable collisions with motorboats.

People have put manatees in danger, so only people can protect them. Many marine biologists agree that areas where the manatees live should be set aside as refuges. That isn't enough, however. Boaters, swimmers, and divers must act responsibly and do whatever they can to save the defenseless manatee. This gentle creature needs and deserves our help.

Grade 5, Lesson 21   **R91**   Persuasive Techniques

Transparency R91

Teach/Model

INTRODUCE PERSUASIVE TECHNIQUES Explain that writers sometimes try to persuade readers to act or think in a particular way, and that writers use various techniques to do this. Display **Transparency R91,** and have a volunteer read aloud the information in the box.

Use the bulleted information below to discuss with students persuasive techniques.

- **Appeal to emotions** uses positive (joy, happiness) or negative (anger, fear) emotions to sway readers.
- **Appeal to logic** uses arguments based on facts or sound reasons to sway readers.
- **Appeal to ethics** uses sense of right and wrong to sway readers.
- **Appeal to authority** uses mention of important person's opinion on the topic to sway readers
- **Word choice** uses words that will influence readers' view on the topic.

Then read aloud the first paragraph. Model recognizing persuasive techniques:

Think Aloud The author's purpose in this paragraph is to persuade readers that protecting the manatee is a good idea. The author uses an appeal to emotions when he says, ". . . sadly, people have put manatee populations at risk in several ways." The word *sadly* tells readers how the author thinks they should feel.

Guided Practice

RECOGNIZE PERSUASIVE TECHNIQUES Have volunteers continue to read the passage on **Transparency R91**. Work with them to identify other examples of persuasive techniques.

Practice/Apply

IDENTIFY PERSUASIVE TECHNIQUES Provide students with science or nature books or science magazines. Ask students to select and read an article, identify the author's viewpoint, and fill in a chart like the one below to show the author's use of persuasive techniques in support of that viewpoint.

Author's Viewpoint on Topic:	
Persuasive Technique Used	**Example from Text**

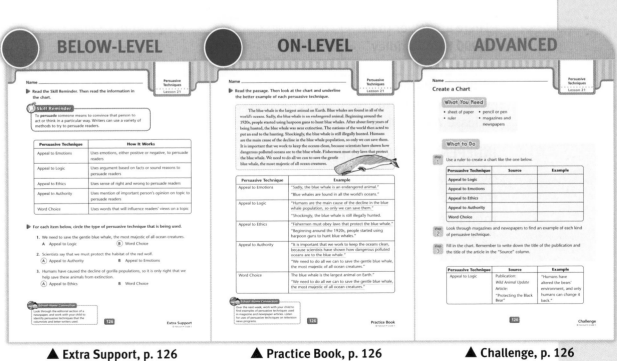

▲ Extra Support, p. 126   ▲ Practice Book, p. 126   ▲ Challenge, p. 126

E L L

• Group students according to academic levels, and assign one of the pages on the left.

• Clarify any unfamiliar concepts as necessary. See *ELL Teacher Guide* Lesson 21 for support in scaffolding instruction.

Make Inferences

Objectives

- *To make inferences about text*
- *To support inferences with text evidence and personal experience*

Skill Trace

 Tested **Make Inferences**

Introduce	pp. T30–T31, Theme 4
Reteach	pp. S2–S3, S12–S13, Theme 4
Review	pp. T66–T67, T116–T117 T144–T145, T326, Theme 4
Test	Theme 4
Maintain	p. T60

Reinforce the Skill

REVIEW MAKING INFERENCES Remind students that sometimes readers need to figure out things in a selection that the author has not stated directly. To do this, readers can use text clues along with prior knowledge and personal experience to make inferences about people and events.

Have a volunteer reread the text on *Student Edition* page 544. Model making an inference:

> **Think Aloud** **This section is titled "Stranded." The text says that the turtle has become confused and its heartbeat has slowed because the temperature in the bay's shallow waters has dropped. These facts could lead to the inference that the turtle should have left the bay before the temperature dropped.**

Practice/Apply

GUIDED PRACTICE Draw on the board a chart like the one below. Guide students to revisit the text to complete it.

Text Evidence	What I Already Know	Inference
There are fewer than 8,000 Kemp's ridley turtles.	That is not a large number for a species.	The Kemp's ridley turtle may become extinct.
Richie looks for safe waters in which to release Yellow-Blue.	Boats and nets can be dangerous for turtles.	Turtles should be released in calm, quiet waters.

INDEPENDENT PRACTICE Ask students to review the selection "Kids in Action." As they revisit the text, ask them to make two inferences about the text. Have them use a graphic organizer like the one above to record their inferences.

Decoding/Word Attack
Structural Analysis: Word Parts in-, out-, down-, up-

Reinforce the Skill

Routine Card 5

DECODE LONGER WORDS Write the word *incomplete* on the board, and read it aloud. Tell students how many syllables are in the word and show them where it should be divided. (3; in/com/plete) Tell students that the word part *in-* forms the first syllable and the root word *complete* forms the next two syllables. Repeat the procedure with *upbeat*, *outdoors*, and *downhill*. Point out the word parts *up*, *out*, and *down* in these words. Tell students to look for these word parts in longer words they encounter.

Practice/Apply

GUIDED PRACTICE Write on the board the following words: *infallible*, *outmaneuver*, *outpatient*, *inhuman*, *downhearted*, *downplay*, *upright*, *upsurge*. Guide students to identify one of the word parts discussed above in each word, break each word into syllables, and then blend the syllables to read the words.

infallible	**outmaneuver**	**outpatient**
in/fal/li/ble	out/ma/neu/ver	out/pa/tient
inhuman	**downhearted**	**downplay**
in/hu/man	down/heart/ed	down/play
upright	**upsurge**	
up/right	up/surge	

INDEPENDENT PRACTICE Have students look in books, magazines, or newspapers to find at least one word with each word part. Have them list the words, divide them into syllables, and read them aloud.

Objectives
• *To use structural analysis to decode longer words*

Skill Trace
Structural Analysis: Word Parts *in-, out-, down-, up-*

Introduce	Grade 2
Maintain	p. T61

Fluency: Expression

15 Min. each

Objectives

- *To demonstrate the characteristics of fluent, effective reading*
- *To read aloud with prosody, using appropriate expression*

 ## MONITOR PROGRESS

Partner Reading

IF students need more support in building fluency and reading with expression,	**THEN** have them echo-read with you, paying close attention to the words you emphasize.

Small-Group Instruction, p. S7:

- ● **BELOW-LEVEL:** Reteach
- ● **ON-LEVEL:** Reinforce
- ● **ADVANCED:** Extend

Fluency Support Materials

 Fluency Builders, Grade 5, Lesson 21

 Audiotext Student Edition selections are available on *Audiotext Grade 5,* CD7.

 Strategic Intervention Teacher Guide, Lesson 21

CHORAL-READ

Routine Card 6 **MODEL EXPRESSION** Model expressive reading with the text on *Student Edition* page 546. Tell students to follow along. Then read the page again. Tell students to pay attention to how you vary your expression to communicate the tone and mood of the text. Then have students choral-read with you.

ECHO-READ

 Routine Card 7 **TRACK PRINT** Have students echo-read *Student Edition* page 546.

- Ask students to put their finger on the beginning of the first sentence.
- Using punctuation and text cues to guide your expression, read aloud the first two paragraphs as students track the print.
- Have students read the sentence aloud, mirroring your expression.
- Continue this process through the rest of the passage.

If students do not read the passage fluently or expressively the first time, have them reread at least three times or until they achieve fluency and appropriate expression.

PARTNER READING

 Routine Card 8 **READ WITH A PARTNER** Pair strong readers with students who need fluency support. Have the strong reader read aloud *Student Edition* page 553 expressively, while the partner listens and follows along in the book. Then have partners switch roles.

 Routine Card 9 Use the sentence frames on *Routine Card 9* to model how to give feedback. Then ask students to provide each other with feedback about their expressiveness. Have partners read the passage to each other again. Encourage students to give each other positive feedback about how their expression improved from the first to the second reading.

Enriching Robust Vocabulary

15 Min. each

5-DAY VOCABULARY	
DAY 1	Vocabulary, pp. T35–T37
DAY 2	Vocabulary Review, p. T55
DAY 3	Reinforce Word Meanings, p. T63
DAY 4	Extend Word Meanings, p. T63
DAY 5	Cumulative Review, p. T63

REINFORCE WORD MEANINGS

Objective
- *To demonstrate knowledge of word meanings*

REVISIT SELECTION VOCABULARY Have students discuss "Interrupted Journey: Saving Endangered Sea Turtles" by responding to these questions. Students should use the Vocabulary Words in their answers.

1. Why would a turtle be **basking** in a bay for three months?

2. Do you think wet sand looks **sleek**? Why or why not?

3. Do you think the cause Max works for is **vital**? Explain.

4. Name something that can **damage** a turtle's shell.

5. What is the purpose of **analyzing** the turtle's blood?

6. What do both Max and the veterinarians **detect** when they observe Yellow-Blue?

EXTEND WORD MEANINGS

Objective
- *To extend meanings of words in context*

CRITICAL THINKING To help extend students' understanding of the Vocabulary Words, have them answer the following questions. Tell students to explain their answers, and encourage discussion.

1. If you are **analyzing** a book, are you looking closely at the details or skimming for big ideas?

2. Describe a day when you might be **basking** in the grass.

3. If a vase was **damaged** during shipping, what did it look like when you received it?

4. What is something that is **vital** for you to do to be successful in school?

5. Name a profession that would involve **detecting** things.

6. Describe an animal that is **sleek**.

CUMULATIVE REVIEW

Objective
- *To use word relationships to determine meaning*

REVIEW VOCABULARY Discuss students' answers to these questions.

1. Do you think it is **appropriate** to be **basking** in the middle of the sidewalk? Explain.

2. What **deduction** could you make about a person who got upset after finding one **measly** dirt speck on his or her **sleek** sports car?

3. When might a **portable** radio be **vital** to your survival?

4. Why is it **vital** for blood to **circulate** through the body?

5. What **damage** might a **boisterous** child cause in a home?

6. Is it **practical** to try **analyzing** the feelings of a **fickle** person?

7. If a captain **scours** the water to **detect** rocks **protruding** from the water, what might he or she be trying to avoid?

Vocabulary **Tested**

Lesson 20		Lesson 21	
appropriate	boisterous	basking	damage
deduction	practical	sleek	analyzing
measly	fickle	vital	detect
portable	scours		
circulate	protrude		

15 Min. each

Spelling: Words with Word Parts
in-, out-, down-, up-

Objective
- *To correctly spell words with the word parts in-, out-, down-, and up-*

Spelling Words

1. **incompetent**	11. **outpatient**
2. **uphold**	12. **outspoken**
3. **inconsiderate**	13. **outwit**
4. **indecisive**	14. **downbeat**
5. **outrank**	15. **downgrade**
6. **inhumane**	16. **downplay**
7. **inorganic**	17. **downtown**
8. **income**	18. **uplift**
9. **invertebrate**	19. **upstage**
10. **outgoing**	20. **uptight**

Challenge Words

21. **insensitive**	24. **downstage**
22. **outcry**	25. **insecure**
23. **upkeep**	

Day 1 — PRETEST/SELF-CHECK

Routine Card 10

ADMINISTER THE PRETEST Use the Dictation Sentences under Day 5. Help students self-check their pretests, using **Transparency LA129.**

Allow students to study the words they misspelled. Have them use the steps *Say, Look, Spell, Write, Check.*

ADVANCED

Challenge Words Provide these Dictation Sentences:

21. Her comment was **insensitive**.

22. There was an **outcry** from the crowd when he dropped the ball.

23. Large yards require **upkeep**.

24. The singer moved **downstage**.

25. He felt **insecure** about his public-speaking ability.

Day 2 — TEACH/MODEL

WORD SORT Display **Transparency LA129** again. Discuss the meanings of the Spelling Words, as necessary. Then have students copy the chart and write each Spelling Word where it belongs.

Write the words *indecisive, outspoken, downplay,* and *uplift* on the board. Ask students to identify the word parts (*in-, out-, down-, up-*) in each word. Point out that when these word parts are added to a base word, the spelling of the base word doesn't change.

HANDWRITING Have students practice writing words with *out-*, being careful to form *o* and *u* properly, with just one stroke between them.

outrank

Transparency LA129

Words with Word Parts *in-, out-, down-, up-*

Spelling Words

1. incompetent	6. inhumane	11. outpatient	16. downplay	
2. uphold	7. inorganic	12. outspoken	17. downtown	
3. inconsiderate	8. income	13. outwit	18. uplift	
4. indecisive	9. invertebrate	14. downbeat	19. upstage	
5. outrank	10. outgoing	15. downgrade	20. uptight	

in-	out-	down-	up-
incompetent	outrank	downbeat	uphold
inconsiderate	outgoing	downgrade	uplift
indecisive	outpatient	downplay	upstage
inhumane	outspoken	downtown	uptight
inorganic	outwit		
income			
invertebrate			

The word parts *in-, out-, down-,* and *up-* can be added to some root words to change their meaning. The spelling of the root word does not change when *in-, out-, down-,* or *up-* is added.

Grade 5, Lesson 21 — LA129 — Spelling

Transparency LA129

▲ Practice Book, p. 127

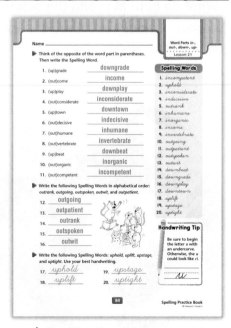

▲ Spelling Practice Book, p. 84

WORD CHAINS Have students work in pairs to create word chains. Have partners begin by writing one Spelling Word. Have them then write another Spelling Word crossing the first word at one letter, and so on. Tell students to create a crossword puzzle by drawing empty boxes for their word chains on graph paper, adding numbers, and writing clues. Have students exchange their puzzles with another pair.

i	n	c	o	m	e			o	
			u					u	
			t					t	
			g			u		r	
		d	o	w	n	p	l	a	y
			i			h		n	
			n			o		k	
			g			l			
						d			

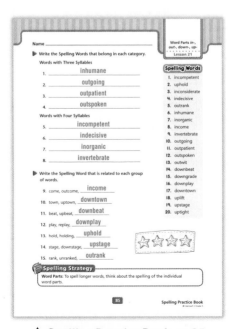

▲ Spelling Practice Book, p. 85

SOUNDS AND LETTERS Tell students that thinking about how letters correspond to sounds can help them correctly spell words. Have students practice adding the word parts to the base words, thinking about the relationships between the letters and the sounds.

APPLY TO WRITING

SOUNDS AND LETTERS Ask students to choose four Spelling Words from the list—one each with the word parts *in-*, *out-*, *down-*, and *up-*. Have them write sentences containing the words and then use the sounds-and-letters strategy to make sure they have spelled the words correctly.

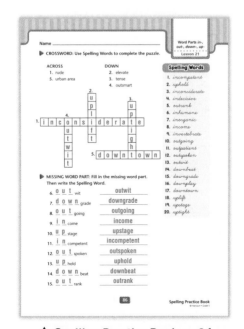

▲ Spelling Practice Book, p. 86

DICTATION SENTENCES

1. The **incompetent** baker burned the bread.
2. She agreed to **uphold** the laws.
3. Talking during a movie is **inconsiderate**.
4. She was **indecisive** about what to do next.
5. Army majors **outrank** corporals.
6. The **inhumane** treatment of animals is wrong.
7. An **inorganic** substance does not contain carbon.
8. Has your **income** increased this year?
9. An **invertebrate** is an animal without a backbone.
10. My brother is very **outgoing**.
11. The **outpatient** went home after seeing his doctor.
12. They are **outspoken** about the importance of education.
13. She tried to **outwit** her older sister.
14. His **downbeat** expression upset me.
15. Did they **downgrade** his condition from serious to critical?
16. She tried to **downplay** her role.
17. Let's go to the library **downtown**.
18. The good news will **uplift** their mood.
19. She moved slowly **upstage**.
20. Don't get **uptight** about the test.

Writing Trait: Sentence Fluency
Persuasive Letter

15 Min. each

Objectives
- *To use a variety of sentence types*
- *To write a persuasive letter*

Writing Trait ▶ Sentence Fluency

- Variety of sentence types used
- Variety of sentence lengths used
- Variety of sentence structures used

Grammar for Writing

As students revise their paragraphs, note whether they need additional support with these skills:
- **Common and Proper Nouns,** pp. T68–T69, Theme 3
- **Punctuation Round-up,** pp. T282–T283, Theme 6
- **Complete, Declarative, and Interrogative Sentences,** pp. T70–T71, Theme 1
- **Action and Linking Verbs,** pp. T68–T69, Theme 5

▲ **Writer's Companion, Lesson 21**

Day 1 TEACH/MODEL

SENTENCE FLUENCY Remind students that they have learned about different types of sentences. Explain that good writers use a variety of sentence types and lengths in their writing to make it more interesting.

ANALYZE THE MENTOR TEXT Display the passage from "Interrupted Journey: Saving Endangered Sea Turtles" on **Transparency LA132**. Have a volunteer read the passage aloud. Then work with students to analyze the sentences in the chart. Point out that the author has used sentences of different types and different lengths.

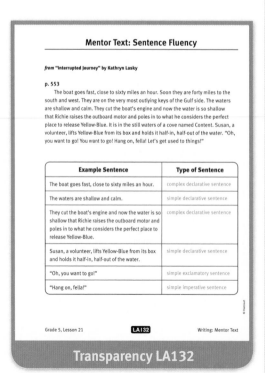

Transparency LA132

Day 2 PRACTICE/APPLY

ANALYZE THE STUDENT MODEL Display **Transparency LA133**. Have a volunteer read the persuasive letter aloud. Review with students correct letter form. Then point out that an effective persuasive letter clearly states the writer's opinion and supports the opinion with details. Have students identify examples of different types of sentences used in the letter. Ask students whether the writer included enough sentence types and lengths to make the letter interesting as well as persuasive.

Transparency LA133

THEME 5 WRITING		
Reading-Writing Connection	Persuasive Essay	Sentence Fluency
LESSON	**FORM**	**TRAIT**
21	Persuasive Letter	Sentence Fluency
22	Persuasive Paragraph	Sentence Fluency
23	Poem	Organization
24	Narrative Composition	Organization
25 REVIEW	Revise and Publish	Sentence Fluency/Organization

Day 3 PREWRITE

WRITING PROMPTS Display **Transparency LA134** and read aloud the prompt to students. Tell students to use a graphic organizer such as the one below to help them plan their letters.

Audience: (name and address)
Type of project:
Why you think it's important:
What you want your audience to do:

Day 4 DRAFT

BEGIN TO DRAFT Have students follow these steps to draft their letters.

1. **Begin** with an appropriate greeting.

2. **Organize** the body of your letter in logical order. Explain the problem. Give your opinion, supported by details. End with a call for action.

3. **Use** a variety of sentence lengths and types.

4. **Close** your letter and sign it.

Day 5 REVISE AND REFLECT

PEER CONFERENCE CHECKLIST Have pairs of students use this checklist to discuss their letters.

• Is the letter formatted correctly?

• Are the problem and the writer's opinion about it clearly stated? Are they supported with details?

• Is there a clear call for action?

• Has the writer used a variety of sentence types and lengths?

• Are action and linking verbs used correctly?

Students may want to keep their revised letters in their portfolios.

Daily Writing Prompts

DAY 1 Writing Prompt:
There are many interesting ocean animals. Choose one that interests you. Write a paragraph that tells about this animal.

DAY 2 Writing Prompt:
"Interrupted Journey" begins with Max Nolan and his mother rescuing Yellow-Blue. Think about what they may have said to each other after finding the turtle. Now write a short dialogue that might have occurred between them.

DAY 3 Writing Prompt:
Most communities have volunteer projects that help the environment. Learn about one such project that you think is important. Write a letter to a friend describing the project and explaining why you think it is important.

DAY 4 Writing Prompt:
"Interrupted Journey" is told from a third-person point of view. Think about how the story would be different if it were told from the turtle's point of view. Write a paragraph describing one event from the story from the turtle's perspective.

DAY 5 Writing Prompt:
Most communities have a landmark or natural area that should be preserved or protected. Think of such a place in your community. Now write a letter to the editor of a local newspaper calling for it to be protected.

Grade 5, Lesson 21   **LA134**   Daily Writing Prompts

Transparency LA134

NOTE: A 4-point rubric appears on page R8.

SCORING RUBRIC						
	6	**5**	**4**	**3**	**2**	**1**
FOCUS	Completely focused, purposeful.	Focused on topic and purpose.	Generally focused on topic and purpose.	Somewhat focused on topic and purpose.	Related to topic but does not maintain focus.	Lacks focus and purpose.
ORGANIZATION	Ideas progress logically; paper conveys sense of completeness.	Organization mostly clear; paper gives sense of completeness.	Organization mostly clear; but some lapses occur; may seem unfinished.	Some sense of organization; seems unfinished.	Little sense of organization.	Little or no sense of organization.
SUPPORT	Strong, specific details; clear, exact language; freshness of expression.	Strong, specific details; clear, exact language.	Adequate support and word choice.	Limited supporting details; limited word choice.	Few supporting details; limited word choice.	Little development; limited or unclear word choice.
CONVENTIONS	Varied sentences; few, if any, errors.	Varied sentences; few errors.	Some sentence variety; few errors.	Simple sentence structures; some errors.	Simple sentence structures; many errors.	Unclear sentence structures; many errors.

REPRODUCIBLE RUBRIC appears on page R7.

Grammar: Verbs
Action and Linking Verbs

Objective
- *To use action and linking verbs correctly in writing and speaking*

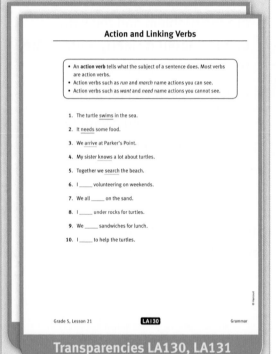

Action and Linking Verbs

- An **action verb** tells what the subject of a sentence does. Most verbs are action verbs.
- Action verbs such as *run* and *march* name actions you can see.
- Action verbs such as *want* and *need* name actions you cannot see.

1. The turtle <u>swims</u> in the sea.
2. It <u>needs</u> some food.
3. We <u>arrive</u> at Parker's Point.
4. My sister <u>knows</u> a lot about turtles.
5. Together we <u>search</u> the beach.
6. I _____ volunteering on weekends.
7. We all _____ on the sand.
8. I _____ under rocks for turtles.
9. We _____ sandwiches for lunch.
10. I _____ to help the turtles.

Grade 5, Lesson 21 **LA130** Grammar

Transparencies LA130, LA131

E L L

Language Structures Help students understand the linking verb *be* by using this model:

- He always helpful. (incorrect)
- He is always helpful. (correct)

See *ELL Teacher Guide* Lesson 21 for support in scaffolding instruction.

Day 1 — TEACH/MODEL

DAILY PROOFREADING

1. Has you ever seen a Sea Turtle? (Have; sea turtle?)
2. He is an friendly, out going person. (a friendly, outgoing)

INTRODUCE THE CONCEPT Display **Transparency LA130**. Read aloud the boxed text. Explain that in sentence 1, *swims* is an **action verb** that names an action you can see. Point out that *needs* in sentence 2 is an action verb that names an action you cannot see.

Have students find and underline the action verbs in sentences 3–5. Then ask them to rewrite sentences 6–10, filling in each blank with an action verb.

✓ LANGUAGE ARTS CHECKPOINT

If students have difficulty with the concepts, see pages S8–S9 to reteach.

Day 2 — TEACH/MODEL

DAILY PROOFREADING

3. We'ell work for an hour and, then eat lunch. (We'll; and then)
4. This organization has two office down-town. (offices; downtown.)

EXTEND THE CONCEPT Display **Transparency LA131**. Read aloud the top box. In sentence 1, the verb *are* links the subject *they* to the word *friends*. In sentence 2, the verb *am* links the subject *I* to the word *proud*. Have students identify each linking verb in sentences 3–4, and tell if it renames or describes the subject.

BUILD LANGUAGE STRUCTURES Have students complete each sentence.

They _____ good volunteers.

The day _____ very interesting.

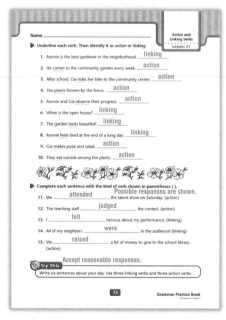

▲ **Grammar Practice Book, p. 73**

Day 3 — TEACH/MODEL

DAILY PROOFREADING

5. She are being undecisive.
(She is; indecisive.)

6. Snakes is unvertebrates.
(Snakes are invertebrates.)

EXTEND THE CONCEPT Display **Transparency LA131** again. Ask students to identify the verbs in sentences 5–8 and tell whether each is an action verb or a linking verb.

Then read aloud the boxed text about the verb *be*. Explain that forms of the verb *be* can act as linking verbs, or as helping verbs for other main verbs.

Then have students write four sentences about a creature that lives in the sea. Ask them to use two forms of *be* as linking verbs and two forms of *be* as helping verbs.

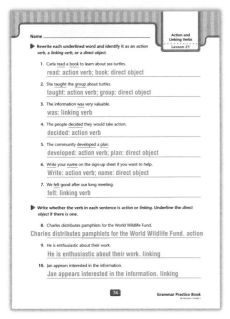

▲ **Grammar Practice Book, p. 74**

Day 4 — APPLY TO WRITING

DAILY PROOFREADING

7. Marco being patient with the unconsiderate woman. (was being; inconsiderate)

8. We have talking about the interestingest animals. (have been; most interesting)

MY VOLUNTEER DIARY Have students imagine that they are volunteering at a beach clean-up. Ask them to write a short diary entry about their experience. Tell them to include both action verbs and linking verbs.

COMMON ERRORS

Error: She **checking** the turtles.
Correct: She **is checking** the turtles.

Error: They **waiting** to swim.
Correct: They **are waiting** to swim.

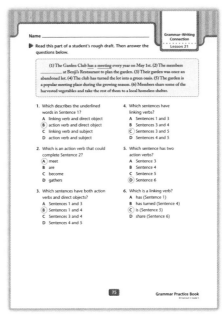

▲ **Grammar Practice Book, p. 75**

Day 5 — REVIEW

DAILY PROOFREADING

9. Wow that is an up lifting story!
(Wow! That; uplifting)

10. We is spreading the word about these unhumane practices.
(We are; inhumane)

PROOFREAD FOR ACTION AND LINKING VERBS Display the following sentences. Explain that each sentence is missing a verb. Have students rewrite each sentence, adding the type of verb called for in parentheses.

1. We to the pet store. (action) (go)

2. My mother pretty. (linking) (is)

3. We about the turtle we brought in. (action) (ask)

4. I concerned about its safety. (linking) (am)

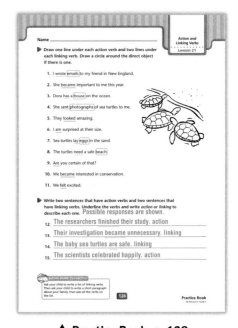

▲ **Practice Book, p. 128**

Speaking & Listening

Give a Persuasive Speech

Objectives
- *To orally present and support a point of view*
- *To use verbal and nonverbal techniques to persuade an audience*

Have students use the persuasive letters they wrote as the source for a persuasive speech they will give to the class. Share these **organizational strategies**:

ORGANIZING CONTENT

- Begin with a statement that clearly identifies the topic and states your point of view about it.
- Organize your points in a logical way, such as from least persuasive to most persuasive.
- End your speech with a call to action.

Before students deliver their persuasive speeches, share with them the following **speaking strategies**:

SPEAKING STRATEGIES

- Speak clearly, using expression to convey your feelings about the topic.
- Make eye contact with your audience. Use your notes only for reference.
- Use correct grammar and a variety of sentences to make your speech clear and engaging.
- Use gestures and pauses to highlight or emphasize important points.

Listen to a Persuasive Speech

Objectives
- *To identify and evaluate a speaker's point of view*
- *To listen and respond to a speaker's verbal and non-verbal cues*

Remind students to listen to find out the reasons the speaker feels as he or she does about the topic. Share these **listening strategies** with students:

LISTENING STRATEGIES

- Show interest in what the speaker is saying.
- Watch for gestures and other signals of important points.
- Make a mental note of anything you do not understand.

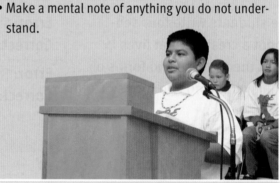

After each speech, have students ask clarifying questions and then tell whether the speech has convinced them to adopt the speaker's viewpoint.

Guide audience members to evaluate each speaker's use of persuasive techniques. Ask
What arguments did the speaker use? Were these arguments effective? What other arguments might get listeners to think or act in the desired way?

RUBRIC See rubric for Presentations on page R5.

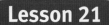

Media Literacy

TECHNOLOGY

Survey of Personal Communication

Objective
• *To understand forms of personal communication*

DISCUSS PERSONAL COMMUNICATION Ask students how they communicate with family and friends when they are apart. (Possible responses: telephone, cell phone, e-mail) Use the chart below to explain three forms of **personal communication** in modern media:

PERSONAL COMMUNICATION

Type	Definition	How Used
e-mail	short for "electronic mail"; a system of exchanging messages through computers	• to send/receive text messages, photos, articles, and other attachments
instant messaging	instant communication between two or more users who are online at the same time	• to send/receive messages in real time
cell phone	short for "cellular"; a mobile phone that can make and receive calls over a wide area	• to talk • to send/receive e-mail, take pictures, play games or music

SURVEY PERSONAL COMMUNICATION USAGE Have students survey friends and relatives about their personal communication usage. Have them record the results in a chart or a graph to show how the forms are used in everyday life.

WEEKLY LESSON TEST

• Selection Comprehension with Short Response
• Focus Skill
• Robust Vocabulary
• Grammar
• Fluency Passage *FRESH READS*
• Podcasting: Assessing Fluency

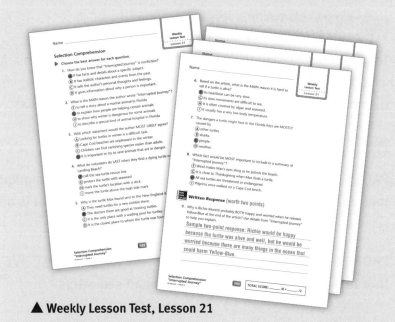

▲ **Weekly Lesson Test, Lesson 21**

GO online For prescriptions, see pp. A2–A6. Also available electronically on *StoryTown Online Assessment* and ExamView®.

Leveled Readers
Reinforcing Skills and Strategies

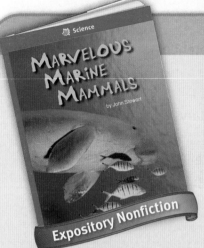

Expository Nonfiction

BELOW-LEVEL

Marvelous Marine Mammals

SUMMARY This selection describes two unique sea mammals: the manatee and the sea otter.

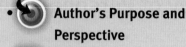

-  **Author's Purpose and Perspective**
- **Summarize**
- **VOCABULARY:** *basking, sleek, vital, damage, analyzing, detect*

Build Background/Set Purpose

Tell students to read the title and look at the photographs. Ask them to predict what they will learn about as they read the book. Remind students that summarizing as they read can help them keep track of main ideas.

Guided Reading

PAGES 3–14 COMPARE AND CONTRAST What is one similarity between manatees and sea otters? (They are both endangered.) **What is one difference?** (Manatees are very large, and sea otters are small.)

PAGES 13–14  **AUTHOR'S PURPOSE AND PERSPECTIVE How does the author feel about protecting manatees and sea otters?** (He thinks it is important to protect these creatures and their habitats.)

After Reading

Have student pairs think of ways to protect endangered animals in their area.

FLUENCY: EXPRESSION Have pairs of students reread a page aloud. Explain that reading with expression can help make information more interesting.

Think Critically *(See inside back cover for questions.)*

1. Sea otters were hunted for their fur.

2. to keep the top layer of their fur ("guard hairs") clean

3. Answers will vary.

4. to inform readers about sea otters and manatees and the dangers they face

5. People accidentally kill them and ruin their habitat.

LEVELED READER TEACHER GUIDE

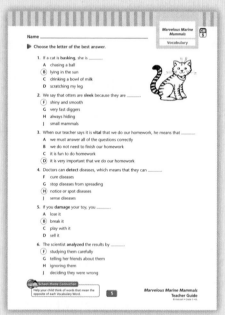

▲ Vocabulary, p. 5

▲ Comprehension, p. 6

ON-LEVEL

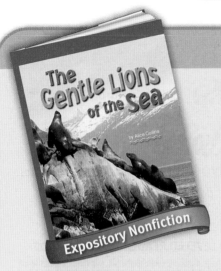

Expository Nonfiction

The Gentle Lions of the Sea

SUMMARY This selection gives facts about sea lions and introduces readers to two sea lions, Guthrie and Ballou, who live at an aquarium.

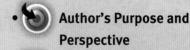

• 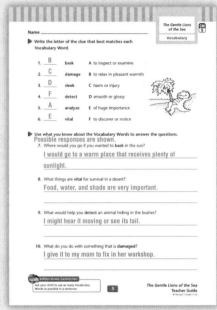 **Author's Purpose and Perspective**

• **Summarize**

• **VOCABULARY:** *basking, sleek, vital, damage, analyzing, detect*

Build Background/Set Purpose

Have students preview the book. Ask students what they think "lions of the sea" are. Then have students set a purpose for reading. Remind students that summarizing can help them keep track of what they read.

Guided Reading

PAGES 4–5 CAUSE AND EFFECT Why do male sea lions gain up to 200 pounds? (to attract a mate)

PAGES 11–13 AUTHOR'S PURPOSE AND PERSPECTIVE How does the author feel about Guthrie and Ballou? How can you tell? (He thinks they are smart and talented because they are obedient and have learned amazing things.)

After Reading

Have pairs of students discuss the main ideas in the selection.

FLUENCY: EXPRESSION Have pairs of students take turns rereading two pages from the book aloud. Ask students to give each other feedback on expression.

Think Critically *(See inside back cover for questions.)*

1. Answers will vary.

2. They get medical treatment and are protected from the dangers of the wild.

3. Compare: They both live at the aquarium and like to eat herring, capelin, and squid. Contrast: Guthrie is larger and more aggressive than Ballou.

4. to inform readers about sea lions and the dangers they face

5. by destroying them for commercial use

LEVELED READER TEACHER GUIDE

▲ Vocabulary, p. 5

▲ Comprehension, p. 6

Leveled Readers
Reinforcing Skills and Strategies

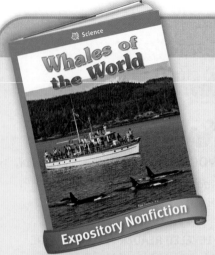

 **ADVANCED**

Whales of the World

SUMMARY This selection describes the physical features and habits of a variety of whales, including dolphins and porpoises.

- 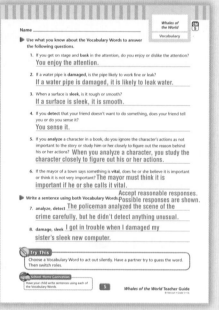 **Author's Purpose and Perspective**
- **Summarize**
- **VOCABULARY:** *basking, sleek, vital, damage, analyzing, detect*

LEVELED READER TEACHER GUIDE

▲ Vocabulary, p. 5

Build Background/Set Purpose

Ask students to share what they know about sea mammals, such as whales, dolphins, and porpoises. Then ask students to preview the book and set a purpose for reading. Remind them to summarize to keep track of main ideas.

During Reading

CREATE A VENN DIAGRAM Distribute the Venn diagram on *Teacher Resource Book* page 82 to pairs of students. Have students complete the diagram by writing the characteristics of land mammals and sea mammals.

After Reading

Have students work in small groups to create a summary of the book. Tell them to include main ideas and important details.

FLUENCY: EXPRESSION Tell students to imagine that they are narrating a documentary. Have student pairs take turns rereading aloud with expression.

Think Critically *(See inside back cover for questions.)*

1. dolphins: beaks, pointed teeth; porpoises: no beaks, shovel-shaped teeth

2. Dolphins make sounds that echo off nearby objects. When the sound comes back, the dolphins feel the vibrations and can tell the location of objects.

3. Both whales are mammals. Baleen whales strain their food from the water. Toothed whales chew their food and are smaller. Baleen whales have two blowholes, but toothed whales only have one.

4. to educate people about different kinds of whales

5. Answers will vary.

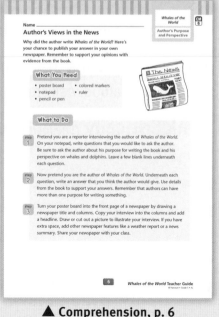

▲ Comprehension, p. 6

E L L

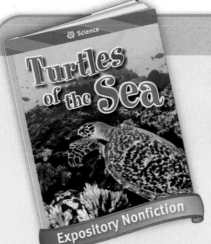

Turtles of the Sea

SUMMARY This selection describes two species of turtles—the Kemp's ridley sea turtle and the loggerhead sea turtle.

- **Build Background**
- **Concept Vocabulary**
- **Scaffolded Language Development**

Build Background/Set Purpose

Preview the book with students. Explain that in this book students will learn about *turtles,* their *nesting* habits, their *shells,* and their *habitats.* Remind students that summarizing as they read can help them remember main ideas.

Guided Reading

As students read, tell them to look for words that signal transitions and connections, such as, *when, if, luckily,* and *so.* Clarify idioms such as *pitch in, over the years,* and *come across.*

PAGES 3–14 **AUTHOR'S PURPOSE AND PERSPECTIVE** **What details tell you that the author cares about protecting sea turtles?** (He mentions helping them survive and claims that we have to protect them.)

PAGES 4–13 **COMPARE AND CONTRAST** **What is one difference between Kemp's ridley and loggerhead sea turtles?** (Kemp's ridleys are endangered, but loggerheads are only threatened.)

After Reading

FLUENCY: EXPRESSION Reread a section aloud with appropriate expression. Then have pairs of students reread a page aloud, focusing on expression.

Encourage students to use concept words such as *endangered species, threatened,* and *extinction* while discussing the book.

Scaffolded Language Development

See inside back cover for teacher-led activity.
Provide additional examples and explanation as needed.

LEVELED READER TEACHER GUIDE

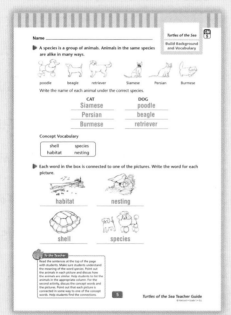

▲ Build Background, p. 5

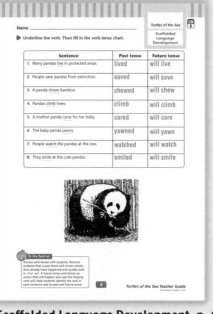

▲ Scaffolded Language Development, p. 6

THEME WRITING OVERVIEW

Reading-Writing Connection ➤ Persuasive Composition

LESSON	FORM	TRAIT
21	Persuasive Letter	Sentence Fluency
22	Persuasive Paragraph	Sentence Fluency
23	Poem	Organization
24	Narrative	Organization
REVIEW 25	Revise and Publish	Sentence Fluency and Organization

Reading-Writing Connection

Persuasive Composition

Focus on

Sentence Fluency and Organization

Students will

- Analyze a persuasive literature model

- Narrow a topic

- Apply outlining skills

- Draft a persuasive composition

- Revise by adding persuasive words

- Proofread

- Self-assess and publish the final version of a persuasive composition

Analyze Writer's Craft: Persuasive Writing

Objectives
- *To analyze writing traits in persuasive writing*
- *To use sentence fluency and organization appropriate to writing persuasive compositions*

Genre Characteristics

DISCUSS PERSUASIVE WRITING   Read aloud the first paragraph on *Student Edition* page 560, and review with students the characteristics of persuasive writing. Then ask a volunteer to read aloud the passage from "Interrupted Journey." As students listen to the passage, have them listen for words intended to persuade readers as to the urgency of the turtles' plight.

Writing Trait > Word Choice

DISCUSS WORD CHOICE   Read aloud the first note on page 560. Ask students what other phrase communicates a sense of urgency. *(right now)*

Writing Trait > Sentence Fluency

DISCUSS SENTENCE FLUENCY   Read aloud the second note on page 560. Point out that the short sentence discussed has a greater impact because it is preceded by a longer sentence.

Reading-Writing Connection

Analyze Writer's Craft: Persuasive Writing

The purpose of **persuasive writing** is to persuade readers to agree with the author's **opinion**. Authors give **reasons** and **examples** to support their arguments. They use powerful language to persuade the reader to take action. Read the paragraph below from "Interrupted Journey" by Kathryn Lasky. Look for ways the author tries to persuade readers to agree with her opinion.

Writing Trait

WORD CHOICE
Carefully chosen words and phrases—*vital, threatened, most endangered of all,* and *vanishing*—give a sense of urgency about saving sea turtles.

Writing Trait

SENTENCE FLUENCY
The writer uses a variety of sentence lengths. Short sentences, such as *They are a vanishing species,* have a strong emotional impact.

> Max and his mother and the other volunteers work for a vital cause. All sea turtles are threatened or endangered; Kemp's ridleys are the most endangered of all. Right now on our planet there are fewer than eight thousand Kemp's ridley turtles left. They are a vanishing species.

560

STAGES OF THE WRITING PROCESS Adjust the pacing to meet students' needs. Guide them back and forth between the steps until the final product meets established criteria.

PREWRITE, pp. T82–T83	DRAFT, pp. T84–T85
Writing Trait > Ideas	**Writing Trait > Ideas**
• Narrowing a Topic	• Supporting Opinions
Writing Trait > Organization	**Writing Trait > Sentence Fluency**
• Outlining	• Writing a Strong Ending

Persuasive Composition

In a **persuasive composition**, a writer states an **opinion** and gives **reasons** that support the opinion. If a writer wants to persuade a reader to do something, the composition may end with a **call to action**. Read this persuasive composition written by a student named Daniel. Notice how Daniel's **word choices** appeal to the reader's emotions.

Student Writing Model

Protect Our Coasts
by Daniel K.

Everyone should help protect the coastlines of the United States. People depend on coastal areas for recreation and for many other things. Fish and other wildlife depend on these areas for food and shelter. Unfortunately, our shorelines are being destroyed.

How do people benefit from coastal areas? Numerous fishing grounds provide delicious foods such as fish, crab, shrimp, and lobster. In addition, some marine organisms are used to make medicines. These organisms need a clean environment to survive, but human activity is poisoning them. Sewage, fertilizers, and trash are killing marine life.

Writing Trait

SENTENCE FLUENCY Daniel begins the second paragraph with an **interrogative sentence** to interact with the reader.

561

Student Writing Model
Persuasive Composition

Introduce the Form

DISCUSS PERSUASIVE COMPOSITIONS Have students read the first paragraph on page 561. Use the following points to summarize the characteristics of a persuasive composition:

- includes a statement of opinion
- gives reasons to support the opinion
- may end with a call to action

READ AND DISCUSS THE STUDENT MODEL Have students read Daniel's persuasive composition on pages 561–562. Discuss the notes on each page.

REVISE, p. T86	PROOFREAD, p. T87	EVALUATE/PUBLISH, pp. T88–T89
Writing Trait → Word Choice • Adding Persuasive Words	Writing Trait → Conventions • Checking Helping Verbs	• Self-Assessment • Publish and Present

Student Writing Model
Persuasive Composition

RESPOND TO THE STUDENT MODEL Ask students the questions below.

1. **What is the topic of Daniel's persuasive composition?** (protecting America's coastlines) **Where does he state his opinion on the topic?** (in the first paragraph)

2. **What reasons does Daniel give to support his opinion?** (People depend on coastal areas; fish and wildlife depend on these areas, too.) **In which paragraphs does he develop these reasons?** (paragraphs 2 and 3)

3. **What is one example of how Daniel has used facts to support his opinion?** (Possible response: He states that marine organisms are used to make medicines; this fact supports the opinion that marine organisms should be protected.)

4. **How does Daniel include a call to action?** (Possible response: He gives examples of ways in which people can help coastal habitats.)

5. **How does Daniel conclude his composition?** (by restating his opinion)

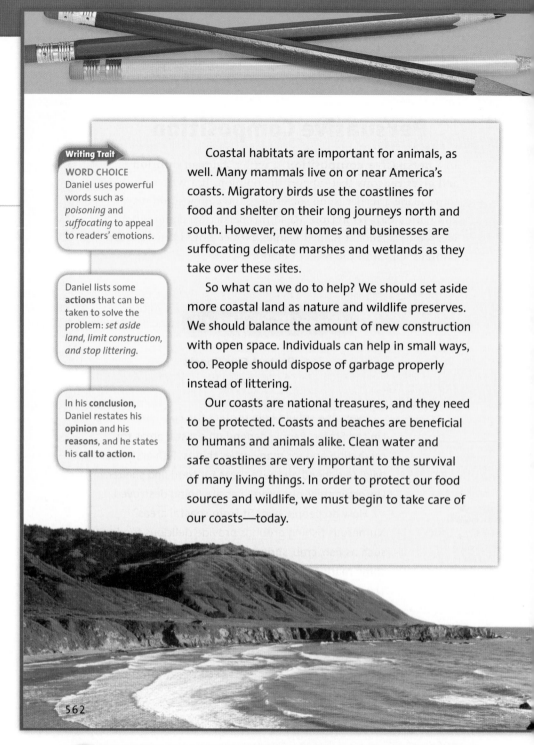

Writing Trait

WORD CHOICE Daniel uses powerful words such as *poisoning* and *suffocating* to appeal to readers' emotions.

Daniel lists some **actions** that can be taken to solve the problem: *set aside land, limit construction, and stop littering.*

In his **conclusion**, Daniel restates his **opinion** and his **reasons**, and he states his **call to action.**

Coastal habitats are important for animals, as well. Many mammals live on or near America's coasts. Migratory birds use the coastlines for food and shelter on their long journeys north and south. However, new homes and businesses are suffocating delicate marshes and wetlands as they take over these sites.

So what can we do to help? We should set aside more coastal land as nature and wildlife preserves. We should balance the amount of new construction with open space. Individuals can help in small ways, too. People should dispose of garbage properly instead of littering.

Our coasts are national treasures, and they need to be protected. Coasts and beaches are beneficial to humans and animals alike. Clean water and safe coastlines are very important to the survival of many living things. In order to protect our food sources and wildlife, we must begin to take care of our coasts—today.

562

BELOW-LEVEL

Paraphrasing Tell students that an effective persuasive composition often ends by restating the opinion stated in the introduction. Remind students that to paraphrase, they can use synonyms and change the word order. Point out the first and last sentences of Daniel's composition, and guide students to recognize that they state the same idea in a slightly different way.

Now look at how Daniel prepared to write his persuasive essay.

Brainstorm Ideas

First, Daniel used an idea web to brainstorm topics he is interested in. Then he chose the topic about which he has the strongest opinions—the beach. Next, Daniel listed his opinions about the beach. He chose *I think everyone should protect our coasts* because he had strong reasons to support this opinion.

Outline Ideas

Then Daniel created an outline to organize his supporting reasons and suggestions for solving the problem.

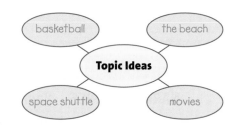

My Opinions About the Beach
  I think California has the best beaches.
* I think everyone should protect our coasts.
  I think surfing is the best sport.

Title: Protect Our Coasts
  I. Introduction
      A. Opinion
      B. Problem
  II. Coasts Are Important to Humans
      A. Benefits
      B. Dangers
  III. Coasts Are Important to Animals
      A. Benefits
      B. Dangers
  IV. Actions to Solve Problem
      A. Create preserves
      B. Cut down on development
      C. Stop littering
  V. Conclusion
      A. Summary
      B. Call to action

563

Discuss Prewriting

DANIEL'S PLANNING AND PREWRITING Have students read page 563. Tell them that before Daniel could start writing his persuasive composition, he had to plan and prewrite. Discuss the following with students.

- **Brainstorm Ideas** Daniel used an idea web to brainstorm topics that interested him. He chose the one for which he has the strongest opinions. Then he listed several opinions about the topic and chose one he had strong reasons to support.

- **Outline Ideas** Daniel made an outline to organize his ideas. He began with an introduction and ended with a conclusion. Then he listed reasons and details in the order in which he would include them in the composition. The first two body paragraphs focus on reasons to support his opinion. The third body paragraph proposes a plan of action.

Tell students that before they begin to write their own persuasive compositions, they will learn how to choose and narrow their topics and make an outline to organize their ideas. (See pp. T82–T83.)

Prewrite

NARROWING A TOPIC
Writing Trait ▸ Ideas

Objective
• *To narrow the focus of a topic*

Teach/Model

NARROWING A TOPIC Tell students that they are going to write a persuasive composition. Students should choose a topic that interests them and about which they have a strong opinion. Draw on the board an inverted triangle such as the one below as you model for students how to narrow a topic.

The Importance of Science

Why Schools Should Support Science

Why Schools Should Fund Science Fairs

Think Aloud The topic "The Importance of Science" is too broad. "Why Schools Should Support Science" is narrower, but most schools already support science. The topic "Why Schools Should Fund Science Fairs" is narrow enough to support with strong, specific reasons.

Guided Practice

NARROW TOPICS Name some other broad topics, such as protecting animals or not being wasteful. Discuss with students narrower topics for each one.

Apply to Writing

CHOOSE A TOPIC Have students brainstorm topics for their persuasive compositions. Make sure students choose a topic they feel strongly about and one they can support with facts or examples.

DISCUSS RUBRIC Distribute to students copies of the writing rubric on page R7. Tell students that their writing will be evaluated on a number of criteria and that they should keep these points in mind as they write their compositions. Point out to students the criteria for a score of 6, an excellent paper.

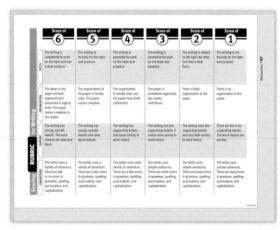

▲ **Teacher Edition, p. R7**

OUTLINING

Writing Trait > Organization

Objective
• *To understand how to develop an outline*

Teach/Model

USE QUESTIONS TO MAKE AN OUTLINE Tell students that Daniel generated questions and made an outline before writing his composition about protecting the coastline. Display **Transparency LA135** and use it to model organizing information in an outline.

Guided Practice

ADD IDEAS TO AN OUTLINE Guide students to use Daniel's answers to the questions to complete the outline.

Think Aloud The questions Daniel asked helped him form an opinion and come up with reasons to support it. To organize his ideas, he made an outline. Each Roman numeral stands for a paragraph in his composition. Each capital letter stands for an idea within a paragraph.

Apply to Writing

CREATE AN OUTLINE Have students ask and answer the questions at the top of **Transparency LA135**. Then have them use their answers to create an outline for their persuasive composition.

CONFERENCE

Outlining Visit with students to check that they understand how to use an outline to plan their persuasive compositions.

**Prewriting a Persuasive Essay:
From Ideas to Outline**

Generating Questions to Get Ideas
• **What** do I have a strong opinion about?
  • Everyone should protect our coasts.
• **Why** do I feel that way?
  • Coasts are important to humans and animals.
• **What** can people do to protect the coasts?
  • People can create preserves, cut down on development, and stop littering.

Organizing Ideas in an Outline
  I. Introduction
      A. Grab readers' attention.
      B. State problem and opinion: Everyone should protect our coasts.
 II. Reason #1:   Coasts are important to humans.
      A. Benefits
      B. Dangers
III. Reason #2:   Coasts are important to animals.
      A. Benefits
      B. Dangers
 IV. Actions to Solve Problem:
      A.   Create preserves.
      B.   Cut down on development.
      C.   Stop littering.
  V. Conclusion
      A. Summarize problem.
      B. Sum up the call to action.

Transparency LA135

Draft

SUPPORTING OPINIONS
Writing Trait ▸ Ideas

Objective
• *To support reasons with facts and examples*

Teach/Model

SUPPORT OPINIONS Display **Transparency LA136**. Read the boxed information at the top of the transparency. Then point out how Daniel's body paragraphs support his opinion with reasons. Use this model:

> **Think Aloud** **The opinion that Daniel wants to support is "Everyone should help protect America's coasts," so he begins his first body paragraph by asking *How do people benefit from the coasts?* Then he gives two facts to show how people benefit—we get food and medicine. He also gives examples of how sea life is threatened.**

Then point out that Daniel states his first reason in the form of a question. Point out that leads like this are effective ways to grab the readers' attention and involve them in your argument. Discuss with students leads that they've found effective in stories or magazine or newspaper articles.

Guided Practice

FROM OUTLINE TO PARAGRAPHS Ask students to read the second paragraph and identify Daniel's reason and the examples he used to support it.

Apply to Writing

BEGIN DRAFTING THE PERSUASIVE COMPOSITION
Have students complete their outlines by adding facts or examples that support each reason. Then have students use their outline to begin drafting. Tell them to focus on one reason in each body paragraph and give examples to support it. Remind students to include an interesting lead to involve readers.

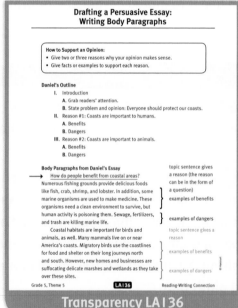

Transparency LA136

CONFERENCE

Writing Body Paragraphs Visit with students to check that they understand the process of taking reasons from an outline and using them to draft body paragraphs that support the opinion they stated in the introduction.

WRITING A STRONG ENDING

Writing Trait ▶ **Sentence Fluency**

Objective
• *To write a strong ending*

Teach/Model

INTRODUCE ENDINGS Display **Transparency LA137**. Read aloud the information at the top of the transparency. Then point out how Daniel's conclusion meets the criteria for a strong ending. Use this model:

Think Aloud **The last two paragraphs of Daniel's composition are the ending. In the second to last paragraph, Daniel explains what he wants people to do. In the final paragraph, he summarizes the problem and restates his call to action.**

Point out that Daniel uses a variety of sentence lengths and sentence types to make the ending engaging and interesting.

Guided Practice

FROM OUTLINE TO ENDING Ask students to identify the sentences in the final paragraph in which Daniel does the following:

• restates his opinion (the first sentence)
• summarizes his reasons (the second and third sentences)
• sums up his call to action (the last sentence)

Apply to Writing

DRAFT AN ENDING Have students complete the first draft of their persuasive composition. Remind them to end their composition by calling readers to action.

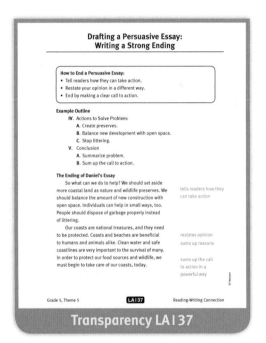

Transparency LA137

CONFERENCE

Writing an Ending Visit with students to check that they are successfully completing their first drafts.

Revise

ADDING PERSUASIVE WORDS
Writing Trait ▷ Word Choice

Objectives
- *To learn strategies for revising a persuasive composition*
- *To revise a persuasive composition*

Teach/Model

INTRODUCE ADDING PERSUASIVE WORDS
Tell students that as they revise their persuasive compositions, they may want to add or change words to make their language more persuasive. Display **Transparency LA138**. Read the information in the box. Tell students that the sentences on the transparency are from an earlier draft of Daniel's composition. Have a volunteer read aloud the first sentence. Then model how to revise the sentence to make the language more persuasive:

Think Aloud The word *can* is not very strong. One way to make this sentence more persuasive is to change the word *can* to *should*. Saying everyone *should* help protect America's coastlines makes it clear that the writer believes that everyone has a responsibility to protect the coastlines.

Guided Practice

ADD PERSUASIVE WORDS Guide students to replace each of the underlined words on **Transparency LA138** with more persuasive language.

Apply to Writing

REVISE THE PERSUASIVE COMPOSITION Have students read the drafts of their persuasive compositions and make any needed revisions. Tell students to replace general verbs and adjectives with more persuasive language.

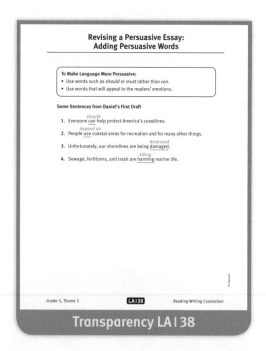

Revising a Persuasive Essay:
Adding Persuasive Words

To Make Language More Persuasive:
- Use words such as *should* or *must* rather than *can*.
- Use words that will appeal to the readers' emotions.

Some Sentences from Daniel's First Draft

should
1. Everyone can help protect America's coastlines.
depend on
2. People use coastal areas for recreation and for many other things.
destroyed
3. Unfortunately, our shorelines are being damaged.
killing
4. Sewage, fertilizers, and trash are harming marine life.

Grade 5, Theme 5   LA138   Reading-Writing Connection

Transparency LA138

CONFERENCE

Routine Card 11 **Adding Persuasive Words** Visit with students to check that they understand how to replace general words with more persuasive ones.

Proofread

CHECKING HELPING VERBS
Writing Trait ▶ Conventions

Objective
- *To proofread a persuasive composition for errors in usage*

Teach/Model

INTRODUCE CHECKING HELPING VERBS Display **Transparency LA139**. Have a volunteer read aloud the first sentence of the paragraph on the transparency. Model for students how to check helping verbs:

Think Aloud The first sentence is a question. The word *can* is being used as a helping verb, but it is in the wrong position. Also, the helping verb *do* is a more powerful choice. The question "How do people benefit from coastal areas?" is a more effective way to begin this paragraph.

Proofreading a Persuasive Essay:
Checking Helping Verbs

How people can benefit from coastal areas?
Numerous fishing grounds provide delicious foods
like fish, crab, shrimp, and lobster. In addition, some
marine organisms is used to make medicine. These
organisms need a clean environment to survive, but
human activity are poisoning them. Sewage, fertilizers,
and trash is killing marine life.

Grade 5, Theme 5   LA139   Reading-Writing Connection

Transparency LA139

Guided Practice

PROOFREAD HELPING VERBS Work with students to proofread the rest of the paragraph. Ask them to find and correct three more helping verb errors.

Apply to Writing

PROOFREAD THE PERSUASIVE COMPOSITION Have students proofread the drafts of their persuasive compositions and make any necessary corrections. Remind students to check that they used helping verbs correctly.

BELOW-LEVEL

Proofreading Support Have partners read aloud each other's compositions. Tell students to listen for sentences that sound incorrect when read aloud. Then have them check those sentences for errors in grammar or usage.

CONFERENCE

Proofreading Conference with students to make sure that they are successfully proofreading their persuasive compositions.

Evaluate/Publish

Objective
• *To self-evaluate a persuasive composition*

Teach/Model

INTRODUCE SELF-ASSESSMENT   Remind students of the writing rubric they received during prewriting. Tell them to use the rubric to assess their compositions before making final copies. Model how to self-assess a persuasive composition:

Think Aloud   **Read the rubric items carefully, and then read your persuasive composition. Ask yourself whether you did well on each item or whether you could do better.**

Guided Practice

USE THE RUBRIC   Guide students to use the rubric to begin a final self-assessment of their persuasive composition. Lead them to recognize any revisions they need to make before making a final copy of their composition.

Apply to Writing

SELF-ASSESS AND PUBLISH   Have students complete the self-assessment of their drafts. Tell them to create a final draft after they have completed revising their persuasive compositions.

CONFERENCE

Using Rubrics Visit with students to check that they understand how to use the rubric to self-assess their persuasive compositions.

NOTE: A 4-point rubric appears on page R8.

SCORING RUBRIC					
6	**5**	**4**	**3**	**2**	**1**
FOCUS Completely focused, purposeful.	Focused on topic and purpose.	Generally focused on topic and purpose.	Somewhat focused on topic and purpose.	Related to topic but does not maintain focus.	Lacks focus and purpose.
ORGANIZATION Ideas progress logically; paper conveys sense of completeness.	Organization mostly clear; paper gives sense of completeness.	Organization mostly clear, but some lapses occur; may seem unfinished.	Some sense of organization; seems unfinished.	Little sense of organization.	Little or no sense of organization.
SUPPORT Strong, specific details; clear, exact language; freshness of expression.	Strong, specific details; clear, exact language.	Adequate support and word choice.	Limited supporting details; limited word choice.	Few supporting details; limited word choice.	Little development; limited or unclear word choice.
CONVENTIONS Varied sentences; few, if any, errors.	Varied sentences; few errors.	Some sentence variety; few errors.	Simple sentence structures; some errors.	Simple sentence structures; many errors.	Unclear sentence structures; many errors.

REPRODUCIBLE RUBRIC appears on page R7.

PUBLISH THE PERSUASIVE COMPOSITION

Objectives
- *To choose a way to publish a persuasive composition*
- *To present the final copy of a persuasive composition*

Publishing Options

DISCUSS PUBLISHING OPTIONS Discuss with students ways in which they could present their persuasive compositions. Then share with them the following ideas:

LETTER TO THE EDITOR Publishing a persuasive composition in letter form and sending it to a local newspaper is a good way to have your opinions heard.

1. Using a word processor, create a final typed copy of your persuasive composition.
2. Locate the name and address of the person to whom you would like to send your letter. This might be the editor of a local newspaper.
3. Put your composition in letter form by adding the date, your address, the name and address of the person to whom you are writing, a salutation, and a complimentary closing.
4. Check that there are no errors in your letter.
5. Send your letter.

PERSUASIVE SPEECH A persuasive speech can convince people that your opinions are valid.

1. List the main ideas of your composition on note cards. Number the note cards and put them in order.
2. Create a persuasive visual aid that supports one of your reasons.
3. Practice giving your presentation several times.
4. Use gestures and dramatizations to emphasize and illustrate important points.

MAKE A FLYER A flyer makes it easier to share your opinions with readers outside your classroom.

1. Using a word processor, create a final typed copy of your persuasive composition.
2. Orient the page of your document horizontally and format your essay into three columns.
3. Print your essay and then fold it into three sections.
4. Add a title and illustration to the cover.

 PORTFOLIO OPPORTUNITY Students may keep their persuasive compositions in their portfolios.

 TECHNOLOGY

Using E-mail If your local newspaper has a website, help interested students locate a contact e-mail address for the appropriate editor. Guide students to create a formal e-mail to send instead of a letter by post.

Writing on Demand: Persuasive Composition

PREPARATION

Objectives

- *To write in response to a persuasive prompt*
- *To organize ideas by making an outline*
- *To revise and proofread for errors in grammar, punctuation, capitalization, and spelling*

Prepare to Write

DISCUSS TIMED WRITING Tell students that on a writing test, they may be asked to write a persuasive composition. Explain that they will probably have 45 minutes to write a focused, organized, well-supported draft. Tell students that they will practice writing a timed persuasive composition.

ANALYZE THE PROMPT Display **Transparency LA140.** Explain that the topic of the prompt is working in a community garden. Point out the words *whether or not,* and tell students that these words indicate that they should defend one side of the issue or the other.

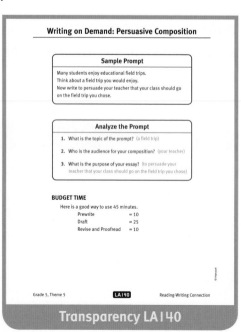

DISCUSS ORGANIZATION Tell students that to do well on a timed writing test such as this one, they must remember the features of a good persuasive composition. Tell them to keep these points in mind as they plan how to answer the prompt:

- The composition includes a statement of opinion.
- The opinion is supported by reasons, facts, and examples.
- The composition ends with a call to action.

Tell students that they may want to make a brief outline to organize their ideas.

DISCUSS BUDGETING TIME Remind students that the test allows 45 minutes to write a composition. Recommend that they budget their time as follows:

Budgeting Time	
Prewrite	10 minutes
Draft	25 minutes
Revise and Proofread	10 minutes

Explain that some students will need more or less time for each step. Ask them to think about how much time they will need to complete each step.

PERSUASIVE COMPOSITION

Write the Composition

RESPOND TO A PROMPT Write the following prompt on the board and have students begin writing. Remind them when the first 20 minutes have passed. At the end of 45 minutes, ask students to stop writing.

PROMPT

Many people do volunteer work to improve their community in some way. Think of something that volunteers could do to improve your community. Now write to persuade people to do that volunteer work. Support your opinion with reasons and examples.

DISCUSS TIMED WRITING Ask students to discuss their experiences during the timed writing assignment. Ask questions such as the following:

- Did you address all parts of the prompt?
- Did you stick to your budgeted time for each step of the writing process?
- In what ways was your prewriting helpful as you wrote your draft?
- What changes did you make as you revised your composition?
- Did you proofread to look for errors in punctuation, capitalization, grammar, and spelling?
- What could you do better the next time you write a timed composition?

EVALUATE Have students revisit the rubric they used when they began to prewrite. Ask students to work independently or in pairs to evaluate their compositions.

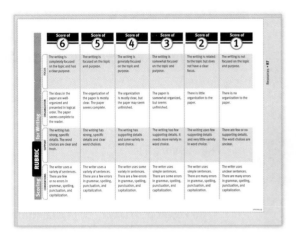

▲ Teacher Edition, p. R7

PORTFOLIO OPPORTUNITY Students may keep their compositions in their work portfolios and compare them with earlier timed writing assignments to assess their progress.

Lesson 22

WEEK AT A GLANCE

✓ **Vocabulary**
somberly, stammers, monopolize, deflated, enraptured, enterprising, cumbersome

✓ **Comprehension**
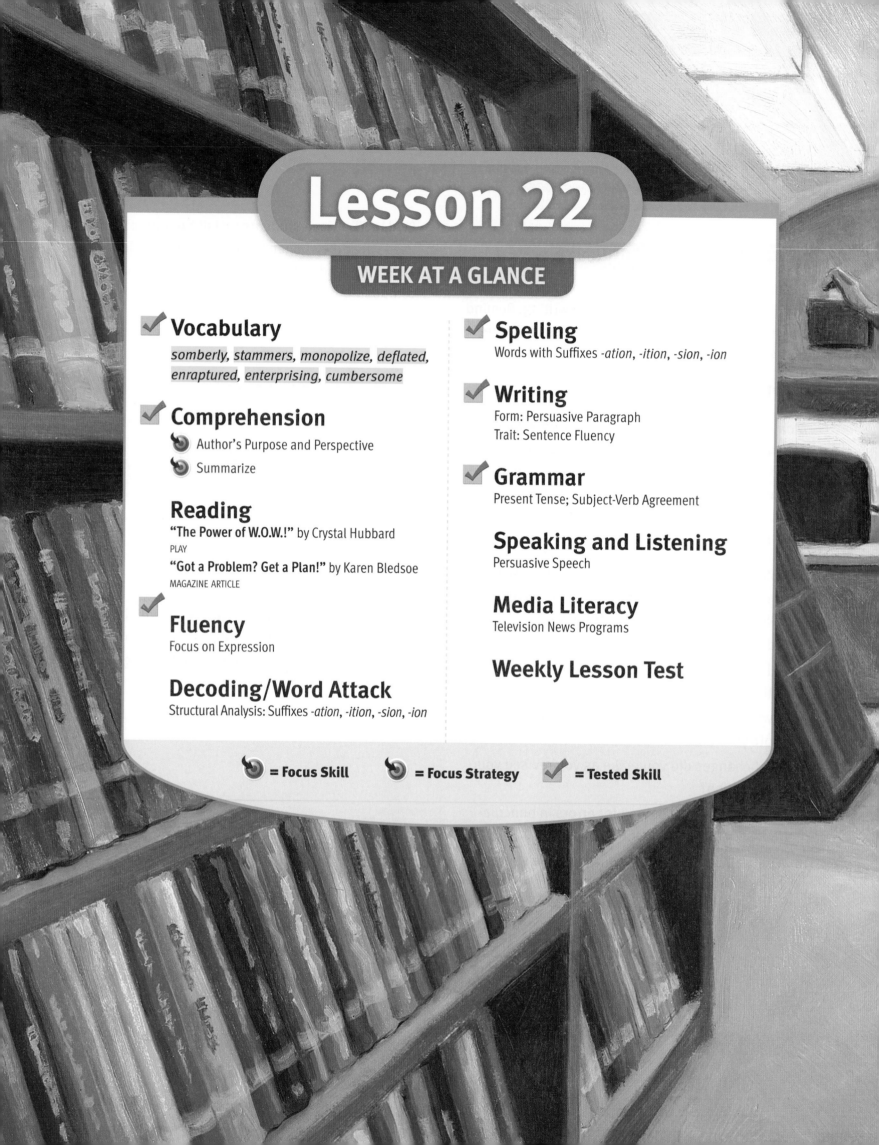 Author's Purpose and Perspective
 Summarize

Reading
"The Power of W.O.W.!" by Crystal Hubbard
PLAY
"Got a Problem? Get a Plan!" by Karen Bledsoe
MAGAZINE ARTICLE

✓ **Fluency**
Focus on Expression

Decoding/Word Attack
Structural Analysis: Suffixes *-ation*, *-ition*, *-sion*, *-ion*

✓ **Spelling**
Words with Suffixes *-ation*, *-ition*, *-sion*, *-ion*

✓ **Writing**
Form: Persuasive Paragraph
Trait: Sentence Fluency

✓ **Grammar**
Present Tense; Subject-Verb Agreement

Speaking and Listening
Persuasive Speech

Media Literacy
Television News Programs

Weekly Lesson Test

 = Focus Skill   = Focus Strategy   ✓ = Tested Skill

One stop
for all
your Digital *needs*

Digital
CLASSROOM

 www.harcourtschool.com/storytown
To go along with your print program

FOR THE TEACHER

Prepare
 Professional Development
in the Online TE

 Videos for Podcasting

Plan & Organize
 Online TE & Planning Resources*

Teach
 Transparencies
access from the Online TE

Assess
 Online Assessment*
with Student Tracking System and Prescriptions

FOR THE STUDENT

Read
 Student eBook*

 Strategic Intervention Interactive Reader

 Leveled Readers

Practice & Apply
 Comprehension Expedition CD-ROM

 *Also available on CD-ROM

Literature Resources

 eBook STUDENT EDITION

STUDENT EDITION

Got a Problem?
GET A PLAN!
by Karen Bledsoe • illustrated by Eric Sturdevant

Genre: Magazine Article

The
Power
of
W.O.W.!

Genre: Play

◀ **Audiotext** *Student Edition selections are available on Audiotext Grade 5, CD7.*

 Accelerated Reader™   ◀ *Practice Quizzes for the Selection*

THEME CONNECTION: MAKING A DIFFERENCE
Comparing Play and Magazine Article

....

Paired Selections

 **MATH**   **The Power of W.O.W.! pp. 570–583**
SUMMARY Author Crystal Hubbard tells about several children who work to save a neighborhood bookmobile program.

 SOCIAL STUDIES   **Got a Problem? Get a Plan! pp. 584–585**
SUMMARY Author Karen Bledsoe explains that an "action plan" is an important part of a community service project.

Support for Differentiated Instruction

LEVELED READERS

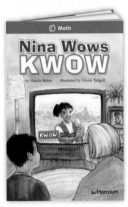

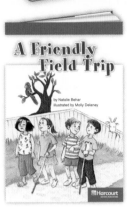

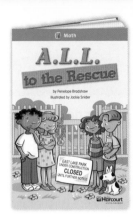

BELOW-LEVEL   **ON-LEVEL**   **ADVANCED**   **ELL**

LEVELED PRACTICE

◀ **Strategic Intervention Resource Kit, Lesson 22**

◀ **Strategic Intervention Interactive Reader, Lesson 22**
Strategic Intervention Interactive Reader Online

◀ **ELL Extra Support Kit, Lesson 22**

◀ **Challenge Resource Kit, Lesson 22**

BELOW-LEVEL
Extra Support Copying Masters, pp. 129, 131–132

ON-LEVEL
Practice Book, pp. 129–134

ADVANCED
Challenge Copying Masters, pp. 129, 131–132

ADDITIONAL RESOURCES

◀ **Picture Card Collection**
◀ **Fluency Builders**
◀ **Literacy Center Kit, Lesson 22**
• Test Prep System
• Writer's Companion, Lesson 22
• Grammar Practice Book, pp. 77–80
• Spelling Practice Book, pp. 87–90
• Phonics Practice Book, pp. 157–162
• Reading Transparencies R92–R96
• Language Arts Transparencies LA141–LA146

ASSESSMENT

✔ **Monitor Progress**

✔ **Weekly Lesson Tests, Lesson 22**
• Comprehension   • Draw Conclusions
• Focus Skill   • Grammar
• Robust Vocabulary • Fluency

✔ **Rubrics, pp. R3–R8**

www.harcourtschool.com/storytown
• Online Assessment
Also available on CD-ROM—ExamView®

Suggested Lesson Planner

90+ Minutes

GO online Online TE & Planning Resources

Step 1 | Whole Group
45-60+ Minutes

Oral Language
- *Question of the Day*
- *Listening Comprehension*

Comprehension
- *Skills and Strategies*

Vocabulary

Reading
- *Fluency*
- *Cross-Curricular Connections*
- *Decoding/Word Attack*

Step 2 | Small Groups
45-60+ Minutes

Step 3 | Whole Group
45+ Minutes

Language Arts
- *Spelling*
- *Writing*
- *Grammar*

Spelling Words

1. acceleration	11. repetition
2. accumulation	12. mansion
3. activation	13. pension
4. alteration	14. passion
5. authorization	15. tension
6. calculation	16. champion
7. cancellation	17. confusion
8. dedication	18. permission
9. organization	19. population
10. demolition	20. companion

Challenge Words

21. presentation	24. decision
22. fixation	25. diversion
23. modernization	

Day 1

QUESTION OF THE DAY *Why are local libraries important community resources?*

READ ALOUD, pp. T104–T105

☑ **COMPREHENSION:**
 Author's Purpose and Perspective, pp. T106–T107

Summarize, pp. T108–T109

☑ **VOCABULARY:**
Introduce Vocabulary, p. T111
Word Detective, p. T113

READ: Vocabulary, pp. T112–T113

FLUENCY: EXPRESSION: Model Oral Fluency, p. T105

DECODING/WORD ATTACK: Structural Analysis: Suffixes *-ation, -ition, -sion, -ion,* p. T137

Day 2

QUESTION OF THE DAY *What do you think were the most important factors contributing to the success of the car wash?*

READ ALOUD, p. T105

☑ **COMPREHENSION:**
Author's Purpose and Perspective, pp. T114–T126

Summarize, pp. T117, T119, T121

☑ **VOCABULARY:**
Vocabulary Review, p. T131

READ: "The Power of W.O.W.!," pp. T114–T127
Options for Reading

▲ Student Edition

FLUENCY: EXPRESSION:
Partner Reading, p. T131

MATH: Calculate a Reasonable Amount, p. T121

Suggestions for Differentiated Instruction *(See pp. T98–T99)*

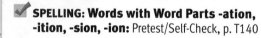
☑ **SPELLING: Words with Word Parts -ation, -ition, -sion, -ion:** Pretest/Self-Check, p. T140

✏ **WRITING: Persuasive Paragraph:** Teach/Model, p. T142

Writing Prompt *Plays have features specific to the genre. Think about how reading a play differs from reading a story or an article. Now write a paragraph comparing and contrasting reading a play with reading another genre.*

☑ **GRAMMAR: Present Tense; Subject-Verb Agreement:** Teach/Model, p. T144

Daily Proofreading

1. Mrs Nguyen do not want to stop running W.O.W. (Mrs.; does not)

2. Ileana sits by herselves to think of a idea. (herself; an)

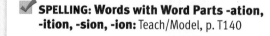
☑ **SPELLING: Words with Word Parts -ation, -ition, -sion, -ion:** Teach/Model, p. T140

✏ **WRITING: Persuasive Paragraph:** Practice/Apply, p. T142

Writing Prompt *The characters in "The Power of W.O.W.!" each had unique personalities. Think of which character you liked best. Now write a descriptive paragraph about this character, telling about his or her personality.*

☑ **GRAMMAR: Present Tense; Subject-Verb Agreement:** Teach/Model, p. T144

Daily Proofreading

3. This organizeation working to save the bookmobile. (organization is working)

4. Hers dedicasion is admirable. (Her dedication)

  = Focus Skill    = Focus Strategy    = Tested Skill

Comprehension	Vocabulary	Fluency	Language Arts

 **Skills at a Glance**

Comprehension

FOCUS SKILL: Author's Purpose and Perspective

FOCUS STRATEGY: Summarize

Vocabulary

somberly   enraptured
stammers   enterprising
monopolize cumbersome
deflated

Fluency

Expression

Language Arts

Writing:
- Trait: Sentence Fluency
- Form: Persuasive Paragraph

Grammar: Present Tense; Subject-Verb Agreement

Day 3

QUESTION OF THE DAY *What does the reaction of the business people to the children's flyers and the news report reveal about their feelings toward the library?*

READ ALOUD, p. T105

COMPREHENSION:
Author's Purpose and Perspective, pp. T132–T133

VOCABULARY:
Reinforce Word Meanings, p. T139

READ: "Got a Problem? Get a Plan!," pp. T128–T129

COMPARING TEXTS, p. T130

 ▲Student Edition

FLUENCY: EXPRESSION:
Choral-Read, p. T138

WRITING: Write a Radio Ad, p. T131

Day 4

QUESTION OF THE DAY *What do you do when you see a friend who looks deflated?*

READ ALOUD, p. T105

SPEAKING AND LISTENING:
Persuasive Speech, p. T146

COMPREHENSION:
Draw Conclusions, pp. T134–T135

VOCABULARY:
Extend Word Meanings, p. T139

FLUENCY: EXPRESSION:
Echo-Read, p. T138

 ▲Student Edition

Day 5

QUESTION OF THE DAY *What does "The Power of W.O.W.!" show about television as an information source?*

READ ALOUD, p. T105

VOCABULARY:
Cumulative Vocabulary, p. T139
Vocabulary Strategies:
Using Word Parts, p. T136

FLUENCY: EXPRESSION:
Partner Reading, p. T138

 ▲Student Edition

MEDIA LITERACY:
Television News Programs, p. T147

 BELOW-LEVEL   ON-LEVEL   ADVANCED   E L L

SPELLING: Words with Word Parts: -ation, -ition, -sion, -ion: Practice/Apply, p. T141

SPELLING: Words with Word Parts: -ation, -ition, -sion, -ion: Spelling Strategies, p. T141

SPELLING: Words with Word Parts: -ation, -ition, -sion, -ion: Posttest, p. T141

 **WRITING: Persuasive Paragraph:** Prewrite, p. T143

Writing Prompt *In the story, people want to save W.O.W. because they consider it an important part of their community. Think of a program like W.O.W. in your community. Now write a persuasive paragraph that supports why you think the program is important.*

 WRITING: Persuasive Paragraph: Draft, p. T143

Writing Prompt *Imagine that you and a group of your friends are holding a fund-raiser for your school. Think about for what you would raise money and how you would accomplish it. Now write a skit describing what you would do.*

 WRITING: Persuasive Paragraph: Revise and Reflect, p. T143

Writing Prompt *Most people have participated in a fund-raiser. Think about why people help raise money for causes. Now write a persuasive ad convincing people to participate in a fund-raiser.*

GRAMMAR: Present Tense; Subject-Verb Agreement: Teach/Model, p. T145

Daily Proofreading

5. Shane and Jason asks for permition. (ask OR asked; permission.)

6. A bee buzzes around Jakes' head. (buzzes; Jake's)

GRAMMAR: Present Tense; Subject-Verb Agreement: Apply to Writing, p. T145

Daily Proofreading

7. Ill set here and wait for you. (I'll sit)

8. By mine calculasions, we have enough money. (my calculations,)

GRAMMAR: Present Tense; Subject-Verb Agreement: Review, p. T145

Daily Proofreading

9. You can lay down here while I call dr Williams. (lie; Dr.)

10. You tries to relieve the tention. (try; tension.)

Suggested Small-Group Planner

45-60+ Minutes

	Day 1	Day 2

 BELOW-LEVEL
15-20+ Minutes

Teacher–Directed
📖 Leveled Readers:
Before Reading, p. T148

Independent
⭐ Word Study Center, p. T102
Extra Support
Copying Masters, p. 129

▲ Leveled Reader

Teacher–Directed
Reread the Selection,
pp. T114–T127

Independent
⭐ Writing Center, p. T103
Audiotext Grade 5, CD7

▲ Student Edition

 **ON-LEVEL**
15-20+ Minutes

Teacher–Directed
📖 Leveled Readers:
Before Reading, p. T149

Independent
⭐ Reading Center, p. T102
Practice Book, p. 129

▲ Leveled Reader

Teacher–Directed
Respond to the Literature,
p. T126

Independent
⭐ Word Study Center,
p. T102

▲ Student Edition

ADVANCED
15-20+ Minutes

Teacher–Directed
📖 Leveled Readers:
Before Reading, p. T150

Independent
⭐ Writing Center, p. T103
Challenge Copying
Masters, p. 129

▲ Leveled Reader

Independent
⭐ Fluency Center, p. T103
Leveled Readers:
Partner Reading, p. T150

▲ Leveled Reader

ELL

English-Language Learners

In addition to the small-group suggestions above, use the ELL Extra Support Kit to promote language development.

LANGUAGE DEVELOPMENT SUPPORT

Teacher–Directed
Leveled Readers:
Build Background, p. T151
ELL Teacher Guide, Lesson 22

Independent
ELL Copying Masters,
Lesson 22

▲ Leveled Reader

LANGUAGE DEVELOPMENT SUPPORT

Teacher–Directed
Scaffold Core Skills
ELL Teacher Guide,
Lesson 22

Independent
Audiotext Grade 5, CD7

▲ ELL Student Handbook

Intervention

▲ Strategic Intervention Resource Kit   ▲ Strategic Intervention Interactive Reader

Strategic Intervention Teacher Guide,
Lesson 22
Strategic Intervention Practice Book,
Lesson 22

Catch a Wave,
Lesson 22
Strategic Intervention
Teacher Guide, Lesson 22

Strategic Intervention
Interactive Reader ▲

       = Literacy Center Cards

MONITOR PROGRESS
Small-Group Instruction

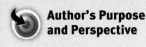

Author's Purpose and Perspective	Selection Comprehension	Robust Vocabulary	Draw Conclusions	Expression	Language Arts
pp. S10–S11	p. S14	pp. S12–S13	pp. S16–S17	p. S15	p. S18–S19

Day 3

Teacher–Directed
Leveled Readers:
During Reading, p. T148

Independent
⭐ Reading Center, p. T102
Extra Support Copying Masters, p. 131

▲ Leveled Reader

Teacher–Directed
Leveled Readers:
During Reading, p. T149

Independent
⭐ Technology Center, p. T103
Practice Book, p. 131

▲ Leveled Reader

Teacher–Directed
Leveled Readers:
During Reading, p. T150

Independent
⭐ Word Study Center, p. T102
Challenge Copying Masters, p. 131

▲ Leveled Reader

LANGUAGE DEVELOPMENT SUPPORT

Teacher–Directed
Leveled Readers:
During Reading, p. T151
ELL Teacher Guide, Lesson 22

Independent
ELL Copying Masters, Lesson 22

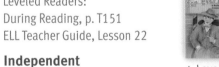
▲ Leveled Reader

Catch a Wave,
Lesson 22
Strategic Intervention
Teacher Guide,
Lesson 22
Strategic Intervention
Practice Book,
Lesson 22

Strategic Intervention
Interactive Reader ▲

Day 4

Teacher–Directed
Leveled Readers:
Guided Fluency, p. T148

Independent
⭐ Technology Center, p. T103
Extra Support Copying Masters, p. 132

▲ Leveled Reader

Teacher–Directed
Leveled Readers:
Guided Fluency, p. T149

Independent
⭐ Fluency Center, p. T103
Practice Book, p. 132

▲ Leveled Reader

Independent
⭐ Reading Center, p. T102
Challenge Copying Masters, p. 132
Classroom Library: Self-Selected Reading

▲ Leveled Reader

LANGUAGE DEVELOPMENT SUPPORT

Teacher–Directed
Leveled Readers:
Guided Fluency, p. T151
ELL Teacher Guide, Lesson 22

Independent
ELL Copying Masters, Lesson 22

▲ Leveled Reader

Catch a Wave,
Lesson 22
Strategic Intervention
Teacher Guide,
Lesson 22

Strategic Intervention
Interactive Reader ▲

Day 5

Teacher–Directed
Leveled Readers:
Responding, p. T148

Independent
⭐ Fluency Center, p. T103
Leveled Readers:
Rereading for Fluency, p. T148

▲ Leveled Reader

Teacher–Directed
Leveled Readers:
Responding, p. T149

Independent
⭐ Writing Center, p. T103
Leveled Readers: Rereading for Fluency, p. T149

▲ Leveled Reader

Teacher–Directed
Leveled Readers:
Responding, p. T150

Independent
⭐ Technology Center, p. T103
Leveled Readers:
Rereading for Fluency, p. T150
Classroom Library: Self-Selected Reading

▲ Leveled Reader

LANGUAGE DEVELOPMENT SUPPORT

Teacher–Directed
Leveled Readers:
Responding, p. T151
ELL Teacher Guide, Lesson 22

Independent
Leveled Readers:
Rereading for Fluency, p. T151

▲ Leveled Reader

Catch a Wave,
Lesson 22
Strategic Intervention
Teacher Guide,
Lesson 22

Strategic Intervention
Interactive Reader ▲

Leveled Readers & Leveled Practice

Reinforcing Skills and Strategies

LEVELED READERS SYSTEM

- ■ **Leveled Readers**
- ■ **Leveled Readers CD**
- ■ **Leveled Reader Teacher Guides**
  - *Vocabulary*
  - *Comprehension*
  - *Oral Reading Fluency Assessment*
- ■ **Response Activities**
- ■ **Leveled Readers Assessment**

See pages T148–T151 for lesson plans.

For extended lesson plans, see *Leveled Reader Teacher Guides*.

T100 • Grade 5, Theme 5

BELOW-LEVEL

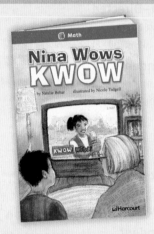

- 🦅 **Author's Purpose and Perspective**
- 🐚 **Summarize**
- ● **Robust Vocabulary**

LEVELED READER TEACHER GUIDE

▲ Vocabulary, p. 5

▲ Comprehension, p. 6

ON-LEVEL

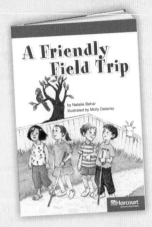

- 🦅 **Author's Purpose and Perspective**
- 🐚 **Summarize**
- ● **Robust Vocabulary**

LEVELED READER TEACHER GUIDE

▲ Vocabulary, p. 5

▲ Comprehension, p. 6

www.harcourtschool.com/storytown

Go online

★ **Leveled Readers Online Database**
Searchable by Genre, Skill, Vocabulary, Level, or Title
★ **Student Activities and Teacher Resources,** *online*

ADVANCED

- 🔊 **Author's Purpose and Perspective**
- 🔊 **Summarize**
- **Robust Vocabulary**

LEVELED READER TEACHER GUIDE

▲ **Vocabulary, p. 5**

▲ **Comprehension, p. 6**

ELL

- **Build Background**
- **Concept Vocabulary**
- **Scaffolded Language Development**

LEVELED READER TEACHER GUIDE

▲ **Build Background, p. 5**

▲ **Scaffolded Language Development, p. 6**

CLASSROOM LIBRARY

for Self-Selected Reading

EASY

▲ *Doña Flor* by Pat Mora.
TALL TALE

AVERAGE

▲ *Eleanor* by Barbara Cooney.
BIOGRAPHY

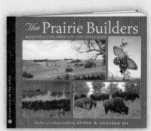

CHALLENGE

▲ *The Prairie Builders: Reconstructing America's Lost Grasslands* by Sneed B. Collard III.
EXPOSITORY NONFICTION

▲ **Classroom Library Books Teacher Guide**

Literacy Centers

15+ Min. each

Management Support

While you provide direct instruction to individuals or small groups, other students can work on these activities.

▲ **Literacy Centers Pocket Chart**

My Activities for the Week

This week I will complete the following:

Literacy Centers
- ☐ **Word Study** Adjective and Adverb Hunt
- ☐ **Reading** Reading Log
- ☐ **Writing** Write a Play
- ☐ **Technology** Find Events
- ☐ **Fluency** Read Aloud

Leveled Readers
- ☐ Reread for Fluency
- ☐ Activities (See inside back cover.)

Practice Book
- ☐ Pages 129–134

▲ **Teacher Resource Book, p. 57**

Homework for the Week

Teacher Resource Book, page 25

The *Homework Copying Master* provides activities to complete for each day of the week.

GO online www.harcourtschool.com/storytown

WORD STUDY

Adjective and Adverb Hunt

Objective
To extend understanding of word meanings

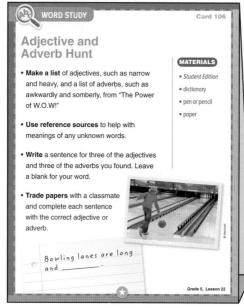

WORD STUDY — Card 106

Adjective and Adverb Hunt

- **Make a list** of adjectives, such as narrow and heavy, and a list of adverbs, such as awkwardly and somberly, from "The Power of W.O.W!"

- **Use reference sources** to help with meanings of any unknown words.

- **Write** a sentence for three of the adjectives and three of the adverbs you found. Leave a blank for your word.

- **Trade papers** with a classmate and complete each sentence with the correct adjective or adverb.

MATERIALS
- Student Edition
- dictionary
- pen or pencil
- paper

Bowling lanes are long and ____.

Grade 5, Lesson 22

⭐ **Literacy Center Kit,** Card 106

Bowling lanes are long and __narrow__.

Lilly danced __awkwardly__ in her platform shoes.

READING

Reading Log

Objective
To select and read books independently

READING — Card 107

Reading Log

- **Look for these books** about community leaders.
- **Choose one** that you find interesting.
- **Use your Reading Log** to keep track of what you read.

MATERIALS
- library book
- My Reading Log
- pen or pencil

Doña Flor by Pat Mora. TALL TALE

Eleanor by Barbara Cooney. BIOGRAPHY

The Prairie Builders: Reconstructing America's Lost Grasslands by Sneed B. Collard III. EXPOSITORY NONFICTION

Grade 5, Lesson 22

⭐ **Literacy Center Kit,** Card 107

www.harcourtschool.com/storytown

★ Additional Literacy Center Activities
★ Resources for Parents and Teachers

● BELOW-LEVEL   ● ADVANCED   ● ON-LEVEL

Differentiated
for Your Needs

WRITING

Write a Play

Objective
To write a play

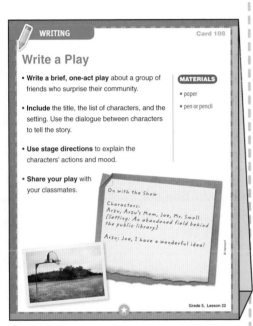

WRITING   Card 108

Write a Play

- **Write** a brief, one-act play about a group of friends who surprise their community.

- **Include** the title, the list of characters, and the setting. Use the dialogue between characters to tell the story.

- **Use stage directions** to explain the characters' actions and mood.

- **Share your play** with your classmates.

MATERIALS
- paper
- pen or pencil

On with the Show

Characters:
Arzu, Arzu's Mom, Joe, Mr. Smoll
(Setting: An abandoned field behind
the public library)

Arzu: Joe, I have a wonderful idea!

Grade 5, Lesson 22

⭐ **Literacy Center Kit,** Card 108

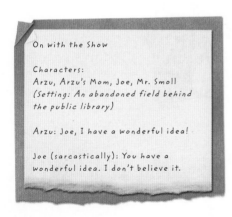

On with the Show

Characters:
Arzu, Arzu's Mom, Joe, Mr. Smoll
(Setting: An abandoned field behind
the public library)

Arzu: Joe, I have a wonderful idea!

Joe (sarcastically): You have a
wonderful idea. I don't believe it.

TECHNOLOGY

Find Events

Objective
To research local events on the Internet

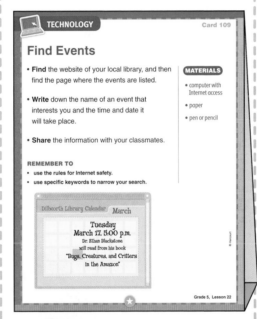

TECHNOLOGY   Card 109

Find Events

- **Find** the website of your local library, and then find the page where the events are listed.

- **Write** down the name of an event that interests you and the time and date it will take place.

- **Share** the information with your classmates.

REMEMBER TO
- use the rules for Internet safety.
- use specific keywords to narrow your search.

MATERIALS
- computer with Internet access
- paper
- pen or pencil

Dillworth Library Calendar March

**Tuesday
March 17, 5:00 p.m.**
Dr. Ethan Blackstone
will read from his book
"Bugs, Creatures, and Critters
in the Amazon"

Grade 5, Lesson 22

⭐ **Literacy Center Kit,** Card 109

Tuesday, March 17

5:00 p.m.
Dr. Ethan Blackstone—
"Bugs, Creatures, and Critters
in the Amazon"

main room of
Dillworth Library

FLUENCY

Read Aloud

Objective
To read aloud with appropriate expression

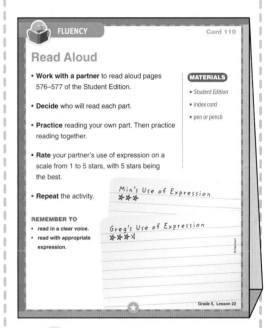

FLUENCY   Card 110

Read Aloud

- **Work with a partner** to read aloud pages 576–577 of the Student Edition.

- **Decide** who will read each part.

- **Practice** reading your own part. Then practice reading together.

- **Rate** your partner's use of expression on a scale from 1 to 5 stars, with 5 stars being the best.

- **Repeat** the activity.

REMEMBER TO
- read in a clear voice.
- read with appropriate expression.

MATERIALS
- Student Edition
- index card
- pen or pencil

Min's Use of Expression
★★★

Greg's Use of Expression
★★★★

Grade 5, Lesson 22

⭐ **Literacy Center Kit,** Card 110

Min's Use of Expression
★★★

Greg's Use of Expression
★★★★

Listening Comprehension *Read-Aloud*

Objectives

- *To determine a purpose for listening*
- *To understand information presented orally*

Genre Study

NARRATIVE NONFICTION

Tell students that they will listen to a narrative nonfiction selection about a unique group of librarians. Remind students that narrative nonfiction

- tells about real people, things, events, or places.
- includes facts about the topic.
- usually has story structure.

Set a Purpose for Listening

LISTEN FOR INFORMATION

Explain to students that when they hear a nonfiction story, they should listen to identify the topic and the main events. Model setting a purpose for listening: *One purpose for listening is to find out what made these librarians special.* Then have students set their own purposes for listening.

Pack Horse Librarians

"Giddyap, Chestnut," the woman urged her horse up the rocky hill. She patted a saddlebag filled with books and magazines. "Lots of people are still waiting for a library visit today."

The woman and her horse had begun their trip before sunrise. They had already stopped at a lonely little house in the woods, a crowded one-room schoolhouse with more students than chairs, and a windowless wood cabin where chickens roamed in the tidy fenced-in yard. They had ten more homes to visit and a long way to go between each stop.

Everywhere they went, the woman left a few books or magazines and picked up the ones she'd delivered two weeks ago. The books weren't new. They were old and tattered, and so were the magazines. But people were glad to get them. ❶

From 1935 to 1943, librarians like this one traveled the mountains of eastern Kentucky on strong horses and mules. Times were hard then, and many people could not find jobs. Families had barely enough money to buy food and clothing. Schools could not afford to buy books. People lived far from towns and neighbors, and had no way to get things to read. ❷

So Kentucky's pack horse librarians journeyed mile after mile across rough, rocky country. There were no roads for them to follow, just a few bumpy dirt paths. They went up and down steep hillsides and crossed through cold creeks and streams.

Sometimes, when the ground was very slippery or uneven, they climbed off their horses and walked. They worked in the rain, snow, and blazing heat, bringing books to thousands of people who loved to read. ❸

Begin the Read-Aloud

MODEL ORAL FLUENCY: EXPRESSION Tell students that good readers

- read aloud with appropriate expression.
- use the volume and intonation of their voice to express the mood and meaning of the passage.

 Display **Transparency R92.** Read the passage aloud with appropriate expression. Have students pay attention to the rise and fall of your voice and to the words you emphasize as you read.

Interact with the Text

Routine Card 1 Continue reading aloud "Pack Horse Librarians." Pause to point out or ask students the following items.

❶ **Who is the woman and what is she doing?** (She is a librarian who is traveling on horseback to bring books to people.) **DRAW CONCLUSIONS**

❷ A *mule* is a pack animal that is half horse and half donkey. **UNDERSTANDING VOCABULARY**

❸ **Why were *pack horse librarians* so important to people living in eastern Kentucky at this time?** (Possible response: Most people could not afford to buy books; many lived in remote places where it was difficult to get books.) **MAIN IDEA**

When you have finished reading the selection, ask:

- **What made the pack horse librarians special?** (Possible responses: They delivered books across Kentucky to people; they rode mules; they were dedicated.) **RETURN TO PURPOSE**

- **Do you think it was easy or difficult to be a pack horse librarian? Explain.** (Possible response: It was difficult because they had to travel over rough country and work in bad weather.) **MAKE JUDGMENTS**

Connect to Reading

Tell students that in this lesson they will read about another traveling library.

Model Oral Fluency

from "Pack Horse Librarians"

"Giddyap, Chestnut," the woman urged her horse up the rocky hill. She patted a saddlebag filled with books and magazines. "Lots of people are still waiting for a library visit today."

The woman and her horse had begun their trip before sunrise. They had already stopped at a lonely little house in the woods, a crowded one-room schoolhouse with more students than chairs, and a windowless wood cabin where chickens roamed in the tidy fenced-in yard. They had ten more homes to visit and a long way to go between each stop.

Everywhere they went, the woman left a few books or magazines and picked up the ones she'd delivered two weeks ago. The books weren't new. They were old and tattered, and so were the magazines. But people were glad to get them.

Grade 5, Lesson 22   **R92**   Model Oral Fluency

Transparency R92

Suggested Daily Read-Aloud

To model fluency and promote listening comprehension, read aloud from one of these books throughout the week:

- *Sea Turtles* by Lorraine A. Jay. NorthWord, 2000.
- *The Kids' Volunteering Book* by Arlene Erlbach. Lerner, 1998.
- *Neighborhood Odes* by Gary Soto. Harcourt, 2005.
- *Chester Cricket's New Home* by George Selden. Random House, 1984.
- *My Backyard Garden* by Carol Lerner. Morrow, 1998.

Author's Purpose and Perspective

Objectives

- *To understand that authors have different purposes for writing*
- *To identify and discuss an author's perspective*

Skill Trace

Tested ✓ Author's Purpose and Perspective

Introduce	pp. T30–T31
Reteach	pp. S2–S3, S10–S11
Review	**pp. T56–T57, T106–T107, T132–T133, T308**
Test	Theme 5
Maintain	p. T274, Theme 6

Teach/Model

REVIEW AUTHOR'S PURPOSE AND PERSPECTIVE Read page 566 with students. Use the points below to summarize:

- An **author's purpose** is his or her reason for writing.

- The **author's perspective** is his or her opinion about the topic of the text. The language the author uses, the details he or she includes, and the author's background can all provide clues to his or her perspective.

Tell students that sometimes authors have more than one purpose for writing, such as to inform and to entertain.

Focus Skill

Author's Purpose and Perspective

You have learned that an **author's purpose** is the author's reason for writing a text. An **author's perspective** is the author's opinion about a subject. You can often identify an author's perspective by thinking about the words the author uses. The details he or she has included in the text also provide clues.

Evidence	Evidence	Evidence

↓

Author's Purpose Author's Perspective

▼ Tip

An author can have more than one purpose for writing something. For example, a story might entertain and teach about a topic.

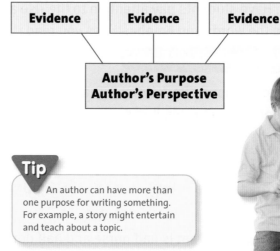

566

BELOW-LEVEL

Discuss Multiple Purposes Tell students that when authors have more than one purpose, there is usually one main purpose. Often the genre can help them identify this purpose. For example, if the genre is expository nonfiction, the author's main purpose is to inform. Humorous or persuasive language can provide clues that an author's secondary purpose is to entertain or persuade.

Read the story below. Then look at the graphic organizer. It shows evidence in the text that can help you identify the author's perspective.

"It's a shame that this park is such a mess!" Tricia said. Every time she and Anita kicked the soccer ball, it hit a piece of trash.

"You're right," Anita agreed. "We should improve it. Let's do something. Let's organize a cleanup day."

Dozens of volunteers participated. The cleanup made the park cleaner and safer for everyone.

Evidence	**Evidence**	**Evidence**
entertaining story about cleaning up a park	the girls organize a cleanup day	dozens of volunteers participate

Author's Purpose
to entertain
Author's Perspective
People should work together to make their community better.

 Try This!

What other purpose might the author have had for writing this story? How does the author's perspective affect the details and word choice in the text?

 www.harcourtschool.com/storytown

567

 MONITOR PROGRESS

Author's Purpose and Perspective

IF students have difficulty determining how the author's perspective affects details and word choice,	**THEN** tell students that showing that the cleanup was a success encourages others to try it.

Small-Group Instruction, pp. S10–S11:

● **BELOW-LEVEL:** Reteach   ● **ON-LEVEL:** Reinforce   ● **ADVANCED:** Extend

---

(TEACH/MODEL CONTINUED) Ask a volunteer to read aloud the passage on page 567. Then model identifying the author's purpose.

Think Aloud This passage is realistic fiction. It uses dialogue and friendly, inviting language to discuss a familiar problem. The author's purpose for writing this passage is to entertain readers with an engaging story.

Guided Practice

DETERMINE THE AUTHOR'S PERSPECTIVE Guide students to discuss how the evidence in the graphic organizer supports the author's perspective.

Practice/Apply

Try This! Students should identify that another purpose is to teach readers how to make a change in their community. They should point out that the author includes details that show the cleanup was a success. Have students discuss how the details and the descriptive words are influenced by the author's perspective.

DURING AND AFTER READING
• Practice the Skill • Apply to Text, pp. T118, T122, T124
• Reinforce the Skill • Practice/Apply, pp. T132–T133

Comprehension Strategy
Summarize

Objectives

- *To use strategies appropriate to the reading selection*
- *To monitor comprehension by summarizing*

Summarize

When you summarize as you read, you state the most important ideas or information from a section of text in one or two sentences. Summarizing as you read can confirm your understanding and help you better remember what you read.

Fiction	Nonfiction
• State the problem in your own words.	• State the main idea in your own words.
• Identify the steps the main character takes to solve it.	• Include only the most important details.
• State the resolution in your own words.	• Use text features, such as headings, to help you identify important details.
• Do not include minor details.	

Grade 5, Lesson 22   R93   Summarize

Transparency R93

"RESEARCH SAYS"

"Summarization training had a significant effect on the recall of major information in a studying task..."

—Rinehart, Stahl, & Erickson, (1986)

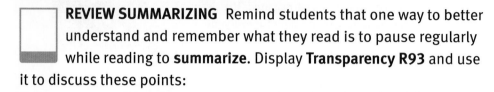
Teach/Model

REVIEW SUMMARIZING Remind students that one way to better understand and remember what they read is to pause regularly while reading to **summarize**. Display **Transparency R93** and use it to discuss these points:

- To summarize, **retell the most important events or ideas**.
- Do not include minor details.
- To **summarize fiction**, identify the problem the main character faces. Look for the steps he or she takes to solve it, and put them in your own words.
- To **summarize nonfiction**, look for the main idea of each section of text and put it in your own words. Use text features, such as headings, to help you.

Display **Transparency R94**. Read aloud the first paragraph. Then model how to pause and summarize the important ideas. Point out to students that they can summarize text in their heads or add the important ideas to a graphic organizer.

Think Aloud This is a realistic fiction story. To summarize the first paragraph, identify the main characters and the problem they face. The Johnson family hosts a car wash every year and donates the money to charity. This year, they cannot agree on which charity to support. Summarize the first paragraph by stating in your own words the problem the Johnsons face.

Guided Practice

SUMMARIZE TEXT Remind students that they should pause regularly to summarize. This may mean stopping after every paragraph or at the end of a section of text, depending on how the text is organized. Display **Transparency R94** again. Ask volunteers to continue reading the story aloud, pausing after each paragraph. Call on students to orally summarize each paragraph. After the reading has been completed, ask a volunteer to summarize the entire passage.

Practice/Apply

PRACTICE SUMMARIZING Have pairs of students select a passage from a fiction book. Have partners take turns reading and summarizing each paragraph or section of the passage.

> **DURING READING**
> • Apply the Focus Strategy, pp. T117, T119, T121
> • Review Comprehension Strategies, p. T123

Summarize

Every year the Johnson family hosts a car wash. Their friends show up to have their cars cleaned and to catch up on community news. Each year, the Johnson family donates the money raised to a different charity. In past years, they have given money to a homeless shelter, a food bank, and an arts organization. This year, however, the members of the family cannot agree on which charity to support.

For a week, the Johnsons have argued at the breakfast table about what to do with the money. Each family member believes strongly in his or her idea.

"I think we should give the money to the Elmwood Hospital," says Mr. Johnson. "They are building a new clinic for children who are very ill."

"We should give to the new home for the elderly," says Mrs. Johnson. "Our senior population is getting larger all the time."

"What about the cancer survivors wellness center?" asks Randy. "That's a worthy cause."

"Well, I think we should support doctors who make home visits," says Amisha.

The day of the car wash is approaching, and they still haven't made a decision. Then Amisha has an idea that she thinks will solve the dilemma. She realizes that each family member wants to support a health-related cause. With her mom's help, Amisha goes on the Internet and learns about Happy Healthy Families, an organization that gives money to many health-related organizations in their community.

"We should donate the money to Happy Healthy Families," Amisha tells her family. "Then we will be supporting all of our interests!"

Grade 5, Lesson 22   R94   Summarize

Transparency R94

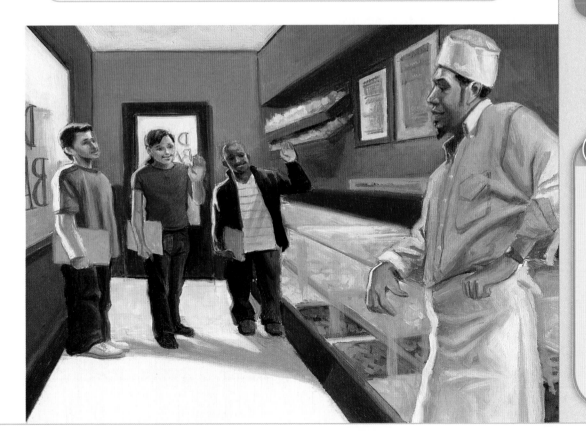

BELOW-LEVEL

Make the Strategy Hands-On
Provide students with self-stick notes cut into narrow strips. Then have them follow along as you read a passage from a story the class read previously. Stop at the end of each paragraph or section and ask students to flag important information. Then have them use the flags to orally summarize as a group.

Build Background

Access Prior Knowledge

CREATE A WEB Discuss with students the different types of fund-raisers they have participated in. Record their responses in a web like the one below. Invite volunteers to share some of the causes for which they have raised funds. Add their ideas to the web.

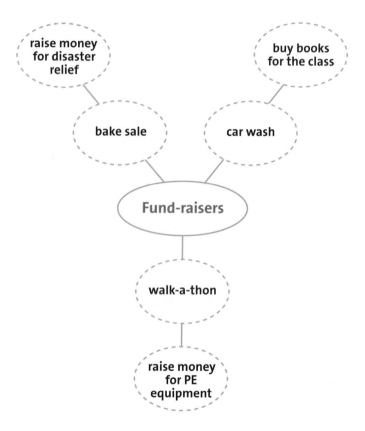

Develop Concepts

DISCUSS FUND-RAISING Use the ideas in the web to develop selection concepts.

- Libraries can benefit from fund-raisers.
- Fund-raisers can help libraries purchase books and audiovisual equipment.
- Fund-raisers can support special programs, such as traveling libraries.

ELL

Selection Background Display *Picture Card 96* and guide students to understand the following concepts.

- You can find books and newspapers in a **library**. (show photos)
- **Bookmobiles** are libraries in vans that bring books to neighborhoods without libraries. (Pantomime putting a book into a van and driving.)

Have students discuss where they go to read books.

Picture Card 96 ▶

See *ELL Teacher Guide* Lesson 22 for support in scaffolding instruction.

Build **Robust Vocabulary**

5-DAY VOCABULARY

DAY 1 Vocabulary, pp. T111–T113
DAY 2 Vocabulary Review, p. T131
DAY 3 Reinforce Word Meanings, p. T139
DAY 4 Extend Word Meanings, p. T139
DAY 5 Cumulative Review, p. T139

Introduce Vocabulary

Routine Card 2

BUILD WORD MEANING Display **Transparency R95.** Ask a volunteer to read aloud the first Vocabulary Word. Have the class repeat the word aloud to practice its pronunciation. Then have the volunteer read aloud the word's explanation. Ask students the first question below. Continue in this way until students have answered a question about each of the Vocabulary Words.

1. What kind of facial expression would you expect to see on a person who is acting **somberly**?

2. What might a person who **stammers** sound like?

3. If you **monopolize** the basketball, what are you doing?

4. Describe a day that would make you feel **deflated**.

5. If a movie **enraptured** you, would you recommend it?

6. Describe an **enterprising** person you know.

7. What would make a backpack **cumbersome** to carry?

INTRODUCE Tested ✓

Vocabulary: Lesson 22

somberly	**enraptured**
stammers	**enterprising**
monopolize	**cumbersome**
deflated	

▼ **Student-Friendly Explanations**

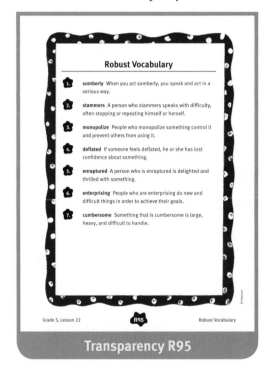

Robust Vocabulary

1. **somberly** When you act somberly, you speak and act in a serious way.

2. **stammers** A person who stammers speaks with difficulty, often stopping or repeating himself or herself.

3. **monopolize** People who monopolize something control it and prevent others from using it.

4. **deflated** If someone feels deflated, he or she has lost confidence about something.

5. **enraptured** A person who is enraptured is delighted and thrilled with something.

6. **enterprising** People who are enterprising do new and difficult things in order to achieve their goals.

7. **cumbersome** Something that is cumbersome is large, heavy, and difficult to handle.

Grade 5, Lesson 22 R95 Robust Vocabulary

Transparency R95

Vocabulary

Build Robust Vocabulary

DEVELOP DEEPER MEANING Have students read the passage on pages 568–569. Then read the passage aloud. Pause at the end of page 568. Ask questions 1–2 about the high-lighted words. Discuss students' answers. Then read page 569 and ask questions 3–7. If students are unable to give reasonable responses, refer them to the explanations on **Transparency R95.**

1. Why do you think Lina enters the room **somberly**?

2. What might make the chair **cumbersome**?

3. What causes Lina to **stammer**?

4. Do you think Lina's volunteer group is **enterprising**? Explain.

5. What **deflated** the group's hopes?

6. Why would it be a problem for a business to **monopolize** a beach?

7. Why do you think Mr. McLane was **enraptured**?

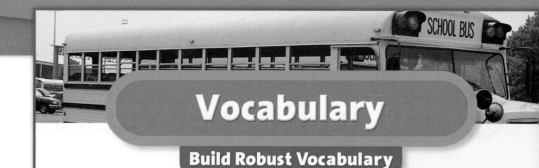

Vocabulary

Build Robust Vocabulary

somberly

cumbersome

stammers

enterprising

deflated

monopolize

enraptured

Safe Swimming

Lina Joyce knocks on Mr. McLane's office door.

"Come in!"

Lina enters the room **somberly**. Mr. McLane frowns at her and nods at a chair in front of his desk. Lina pulls out the **cumbersome** chair and sits. She fiddles with the folder in her hand.

568

ELL

Clarify Meanings Use facial expressions to clarify the meanings of *somberly, enraptured,* and *deflated.* Demonstrate *stammering,* and pantomime carrying something *cumbersome.* Give examples of being *enterprising* and of *monopolizing* something.

See *ELL Teacher Guide* Lesson 22 for support in scaffolding instruction.

"I. . . you. . . I mean. . . ," Lina **stammers**. Then she takes a deep breath, and begins again. "I belong to an **enterprising** volunteer group that wants to make Silver Beach a safe public swimming spot. When we read about your plans for an oyster farm there, our hopes were **deflated**. We're afraid your farm will **monopolize** the beach. We believe Doan Beach is a better spot for your farm. We also think that location will save you money." Lina hands the folder to Mr. McLane.

Mr. McLane looks through the papers inside. Then he smiles at Lina. "Tell me more about your idea!" he exclaims, **enraptured**.

GO online www.harcourtschool.com/storytown

Word Detective

Your mission this week is to look for the Vocabulary Words outside your classroom. Be alert for them when you read novels, textbooks, magazines, and newspapers and as you watch television. Each time you see or hear a Vocabulary Word, write it in your vocabulary journal. Don't forget to record where or how you encountered the word.

569

Word Detective

Search for Words Suggest that students keep a list of the Vocabulary Words with them. Encourage them to think creatively about places where they might find the words, including billboards, e-mails, and advertisements. At the week's end, have students share where they saw or heard the words.

HOMEWORK/INDEPENDENT PRACTICE

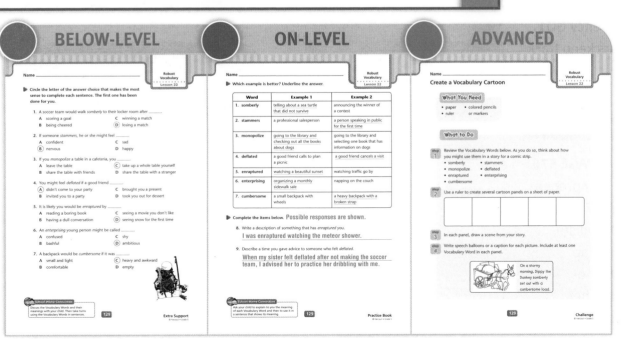

▲ Extra Support, p. 129   ▲ Practice Book, p. 129   ▲ Challenge, p. 129

ELL

• Group students according to academic levels, and assign one of the pages on the left.

• Clarify any unfamiliar concepts as necessary. See *ELL Teacher Guide* Lesson 22 for support in scaffolding instruction.

MATH

Read the Selection

Objective
- *To identify the distinguishing characteristics of a play*

Genre Study

DISCUSS PLAYS: PAGE 570 Have students read the genre information on page 570. Discuss with them the characteristics of a play, including the division of text into acts and scenes and the location and use of stage directions. Then have them look at pages 570–572 and identify features that show this selection is a play.

LIST GENRE FEATURES Guide students to compare and contrast the characteristics of plays with those of fiction stories. If necessary, point out that while both have plots with conflicts and resolutions, the plot events in a play are revealed in dialogue and stage directions rather than through description. Then display **Transparency GO1**. Use the story map to help students keep track of story elements.

Comprehension Strategy

DISCUSS SUMMARIZING: PAGE 570 Have students read the Comprehension Strategy information on page 570. Then distribute *Practice Book* page 130. Tell students that they will fill in the story map as they read to help them keep track of important information and monitor their comprehension. See page T127 for the completed *Practice Book* page.

The Power of W.O.W.!
Play

Genre Study

A play is a story that can be performed for an audience. As you read, look for

- plot events organized into acts and scenes.
- characters' actions and feelings shown through dialogue.

```
Characters        Setting
        Conflict
      Plot Events
      Resolution
```

Comprehension Strategy

Summarize the main ideas and the most important details of the selection as you read.

570

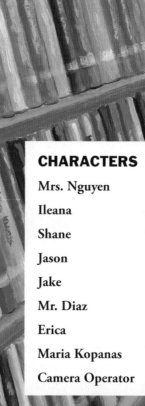

CHARACTERS

Mrs. Nguyen

Ileana

Shane

Jason

Jake

Mr. Diaz

Erica

Maria Kopanas

Camera Operator

▲ Practice Book, p. 130

TECHNOLOGY

eBook "The Power of W.O.W.!" is available in an eBook.

Audiotext "The Power of W.O.W.!" is available on *Audiotext Grade 5*, CD7 for subsequent readings.

The Power of W.O.W.!

by Crystal Hubbard
illustrated by Eric Velasquez

571

Preview/Set a Purpose

 Routine Card 3

PREVIEW AND PREDICT Remind students that they can set a purpose for reading based on their preview of a selection, plus what they know about the genre. Have students read the title and the introduction to Act One, Scene One on page 572. Ask them to look at the first few illustrations. Then have them predict who and what the play will be about.

MODEL SETTING A PURPOSE Ask students to use their preview to set a purpose for reading. You may want to use this model:

Think Aloud The title has the initials W.O.W. These letters stand for Words on Wheels and also spell the exclamation "Wow!" One purpose for reading is to find out what the power of W.O.W. is and what it has to do with Words on Wheels.

Options for Reading

BELOW-LEVEL	ON-LEVEL	ADVANCED
Small Group Preview the selection with students. Model how to use the preview and the genre information to set a purpose for reading.	**Whole Group/Partner** Use the Monitor Comprehension questions as students read the selection, or have partners read the selection together and complete *Practice Book* page 127.	**Independent** Have students read the selection independently, using *Practice Book* page 130 to monitor their comprehension and keep track of the information in the selection.

Monitor Comprehension

1 **CHARACTER'S FEELINGS**
How is Mrs. Nguyen feeling as she talks to Ileana? How do you know? (sad; discouraged; she speaks somberly, forces a smile, sighs, and slumps her shoulders)

2 **PLOT: CONFLICT AND RESOLUTION**
What problem does the W.O.W. program face? (The library does not have any more money to pay for the program, so it will end in another week.)

3 **MAKE PREDICTIONS**
Do you think W.O.W. will be saved?
(Responses will vary.)

 See *Questioning the Author Comprehension Guide,* Lesson 22, as an alternate questioning strategy to guide student interaction with the text.

Questioning the Author Comprehension Guide, Lesson 22 ▶

ACT ONE

SCENE ONE
Time: *Present*
Setting: *Inside a bus that has been converted into a bookmobile—a traveling library. Mrs. Nguyen [WIN] sits at a narrow checkout counter. Ileana boards the bus and awkwardly sets a heavy stack of books on the checkout counter.*

Mrs. Nguyen: Hi, Ileana! Did you enjoy the books I recommended last week?
Ileana: (Displays top book) I didn't think I'd like Greek mythology, and I didn't. I loved it!
Mrs. Nguyen: Which myth was your favorite?

572

E L L

Clarify Expressions Use simple explanations and definitions to help students understand the following expressions:

- **golden touch**—refers to the myth about King Midas; means "being able to make something good happen"
- **pilot program**—a new program that is being tried out and usually has enough money to run for a specific period of time only
- **funded**—gave money to pay for a specific program or effort

Accepting donations for new library books.

Ileana: The one about King Midas and how he wished that everything he touched would turn to gold. Boy, did that turn out to be a bad wish.

Mrs. Nguyen: (Speaks somberly) I don't think I'd mind having the golden touch, just for a minute.

Ileana: Is something wrong?

Mrs. Nguyen: (Forces herself to smile) Nothing you need to worry about. I'll just check your books in while you browse the shelves. We've got the latest book about Sam Thorne, Fifth-Grade Detective. It's called "The Case of the Missing Monkey's Paw."

Ileana: Now I know something's wrong. You're trying to distract me.

Mrs. Nguyen: (Sighs, and her shoulders slump) Words on Wheels won't be back after next week. ❶

Ileana: Why not?

Mrs. Nguyen: Words On Wheels is just a pilot program. The library funded W.O.W. for one year, and the year's almost up. There's no more money to pay for gas and repairs, to pay the driver, or to buy new books. I'll have to go back to the library downtown.

Ileana: (Stammers in worry) B-but that's so far away! How will my neighborhood get books? The only time my grandmother can use a computer is when the W.O.W. bus comes. And I'll never get to see you, Mrs. Nguyen. Can't the library give you some more money?

Mrs. Nguyen: The library does the best it can, but the money it receives just doesn't go as far as we'd like. We rely on community support, and people just don't seem to be interested in contributing to W.O.W.

Ileana: I have some money saved. You can have it—all of it.

Mrs. Nguyen: That's very generous, Ileana, but I'm afraid you and I together wouldn't have nearly enough money to save W.O.W. It's an expensive program. I'm sorry. ❷ ❸

573

Apply Comprehension Strategies

Summarize

USE STORY ELEMENTS TO SUMMARIZE Ask students to think about the information they would include in a summary of pages 572–573, such as story elements. Model identifying the key story elements:

Think Aloud **This first scene introduces the story conflict—the W.O.W. program is going to end because there is not enough funding. The conflict of a story should be included in a summary.**

Guide students to restate the conflict of the story in their own words. Remind them that pausing to summarize important developments in the plot can help them understand and better remember what they read.

ANALYZE WRITER'S CRAFT

Acronyms Tell students that W.O.W. is an acronym for Words on Wheels. Explain that an acronym is a word made up by combining the first letter or letters of a series of words. Explain that authors often use acronyms to save space or to avoid repetition of phrases.

Monitor Comprehension

4 **MAKE INFERENCES**

Why does Ileana say "It's not funny, Shane"? (Possible response: She thinks Shane isn't taking the situation seriously because he makes a joke by using the exclamation "Wow!" and the acronym W.O.W. in the same sentence.)

5 **MAKE INFERENCES**

Is Ileana the only person who values W.O.W.? How do you know? (Possible response: No; Shane, Jason, and Jake all want to help save the program.)

6 **AUTHOR'S PURPOSE AND PERSPECTIVE**

What is the author's perspective about the importance of community programs? How do you know? (Possible response: She is writing about students who want to save a community program, so she thinks they are important.)

7 **MAKE PREDICTIONS**

What do you think Ileana and her friends will do to try to save the W.O.W. program? (Responses will vary.)

SCENE TWO

Setting: *Shane's backyard. Ileana, Shane, and Jason are sitting at a picnic table, sipping juice and munching snacks.*

Shane: (Shaking his head) Wow. That's bad news about W.O.W..
Ileana: It's not funny, Shane. **4**
Jason: What did Mrs. Nguyen mean when she said W.O.W. needs community support?
Ileana: Donations from people in the community pay for the library's special programs.
Jason: Well, we're the community, and if we want to save W.O.W., we have to find a way to make money to pay for it.
Ileana: I wish I had King Midas's golden touch. I could turn this picnic table into gold, and then we could sell it to pay for W.O.W..
Jason: Maybe we could sell something else.
Shane: I can't sell my bike. I need it to get to school.
Ileana: What if we sell our skills?
Jason: Our what?
Ileana: Our skills. Isn't there something we could do to raise money?
Shane: Let's ask Jake. He and his friends raised money for their school picnic last year. We could ask him how they did it.
Jake: (Calls to Shane from back door) Hey, Squirt. Mom wants to know if your little friends want to stay for dinner. We're having mutant chicken.
Ileana: (Exchanging a look of confusion with Jason) Mutant chicken?
Shane: Jake and I used to fight over the drumsticks, so my mom uses skewers to attach extra legs to a regular chicken. (To Jake) Could we ask you a question, Jake?
Jake: (Sits at picnic table) What's up?
Ileana: We need to make a lot of money really quickly. Mrs. Nguyen won't be coming to our neighborhood anymore because the W.O.W. program ran out of money.
Jake: (Thoughtfully) I never would have gotten an A on my science project if Mrs. Nguyen hadn't let me monopolize the W.O.W. computer. She showed me how to use a software program to create diagrams of the chemical compounds I wrote about in my report. **5**
Shane: You're on your own for your next project if we can't figure out a way to save W.O.W.. How did your class pay for last year's picnic? **6**

574

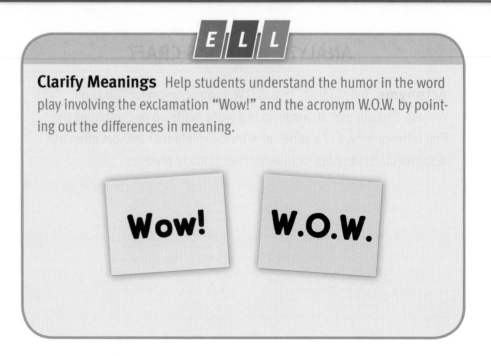

E L L

Clarify Meanings Help students understand the humor in the word play involving the exclamation "Wow!" and the acronym W.O.W. by pointing out the differences in meaning.

Jake: We did a lot of things. (Picks up a handful of snacks and gobbles them) You could have a bake sale.

Jason: Is that what you and your friends did?

Jake: (Laughs) Bake sales are for kids. We held a car wash one Saturday morning, and we earned enough money to pay for the picnic.

Ileana: (Perking up) A car wash!

Shane: That's perfect!

Jason: That would be so much fun!

Jake: Hold on. You can't just stand on the street and yell "Car Wash." You have to organize it. You need a place to have it and supplies to wash the cars. You especially need a water source, and you have to advertise.

Shane: (Somewhat deflated) Wow. It's going to take a lot of work to save W.O.W.

Ileana: Shane, you're doing it again.

Shane: I'm sorry. I really don't mean to.

Jake: (To Ileana and Jason) If you guys stay for mutant chicken, we can discuss ways to save W.O.W. **7**

575

Apply Comprehension Strategies

Summarize

IDENTIFY IMPORTANT INFORMATION Remind students that when they summarize, they should include important information only. Model deciding which details from pages 574–575 should be included in a summary:

Think Aloud Only include the important events in a summary. Jake's suggestion to hold a car wash to raise money is an important event and belongs in a summary. Shane's joking around about the word *wow* should not be included.

Ask students to suggest other events and details on pages 574–575 to include in a summary.

ANALYZE WRITER'S CRAFT

Humor Tell students that writers often use humor to make writing entertaining and enjoyable. Guide students in a discussion about humor, using the following points:

- Shane makes a joke by using the exclamation "Wow!" and the acronym W.O.W. in the same sentence.
- The children discuss the idea of a mutant chicken.
- Have students evaluate how the author's use of humor adds to the overall quality of the work.

Monitor Comprehension

⑧ CHARACTER'S MOTIVES

What are some reasons why Mr. Diaz is willing to help the children? (Possible responses: He uses and appreciates W.O.W. resources. He likes Mrs. Nyguyen.)

⑨ MAKE INFERENCES

What does Shane mean when he says "the power of W.O.W."? (He is referring to the ideas about fundraising that he and his friends learned from materials they got from the bookmobile.)

⑩ SEQUENCE

What are the steps of the children's plan to have a successful car wash? (Get cleaning supplies from their parents; make advertisements with the W.O.W. computer and printer; convince Mr. Diaz to let them use his parking lot for the car wash; advertise in local businesses)

ACT TWO

SCENE ONE

Setting: *Diaz Bakery. Mr. Diaz stands beside a counter next to a glass case filled with scrumptious-looking desserts. Ileana, Shane, and Jason enter the shop wearing hand-lettered buttons that read P.O.W.W.O.W.. Each one carries a stack of papers of assorted colors.*

Mr. Diaz: *Hola, niños.*[1] (Reads buttons) What's "pow-wow"?

Shane: It stands for "Please Open Wallets for Words On Wheels." Ileana thought of it.

Ileana: (Clears her throat and speaks formally) We'd like to ask you for help, Uncle Carlos. Words on Wheels needs money to keep coming to our neighborhood.

Jason: W.O.W. brings the library to us when our parents can't take us to the library.

Ileana: We'd like to have a car wash this Saturday to raise money. Our parents donated all the cleaning supplies, and we used the W.O.W. computer and printer to make advertisements. (She hands Mr. Diaz a bright-blue flyer, which he reads.)

Jason: All we need now is a place to hold the car wash.

Mr. Diaz: (Chuckles softly) And that's where I come in, right?

Ileana: Well, you are a part of the community, Uncle Carlos. Mrs. Nguyen always stops the bookmobile right here in front of your shop so you can look up new cake recipes on the Internet.

Mr. Diaz: The orange chiffon cake recipe I found online last month has been one of my best sellers. And I always enjoy having coffee with Mrs. Nguyen. She loves my chocolate cake. (Thoughtfully strokes his chin) You can use my parking lot. You can hook up your hose right to the building.

Ileana: (Slaps high-fives with Shane, Jason, and Mr. Diaz) *Gracias,*[2] Uncle Carlos! Thank you!

Shane: *Gracias,* Señor Diaz. You won't be sorry. Just think of all the people who'll want to buy pies and cakes and cookies while we're washing their cars.

---

[1] *Hola, niños.*: Hi, kids.
[2] *gracias*: Thank you.

576

Jason: (Turns to Ileana and Shane) The next step is to get the word out. We have to add the location to these flyers and hand them out. Let's stick to the places that we know. I'll go to the Busy Bee Cleaners across the street and to the Split Ends Barbershop and see if we can put flyers there. Mr. Diaz, may I leave a stack of flyers for your customers?

Mr. Diaz: Of course, and I'll give a free coffee to anyone who lets you wash their car.

Jason: *Muchas gracias,*[3] Mr. Diaz.

Mr. Diaz: *De nada,*[4] Jason.

Shane: I'll go to the Sweet Delights Candy Shop and the Clickety-Clack Toy Store.

Ileana: And I'll take my flyers to Mrs. Romero's market, the Twinkle Time Bead Shop, and Flora's Glorious Florals.

Mr. Diaz: (Impressed) You're very organized.

Ileana: The bookmobile has a lot of information on fund-raising.

Shane: That's the power of W.O.W.. **9**

Mr. Diaz: After you finish handing out your flyers, meet back here and I'll show you the power of orange chiffon cake! **10**

---

[3] *muchas gracias*: Thank you very much.
[4] *de nada*: You're welcome.

577

Apply Comprehension Strategies

Summarize

USE SEQUENCE If students have difficulty responding to question 10, remind them to summarize ideas in the same order as they appear in the selection. Draw a sequence chart like the one shown below. Guide students to complete it by using information from pages 576–577.

> **First,** the children get cleaning supplies from their parents.
>
> ↓
>
> **Next,** they use the W.O.W. computer and printer to make advertisements.
>
> ↓
>
> **Then,** they ask Mr. Diaz to let them use the bakery parking lot for the car wash.
>
> ↓
>
> **Finally,** they divide up places to go to hand out flyers.

 **MATH**   **SUPPORTING STANDARDS**

Calculate a Reasonable Amount Ask students to work in pairs to figure out what amount of money the children can reasonably expect to earn from a one-day car wash. You might prompt them with the following questions:

- How much can the children charge per car?
- How many cars can they wash in an hour?
- How many hours total will they work?

Once students have finished their calculations, have partners compare their results with other pairs.

Monitor Comprehension

11 **MAKE INFERENCES**

Why are Ileana and Erica disappointed after the first three hours of the car wash? (Possible response: Not many cars have come by so far.)

12 **PLOT: CONFLICT AND RESOLUTION**

What is an unexpected result of delivering the flyers to neighborhood businesses? (Possible response: The owner of the Busy Bee Cleaners has told her niece, Maria Kopanas, about the car wash, and Maria has come to do a report on it.)

13 **AUTHOR'S PURPOSE AND PERSPECTIVE**

Focus Skill

Why do you think the author uses the television reporter in the story? (Possible responses: to make the events seem more important; to help resolve the story problem.)

14 **CAUSE AND EFFECT**

What do you think the effect of the news report will be on the car wash? (Possible response: People will see the report and will come out to support the car wash.)

SCENE TWO

Setting: Parking lot of Diaz Bakery. Jake uses a water hose to rinse his father's car. Shane and Jason towel-dry a car they have just finished washing. Erica accepts a few bills from the driver and hurries the money over to Ileana, who holds the cash jar.

Erica: (Excitedly) That man gave us five whole dollars extra! How much do we have so far?

Ileana: We've washed Uncle Carlos's car and all of our parents' cars, and with that last customer, we have a whopping sixty-five dollars.

Erica: We've been out here for three hours, and that's it? **11**

Ileana: I thought for sure we'd have tons of cars. I guess. . . (Voice trails off as she stares over Erica's shoulder.)

578

E L L

Use Prefixes Point to the word *co-organizer* on page 579. Tell students that *co-* is a prefix that means "together." A co-organizer is someone who organizes an event with others. Then ask students what they think *cochampion* and *co-owner* might mean. Explain that using their knowledge of prefixes can help them determine the meaning of unfamiliar words.

Erica: (Turns to see what has Ileana enraptured) There's a van coming. We should charge extra to wash that big silver pole on top.

Jake: (Jogs over to Ileana and Erica, with Shane and Jason on his heels) That's a television van! (Shoves the cash from his father into the money jar) I've seen that lady on the news.

Maria Kopanas: (Holding a microphone, she exits the passenger side of the van. She uses her index finger to polish her teeth in the side-view mirror while the driver retrieves a heavy camera from the back of the van. The two approach the children.) Hello, my name is Maria Kopanas, and I'm a roving reporter for Channel 7. My aunt owns the Busy Bee Cleaners, and she told me about the car wash today to raise money for the Words on Wheels bookmobile. May I speak to the organizer of today's event? **12**

Ileana: (Reluctantly allows Shane, Jason, Jake, and Erica to push her forward; reporter holds microphone toward her.)

Maria: You're the organizer of . . . (Checks flyer in her pocket) . . . Please Open Wallets for Words on Wheels?

Shane: (Leans toward microphone) Co-organizer.

Camera Operator: (Stands back and aims camera toward Maria and the group of children, who crowd close together) We're on the air in five . . . four . . . three . . . (Raises two fingers and then one; then points to Maria)

Maria: (Smiles widely and speaks loudly and clearly) I'm Maria Kopanas reporting live from the parking lot of Diaz Bakery. I'm with some enterprising young people who decided to do something when they learned that their beloved bookmobile, Words on Wheels, no longer had the money to operate. I'll let the children introduce themselves. (Holds microphone to each)

Ileana: Hi. I'm Ileana, and this is my sister Erica. (Puts an arm around her shoulders)

Erica: (Shrugs off Ileana's arm) I can say my own name! (Sweetly, to camera) I'm Erica. And Diaz Bakery makes the best orange chiffon cake in town!

Shane: I'm Shane. (Waves) Hi, Mom!

Jason: I'm Jason.

Jake: I'm Jake.

Shane: (Pulling microphone from Jake's face to his own) He's my brother. He wants to be a veterinarian. **13 14**

579

Apply Comprehension Strategies

Use Story Structure

IDENTIFY THE RESOLUTION If students have difficulty answering question 12, remind them that thinking about the parts of a story can help them better understand what they read. Point out that as they read, they should look for how the conflict will be resolved. Explain that the children appearing on television is an important step toward the resolution. You may want to use this model:

Think Aloud Ileana is upset that they haven't raised as much money as she thought they would. She said that she thought there would be more cars. Then Maria Kopanas arrives to put the children on the news. Many people watch the news, so it is very likely that the news report will attract people to the car wash and help the children raise money.

ANALYZE WRITER'S CRAFT

Developing Realistic Characters Guide students to analyze the stage directions on pages 578–579 to identify

- how the characters are feeling.
- how the characters are reacting to each other.

Then ask students to tell whether they think the author has done a good job of creating a realistic scene and to explain why or why not.

Monitor Comprehension

15 **PERSONAL OPINION**
Do you agree with Ileana and her friends that a book "isn't just a bunch of pages"? Explain. (Reponses will vary.)

16  **AUTHOR'S PURPOSE AND PERSPECTIVE**
What do you think is the author's perspective about children's ability to make a difference in their communities? How do you know? (Possible response: The author believes that children can make a difference in their communities; she has written a story in which children organized and saved a valued program in their community.)

17 **CONFIRM PREDICTIONS**
Did the plan to save W.O.W. turn out as you thought it would? (Responses will vary.)

Maria: (Speaking into microphone) How have you done so far?
Ileana: (Uncomfortably) Not too well, actually. There haven't been that many cars.
Maria: Why's the bookmobile so important to you?
Ileana: It's the only way the kids in my neighborhood can get library books and use a computer. The library downtown is too far away, so it's nice to have a library that comes to us. P.O.W. stands for Please Open Wallets, but it could also stand for Power of Words. A book isn't just a bunch of pages. A book can give you an adventure. **15**
Shane: Or make you laugh.
Erica: Or make you scared, but in a good way.
Jason: Or teach you something.
Jake: Books mean a lot of different things to different people, and we want to make sure that books keep coming to us.
Maria: (Speaks directly into camera) It's a beautiful day for a car wash, folks, and I hope to see you and your dirty cars down here to help the power of words remain in this dedicated community.
Camera Operator: (Shuts off camera) And we're out, Maria. Good job, kids.
Maria: (Hands him her microphone) Before we head back to the station, I think the news van could use a good wash.
Shane: Wow! A reporter's going to help out W.O.W.!
Ileana: Shane!

580

Clarify the Resolution Make sure that students understand that in addition to the money raised from washing cars, many people wrote checks to donate money. The combination of the two generated enough money to keep W.O.W. running.

SCENE THREE

Setting: *Parking lot of Diaz Bakery. Shane, Jason, Jake, their parents, and the camera operator are washing a long line of cars. Erica ferries the money to Ileana, who has to mash the cash down in the overfilled money jar. The W.O.W. bus lumbers into the parking lot. Drivers honk their horns as Mrs. Nguyen exits the bookmobile.*

Ileana: (*Ecstatic*) Look, Mrs. Nguyen! (*Meets her halfway with the money jar hugged to her body*) This is for W.O.W.

Mrs. Nguyen: (*Accepts jar*) Ileana, this is unbelievable!

Ileana: We started out really slowly, but after Maria Kopanas put us on the news, all of a sudden tons of cars showed up. We had to call our families to help us. I don't know if there's enough money here to save W.O.W., but it looks like a good start, doesn't it?

Mrs. Nguyen: That's what I came to tell you, Ileana. Many people in the community picked up your flyers and saw you on television, and they've promised to do something to help. (*Sets cumbersome jar on the asphalt and pulls envelopes from her pocket*) All of these contain checks! They're from Busy Bee Cleaners, Split Ends Barbershop, Sweet Delights, Clickety-Clack Toy Store, Twinkle Time Bead Shop, Flora's Glorious Florals, Mrs. Romero's market, Channel 7, your parents, and so many other people in the neighborhood. Oh, Ileana! W.O.W. can keep running for a long time to come!

Ileana: (*Jumps for joy and shouts to her friends*) Wow! We saved W.O.W.!

581

Additional Related Reading

Students interested in communities and volunteering may want to locate these titles.

- *Serving Your Community* by Christin Ditchfield. Children's Press, 2004.
  EASY

- *What is a Community?: From A to Z* by Bobbie Kalman. Crabtree, 2000.
  AVERAGE

- *The Kids' Volunteering Book* by Arlene Erlbach. Lerner, 1998.
  CHALLENGE

ANALYZE AUTHOR'S PURPOSE

Author's Purpose Remind students that authors have a purpose, or reason, for writing. After students have finished "The Power of W.O.W.!," ask them:

Why do you think the author chose to write this play?

- **To explain the history of bookmobiles**

- **To persuade people to visit a library**

- To entertain with a play about the power of community

- **To inform readers about how to hold a car wash**

Think Critically

Respond to the Literature

Have students discuss or write their responses to the questions on page 582.

1 Possible response: The W.O.W. program provides them with books and computer access. **NOTE DETAILS**

2 Responses will vary. **MAKE JUDGMENTS**

3 Responses will vary. **EXPRESS PERSONAL OPINIONS**

4 Possible response: The author believes that the public library plays an important role in a community because she wrote a story about characters who fight to have access to a library. 🔄 **AUTHOR'S PURPOSE AND PERSPECTIVE**

5 ✏️ **WRITE** Students' responses should answer the questions *who*, *what*, *where*, *when*, *why*, and *how*. They should explain that the car wash was held to save W.O.W. and that the children achieved their goal. **SHORT RESPONSE**

RUBRIC For additional support in scoring this item, see the rubric on page R6.

Think Critically

1 In what ways is the W.O.W. program important to Ileana and her friends?
NOTE DETAILS

2 Is it believable that people change their minds quickly about supporting the W.O.W. program? Explain. MAKE JUDGMENTS

3 What are some community programs that help people in your city or town? Why is each important? EXPRESS PERSONAL OPINIONS

4 What is the author's opinion about the role of the public library in a community? How do you know? 🔄 AUTHOR'S PURPOSE AND PERSPECTIVE

5 **WRITE** Write a brief news story about the P.O.W.W.O.W. car wash for the next morning's newspaper. Tell why the car wash was held and what the outcome was. ✏️ SHORT RESPONSE

582

BELOW-LEVEL

Express Personal Opinions If students have difficulty explaining whether or not they think it's believable that people would change their minds about supporting W.O.W., you might want to guide them by asking these questions:

• Do people like to support children who are working for a good cause?

• Do people think libraries are important?

• Can the media influence the way people act or make them aware of a problem or event?

About the Author

Crystal Hubbard

As a child growing up in St. Louis, Missouri, Crystal Hubbard dreamed of being a writer. She worked toward that dream when she wrote for her college newspaper and, later, for Boston-area newspapers. She lives in Wakefield, Massachusetts, with her husband, their children, and two goldfish named Eyeballs and Rocks.

 www.harcourtschool.com/storytown

About the Illustrator

Eric Velasquez

Eric Velasquez inherited a love of drawing from his mom, a love of film from his dad, and an appreciation of music from his grandmother. He said, "Becoming an artist was a natural choice for me. I have never thought of being anything else." He has illustrated more than 300 book jackets, and several of his own picture books have been published. He lives in Hartsdale, New York.

583

Check Comprehension

Retell and Summarize

DISCUSS AUTHOR AND ILLUSTRATOR: PAGE 583 Have students read the information and discuss how writing for newspapers might help a children's book author.

RETELL Students may refer to the story map on *Practice Book* page 130 that they completed during reading to help them retell "The Power of W.O.W.!"

 Routine Card 4

WRITE A SUMMARY Ask students to write a summary of the selection. Share the following tips:

- Begin with the selection title and its genre.
- Describe the conflict, events, and resolution in story order.
- Explain the author's message.

RUBRIC See rubric for Retelling and Summarizing on page R3.

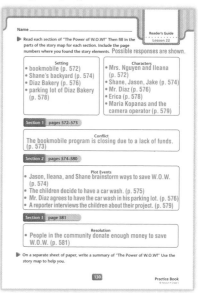

▲ Practice Book, p. 130

MONITOR PROGRESS

Summarize

IF students have difficulty writing a summary,	**THEN** help them list the steps the students took to save W.O.W.

Small-Group Instruction, p. S14:

● **BELOW-LEVEL:** Reteach   ● **ON-LEVEL:** Reinforce   ● **ADVANCED:** Extend

SOCIAL STUDIES

Paired Selection

Objective
- *To recognize the distinguishing characteristics of a magazine article*

Genre Study

PREVIEW THE ARTICLE Point out that a magazine article gives information about a topic. It may contain headings and graphics that give more information about the topic. Ask students to read the title and the heading above the directions and to look at the illustration. Have students predict what they will learn from reading this article. (Possible response: how to organize a community project)

ANALYZE THE ARTICLE Have students read the article. Ask them what the author thinks people should do if they see a problem in their community. (Possible responses: organize to solve the problem; create an action plan) Then have students restate the steps the author suggests.

Social Studies

Magazine Article

KIDS CAN Change the World

Got a Problem? GET A PLAN!

by Karen Bledsoe • illustrated by Eric Sturdevant

Your school's jogging path is worn out, there's litter in the park, and the animal shelter needs new doghouses. Someone should do something! That someone could be you.

You, your family, or your class can carry out service projects to solve problems in your community. But before you begin, you need a good action plan.

An action plan is a detailed plan of your project from beginning to end. A good plan helps you decide exactly what needs to be done and how to do it, so there won't be any unpleasant surprises.

584

ELL

Use Demonstrations and Gestures After you read each step, pause to use gestures or demonstration to clarify it. For example, after reading step 1, you might list project ideas and then circle one. Then have students restate or demonstrate each step to confirm their understanding.

Follow these steps to create your action plan:

1. Brainstorm ideas for your project. Decide on something that you want to do.
2. Find out whom to call to get permission to carry out the project.
3. Write down exactly what needs to be done. Make sure everyone understands.
4. Decide how many people you will need. Recruit volunteers to help.
5. List any materials you will need. Find out where to get them and how much they will cost. (Don't forget tools, drinks, snacks, and a first-aid kit.)
6. Figure out how long your project will take. Choose a starting date.
7. List the things your helpers will need to bring, such as work gloves and lunch.
8. Give your helpers a reminder call one or two days before the starting date of the project.
9. On the day you begin, make sure you're the first one there. That way, you can answer any questions people have about what you are doing, and you can help volunteers get started as soon as they arrive.
10. When the project is over, celebrate! And remember to give a big "thanks" to all your helpers. You couldn't have done it without them!

585

 SOCIAL STUDIES SUPPORTING STANDARDS

Taking Action Lead students in a discussion about national issues that concern them, such as protecting the national parks, or conserving energy or water. List ideas on the board, and then have the class vote on one. Work with students to create an imaginary action plan for getting involved with the issue. Such a plan might begin with corresponding with their representative in Congress.

Respond to the Article

Ask students to reread the article silently, paying careful attention to the information about action plan steps. Then ask:

1. MAIN IDEA **Why do people who participate in service projects need a detailed action plan?** (Possible response: so that they know exactly what needs to be done and how to do it)

2. SEQUENCE **What must you do before you can decide how many volunteers you'll need?** (Write down exactly what needs to be done.) **Why is this step important?** (Possible response: It helps you figure out whether you have enough volunteers for the amount of work there is to do.)

3. SOCIAL STUDIES **CONNECTING TEXTS Do you think Ileana and her friends in "The Power of W.O.W!" would agree with the author's advice in "Got a Problem? Get a Plan!"? Why or why not?** (Possible response: Yes, because they seem to have had a specific plan for raising money for the W.O.W. program.)

WRITE AN E-MAIL Have students think of projects they would like to work on in your community. Help them to find out whom to contact to get information. Then have them write an e-mail requesting information about ways to participate in the project. **WRITING**

Comparing Texts

Answers:

1. Reponses will vary. **TEXT TO SELF**

2. Possible response: People can work together to make their community better. **TEXT TO TEXT**

3. Possible responses: show enthusiasm for the cause yourself; use various techniques to persuade people to be interested **TEXT TO WORLD**

Connections

Comparing Texts

1. The young people in "The Power of W.O.W!" raise money for something they believe in. Describe a group activity you would like to participate in for a good cause.

2. What is the theme of both "The Power of W.O.W!" and "Got a Problem? Get a Plan!"?

3. What are some ways to get people interested in a cause?

Vocabulary Review

The enterprising student enraptured everyone with her plan.

Word Pairs

Work with a partner. Write the Vocabulary Words on index cards. Place the cards face down. Take turns flipping over two cards and writing a sentence using both words. Read the sentences aloud to your partner. You must use both words correctly to keep the cards. The player with the most cards wins.

somberly

stammers

monopolize

deflated

enraptured

enterprising

cumbersome

586

Fluency Practice

Partner Reading

Work with a partner. Choose a section of the play that has two to four speaking roles, and decide which roles each of you will take. Discuss how the characters you have chosen might feel at that point in the play and what they might sound like. Read aloud the text you have chosen, focusing on expression. Repeat the process until you are satisfied with your expression.

 ## Writing

Write a Radio Ad

Think about someone who makes a difference in your community. Write a radio ad to help the people in your community become aware of the work this person does.

Who?	
What?	
When?	
Where?	
Why?	
How?	

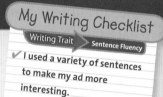

My Writing Checklist

Writing Trait ▶ Sentence Fluency

✓ I used a variety of sentences to make my ad more interesting.

✓ I used a graphic organizer to plan my writing.

✓ I used persuasive language in my ad.

587

 ## VOCABULARY REVIEW

Word Pairs Remind students to write sentences that are clear and descriptive. Suggest that they think about what the words they choose have in common that would help them work together in a sentence.

 ## FLUENCY PRACTICE

Partner Reading: Expression Have each partner silently read his or her section of the play before reading it aloud. Tell students to focus on making their character sound as if he or she is speaking naturally. Have students practice until they are satisfied with their expression. *For additional fluency practice, see p. T138.*

WRITING

 Write a Radio Ad Have students discuss radio ads they have heard that they think are effective. Point out that radio ads are usually brief and state the message clearly, in an attention-grabbing way. Tell students to use the checklist to evaluate their writing.

PORTFOLIO OPPORTUNITY Students may choose to place their radio ads in their portfolios.

 ## MONITOR PROGRESS

Vocabulary Review

IF students have difficulty writing sentences,

THEN provide them with this example: *She felt deflated when her brother monopolized play time with the new puppy.*

Small-Group Instruction, pp. S12–S13:

● **BELOW-LEVEL:** Reteach

● **ON-LEVEL:** Reinforce

● **ADVANCED:** Extend

Author's Purpose and Perspective

Objectives

- *To understand that authors have different purposes for writing*
- *To identify and discuss an author's perspective*

Skill Trace

 Tested **Author's Purpose and Perspective**

Introduce	pp. T30–T31
Reteach	pp. S2–S3, S10–S11
Review	**pp. T56–T57, T106–T107, T132–T133, T308**
Test	Theme 5
Maintain	p. T274, Theme 6

ADVANCED

Discuss Author's Background

Have students choose a story they recently read that they enjoyed. Ask them to tell the author's purpose and perspective. Then have them look for biographical information about the author, on the book jacket or the Internet, to see how the author's background may have influenced his or her perspective. Have them share the information they find.

Reinforce the Skill

REVIEW AUTHOR'S PURPOSE AND PERSPECTIVE Remind students that authors write for different purposes and that they sometimes reveal their perspective, or opinion, about the topic. Review these points:

- An author may have more than one **purpose** for writing a text. For example, an author's main purpose for writing a fiction story may be to entertain, but he or she may also intend to teach a lesson.

- Readers can determine an **author's perspective** by paying attention to the language the author uses, the details he or she includes, and the author's background.

Guided Practice

APPLY TO LITERATURE Work with students to revisit "The Power of W.O.W!" and find clues that indicate the author's purpose and perspective. Have students reread the sections listed below and answer the questions.

- **Pages 574–576** Why do you think the author includes the parts where Jake and Mr. Diaz reveal how helpful W.O.W. has been to them? (Possible response: to show that programs like W.O.W. can have an impact on many different kinds of people)

- **Page 580** How do you think the author feels about books and reading? (Possible response: Reading can be a powerful experience and affect different people in different ways.) What details on this page reveal her perspective? (Possible response: The dialogue includes characters' comments that reveal the author's perspective, including *A book can give you an adventure; or make you laugh; or make you scared; or teach you something.*)

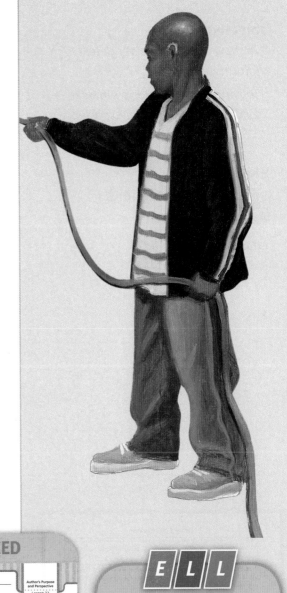

Practice/Apply

IDENTIFY AUTHOR'S PURPOSE AND PERSPECTIVE Distribute three different types of reading materials, such as a social studies textbook, a biography, or a fiction story, to pairs of students. Tell partners to preview each by reading its title, introduction, and any captions, and by viewing its illustrations and other visuals.

Then ask students to complete a chart like the one below. When their charts are complete, partners should present their findings to the class.

Author's Purpose	Author's Perspective	Details

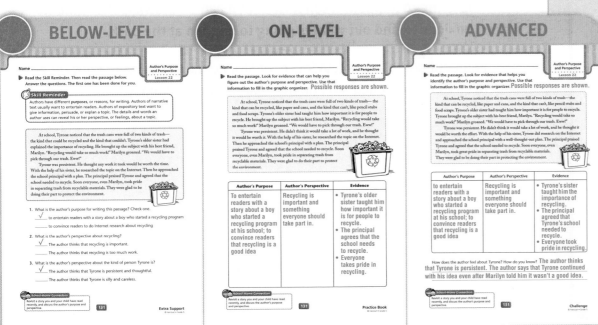

▲ Extra Support, p. 131   ▲ Practice Book, p. 131   ▲ Challenge, p. 131

ELL

- Group students according to academic levels, and assign one of the pages on the left.

- Clarify any unfamiliar concepts as necessary. See *ELL Teacher Guide* Lesson 22 for support in scaffolding instruction.

Draw Conclusions

Objectives

- *To draw conclusions about text information*
- *To support conclusions with text evidence and personal experience*

Skill Trace

Tested **Draw Conclusions**

Introduce	pp. T134–T135
Reteach	pp. S16–S17
Review	pp. T256, T311
Test	Theme 5
Maintain	p. T209, Theme 6

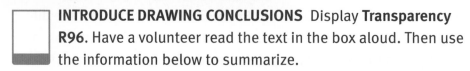 **Teach/Model**

INTRODUCE DRAWING CONCLUSIONS Display **Transparency R96**. Have a volunteer read the text in the box aloud. Then use the information below to summarize.

- Authors don't always explain everything in a story. Readers must **draw conclusions** to figure out things the author does not directly state.

- To figure out something not explained by the author, readers can use information given in the story along with their prior knowledge and experience.

- For a conclusion to be valid, it must be supported by textual evidence.

Point out that using a graphic organizer like the one on the transparency can help students keep track of conclusions they draw as they read.

DRAW A CONCLUSION Read aloud the passage on **Transparency R96**. Then model drawing a conclusion:

> **Think Aloud** The story says that Hindatu was up early. She was eager to get to the park. Often, when people are anxious and in a hurry to get somewhere, they are anticipating that something important is going to happen. A conclusion that can be drawn is that Hindatu is anxious to find out what is going to happen at the park.

Point out other textual evidence, or story details. Use prior knowledge to support the conclusion on the chart on **Transparency R96**.

Draw Conclusions

Sometimes readers must **draw conclusions** by using **story details** and **their own knowledge** to understand story events.

Even though the sun had yet to rise, Hindatu was already brushing her teeth. She was so anxious that she could barely tie her shoes. When she went downstairs, her mom was waiting for her in the kitchen.

"You have to eat before you go," her mom said.

"I don't have time, Mom. May I just take some toast to go?"

Hindatu's mom understood. Today was the day bulldozers were supposed to tear up Happy Meadows Park. In the last few weeks, her daughter had spent all her free time talking about the park. Her mother handed Hindatu a slice of toast and gave her a goodbye hug.

As Hindatu rode her bike to the park, the morning air relaxed her. From two blocks away, she saw a crowd of familiar faces gathered around the park entrance. She saw her teacher and her best friend holding signs saying *People Need Parks, Not Parking Lots*. Hindatu smiled. There were a lot of people hoping to save the park, and more would be coming.

Story Details	What I Know	Conclusions
• Hindatu is up early. • She's anxious. • She wants to skip breakfast and get to the park.	People who are anxious are eager to find out what is going to happen. They are in a hurry because they are expecting something big to happen.	Hindatu wants to find out what is going to happen at the park.
• Bulldozers are supposed to tear up the park. • People have gathered with signs at the entrance.	People who want to save a place may gather together and express their opinions peacefully.	Hindatu and her friends are hoping to save the park.

Grade 5, Lesson 22   **R96**   Draw Conclusions

Transparency R96

Guided Practice

DRAW CONCLUSIONS Have students reread the passage on **Transparency R96.** Then work with them to draw a conclusion about what Hindatu is hoping will happen at Happy Meadows Park. Record the conclusion in the third row on the chart.

Practice/Apply

DRAW CONCLUSIONS Have students review the sections listed below in "The Power of W.O.W!" and draw conclusions about the story elements described. Tell them to use a chart like the one on **Transparency R96** to show how they arrived at their conclusions.

- **Pages 572–573** Ileana's relationship with Mrs. Nguyen
- **Pages 579–580** Maria Kopanas's opinion about the value of community service projects

MONITOR PROGRESS

Draw Conclusions

IF students have difficulty drawing conclusions in the Practice/Apply activity,	**THEN** help them identify story details they can use to draw a conclusion.

Small-Group Instruction, pp. S16–S17:

- **BELOW-LEVEL:** Reteach
- **ON-LEVEL:** Reinforce
- **ADVANCED:** Extend

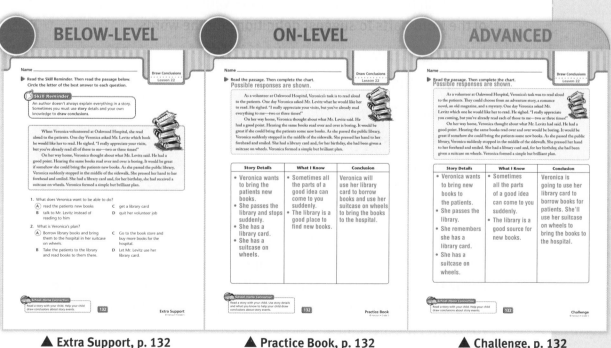

▲ Extra Support, p. 132   ▲ Practice Book, p. 132   ▲ Challenge, p. 132

ELL

- Group students according to academic levels, and assign one of the pages on the left.
- Clarify any unfamiliar concepts as necessary. See *ELL Teacher Guide* Lesson 22 for support in scaffolding instruction.

Vocabulary Strategies: Using Word Parts

Objectives

- *To use knowledge of prefixes, suffixes, and roots to analyze longer words*
- *To use reference aids to clarify meanings of longer words*

Skill Trace

Tested **Vocabulary Strategies: Using Word Parts**

Introduce	pp. T202–T203, Theme 3
Reteach	pp. S28–S29
Review	pp. T264, T320, Theme 3
Test	Theme 3
Maintain	p. T136

Reinforce the Skill

REVIEW WORD PARTS Remind students that their knowledge of word parts can help them determine the meaning of unfamiliar words. Remind them that a **root** or **root word** is the basic part of a word; a **prefix** is a word part added to the beginning of a root or root word; a **suffix** is a word part added to the end of a root or root word.

Have students share prefixes, suffixes, and roots they have learned. Record these in a chart on the board along with the ones below.

Prefix (Meaning)	Suffix (Meaning)	Root Word (Meaning)
im-, *in-* ("not") *trans-* ("across") *dis-* ("opposite of"; "not")	*-ful* ("full of") *-able* ("able to be") *-less* ("without")	port ("to carry") spire ("to breathe")

Practice/Apply

GUIDED PRACTICE Help students identify the prefixes, root words, and suffixes in the words below. Then work with them to use the meanings of the word parts to suggest definitions for the words.

- **transportable** (*trans-*, *port*, *-able*; "can be carried from place to place")
- **distrustful** (*dis-*, *trust*, *-ful*; "the opposite of *trusting*")
- **indisputable** (*in-*, *dispute*, *-able*; "not able to be disputed")
- **meaningless** (*meaning*, *-less*; "without meaning")
- **transpire** (*trans-*, *spire*; "to give off a vapor")

Ask students to use a dictionary to confirm each word's meaning.

INDEPENDENT PRACTICE Have students scan "The Power of W.O.W!" and "Got a Problem? Get a Plan!" and find at least three words with prefixes or suffixes. Have them identify and list the word parts and word meanings. When they have finished, ask them to use a dictionary to confirm the meanings.

Decoding/Word Attack
Structural Analysis: Word Parts -ation, -ition, -sion, -ion

Reinforce the Skill

Routine Card 5

DECODE LONGER WORDS Write the following chart on the board:

-ation	-ition	-sion	-ion
in/vi/ta/tion	con/tri/tion	im/pres/sion	sus/pi/cion
nar/ra/tion	au/di/tion	ad/mis/sion	cham/pi/on
ex/cla/ma/tion	ex/pe/di/tion	com/pres/sion	re/un/ion

Remind students that:

- The word parts *-tion, -sion,* and *-ion* are unaccented syllables that form the last syllable of a word. They are usually pronounced /shən/or /zhən/.

Then read aloud each word and demonstrate how to divide each word into syllables. Guide students to blend the syllables to pronounce the words.

Practice/Apply

GUIDED PRACTICE List the following story-related words on the board: *donation, television, permission,* and *confusion.* Guide students to divide the words into syllables, and then blend the syllables to read the words.

INDEPENDENT PRACTICE Have partners look through content-area text-books for five words that have the word parts *-tion, -sion,* or *-ion.* Tell them to write the words they find, divide them into syllables, and read the words aloud.

Objective
- *To review word parts -ation, -ition, -sion, -ion*
- *To use knowledge of word parts to decode longer words*

Skill Trace
Structural Analysis: Word Parts *-ation, -ition, -sion, -ion*

Introduce	Grade 2
Maintain	p. T137

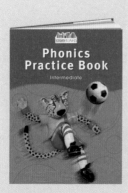

▲ **Phonics Practice Book, pp. 157–162**

Fluency: Expression

15 Min. each

Objectives

- *To read a play with grade-appropriate fluency*
- *To read aloud with prosody, using appropriate expression*

MONITOR PROGRESS

Partner Reading

IF students need more support in building fluency and in using appropriate expression,	THEN have them echo-read with you, matching your expression.

Small-Group Instruction, p. S15:

- ● **BELOW-LEVEL:** Reteach
- ● **ON-LEVEL:** Reinforce
- ● **ADVANCED:** Extend

Fluency Support Materials

Fluency Builders, Grade 5, Lesson 22

Audiotext *Student Edition* selections are available on *Audiotext Grade 5,* CD7.

Strategic Intervention Teacher Guide, Lesson 22

CHORAL-READ

Routine Card 6 **MODEL EXPRESSION** Model expressive reading with the text on *Student Edition* page 581. Tell students to follow along. Then read the passage again. Tell students to pay attention to the way you match your expression to the characters' feelings as well as the overall mood of the passage. Have students choral-read the passage with you.

ECHO-READ

Routine Card 7 **TRACK PRINT** Have students echo-read the passage on *Student Edition* page 581.

- Ask students to put their finger on the beginning of the first sentence.
- Read the sentence aloud as students track the print. Point out that the exclamation point signals you to read with excitement.
- Have students read the sentence aloud, mirroring your vocal expression.
- Continue this process through the rest of the passage.

If students do not read the passage fluently or expressively the first time, have them reread until they achieve fluency and appropriate expression.

PARTNER READING

Routine Card 8 **READ WITH A PARTNER** Pair strong readers with students who need fluency support. Have the strong reader read aloud *Student Edition* page 575 expressively, while the partner listens and follows along in the book. Then have partners switch roles.

Routine Card 9 Use the sentence frames on *Routine Card 9* to model how to give feedback. Then ask students to provide each other with feedback about their expressiveness, focusing on the way the reader changed his or her expression to match the character's feelings.

Have partners read the whole passage to each other again. Encourage students to give each other positive feedback about how their expression improved from the first to the second reading.

15 Min. each

Enriching Robust Vocabulary

5-DAY VOCABULARY

DAY 1 Vocabulary, pp. T111–T113
DAY 2 Vocabulary Review, p. T131
DAY 3 Reinforce Word Meanings, p. T139
DAY 4 Extend Word Meanings, p. T139
DAY 5 Cumulative Review, p. T139

REINFORCE WORD MEANINGS

Objective
- *To demonstrate knowledge of word meanings*

REVISIT SELECTION VOCABULARY
Have students discuss "The Power of W.O.W!" by responding to these questions.

1. Why did Mrs. Nguyen speak **somberly**?

2. What made Ileana **stammer**?

3. Why did Jake **monopolize** the computer?

4. Why did Shane feel **deflated** about the car wash idea?

5. Why was Ileana **enraptured** by the van?

6. Why would Maria say that the friends were **enterprising**?

7. What made the money jar **cumbersome**?

EXTEND WORD MEANINGS

Objective
- *To extend meanings of words in context*

CRITICAL THINKING To help extend students' understanding of the Vocabulary Words, have them answer the following questions. Tell them to explain their answers.

1. To what kind of movie would you react **somberly**?

2. Why might you **stammer** if you walked into a surprise birthday party?

3. Why is it unfair to **monopolize** a computer that others are waiting for?

4. Why do you think the word **deflated** can be used to describe both people and balloons?

5. Describe something in nature that has **enraptured** you.

6. If an **enterprising** friend needed money, what would you suggest?

7. Would carrying a large stack of books home from school be **cumbersome**? Why?

CUMULATIVE REVIEW

Objective
- *To use word relationships to determine meaning*

REVIEW VOCABULARY Discuss students' answers to these questions.

1. If the forecaster speaks **somberly** after **analyzing** the storm data and says that it is **vital** for people to evacuate, is the storm likely to be serious?

2. Would you expect a person to **stammer** while apologizing for **damage** he or she did?

3. Do you prefer to **bask** on the beach or **monopolize** the shade? Explain.

4. How can you **detect** when someone feels **deflated**?

5. What job would be good for someone who is **enraptured** by **analyzing** things?

6. Would an **enterprising** salesperson sell clothes that are **cumbersome** or **sleek**? Explain.

 Tested

Vocabulary ✓

Lesson 21		Lesson 22	
analyzing	basking	somberly	enraptured
vital	detect	stammers	enterprising
damage	sleek	monopolize	cumbersome
		deflated	

15 Min. each

Spelling: Words with Word Parts -ation, -ition, -sion, -ion

Objective
- *To correctly spell words with the word parts* -ation, -ition, -sion, *and* -ion

Spelling Words

1. acceleration	11. repetition
2. accumulation	12. mansion
3. activation	13. pension
4. alteration	14. passion
5. authorization	15. tension
6. calculation	16. champion
7. cancellation	17. confusion
8. dedication	18. permission
9. organization	19. population
10. demolition	20. companion

Challenge Words

21. presentation	24. decision
22. fixation	25. diversion
23. modernization	

Day 1 — PRETEST/SELF-CHECK

Routine Card 10

ADMINISTER THE PRETEST Use the Dictation Sentences under Day 5. Help students self-check their pretests, using **Transparency LA141**.

Allow time for students to study the words they misspelled. Have them use the steps *Say, Look, Spell, Write, Check.*

ADVANCED

Challenge Words Provide these Dictation Sentences:

21. Tim's **presentation** went well.

22. My cat has a **fixation** with string.

23. The **modernization** of the town included paving the dirt road.

24. We made the **decision** together.

25. The picnic was a pleasant **diversion**.

Day 2 — TEACH/MODEL

WORD SORT Display **Transparency LA141** again. Review the meanings of each suffix. Then ask students to copy the chart and write each Spelling Word where it belongs. Discuss word meanings as needed.

Write the word *alteration* on the board, and underline the word part *-ation*. Then have a volunteer circle the base word *alter*. Ask the class whether a spelling change was made to the base word before the word part was added. (no) Repeat this process with the word *acceleration*.

HANDWRITING Remind students that the letter *l* has a loop in it and the letter *t* does not.

late

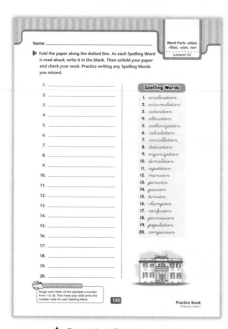
▲ Practice Book, p. 133

▲ Spelling Practice Book, p. 88

Transparency LA141

PARTNER SPELLING BEE Have students form pairs. Direct students to write each Spelling Word on a separate index card. Have one student draw a card and read the word aloud, and have the other spell the word. Partners should then switch roles. When a student spells a word correctly, he or she should initial the index card and return it to the pile. Students should work through the pile twice, or until each student has had a chance to spell each of the words. Have students write down each word they misspell to study later.

▲ Spelling Practice Book, p. 89

WORD PARTS Write the following root words and suffixes on the board:

authorize (-ation)   **tense (-ion)**

dedicate (-ation)   **confuse (-ion)**

organize (-ation)   **company (-ion)**

Ask students to add each word part to the base word to form a new word. Then have students explain the spelling change they made to the base word before adding the word parts.

APPLY TO WRITING

CHECK WORD PARTS Have students use the Word Parts strategy to check that they have correctly spelled words ending in the word parts *-ation*, *-ition*, *-sion*, and *-ion* in a recently completed piece of writing.

▲ Spelling Practice Book, p. 90

DICTATION SENTENCES

1. This car has good **acceleration**.
2. There was an **accumulation** of snow on the ground.
3. The **activation** of the account involves entering a password.
4. The **alteration** of the suit took two weeks.
5. Carlos needs **authorization** from his coach to attend soccer camp.
6. The manager helped Ed with the **calculation** of the sales tax.
7. We were disappointed by the **cancellation** of the swim meet.
8. Claire's **dedication** is admirable.
9. That **organization** works to reduce pollution.
10. The **demolition** of the building is scheduled for Saturday.
11. The **repetition** of the lyrics made the song easy to remember.
12. The **mansion** has 26 rooms in it.
13. Our grandmother receives a **pension** from her last job.
14. Sam's **passion** is drawing.
15. Exercise can relieve **tension**.
16. Sonya is a **champion** athlete.
17. There was some **confusion** about where to meet.
18. Ask your parents for **permission**.
19. What is the city's **population**?
20. Her dog is a faithful **companion**.

Writing Trait: Sentence Fluency
Persuasive Paragraph

15 Min. each

Objectives

- *To demonstrate an understanding of sentence fluency*
- *To write a persuasive paragraph*

Writing Trait ▸ Sentence Fluency

- Variety of sentence types used
- Variety of sentence lengths used
- Variety of sentence structures used

Grammar for Writing

As students revise their paragraphs, note whether they need additional support with these skills:

- **Complete, Declarative, and Interrogative Sentences,** pp. T70–T71, Theme 1
- **Adverbs,** pp. T218–T219, Theme 6
- **Present Tensse; Subject-Verb Agreement,** pp. T144–T145, Theme 5

▲ **Writer's Companion, Lesson 22**

Day 1 — TEACH/MODEL

SENTENCE FLUENCY Tell students that persuasive text should engage readers and convince them to think or feel a certain way. Tell students that using effective reasons, details, and examples in a variety of sentence types and lengths is important when writing a persuasive paragraph.

ANALYZE THE MENTOR TEXT Display the passage from "The Power of W.O.W.!" on **Transparency LA144**. Have a volunteer read the passage aloud. Then work with students to identify the examples in the chart as simple or compound sentences. Then point out Shane's, Erica's, and Jason's lines. Discuss how the short, longer, short pattern of the sentences makes the writing more interesting.

Day 2 — PRACTICE/APPLY

ANALYZE THE STUDENT MODEL Display **Transparency LA145**. Tell students that this is an example of a persuasive paragraph. Have a volunteer read the paragraph aloud. Point out that a persuasive paragraph establishes a controlling idea and develops it with the use of examples, reasons, and details.

Then guide students to complete the chart with an example of a simple sentence, a complex sentence, and a compound sentence. Discuss how using a variety of sentences keeps the reader engaged.

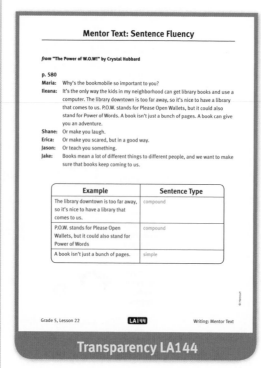

Mentor Text: Sentence Fluency

from "The Power of W.O.W!" by Crystal Hubbard

p. 580

Maria: Why's the bookmobile so important to you?

Ileana: It's the only way the kids in my neighborhood can get library books and use a computer. The library downtown is too far away, so it's nice to have a library that comes to us. P.O.W. stands for Please Open Wallets, but it could also stand for Power of Words. A book isn't just a bunch of pages. A book can give you an adventure.

Shane: Or make you laugh.

Erica: Or make you scared, but in a good way.

Jason: Or teach you something.

Jake: Books mean a lot of different things to different people, and we want to make sure that books keep coming to us.

Example	Sentence Type
The library downtown is too far away, so it's nice to have a library that comes to us.	compound
P.O.W. stands for Please Open Wallets, but it could also stand for Power of Words	compound
A book isn't just a bunch of pages.	simple

Grade 5, Lesson 22 — LA144 — Writing: Mentor Text

Transparency LA144

Student Model: Persuasive Paragraph

The Sweet Sound Center's after-school music program is one of the most important education programs in our city. The program provides music instruction to students, in addition to hosting performance events. What if young people can't afford their own instruments? They can use the ones at the center free of charge. Some schools do not provide any music instruction, so the after-school program at the Sweet Sound Center gives kids at all schools the opportunity to receive instruction from talented, experienced musicians. At the center students also learn other important skills, such as discipline and creativity, which can help them succeed in other subjects and activities. For these reasons, the after-school music program at the Sweet Sound Center should be supported by everyone in the community.

Sentence Type	Example
simple	The Sweet Sound Center's after-school music program is one of the most important education programs in our city.
complex	The program provides music instruction to students in addition to hosting performance events.
compound	Some schools do not provide any music instruction, so the after-school program at the Sweet Sound Center gives kids at all schools the opportunity to receive instruction from talented, experienced musicians.

Grade 5, Lesson 22 — LA145 — Writing: Student Model

Transparency LA145

THEME 5 WRITING		
Reading-Writing Connection	Persuasive Composition	Sentence Fluency
LESSON	**FORM**	**TRAIT**
21	Persuasive Letter	Sentence Fluency
22	**Persuasive Paragraph**	**Sentence Fluency**
23	Poem	Organization
24	Narrative	Organization
25 REVIEW	Revise and Publish	Sentence Fluency/Organization

 Day 3 PREWRITE

WRITING PROMPTS Display **Transparency LA146** and read aloud the prompt for Day 3. Have students use a graphic organizer like the one below to plan their paragraphs.

> Purpose/Controlling Idea: _____
> _____
> Reason 1: _____
> Reason 2: _____
> Reason 3: _____
> Restatement of purpose: _____

Tell students to clearly state their purpose for writing; keep their audience in mind; and to use a variety of sentence lengths and types. Remind students to use a dictionary or thesaurus to locate alternate word choices to make their arguments stronger.

Daily Writing Prompts

DAY 1 Writing Prompt:
Plays have features specific to the genre. Think about how reading a play differs from reading a story or an article. Now write a paragraph comparing and contrasting reading a play with reading another genre.

DAY 2 Writing Prompt:
The characters in "The Power of W.O.W!" each had unique personalities. Think of which character you liked best. Now write a descriptive paragraph about this character, telling about his or her personality.

DAY 3 Writing Prompt:
In the story, people want to save W.O.W. because they consider it an important part of their community. Think of a program like W.O.W. in your community. Now write a persuasive paragraph that supports why you think the program is important.

DAY 4 Writing Prompt:
Imagine that you and a group of your friends are holding a fundraiser for your school. Think about for what you would raise money and how you would accomplish it. Now write a skit describing what you would do.

DAY 5 Writing Prompt:
Most people have participated in a fundraiser. Think about why people help raise money for causes. Now write a persuasive ad convincing people to participate in a fundraiser.

Grade 5, Lesson 22   LA146   Daily Writing Prompts

Transparency LA146

 Day 4 DRAFT

BEGIN TO DRAFT Have students follow these steps to draft their paragraphs.

1. **Introduce** your opinion in a clear topic sentence.

2. **Organize** ideas in an order that makes sense.

3. **Develop** your idea with supporting details.

4. **Conclude** by restating your opinion.

NOTE: A 4-point rubric appears on page R8.

 Day 5 REVISE AND REFLECT

PEER CONFERENCE CHECKLIST
Have pairs of students use this checklist to discuss their paragraphs.

- Does the paragraph have a topic sentence that states an opinion?

- Does the paragraph include reasons and details in a logical order?

- Does the paragraph conclude by restating the opinion?

- Has the writer used a variety of sentence lengths and types?

Students may want to keep revised paragraphs in their portfolios.

SCORING RUBRIC						
	6	**5**	**4**	**3**	**2**	**1**
FOCUS	Completely focused, purposeful.	Focused on topic and purpose.	Generally focused on topic and purpose.	Somewhat focused on topic and purpose.	Related to topic but does not maintain focus.	Lacks focus and purpose.
ORGANIZATION	Ideas progress logically; paper conveys sense of completeness.	Organization mostly clear; paper gives sense of completeness.	Organization mostly clear, but some lapses occur; may seem unfinished.	Some sense of organization; seems unfinished.	Little sense of organization.	Little or no sense of organization.
SUPPORT	Strong, specific details; clear, exact language; freshness of expression.	Strong, specific details; clear, exact language.	Adequate support and word choice.	Limited supporting details; limited word choice.	Few supporting details; limited word choice.	Little development; limited or unclear word choice.
CONVENTIONS	Varied sentences; few, if any, errors.	Varied sentences; few errors.	Some sentence variety; few errors.	Simple sentence structures; some errors.	Simple sentence structures; many errors.	Unclear sentence structures; many errors.

REPRODUCIBLE RUBRIC appears on page R7.

Grammar: Verbs
Present Tense; Subject-Verb Agreement

Objectives
- *To use correct subject-verb agreement*
- *To identify forms of the verb* be

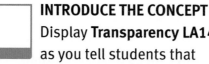

Present-Tense Verbs; Subject-Verb Agreement

- A verb's **tense** helps tell when something happened.
- **Present-tense** verbs can indicate that an action is happening right now.

1. The bookmobile *stops* in the street.
2. Ileana and Mrs. Nguyen *talk* about mythology.
3. Mr. Diaz *owns* a bakery.
4. The five friends *organize* a car wash.
5. A news crew *films* the group.
6. Drivers *give* Erica money.

A verb must agree in number with its subject.

Subject	Rule	Example
plural	Do not add an ending.	Ileana and Shane **devise** a strategy.
I or *you* singular	Do not add an ending. Add *s* to most verbs.	You **see** the bookmobile. Jason **eats** mutant chicken.
	Add *es* to verbs that end with *sh, ch, s, ss, x, z,* or *zz.*	He **relaxes** outside with his friends.
	Change *y* to *i* and add *es* to verbs that end with a consonant and *y.*	The group **tries** to think of a plan.

7. Ileana, Shane, and Jake *asked* the community for help. (ask)
8. Jason *washed* cars with them. (washes)
9. Lynn *pushed* the swing. (pushes)
10. A helicopter *flew* overhead. (flies)

Grade 5, Lesson 22   LA142   Grammar

Transparencies LA142, LA143

Language Structures Help
students understand verb tense by using this model:

- Today I <u>learn</u>. (present)
- Yesterday I <u>learned</u>. (past)
- Tomorrow I <u>will learn</u>. (future)

See *ELL Teacher Guide* Lesson 22 for support in scaffolding instruction.

Day 1 TEACH/MODEL

DAILY PROOFREADING

1. Mrs Nguyen do not want to stop running W.O.W. (Mrs.; does not)

2. Ileana sits by herselves to think of a idea. (herself; an)

INTRODUCE THE CONCEPT
Display **Transparency LA142** as you tell students that

- the **tense** of a verb helps show the time of the action. A verb in **present tense** can indicate that the action is happening now.

- in sentence 1, the verb *stops* is a present-tense verb.

- in sentence 2, the verb *talk* is a present-tense verb.

Have students identify the present-tense verbs in sentences 3–6.

✓ LANGUAGE ARTS CHECKPOINT

If students have difficulty with the concepts, see pages S18–S19 to reteach.

Day 2 TEACH/MODEL

DAILY PROOFREADING

3. This organizeation working to save the bookmobile. (organization is working)

4. Hers dedicasion is admirable. (Her dedication)

EXTEND THE CONCEPT Display **Transparency LA142.** Read the information in the second box and discuss the examples in the chart. Then have students replace the underlined past-tense verbs in items 7–10 with present-tense verbs.

BUILD LANGUAGE STRUCTURES Have students complete the following sentences with present-tense verbs.

- I _____ to the car wash.
- Jake and Jason _____ mutant chicken.
- Everyone _____ and _____ the cars.

Present Tense; Subject-Verb Agreement
Lesson 22

Name _____

▶ Write the correct present-tense form of the verb in parentheses ( ).

1. Marie and Sal (come) to the car wash to help. **come**
2. Donna (carry) water and soap over to the car. **carries**
3. Gordon (place) his sponge in the bucket. **places**
4. Wilma (wash) the tires. **washes**
5. Clare (fill) the bucket with water again. **fills**
6. The man in the blue car (drive) onto the lot. **drives**
7. The car's engine (purr) like a kitten. **purrs**
8. He (watch) the kids working. **watches**
9. More cars (wait) in line. **wait**
10. The children (make) money for their project. **make**

▶ Rewrite each sentence, correcting each present-tense verb to agree with its subject.

11. The kids listens to John's ideas for raising money.
The kids listen to John's ideas for raising money.

12. He want to have a bake sale.
He wants to have a bake sale.

13. Greg and Paul decides they will bake muffins.
Greg and Paul decide they will bake muffins.

14. Tamika greet everyone with a smile.
Tamika greets everyone with a smile.

15. She thank them for giving money to their school.
She thanks them for giving money to their school.

77   Grammar Practice Book

▲ **Grammar Practice Book, p. 77**

Day 3 — TEACH/MODEL

DAILY PROOFREADING

5. Shane and Jason asks for permition. (ask or asked; permission.)

6. A bee buzzs around Jakes' head. (buzzes; Jake's)

EXTEND THE CONCEPT Display **Transparency LA143**. Discuss the information in the box. Have students complete items 1–6 by choosing the correct verb in each sentence.

Then have students write three sentences about libraries, using an easily confused present-tense verb—such as *lie, sit,* or *rise*—in each sentence.

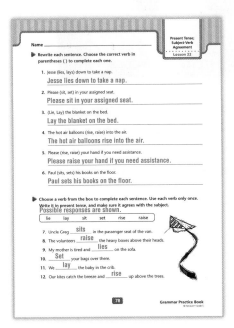

▲ Grammar Practice Book, p. 78

Day 4 — APPLY TO WRITING

DAILY PROOFREADING

7. Ill set here and wait for you. (I'll sit)

8. By mine calculasions, we have enough money. (my calculations,)

HELPING OUT Have students write a short paragraph describing a fund-raising event as if it were happening now. Have students include two easily confused verbs in their paragraphs.

> #### COMMON ERRORS
>
> **Error:** Ileana **crys**, "We saved the bookmobile!"
> **Correct:** Ileana **cries**, "We saved the bookmobile!"
>
> **Error:** I will **rise** my hand.
> **Correct:** I will **raise** my hand.

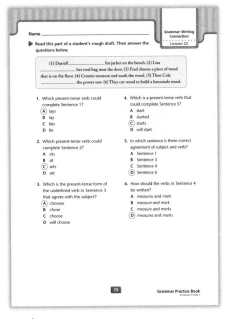

▲ Grammar Practice Book, p. 79

Day 5 — REVIEW

DAILY PROOFREADING

9. You can lay down here while I call dr Williams. (lie; Dr.)

10. You tries to relieve the tention. (try; tension.)

CHOOSE THE PRESENT-TENSE VERB

Display the following sentences. Have students rewrite each sentence, filling in the blank with the correct present-tense form of the verb in parentheses. For item 4, have them choose the correct verb.

1. The reporter <u>guesses</u> what might happen next. (guess)

2. The children <u>wait</u> for customers to arrive. (wait)

3. Ileana <u>laughs</u> at Shane's joke. (laugh)

4. You can (lie/lay) the book down on the table. (lay)

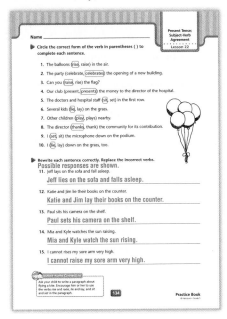

▲ Practice Book, p. 134

Speaking & Listening

SPEAKING

Give a Persuasive Speech

Objectives
- *To present a persuasive speech*
- *To use strategies to engage listeners*

Have students publish their persuasive paragraphs by giving a persuasive speech. Share these **organizational strategies**:

ORGANIZING CONTENT
- Open with a clear opinion statement that will capture your listeners' interest.
- Use language that is appropriate for your purpose and audience.
- End with a strong restatement of your opinion and a call to action that urges your audience to join your side.

Before students give their speeches to a small group, share with them the following **speaking strategies:**

SPEAKING STRATEGIES
- Pace yourself while speaking.
- Speak clearly and use an engaging tone.
- Make eye contact with your audience.
- Use natural gestures to emphasize your points.

speak clearly

Students may use props, such as handmade posters or advertisements, to increase the impact of their speech.

LISTENING

Listen to a Persuasive Speech

Objectives
- *To eliminate barriers to effective listening*
- *To respond appropriately to speakers*

Have students listen to the persuasive speeches. Share these **listening strategies** with students:

LISTENING STRATEGIES
- Show interest in what the speaker is saying.
- Watch for gestures or other signals.
- Wait until the speaker is finished to ask questions and give feedback.

After each speaker is finished, have listeners respond by giving feedback on the effectiveness of the speech.

RUBRIC See rubric for Presentations on page R5.

Media Literacy

RESEARCH

Television News Programs

Objective
- *To understand the organization of television news programs*

ORGANIZATION OF A NEWS PROGRAM Tell students that television news programs are an important source of local, national, and international news.

On the board, list these parts of a television news program and then discuss the types of information that can be seen and heard in each segment:

- local news
- business and technology
- health, education, arts
- breaking news
- traffic and weather
- sports
- national news
- international news
- human interest

You may want to model why the P.O.W.W.O.W. event was a good television news story:

> **Think Aloud** Maria gave an "on location," live report. Television viewers learned about what was happening in Mr. Diaz's parking lot, and they could respond immediately by going to the car wash or giving money. The human interest report showed young people doing something positive for their community.

WATCH A NEWS PROGRAM Have students watch part of a local news program. Have them identify the different segments of the program and tell which parts of the news gave information that was most useful to them.

- Selection Comprehension with Short Response
- Focus Skill
- Robust Vocabulary
- Draw Conclusions
- Grammar
- Fluency Passage *FRESH READS*
- Podcasting: Assessing Fluency

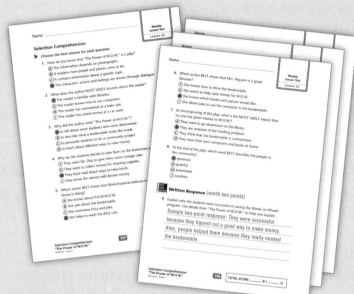

▲ Weekly Lesson Test, Lesson 22

GO online For prescriptions, see pp. A2–A6. Also available electronically on *StoryTown Online Assessment* and ExamView®.

Leveled Readers
Reinforcing Skills and Strategies

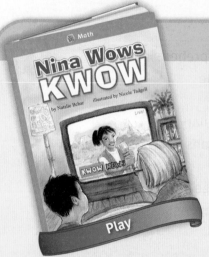

BELOW-LEVEL

Nina Wows KWOW

SUMMARY Nina wants to be a news reporter. Unfortunately, the television station thinks that she is too young for the job—until an unexpected event gives Nina the opportunity to prove her abilities.

-  Author's Purpose and Perspective
- Summarize
- **VOCABULARY:** *somberly, stammers, monopolize, deflated, enraptured, enterprising, cumbersome*

LEVELED READER TEACHER GUIDE

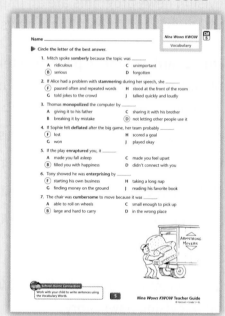

▲ Vocabulary, p. 5

Build Background/Set Purpose

Have students page through the play and look at the illustrations. Ask them what they think it will be about. Remind students that summarizing as they read can help them keep track of story events.

Guided Reading

PAGES 7–8 MAKE JUDGMENTS **Was it wise for Nina to say that she was going to be on the news before she applied for the job? Why or why not?** (no, because she didn't know if the station was hiring or if she was qualified)

PAGES 3–14 AUTHOR'S PURPOSE AND PERSPECTIVE **What is one message the author is trying to get across in the story?** (If you want something, you should go after it even if you've been rejected.)

After Reading

Have students work in pairs to discuss the play.

FLUENCY: EXPRESSION Have pairs of students take turns rereading sections aloud. Tell them to give each other feedback on expression.

Think Critically *(See inside back cover for questions.)*

1. Yes. She has varied interests and likes speech and communication.

2. Answers will vary.

3. She will probably try anyway.

4. Nina's friends are supportive of her ideas.

5. to entertain and to encourage readers to believe in themselves

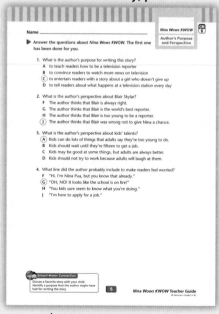

▲ Comprehension, p. 6

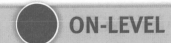 **ON-LEVEL**

A Friendly Field Trip

SUMMARY Ms. Price's students exchange letters with a class of sight-impaired students. When the two groups go on a field trip together, the sighted students learn about other ways to "see."

• ⟳ **Author's Purpose and Perspective**

• ⟳ **Summarize**

• **VOCABULARY:** *somberly, stammers, monopolize, deflated, enraptured, enterprising, cumbersome*

Build Background/Set Purpose

Ask students to read the title and look at the illustrations. Then ask them to predict what they think the play will be about. Remind students that summarizing as they read can help them keep track of main events.

Guided Reading

PAGES 8–9 CAUSE AND EFFECT How has Ian's relationship with Syd changed the way he views sight-impaired people? (It has made him more sensitive and understanding.)

PAGES 10–14 ⟳ AUTHOR'S PURPOSE AND PERSPECTIVE Why do you think the author set the last part of the play at a petting zoo? (Both sighted and sight-impaired students can learn about animals there.)

After Reading

Have student pairs work together to write a short summary of the play.

FLUENCY: EXPRESSION Have pairs of students reread a section aloud. Tell them that using lively expression helps bring the characters to life.

Think Critically *(See inside back cover for questions.)*

1. Answers will vary.

2. Compare: They are both in Ms. Price's class. Contrast: Ian is eager to get to know the new class, while Tracey avoids spending time with her partner.

3. Tracey will probably be kinder because of her experience.

4. to inform readers about different ways of living and learning

5. Blind students have different talents than sighted students.

LEVELED READER TEACHER GUIDE

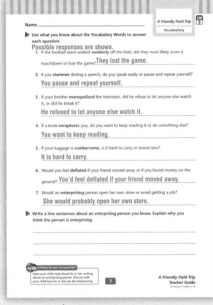

▲ Vocabulary, p. 5

▲ Comprehension, p. 6

Leveled Readers
Reinforcing Skills and Strategies

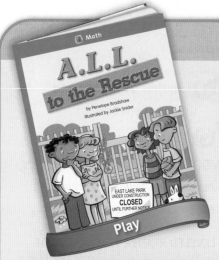

ADVANCED

A.L.L. to the Rescue

SUMMARY When a park closes, a group of friends must find a new place to play. Their enterprising solution benefits everyone.

- Author's Purpose and Perspective
- Summarize
- **VOCABULARY:** *somberly, stammers, monopolize, deflated, enraptured, enterprising, cumbersome*

LEVELED READER TEACHER GUIDE

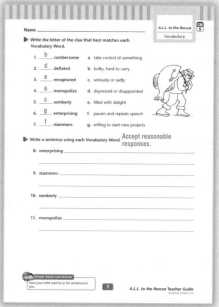

▲ Vocabulary, p. 5

Build Background/Set Purpose

Write the word *litter* on the board. Ask students to define it, give examples of it, and suggest ways to fix litter problems. Then ask students to preview the play and predict what it will be about. Remind them that summarizing as they read can help them keep track of what is happening in the play.

During Reading

COMPLETE A SEQUENCE CHART Distribute the sequence chart on *Teachers Resource Book* page 84 to pairs of students. Have students fill in the sequence chart with the steps the children take to find a new place to play.

After Reading

Have students work in pairs to discuss the play and write a short summary.

FLUENCY: EXPRESSION Tell students to imagine that they are performing this play. Have them adopt roles and reread the play aloud, using lively expression.

Think Critically *(See inside back cover for questions.)*

1. They are helpful, resourceful, and eager to improve their community.

2. Answers will vary.

3. good, because it gave the group a chance to clean Mr. Jenkins's lot and help his business as a result

4. The stage directions say that Mr. Jenkins was "downcast" and looked as though he had a "cumbersome burden on his mind." They also note that there was no one in the store.

5. to entertain and tell about the value of respecting our environment

▲ Comprehension, p. 6

E L L

Realistic Fiction

A Play for Everyone

SUMMARY Diego wants to see a play that is coming to his town, but he needs to find a chaperone and a way to pay for the ticket.

- **Build Background**
- **Concept Vocabulary**
- **Scaffolded Language Development**

Build Background/Set Purpose

Discuss the different parts of a play with students. Tell students that the *author* of a play is a *playwright* and actors must *rehearse* and perform in front of an *audience*. Remind students that summarizing helps them keep track of main events.

Guided Reading

As students read, tell them to look for words that signal transitions and connections such as *when, finally, however,* and *also*. Clarify the idiom *raise money*.

PAGES 4–7 CHARACTER'S EMOTIONS Why is Diego so excited about seeing *Our Town*? (The play is written by his favorite playwright.)

PAGES 3–14 AUTHOR'S PURPOSE AND PERSPECTIVE What was the author's purpose in writing this story? (to entertain readers and give the message that creative thinking can solve problems)

After Reading

FLUENCY: EXPRESSION Reread the story aloud. Tell students to focus on your expression. Then have pairs of students take turns rereading a page of the story aloud, using appropriate expression.

Encourage students to use the concept words *rehearse, audience, tickets,* and *donations* while discussing the story.

Scaffolded Language Development

See inside back cover for teacher-led activity.
Provide additional examples and explanation as needed.

LEVELED READER TEACHER GUIDE

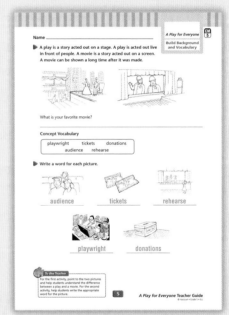

▲ Build Background, p. 5

▲ Scaffolded Language Development, p. 6

Lesson 23

WEEK AT A GLANCE

✔ **Vocabulary**

gouges, desolate, bustles, fervor, immaculate, assuage

✔ **Comprehension**

 Literary Devices

 Answer Questions

Reading

"Any Small Goodness" by Tony Johnston
REALISTIC FICTION

"The Ant and the Dove; The Lion and the Mouse"
retold by Ann McGovern
FABLE

✔ **Fluency**
Focus on Pace

Decoding/Word Attack
Silent Letters

✔ **Spelling**
Words with Silent Letters

✔ **Writing**
Form: Poem
Trait: Organization

✔ **Grammar**
Past and Future Tenses

Speaking and Listening
Poetry Reading

Media Literacy
Compare News Media

Weekly Lesson Test

 = Focus Skill   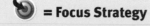 = Focus Strategy   = Tested Skill

One stop

for all

your **Digital** *needs*

Lesson 23

Digital
CLASSROOM

 www.harcourtschool.com/storytown
To go along with your print program

FOR THE TEACHER

Prepare   Professional Development

in the Online TE

 Videos for Podcasting

Plan & Organize   Online TE & Planning Resources*

Teach   Transparencies

access from the Online TE

Assess   Online Assessment*

with Student Tracking System and Prescriptions

FOR THE STUDENT

Read  Student eBook*

 Strategic Intervention Interactive Reader

 Leveled Readers

Practice & Apply   Comprehension Expedition CD-ROM

 Also available on CD-ROM

Lesson 23 • **T153**

STUDENT
EDITION

GO online | eBook STUDENT EDITION

TONY JOHNSTON
Any Small Goodness
a novel of the barrio

Genre: Realistic Fiction

APPLE Classics

retold by Ann McGovern

Aesop's Fables

Genre: Fable

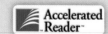

◀ **Audiotext** *Student Edition selections are available on Audiotext Grade 5, CD7.*

Accelerated Reader™ ◀ *Practice Quizzes for the Selection*

THEME CONNECTION: MAKING A DIFFERENCE
Comparing Realistic Fiction and Fable

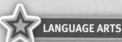

Paired Selections

🌐 SOCIAL STUDIES **Any Small Goodness, pp. 594–607**
SUMMARY Author Tony Johnston explains how a family's search for their lost cat leads them to discover a man of good character.

⭐ LANGUAGE ARTS **The Ant and the Dove; The Lion and the Mouse, pp. 608–609**
SUMMARY By retelling two of Aesop's fables, author Ann McGovern writes about a world where animals take the opportunity to help one another.

Support for Differentiated Instruction

 LEVELED READERS

BELOW-LEVEL

ON-LEVEL

ADVANCED

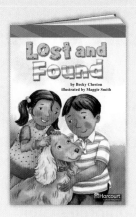

E L L

LEVELED PRACTICE

◀ **Strategic Intervention Resource Kit, Lesson 23**

◀ **Strategic Intervention Interactive Reader, Lesson 23**
Strategic Intervention Interactive Reader Online

◀ **ELL Extra Support Kit, Lesson 23**

◀ **Challenge Resource Kit, Lesson 23**

BELOW-LEVEL
Extra Support Copying Masters, pp. 135, 137

ON-LEVEL
Practice Book, pp. 135–139

ADVANCED
Challenge Copying Masters, pp. 135, 137

ADDITIONAL RESOURCES

◀ **Picture Card Collection**
◀ **Fluency Builders**
◀ **Literacy Center Kit, Lesson 23**
• Test Prep System
• Writer's Companion, Lesson 23
• Grammar Practice Book, pp. 81–84
• Spelling Practice Book, pp. 91–94
• Reading Transparencies R97–R100
• Language Arts Transparencies LA147–LA152

ASSESSMENT

✔ **Monitor Progress**

✔ **Weekly Lesson Tests, Lesson 23**
• Comprehension
• Focus Skill
• Robust Vocabulary
• Literary Patterns and Symbols
• Grammar
• Fluency

✔ **Rubrics, pp. R3–R8**

 www.harcourtschool.com/storytown
• Online Assessment
Also available on CD-ROM—ExamView®

Suggested Lesson Planner

90+ Minutes

GO online Online TE & Planning Resources

	Day 1	**Day 2**
Step 1 Whole Group 45-60+ Minutes		

Step 1 Whole Group *45-60+ Minutes*

Oral Language
- *Question of the Day*
- *Listening Comprehension*

Comprehension
- *Skills and Strategies*

Vocabulary

Reading
- *Fluency*
- *Cross-Curricular Connections*
- *Decoding/Word Attack*

Day 1

QUESTION OF THE DAY *What story have you read that teaches you a valuable lesson about life? What lesson does it teach?*

READ ALOUD, pp. T164–T165

 COMPREHENSION:
Literary Devices, pp. T166–T167
Answer Questions, pp. T168–T169

VOCABULARY:
Introduce Vocabulary, p. T171
Word Champion, p. T173

READ: Vocabulary, pp. T172–T173

FLUENCY: PACE: Model Oral Fluency, p. T165

DECODING/WORD ATTACK:
Silent Letters, p. T197

Day 2

QUESTION OF THE DAY *What evidence is there in the selection to suggest that the family will keep in touch with Leo Love?*

READ ALOUD, p. T165

 COMPREHENSION:
Literary Devices, pp. T174–T186
Answer Questions, pp. T177, T181, T183

VOCABULARY:
Vocabulary Review, p. T191

READ: "Any Small Goodness," pp. T174–T187
Options for Reading

 ▲ Student Edition

FLUENCY: PACE:
Partner Reading, p. T191

SCIENCE: Domestic Cats, p. T177

 Step 2 Small Groups *45-60+ Minutes*

Step 3 Whole Group *45+ Minutes*

Language Arts
- *Spelling*
- *Writing*
- *Grammar*

Suggestions for Differentiated Instruction *(See pp. T158–T189.)*

Day 1	**Day 2**
SPELLING: Words with Silent Letters: Pretest/Self-Check, p. T200	**SPELLING: Words with Silent Letters:** Teach/Model, p. T200

WRITING: Poem: Teach/Model, p. T202

Writing Prompt *People are often kind to one another. Think of a time when a friend or stranger helped you in some way. Write a letter or e-mail to the person, thanking him or her for the assistance.*

WRITING: Poem: Practice/Apply, p. T202

Writing Prompt *Mr. Leo Love did something good "when no eyes were upon him." Think of a time when you did something good when no one was looking. Write a paragraph describing your actions.*

GRAMMAR: Past and Future Tenses: Teach/Model, p. T204

Daily Proofreading
1. The cat were an irriplacable part of the family. (was; irreplaceable)
2. Most cats, do not respond to a wissle. (cats do; whistle)

GRAMMAR: Past and Future Tenses: Teach/Model, p. T204

Daily Proofreading
3. The music, it was the most loud I ever heard. (music was; the loudest)
4. Mr Leo Love kneaded a companyun. (Mr.; needed; companion)

Spelling Words
1. assign	11. knowledge
2. autumn	12. lightning
3. column	13. resign
4. crumb	14. rhyme
5. debris	15. solemn
6. delight	16. thorough
7. design	17. scenery
8. glisten	18. whirl
9. hasten	19. wreath
10. knead	20. wrestled

Challenge Words
21. scenic	24. rhythm
22. yacht	25. handkerchief
23. aisle	

 = **Focus Skill**   = **Focus Strategy**   = **Tested Skill**

Comprehension	Vocabulary	Fluency	Language Arts
Skills at a Glance **FOCUS SKILL:** Literary Devices **FOCUS STRATEGY:** Answer Questions	gouges immaculate desolate assuage bustles fervor	Pace	**Writing:** - Trait: Organization - Form: Poem **Grammar:** Past and Future Tenses

Day 3

QUESTION OF THE DAY *What, besides a sad mood, could the word* desolate *be used to describe?*

READ ALOUD, p. T165

COMPREHENSION:

 Literary Devices, pp. T192–T193

VOCABULARY: Reinforce Word Meanings, p. T199

READ: "The Ant and the Dove; The Lion and the Mouse," pp. T188–T189

▲Student Edition

COMPARING TEXTS, p. T190

FLUENCY: PACE: Choral-Read, p. T198

WRITING: Write a Descriptive Paragraph, p. T191

Day 4

QUESTION OF THE DAY *If you wanted to describe a day in the park, what kind of imagery might you use to appeal to the five senses?*

READ ALOUD, p. T165

SPEAKING AND LISTENING: Poetry Reading, p. T206

VOCABULARY: Extend Word Meanings, p. T199

FLUENCY: PACE: Echo-Read, p. T198

▲Student Edition

Day 5

QUESTION OF THE DAY *How has modern technology made it easier to find lost pets?*

READ ALOUD, p. T165

COMPREHENSION: Literary Patterns and Symbols, p. T194 Persuasive Techniques, p. T195 Main Idea and Details, p. T196

VOCABULARY: Cumulative Review, p. T199

FLUENCY: PACE: Partner Reading, p. T198

MEDIA LITERACY: Compare News Media, p. T207

▲Student Edition

● BELOW-LEVEL   ● ON-LEVEL   ● ADVANCED   E L L

SPELLING: Words with Silent Letters: Practice/Apply, p. T201

 WRITING: Poem: Prewrite, p. T203

Writing Prompt *People use various types of writing to persuade others to do something. Think of an issue or idea that is important to you. Write a poem that tries to persuade readers to agree with you.*

GRAMMAR: Past and Future Tenses: Teach/Model, p. T205

Daily Proofreading

5. Luis' band will practices tonight. (Luis's; practice)

6. Leo Love wait two weaks before calling. (waited; weeks)

SPELLING: Words with Silent Letters: Spelling Strategies, p. T201

 WRITING: Poem: Draft, p. T203

Writing Prompt *Almost everyone holds another person in high esteem. Think of a person whom you admire. Then write a short composition in which you explain why that person is* estimado, *or esteemed.*

GRAMMAR: Past and Future Tenses: Apply to Writing, p. T205

Daily Proofreading

7. The cat rubed against Mamis leg. (rubbed; Mami's)

8. We eat the delishous soup in an hour. (will eat; delicious)

SPELLING: Words with Silent Letters: Posttest, p. T201

 WRITING: Poem: Revise and Reflect, p. T203

Writing Prompt *Vivid descriptions of characters help stories come alive for readers. Think of how Huitla is described in "Any Small Goodness." Now write a more vivid description of Huitla.*

GRAMMAR: Past and Future Tenses: Review, p. T205

Daily Proofreading

9. Leo Love climb the tree although it was hazerdous. (climbed; tree,; hazardous)

10. When the door opened the cat hurryed out. (opened,; hurried)

Suggested Small-Group Planner

45-60+ Minutes

 BELOW-LEVEL — 15-20+ Minutes

 ON-LEVEL — 15-20+ Minutes

 ADVANCED — 15-20+ Minutes

Day 1

Day 2

BELOW-LEVEL

Day 1

Teacher–Directed
🔖 Leveled Readers:
Before Reading, p. T208

Independent
⭐ Word Study Center, p. T162
Extra Support
Copying Masters, p. 135

▲ Leveled Reader

Day 2

Teacher–Directed
Reread the Selection,
pp. T174–T187

Independent
⭐ Writing Center, p. T163
Audiotext Grade 5, CD7

▲ Student Edition

ON-LEVEL

Day 1

Teacher–Directed
🔖 Leveled Readers:
Before Reading, p. T209

Independent
⭐ Reading Center, p. T162
Practice Book, p. 135

▲ Leveled Reader

Day 2

Teacher–Directed
Respond to the Selection,
p. T186

Independent
⭐ Word Study Center,
p. T162

▲ Student Edition

ADVANCED

Day 1

Teacher–Directed
🔖 Leveled Readers:
Before Reading, p. T210

Independent
⭐ Writing Center, p. T163
Challenge Copying
Masters, p. 135

▲ Leveled Reader

Day 2

Independent
⭐ Fluency Center, p. T163
Leveled Readers: Partner
Reading, p. T210

▲ Leveled Reader

 ELL

English-Language Learners

In addition to the small-group suggestions above, use the ELL Extra Support Kit to promote language development.

LANGUAGE DEVELOPMENT SUPPORT

Teacher–Directed
Leveled Readers:
Build Background, p. T211
ELL Teacher Guide, Lesson 23

Independent
ELL Copying Masters,
Lesson 23

▲ Leveled Reader

LANGUAGE DEVELOPMENT SUPPORT

Teacher–Directed
Scaffold Core Skills
ELL Teacher Guide,
Lesson 23

Independent
Audiotext Grade 5, CD7

▲ ELL Student Handbook

Intervention

▲ Strategic Intervention Resource Kit

▲ Strategic Intervention Interactive Reader

Strategic Intervention Teacher Guide,
Lesson 23
Strategic Intervention Practice Book,
Lesson 23

Catch a Wave,
Lesson 23
Strategic Intervention
Teacher Guide,
Lesson 23

Strategic Intervention Interactive Reader ▲

 = Literacy Center Cards

MONITOR PROGRESS

Small-Group Instruction

 Literary Devices	Selection Comprehension	Robust Vocabulary	Fluency	Language Arts
pp. S20–S21	p. S24	pp. S22–S23	p. S25	p. S26–S27

Day 3

Teacher–Directed
Leveled Readers:
During Reading, p. T208

Independent
⭐ Reading Center, p. T162
Extra Support Copying Masters, p. 137

▲ Leveled Reader

Teacher–Directed
Leveled Readers:
During Reading, p. T209

Independent
⭐ Technology Center, p. T163
Practice Book, p. 137

▲ Leveled Reader

Teacher–Directed
Leveled Readers:
During Reading, p. T210

Independent
⭐ Word Study Center, p. T162
Challenge Copying Masters, p. 137

▲ Leveled Reader

LANGUAGE DEVELOPMENT SUPPORT

Teacher–Directed
Leveled Readers:
During Reading, p. T211
ELL Teacher Guide, Lesson 23

Independent
ELL Copying Masters, Lesson 23

▲ Leveled Reader

Catch a Wave,
Lesson 23
Strategic Intervention
Teacher Guide,
Lesson 23
Strategic Intervention
Practice Book,
Lesson 23

Strategic Intervention
Interactive Reader ▲

Day 4

Teacher–Directed
Leveled Readers:
Guided Fluency, p. T208

Independent
⭐ Technology Center, p. T163

▲ Leveled Reader

Teacher–Directed
Leveled Readers:
Guided Fluency, p. T209

Independent
⭐ Fluency Center, p. T163

▲ Leveled Reader

Independent
⭐ Reading Center, p. T162
Classroom Library:
Self-Selected Reading

▲ Leveled Reader

LANGUAGE DEVELOPMENT SUPPORT

Teacher–Directed
Leveled Readers:
Guided Fluency, p. T211
ELL Teacher Guide, Lesson 23

Independent
ELL Copying Masters, Lesson 23

▲ Leveled Reader

Catch a Wave,
Lesson 23
Strategic Intervention
Teacher Guide,
Lesson 23

Strategic Intervention
Interactive Reader ▲

Day 5

Teacher–Directed
Leveled Readers:
Responding, p. T208

Independent
⭐ Fluency Center, p. T163
Leveled Readers:
Rereading for Fluency, p. T208

▲ Leveled Reader

Teacher–Directed
Leveled Readers:
Responding, p. T209

Independent
⭐ Writing Center, p. T163
Leveled Readers: Rereading for Fluency, p. T209

▲ Leveled Reader

Teacher–Directed
Leveled Readers:
Responding, p. T210

Independent
⭐ Technology Center, p. T163
Leveled Readers:
Rereading for Fluency, p. T210
Classroom Library: Self-Selected Reading

▲ Leveled Reader

LANGUAGE DEVELOPMENT SUPPORT

Teacher–Directed
Leveled Readers:
Responding, p. T211
ELL Teacher Guide, Lesson 23

Independent
Leveled Readers:
Rereading for Fluency, p. T211

▲ Leveled Reader

Catch a Wave,
Lesson 23
Strategic Intervention
Teacher Guide,
Lesson 23

Strategic Intervention
Interactive Reader ▲

Leveled Readers & Leveled Practice
Reinforcing Skills and Strategies

LEVELED READERS SYSTEM

- **Leveled Readers**
- **Leveled Readers CD**
- **Leveled Reader Teacher Guides**
  - *Vocabulary*
  - *Comprehension*
  - *Oral Reading Fluency Assessment*
- **Response Activities**
- **Leveled Readers Assessment**

See pages T208–T211 for lesson plans.

For extended lesson plans, see *Leveled Reader Teacher Guides.*

T160 • Grade 5, Theme 5

BELOW-LEVEL

- Literary Devices
- Answer Questions
- Robust Vocabulary

LEVELED READER TEACHER GUIDE

▲ Vocabulary, p. 5

▲ Comprehension, p. 6

ON-LEVEL

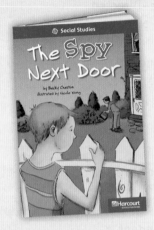

- Literary Devices
- Answer Questions
- Robust Vocabulary

LEVELED READER TEACHER GUIDE

▲ Vocabulary, p. 5

▲ Comprehension, p. 6

ADVANCED

🎧 **Literary Devices**
🎧 **Answer Questions**
• **Robust Vocabulary**

LEVELED READER TEACHER GUIDE

▲ **Vocabulary, p. 5**

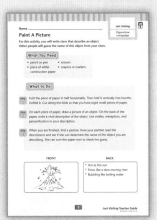

▲ **Comprehension, p. 6**

E L L

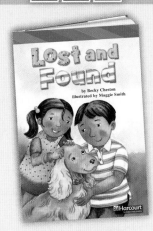

• **Build Background**
• **Concept Vocabulary**
• **Scaffolded Language Development**

LEVELED READER TEACHER GUIDE

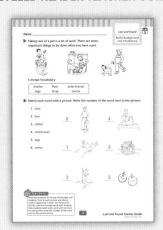

▲ **Build Background, p. 5**

▲ **Scaffolded Language Development, p. 6**

CLASSROOM LIBRARY

for Self-Selected Reading

EASY

▲ *Doña Flor* **by Pat Mora.**
TALL TALE

AVERAGE

▲ *Eleanor* **by Barbara Cooney.**
BIOGRAPHY

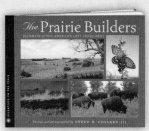

CHALLENGE

▲ *The Prairie Builders: Reconstructing America's Lost Grasslands* **by Sneed B. Collard III.**
EXPOSITORY NONFICTION

▲ **Classroom Library Books Teacher Guide**

Literacy Centers

15+ Min. each

Management Support

While you provide direct instruction to individuals or small groups, other students can work on these activities.

▲ Literacy Centers Pocket Chart

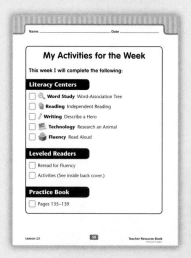

My Activities for the Week

This week I will complete the following:

Literacy Centers
- ☐ 🔍 **Word Study** Word-Association Tree
- ☐ 📖 **Reading** Independent Reading
- ☐ ✏️ **Writing** Describe a Hero
- ☐ 💻 **Technology** Research an Animal
- ☐ 📗 **Fluency** Read Aloud

Leveled Readers
- ☐ Reread for Fluency
- ☐ Activities (See inside back cover.)

Practice Book
- ☐ Pages 135–139

Lesson 23   5R   Teacher Resource Book

▲ Teacher Resource Book, p. 58

Homework for the Week

Teacher Resource Book, page 26

The *Homework Copying Master* provides activities to complete for each day of the week.

GO online www.harcourtschool.com/storytown

WORD STUDY

Shades of Meaning

Objective
To extend understanding of word meanings

WORD STUDY   Card 111

Shades of Meaning

- **Use a thesaurus** to help you create a list of synonyms for each Vocabulary Word.

- **Look up the synonyms** in a dictionary and compare their meanings to those of the Vocabulary Words.

- **Use a thesaurus** to help you find a word that is related to the Vocabulary Word and write a word in each branch.

- **Rank the Vocabulary Word** and its synonyms by their shades of meaning from the strongest meaning to the weakest meaning.

MATERIALS
- thesaurus
- dictionary
- paper
- pencil or pen

strongest meaning   weakest meaning

immaculate   clean

Grade 5, Lesson 23

⭐ **Literacy Center Kit,** Card 111

strongest meaning   weakest meaning

immaculate   pure   spotless   clean

READING

Reading Log

Objective
To select and read books independently

READING   Card 112

Reading Log

- **Look for these books** about being a helpful member of the natural world.

- **Choose one** that you find interesting.

- **Use your Reading Log** to keep track of what you read.

MATERIALS
- library book
- My Reading Log
- pen or pencil

Doña Flor by Pat Mora. TALL TALE

Eleanor by Barbara Cooney. BIOGRAPHY

The Prairie Builders: Reconstructing America's Lost Grasslands by Sneed B. Collard III. EXPOSITORY NONFICTION

Grade 5, Lesson 23

⭐ **Literacy Center Kit,** Card 112

www.harcourtschool.com/storytown

Go online

★ Additional Literacy Center Activities
★ Resources for Parents and Teachers

● BELOW-LEVEL ● ADVANCED ● ON-LEVEL

Differentiated *for Your Needs*

WRITING

Describe a Hero

Objective
To write a descriptive paragraph

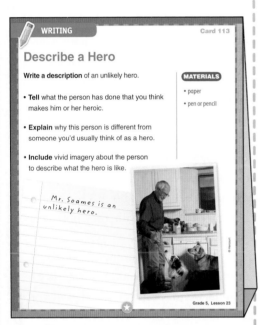

WRITING — Card 113

Describe a Hero

Write a description of an unlikely hero.

- **Tell** what the person has done that you think makes him or her heroic.
- **Explain** why this person is different from someone you'd usually think of as a hero.
- **Include** vivid imagery about the person to describe what the hero is like.

Mr. Soames is an unlikely hero.

MATERIALS
- paper
- pen or pencil

Grade 5, Lesson 23

⭐ **Literacy Center Kit,** Card 113

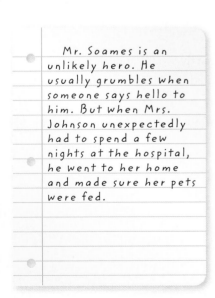

Mr. Soames is an unlikely hero. He usually grumbles when someone says hello to him. But when Mrs. Johnson unexpectedly had to spend a few nights at the hospital, he went to her home and made sure her pets were fed.

TECHNOLOGY

Research an Animal

Objective
To use electronic resources to gather information on a topic

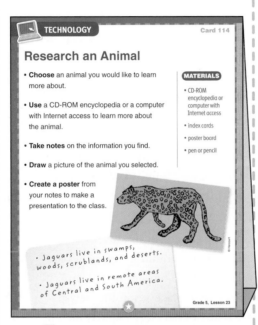

TECHNOLOGY — Card 114

Research an Animal

- **Choose** an animal you would like to learn more about.
- **Use** a CD-ROM encyclopedia or a computer with Internet access to learn more about the animal.
- **Take notes** on the information you find.
- **Draw** a picture of the animal you selected.
- **Create a poster** from your notes to make a presentation to the class.

MATERIALS
- CD-ROM encyclopedia or computer with Internet access
- index cards
- poster board
- pen or pencil

· Jaguars live in swamps, woods, scrublands, and deserts.

· Jaguars live in remote areas of Central and South America.

Grade 5, Lesson 23

⭐ **Literacy Center Kit,** Card 114

The biggest population of jaguars is in the Amazon Rainforest.

FLUENCY

Read Aloud

Objective
To read aloud with appropriate pace

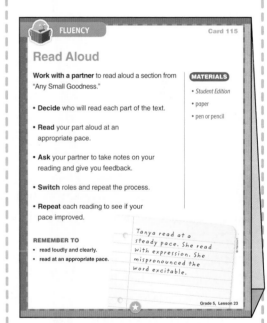

FLUENCY — Card 115

Read Aloud

Work with a partner to read aloud a section from "Any Small Goodness."

- **Decide** who will read each part of the text.
- **Read** your part aloud at an appropriate pace.
- **Ask** your partner to take notes on your reading and give you feedback.
- **Switch** roles and repeat the process.
- **Repeat** each reading to see if your pace improved.

REMEMBER TO
- read loudly and clearly.
- read at an appropriate pace.

MATERIALS
- Student Edition
- paper
- pen or pencil

Tanya read at a steady pace. She read with expression. She mispronounced the word excitable.

Grade 5, Lesson 23

⭐ **Literacy Center Kit,** Card 115

Listening Comprehension *Read-Aloud*

Objectives
• *To determine a purpose for listening*
• *To understand information presented orally*

Genre Study

EXPOSITORY NONFICTION Tell students that they will listen to an expository selection called "Dog Gone." Remind students that expository nonfiction

• gives facts about a topic.

• is usually organized by main ideas and details.

Set a Purpose for Listening

LISTEN TO LEARN Tell students that when they listen to expository nonfiction, they should listen to learn facts about the topic. Model setting a purpose for listening: *The title is "Dog Gone." A good purpose for listening is to find out what the selection says about dogs.* Then have students set their own purposes for listening.

Dog Gone
by Charles Downey

A rare Burmese mountain dog was found in the Texas woods, skinny, dirty, his coat full of weeds. He had been on his own for months.

But the animal warden knew of no report on a lost, valuable dog. So he called Mary Packwood.

Packwood, a real-life pet detective, looked through her old files and records of lost and found dogs. Sure enough, more than a year before, a woman who had visited Dallas reported that her valuable show dog ran away. She was overjoyed when Packwood called to tell her she could pick up her pet.

According to the National Dog Registry, about two million dogs are lost each year. Fewer than 60,000 are ever found. And you won't believe some of the wacky ways pet owners are finding their missing mutts. ❶

Doggie Detectives

Packwood, who has found lost pooches for 17 years, takes about 50 reports a day from frantic owners. She'll place ads in the newspaper, then see if any of her "lost" reports match her "found" reports.

Micky Flynn, a pet detective from San Diego, Calif., goes one step further. He visits animal shelters with a video camera to film the lost pooches.

People send Flynn pictures of their lost dogs and tell him the date their pet disappeared. Flynn then looks at his videos. If a photograph matches a dog on the tape, bingo! The pet is reunited with its owner.

Even if a lost pooch has been adopted out of an animal shelter, the pet could still show up on the video. That way, the new owners can be found and the dog returned to the original owner. ❷

Flynn's process is working. His first month in business, he returned four missing dogs to their owners.

Other pet detectives are putting their magnifying glasses on the Internet. The U.S. Department of Agriculture's Missing and Found Animal Page posts lost and found pets from around the country.

Calling Codemaster

You wouldn't think a dog would have a tattoo on its chest. But for some owners, it's the only way they can find their lost pets.

Take Star, a 28-pound sheltie who ran off from his Las Vegas, Nev., home. The family had given up hope of ever finding him.

But four months after Star disappeared, two men four-wheeling in the desert found a dog caught in a steel leg-hold trap, near death. When they gave the dog a bath, they noticed a strange marking on his skin.

It was an identification number tattooed on the animal by the National Dog Registry (NDR). Sound weird? Association officials say about six million dogs in North America carry one of its secret codes that match the animal with its owner. Another organization, Tattoo-A-Pet, returns 10 to 25 lost dogs on a typical day.

That's exactly what happened to Star. When the men called the identification mark in to NDR, workers there knew just where to find the dog's family and sent the pooch home. ❸

Read-Aloud is continued on page T327.

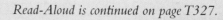

Begin the Read-Aloud

MODEL ORAL FLUENCY: PACE Tell students that good readers

- read aloud with appropriate pace.
- match their reading speed to the type of text they are reading.

Display **Transparency R97.** Read the passage aloud with appropriate pace as students follow along. Point out how your pace slows down as you read important facts in the text.

Interact with the Text

Routine Card 1

Continue reading aloud "Dog Gone." Pause to point out or ask students the following items.

❶ **About how many dogs are lost each year?** (2 million) **How many are found?** (fewer than 60,000) **NOTE DETAILS**

❷ **How does Micky Flynn use a video camera to find pets?** (He films lost pets at animal shelters and compares the pictures with photographs people send him of their lost pets.) **MAIN IDEA**

❸ **What is one advantage and one disadvantage of tattooing a pet?** (Advantage: permanent mark; Disadvantage: may not be seen under fur) **MAKE JUDGMENTS**

❹ **What is one disadvantage of having a microchip put in your pet?** (People may not know it's there; it may not be read by scanner.) **MAKE JUDGMENTS**

When you have finished reading the selection, ask:

- **Why do you think the author wrote this selection?** (to give facts about how pets are found) **RETURN TO PURPOSE**

- **What is the best way to avoid losing a pet?** (Make sure it has identification tags.) **MAIN IDEA**

Connect to Reading

Tell students that in this lesson they will read about a lost cat.

Model Oral Fluency

from "Dog Gone" by Charles Downey

A rare Burmese mountain dog was found in the Texas woods, skinny, dirty, his coat full of weeds. He had been on his own for months.

But the animal warden knew of no report on a lost, valuable dog. So he called Mary Packwood.

Packwood, a real-life pet detective, looked through her old files and records of lost and found dogs. Sure enough, more than a year before, a woman who had visited Dallas reported that her valuable show dog ran away. She was overjoyed when Packwood called to tell her she could pick up her pet.

According to the National Dog Registry, about two million dogs are lost each year. Fewer than 60,000 are ever found. And you won't believe some of the wacky ways pet owners are finding their missing mutts.

Grade 5, Lesson 23   R97   Model Oral Fluency

Transparency R97

Suggested Daily Read-Aloud

To model fluency and promote listening comprehension, read aloud from one of these books throughout the week:

- *Sea Turtles* by Lorraine A. Jay. NorthWord, 2000.
- *The Kids' Volunteering Book* by Arlene Erlbach. Lerner, 1998.
- *Neighborhood Odes* by Gary Soto. Harcourt, 2005.
- *Chester Cricket's New Home* by George Selden. Random House, 1984.
- *My Backyard Garden* by Carol Lerner. Morrow, 1998.

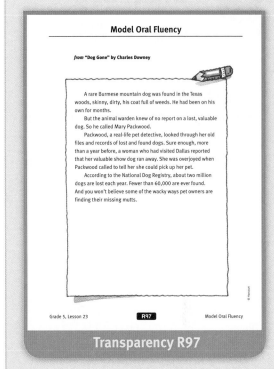

Literary Devices

Objectives

- *To recognize and understand literary devices*
- *To identify and use sensory language*

Skill Trace

 Literary Devices

Introduce	pp. T166–T167
Reteach	pp. S20–S21, S28–S29
Review	pp. T192–T193, T226–T227, T254–T255, T309
Test	Theme 5
Maintain	p. T144, Theme 6

Teach/Model

INTRODUCE LITERARY DEVICES Read page 590 with students. Then use these points to summarize:

- **Imagery** uses vivid language to describe people, places, things, and ideas.
- Imagery appeals to the five senses: sight, hearing, smell, taste, and touch.

Tell students that imagery can help readers picture, or visualize, all the elements of a story: *characters*, *setting*, and *plot events*.

Focus Skill

 Literary Devices

Authors use many kinds of literary devices to make their writing vivid and interesting. **Imagery** is a literary device that uses vivid language to describe people, places, things, and ideas. Imagery appeals to the senses of sight, hearing, smell, taste, and touch.

Text Example	Sense It Appeals To

Tip

Literary devices, such as imagery, help readers create images in their minds.

590

E L L

Categorize Images To help students understand how images appeal to the senses, write the following images on the board and ask students which sense each image appeals to.

- the flowery **perfume** of roses
- sun **glittering** on water
- a **cool** breeze blowing
- wind **whispering** through pine trees
- a bowl of **sweet ripe** mango slices

sight	
smell	
touch	
hearing	
taste	

Read the paragraph below. The graphic organizer lists examples of imagery and the senses they appeal to.

Val watched her cat, Mr. Meow, hunt stray beams of sunlight that cut across the yard. Finally, bored or tired, he headed to where Val sat. His soft, silent walk didn't make a single leaf rustle. He hopped onto her lap and licked her hand with his sandpaper-rough tongue. Val giggled and petted him. Mr. Meow purred loudly at first and then softly as he settled into a catnap.

Text Example	Sense It Appeals To
stray beams of sunlight	sight
didn't make a leaf rustle	sound

Reread the paragraph. Look for an example of imagery that appeals to the sense of touch.

www.harcourtschool.com/storytown

591

 MONITOR PROGRESS

Literary Devices

IF students have difficulty finding an example of imagery that appeals to the sense of touch,	**THEN** explain that the cat's "sandpaper-rough" tongue on Val's hand helps readers imagine how the cat's tongue felt to Val.

Small-Group Instruction, pp. S20–S21:

● **BELOW-LEVEL:** Reteach   ● **ON-LEVEL:** Reinforce   ● **ADVANCED:** Extend

(TEACH/MODEL CONTINUED) Ask a volunteer to read aloud the paragraph on *Student Edition* page 591. Model how to recognize and understand imagery.

Think Aloud The phrase *stray beams of sunlight* is imagery that appeals to the sense of sight. It helps you picture how the sun hits the ground in some spots and not others.

Guided Practice

IDENTIFY IMAGERY Call on another volunteer to read the paragraph again. Ask:

- **What do you picture the cat doing when you read about him hunting stray beams of sunlight?** (Possible response: I picture him sneaking up on a beam of sunlight and then pouncing on it.)

- **What sense does this image appeal to?** (sight)

- **Which sense does the description of the cat's soft, silent walk appeal to?** (hearing)

Practice/Apply

Try This Have students read the paragraph to find an example of imagery that appeals to the sense of touch.

DURING AND AFTER READING
- Practice the Skill • Apply to Text, pp. T178, T180, T182
- Reinforce the Skill • Practice/Apply, pp. T192–T193

(*Student Edition*, page 591) Lesson 23 • **T167**

Comprehension Strategy
Answer Questions

Objectives

- *To identify types of question-answer relationships*
- *To use strategies for answering questions*

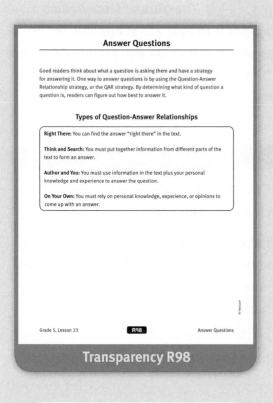

Transparency R98

Answer Questions

Good readers think about what a question is asking them and have a strategy for answering it. One way to answer questions is by using the Question-Answer Relationship strategy, or the QAR strategy. By determining what kind of question a question is, readers can figure out how best to answer it.

Types of Question-Answer Relationships

Right There: You can find the answer "right there" in the text.

Think and Search: You must put together information from different parts of the text to form an answer.

Author and You: You must use information in the text plus your personal knowledge and experience to answer the question.

On Your Own: You must rely on personal knowledge, experience, or opinions to come up with an answer.

Grade 5, Lesson 23   R98   Answer Questions

Professional Development

 Podcasting: Answer Questions

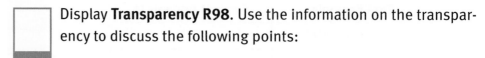
Teach/Model

INTRODUCE THE ANSWER QUESTIONS STRATEGY Tell students that determining the kind of information a question asks for will help them answer it more easily. The Question-Answer Relationship, or QAR, Strategy can help them identify where to look for information to answer questions.

Display **Transparency R98**. Use the information on the transparency to discuss the following points:

- A question that asks about a specific detail is a **Right There** question. The answer will appear in one place in the text.

- A question that asks you to relate two or more ideas is a **Think and Search** question. The answer will be in at least two places.

- A question that asks you to draw conclusions is an **Author and You** question. Combine text information with prior knowledge to answer.

- Questions that ask you to form an opinion or make a judgment are **On Your Own** questions. Use what you know to answer these questions.

Display **Transparency R99.** Ask a volunteer to read the first paragraph aloud. Then ask the first question in the chart. Model using the strategy to answer the question.

 **This question is an Author and You question because the next sentence you have to connect the sound with the rabbit emerging from the hole in the fence and infer that the "scritch-scritch" sound is made by the rabbit.**

Guided Practice

ANSWER QUESTIONS Call on volunteers to take turns reading the remaining paragraphs on **Transparency R99**. Ask the following questions:

- **Why doesn't the rabbit run away?**
- **Why don't the children notice the rabbit at first?**
- **Why can't they keep the rabbit right away?**

Guide students to identify each question type and then answer the questions from their own knowledge or by drawing on details from the text. Add their answers to the chart.

Practice/Apply

MONITOR COMPREHENSION Make available to students an online or print encyclopedia article about an animal-related topic. Have them read the text and generate a question for each type of question-answer relationship. Have students exchange questions with a partner, identify each kind of question, and write answers to the questions.

> **DURING READING**
> - Apply the Focus Strategy, pp. T177, T181, T183
> - Review Comprehension Strategies, p. T179

Answer Questions

The Wong family was relaxing under the oak tree in their backyard. Mr. Wong read a book while Mrs. Wong pulled weeds. The children squealed as they played on the swings. Then Mrs. Wong heard a *scritch-scritch* from the other side of the fence. Suddenly a rabbit emerged through a hole in the fence. He was pale gray with white paws. He hopped over to a clump of dandelion weeds and began nibbling.

"Jim, come look," Mrs. Wong called softly to her husband. He crouched down next to the rabbit. The rabbit continued dining on dandelions. He gently stroked the rabbit's soft fur. It stopped eating, but it didn't run away.

"He's obviously tame—probably a neighbor's pet," Mr. Wong said.

The children rushed over to inspect the visitor. "Can we keep him, Dad?" asked Billy.

"Let's try to find his owner first," Dad answered. "We'll post signs around the neighborhood. If no one claims him, we'll keep him."

Question	Question-Answer Relationship	Answer
What is the "scritch-scritch" sound?	Author and You	The sound is a rabbit digging.
Why doesn't the rabbit run away?	Right There	The rabbit is tame.
Why can't they keep the rabbit?	Think and Search	The rabbit may belong to someone.
Why do you think someone would keep a rabbit as a pet?	On Your Own	Responses will vary.

Grade 5, Lesson 23   **R99**   Answer Questions

Transparency R99

BELOW-LEVEL

Clarify Understanding

Students may have difficulty distinguishing between "Right There" and "Think and Search" questions. Tell them that questions that ask about more than one character, event, or idea, such as sequence, cause and effect, or comparison and contrast questions, are usually "Think and Search."

What will this character do next?

 Build Background

Access Prior Knowledge

CREATE A LIST Tell students that the next story they will read is about a family whose cat suddenly disappears. Ask students to share their knowledge of what steps people take when a pet is missing, and the order in which they do them. Create a sequence chart on the board similar to the one below.

Steps for Finding a Lost Pet

First, look in the house, yard, and known hiding places while calling the pet's name.

↓

Next, ask neighbors if they've seen the pet.

↓

Then, post MISSING notices around the neighborhood.

↓

After that, call local animal shelters.

↓

Finally, put an ad in the newspaper.

Develop Concepts

DISCUSS NEIGHBORHOODS Use ideas from the sequence chart as the starting point for a discussion of key concepts from the selection. Focus on how people in a neighborhood interact:

• News travels fast in a neighborhood.

• People in neighborhoods look out for each other's children and pets.

• Neighbors help each other in times of trouble.

• Neighbors respect one another's property and belongings.

E L L

Selection Background Use *Picture Card 68*, along with gestures, sketches, and simple explanations, to scaffold background and vocabulary as needed:

• A **house** is a building where a family lives. A house can be a **home** to a large family or to a person living alone. (show photo)

• Many houses together form a **neighborhood**. (show photo)

Have students share any experiences they have had living in a **neighborhood**.

Picture Card 68 ▶

See *ELL Teacher Guide* Lesson 23 for support in scaffolding instruction.

5-DAY **VOCABULARY**

DAY 1 Vocabulary, pp. T171–T173
DAY 2 Vocabulary Review, p. T191
DAY 3 Reinforce Word Meanings, p. T199
DAY 4 Extend Word Meanings, p. T199
DAY 5 Cumulative Review, p. T199

Build **Robust Vocabulary**

Introduce Vocabulary

Routine Card 2

BUILD WORD MEANING Display **Transparency R100**. Have a volunteer read aloud the first Vocabulary Word, and have the class repeat the word aloud to practice its pronunciation. Then have the volunteer read the explanation for the word. Ask students the first question below. Continue in this way until students have answered a question about each of the Vocabulary Words.

1. If a person **gouges** something, does he or she poke it hard or touch it gently?

2. Would you be **desolate** if you learned that you and your family would be moving to another state? Why or why not?

3. If a student **bustles** to get to class on time, would you expect him to be late? Explain.

4. Would you be more likely to speak with **fervor** about your favorite sports team or a movie during which you fell asleep?

5. Do you think it is important to keep your room **immaculate**? Why or why not?

6. What could someone do to **assuage** his guilt about losing something that belonged to a friend?

▼ Dogs running with **fervor**.

INTRODUCE ✓ Tested

Vocabulary: Lesson 23

gouges	fervor
desolate	immaculate
bustles	assuage

▼ **Student-Friendly Explanations**

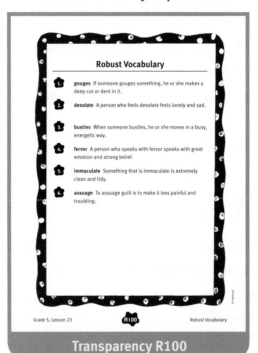

Robust Vocabulary

1. **gouges** If someone gouges something, he or she makes a deep cut or dent in it.

2. **desolate** A person who feels desolate feels lonely and sad.

3. **bustles** When someone bustles, he or she moves in a busy, energetic way.

4. **fervor** A person who speaks with fervor speaks with great emotion and strong belief.

5. **immaculate** Something that is immaculate is extremely clean and tidy.

6. **assuage** To assuage guilt is to make it less painful and troubling.

Grade 5, Lesson 23   R100   Robust Vocabulary

Transparency R100

Vocabulary

Build Robust Vocabulary

DEVELOP DEEPER MEANING Have students read the passage on pages 592–593. Then read the passage aloud. Pause at the end of page 592. Ask questions 1–2 about the high-lighted words. Discuss students' answers. Then read page 593 and discuss students' answers to questions 3–6. If students are unable to give reasonable responses, refer them to the explanations on **Transparency R100**.

1. Where does Delilah the cat usually **bustle** around each day?

2. What does Delilah enjoy **gouging** her claws into?

3. What causes Delilah's family to feel **desolate**?

4. Why does nothing **assuage** the sorrow that Delilah's family feels?

5. What might have happened to Delilah if the ship had been in **immaculate** condition?

6. Why do you think Delilah devours her snack with such **fervor**?

Vocabulary

Build Robust Vocabulary

Curious Cat Sets Sail

bustles

gouges

desolate

assuage

immaculate

fervor

Delilah the cat normally **bustles** around her Wisconsin home and neighborhood each day. She **gouges** claw marks into a fence post as she makes her way through her hometown.

One day, though, Delilah sneaked into a warehouse full of cargo containers. Little did she know that she was about to take a three-week ocean voyage. Delilah hopped inside one of the huge containers. Before she could get out, it was loaded onto a ship on its way to France!

Newscasters around the world spoke about Delilah's amazing sea adventure.

592

E L L

Synonyms Use the synonyms to clarify the Vocabulary Words:

Vocabulary Word	Synonym
gouges	dents
desolate	sad
bustles	hurries
fervor	excitement
immaculate	spotless
assuage	soothe

See *ELL Teacher Guide* Lesson 23 for support in scaffolding instruction.

Back home, Delilah's family felt lonely and **desolate**. Nothing could **assuage** their sorrow at Delilah's disappearance.

When the ship landed in France, dockworkers were shocked to find Delilah aboard. Fortunately, she was wearing identification tags. The workers quickly called her family in the United States. Imagine how surprised they were!

Delilah's family is glad the ship was not in **immaculate** condition. They suspect Delilah survived the voyage by catching mice. Delilah is probably one of the few cats to have traveled internationally on her own.

GO online www.harcourtschool.com/storytown

Delilah devours a snack with **fervor** before flying home.

Word Champion

Your challenge this week is to use Vocabulary Words outside your classroom. Keep the list of words in a place at home where you can see it. Use as many of the Vocabulary Words as you can when you speak with family members and friends. For example, you might tell your brother that you think his room is immaculate. Write in your vocabulary journal the words you used, and tell how you used them.

593

Word Champion

Use Words in Everyday Speech Have students post a list of the Vocabulary Words where they will see it often. Challenge them to use two words from the list in conversation each day and then record how they used them in their vocabulary journals. At the end of the week, call on volunteers to share the sentences they wrote in their vocabulary journals.

HOMEWORK/INDEPENDENT PRACTICE

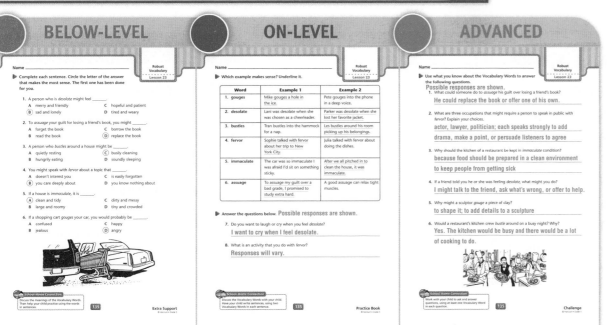

BELOW-LEVEL

▲ Extra Support, p. 135

ON-LEVEL

▲ Practice Book, p. 135

ADVANCED

▲ Challenge, p. 135

ELL

• Group students according to academic levels, and assign one of the pages on the left.

• Clarify any unfamiliar concepts as necessary. See *ELL Teacher Guide* Lesson 23 for support in scaffolding instruction.

SOCIAL STUDIES

Read the Selection

Objective
- *To recognize the distinguishing characteristics of realistic fiction*

Genre Study

DISCUSS REALISTIC FICTION: PAGE 594 Have students read the genre information on page 594. Discuss with students each of the characteristics of realistic fiction. Have students scan the illustrations for clues that this selection is about believable characters and situations.

LIST GENRE FEATURES Write on the board the titles of some other realistic fiction stories students may be familiar with. Have them contrast the features of realistic fiction with the features of folktales or fantasies. Then display **Transparency GO3**. Use the story map to review story structure with students.

Comprehension Strategy

ANSWER QUESTIONS STRATEGY: PAGE 594 Have students read the Comprehension Strategy information on page 594. Then distribute *Practice Book* page 136. Tell students that a story map is a useful tool for remembering the elements in a story. Have students use the story map to record the characters, setting, conflict, plot events, and resolution as they read. See page T187 for the completed *Practice Book* page.

Realistic Fiction

Genre Study

Realistic fiction has characters and events that are like people and events in real life. As you read, look for

- challenges and problems that might happen in real life.
- characters with realistic traits.

Character

Comprehension Strategy

Answer questions you have by looking in the story and thinking about what you already know.

594

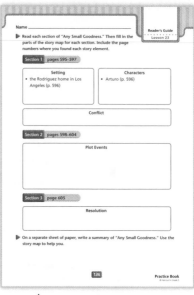

▲ Practice Book, p. 136

TECHNOLOGY

eBook "Any Small Goodness: A Novel of the Barrio" is available in an eBook.

Audiotext "Any Small Goodness: A Novel of the Barrio" is available on *Audiotext Grade 5*, CD7 for subsequent readings.

Any Small Goodness
A Novel of the Barrio
by Tony Johnston • • • • illustrated by Raúl Colón

It has been three years since Arturo Rodriguez and his family moved from Mexico to Los Angeles, California, and they are slowly adjusting to life in the United States. Arturo's older brother, Luis, has formed a band that practices in the garage. No one notices the cat, Huitla (WEET•lah), napping in the garage until she flies out, scared by the band's first blast of song. Arturo forgets about Huitla's wild escape until that night.

595

Preview/Set a Purpose

Routine Card 3

PREVIEW AND PREDICT Have students read the title of the selection. Read aloud the introduction on page 595. Ask students to predict what they think the story will be about.

MODEL SETTING A PURPOSE Remind students that good readers set a purpose for reading a story, based on their preview and what they know about the genre. Have students set their own purpose for reading "Any Small Goodness: A Novel of the Barrio." You may want to use the following model:

Think Aloud The introduction on page 595 and the illustration of the cat indicate that Huitla's escape will probably be important to the story. One purpose for reading might be to find out whether the family finds Huitla.

Options for Reading

BELOW-LEVEL
Small Group Preview the selection with students. Model how to use the preview and the genre information to set a purpose for reading.

ON-LEVEL
Whole Group/Partner Use the Monitor Comprehension questions as students read the selection, or have partners read the selection together and complete *Practice Book* page 136.

ADVANCED
Independent Have students read the selection independently, using *Practice Book* page 136 to monitor their comprehension and keep track of the information in the selection.

Monitor Comprehension

1 PLOT: CONFLICT AND RESOLUTON
What is the problem in the story?
(The family has lost its cat.)

2 CHARACTER'S EMOTIONS
How does the family feel about Huitla's escape? How do you know? (Possible response: Everyone is sad. They talk about Huitla, Rosa wanders through the house calling her, and the family searches for her everywhere.)

3 MAKE PREDICTIONS
Do you think the family will find Huitla?
(Responses will vary.)

See *Questioning the Author Comprehension Guide,* Lesson 23, as an alternate questioning strategy to guide student interaction with the text.

Questioning the Author Comprehension Guide, Lesson 23 ▶

Mami's stirring the various pots that will become dinner. "Where's Huitla?" she asks. Because that cat has always twined around her legs when food's available, nearly tripping her sometimes. Mami doesn't mind. She always stops cooking, stoops her dove-shaped body down, giving Huitla a little pat. "*Ay,*[1] Huitla, old black lump," she croons gently. "One day you will simply break Mami's old neck. Then what will those greedy ones do for a cook?" She chuckles a lot, she finds herself so humorous.

"That Huitla," Mami repeats. "*¿Dónde está?*"[2]

Luis gouges a taste of refried beans from a saucepan. "*No sé.*"[3] He grunts.

"She took off," I say, in explanation of everything.

Things are pretty quiet at dinner. Except for cat questions. We're all wondering where Huitla's gone. Rosa wanders from room to room. "Huitla!" She calls over and over. "*Ven,*[4] kitty! Come!"

But she doesn't. Not tonight. Not any night. **1**

From the start we search everywhere. All of Huitla's favorite spots. Like beside the scarecrow in the corn plot, where she loves to plop her lazy self down, in the fullest sun. The neighbors help. They love our little cat for her sweetness. And for her funky stuck-out tongue.

With crayons, Rosa makes a sign. Just the face of a little black cat, poking out the tip of its tongue. MY KITTY IS LOST, she writes, with our help, and gives the number of our telephone. **2** **3**

---

1   *ay:* oh
2   *¿Dónde está?:* Where is she?
3   *No sé.:* I don't know.
4   *ven:* come

596

BELOW-LEVEL

Footnotes Point out the words in italic type on page 596 that have numbers after them. Tell students that each number corresponds to a footnote at the bottom of the page. Explain that footnotes are used to define words without interrupting the flow of the story. Have students identify the footnote that goes with each italicized word or phrase and take turns reading the translations aloud.

Ven means "come" in Spanish.

597

Answer Questions

QUESTION-ANSWER RELATIONSHIPS Remind students of the four types of questions:

- **Right There:** The reader finds the answer "right there" in the text.

- **Think and Search:** The reader puts together information from different parts of the selection to find the answer.

- **Author and You:** The reader uses information in the selection and personal knowledge to find an answer.

- **On Your Own:** The reader relies on personal knowledge rather than the text to find an answer.

Then ask:

What steps do the Rodriguez family take to find Huitla? (Possible responses: Rosa searches the house, calling her name; the whole family searches Huitla's favorite spots; they ask the neighbors to help; Rosa makes a sign.)

Model the thinking:

Think Aloud This is a Think and Search question. The answer can be found in the last two paragraphs on page 596. You must combine information from these paragraphs to answer the question.

SCIENCE SUPPORTING STANDARDS

Domestic Cats Explain to students that house cats have adapted to living with humans while still retaining many of their wild traits. For example, cats are carnivores, so both wild cats and pet cats have sharp teeth to help them chew food in preparation for digestion. Have students complete a Venn diagram comparing the characteristics of a house cat with those of a cat living in the wild.

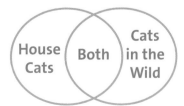

House Cats — Both — Cats in the Wild

Monitor Comprehension

4 LITERARY DEVICES
In the first paragraph on page 599, how does the author use imagery to help readers understand how the mood in the house has changed since Huitla disappeared? (Possible response: The author says that a "little silence" moves through the house.)

5 AUTHOR'S CRAFT
How does the author make the Rodriguez family seem realistic? (She refers to real parts of American culture and uses casual language and a mix of Spanish and English to show how the family members speak to one another.)

6 CHARACTER'S TRAITS
What do you think Leo Love will be like, based on the way he speaks on the phone? (Possible response: nervous; shy)

ELL

Cultural References and Slang Point out to students that the narrator, the person who is telling this story, uses a mix of standard English, English slang, and Spanish words. Also point out that she refers to things that are part of popular American culture. Clarify the following words and phrases as necessary:

- **squeaking like Alvin the Chipmunk** – speaking in a fast, high voice like a cartoon chipmunk named Alvin
- **dibs not answering** – I claim the right to not answer the phone.
- **speak face-to-face** – talk to a person who is in the room with you
- **dash up** – run quickly toward something

It's two weeks since we've seen her. Now a little silence moves through the house, as if filling Huitla's space. Nobody ever says so, but maybe we guess she's dead. Or at least that she won't return.

Abuelita has her words of comfort to say. "We will find her." **4**

Rosa's the one most <u>desolate</u>. She sometimes crawls into my lap and says nothing, just sucks her thumb.

· · · · · ·

It's a typical night at home. Rosa's blabbling into a big plastic bottle, squeaking like Alvin the Chipmunk. Luis's blazing out "*Chango*" on the radio.

"Turn it down, I'm trying to study!" I shout.

"Well, try harder!"

Above the blare, the phone rings.

"¡*Zafo*!" Luis yells, which means "dibs not answering."

"¡*Zafo*!" Rosa echoes.

Though she's sitting close, Abuelita also refuses to answer. *Or speak face-to-face, or don't speak at all,* is her thought on the subject of telephones. Given the chance, she'd throw it off a cliff. **5**

I dash up and take the call. At first, there's only breathing on the line.

"Hello?"

At last a voice comes. "Hello. This is Leo Love speaking."

This is Leo Love breathing, I think.

Leo Love! It's got to be one of those crank romantic calls you hear about sometimes! I don't want to become involved in anything weird, so I nearly hang up.

"I've got Hoo—Hoo—" The voice makes frustrated-owl calls, then just blurts, "I've got your cat." **6**

599

SCIENCE **CONTENT-AREA VOCABULARY**

Word Bank: Science Point out the word *radio* on page 599. Tell students that a radio uses electromagnetic waves to send out or receive electric signals. Explain that *radio* comes from the Latin word *radius*, meaning "ray," and that many words that have to do with rays or energy that radiates also have this root. Make a word web like the one below.

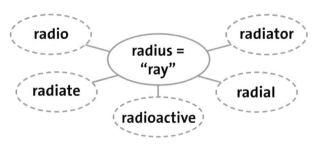

Apply Comprehension Strategies

Use Story Structure

STORY ELEMENTS Remind students that paying attention to story elements can help them keep track of the important information in a story. To help students identify key story elements, ask:

- **What is the setting of this story?**

- **Who are the main characters in the story?**

- **What is the problem in the story?**

Then guide students to use their responses to the questions to fill in a story map.

Character	Setting
Mami, Abuelita, Arturo, Rosa, Luis	the Rodriguez home in Los Angeles, California

Conflict
The family cat escaped and has been missing for two weeks.

Remind students that they may be introduced to new characters as the story moves forward and the setting may change to match the unfolding action. Suggest that students use a story map to keep track of the main plot events as the story unfolds.

Monitor Comprehension

7 PLOT: CONFLICT AND RESOLUTION

What is the resolution to the story's problem? (Leo Love phones to say he has the family's cat.)

8 LITERARY DEVICES

FocusSkill **How does the author use imagery to help you understand how the family feels on the way to Leo Love's house?** (Possible response: The author uses words like *laughing, ecstatic, crying, jittering, slowing, speeding up*, and *anxious*.)

9 CHARACTER'S EMOTIONS

How do you think Leo Love feels when he sees the whole family at his door? (Possible response: overwhelmed, confused, amazed)

10 CAUSE AND EFFECT

Why does Leo Love sneeze? (He is allergic to cats.)

11 COMPARE AND CONTRAST

How is Leo Love different from the Rodriguez family? (Leo Love is shy, quiet, and reserved, while the Rodriguez family is loud, outgoing, and energetic.)

"Huitlacoche!" I shout into the receiver.

"Yes, Hootlecooch," the man agrees.

Over a series of explosions of joy in the room, I take the guy's *datos*[5] down. Name, address, telephone. I say, "We're on our way." **7**

And we are, all of us piling into Papi's car, Valentín. Laughing, all ecstatic. And crying.

Valentín goes jittering down the streets, slowing, speeding up, sometimes stopping in full so we can check the directions. We're all so anxious. When we reach the given address, it seems like we've been driving forever. Actually, it's not many blocks. **8**

Mr. Leo Love doesn't need to hear his doorbell. We arrive in such an excitement, he can't miss us. He opens the door. **9**

He's an old white guy, wire-bearded and small. No Mr. Universe, but more with the build of a sparrow. Pants creased sharp enough to slice *chorizo*.[6] Dressed in tweed, so he looks like he's wrapped in tree bark. He talks stiff as bark, too. Like every word makes a difference to his life.

Then, suddenly, he nearly blasts his bark off with a sneeze. A chorus of *saluds*[7] follows.

Quickly, Abuelita holds out a lime from her lumpy purse. She never travels without limes.

Leo Love looks surprised.

---

5 *datos*: information
6 *chorizo*: a type of sausage
7 *salud*: bless you

600

E L L

Clarify Figurative Language Have a volunteer read the seventh and eighth paragraphs on page 600. Explain that tweed is a woolen material used in many suits and coats, and bark is the brown outer coating of a tree. Discuss with students the image that this passage conveys of Leo Love. (His suit is brown and he holds himself straight and stiff like a tree.) Then ask what image the phrase "nearly blasts his bark off" gives students. (He sneezes so hard that if he were a tree, his bark would have peeled off.)

"You take this," she orders him. "Good for all things."

He lamely takes the lime.

"I am allergic to cats," he says, embarrassed, holding out Huitla.

"*Limones*[8] good also for that," says Abuelita.

By now, Rosa's popcorning up and down so much that for safety, Leo Love hands the cat to Mami.

Squashed-in face. Tip of pink tongue flagging out. It's our cat, all right.

"Hey, Fish Breath," Luis greets her. Words of love, for him.

What's the next step? Everyone's in confusion. Everyone except Abuelita. She bustles up and embraces this stranger. Plants kisses on his tortilla-white cheeks.

"*Estimado*[9] Señor Mister Leo Love," she says with fervor, "you are a most very good hero."

Señor Mister Leo Love seems amazed by that. And touched. In confusion, he invites us into his immaculate house. Everyone sits in a perched position, the furnishings are so clean. Mami's eyes survey the room. They say that she loves his housekeeping. **11**

8 *limones:* limes
9 *estimado:* esteemed

Answer Questions

Focus Strategy

THINK AND SEARCH If students have difficulty answering question 11, remind them that identifying the question type can help them determine how to answer it. Model the thinking:

Think Aloud **Question 11 is a Think and Search question because you must look in different parts of the text to find what Leo Love is like and what the Rodriguez family is like. Then you can put this information together to answer the question.**

Remind students to use Question-Answer Relationships to answer questions as they read the remainder of the text.

ANALYZE WRITER'S CRAFT

Vivid Details and Imagery Direct students' attention to the details and imagery that make the author's description of Leo Love so effective. Discuss the following: *frustrated-owl calls; pants creased sharp enough to slice chorizo; … looks like he's wrapped in tree bark; talks stiff as bark … like every word makes a difference to his life.* Invite students to describe their mental image of Leo Love and his immaculate house.

Monitor Comprehension

12  **LITERARY DEVICES**
What does the author mean when she describes the conversation as a "thick braid"? (Possible response: She means that many people were talking at once so it was difficult to keep track of what was being said.)

13 **MAKE INFERENCES**
What question is Papi meaning to ask when he says "But two weeks—"? (He means to ask Leo Love why he waited two weeks before calling them to say that he'd found their cat.)

14 **CAUSE AND EFFECT**
Why didn't Leo Love call the family sooner? (The cat's identification tags had fallen off when the cat lost her collar.)

Leo Love offers coffee. We all accept. In her excitement, even Rosa. This is a happy time. I guess that's why Mami allows it. Anyway, when Rosa's done, it's not coffee. Just some pale gunk, mainly sugar, so thick it could hold bricks together.

While Rosa glugs this down, she never lets go of Huitla. (Now that she's semi-settled down, Mami allows Rosa to hold the cat.)

On her chair, Abuelita leans forward. Like a small and eager bird. We await the prize words that are surely coming.

"Now, Señor Mister Leo Love," she says with respect and careful words, like taking careful steps on stairs, "how arrived our sweet little *gatita*[10] to your door?"

Somehow Leo Love has followed this thick braid of conversation. He sips his coffee and says, "Actually, she did not arrive at the door. I discovered her near my avocado tree." **12**

"I do not wish to seem rude," says Papi, who has never seemed rude in his whole life. "But two weeks—" **13**

Leo Love nods his head. "Yes. It is certainly a long time not to communicate. However, there was nothing to identify her."

Huitla has tags. From the vet. He even had to make them two times, because of problems of spelling.

"She had no tags," he continues. "And I have allergies. But, what could I do? I decided that at my age, I had earned the right to throw caution away. I decided to keep the little creature. I hadn't much else to offer, so I fed her trout." **14**

A shadow skims Mami's face. It seems to mean, *I cannot compete with trout.* Leo Love goes on.

"However, all the trout in the world could not assuage my guilt. Someone must miss her terribly. A child, most probably. Today, I searched the rescue site again, and by good fortune found the cat's collar. Broken. It was precisely then that I dialed your number."

At that, Abuelita perks up. She puts two and two together fast. "You believe in God?" She bores into him, all energized.

Leo Love looks at her as if seeing a blink of new light about his situation. He says, "It is something always worth considering."

For the moment, that satisfies Abuelita.

---

10 *gatita:* kitty

602

E L L

Sentence Fragments Point out that complete sentences have a subject and predicate. However, authors sometimes use sentence fragments, or sentences that lack either a subject or a verb, to make their characters' dialogue and their narrator's voice sound natural. Help students identify the fragments and, if necessary, restate them as complete sentences.

A child, most probably.

Then, like a meteor shooting on a wild course, Rosa asks, "Will you be my pen pal?"

Even though he lives so close she could spit about as far as his house, he agrees.

When we leave, Leo Love asks, "Hootlecooch, what sort of name is that?"

Abuelita explains, "It's Mexico—for corn fungus."

Leo Love looks stunned.

"Soon I bring you some."

And she will. And she'll see that he eats it, too.

Apply Comprehension Strategies

Focus Strategy

Answer Questions

USE MULTIPLE STRATEGIES Review with students the four types of questions in the Question-Answer Relationships strategy:

> **The 4 Kinds of Question-Answer Relationships**
>
> - **Right There**
> - **Think and Search**
> - **Author and You**
> - **On Your Own**

Remind students that good readers monitor their comprehension of a selection by asking themselves questions and then using the Answer Questions strategy to answer them. For example, they might ask why the family named the cat Huitlacoche. Model the thinking:

Think Aloud The story says that Huitlacoche means "corn fungus" and that Abuelita will take some to Leo Love. This might make you ask yourself whether corn fungus is good to eat. This is an On Your Own question because the answer isn't given in the text. You might draw the conclusion that corn fungus is good, just as Huitlacoche, the cat, is good for the Rodriguez family.

Monitor Comprehension

15 **AUTHOR'S CRAFT**

Why did the author put the newspaper boy in the story? (Possible response: to let the family know what Leo Love didn't tell them about how he rescued Huitla)

16 **CHARACTER'S MOTIVES**

Why do you think Leo Love didn't tell the whole story of how he found Huitla? (Possible responses: He didn't want to call attention to himself; he didn't want the Rodriguez family to know that he and the cat had to be rescued by the fire department.)

17 **PARAPHRASE**

What does Papi mean when he says, "When no eyes are upon him, that is a person's true test"? (Possible response: The way a person acts when no one is looking shows what that person is really like.)

18 **CONFIRM PREDICTIONS**

Did the story turn out the way you thought it would? If not, how was it different from what you expected? (Responses will vary.)

We've thanked Leo Love so much, he's retreated. We're outside the house, standing under the avocado tree. A slight breeze breathes by. The rustle of leaves sounds like I'm inside a flight of birds.

The newspaper boy wheels up in a gravelly crunch.

"That your cat?" he asks, eyeing Huitla.

"Yeah."

"What a pain!"

We all ask what he means.

"Mr. Love spent a whole night in that tree," he says, pointing to where we are. "Baby-sitting the cat. He's kinda old. And a handful of cat—plus fear of falling—kept him up there."

"How do you know this?" Papi asks.

"I found him. Next morning. Firemen got 'em down." **15** **16**

604

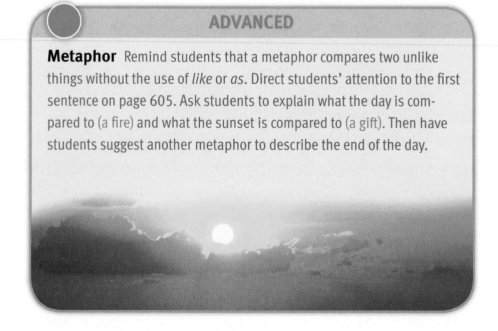

The day flames out in a smog-sunset, a wild gift of L.A.

On the way home Papi says, "This Leo Love is a brave man. In spite of fear he saved Huitla. When no eyes are upon him, that is a person's true test."

I file this inside of myself. Maybe one day when no eyes are on me, I'll have a true test, too.

· · · · · ·

Now Huitla's home. Sleeping on the sofa in a happy sprawl of fur. I sit beside her, totally sunken down. Our sofa's so soft, sitting on it's like being swallowed by a clam. I think about old Leo Love, who Abuelita now calls *El Estimado*, The Esteemed One. Going against allergies and dizziness and possible broken bones to save our cat.

You could do worse than be like such a person. **18**

Additional Related Reading

Students interested in cats or neighborhood stories may want to locate these titles.

- *Why Do Cats Do That?: Facts About Real Cats and Why They Act the Way They Do!* by Nancy White. Scholastic, 1997.
  EASY

- *How to Talk to Your Cat* by Jean Craighead George. HarperTrophy, 2003.
  AVERAGE

- *Neighborhood Odes* by Gary Soto. Harcourt, 2005.
  CHALLENGE

ANALYZE AUTHOR'S PURPOSE

Author's Purpose Remind students that authors always have a purpose, or reason, for writing. After students have finished "Any Small Goodness: A Novel of the Barrio," ask them:

Why do you think Tony Johnston wrote this story?

- **to describe a family pet**

- **to explain how to rescue a cat**

- to entertain while teaching a life lesson

- **to persuade people to get tags for their pets**

Think **Critically**

Respond to the Literature

Have students discuss or write their responses to the questions on page 606.

1 Possible response: She crawls onto Arturo's lap and sucks her thumb. **CHARACTER'S EMOTIONS**

2 Possible response: Sound; I can picture the boy putting on the brakes and hear the crunch of the gravel under his wheels.  **LITERARY DEVICES**

3 Possible response: Yes, he puts aside his own fears and safety to help a cat without expecting anything in return. **MAKE JUDGMENTS**

4 Possible responses: I would check to see if the animal had tags; I would ask the neighbors if anyone had lost a pet; I would put up flyers describing the animal I found. **MAKE CONNECTIONS**

5 **WRITE** Students should explain how Arturo might now define a hero, and should support their responses with information from the text. **SHORT RESPONSE**

RUBRIC For additional support in scoring this item, see the rubric on p. R6.

Think Critically

1 How do Rosa's actions reveal her feelings when Huitla is missing?
CHARACTER'S EMOTIONS

2 On page 604, the author describes the newspaper boy "wheeling up in a gravely crunch." Which sense helps you visualize this scene, and how?
LITERARY DEVICES

3 Do you agree with Papi that Leo Love is brave? Why or why not?
MAKE JUDGMENTS

4 What would you do if you found a lost animal? Explain your actions.
MAKE CONNECTIONS

5 **WRITE** How might meeting Leo Love change Arturo's definition of a hero? Use information and details from the selection to explain.
SHORT RESPONSE

606

BELOW-LEVEL

Before and After Tell students that the most important word in question 5 is *change*. Students should think about how Arturo would have defined a hero before meeting Leo Love and after. Guide them to fill in a chart like the one below.

Before	After
• does daring things • has exciting adventures	• does something difficult, even if it isn't exciting • acts courageously even when no one is looking

About the Author
Tony Johnston

When Tony Johnston was growing up, she wanted to be a "bugologist" because she was fascinated by every insect that flew or crawled. Instead, she became a writer who has now written more than one hundred books. Many of her stories have been published in Spanish. Tony Johnston grew up in Los Angeles. Later she lived in Mexico for fifteen years. In Mexico, her passion was collecting hand-woven sashes and recording the history of the craftspeople who made them. Her advice to young readers is, "Read your brains loose!"

About the Illustrator
Raúl Colón

As a young boy, Raúl Colón was often ill with asthma and had to stay indoors for days at a time. He spent that time filling notebook after notebook with his drawings. Raúl Colón knew early on that he wanted to be an artist. Now that he's accomplished that goal, he hopes that one of his other childhood dreams will come true—traveling to the moon.

 www.harcourtschool.com/storytime

Check Comprehension

Retell and Summarize

DISCUSS AUTHOR AND ILLUSTRATOR: PAGE 607: Have students read about the author and illustrator independently. Ask them how an author with an interest in bugs may have come to create an unlikely hero like Leo Love.

RETELL Students may refer to the story map on *Practice Book* page 136 that they completed during reading to help them retell "Any Small Goodness: a Novel of the Barrio."

 WRITE A SUMMARY Ask students to write a summary of "Any Small Goodness: A Novel of the Barrio." Share the following tips:
Routine Card 4

- Describe the conflict, main events, and resolution.
- Tell the lesson the story teaches.

RUBRIC See rubric for Retelling and Summarizing on page R3.

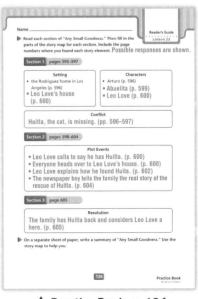

▲ Practice Book, p. 136

MONITOR PROGRESS

Summarize

IF students have difficulty writing a complete summary of "Any Small Goodness: A Novel of the Barrio,"	**THEN** work with them to identify the story elements on *Practice Book* page 136 that should be included in a summary.

Small-Group Instruction, p. S24:

● **BELOW-LEVEL:** Reteach ● **ON-LEVEL:** Reinforce ● **ADVANCED:** Extend

SOCIAL STUDIES

Paired Selection

Objectives

- *To read and understand a variety of texts*
- *To recognize the distinguishing features of a fable*

Genre Study

DISCUSS FABLES Tell students that they will now read two fables by Aesop. Explain that Aesop was an ancient Greek storyteller who lived about 3,000 years ago. Remind students that fables

- **teach a lesson.**

- **have animal characters that act like humans.**

- **have characters that represent a simple trait, such as good or evil, wisdom or foolishness, strength or weakness.**

Have students preview the selection by reading the introduction and looking at the illustrations. Ask them to predict what traits each character will represent.

IDENTIFY THE MORAL Remind students that fables have a moral, or lesson about life. Have students read "The Ant and the Dove" and "The Lion and the Mouse" and identify the moral in each. (One good turn deserves another; In time of need, the weak may help the strong.)

Social Studies

Fable

AESOP'S

Aesop lived in Greece about 3,000 years ago. He became famous for the clever animal fables through which he showed the wise and foolish behavior of people. Today, there are many versions of the tales that Aesop told so long ago.

THE ANT AND THE DOVE

A thirsty Ant went to the river to drink. To reach the river he had to climb down the steep bank on a blade of grass. Halfway down he slipped and fell into the swirling waters.

A Dove, perched in a nearby tree, saw the Ant's desperate plight. Quickly she plucked a leaf from the tree and dropped it into the river, close to the Ant. The Ant was able to climb up on the leaf and float safely to shore.

As soon as he was on dry land, the Ant saw a hunter of birds hiding behind a tree with a net in his hand. Seeing that the Dove was in danger, he crawled up to the hunter and bit him on his heel. The startled hunter dropped his net, and the Dove flew off.

The Dove, perched safely in the tree, called down to the Ant, "Thank you, my little friend."

"Not at all," said the Ant. *"One good turn deserves another."*

608

E L L

Develop Vocabulary Write the nouns and verbs below on the board and use brief definitions or synonyms to discuss their meanings with students before they read the fables.

Nouns	Verbs
• **bank:** the ground that borders a river	• **perched:** seated
• **plight:** a dangerous situation	• **plucked:** pulled hard
• **misery:** suffering	• **spare (my life):** let me go
• **captor:** a person who takes and holds another person	• **gnaw:** bite or chew

FABLES

retold by Ann McGovern
illustrated by Todd Kale

THE LION AND THE MOUSE

A Lion was awakened from sleep by a Mouse running across his face. With a terrible roar, the Lion seized the Mouse with his paw and was about to kill him.

"Oh please," the Mouse begged. "Spare my life! I will be sure to repay your kindness."

The King of Beasts was so amused at the thought of a Mouse being able to help *him* that he let the frightened creature go.

Shortly afterward the Lion fell into a trap set by some hunters and was hopelessly caught in strong ropes. In his misery the Lion roared so loudly that all the beasts in the forest heard him.

The Mouse recognized the roar of his former captor and ran to the place where the Lion lay trapped. At once the Mouse began to gnaw the ropes with his teeth. He gnawed rope after rope until at last the Lion was free.

"Thank you," said the grateful Lion. "I know now that *in time of need the weak may help the strong.*"

609

ABOUT THE AUTHOR

Ann McGovern has written more than 50 books. She says, "Looking backwards (and forwards) to my books, I realize that they reflect my life in three parts: 1) ideas I strongly believe in; 2) desire for knowledge; 3) exciting personal experiences." She has traveled to all seven continents in search of adventure.

Other books by Ann McGovern include these:

• *The Secret Soldier: The Story of Deborah Sampson.* Scholastic, 1999.
• *Adventures of the Shark Lady: Engenie Clark Around the World.* Scholastic, 1998.
• *Stone Soup.* Scholastic, 1986.

Respond to the Fables

Have students reread the fables silently. Then ask:

1. **MAKE INFERENCES Why did the Lion think the Mouse's promise to help him someday was so funny?** (Possible response: He didn't understand how a tiny little mouse could ever help a big, strong lion.)

2. **PERSONAL RESPONSE Which fable did you like best? Why?** (Responses will vary.)

3. **SOCIAL STUDIES CONNECTING TEXTS What do "The Ant and the Dove" and "The Lion and the Mouse" tell you about the values of the ancient Greeks?** (Possible response: The ancient Greeks thought it was important to help others.)

WRITE A FABLE Have students write a fable. Tell them to decide what lesson they want to teach and then pick the animal characters and the situation that will best teach it. Suggest that they use "The Ant and the Dove" or "The Lion and the Mouse" as models. **WRITING**

Comparing Texts

Answers:

1. Responses will vary. **TEXT TO SELF**

2. Possible response: The theme of "Any Small Goodness" is that you don't have to look like a hero to be one; the theme of "The Ant and the Dove" is that if you do something good, something good will be done for you; and the theme of "The Lion and the Mouse" is that the weak can help the strong. The themes are alike in that Leo Love, the Ant, and the Mouse are all seemingly weak creatures who do great things. **TEXT TO TEXT**

3. Responses will vary. **TEXT TO WORLD**

Comparing Texts

1. The members of Arturo's family share a love for Huitla. Describe something that you have in common with your friends or family members.

2. "Any Small Goodness" and the two fables by Aesop all have similar themes. What are the themes, and how are they alike?

3. Leo Love and Arturo's family might never have met if Huitla hadn't gotten stuck in Leo Love's tree. How can difficult situations sometimes bring people closer together?

Vocabulary Review

Word Sort

Work in a group. Sort the Vocabulary Words into categories. Discuss your sorted words with the group, explaining your choices. Then choose at least one Vocabulary Word from each category. Write a sentence for each word.

gouges

desolate

bustles

fervor

immaculate

assuage

Feelings	Actions	Appearance

610

Fluency Practice

Partner Reading

Work with a partner. Choose a section of "Any Small Goodness" to read aloud. Focus on your pace as you read. Ask your partner to tell you if you are reading too quickly or too slowly to match the mood and the action. Then switch roles with your partner and repeat the procedure.

Writing

Write a Descriptive Paragraph

Write a descriptive paragraph about an everyday event. Use imagery that appeals to the senses to help the reader picture what you are describing.

My Writing Checklist

Writing Trait ▶ Organization

✓ I organized the details of my topic.

✓ I used a graphic organizer to develop sensory language.

✓ I chose words that appealed to the senses.

Example	Sense It Appeals To

611

VOCABULARY REVIEW

Word Sort After students have sorted the Vocabulary Words, tell them to use the categories as a guide for correctly using the words in sentences. Invite volunteers to share their sentences with the class.

FLUENCY PRACTICE

Partner Reading: Pace Each student should listen and follow the text carefully to note whether his or her partner's pace is appropriate and corresponds to the action in the passage. Encourage partners to give feedback on pace as needed. *For additional fluency practice, see p. T198.*

WRITING

Write a Descriptive Paragraph

After students have chosen an everyday event to write about, have them record the sensory imagery in the graphic organizer to help them plan their ideas. Encourage them to use the checklist to evaluate their writing.

PORTFOLIO OPPORTUNITY Students may choose to place their paragraphs in their portfolios.

✓ MONITOR PROGRESS

Vocabulary Review

IF students have difficulty writing sentences for the Vocabulary Words,

THEN suggest simple categories, such as parts of speech. Guide students to explain why each word belongs in a particular category.

Small-Group Instruction, pp. S22–S23:

- ● **BELOW-LEVEL:** Reteach
- ● **ON-LEVEL:** Reinforce
- ● **ADVANCED:** Extend

Literary Devices

Objectives

- *To recognize and understand literary devices*
- *To identify and use sensory language*

Skill Trace

 Tested **Literary Devices**

Introduce	pp. T166–T167
Reteach	pp. S20–S21, S28–S29
Review	**pp. T192–193, T226–T227, T254–T255, T309**
Test	Theme 5
Maintain	p. T144, Theme 6

 BELOW-LEVEL

Imagery Write the following pairs of sentences on the board. Ask students which sentence from each pair evokes a stronger image.

- The man towered above the crowd, making everyone else look like children.
- The man was the tallest individual I'd ever seen.
- The stew had a nice aroma.
- The stew bubbled in its pot, filling the kitchen with a rich, tangy aroma.

Reinforce the Skill

REVIEW LITERARY DEVICES Remind students that authors often use literary devices such as imagery to make their writing more interesting and colorful. Review imagery with students:

- **Imagery** uses vivid language to describe people, places, things, and ideas.
- **Imagery** includes **sensory language,** or language that appeals to the five senses: sight, hearing, smell, taste, and touch.

Guided Practice

APPLY TO LITERATURE Have students reread these passages in the *Student Edition*. Ask them to find an example of imagery in each passage and tell what sense or senses it appeals to.

- **Page 599, fourth paragraph** (Rosa blabbling and squeaking; Luis blazing out a song on the radio; sense of hearing)
- **Page 600, seventh paragraph** (description of Leo Love, including how he dresses and how he talks—senses of sight and hearing)
- **Page 604, paragraph 1** (breeze breathes by, the rustle of leaves—senses of touch and hearing)

Then have students find one additional example of imagery. Invite volunteers to share their examples with the class.

Practice/Apply

RECOGNIZE IMAGERY Remind students that authors of realistic fiction often use imagery to help readers picture people, places, and events in their stories and to make their descriptions more interesting and entertaining.

Have students choose a page in a realistic fiction story they have already read. Have them identify each example of imagery on the page and tell which sense it appeals to. Tell them to enter this information in a chart like the one below.

Example of Imagery	Sense It Appeals to

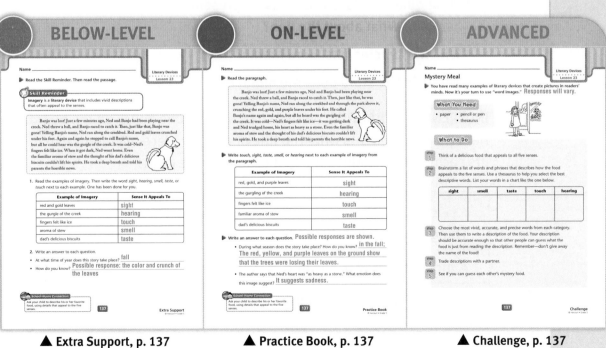

▲ Extra Support, p. 137   ▲ Practice Book, p. 137   ▲ Challenge, p. 137

E L L

- Group students according to academic levels, and assign one of the pages on the left.

- Clarify any unfamiliar concepts as necessary. See *ELL Teacher Guide* Lesson 23 for support in scaffolding instruction.

Literary Patterns and Symbols

Objective
- *To identify and evaluate archetypal patterns and symbols in literary texts*

Skill Trace

 Tested Literary Patterns and Symbols

Introduce	pp. T68–T69, Theme 4
Reteach	pp . S8–S9, Theme 4
Review	**pp. T194, T310**
Test	Theme 4
Maintain	p. T210, Theme 6

Teach/Model

REVIEW LITERARY PATTERNS AND SYMBOLS IN LITERATURE Remind students that many folktales and fables follow similar patterns. Review these patterns and symbols:

- Characters in fables are usually animals that act like humans and represent certain human qualities.
- Fables have a moral or lesson that usually comes at the end.
- Often the events in folktales happen in "threes."

Model identifying the literary patterns and symbols in "The Ant and the Dove."

Think Aloud In "The Ant and the Dove," two animals help each other escape from life-threatening situations. Each character represents good and does something heroic. The lesson is "one good turn deserves another."

Practice/Apply

GUIDED PRACTICE Help students identify the literary patterns and symbols in "The Lion and the Mouse." Ask

- **What qualities does the mouse represent?** (kindness, gratefulness, heroism) **What about the lion?** (strength, pridefulness)
- **Which character acts more heroic?** (the mouse)
- **Where in the story does the moral become clear?** (at the end)

INDEPENDENT PRACTICE Write a chart like the one below on the board. Have pairs of students write the title of another piece of literature that fits each of the criteria in the first column of the chart.

Pattern or Symbol	Title of Story
Things happen in "threes."	
A moral is stated at the end.	
A character learns a lesson.	

Persuasive Techniques

Objectives
- *To understand the characteristics of persuasive writing*
- *To identify techniques of persuasion*

Skill Trace
Persuasive Techniques

| Introduce | pp. T58–T59 |
| Review | p. T195 |

Reinforce the Skill

REVIEW PERSUASIVE TECHNIQUES Remind students that sometimes authors try to persuade readers to do, think, or believe something. To do this, authors use certain persuasive techniques. Model the thinking involved in recognizing an author's use of persuasive techniques:

Think Aloud **When you read, think about the author's purpose. Is the author writing to give facts or to tell a story? Or is there a deeper message the writer wants to persuade you to believe? The topics an author chooses, the author's word choice, and the opinions an author expresses are all important clues to whether an author is trying to persuade you to think or believe something.**

Practice/Apply

GUIDED PRACTICE Have students revisit "The Lion and the Mouse." Ask them to identify the words the Mouse uses to persuade the Lion to spare his life. ("I will be sure to repay your kindness.") Then ask students to discuss why these words are persuasive. (Possible response: People are more likely to do something if they believe there is a benefit in it for them.)

INDEPENDENT PRACTICE Have pairs of students look for examples of persuasive techniques in advertisements. Then have partners write an advertisement for a new product. Remind students to use persuasive techniques, such as word choice or emotional appeal, to convince buyers to purchase the product.

Text	Author's Purpose	Persuasive Techniques

Main Idea and Details

Objectives

- *To recognize the main idea of a text*
- *To identify details that support the main idea*

Skill Trace

 Tested Main Idea and Details

Introduce	pp. T178–T179, Theme 4
Reteach	pp. S22–S23, S32–S33, Theme 4
Review	pp. T206–T207, T240–T241, T270–T271, T327, Theme 4
Test	Theme 4
Maintain	p. T196

Reinforce the Skill

REVIEW MAIN IDEA AND DETAILS Remind students that authors often organize stories by using main idea and details. Review with them how to recognize the main idea.

- The main idea is the most important idea in a passage or a selection. It may be directly stated or implied.
- Details support the main idea by giving information about characters, providing background, explaining causes or effects, and expanding on descriptions of events.
- Identify an unstated main idea by thinking about what the details in a paragraph or section of text have in common.

Practice/Apply

GUIDED PRACTICE Point out that the author of "Any Small Goodness: A Novel of the Barrio" does not state what the story characters are like; instead, she reveals their traits through details. Ask students to help you fill in a main-idea-and-details chart for Abuelita.

Detail	Detail	Detail	Detail
She realizes that Mr. Leo Love is a hero right away.	She kisses Leo Love for rescuing the cat.	She refuses to talk on the phone.	The family looks up to Abuelita.

Main Idea
Abuelita is a good judge of character, values kindness, and is a little old-fashioned.

INDEPENDENT PRACTICE Have students create a similar chart for the character of Papi, Rosa, or Mr. Leo Love.

Decoding/Word Attack
Silent Letters

Reinforce the Skill

Routine Card 5

DECODE WORDS WITH SILENT LETTERS Write the words *whistle*, *assign*, and *kneel* on the board. Circle the *t* in *whistle* and remind students that some consonants are silent. Say *whistle* aloud and ask students if they hear a *t* sound. (no) Repeat the process with the silent *g* in *assign* and the silent *k* in *kneel*.

Practice/Apply

GUIDED PRACTICE List the following words on the board. Read each word aloud and guide students to identify the silent consonant(s).

science (c)	**crumb** (b)	**lightning** (gh)	**numb** (b)	**fighting** (gh)
knead (k)	**autumn** (n)	**know** (k)	**column** (n)	**scenery** (c)

Then guide students to read each word aloud.

INDEPENDENT PRACTICE Ask pairs of students to look through their content-area textbooks for three other examples of words with silent consonants. Have partners list the words on a sheet of paper and then take turns saying the words. Then have partners switch papers with another pair and read those words.

Objectives
- *To correctly pronounce words with silent letters*
- *To apply knowledge of letter-sound correspondences to recognize words*

Skill Trace
Silent Letters

Introduce	Grade 2
Maintain	p. T197

Fluency: Pace

15 Min. each

Objectives
- *To demonstrate characteristics of fluent, effective reading*
- *To read aloud with prosody, using appropriate pace*

MONITOR PROGRESS

Partner Reading

IF students need more support in building fluency and in using appropriate pace,	**THEN** have them echo-read with you, noting how you change your pace to reflect the action in the story.

Small-Group Instruction, p. S25:

- ● **BELOW-LEVEL:** Reteach
- ● **ON-LEVEL:** Reinforce
- ● **ADVANCED:** Extend

Fluency Support Materials

 Fluency Builders, Grade 5, Lesson 23

 Audiotext *Student Edition* selections are available on *Audiotext Grade 5,* CD7.

 Strategic Intervention Teacher Guide, Lesson 23

CHORAL-READ

Routine Card 6 **MODEL PACE** Model appropriate pace by reading the first seven paragraphs on *Student Edition* page 600. Tell students to follow along. Then read the passage again. Tell students to notice how the actions and feelings described in the story affect the pace at which you read. Then have students choral-read the passage with you.

ECHO-READ

Routine Card 7 **TRACK PRINT** Have students echo-read the passage on *Student Edition* page 600.

- Ask students to put their finger on the beginning of the first sentence.
- Read the sentence aloud as students track the print.
- Have students read the sentence aloud, matching your pace.
- Continue through the rest of the passage, adjusting your pace to match the action in the story.

If students do not read the passage with appropriate pace the first time, have them read the passage until they read it fluently and with appropriate pace.

PARTNER READING

Routine Card 8 **READ WITH A PARTNER** Pair strong readers with students who need fluency support. Have the strong reader read aloud the passage on *Student Edition* page 601 while the partner listens and follows along in the book. Then have partners switch roles.

Routine Card 9 Use the sentence frames on *Routine Card 9* to model for students how to give feedback. Then ask students to provide each other with feedback about pace. Encourage students to give each other positive feedback about how their pace improved from the first to the second reading.

"RESEARCH SAYS"

"Adequate process in learning to read English beyond the initial level depends on... sufficient practice in reading to achieve fluency with different kinds of texts written for different purposes."

—Snow, Burns, & Griffin (1998)

Enriching Robust Vocabulary

5-DAY VOCABULARY	
DAY 1	Vocabulary, pp. T171–T173
DAY 2	Vocabulary Review, p. T191
DAY 3	Reinforce Word Meanings, p. T199
DAY 4	Extend Word Meanings, p. T199
DAY 5	Cumulative Review, p. T199

REINFORCE WORD MEANINGS

Objective
- *To demonstrate knowledge of word meanings*

REVISIT SELECTION VOCABULARY Have students discuss "Any Small Goodness" by responding to these questions.

1. Do you think Mami is surprised when Luis **gouges** refried beans from the pan? Why or why not?

2. How did Rosa show that she was **desolate**?

3. Why is Leo Love surprised when Abuelita **bustles** up to him?

4. Why did Abuelita speak to Leo Love with such **fervor**?

5. Did it surprise you that Leo Love's house was **immaculate**? Why or why not?

6. How did Leo Love finally **assuage** his guilt about keeping the cat for two weeks?

EXTEND WORD MEANINGS

Objective
- *To extend meanings of words in context*

CRITICAL THINKING Have students answer the following questions. Have them explain their answers, and encourage discussion.

1. Would you pay full price for a piece of furniture that had been **gouged**?

2. What might cause someone to feel **desolate**?

3. When might you **bustle** around?

4. If someone speaks about a topic with **fervor**, how does he or she feel about it?

5. What is one place that should be kept **immaculate**?

6. What could you do to **assuage** your sadness over moving to a new place?

CUMULATIVE REVIEW

Objective
- *To use word relationships to determine meaning*

REVIEW VOCABULARY Discuss students' answers to these questions.

1. What would be heavy and **cumbersome** enough to **gouge** a dent in a wood floor?

2. Would a **desolate** person speak excitedly or **somberly**? Explain.

3. Why might **enterprising** people **bustle** about as they work?

4. When would it be all right to speak with such **fervor** that you **monopolize** a conversation?

5. Would you feel **enraptured** or **deflated** if your puppy dirtied your **immaculate** room? Why?

6. Why might you **stammer** a confession if you wanted to **assuage** your guilt?

Vocabulary Tested

Lesson 22		Lesson 23	
cumbersome	enraptured	gouges	immaculate
somberly	deflated	desolate	assuage
enterprising	stammers	bustles	
monopolize		fervor	

Spelling: Words with Silent Letters

15 Min. each

Objective
- *To spell correctly words with silent letters*

Spelling Words

1. **assign**	11. **knowledge**
2. **autumn**	12. **lightning**
3. **column**	13. **resign**
4. **crumb**	14. **rhyme**
5. **debris**	15. **solemn**
6. **delight**	16. **thorough**
7. **design**	17. **scenery**
8. **glisten**	18. **whirl**
9. **hasten**	19. **wreath**
10. **knead**	20. **wrestled**

Challenge Words

21. **scenic**	24. **rhythm**
22. **yacht**	25. **handkerchief**
23. **aisle**	

Day 1 — PRETEST/SELF-CHECK

Routine Card 10

ADMINISTER THE PRETEST Use the Dictation Sentences under Day 5. Help students self-check their pretests, using **Transparency LA147.**

Give students time to study the words they misspelled. Have them use the steps *Say, Look, Spell, Write, Check.*

ADVANCED

Challenge Words Use the Challenge Words in these Dictation Sentences:

21. We took the **scenic** route.

22. A fancy **yacht** sailed into port.

23. I prefer a seat on the **aisle.**

24. The song's **rhythm** makes me want to dance.

25. I always carry a **handkerchief.**

Day 2 — TEACH/MODEL

WORD SORT Display **Transparency LA147.** Discuss the meanings of the Spelling Words, as necessary. Ask students to copy the chart and write each Spelling Word where it belongs.

Point out the words *knowledge, wrestled,* and *crumb.* Identify the silent letter or letters in each, and explain that a silent letter can come at the beginning, middle, or end of a word.

Point out that some words, such as *wrestled* and *knowledge,* have more than one silent letter.

HANDWRITING When *n* follows *m,* students should be sure to finish writing the *m* before beginning the *n.*

autumn

Transparency LA147

Words with Silent Letters

Spelling Words

1. assign	6. delight	11. knowledge	16. thorough
2. autumn	7. design	12. lightning	17. scenery
3. column	8. glisten	13. resign	18. whirl
4. crumb	9. hasten	14. rhyme	19. wreath
5. debris	10. knead	15. solemn	20. wrestled

Silent First Letter	Silent Last Letter	Silent *g* or *gh*	Other Silent Letter
knead	autumn	assign	glisten
knowledge	column	delight	hasten
wreath	crumb	design	knowledge
wrestled	debris	lightning	rhyme
	solemn	resign	scenery
		thorough	whirl
			wrestled

- The first letter is silent when *w* is followed by *r,* as in *wreath,* and when *k* is followed by *n,* as in *knead.*
- The final letter is silent when *n* or *b* follow *m,* as in *autumn* and *crumb.* The word *debris* is special because it is a borrowed word and we still use its French pronunciation.
- The letters *g* and *gh* are often silent, as in *assign* and *delight.*

Grade 5, Lesson 23 — **LA147** — Spelling

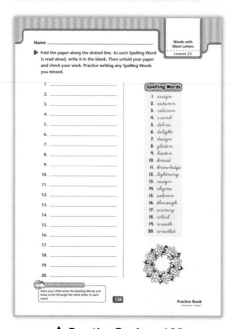

▲ Practice Book, p. 138

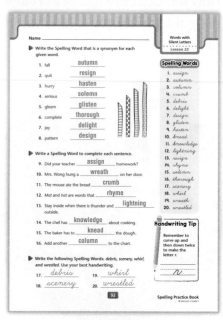

▲ Spelling Practice Book, p. 92

SPELLING PASSWORD Have groups of four students form Team A and Team B with two players each. Before beginning to play, the group should make a set of 20 cards with a different Spelling Word written on each.

To initiate play, have each team choose 10 cards. A student on Team A will say a word. The other member of Team A must then correctly spell the word to get a point. If the player misspells the word, the card is passed to Team B. The team with more points wins.

knead

rhyme

CHECK THE DICTIONARY Tell students that words with silent letters are easy to misspell because many of these words are homophones. They sound exactly like other words that have a different spelling. Use these examples: *knead/need, scene/seen.* Tell students that they should check a dictionary whenever they are unsure of how to spell a word with silent letters.

APPLY TO WRITING

CHECK THE DICTIONARY Have students use the strategy of checking a dictionary as they proofread their writing. Tell them if they cannot find a word under the letter of its initial sound, it may have a silent first letter. Have students proofread their writing for words with silent letters.

DICTATION SENTENCES

1. Our teacher will **assign** a story for us to read.
2. I love the colors of the leaves in **autumn**.
3. The **column** has a statue on top of it.
4. The mouse ate every last **crumb**.
5. The city workers cleaned up the **debris**.
6. It was a **delight** to hear her sing.
7. Bill's **design** won first prize.
8. Diamonds **glisten** in the light.
9. Irina must **hasten** to catch up.
10. You must **knead** the bread dough for ten minutes.
11. A quiz tests your **knowledge**.
12. We heard thunder and saw **lightning**.
13. Mr. Jones will **resign** from his job.
14. Many words **rhyme** with *moon*.
15. Graduation is both a **solemn** and a happy occasion.
16. We did a **thorough** job of cleaning.
17. The mountain **scenery** is beautiful.
18. Leaves **whirl** in the breeze.
19. We hung a **wreath** on our door.
20. Two puppies **wrestled** on the grass.

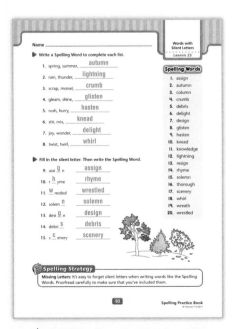

▲ Spelling Practice Book, p. 93

▲ Spelling Practice Book, p. 94

Writing Trait: Organization
Poem

15 Min. each

Day 1 TEACH/MODEL

Day 2 PRACTICE/APPLY

Objectives
- *To use strong, specific details to develop writing*
- *To write poetry with a persuasive element*

Writing Trait ▸ Organizations

- Topic presented near beginning of poem
- Specific details and examples organized in a logical way, such as weakest to strongest
- Poem ends with an appeal to the reader

Grammar for Writing

As students revise their poems, note whether they need additional support with these skills:
- **Adjectives and Articles,** pp. T218–T219, Theme 4
- **Adverbs,** pp. T218–T219, Theme 6
- **Past and Future Tenses,** pp. T204–T205, Theme 5

Writer's Companion
Grade 5

▲ **Writer's Companion, Lesson 23**

DEVELOPMENT: SPECIFIC DETAILS AND EXAMPLES Tell students that persuasive writing is organized to clearly present the writer's point of view. Persuasive writing clearly states the writer's opinion, provides details to support the opinion, and ends with an appeal to the reader.

ANALYZE THE MENTOR TEXT Display **Transparency LA150** and read the text aloud. Point out that the writer clearly states that Leo Love is brave. Then guide students to name the details and examples the author gives to support this idea. Tell students that the writer effectively organizes the supporting ideas by arranging them from general details about Leo Love's actions to more specific ones.

ANALYZE THE STUDENT MODEL Display **Transparency LA151**. Tell students that the poem is one student's attempt to write a persuasive poem. Have a volunteer read the poem aloud. Discuss what the writer is trying to persuade readers to do. (have their pets wear ID tags)

Discuss with students how the poet organizes the poem. Point out that the poet effectively organizes the poem by ending with a strong call to a action.

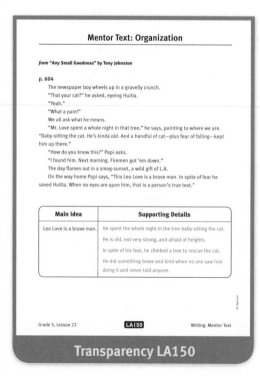

Transparency LA150

Transparency LA151

THEME 5 WRITING		
Reading-Writing-Connection	Persuasive Composition	Sentence Fluency
LESSON	**FORM**	**TRAIT**
21	Persuasive Letter	Sentence Fluency
22	Persuasive Paragraph	Sentence Fluency
23	**Poem**	**Organization**
24	Narrative	Organization
25 REVIEW	Revise and Publish	Sentence Fluency/Organization

 Day 3 PREWRITE

 Day 4 DRAFT

 Day 5 REVISE AND REFLECT

Day 3 — PREWRITE

WRITING PROMPT Display **Transparency LA152** and read aloud the prompt for Day 3.

You might suggest these topics and help students brainstorm others:

- why a local park should be saved
- the importance of exercise

Have students use a chart like this to help them organize their poems.

Opinion

Reasons and Details
1.
2.
3.

Call to Action

Daily Writing Prompts

DAY 1 Writing Prompt:
People are often kind to one another. Think of a time when a friend or a stranger helped you in some way. Write a letter or e-mail to the person, thanking him or her for the assistance.

DAY 2 Writing Prompt:
Mr. Leo Love did something good "when no eyes were upon him." Think of a time you did something good when no one was looking. Write a paragraph describing your actions.

DAY 3 Writing Prompt:
People use various types of writing to persuade others to do something. Think of an issue or idea that is important to you. Write a poem that tries to persuade readers to agree with you.

DAY 4 Writing Prompt:
Almost everyone holds another person in high esteem. Think of a person whom you admire. Then write a short composition in which you explain why that person is *estimado*, or esteemed.

DAY 5 Writing Prompt:
Vivid descriptions of characters help stories come alive for readers. Think of how Huitla is described in "Any Small Goodness." Now write a more vivid description of Huitla.

Grade 5, Lesson 23   **LA152**   Daily Writing Prompts

Transparency LA152

Day 4 — DRAFT

BEGIN TO DRAFT Have students follow these steps to draft their poems.

1. **Introduce** the topic at the beginning of the poem.

2. **Make** sure that your opinion is clearly stated.

3. **Develop** the poem, using strong details and examples that will appeal to readers' emotions.

4. **Conclude** with a call to action.

NOTE: A 4-point rubric appears on page R8.

Day 5 — REVISE AND REFLECT

PEER CONFERENCE CHECKLIST Have student pairs use this checklist to discuss their poems. Provide these questions:

- Does the first stanza introduce the topic?
- Do all the details and examples support and develop the author's opinion?
- Does the writer include persuasive techniques?
- Does the writer end with a call to action?
- Does the writer correctly use simple verb tenses?

Students may want to keep their revised poems in their work portfolios.

SCORING RUBRIC

	6	5	4	3	2	1
FOCUS	Completely focused, purposeful.	Focused on topic and purpose.	Generally focused on topic and purpose.	Somewhat focused on topic and purpose.	Related to topic but does not maintain focus.	Lacks focus and purpose.
ORGANIZATION	Ideas progress logically; paper conveys sense of completeness.	Organization mostly clear; paper gives sense of completeness.	Organization mostly clear, but some lapses occur; may seem unfinished.	Some sense of organization; seems unfinished.	Little sense of organization.	Little or no sense of organization.
SUPPORT	Strong, specific details; clear, exact language; freshness of expression.	Strong, specific details; clear, exact language.	Adequate support and word choice.	Limited supporting details; limited word choice.	Few supporting details; limited word choice.	Little development; limited or unclear word choice.
CONVENTIONS	Varied sentences; few, if any, errors.	Varied sentences; few errors.	Some sentence variety; few errors.	Simple sentence structures; some errors.	Simple sentence structures; many errors.	Unclear sentence structures; many errors.

REPRODUCIBLE RUBRIC appears on page R7.

15 Min. each

Grammar: Verbs
Past and Future Tenses

Objective
- *To use past-, present-, and future-tense verbs correctly in speaking and writing*

Past and Future Tenses

The **tense** of a verb tells the time of the action.
- A **past-tense verb** tells about an action that happened in the past.
- Add *-ed* to regular verbs to form the past tense. Most verbs are regular.

Rule	Example	
Add *-ed* to most regular verbs.	reach	reached
If a verb ends in *e*, drop the *e* before adding *-ed*.	arrive	arrived
If a verb ends with a consonant and a *y*, change *y* to *i* before adding *-ed*.	deny	denied
If a verb ends with a vowel and a consonant, double the final consonant before adding *-ed*.	stun	stunned

1. Mami searched for the missing cat.
2. Rosa hurried to the door.
3. I dashed to the telephone.
4. We identified our lost cat.
5. I turn down the radio. (turned)
6. Everyone loves the little black cat. (loved)
7. We worry about the cat. (worried)
8. Our cat naps in the garage. (napped)

Grade 5, Lesson 23   **LA148**   Grammar

Transparencies LA148, LA149

E L L

Language Structures Use this model to demonstrate subject-verb agreement:

- Mom <u>cooks</u> every day. (one subject)
- Mom and Dad <u>cook</u> every day. (two subjects)
- Mom (and Dad) <u>cooked</u> yesterday. (one or two subjects)

See *ELL Teacher Guide* Lesson 23 for support in scaffolding instruction.

Day 1 — TEACH/MODEL

DAILY PROOFREADING

1. The cat were an irriplacable part of the family. (was; irreplaceable)

2. Most cats, do not respond to a wissle. (cats do; whistle.)

INTRODUCE THE CONCEPT Display **Transparency LA148** and read the information in the two boxes. Explain to students that in sentence 1, the verb *searched* is in the past tense; it ends in *-ed*. Point out that in sentence 2, *hurried* is also in the past tense. Tell students that the *y* in *hurry* was changed to *i* before adding *-ed*.

Have students identify the past-tense verb in sentences 3 and 4. Then have students identify the verbs in sentences 5–8, and change each verb from the present tense to the past tense.

✓ LANGUAGE ARTS CHECKPOINT

If students have difficulty with the concepts, see pages S26–S27 to reteach.

Day 2 — TEACH/MODEL

DAILY PROOFREADING

3. The music, it was the most loud I ever heard. (music was; the loudest)

4. Mr Leo Love kneaded a companyun. (Mr.; needed; companion.)

EXTEND THE CONCEPT Display **Transparency LA149** and read the information in the box at the top. Explain that in sentence 1, *will play* is in the future tense. Tell students to rewrite sentences 2–5 in the future tense.

BUILD LANGUAGE STRUCTURES Have students complete each sentence with a future-tense verb.

- Next week I _____ a new job.
- Tomorrow I _____ to school.
- In five years I _____ to drive.

Name _____

Past and Future Tenses
Lesson 23

▶ Rewrite each sentence. Change the verbs from the present tense to the past tense.

1. We move from Mexico to California.
   We moved from Mexico to California.
2. I pack my belongings and load them on the train.
   I packed my belongings and loaded them on the train.
3. There is a whistle, and the train starts moving.
   There was a whistle, and the train started moving.
4. My mother and father seem happy and excited.
   My mother and father seemed happy and excited.
5. My sister sits next to me and rests her head on my shoulder.
   My sister sat next to me and rested her head on my shoulder.

▶ Write a sentence using each verb in the box. Use each verb in its future tense.

| visit | fly | care | entertain | play | be | drive |

Possible responses are shown.
6. I will fly to Mexico next week.
7. I will visit my family in Mexico City.
8. My father will drive me to the airport.
9. Keisha will care for my cats while I am away.
10. My brother and I will play with our cousins.
11. Juan and Carlos will entertain us with a song.
12. I will be sad to leave when the visit is over.

81   Grammar Practice Book

▲ **Grammar Practice Book, p. 81**

Day 3 — TEACH/MODEL

DAILY PROOFREADING

5. Luis' band will practices to-night. (Luis's; practice)

6. Leo Love wait two weaks be-fore calling. (waited; weeks)

EXTEND THE CONCEPT Display **Transparency LA149** again and read the information at the bottom. Then write the following sentence frames on the board. Have students complete them with the correct form of *look*.

She <u>looks</u> for the cat every night.

She <u>looked</u> for the cat yesterday.

We <u>will look</u> for the cat tomorrow.

Then have students write six sentences with the word *lose*. Tell them to include verbs in all the simple tenses.

Day 4 — APPLY TO WRITING

DAILY PROOFREADING

7. The cat rubed against Mamis leg. (rubbed; Mami's)

8. We eat the delishous soup in an hour. (will eat; delicious)

CATS AND DOGS Have students write 4–6 sentences about whether they are a "cat person" or a "dog person." Tell them to include verbs in all the simple tenses—present, past, and future. Remind students to use the correct form of each verb.

> **COMMON ERRORS**
>
> **Error:** Our cat **play** with a toy mouse.
> **Correct:** Our cat **plays** with a toy mouse.
>
> **Error:** Yesterday we **rescue** our cat.
> **Correct:** Yesterday we **rescued** our cat.

Day 5 — REVIEW

DAILY PROOFREADING

9. Leo Love climb the tree although it was hazardous. (climbed; tree,; hazardous.)

10. When the door opened the cat hurryed out. (opened,; hurried)

PROOFREAD VERB TENSE AND FORM Display the following sentences. Have students copy them and correct any errors.

1. The doctor insert a chip in our cat's ear last week. (inserted)

2. If the cat gets lost someday, information on the chip identified her. (will identify)

3. Rosa claim her cat is the smartest in the world. (claims)

4. Abuelita and Mami always laughs at the cat's tricks. (laugh)

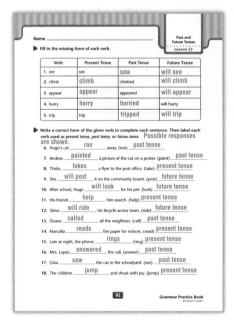

▲ Grammar Practice Book, p. 82

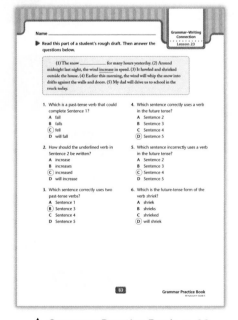

▲ Grammar Practice Book, p. 83

▲ Practice Book, p. 139

Speaking & Listening

SPEAKING

Give a Poetry Reading

Objectives
- *To read aloud a poem*
- *To emphasize imagery in poetry*

Tell students that they are going to organize and present a class poetry reading. Explain that they can read the poem they wrote or another poem of their choosing. Share these **organizational strategies**:

ORGANIZING CONTENT
- Read the title and author of the poem first.
- Write the poem on a notecard. Underline words and ideas you want to emphasize.

Before students read their poems aloud, share with them the following **speaking strategies**:

SPEAKING STRATEGIES
- Read the poem loudly and clearly so that everyone in the room can hear you. Vary your pace and intonation.
- Emphasize the literary language and imagery of the poem.
- Remember to use eye contact and appropriate gestures.

LISTENING

Listen to a Poetry Reading

Objectives
- *To understand information presented orally*
- *To appreciate imagery in poetry*

Have students listen as other students read their poems aloud. Share these **listening strategies**:

LISTENING STRATEGIES
- As you listen, monitor your understanding of the poem. Make a mental note of any questions you want to ask the presenter.
- Think about how the literary language, such as rhyme, rhythm, and imagery, affects the language and the listener.
- Consider whether you agree or disagree with the opinions or ideas expressed in the poems.

After students have finished reading, invite the audience to comment. Have students tell what they liked about the poems, describe how the language of the poems affected them, tell whether they were persuaded by the opinions offered in the poems, and ask questions to clarify anything they did not understand.

RUBRIC See rubric for Presentations on page R5.

Media Literacy

RESEARCH

Compare News Media

> ### Objectives
> - *To identify sources of local news*
> - *To read and compare accounts of the same local event*

DISCUSS LOCAL NEWS MEDIA Ask students to describe the forms of media that people in their community use to find out about news. Explain that

- newspapers cover many kinds of news, including local, national, and international events.

- a local newspaper covers noteworthy events in and around the community.

- many newspapers have a website where daily news is covered and old articles are stored in an electronic archive.

- a newspaper's website can be searched by category (weather; business; sports), by name (Mayor Garcia), or by date.

IDENTIFY A LOCAL EVENT Help students identify local events that are related to the theme of "Any Small Goodness: A Novel of the Barrio." You might look for stories about something valuable that was lost and then found, a good deed, an animal rescue, or a local hero.

READ ALL ABOUT IT Have pairs of students locate two different accounts of the event in two different sources of local news, such as the newspaper, an online news magazine, the radio, or a television news report. Ask students to read or listen to the two accounts and compare how the two sources presented the story.

- Selection Comprehension with Short Response
- Focus Skill
- Robust Vocabulary
- Literary Patterns and Symbols
- Grammar
- Fluency Passage *FRESH READS*
- Podcasting: Assessing Fluency

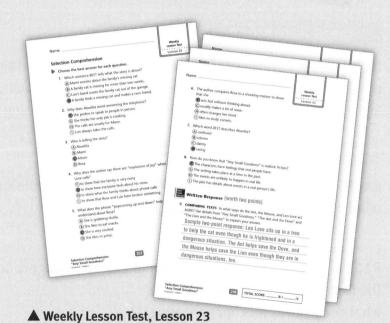

▲ **Weekly Lesson Test, Lesson 23**

GO online For prescriptions, see pp. A2–A6. Also available electronically on *StoryTown Online Assessment* and ExamView®.

Leveled Readers
Reinforcing Skills and Strategies

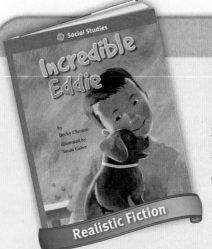

BELOW-LEVEL

Incredible Eddie

SUMMARY Eddie and his family visit the animal shelter to bring home a new puppy, but Eddie has a hard time choosing one dog over the others.

- Literary Devices
- Answer Questions
- **VOCABULARY:** *gouges, desolate, bustles, fervor, immaculate, assuage*

Build Background/Set Purpose

Have students preview the book by reading the title and examining the illustrations. Ask students what they think the book will be about. Remind them that answering questions while reading can clear up confusing text.

Guided Reading

PAGES 3–5 MAKE INFERENCES **Why do you think Eddie's mother changed her mind about letting him adopt a dog?** (She works at home and thinks that a dog might be good company.)

PAGE 9 LITERARY DEVICES **What example imagery does the author use in the first paragraph on page 9?** ("sadness brushed lightly against him . . .") **To what sense does this imagery appeal?** (touch)

After Reading

Have students work in pairs to discuss pets they own or would like to own.

FLUENCY: PACE Have pairs of students choose a page of the text to reread aloud. As students read, they should give each other feedback on pace.

Think Critically *(See inside back cover for questions.)*

1. He didn't want to hurt the dogs' feelings by choosing just one.
2. He compares Mama's face to a full moon; it describes how her face "lit up."
3. Eddie is caring, sympathetic, and helpful.
4. She wanted Eddie to have a dog and knew he couldn't choose one.
5. Answers will vary.

LEVELED READER TEACHER GUIDE

▲ Vocabulary, p. 5

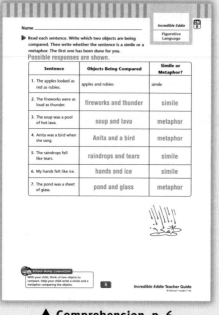

▲ Comprehension, p. 6

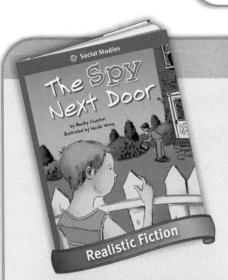

Realistic Fiction

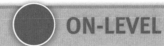
ON-LEVEL

The Spy Next Door

SUMMARY Jeff's brother Nick is convinced that their neighbor is a spy, but Nick's family doesn't believe him.

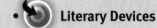 **Literary Devices**

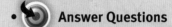 **Answer Questions**

• **VOCABULARY:** *gouges, desolate, bustles, fervor, immaculate, assuage*

Build Background/Set Purpose

Have students preview the book by reading the title and looking at the illustrations. Ask them to predict what they think it will be about. Tell students to answer questions as they read if they encounter confusing text.

Guided Reading

PAGES 4–5 CAUSE AND EFFECT **What effect does Nick's game "Spies and Secret Agents" have on him?** (The game makes him imaginative and makes him think his neighbor is a spy.)

PAGE 4 LITERARY DEVICES **What example of imagery does the author use to describe Dr. Ross's yard?** (tall, brown grass; scraggly weeds and dandelions; solitary sunflower)

After Reading

Have students work in pairs to summarize the story.

FLUENCY: PACE Have partners take turns rereading two pages of the book aloud. Tell them to give each other feedback about reading pace.

Think Critically *(See inside back cover for questions.)*

1. Nick says that Dr. Ross has a walkie-talkie.

2. It is the only form of life in a barren backyard. It conveys feelings of isolation and loneliness and shows that Dr. Ross is rarely home.

3. Jeff is a caring older brother who is sometimes annoyed by Nick.

4. Jeff and his dad know that Nick has a powerful imagination.

5. Answers will vary.

LEVELED READER TEACHER GUIDE

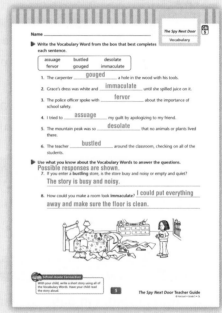

▲ Vocabulary, p. 5

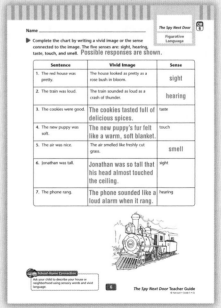

▲ Comprehension, p. 6

Leveled Readers
Reinforcing Skills and Strategies

ADVANCED

Just Visiting

SUMMARY Becca is annoyed at having to walk her dog, Arwen, but her mood changes when she realizes the effect Arwen has on the people they meet.

- ◗ **Literary Devices**
- ◗ **Answer Questions**
- **VOCABULARY:** *gouges, desolate, bustles, fervor, immaculate, assuage*

Build Background/Set Purpose

Ask students to brainstorm a list of different ways animals help humans. (guide dogs, visiting dogs, herding dogs, companions) Then have students preview the book and set a purpose for reading. Remind them to answer questions while reading to help clear up confusion.

During Reading

COMPLETE A SEQUENCE CHART Distribute the sequence chart on *Teacher Resource Book* page 84 so pairs of students can complete it as they read.

After Reading

Have students work in pairs to summarize the book. Then ask them to write three questions about it, trade questions with a partner, and answer them.

FLUENCY: PACE Have students take turns rereading portions of the book aloud. Tell them to vary their pace as they read.

Think Critically *(See inside back cover for questions.)*

1. Her brother, who used to walk Arwen, is now busy at soccer practice.

2. The image works because it tells how Becca travels from one negative thought to another in her mind.

3. Arwen's visit is the high point of their day. When she walks by, their mood changes and they forget their negative feelings.

4. She feels uneasy because she realizes that her neighbors will miss Arwen. This shows that Becca cares about the feelings of others.

5. Answers will vary.

LEVELED READER TEACHER GUIDE

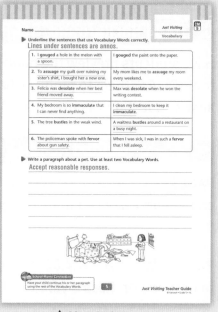

▲ Vocabulary, p. 5

▲ Comprehension, p. 6

ELL

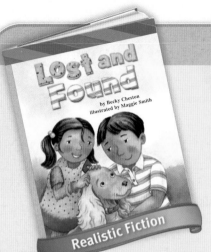

Lost and Found
by Becky Cheston
illustrated by Maggie Smith

Realistic Fiction

Lost and Found

SUMMARY Marco and Donna wish they had a pet. When a stray follows Donna home, their wish may come true.

- Build Background
- Concept Vocabulary
- Scaffolded Language Development

Build Background/Set Purpose

Discuss with students what might happen if they found a lost dog. Use the words *veterinarian, shelter, tags, owner,* and *pet* in your discussion. Then have students preview the book. Remind them that answering questions can help them clear up confusing text.

Guided Reading

As students read, tell them to look for words that signal transitions, such as *later, however,* and *when.* Clarify the idioms *fast asleep* and *get used to.*

PAGE 9 LITERARY DEVICES **What example of imagery does the author use to describe what it is like in Marco's room?** (Sammy curled up beside the bed; Marco listened to the sound of Sammy breathing.)

PAGES 10–13 CHARACTER'S MOTIVES **What made Marco decide to show the flyer to his mother?** (He thought about Sammy's owners.)

After Reading

FLUENCY: PACE Reread the selection aloud at an appropriate pace. Then have pairs of students take turns rereading a page from the book aloud. As students read, partners should give feedback on pace.

Encourage students to use the concept words *stray, tags, owner,* and *pet* while discussing the story.

Scaffolded Language Development

See inside back cover for teacher-led activity.
Provide additional examples and explanation as needed.

LEVELED READER TEACHER GUIDE

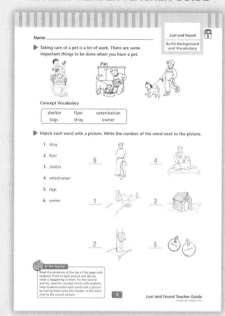

▲ Build Background, p. 5

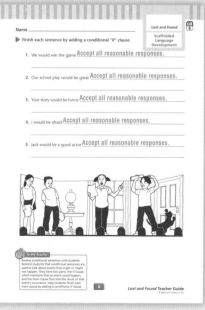

▲ Scaffolded Language Development, p. 6

Lesson 24

WEEK AT A GLANCE

✔ **Vocabulary**

excursions, giddy, pinnacle, gleeful, panic, turbulent, precious

✔ **Comprehension**

 Literary Devices

 Answer Questions

Reading

"Chester Cricket's Pigeon Ride" by George Selden
FANTASY

"Central Park" by John J. Bonk
POETRY

✔ **Fluency**

Focus on Pace

Decoding/Word Attack

Structural Analysis: Unusual Plurals

✔ **Spelling**

Words with Unusual Plurals

✔ **Writing**

Form: Narrative Composition
Trait: Organization

✔ **Grammar**

Perfect Tenses

Speaking and Listening

Travel Description

Media Literacy

Using Media to Locate Facts

Weekly Lesson Test

 = Focus Skill   = Focus Strategy   = Tested Skill

One stop
for all
your **Digital** *needs*

Digital
CLASSROOM

 www.harcourtschool.com/storytown
To go along with your print program

FOR THE TEACHER

Prepare **Professional Development**
in the Online TE

 Videos for Podcasting

Plan & Organize **Online TE & Planning Resources***

Teach **Transparencies**
access from the Online TE

Assess **Online Assessment***
with Student Tracking System and Prescriptions

FOR THE STUDENT

Read  **Student eBook***

 Strategic Intervention Interactive Reader

 **Leveled Readers**

Practice & Apply **Comprehension Expedition CD-ROM**

 Also available on CD-ROM

Literature Resources

eBook STUDENT EDITION

STUDENT EDITION

Chester Cricket's Pigeon Ride

by George Selden

Pictures by Garth Williams

Genre: Fantasy

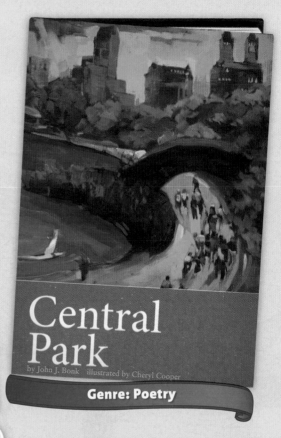

Central Park

by John J. Bonk   illustrated by Cheryl Cooper

Genre: Poetry

◀ **Audiotext** *Student Edition selections are available on Audiotext Grade 5, CD8.*

Accelerated Reader™   ◀ *Practice Quizzes for the Selection*

THEME CONNECTION: MAKING A DIFFERENCE
Comparing Fantasy and Poetry

....

Paired Selections

🌐 **SOCIAL STUDIES** **Chester Cricket's Pigeon Ride, pp. 618–631**

SUMMARY As author George Selden explains, Lulu Pigeon is proud of her city and wants to show Chester Cricket some unforgettable New York City views. Feeling excitement and fear, Chester climbs aboard for a thrilling ride.

🌐 **SOCIAL STUDIES** **Central Park, pp. 632–635**

SUMMARY Poet John Bonk imagines many of the ways that people spend time in Central Park.

Support for Differentiated Instruction

LEVELED READERS

BELOW-LEVEL

ON-LEVEL

ADVANCED

E L L

LEVELED PRACTICE

◀ **Strategic Intervention Resource Kit,**
Lesson 24

◀ **Strategic Intervention Interactive**
Reader, Lesson 24
Strategic Intervention Interactive Reader
Online

◀ **ELL Extra Support Kit, Lesson 24**

◀ **Challenge Resource Kit, Lesson 24**

● **BELOW-LEVEL**
Extra Support Copying Masters,
pp. 140, 142

● **ON-LEVEL**
Practice Book, pp. 140–144

● **ADVANCED**
Challenge Copying Masters,
pp. 140, 142

ADDITIONAL RESOURCES

◀ **Picture Card Collection**
◀ **Fluency Builders**
◀ **Literacy Center Kit, Lesson 24**
• Test Prep System
• Writer's Companion, Lesson 24
• Grammar Practice Book, pp. 85–88
• Spelling Practice Book, pp. 95–98
• Phonics Practice Book, pp 25–26
• Reading Transparencies R101–R104
• Language Arts Transparencies
 LA153–LA158

✓ ASSESSMENT

✓ **Monitor Progress**

✓ **Weekly Lesson Tests, Lesson 24**
 • Comprehension   • Draw Conclusions
 • Focus Skill   • Grammar
 • Robust Vocabulary   • Fluency

✓ **Rubrics, pp. R3–R8**

 www.harcourtschool.com/storytown
• Online Assessment
Also available on CD-ROM—ExamView®

Suggested Lesson Planner

 Online TE & Planning Resources

 Step 1 | **Whole Group**

Oral Language
- *Question of the Day*
- *Listening Comprehension*

Comprehension
- *Skills and Strategies*

Vocabulary

Reading
- *Fluency*
- *Cross-Curricular Connections*
- *Decoding/Word Attack*

Day 1

QUESTION OF THE DAY *Do you feel more comfortable in a big city or in the country? Why?*

READ ALOUD, pp. T224–T225

✔ **COMPREHENSION:**
 Literary Devices, pp. T226–T227
 Answer Questions, pp. T228–T229

✔ **VOCABULARY:**
Introduce Vocabulary, p. T231
Word Scribe, p. T233

READ: Vocabulary, pp. T232–T233

FLUENCY: PACE: Model Oral Fluency, p. T225

DECODING/WORD ATTACK: Structural Analysis: Unusual Plurals, p. T257

Day 2

QUESTION OF THE DAY *How might Chester's feelings about New York have changed as a result of flying around the city with Lulu?*

READ ALOUD, p. T225

✔ **COMPREHENSION:**
 Literary Devices, pp. T234–T246
 Answer Questions, pp. T237, T239, T243, T249

✔ **VOCABULARY:**
Vocabulary Review, p. T253

READ: "Chester Cricket's Pigeon Ride," pp. T234–T247
Options for Reading

FLUENCY: PACE:
Repeated Reading, p. T253

SOCIAL STUDIES: New York, p. T237

▲Student Edition

 Step 2 | **Small Groups**

 Step 3 | **Whole Group**

Language Arts
- *Spelling*
- *Writing*
- *Grammar*

Suggestions for Differentiated Instruction *(See pp. T218–T219.)*

✔ **SPELLING: Words with Unusual Plurals:** Pretest/Self-Check, p. T260

✏ **WRITING: Narrative:** Teach/Model, p. T262

Writing Prompt *Many people have imagined what it would be like to fly as birds do. Imagine that you could fly like a bird. Write a description of what you would see and do around your community.*

✔ **GRAMMAR: Perfect Tenses:** Teach/Model, p. T264

Daily Proofreading

1. Lulu will takes Chester to Central Park? (will take; Park.)

2. We will goes to new york city. (will go; New York City.)

✔ **SPELLING: Words with Unusual Plurals:** Teach/Model, p. T260

✏ **WRITING: Narrative:** Practice/Apply, p. T262

Writing Prompt *Chester Cricket had to adjust to a different life. Think about what it was like for him to move from the fields of Connecticut to Times Square in New York City. Write a biographical paragraph describing Chester's life.*

✔ **GRAMMAR: Perfect Tenses:** Teach/Model, p. T264

Daily Proofreading

3. They has flown over the cars and busses. (have flown; buses.)

4. Together, they have view New York Citys skyline. (have viewed; City's)

Spelling Words
1. addresses	11. radios
2. armies	12. halves
3. calves	13. hooves
4. countries	14. knives
5. leaves	15. taxes
6. buses	16. tomatoes
7. videos	17. opportunities
8. echoes	18. volcanoes
9. shelves	19. stitches
10. studios	20. wolves

Challenge Words
21. tornadoes	24. vetoes
22. patios	25. crises
23. quizzes	

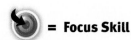 = **Focus Skill**    = **Focus Strategy**   ✔ = **Tested Skill**

Comprehension	Vocabulary	Fluency	Language Arts
FOCUS SKILL: Literary Devices **FOCUS STRATEGY:** Answer Questions	excursions panic giddy turbulent pinnacle precious gleeful	Pace	**Writing:** - Trait: Organization - Form: Narrative Composition **Grammar:** Perfect Tenses

Day 3

QUESTION OF THE DAY *Would a turbulent boat ride make you feel gleeful? Why or why not?*

READ ALOUD, p. T225

✔ **COMPREHENSION:**
 Literary Devices, pp. T254–T255

✔ **VOCABULARY:**
Reinforce Word Meanings, p. T259

READ: "Central Park," pp. T248–T251

COMPARING TEXTS, p. T252

FLUENCY: PACE:
Choral-Read, p. T258

WRITING: Write a Journal Entry, p. T253

▲Student Edition

Day 4

QUESTION OF THE DAY *Many people call New York City "the city that never sleeps." What type of figurative language is this? What do you think this statement means?*

READ ALOUD, p. T225

SPEAKING AND LISTENING:
Travel Description, p. T266

✔ **VOCABULARY:**
Extend Word Meanings, p. T259

FLUENCY: PACE:
Echo-Read, p. T258

▲Student Edition

Day 5

QUESTION OF THE DAY *What are some benefits to living in a large city? What are some disadvantages?*

READ ALOUD, p. T225

✔ **COMPREHENSION:**
Draw Conclusions, p. T256

✔ **VOCABULARY:**
Cumulative Vocabulary, p. T259

FLUENCY: PACE:
Partner Reading, p. T258

MEDIA LITERACY:
Using Media to Locate Facts, p. T267

▲Student Edition

● BELOW-LEVEL ● ON-LEVEL ● ADVANCED **ELL**

✔ **SPELLING: Words with Unusual Plurals:**
Practice/Apply, p. T261

✔ **SPELLING: Words with Unusual Plurals:**
Spelling Strategies, p. T261

✔ **SPELLING: Words with Unusual Plurals:**
Posttest, p. T261

 WRITING: Narrative: Prewrite, p. T263

Writing Prompt *Plan a narrative composition about an adventure shared by two friends. Think about the characters, setting, conflict, and resolution. Then write the beginning of the story of the friends' adventure.*

 WRITING: Narrative: Draft, p. T263

Writing Prompt *People often enjoy visiting new places. Think of a time when you took a trip somewhere. Write a journal entry detailing one day of your trip.*

 WRITING: Narrative: Revise and Reflect, p. T263

Writing Prompt *Think about the beginning of the story you wrote on Day 3. Complete your story by adding plot events and concluding with a resolution. Develop your plot events with descriptive details and figurative language.*

✔ **GRAMMAR: Perfect Tenses:** Teach/Model, p. T265

Daily Proofreading

5. Will there be opportunitys for taking pictures? (opportunities)

6. We had tunes both radioes (had tuned; radios.)

✔ **GRAMMAR: Perfect Tenses:** Apply to Writing, p. T265

Daily Proofreading

7. Chester had never saw a like glissen like that. (had never seen; glisten)

8. The leafs on the trees is changing. (leaves; are changing.)

✔ **GRAMMAR: Perfect Tenses:** Review, p. T265

Daily Proofreading

9. Chester will have watch the sun rise over downton. (will have watched; downtown.)

10. Chester had never enjoy such spontaneus travel before. (enjoyed; spontaneous)

Suggested Small-Group Planner

45-60+ Minutes

	Day 1	Day 2

 BELOW-LEVEL
15-20+ Minutes

Day 1

Teacher–Directed
 Leveled Readers:
Before Reading, p. T268

Independent
 Word Study Center, p. T222
Extra Support
Copying Masters, p. 140

▲ Leveled Reader

Day 2

Teacher–Directed
Reread the Selection,
pp. T234–T247

Independent
 Writing Center, p. T223
Audiotext Grade 5, CD8

▲ Student Edition

 ON-LEVEL
15-20+ Minutes

Day 1

Teacher–Directed
 Leveled Readers:
Before Reading, p. T269

Independent
 Reading Center, p. T222
Practice Book, p. 140

▲ Leveled Reader

Day 2

Teacher–Directed
Respond to the Selection,
p. T246

Independent
 Word Study Center,
p. T222

▲ Student Edition

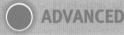 **ADVANCED**
15-20+ Minutes

Day 1

Teacher–Directed
 Leveled Readers:
Before Reading, p. T270

Independent
 Writing Center, p. T223
Challenge Copying
Masters, p. 140

▲ Leveled Reader

Day 2

Independent
 Fluency Center, p. T223
Leveled Readers: Partner
Reading, p. T270

▲ Leveled Reader

 ELL

English-Language Learners

In addition to the small-group suggestions above, use the ELL Extra Support Kit to promote language development.

LANGUAGE DEVELOPMENT SUPPORT

Teacher–Directed
Leveled Readers:
Build Background, p. T271
ELL Teacher Guide, Lesson 24

Independent
ELL Copying Masters,
Lesson 24

▲ Leveled Reader

LANGUAGE DEVELOPMENT SUPPORT

Teacher–Directed
Scaffold Core Skills
ELL Teacher Guide,
Lesson 24

Independent
Audiotext Grade 5, CD8

▲ ELL Student Handbook

Intervention

▲ Strategic Intervention Resource Kit

▲ Strategic Intervention Interactive Reader

Strategic Intervention Teacher Guide,
Lesson 24
Strategic Intervention Practice Book,
Lesson 24

Catch a Wave,
Lesson 24
Strategic Intervention
Teacher Guide,
Lesson 24

Strategic Intervention
Interactive Reader ▲

 = **Literacy Center Cards**

MONITOR PROGRESS

Small-Group Instruction

 Literary Devices	Selection Comprehension	Robust Vocabulary	Fluency	Language Arts
pp. S28–S29	p. S32	pp. S30–S31	p. S33	p. S34–S35

Day 3

Teacher–Directed
Leveled Readers:
During Reading, p. T268

Independent
⭐ Reading Center, p. T222
Extra Support Copying Masters,
p. 142

▲ Leveled Reader

Teacher–Directed
Leveled Readers:
During Reading, p. T269

Independent
⭐ Technology Center, p. T223
Practice Book, p. 142

▲ Leveled Reader

Teacher–Directed
Leveled Readers:
During Reading, p. T270

Independent
⭐ Word Study Center, p. T222
Challenge Copying Masters,
p. 142

▲ Leveled Reader

LANGUAGE DEVELOPMENT SUPPORT

Teacher–Directed
Leveled Readers:
During Reading, p. T271
ELL Teacher Guide, Lesson 24

Independent
ELL Copying Masters,
Lesson 24

▲ Leveled Reader

Catch a Wave,
Lesson 24
Strategic Intervention
Teacher Guide,
Lesson 24
Strategic Intervention
Practice Book
Lesson 24

Strategic Intervention
Interactive Reader ▲

Day 4

Teacher–Directed
Leveled Readers:
Guided Fluency, p. T268

Independent
⭐ Technology Center, p. T223

▲ Leveled Reader

Teacher–Directed
Leveled Readers:
Guided Fluency, p. T269

Independent
⭐ Fluency Center, p. T223

▲ Leveled Reader

Independent
⭐ Reading Center, p. T222
Classroom Library:
Self-Selected Reading

▲ Leveled Reader

LANGUAGE DEVELOPMENT SUPPORT

Teacher–Directed
Leveled Readers:
Guided Fluency, p. T271
ELL Teacher Guide, Lesson 24

Independent
ELL Copying Masters,
Lesson 24

▲ Leveled Reader

Catch a Wave,
Lesson 24
Strategic Intervention
Teacher Guide,
Lesson 24

Strategic Intervention
Interactive Reader ▲

Day 5

Teacher–Directed
Leveled Readers:
Responding, p. T268

Independent
⭐ Fluency Center, p. T223
Leveled Readers:
Rereading for Fluency, p. T268

▲ Leveled Reader

Teacher–Directed
Leveled Readers:
Responding, p. T269

Independent
⭐ Writing Center, p. T223
Leveled Readers: Rereading for
Fluency, p. T269

▲ Leveled Reader

Teacher–Directed
Leveled Readers:
Responding, p. T270

Independent
⭐ Technology Center, p. T223
Leveled Readers:
Rereading for Fluency, p. T270

Classroom Library: Self-Selected Reading

▲ Leveled Reader

LANGUAGE DEVELOPMENT SUPPORT

Teacher–Directed
Leveled Readers:
Responding, p. T271
ELL Teacher Guide, Lesson 24

Independent
Leveled Readers:
Rereading for Fluency, p. T271

▲ Leveled Reader

Catch a Wave,
Lesson 24
Strategic Intervention
Teacher Guide,
Lesson 24

Strategic Intervention
Interactive Reader ▲

Leveled Readers & Leveled Practice

Reinforcing Skills and Strategies

LEVELED READERS SYSTEM

- **Leveled Readers**
- **Leveled Readers CD**
- **Leveled Reader Teacher Guides**
  - *Vocabulary*
  - *Comprehension*
  - *Oral Reading Fluency Assessment*
- **Response Activities**
- **Leveled Readers Assessment**

See pages T268–T271 for lesson plans.

For extended lesson plans, see *Leveled Reader Teacher Guides.*

T220 • Grade 5, Theme 5

BELOW-LEVEL

- 🔖 **Literary Devices**
- 🔖 **Answer Questions**
- • **Robust Vocabulary**

LEVELED READER TEACHER GUIDE

▲ **Vocabulary, p. 5**

▲ **Comprehension, p. 6**

ON-LEVEL

- 🔖 **Literary Devices**
- 🔖 **Answer Questions**
- • **Robust Vocabulary**

LEVELED READER TEACHER GUIDE

▲ **Vocabulary, p. 5**

▲ **Comprehension, p. 6**

ADVANCED

Social Studies

Best Bugs

by Becky Cheston
Illustrated by Marsha Slomowitz

Harcourt

- 🎯 Literary Devices
- 🎯 Answer Questions
- • Robust Vocabulary

LEVELED READER TEACHER GUIDE

▲ **Vocabulary, p. 5**

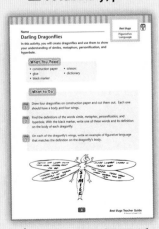

▲ **Comprehension, p. 6**

ELL

Social Studies

CALLING ALL Crickets

by Trish Marx   Harcourt

- • Build Background
- • Concept Vocabulary
- • Scaffolded Language Development

LEVELED READER TEACHER GUIDE

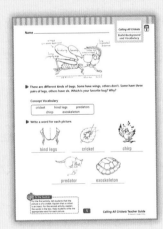

▲ **Build Background, p. 5**

▲ **Scaffolded Language Development, p. 6**

CLASSROOM LIBRARY
for Self-Selected Reading

DOÑA FLOR

EASY

▲ *Doña Flor* by Pat Mora.
TALL TALE

Eleanor
Story and pictures by
BARBARA COONEY

AVERAGE

▲ *Eleanor* by Barbara Cooney.
BIOGRAPHY

SHIPS
OF THE AIR

LYNN CURLEE

CHALLENGE

▲ *Ships of the Air* by Lynn Curlee.
NARRATIVE NONFICTION

Classroom
Library Books
Teacher Guide

▲ **Classroom Library Books Teacher Guide**

Literacy Centers

15+ Min. each

Management Support

While you provide direct instruction to individuals or small groups, other students can work on these activities.

▲ Literacy Centers Pocket Chart

My Activities for the Week

This week I will complete the following:

Literacy Centers
- ☐ **Word Study** Add a Word
- ☐ **Reading** Reading Log
- ☐ **Writing** Write a Letter
- ☐ **Technology** Map a Place
- ☐ **Fluency** Timed Reading

Leveled Readers
- ☐ Reread for Fluency
- ☐ Activities (See inside back cover.)

Practice Book
- ☐ Pages 140–144

▲ Teacher Resource Book, p. 59

Homework for the Week

Teacher Resource Book, page 27

The *Homework Copying Master* provides activities to complete for each day of the week.

GO online www.harcourtschool.com/storytown

WORD STUDY

Add a Word

Objective
To extend understanding of word usage

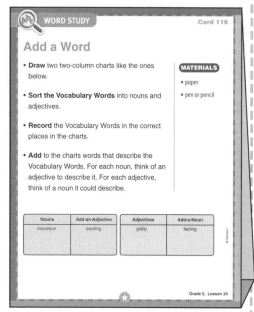

WORD STUDY — Card 116

Add a Word

- **Draw** two two-column charts like the ones below.
- **Sort** the Vocabulary Words into nouns and adjectives.
- **Record** the Vocabulary Words in the correct places in the charts.
- **Add** to the charts words that describe the Vocabulary Words. For each noun, think of an adjective to describe it. For each adjective, think of a noun it could describe.

MATERIALS
- paper
- pen or pencil

Nouns	Add-an-Adjective	Adjectives	Add-a-Noun
excursion	exciting	giddy	feeling

Grade 5, Lesson 24

⭐ **Literacy Center Kit,** Card 116

Nouns	Add-an-Adjective
excursion	exciting
pinnacle	
panic	

Adjectives	Add-a-Noun
giddy	feeling
gleeful	
turbulent	
precious	

READING

Reading Log

Objective
To select and read books independently

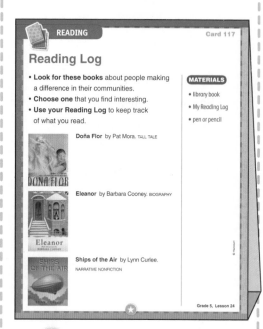

READING — Card 117

Reading Log

- **Look for these books** about people making a difference in their communities.
- **Choose one** that you find interesting.
- **Use your Reading Log** to keep track of what you read.

MATERIALS
- library book
- My Reading Log
- pen or pencil

Doña Flor by Pat Mora. TALL TALE

Eleanor by Barbara Cooney. BIOGRAPHY

Ships of the Air by Lynn Curlee. NARRATIVE NONFICTION

Grade 5, Lesson 24

⭐ **Literacy Center Kit,** Card 117

Go online

www.harcourtschool.com/storytown

★ Additional Literacy Center Activities
★ Resources for Parents and Teachers

● BELOW-LEVEL   ● ADVANCED   ● ON-LEVEL

Differentiated *for Your Needs*

 WRITING

Write Directions

Objective
To write directions

⭐ **Literacy Center Kit,** Card 118

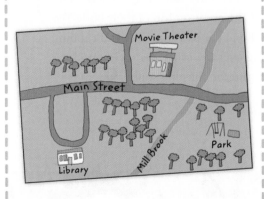

 TECHNOLOGY

Map a Place

Objective
To use electronic resources to gather information

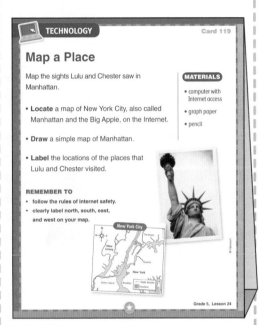

⭐ **Literacy Center Kit,** Card 119

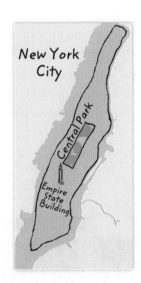

FLUENCY

Timed Reading

Objective
To read aloud with appropriate pace

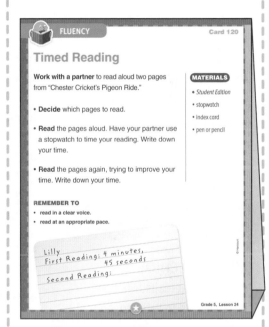

⭐ **Literacy Center Kit,** Card 120

Listening Comprehension *Read-Aloud*

Objectives
- *To determine a purpose for listening*
- *To understand information presented orally*

Genre Study

REALISTIC FICTION Tell students that they will listen to a realistic fiction story called "Keeping Cool with Crickets." Remind students that a realistic fiction story

- is made up by an author.
- has characters, settings, and events that could exist in real life.

Set a Purpose for Listening

LISTEN TO ENJOY Tell students that realistic fiction is usually fun to listen to, and that some realistic fiction stories also give information about a topic. Model setting a purpose: *One purpose for listening to this story is to find out how crickets keep people cool.* Then have students set their own purposes for listening.

Keeping Cool With Crickets
by Lois Jacobson

"KONNICHIWA" ("Good Afternoon"), my Japanese neighbor called through the door. "I have brought a present to welcome you to Japan."

The package was very small and tied with delicately curled ribbons. What could such a tiny box contain? Puzzled, I lifted the lid, and there, nestled in whisper-thin tissue paper, was a blue-and-white dish. It was shaped like a miniature bottle cap, and its cracked, glazed surface made it look very old—and very special.

"It's a water dish for crickets." My new friend's voice almost chirped with delight.

"What does one do with a water dish for crickets?" I asked.

"You put it inside a cricket house."

"Cricket house?"

"If you are going to live in Tokyo during the heat of summer," said my neighbor, "you must learn to keep cool with crickets!"

Now my curiosity was aroused, and I soon learned that in the Far East, people have kept crickets as pets for centuries. In the past they housed them in cages made of bamboo or delicately carved jade, which they hung from the eaves or porches of their weathered homes. Bamboo cages are still used today, but most children keep their crickets in plastic cages the colors of cool lime or raspberry sherbet. ❶

During the hot, breathless summer months, Japanese parks teem with laughing children and parents, armed with butterfly nets and small towels, pursuing their prey. The crickets are hard to catch because their hind legs are well developed for jumping. But once trapped in a net or under a small towel, they can be transferred to cages or small glass jars with air holes in the lids.

For people who can't catch their own, there are cricket vendors who carry on a thriving business. I soon found myself at a market stall eyeing a plump, brownish black cricket. The vendor put my selection in a cardboard container. From the vibrations, I knew that my cricket didn't like being shut up inside. He needed a house. ❷

He and I scouted out the local cricket real-estate market. Our search ended in a cluttered stall filled with bamboo wares. Tucked in a corner, amid baskets and flower containers, was a miniature Japanese house made of slender bamboo reeds. It was just right for the antique water dish—and, of course, for my cricket.

Using many hand gestures, the kimono-clad shopkeeper explained that the bottom of the house must be layered with just enough soil to anchor the filled water dish. Crickets, she added, love raw potatoes, cucumbers, bits of water-soaked bread, and leafy greens—all in cricket-size portions.

Charlie and I were eager to move in. I knew he was a Charlie because only male crickets chirp. Crickets have four wings that lie flat, one pair over the other on top of their body. By raising the upper pair of wings and rubbing one wing over the other, the males produce their singing or chirping sound. ❸

Read-Aloud is continued on page T327.

Begin the Read-Aloud

MODEL ORAL FLUENCY: PACE Remind students that good readers

- read aloud at a steady, even pace.

- read text slowly and clearly so that listeners can understand it.

Display **Transparency R101**. Read the passage aloud as students follow along. Point out the steady, even pace with which you read.

Interact with the Text

Routine Card 1

Continue reading "Keeping Cool with Crickets." Pause to point out or ask students the following.

❶ How can you tell that the narrator is unfamiliar with keeping crickets as pets? (Possible response: The narrator doesn't know what to do with a water dish for crickets.) **DRAW CONCLUSIONS**

❷ A *vendor* is a person who sells things. **UNDERSTANDING VOCABULARY**

❸ Do you think the narrator is eager to get the cricket house set up? Why do you think this? (Yes; the narrator gets a cricket and a cricket house right away and also gives the cricket a name.) **CHARACTER'S EMOTIONS**

When you have finished reading the story, ask:

- **What facts did you learn about crickets?** (Possible responses: Their strong hind legs help them jump; they make noise by rubbing their wings together; they like cucumbers and potatoes.) **NOTE DETAILS**

- **Why do you think the cricket helps people stay cool in summer?** (Possible response: Their sound calms people.) **RETURN TO PURPOSE**

Connect to Reading

Tell students that in the next story they will read about a cricket and his adventures.

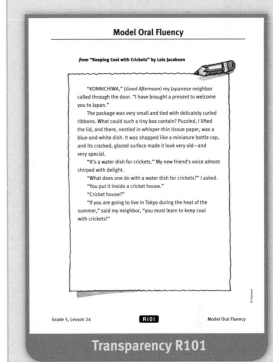

Model Oral Fluency

from "Keeping Cool with Crickets" by Lois Jacobson

"KONNICHIWA," (*Good Afternoon*) my Japanese neighbor called through the door. "I have brought a present to welcome you to Japan."

The package was very small and tied with delicately curled ribbons. What could such a tiny box contain? Puzzled, I lifted the lid, and there, nestled in whisper-thin tissue paper, was a blue-and-white dish. It was shapped like a miniature bottle cap, and its cracked, glazed surface made it look very old—and very special.

"It's a water dish for crickets." My new friend's voice almost chirped with delight.

"What does one do with a water dish for crickets?" I asked.

"You put it inside a cricket house."

"Cricket house?"

"If you are going to live in Tokyo during the heat of the summer," said my neighbor, "you must learn to keep cool with crickets!"

Grade 5, Lesson 24   **R101**   Model Oral Fluency

Transparency R101

Suggested Daily Read-Aloud

To model fluency and promote listening comprehension, read aloud from one of these books throughout the week:

- *Sea Turtles* by Lorraine A. Jay. NorthWord, 2000.

- *The Kids' Volunteering Book* by Arlene Erlbach. Lerner, 1998.

- *Neighborhood Odes* by Gary Soto. Harcourt, 2005.

- *Chester Cricket's New Home* by George Selden. Random House, 1984.

- *My Backyard Garden* by Carol Lerner. Morrow, 1998.

Lesson 24 • **T225**

Literary Devices

Objectives

- *To recognize and understand literary devices*
- *To identify and use sensory language*

Skill Trace

Tested ✓ **Literary Devices**

Introduce	pp. T166–T167
Reteach	pp. S20–S21, S28–S29
Review	**pp. T192–T193, T226–T227, T254–T255, T309**
Test	Theme 5
Maintain	p. T144, Theme 6

Teach/Model

REVIEW LITERARY DEVICES Read page 614 with students. Then use these points to summarize:

- **Figurative language** is language that has a meaning other than its literal meaning.

- A **simile** compares two things by using the word *like* or *as.*

- A **metaphor** compares two things by saying one thing *is* the other.

- **Personification** gives human traits to animals or objects.

Point out that similes and metaphors are similar, but if the word *like* or *as* is used, then the expression is a simile.

Focus Skill

 Literary Devices

You have learned that imagery is one kind of literary device. Authors use it to appeal to the senses. **Figurative language** expressions are another type of literary device. These expressions have meanings that are different from the literal meanings of the words that make them up. The following are three kinds of figurative language.

- A **simile** compares two things by using the word *like* or *as.*
- A **metaphor** compares two things by saying that one thing is the other. Metaphors do not use the words *like* or *as.*
- **Personification** gives human traits to animals or objects.

Text Example	Type of Figurative Language	Meaning

Tip
Look for the word *like* or *as* to identify a *simile.*

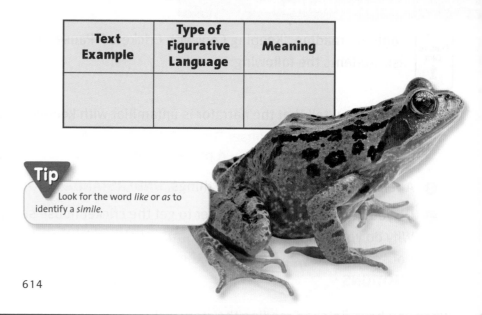

614

E L L

Figurative vs. Literal Help students understand the difference between **figurative** and **literal** statements by guiding them to create real-life examples of figurative language. Make a chart showing the figurative phrases and their literal meanings.

Figurative	Literal
simile: My brother eats like a hungry lion.	My brother eats a lot.
metaphor: The Internet is an information superhighway.	The Internet carries huge amounts of information.
personification: Our house welcomes strangers and friends.	Everyone is welcome in our house.

Read the paragraph below. The graphic organizer shows examples of personification and simile from the paragraph and tells what they mean.

> When I stay at Aunt Judy's farm, the night keeps me awake with all of its noises. Frogs sing a chorus of croaks, and crickets join in with their chirps. Cats screech and fight. Not even a pillow over my head blocks out the noise! Then, even before the sun rises, the rooster starts crowing. He sounds like a car alarm, yelling at the day to make it wake up!

Text Example	Type of Figurative Language	Meaning
Frogs sing a chorus	personification	The frogs croak as if singing a song.
He sounds like a car alarm	simile	The rooster is loud and annoying, like a car alarm.

 Try This!

How is "the night keeps me awake with all of its noises" an example of personification?

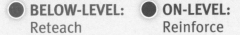 www.harcourtschool.com/storytown

615

(TEACH/MODEL CONTINUED) Ask a volunteer to read aloud the paragraph on *Student Edition* page 615. Model how to recognize and understand figurative language.

Think Aloud "Frogs sing a chorus of croaks" is an example of personification. Frogs do croak, but they don't really sing in a chorus, as people do.

Guided Practice

IDENTIFY IMAGERY Call on another volunteer to reread the paragraph again. Ask:

What type of figurative language is "crickets join in"? Why? (personification; The crickets don't really join in with the frogs; they just happen to sing at the same time.)

Why is "he sounds like a car alarm" a simile and not a metaphor? (It uses the word *like*.)

Practice/Apply

Try This! Have students reread the paragraph and explain why "the night keeps me awake with all its noises" is an example of personification. (Possible response: It gives the night a human quality—the ability to keep someone awake.)

> **DURING AND AFTER READING**
> • Practice the Skill • Apply to Text, pp. T236, T238, T240, T244
> • Reinforce the Skill • Practice/Apply, pp. T254–T255

 MONITOR PROGRESS

 **Literary Devices**

IF students have difficulty understanding how "the night keeps me awake" is an example of personification,

THEN explain that this phrase gives nighttime a human quality—the ability to keep someone awake on purpose.

Small-Group Instruction, pp. S28–S29:

● **BELOW-LEVEL:** Reteach ● **ON-LEVEL:** Reinforce ● **ADVANCED:** Extend

Comprehension Strategy
Answer Questions

Objectives

- *To identify types of question-answer relationships*
- *To use strategies for answering questions*

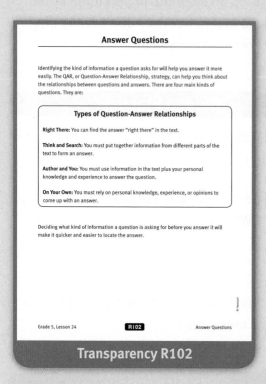

Transparency R102

Professional Development

 Podcasting: Answer Questions

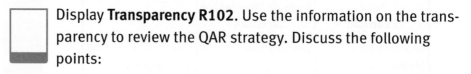
Teach/Model

REVIEW ANSWER QUESTIONS STRATEGY Remind students that identifying the kind of information a question asks for will help them answer it more easily. Remind them that the Question-Answer Relationship, or QAR, strategy can help them answer a question more quickly and easily.

Display **Transparency R102**. Use the information on the transparency to review the QAR strategy. Discuss the following points:

- The answer to a **Right There** question will appear in one place in a text.

- **Think and Search** questions ask you to tell how one idea relates to another. The answer will be in at least two places.

- **Author and You** questions ask you to draw conclusions, using clues the author gives you and your own knowledge.

- **On Your Own** questions ask you to express an opinion or make a judgment based on what you already know.

Display **Transparency R103**. Ask a volunteer to read aloud the first paragraph. Then ask the first question and model answering it:

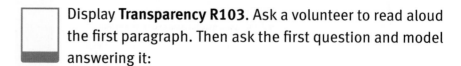 **Think Aloud** **The question asks when the story takes place. The first sentence says that it is the day of Jack's first race. This is a Right There question because the answer can be found in one place in the text.**

Guided Practice

ANSWER QUESTIONS Ask the remaining questions and guide students to identify the Question-Answer Relationships and answer the questions. Record their responses in the chart on **Transparency R103**.

Practice/Apply

APPLY THE QAR STRATEGY Have students work in small groups to read the first few pages of another fantasy or realistic fiction selection. Ask them to generate one question for each type of question-answer relationship. Groups should exchange questions, identify each kind of Question-Answer Relationship, and write answers to the questions.

> **DURING READING**
> • Apply the Focus Strategy, pp. T237, T239, T243, T249
> • Review Comprehension Strategies, p. T241

Answer Questions

It was the day of Jack's first race. He had come a long way since he first became interested in racing pigeons. In a pigeon race, the birds are taken far away from their lofts and set free. Then the birds fly back to their lofts. The bird that finds its way home the fastest is the winner.

Jack was proud of his pigeons. He had carefully trained the young birds for his racing team. His pigeons had found their way home from distances of as great as 100 miles, but this race would be 300 miles. Jack approached the release point. He wondered if all of his birds would find their way back.

At the release point, the birds had rubber bands and identification tags placed on their legs to show that they were part of the race. The clocks were set, the starting time noted, and the birds released. Back at the loft, the birds' arrival time would be recorded on a tamper-proof clock. Then the waiting would begin to see which bird found its way home the fastest. Jack hoped one of his pigeons would win.

Question	Type of Question-Answer Relationship	Answer
What special day is it?	Right There	The day of Jack's first race.
What happens before and after the starting time is noted?	Think and Search	The clocks are set and the birds are released.
Why does Jack wonder if all his birds will find their way back?	Author and You	The race is a greater distance than his birds had ever flown.
Would you enjoy participating in a pigeon race?	On Your Own	Responses will vary.

Grade 5, Lesson 24   R103   Answer Questions

Transparency R103

BELOW-LEVEL

Support Think and Search Answers To help students answer questions that require them to Think and Search, give each student some self-stick notes. Have students put a note next to each place in the text where they find part of the answer. Then tell students to use the self-stick notes as a guide when they answer the question. Explain to students that this process will help them give complete answers to Think and Search questions.

Build Background

Access Prior Knowledge

COMPLETE A CHART Tell students that the story they are going to read takes place in New York City. Ask students to share what they know about big cities in general and New York City in particular. Work with students to complete a chart like the one below.

Big Cities	New York City
• cars, taxis, buses • tall buildings (skyscrapers) • neighborhood or city parks • many pigeons • many people • crowded, noisy	• largest city in the U.S. • located on the East Coast • Central Park, a large park located in Manhattan • Empire State Building, once the world's tallest building • Statue of Liberty

Develop Concepts

DISCUSS NEW YORK CITY Draw on information from the chart to develop concepts related to the selection. Explain to students that

- New York City is the largest city in the United States and among the largest in the world. It is made up of five areas, or boroughs: Manhattan, the Bronx, Brooklyn, Queens, and Staten Island.

- Central Park is a huge park in Manhattan. It has several lakes and is home to many animals.

- The Statue of Liberty was a gift to our country from France. It is located near Ellis Island and is a symbol of freedom to newcomers to the United States.

ELL

Selection Background Display *Picture Card 26*, along with visuals from the *Student Edition*, to scaffold background and vocabulary as needed. Discuss these points:

- New York is a big **city.** (show photo)

- New York City has tall buildings called **skyscrapers.** (show photo)

Discuss with students other things they would expect to see in a big city.

Picture Card 26 ▶

See *ELL Teacher Guide* Lesson 24 for support in scaffolding instruction.

Build **Robust Vocabulary**

5-DAY VOCABULARY
DAY 1 Vocabulary, pp. T231–T233
DAY 2 Vocabulary Review, p. T253
DAY 3 Reinforce Word Meanings, p. T259
DAY 4 Extend Word Meanings, p. T259
DAY 5 Cumulative Review, p. T259

Introduce Vocabulary

Routine Card 2

BUILD WORD MEANING Display **Transparency R104.** Have a volunteer read aloud the first Vocabulary Word, and have the class repeat the word aloud to practice its pronunciation. Then have the volunteer read the explanation for the word. Ask students the first question below. Continue in this way until students have answered a question about each of the Vocabulary Words.

1. What are some **excursions** you've been on?

2. Which would make you feel **giddy**—winning a free vacation or falling asleep during a movie? Why?

3. Where is the **pinnacle** of a building?

4. How does a person who is feeling **gleeful** act?

5. What might cause people at a zoo to feel **panic**?

6. Where would water be **turbulent**—in a quiet pond or at the bottom of a waterfall? Explain.

7. What would be **precious** to someone stranded on a desert island?

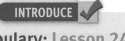

INTRODUCE Tested ✓

Vocabulary: Lesson 24

excursions	panic
giddy	turbulent
pinnacle	precious
gleeful	

▼ **Student-Friendly Explanations**

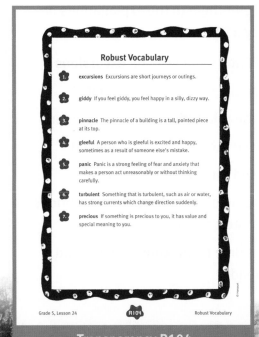

Robust Vocabulary

1. **excursions** Excursions are short journeys or outings.

2. **giddy** If you feel giddy, you feel happy in a silly, dizzy way.

3. **pinnacle** The pinnacle of a building is a tall, pointed piece at its top.

4. **gleeful** A person who is gleeful is excited and happy, sometimes as a result of someone else's mistake.

5. **panic** Panic is a strong feeling of fear and anxiety that makes a person act unreasonably or without thinking carefully.

6. **turbulent** Something that is turbulent, such as air or water, has strong currents which change direction suddenly.

7. **precious** If something is precious to you, it has value and special meaning to you.

Grade 5, Lesson 24   R104   Robust Vocabulary

Transparency R104

Vocabulary

Build Robust Vocabulary

DEVELOP DEEPER MEANING Have students silently read the passage on pages 616–617. Then read the passage aloud. Pause at the end of page 616. Ask questions 1–5 about the highlighted words. Discuss students' answers. Then read page 617 and discuss students' answers to questions 6–7. If students are unable to give reasonable responses, refer them to the explanations on **Transparency R104**.

1. When did Frida usually go on **excursions**?

2. What made the shy spider feel **giddy**?

3. Why was the ride **turbulent** for the spider?

4. What caused the spider to feel **gleeful**?

5. What caused the spider to feel **panic**?

6. How did being on the **pinnacle** of the bridge help Frida see a trash can?

7. Why might time be **precious** to Frida and her cat friends?

Vocabulary

Build Robust Vocabulary

Nights on the Prowl

excursions

giddy

turbulent

gleeful

panic

pinnacle

precious

Frida and I are an unlikely pair. She is a plump, noisy cat who spends the darkest parts of the night outdoors. I am a shy spider who minds my own business.

One night, Frida invited me to join her on one of her nighttime **excursions**. I spun a line of silk around her left ear and hung on tight. I felt **giddy**! It was a **turbulent**, thrilling ride. After I got over feeling dizzy, I was **gleeful**! I'd never had so much fun.

Another night, Frida offered to introduce me to the cats who go trash-tasting with her. **Panic** set in. I worried her friends wouldn't like me and might hurt me.

Unlike Frida, I usually spend my nights indoors.

616

E L L

Meaning Reminders Have students list the Vocabulary Words on a separate sheet of paper. Next to each word, have them write a word or phrase or draw a simple sketch to remind them of the meaning of the word. For example, next to **pinnacle,** they might draw a mountain peak. Next to **panic,** they might write the word *fear.*

See *ELL Teacher Guide* Lesson 24 for support in scaffolding instruction.

Pinnacle

We crossed the bridge that arched over the river. From the **pinnacle** of the bridge, Frida spotted a new trash can. We raced to it. I crawled up the can and peeked inside, discovering the remains of a tasty meal. The cats knocked over the can and dined. During the rest of the night I quickly crawled up and looked inside each can, saving the cats **precious** time. They were so pleased that they invited me to their next trash-tasting!

GO online www.harcourtschool.com/storytown

Word Scribe

This week, your task is to use the Vocabulary Words in your writing. In your vocabulary journal, write sentences to show the meanings of the words. For example, you could write about excursions you went on, or you could tell about something that makes you feel gleeful. Use as many of the Vocabulary Words as you can. Share your writing with your classmates.

617

Word Scribe

Use Words in Writing Have students review the Vocabulary Words before they begin writing in their vocabulary journals. If students have difficulty using any of the words in their writing, suggest that they discuss the word with a classmate before writing in their vocabulary journal.

HOMEWORK/INDEPENDENT PRACTICE

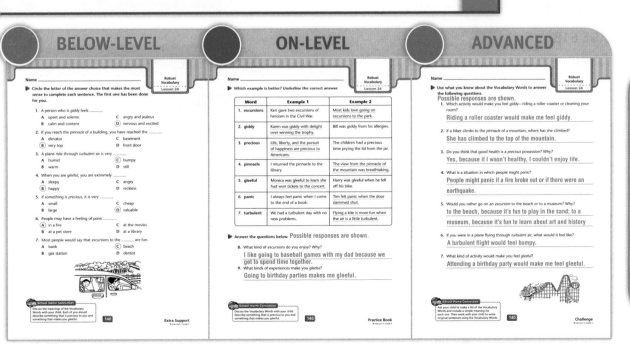

▲ Extra Support, p. 140   ▲ Practice Book, p. 140   ▲ Challenge, p. 140

E L L

• Group students according to academic levels, and assign one of the pages on the left.

• Clarify any unfamiliar concepts as necessary. See *ELL Teacher Guide* Lesson 24 for support in scaffolding instruction.

(*Student Edition*, page 617) Lesson 24 • **T233**

SOCIAL STUDIES

Read the Selection

Award-Winning Author

Chester Cricket's Pigeon Ride

by George Selden

Pictures by Garth Williams

Fantasy

Objective

- *To identify the distinguishing features of fantasy*

Genre Study

DISCUSS FANTASY: PAGE 618 Have students read the genre information on page 618. Discuss each characteristic of fantasy. Have students view the opening spread and identify details in the illustration that make the characters seem unrealistic.

LIST GENRE FEATURES Have students page through the selection. Discuss why a story about animals who take a journey would be a fantasy. Then display **Transparency GO1**. You may want to use the story map to help students keep track of story elements.

Comprehension Strategy

ANSWER QUESTIONS: PAGE 618 Have students read the Comprehension Strategy information on page 618. Then distribute *Practice Book* page 141. Tell students that they will fill in the graphic organizer as they read to help them keep track of important information and monitor their comprehension. See page T247 for the completed *Practice Book* page.

Genre Study

A fantasy is an imaginative story that may have unrealistic characters and events. As you read, look for

- story events or settings that could not happen in real life.

- characters that behave in an unrealistic way.

Characters	Setting

Conflict

↓

Plot Events

↓

Resolution

Comprehension Strategy

Answer questions about a story by looking in the text and thinking about what you already know.

618

▲ **Practice Book, p. 141**

TECHNOLOGY

GO online **eBook** "Chester Cricket's Pigeon Ride" is available in an eBook.

Audiotext "Chester Cricket's Pigeon Ride" is available on *Audiotext Grade 5*, CD8 for subsequent readings.

Chester Cricket's Pigeon Ride

by George Selden
illustrated by Garth Williams

Chester Cricket finds life in New York City thrilling. Mario, the boy who found Chester his first night in the city, has taken him to many places, but Chester is homesick. He longs for the fields and trees of his Connecticut home. In Times Square, Chester meets a new friend, Lulu Pigeon. She takes him on a wild ride, and he finds a little bit of the country he's been missing.

619

Preview/Set a Purpose

Routine Card 3

PREVIEW AND PREDICT Explain to students that the story they are about to read is an excerpt from a book called *Chester Cricket's Pigeon Ride*. Have a volunteer read aloud the story title and the introduction on page 619. Ask students to predict where the main characters might go on their wild ride.

MODEL SETTING A PURPOSE Remind students that good readers set a purpose for reading, based on the genre and what they think the story will be about. Have students set their own purpose for reading. You might want to use this model:

Think Aloud The illustration on page 619 shows a cricket on the back of a pigeon. Based on the title and the introduction, Chester Cricket is probably the main character. A purpose for reading this story could be to find out where Chester goes on his ride.

Options for Reading

BELOW-LEVEL

Small Group Preview the selection with students. Model how to use the preview and the genre information to set a purpose for reading.

ON-LEVEL

Whole Group/Partner Use the Monitor Comprehension questions as students read the selection, or have partners read the selection together and complete *Practice Book* page 141.

ADVANCED

Independent Have students read the selection independently, using *Practice Book* page 141 to monitor their comprehension and keep track of the information in the selection.

Monitor Comprehension

1 **CHARACTER'S MOTIVES**

Why does Lulu offer to give Chester a tour of New York? (Possible responses: to make him feel at home; to cheer him up)

2 **LITERARY DEVICES**

When Lulu says, "Sorry for the bumpy takeoff," what is she comparing herself to? (an airplane pilot or an airplane) **What type of figurative language is this?** (metaphor)

3 **MAKE INFERENCES**

Why is Chester thrilled by Central Park? (It reminds him of home.)

4 **MAKE PREDICTIONS**

How do you predict Chester will feel about New York after his flight? (Responses will vary.)

See *Questioning the Author Comprehension Guide,* Lesson 24, as an alternate questioning strategy to guide student interaction with the text.

Questioning the Author Comprehension Guide, Lesson 24 ▶

"You don't know where Central *Park* is?" said Lulu. "Big beautiful Central Park!—the best place in the city—"

"I guess I don't," Chester apologized. He explained that Mario had taken him on several excursions, but not, as yet, to Central Park.

"Say!" exclaimed Lulu. "How would you like a real tooor of Nooo York? One that only a pigeon could give."

"Well, I'd love one," said Chester, "but—"

"Hop on my back, just behind my neck. Nope—" Lulu bobbed her head jerkily, trying to think. "—Yooo couldn't see down through my wings too well." Then she gave a big scratch and exclaimed, "I got it! You sit on my claw—take the left one there—and wrap a couple of feelers around." Chester hesitated a minute or two. He was quite sure no cricket had ever done *this* before.

"Go on! Get on!" Lulu ordered. "You're in for a thrill."

"All right—" Chester mounted the pigeon's claw, with a feeling that was partly excitement, partly fear, and held on tight.

620

Extended Metaphor Remind students that a **metaphor** is a comparison between two things that does not use *like* or *as*. Explain that an **extended metaphor** is a metaphor developed at great length. Point out that this story presents an extended metaphor that compares Lulu to an airplane. As students read the story, have them note and record words and phrases that support this metaphor, using this chart.

Lulu compared to an airplane	
• bumpy takeoff—p. 621	

"First I gotta rev up." Lulu flapped her wings a few times. And then—before Chester could gasp with delight—*they were flying*!

To fly—oh, be flying!

"Sorry for the bumpy takeoff," **2** said Lulu.

But it hadn't seemed bumpy to Chester at all.

"It'll be better when I gain altitoode."

Back in Connecticut, in the Old Meadow, when Chester made one of his mightiest leaps—usually showing off in front of a friend like Joe Skunk—he sometimes reached as high as six feet. But in seconds Lulu had passed that height, and in less than a minute she was gliding along at the level of the tops of the sycamore trees.

"Okay down there?" she called into the rush of air they sped through.

"Oh—oh, sure—I mean, I guess—" There are times when you don't know whether you feel terror or pleasure—or perhaps you feel both all at once, all jumbled together wonderfully! "I'm fine!" the cricket decided, and held on to Lulu's leg even tighter. Because now they were far above even the tops of the trees, and Chester could see whole blocks of buildings below him. He suddenly felt all giddy and free.

"How about a spin up to Central Park first?"

"Great, Lulu! I want to see *everything*!"

The pigeon flew east, to Fifth Avenue, and then due north. High though they were flying, Chester could see how beautiful the store windows were in the street beneath. The finest shops in all the world are on Fifth Avenue, and the cricket would have liked to fly a bit lower, to get a closer look. But he thought better of it and decided to leave all the navigating to Lulu. Besides, there was something strange up ahead. A huge rectangle of dark was sliding toward them—close, then closer, then under them.

"Here's Central Park," Lulu screeched against the wind.

And now Chester had another thrill. For there weren't only sycamore trees in the park. The cricket could smell birches, beeches, and maples—elms, oaks—almost as many kinds of trees as Connecticut itself had to offer. And there was the moon!—the crescent moon—reflected in a little lake. Sounds, too, rose up to him: the shooshing of leaves, the nighttime countryside whispering of insects and little animals, and—best of all—a brook that was arguing with itself, as it splashed over rocks. The miracle of Central Park, a sheltered wilderness in the midst of the city, pierced Chester Cricket's heart with joy. **3** **4**

621

 SOCIAL STUDIES SUPPORTING STANDARDS

New York Remind students that New York was one of the 13 original colonies. It was originally called New Amsterdam but became known as New York when control passed to the Duke of York. The city grew in importance as a trading port, and it still is today. Ask students why they think New York City makes a good trading port.

Apply Comprehension Strategies

 Answer Questions

REVIEW ANSWER QUESTIONS Remind students that they can ask and answer questions to help them monitor their comprehension. Review these Question-Answer Relationships with students:

> ### The 4 Kinds of Question-Answer Relationships
>
> - **Right There**
> - **Think and Search**
> - **Author and You**
> - **On Your Own**

Then ask: **Why does the author spell *tour* and *New* with three *o*'s?** Model using Question-Answer Relationships to answer the question:

> **Think Aloud** This is an *Author and You* question. The answer is not directly stated, so you must use your own experience and knowledge to answer it. A pigeon makes a coo-coo sound, so the author spells words with the sound of /$\overline{oo}$/ this way to make Lulu's voice sound like that of a real pigeon.

Remind students to use Question-Answer Relationships to answer questions as they read.

Monitor Comprehension

5 **CHARACTER'S MOTIVES**

Why does Chester want to go down to Central Park? (Possible response: The park reminds him of home, so he wants to experience it.)

6 **USE CONTEXT CLUES**

What does the phrase *call on* mean? (It means "visit.")

7  **LITERARY DEVICES**

Is the statement "Lulu Pigeon coasted down through the air, as swiftly and neatly and accurately as a little boy's paper airplane" a simile or a metaphor? How do you know? (It's a simile. It uses the word *as* to compare two things.)

8 **USE CONTEXT CLUES**

What can the word *rose* mean? What does it mean in this paragraph? (*Rose* can be a flower or it can mean "to move upward." In this paragraph it means "to move upward.")

9 **USE CONTEXT CLUES**

What does the word *acrophobia* mean? (It means "fear of heights.") **How do you know?** (Possible response: The author provides the explanation right after the word.)

"Oh, can we go down?" he shouted up. **5** "Lulu?—please!"

"'Course, Chester C." The pigeon slowed and tilted her wings. "Anything you want. But let's not call on my relatives. They're a drag, and they're all asleep by now anyway." **6**

"I don't want to *visit* anybody!" said Chester, as Lulu Pigeon coasted down through the air, as swiftly and neatly and accurately as a little boy's paper airplane, and landed beside the lake. "All I want is—is—" He didn't know how to say it exactly, but all Chester wanted was to sit beside that shimmering lake—a breeze ruffled its surface—and look at the jiggling reflection of the moon, and enjoy the sweet moisture and the tree-smelling night all around him. **7**

BELOW-LEVEL

Reality vs. Fantasy Create a chart such as the one below to help students follow the interplay of realistic and unrealistic elements in the story.

Realistic	Unrealistic
• setting • descriptions of New York • animals' physical appearance	• The animals can talk. • A pigeon gives a cricket a tour of New York. • Lulu knows things about New York that only people would know.

And chirp. Above all, Chester wanted to chirp. Which he did, to his heart's content. And to Lulu Pigeon's heart's content, too.

But even the loveliest intervals end. Song done—one moment more of silent delight—and then Lulu said, "Come on, Chester C., let me show you some more of my town"—by which she meant New York.

"Okay," said Chester, and climbed on her claw again.

"I want you to see it *all* now!" said Lulu. Her wings were beating strongly, rhythmically. "And the best place for that is the Empire State Building."

They rose higher and higher. And the higher they went, the more scared Chester got. Flying up Fifth Avenue had been fun as well as frightening, but now they were heading straight for the top of one of the tallest buildings in all the world. **8**

Chester looked down—the world swirled beneath him—and felt as if his stomach turned over. Or maybe his brain turned around. But something in him felt queasy and dizzy. "Lulu—" he began anxiously, "—I think—"

"Just hold on tight!" Lulu shouted down. "And trust in your feathered friend!"

What Chester had meant to say was that he was afraid he was suffering from a touch of acrophobia—fear of heights. (And perched on a pigeon's claw, on your way to the top of the Empire State, is not the best place to find that you are afraid of great heights.) But even if Lulu hadn't interrupted, the cricket couldn't have finished his sentence. His words were forced back into his throat. For the wind, which had been just a breeze beside the lake, was turning into a raging gale as they spiraled upward, around the building, floor past floor, and approached their final destination: the television antenna tower on the very top. **9**

And they made it! Lulu gripped the pinnacle of the TV antenna with both her claws, accidentally pinching one of Chester's legs as she did so. The whole of New York glowed and sparkled below them.

623

Apply Comprehension Strategies

Answer Questions

IDENTIFY QUESTION-ANSWER RELATIONSHIPS If students have trouble answering question 5, guide them to draw on their own experiences and on story clues to arrive at an answer. If necessary, provide the following model:

Think Aloud Chester has been homesick for Connecticut. People who feel homesick long to be home or in a place that feels like home. Chester wants to sit in Central Park and chirp because the park looks, feels, and smells like home.

ANALYZE WRITER'S CRAFT

Changes in Vocabulary and Language Patterns Call students' attention to the phrase *call on* on page 622 and the phrases *suffering from a touch of acrophobia* and *the whole of New York* on page 623. Ask students what words they would use to mean the same as the phrases. (Possible responses: *visit, feeling acrophobic, all of New York*) Then discuss with students how these changes in vocabulary may have come about, and how the use of these particular language patterns gives the story an old-fashioned feel.

Monitor Comprehension

10 🎯 **LITERARY DEVICES**

What do people look like to Chester from his position on the Empire State Building? (like bugs moving up and down the sidewalks) **What type of figurative language is this?** (simile)

11 **CAUSE AND EFFECT**

What two events cause Chester to fall after Lulu lifts her claw? (A plane landing at LaGuardia Airport makes him dizzy, and a gust of wind blows against Lulu and him.)

12 **AUTHOR'S CRAFT**

How does the author add humor to break the suspense of Chester's fall? (Possible response: He has Chester think that falling off the Empire State Building probably hasn't happened to many crickets and that he wishes it weren't happening to him.)

Now it is strange, but it is true, that although there are many mountains higher than even the tallest buildings, and airplanes can fly much higher than mountains, *nothing* ever seems quite so high as a big building that's been built by men. It suggests our own height to ourselves, I guess.

Chester felt as if not only a city but the entire world was down there where he could look at it. He almost couldn't see the people. 'My gosh!' he thought. 'They look just like bugs.' And he had to laugh at that: like bugs—perhaps crickets—moving up and down the sidewalks. And the cars, the buses, the yellow taxis, all jittered along like miniatures. He felt that kind of spinning sensation inside his head that had made him dizzy on the way up. But he refused to close his eyes. It was too much of an adventure for that. **10**

"Lulu, my foot," said Chester, "you're stepping on it. Could you please—"

"Ooo, I'm sorry," the pigeon apologized. She lifted her claw.

And just at that moment two bad things happened. The first was, Chester caught sight of an airplane swooping low to land at LaGuardia Airport across the East River. The dip of it made his dizziness worse. And the second—worse yet—a sudden gust of wind sprang up, as if a hand gave them both a push. Lulu almost fell off the Empire State.

Lulu *almost* fell off—but Chester *did*! In an instant his legs and feelers were torn away from the pigeon's leg, and before he could say, 'Old Meadow, farewell!' he was tumbling down through the air. One moment the city appeared above him—that meant that he was upside down; then under him—he was right side up; then everything slid from side to side. **11**

He worked his wings, tried to hold them stiff to steady himself—no use, no use! The gleeful wind was playing with him. It was rolling him, throwing him back and forth, up and down, as a cork is tossed in the surf of a storm. And minute by minute, when he faced that way, the cricket caught glimpses of the floors of the Empire State Building plunging upward as he plunged down.

Despite his panic, his mind took a wink of time off to think: 'Well, *this* is something that can't have happened to many crickets before!' (He was right, too—it hadn't. And just at that moment Chester wished that it wasn't happening to *him*.) **12**

624

Cause and Effect If students have trouble answering question 11, use a cause-and-effect diagram to help them.

Cause	Effect
Chester sees a plane land and it makes him dizzy.	**Chester falls from the Empire State Building.**
A big gust of wind blows against Lulu and Chester.	

Apply Comprehension Strategies

Use Graphic Organizers

SEQUENCE Remind students that in fictional narratives, authors usually organize events in the order in which they occur. Remind students that keeping track of the **sequence of plot events** can help them follow a story. Ask:

- **What is the first plot event?** (Lulu invites Chester on a tour of New York City.)
- **What is the second event?** (Lulu and Chester visit Central Park, and Chester chirps there.)
- **What is the third event?** (Lulu takes Chester to the top of the Empire State Building, and a big gust of wind sweeps him off the building.)

You may want to have students record the important events in a sequence chart like the one below.

First Event

↓

Next Event

↓

Last Event

MATH **SUPPORTING STANDARDS**

Compare Building Heights Tell students the Empire State Building is one of the tallest buildings in the world. Provide students with these building heights, and work with them to represent the information in a bar graph.

Petronas Towers—1,483 ft.
Sears Tower—1,454 ft.
Empire State Building—1,250 ft.
Eiffel Tower—986 ft.

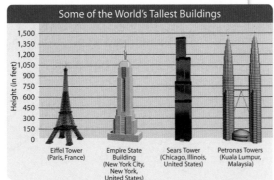

Some of the World's Tallest Buildings

Monitor Comprehension

13 **NOTE DETAILS**

How does Lulu save Chester? (She flies around the Empire State Building until she finds him. Then she swoops beneath him.)

14 **COMPARE AND CONTRAST**

Contrast the way Lulu and Chester each feel about continuing the tour. (Possible response: Chester is tired and wants to go back to the drainpipe. Lulu is still having fun and wants to continue.)

15 **DRAW CONCLUSIONS**

What clue does Chester use to draw the conclusion that he and Lulu are on a rather long flight? (Possible response: Lulu's wingbeats are strong and regular.)

He guessed, when New York was in the right place again, that he was almost halfway down. The people were looking more and more like people—he heard the cars' engines—and the street and the sidewalk looked *awfully* hard! Then—

Whump! He landed on something both hard and soft. It was hard inside, all muscles and bones, but soft on the surface—feathers!

"Grab on!" a familiar voice shouted. "Tight! Tighter! That's it."

Chester gladly did as he was told.

"Whooooey!" Lulu breathed a sigh of relief. "Thought I'd never find you. Been around this building at least ten times." **13**

Chester wanted to say, 'Thank you, Lulu,' but he was so thankful he couldn't get one word out till they'd reached a level where the air was friendly and gently buoyed them up.

But before he could even open his mouth, the pigeon— all ready for another adventure—asked eagerly, "Where now, Chester C.?"

"I guess I better go back to the drainpipe, Lulu. I'm kind of tired."

626

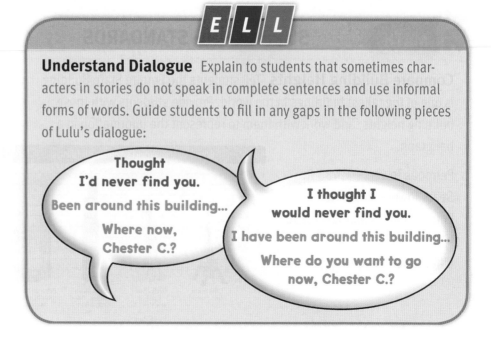

"Aw, no—!" complained Lulu, who'd been having fun. **14**

"You know, I'm really not all that used to getting blown off the Empire State Building—"

"Oh, all right," said the pigeon. "But first there's one thing you *gotta* see!"

Flying just below the level of turbulent air—good pilot that she was—Lulu headed south, with Chester clinging to the back of her neck. He felt much safer up there, and her wings didn't block out as much of the view as they'd thought. He wanted to ask where they were going, but he sensed from the strength and regularity of her wingbeats that it was to be a rather long flight. And the wind was against them too, which made the flying more difficult. Chester held his peace, and watched the city slip beneath them. **15**

They reached the Battery, which is that part of lower New York where a cluster of skyscrapers rise up like a grove of steel trees. But Lulu didn't stop there.

627

Apply Comprehension Strategies

Answer Questions

MODEL ANSWERING QUESTIONS Ask **If you were Chester, would you want to continue the journey? Why or why not?**

If students have difficulty answering, model the strategy:

Think Aloud This question asks you to make a judgment based on what you've read. It is an *Author and You* question. To answer this question, ask yourself how you would feel if you were Chester.

ANALYZE WRITER'S CRAFT

Sensory Details Remind students that one way authors develop their stories is to include **sensory details**. Have students look back at the text on pages 626–627 and find examples of sensory details George Selden included to develop this part of the story. Ask them to evaluate whether his imagery is effective in helping them picture the city.

Sight	Sound	Touch
• watched the city slip beneath them • skyscrapers rise up like a grove of steel trees	• cars' engines • Whump! • Whooooey!	• landed on something hard and soft • just below the level of turbulent air

Monitor Comprehension

16  **LITERARY DEVICES**
To what does the author compare Lulu's wings? (beautiful, trustworthy machines) **How are her wings like machines?** (Possible response: They seem tireless and powerful.)

17 **CHARACTER'S MOTIVES**
Why does Lulu take Chester to the Statue of Liberty? (Possible responses: The view of New York City is so beautiful from there; Lulu is proud of her city.)

18 **PLOT: CONFLICT AND RESOLUTION**
Do you think Chester's conflict is beginning to be resolved? Explain. (Possible response: Yes. He doesn't feel so homesick anymore because he has found a place that reminds him of home and Lulu has shown him her favorite places in New York.)

19 **CONFIRM PREDICTIONS**
How does the story compare to your predictions about it? (Responses will vary.)

BELOW-LEVEL

National Symbols Tell students that the Statue of Liberty is a national symbol, or an object that represents beliefs that are important to many Americans. Explain that the Statue of Liberty, a gift from France, represents freedom and the tradition of welcoming immigrants. The statue stands near Ellis Island, which for many years was the main immigration station on the East Coast of the United States.

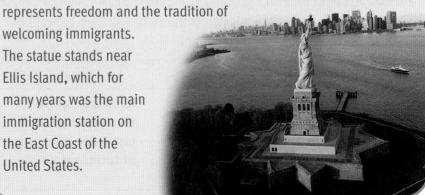

With a gasp and an even tighter hold on her feathers, Chester realized that they'd flown right over the end of Manhattan. There was dark churning water below them. And this was no tame little lake, like the one in Central Park. It was the great deep wide bay that made New York such a mighty harbor. But Lulu showed no sign whatsoever of slowing. Her wings, like beautiful trustworthy machines, pumped on and on and on and on. **16**

At last, Chester saw where the pigeon was heading. On a little island, off to the right, Chester made out the form of a very big lady. Her right hand was holding something up. Of course it was the Statue of Liberty, but Chester had no way of knowing that. In the Old Meadow in Connecticut he never had gone to school—at least not to a school where the pupils use books. His teacher back there had been Nature herself.

Lulu landed at the base of the statue, puffing and panting to get back her breath. She told him a little bit about the lady—a gift from the country of France, it was, and very precious to America—but she hadn't flown him all that way just to give him a history lesson.

"Hop on again, Chester C.!" she commanded—and up they flew to the torch that the lady was holding. Lulu found a perch on the north side of it, so the wind from the south wouldn't bother them.

"Now, just look around!" said Lulu proudly, as if all of New York belonged to her. "And don't anybody ever tell *this* pigeon that there's a more beautiful sight in the world." **17**

Chester did as he was told. He first peered behind. There was Staten Island. And off to the left, New Jersey. To the right, quite a long way away, was Brooklyn. And back across the black water, with a dome of light glowing over it, the heart of the city—Manhattan. **18 19**

629

Additional Related Reading

Students interested in New York's landmarks or Chester Cricket's other adventures may want to locate these titles.

- *The Brooklyn Bridge: The Story of the World's Most Famous Bridge and the Remarkable Family That Built It* by Elizabeth Mann. Mikaya, 2006.
  EASY

- *Liberty* by Lynn Curlee. Aladdin, 2003.
  AVERAGE

- *Chester Cricket's New Home* by George Selden. Random House, 1984.
  CHALLENGE

ANALYZE AUTHOR'S PURPOSE

Author's Purpose Remind students that authors have a purpose, or reason, for writing. After students have finished reading, ask them:

Why did the author write "Chester Cricket's Pigeon Ride"?

- to entertain readers with an exciting story
- **to explain why pigeons are such good fliers**
- **to persuade readers to take a flying tour of New York City**
- **to inform readers about the Empire State Building**

Think **Critically**

Respond to the Literature

Have students discuss or write their responses to the questions on page 630.

1 Possible response: He is homesick, and he is rather curious about the city. He is also polite and doesn't want to refuse Lulu's kind offer. **CHARACTER'S MOTIVES**

2 Possible response: It is personification. The author means that the brook is making noises that sound like human speech as it splashes over the rocks. **LITERARY DEVICES**

3 Possible response: She loves New York City. She is very excited about the opportunity to show Chester her favorite places. **CHARACTER'S EMOTIONS**

4 Responses will vary. **PERSONAL RESPONSE**

5 ✏️ **WRITE** Students should identify the locations Chester and Lulu visit, describe Chester's emotional response to each, and support their answer with information from the text. **EXTENDED RESPONSE**

RUBRIC For additional support in scoring this item, see the rubric on p. R6.

Think Critically

1 Why does Chester Cricket decide to go for a ride with Lulu? CHARACTER'S MOTIVES

2 The author writes that in Central Park there is *a brook that was arguing with itself*. What kind of figurative language is this, and what does it mean? 🐚 LITERARY DEVICES

3 How does Lulu feel about New York City? How do you know? CHARACTER'S EMOTIONS

4 Lulu is very outgoing, and Chester is quiet and timid. Which character are you more like? Explain. PERSONAL RESPONSE

5 **WRITE** How does Chester feel about each of the places where Lulu takes him? Use information from the story to support your answer. ✏️ EXTENDED RESPONSE

630

BELOW-LEVEL

Think and Search Explain to students that question 5 is a **Think and Search** question. To answer the question, students should look back at the story to recall the places that Chester visits. Then they should think about how he feels in each place and use this information to plan their response.

You may want to have students mark with self-stick notes the different portions of text that contain part of the answer.

About the Author

George Selden

Like Chester Cricket, George Selden came from Connecticut. In New York City, he heard a cricket chirp in the subway, and immediately had an idea. "The story formed in my mind within minutes," he said. "An author is very thankful for minutes like those, although they happen all too infrequently." George Selden wanted his readers to be able to connect with the animal characters he created. To make this possible, he gave his characters emotions and feelings similar to those of real people.

About the Illustrator

Garth Williams

Garth Williams grew up in a family of artists. "Everybody in my house was always either painting or drawing," he said. "So I thought there was nothing else to do in life but make pictures."

Garth Williams spent a lot of time studying the animals he drew in his books. He said, "I start with the real animal, working over and over until I can get the effect of human qualities and expression and poses."

www.harcourtschool.com/storytown

Check Comprehension

Retell and Summarize

DISCUSS AUTHOR: PAGE 631 Have students read the author information on page 631. Discuss how the author and illustrator worked to help readers connect with the animal characters.

RETELL Students may refer to the story map on *Practice Book* page 141 to help them retell "Chester Cricket's Pigeon Ride."

Routine Card 4 **WRITE A SUMMARY** Ask students to write a summary of "Chester Cricket's Pigeon Ride." Remind them to

- include the title of the story.
- identify the characters and setting.
- state the conflict.
- retell the most important plot events in sequence.
- state the resolution.

RUBRIC See rubric for Retelling and Summarizing on page R3.

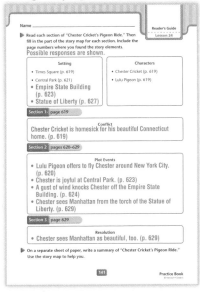

▲ Practice Book, p. 141

 MONITOR PROGRESS

Summarize

IF students have difficulty writing a complete summary,	**THEN** work with them to list the places Chester and Lulu visit on their wild ride.

Small-Group Instruction, p. S32:

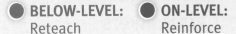 **BELOW-LEVEL:** Reteach   **ON-LEVEL:** Reinforce   **ADVANCED:** Extend

SOCIAL STUDIES

Paired Selection

Objectives
- *To read and understand a variety of texts*
- *To recognize the uses of language in literature*

Genre Study

PREVIEW THE POEM Have students preview the poem by reading the title and looking at the illustrations. Ask students to predict what kinds of activities people do in Central Park.

MODEL RHYTHMIC LANGUAGE IN POETRY Model the rhythmic language in the poem by reading it aloud to students. Then have them join you as you read the poem again.

ANALYZE THE POEM Ask students what the mood of the poem is. (Possible responses: joyful, lively, active) Have students identify words and phrases that create a joyful or lively feeling. Then discuss how the rhythm also helps communicate the poem's mood.

Social Studies

New York City

Poetry

Central Park

by John J. Bonk   illustrated by Cheryl Cooper

Whisk me away to a tree-covered world
 and surround me with nothing but
  green.
Squawking ducks in a lake, and long walks
 we could take,
Where the air is all dewy and clean.

Pack up a lunch and we'll picnic till dusk
 on a hill overlooking a stream.
In the distance the sound of a merry-go-
  round.
Faces covered with smiles and ice cream.

ELL

Nouns and Verbs Read aloud the line *Joggers jog, hikers hike, skaters skate, bikers bike.* Explain that the poet has used these noun and verb pairs to create rhythm and rhyme in the poem. Tell students that *-er* is a suffix that can mean "one who." (For example, a jogger is one who jogs.)

Have students make a list of the noun and verb pairs the poet uses. Encourage students to suggest others he could have used, such as *riders ride* and *walkers walk.*

jog + ers = joggers
hike + ers = hikers

Kick off your shoes and we'll tickle our toes
    as we frolic through crispy tall grass.
Then we'll rest for a bit, find a nice bench
    and sit,
As we watch all the passersby pass.

Horses clop by pulling tourist-filled carriages
    driven by men in top hats.
Sweethearts stroll hand in hand toward the
    souvenir stand.
Muddy kids lug their baseballs and bats.

People on skateboards, and babies in
    buggies,
    and grandmothers having long talks.
Joggers jog, hikers hike, skaters skate, bikers
    bike,
Barking dogs take their owners for walks.

Artists at easels are capturing scenery,
    sunbathers soak up the sun.
Little children aglow at a free puppet show,
Crowds are cheering a marathon run.

633

Apply Comprehension Strategies

Answer Questions

IDENTIFY QUESTION-ANSWER RELATION-SHIPS Ask: **What are some things people enjoy doing in Central Park?** (Possible responses: picnicking, resting, strolling, exercising, talking, sunbathing, watching puppet shows, cheering) **What kind of Question-Answer Relationship is this?** (Think and Search) If students have difficulty answering, model the strategy:

> Think Aloud **This is a *Think and Search* question because the author lists activities people do in Central Park throughout the poem.**

Respond to the Poem

Ask students to read the poem silently and to think about the pictures that the words create in their minds as they read. Then ask:

1. **AUTHOR'S PERSPECTIVE If you asked the poet how he felt about Central Park, what do you think he would say?** (Possible responses: It's a great place to visit; it has many things to do.) **How does the poet's perspective influence the poem?** (Possible response: Since the poet likes Central Park, he only mentions the positive, fun, and interesting aspects of it.)

2. *(Focus Skill)* **LITERARY DEVICES What type of figurative language is "Faraway skyscrapers seem to be stretching their necks for a peek in the park"? What does it mean?** (personification; the skyscrapers are being compared to curious people.)

3. *(SOCIAL STUDIES)* **CONNECTING TEXTS How would an article about Central Park in a social studies textbook be different from this poem?** (Possible response: A textbook article would give facts about the park and its history. The poem describes what the park means to people.)

634

BELOW-LEVEL

Sequence Help students see that the poet has organized the descriptions of the activities in Central Park in chronological order, beginning in the late morning and ending in the late evening. Help students construct a simple time line of the day's events.

late morning: arrive at the park
noon: picnic on a hill
afternoon: frolic, rest, watch people go by, free puppet show, marathon, musicians
early evening: riders return to stables, bird-watchers quit, hot dog vendors roll away
night: concert, play, fireworks, thunderstorm, good-bye

People applaud for a man with a saxophone
    playing a medley of tunes.
Toss some coins in his case, watch it light
    up his face,
And we'll spend all the rest on balloons.

Faraway skyscrapers seem to be stretching
    their necks
    for a peek in the park.
They pop over the trees just as if to say,
    "Please,
Hurry home now before it gets dark!"

Riders on horseback head back to the stables,
    and bird watchers call it a day.
Games of chess disappear as the evening
    grows near.
Hot dog vendors are rolling away.

Wait, not so fast! There are still things to see
    like an outdoor Shakespearean play.
There are concerts at night under stars and
    moonlight,
Ending under a fireworks display.

Shaking the ground comes a rumbling of
    thunder
    and lightning is piercing the sky.
Grab your stuff! Better run! We've had
    nothing but fun.
But for now, Central Park, it's good-bye!

635

Write a Poem

Have students write a poem about a place in their community. Suggest that they use the verses in "Central Park" as models. Tell students to use figurative language in their poems, as well as rhythm to set a mood. After students finish writing, have volunteers read their poems aloud to the class or to small groups. **WRITING**

WRITER'S CRAFT

Rhythm Explain that one way that poets create rhythm is by using a variety of sentence lengths and types. Point out that following the longer line "shaking the ground comes a rumbling of /thunder/ and lightning is piercing the sky." with the shorter lines "Grab your stuff! Better run! We've had /nothing but fun." changes the tempo of the poem and creates a sense of urgency. Have students give examples of other places where the poet varied his sentence length.

Comparing Texts

Answers:

1. Responses will vary. **TEXT TO SELF**

2. Possible response: Both George Selden and John J. Bonk use figurative language that appeals to the senses to help readers picture Central Park. **TEXT TO TEXT**

3. Possible response: A friend like Lulu would help someone get to know a new place so it wouldn't feel too strange. Also, a new friend would help someone feel less lonely or homesick. **TEXT TO WORLD**

Connections

Comparing Texts

1. On Chester's first flight, he feels the thrill of excitement and fear "all jumbled together wonderfully." Describe a time when you felt that way.

2. Compare how George Selden and John J. Bonk use figurative language to describe Central Park.

3. Why might someone who is moving to a new place feel at ease after meeting a friend like Lulu?

Vocabulary Review

Rate a Situation

With a partner, read aloud each sentence below. Point to a spot on the line to show how happy you would feel in each situation. Explain your choices.

Least Happy ——————————————— Most Happy

- Your airplane ride is **turbulent**.
- The swim meet is the **pinnacle** of your summer.
- You must stop your **excursions** to the park.
- You feel **giddy** after winning a contest.

| excursions |
| giddy |
| pinnacle |
| gleeful |
| panic |
| turbulent |
| precious |

636

Fluency Practice

Repeated Reading

Read the passage on page 629 that begins, "Lulu landed at the base of the statue." Pay careful attention to your pace, matching it to the action of the story. Read the passage several times until you feel you have the correct pace. Then read the passage aloud to a partner.

Writing

Write a Journal Entry

Imagine that Chester Cricket is flying over your city or town for the first time. Write a journal entry that describes Chester's experience of flying over your city.

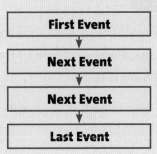

My Writing Checklist

Writing Trait ▸ Organization

✓ I organized the information sequentially.

✓ I used a graphic organizer to plan my journal entry.

✓ I used the correct format for a journal entry.

```
First Event
   ↓
Next Event
   ↓
Next Event
   ↓
Last Event
```

637

 ● **VOCABULARY REVIEW** ●

Rate a Situation Have students work with a partner to rate each situation. Before students begin, you may want to help them decide which words are generally positive and which words are generally negative. Ask them to explain their rankings.

 FLUENCY PRACTICE

Repeated Reading: Pace Tell students to pay attention to events in the story and to use them to guide their pace. After they have practiced reading the passage individually, have them take turns reading and giving feedback on the pace at which their partner reads the story. Encourage students to be specific when providing feedback. *For additional fluency practice, see p. T258.*

 WRITING

Write a Journal Entry Tell students to draw a chart like the one on *Student Edition* page 637 to plan their writing. Tell students to include at least one type of figurative language in their entry. Have students use the checklist to evaluate their writing.

PORTFOLIO OPPORTUNITY Students may choose to place their journal entries in their portfolios.

✓ **MONITOR PROGRESS**

Vocabulary Review

IF students have difficulty rating the situations, | **THEN** paraphrase each situation and have students explain how they would feel and why, and then review with students the Student-Friendly Explanations on **Transparency R104**. (See page T231.)

Small-Group Instruction, pp. S30–S31:

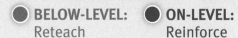 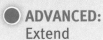

● **BELOW-LEVEL:** Reteach   ● **ON-LEVEL:** Reinforce   ● **ADVANCED:** Extend

Literary Devices

Objectives

- *To recognize and understand literary devices*
- *To identify and use sensory language*

Skill Trace

 Tested **Literary Devices**

Introduce	pp. T166–T167
Reteach	pp. S20–S21, S28–S29
Review	**pp. T192–T193, T226–T227, T254–T255, T309**
Test	Theme 5
Maintain	p. T144, Theme 6

BELOW-LEVEL

Write the following sentences on the board. Guide students to identify the type of figurative language each represents. Point out signal words, such as *like*.

- Lulu flew like a jet. (simile)

- The wind treated them rudely. (personification)

- The streets were a river of moving people. (metaphor)

Reinforce the Skill

REVIEW FIGURATIVE LANGUAGE Remind students that authors often use literary devices such as figurative language to make their writing more interesting and colorful. Review these forms of figurative language with students:

- **simile:** a comparison that uses *like* or *as*

- **metaphor:** a comparison that talks about one thing as if it were another, without using *like* or *as*

- **personification:** a description that gives human qualities to animals or objects

Guided Practice

APPLY TO LITERATURE Have students reread these passages in the *Student Edition*. Ask students to find at least one example of figurative language in each passage and tell what kind it is.

- **Page 624, paragraph 2** ("'They look just like bugs!'"—simile; "And the cars, the buses, the yellow taxis, all jittered along like miniatures."—simile)

- **Page 624, next-to-last paragraph** ("The gleeful wind was playing with him."—personification)

- **Page 626, paragraph 6** (". . . where the air was friendly and gently buoyed them up."—personification)

- **Page 627, last paragraph** (". . . where a cluster of skyscrapers rise up like a grove of steel trees."—simile)

- **Page 629, paragraph 2** ("His teacher back there had been Nature herself."—personification or metaphor)

Practice/Apply

RECOGNIZE FIGURATIVE LANGUAGE Have students choose a passage from a fiction story they have already read, or have them revisit the poem "Central Park." Then ask students to find at least two examples of figurative language in the passage or poem and tell what type each is, along with its meaning. Ask them to record this information in a chart.

Example	Type of Figurative Language	Meaning

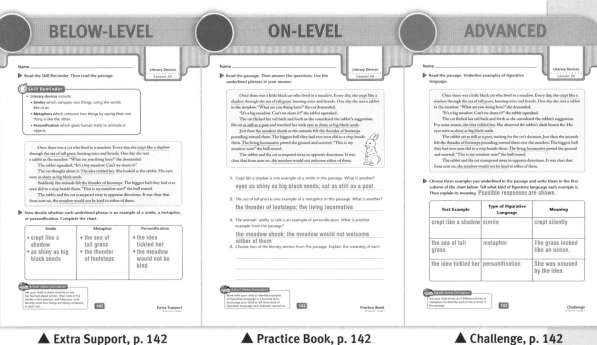

▲ Extra Support, p. 142   ▲ Practice Book, p. 142   ▲ Challenge, p. 142

ELL

- Group students according to academic levels, and assign one of the pages on the left.

- Clarify any unfamiliar concepts as necessary. See *ELL Teacher Guide* Lesson 24 for support in scaffolding instruction.

Draw Conclusions

Objectives

- *To draw conclusions about text information*
- *To support conclusions with text evidence and personal experience*

Skill Trace

 Tested **Draw Conclusions**

Introduce	pp. T134–T135
Reteach	pp. S16–S17
Review	**pp. T256, T311**
Test	Theme 5
Maintain	p. T209, Theme 6

Reinforce the Skill

REVIEW DRAW CONCLUSIONS Remind students that because authors do not explain everything in stories, readers must figure out some things for themselves. Review the steps in drawing a conclusion:

- Begin with the information given in the story.
- Think about what you know from real life about the topic.
- Combine the story information and your prior knowledge.

Practice/Apply

GUIDED PRACTICE Write the following question on the board: **How would you describe Lulu Pigeon's character traits?**

Point out that the author doesn't tell readers what Lulu is like; he uses details such as Lulu's words and actions to help them draw conclusions about her. Write on the board a chart like the one below and work with students to fill it in, using details from the story and what they know about people.

Lulu's Traits		
Text Clues	**What I Know**	**Conclusions**
Chester is tired, but Lulu wants to continue the tour.	Hardworking people keep on going.	energetic
She tries to make Chester feel better and offers to show him the sights.	Kind people always try to help.	compassionate
She goes around and around the Empire State Building until she sees Chester and catches him.	Persistent people don't give up.	determined

INDEPENDENT PRACTICE Have students choose a piece of narrative fiction or narrative nonfiction they have read recently. Ask students to use text information and their own knowledge to draw a conclusion about one or more characters or events in the narrative.

Decoding/Word Attack
Structural Analysis: Unusual Plurals

Reinforce the Skill

Routine Card 5

DECODE LONGER WORDS Write the word pairs *cricket/crickets,* *beech/beeches,* and *mystery/mysteries* on the board, and read them aloud. Tell students that *-s* and *-es* are inflections that are added to words to make them plural. Then point out that

- the ending *-es* forms its own syllable when it follows a consonant.
- in words that end in a consonant plus *y,* the *y* changes to *i* when *-es* is added.
- in many words that end in *f* or *fe,* the *f* changes to *v* when *-es* is added. The /f/ sound becomes /v/ and the *-es* ending is pronounced /z/.

Practice/Apply

GUIDED PRACTICE Display the following words. Guide students to divide each word into syllables, read it aloud, and tell whether the ending forms its own syllable. Have them write the words in a chart like the one below.

wishes	scratches	miniatures	buildings	feelers	knives
wish-es	scratch-es	min-i-a-tures	build-ings	feel-ers	knives

Ending adds a syllable	Ending does not add a syllable	
wishes	miniatures	feelers
scratches	buildings	knives

INDEPENDENT PRACTICE Have students look through their *Student Edition* and find six examples of words with the *-s* or *-es* ending. Have students pronounce each word and write it in the chart under the appropriate heading.

Objective
- *To decode longer words with unusual plurals*

Skill Trace
Structural Analysis: Unusual Plurals

Introduce	Grade 2
Maintain	p. T257

▲ Phonics Practice Book, pp. 25–26

Lesson 24 • **T257**

Fluency: Pace

15 Min. each

Objectives
- *To read fantasies with grade-appropriate fluency*
- *To read aloud with prosody, using appropriate pace*

MONITOR PROGRESS

Partner Reading

IF students need more support in building fluency and in reading at an appropriate pace,	THEN have them echo-read with you, paying close attention to how ideas and events in the story affect the pace.

Small-Group Instruction, p. S33:

- ● **BELOW-LEVEL:** Reteach
- ● **ON-LEVEL:** Reinforce
- ● **ADVANCED:** Extend

Fluency Support Materials

Fluency Builders, Grade 5, Lesson 24

Audiotext *Student Edition* selections are available on *Audiotext Grade 5,* CD8.

Strategic Intervention Teacher Guide, Lesson 24

CHORAL-READ

 Routine Card 6

MODEL PACE Model appropriate pace by reading aloud the passage on *Student Edition* page 622. Tell students to follow along. Then read the passage again. Tell students to pay attention to how you increase or decrease your reading pace, based on what is happening in the story. Then have students choral-read the passage with you.

ECHO-READ

Routine Card 7

TRACK PRINT Have students echo-read the passage on *Student Edition* page 622.

- Ask students to put their finger on the beginning of the first sentence.
- Read the sentence aloud as students track the print.
- Have students read the sentence aloud, matching your pace.
- Continue through the rest of the passage.

If students do not read the passage with appropriate pace, work with them to identify places where they should speed up or slow down. Then have them read the passage at least three more times or until they can read it fluently at an appropriate pace.

PARTNER READING

 Routine Card 8

READ WITH A PARTNER Pair strong readers with students who need fluency support. Have the strong reader read aloud *Student Edition* page 626, while the partner listens and notes places where the reader sped up and slowed down. Then have partners switch roles.

 Routine Card 9

Use the sentence frames on *Routine Card 9* to model for students how to give feedback. Ask them to provide each other with feedback about pace.

Have partners read the complete page to each other again. Encourage students to give each other positive feedback about how their pace improved from the first to the second reading.

"RESEARCH SAYS"

"Repeated reading provides students with the necessary practice to build fluency, acquire new information, and maintain established information."

—O'Shea, Sindelan, & O'Shea (1985)

Enriching Robust Vocabulary

15 Min. each

5-DAY VOCABULARY

DAY 1	Vocabulary, pp. T231–T233
DAY 2	Vocabulary Review, p. T253
DAY 3	Reinforce Word Meanings, p. T259
DAY 4	Extend Word Meanings, p. T259
DAY 5	Cumulative Review, p. T259

REINFORCE WORD MEANINGS

Objective
• *To demonstrate knowledge of word meanings*

REVISIT SELECTION VOCABULARY
Have students discuss "Chester Cricket's Pigeon Ride" by responding to these questions.

1. On what kind of **excursion** did Lulu take Chester?

2. Why did Chester feel **giddy** on his ride?

3. What could Lulu and Chester see as they perched on the **pinnacle** of the Empire State Building?

4. Why did the sight of Central Park make Chester feel **gleeful**?

5. What situation caused Chester to feel **panic**?

6. On the way to the Statue of Liberty, why did Lulu fly below the level of **turbulent** air?

7. What monument did Lulu describe as **precious** to Americans?

EXTEND WORD MEANINGS

Objective
• *To extend meanings of words in context*

CRITICAL THINKING Have students answer the following questions. Have them explain their answers, and encourage discussion.

1. What is one thing that is **precious** to you?

2. Would you want to go rafting on a **turbulent** river? Explain.

3. What might make you **gleeful** on a rainy day?

4. What kind of **excursions** are fun to go on on your own?

5. What would make you feel **giddy**?

6. Why is it wise not to **panic** in an emergency?

7. What kinds of natural geographic features have a **pinnacle**?

CUMULATIVE REVIEW

Objective
• *To use word relationships to determine meaning*

REVIEW VOCABULARY Discuss students' answers to these questions.

1. Why might **bustling** around, preparing for an **excursion**, make you feel **giddy**?

2. Would you feel **desolate** if you failed to reach the **pinnacle** of a mountain?

3. If someone cleaned a room with **fervor**, would he or she feel **gleeful** if someone said the room was **immaculate**? Explain.

4. What might you say to **assuage** someone's **panic** on a **turbulent** airplane ride?

5. How would you feel if you **gouged** a **precious** object?

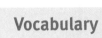

Vocabulary

Lesson 23		Lesson 24	
bustles	immaculate	excursions	panic
desolate	assuage	giddy	turbulent
fervor	gouges	pinnacle	precious
		gleeful	

Spelling: Words with Unusual Plurals

Objective
- *To spell correctly words with unusual plural forms*

Spelling Words

1. addresses	11. radios
2. armies	12. halves
3. calves	13. hooves
4. countries	14. knives
5. leaves*	15. taxes
6. buses*	16. tomatoes
7. videos	17. opportunities
8. echoes	18. volcanoes
9. shelves	19. stitches
10. studios	20. wolves

Challenge Words

21. tornadoes	24. vetoes
22. patios	25. crises
23. quizzes	

*Words from "Chester Cricket's Pigeon Ride"

Day 1 — PRETEST/SELF-CHECK

Routine Card 10

ADMINISTER THE PRE-TEST Use the Dictation Sentences under Day 5. Help students self-check their pre-tests, using **Transparency LA153.**

Allow time for students to study the words they misspelled. Have them use the steps *Say, Look, Spell, Write, Check.*

ADVANCED

Challenge Words Provide these Dictation Sentences:

21. **Tornadoes** cause great damage.

22. The houses have **patios**.

23. We took two **quizzes** this week.

24. The mayor's **vetoes** made some people angry.

25. Your quick thinking prevented a number of **crises**.

Day 2 — TEACH/MODEL

WORD SORT Display **Transparency LA153.** Discuss the meanings of the Spelling Words as necessary. Then have students copy and complete the chart from the transparency.

Write the word *radios* on the board. Tell students that this plural was formed by adding *s* to the word *radio*. Repeat with *taxes, armies,* and *leaves*. Ask students to tell the letters that were added to each word to change it to a plural.

HANDWRITING Demonstrate how to bring the first upstroke of the letter s to a point so that the *s* doesn't look like an *a*.

addresses

▲ Practice Book, p. 143

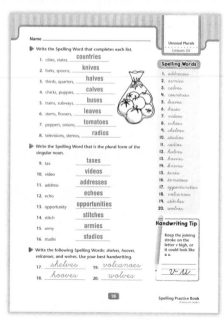

▲ Spelling Practice Book, p. 96

SPELLING CHALLENGE Have small groups of 4 to 6 students choose 10 Spelling Words and write them on a sheet of paper. Have one team challenge another team to spell one of the words on their list. Teams get a point for every correctly spelled word. Have teams take turns challenging one another.

armies
leaves
videos
echoes
studios
halves
hooves
tomatoes
wolves

▲ Spelling Practice Book, p. 97

COMPARING SPELLINGS Write the following sentences on the board:

**Jon did research on (wolfs/wolves).
I don't like (tomatoes/tomatos).**

Ask students to compare the spellings of the words in parentheses and determine which spelling is correct. Tell students that if they are unsure of how to spell a word, they can try different spellings and then compare to see which one looks correct.

APPLY TO WRITING

PROOFREADING Have students look for unusual plurals in a piece of writing they have completed recently. Tell students to use the strategy of comparing spellings to make sure that they have spelled each plural form correctly.

▲ Spelling Practice Book, p. 98

DICTATION SENTENCES

1. The guests' **addresses** have been updated.
2. The **armies** prepared for battle.
3. There are two **calves** in the barn.
4. We plan to visit several **countries** in Central America.
5. Dan swept the **leaves** from the driveway.
6. The **buses** will arrive at noon.
7. Please return the **videos**.
8. I heard the **echoes** of voices.
9. Please put the books on the **shelves**.
10. The dance **studios** are on the same street.
11. Kyle has two **radios** in his room.
12. Helene cut the apple into **halves**.
13. You must sometimes clean a horse's **hooves**.
14. Please handle the **knives** carefully.
15. Our **taxes** are due in April.
16. I grew **tomatoes** this year.
17. We had several **opportunities** to visit the park.
18. Those **volcanoes** are inactive.
19. The **stitches** of the hem ripped.
20. I heard **wolves** howling.

Writing Trait: Organization
Narrative

15 Min. each

Objectives
- *To organize a story in chronological order*
- *To write a narrative*

Writing Trait ▶ **Organizations**

- Characters, setting, and conflict are introduced in the beginning
- Events in the middle are told in order
- Ends with a satisfying conclusion

Grammar for Writing

As students revise their narratives, note whether they need additional support with these skills:

- **Complete, Declarative, and Interrogative Sentences,** pp. T70–T71, Theme 1
- **Common and Proper Nouns,** pp. T68–T69, Theme 3
- **Punctuation Round-up,** pp. T282–T283, Theme 6
- **Perfect Tenses,** pp. T264–T265, Theme 5

Writer's Companion Grade 5

▲ **Writer's Companion, Lesson 24**

Day 1 — TEACH/MODEL

ORGANIZATION Tell students that writers of fictional narratives organize their story lines in a way that is easy for readers to follow. The characters, setting, and conflict are introduced at the beginning. The important story events are told in sequence, and the story ends with a satisfying conclusion.

ANALYZE THE MENTOR TEXT Display **Transparency LA156** and read the text aloud. Point out the way the author organized events in the order in which they occurred. Then point out the signal words the author used to help readers recognize the order of events. Guide students to complete the graphic organizer.

Mentor Text: Organization

from "Chester Cricket's Pigeon Ride" by George Selden

p. 624

And just at that moment, two bad things happened. The first was, Chester caught sight of an airplane swooping low to land at LaGuardia Airport across the East River. The dip of it made his dizziness worse. And the second—worse yet—a sudden gust of wind sprang up, as if a hand gave them both a push. Lulu almost fell off the Empire State.

Lulu *almost* fell off—but Chester *did*! In an instant his legs and feelers were torn away from the pigeon's leg, and before he could say 'Old meadow, farewell!' he was tumbling down through the air. One moment the city appeared above him—that meant he was upside down; then under him—he was right side up; then everything slid from side to side.

> First, the sight of an airplane makes Chester dizzier.

> Then a wind springs up.

> Last, Chester falls off the Empire State Building.

Grade 5, Lesson 24   **LA156**   Writing: Mentor Text

Transparency LA156

Day 2 — PRACTICE/APPLY

ANALYZE THE STUDENT MODEL Display **Transparency LA157.** Tell students that this is the beginning of one student's fictional narrative. Have a volunteer read the composition aloud. Point out that the writer organized the composition by introducing the characters, setting, and conflict. Then the writer tells in order the steps the characters take to resolve the conflict. Have students complete the sequence chart to show the steps in Penny's plan. Tell them to use the signal words to help them.

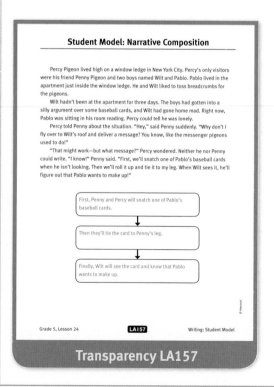

Student Model: Narrative Composition

Percy Pigeon lived high on a window ledge in New York City. Percy's only visitors were his friend Penny Pigeon and two boys named Wilt and Pablo. Pablo lived in the apartment just inside the window ledge. He and Wilt liked to toss breadcrumbs for the pigeons.

Wilt hadn't been at the apartment for three days. The boys had gotten into a silly argument over some baseball cards, and Wilt had gone home mad. Right now, Pablo was sitting in his room reading. Percy could tell he was lonely.

Percy told Penny about the situation. "Hey," said Penny suddenly. "Why don't I fly over to Wilt's roof and deliver a message? You know, like the messenger pigeons used to do!"

"That might work—but what message?" Percy wondered. Neither he nor Penny could write. "I know!" Penny said. "First, we'll snatch one of Pablo's baseball cards when he isn't looking. Then we'll roll it up and tie it to my leg. When Wilt sees it, he'll figure out that Pablo wants to make up!"

> First, Penny and Percy will snatch one of Pablo's baseball cards.

> Then they'll tie the card to Penny's leg.

> Finally, Wilt will see the card and know that Pablo wants to make up.

Grade 5, Lesson 24   **LA157**   Writing: Student Model

Transparency LA157

THEME 5 WRITING		
Reading-Writing Connection	Persuasive Composition	Sentence Fluency
LESSON	**FORM**	**TRAIT**
21	Persuasive Letter	Sentence Fluency
22	Persuasive Paragraph	Sentence Fluency
23	Poetry	Organization
24	**Narrative**	**Organization**
25 REVIEW	Revise and Publish	Sentence Fluency/Organization

Day 3 PREWRITE

WRITING PROMPT Display **Transparency LA158** and read aloud the prompt for Day 3 to students. Have students use a graphic organizer like the one below to organize their story. Then have them think about signal words they could use to show the order of events.

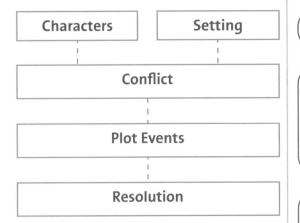

Characters	Setting

Conflict

Plot Events

Resolution

Transparency LA158

Day 4 DRAFT

BEGIN TO DRAFT Have students follow these steps to draft their narratives.

1. **Introduce** the setting, the characters, and a conflict at the beginning of the story.

2. **Organize** events in sequence.

3. **Develop** characters, setting, and plot events through strong supporting details, including figurative language.

4. **Conclude** by suggesting how the conflict may be resolved.

NOTE: A 4-point rubric appears on page R8.

Day 5 REVISE AND REFLECT

PEER CONFERENCE CHECKLIST Have pairs of students use this checklist to discuss their narratives.

• Does the narrative include a setting, characters, and a conflict?

• Are events organized in sequence?

• Are there signal words to show the order of events?

• Are there enough supporting details, including figurative language, to help form mental pictures of the setting, characters, and plot events?

• Has the writer used perfect-tense verbs correctly?

Students may want to keep their revised narratives in their work portfolios.

SCORING RUBRIC

	6	5	4	3	2	1
FOCUS	Completely focused, purposeful.	Focused on topic and purpose.	Generally focused on topic and purpose.	Somewhat focused on topic and purpose.	Related to topic but does not maintain focus.	Lacks focus and purpose.
ORGANIZATION	Ideas progress logically; paper conveys sense of completeness.	Organization mostly clear; paper gives sense of completeness.	Organization mostly clear, but some lapses occur; may seem unfinished.	Some sense of organization; seems unfinished.	Little sense of organization.	Little or no sense of organization.
SUPPORT	Strong, specific details; clear, exact language; freshness of expression.	Strong, specific details; clear, exact language.	Adequate support and word choice.	Limited supporting details; limited word choice.	Few supporting details; limited word choice.	Little development; limited or unclear word choice.
CONVENTIONS	Varied sentences; few, if any, errors.	Varied sentences; few errors.	Some sentence variety; few errors.	Simple sentence structures; some errors.	Simple sentence structures; many errors.	Unclear sentence structures; many errors.

REPRODUCIBLE RUBRIC appears on page R7.

Lesson 24 • T263

Grammar: Verbs
Perfect Tenses

Objectives
- *To use perfect-tense verbs correctly in speaking and writing*
- *To conjugate verbs correctly*

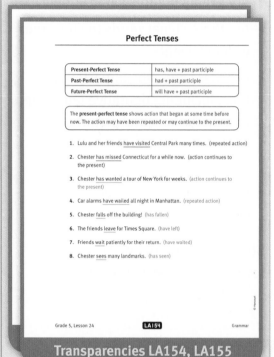

Perfect Tenses

Present-Perfect Tense	has, have + past participle
Past-Perfect Tense	had + past participle
Future-Perfect Tense	will have + past participle

The **present-perfect tense** shows action that began at some time before now. The action may have been repeated or may continue to the present.

1. Lulu and her friends <u>have visited</u> Central Park many times. (repeated action)
2. Chester <u>has missed</u> Connecticut for a while now. (action continues to the present)
3. Chester <u>has wanted</u> a tour of New York for weeks. (action continues to the present)
4. Car alarms <u>have wailed</u> all night in Manhattan. (repeated action)
5. Chester <u>falls</u> off the building! (has fallen)
6. The friends <u>leave</u> for Times Square. (have left)
7. Friends <u>wait</u> patiently for their return. (have waited)
8. Chester <u>sees</u> many landmarks. (has seen)

Grade 5, Lesson 24   **LA154**   Grammar

Transparencies LA154, LA155

Language Structures Help students understand how the present tense differs from the present-perfect tense by using this model:

I <u>walk</u> to school every day.

I <u>have walked</u> to school all year.

See *ELL Teacher Guide* Lesson 24 for support in scaffolding instruction.

Day 1 TEACH/MODEL

DAILY PROOFREADING

1. Lulu will takes Chester to Central Park? (will take; Park.)
2. We will goes to new york city. (will go; New York City.)

INTRODUCE THE CONCEPT Display **Transparency LA154** and read the information in the box. Tell students that in sentence 1, the present perfect is formed with the helping verb *have* and the past participle of the verb *visit*. In sentence 2, the present perfect is formed with the helping verb *has* and the past participle of the verb *miss*. Point out that the action in sentence 1 is repeated and the action in sentence 2 continues to the present.

Have students identify the present-perfect-tense verbs in sentences 3 and 4 and explain whether the action is repeated or continues to the present. Then ask students to rewrite sentences 5–8, changing each verb from the present tense to the present-perfect tense.

✓ LANGUAGE ARTS CHECKPOINT

If students have difficulty with the concepts, see pages S34–S35 to reteach.

Day 2 TEACH/MODEL

DAILY PROOFREADING

3. They has flown over the cars and busses. (have flown; buses.)
4. Together, they have view New York Citys skyline. (have viewed; City's)

EXTEND THE CONCEPT Display **Transparency LA155** and read the top box. Explain that in sentence 1, *had taken* is in the past-perfect tense. In sentence 2, the word *never* comes between the helping verb *had* and the main verb *seen*. Tell students to rewrite sentences 3 and 4 in the past-perfect tense.

BUILD LANGUAGE STRUCTURES Have students complete these sentences.

- I _____ by the time school started.
- We _____ before the movie ended.

▲ Grammar Practice Book, p. 85

Day 3 — TEACH/MODEL

DAILY PROOFREADING

5. Will there be opportunitys for taking pictures? (opportunities)

6. We had tunes both radioes. (had tuned; radios.)

EXTEND THE CONCEPT Display **Transparency LA155**, and read the information in the second box. Point out the future-perfect tense verb and the time clue in sentence 5. Have students rewrite sentences 6–8, putting each verb in parentheses in the future-perfect tense. Then have students complete these sentence frames with a verb in the future-perfect tense.

I _____ by next week.

He _____ by the end of the year.

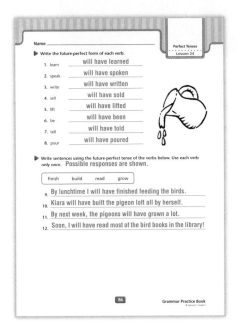

▲ Grammar Practice Book, p. 86

Day 4 — APPLY TO WRITING

DAILY PROOFREADING

7. Chester had never saw a lake glissen like that. (had never seen; glisten)

8. The leafs on the trees is changing. (leaves; are changing.)

FLYING OVER HOME Tell students to imagine that they are able to fly over their home city like Chester and Lulu flew over New York City. Have them write 5 sentences describing the experience. Ask them to use perfect tenses.

COMMON ERRORS

Error: We **been** here an hour.
Correct: We **have been** here an hour.

Error: By noon, they **had went** home.
Correct: By noon, they **had gone** home.

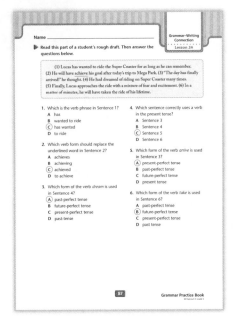

▲ Grammar Practice Book, p. 87

Day 5 — REVIEW

DAILY PROOFREADING

9. Chester will have watch the sun rise over downton. (watched; downtown.)

10. Chester had never enjoy such spontaneus travel before. (enjoyed; spontaneous)

PROOFREAD FOR CORRECT VERB TENSE Display the following sentences. Have students copy them and correct any errors.

1. The friends has gathered at the station. (have gathered or had gathered)

2. Chester has chirped for an hour before Mario came. (had chirped)

3. Lulu will had flown around the park many times this year. (will have flown)

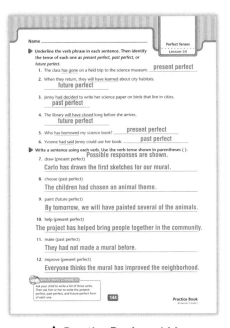

▲ Practice Book, p. 144

Speaking & Listening

SPEAKING

Present a Travel Description

Objectives
- *To effectively organize a speech*
- *To demonstrate effective communication skills*

Have students think about a trip they have taken or would like to take. Tell them that they will be presenting an oral description of this real or imaginary trip. Share these **organizational strategies**:

ORGANIZING CONTENT

- Start your travel description by naming the place you visited or would like to visit.
- Organize trip details in a logical sequence, such as the order in which you did or would do things.
- End with a statement that sums up the experience.

Before students present their travel descriptions, share with them the following **speaking strategies**:

SPEAKING STRATEGIES

- Practice presenting your travel description until you are familiar with the information.
- Use figurative and descriptive language to engage your audience.
- Prepare a visual aid and plan when and how you will display it.

Grand Canyon, Arizona

LISTENING

Listen to a Travel Description

Objectives
- *To listen attentively to the speaker*
- *To understand information presented orally*

Have students listen for vivid descriptions and examples of figurative language that the speaker may use. Share these **listening strategies** with students:

LISTENING STRATEGIES

- Pay close attention to the speaker.
- Try to visualize the places the speaker is describing.
- Look at the visual aid and connect it with the speaker's descriptions.
- Write down notes and questions that you would like to ask the speaker.

After speakers present their travel descriptions, have students in the audience ask questions for clarification. Then invite listeners to give the speaker feedback about which parts of the travel description they liked best.

RUBRIC

See rubric for Presentations on page R5.

Media Literacy

WEEKLY LESSON TEST

RESEARCH

Using Media to Locate Facts

Objective
- *To use criteria to choose different types of media*

DISCUSS MEDIA Tell students that if they wanted to learn more about a place that interests them, they could use different kinds of media to locate facts. Work with students to create a chart like the one below.

	News-papers	TV news	Internet	Nonfiction books
local weather news		✓	✓	
history			✓	✓
maps			✓	✓
movie schedules	✓		✓	

MODEL CHOOSING MEDIA Model selecting the right kind of media for specific tasks:

Think Aloud **If you want background information about a place, the Internet or a nonfiction book might give you the facts you need. Newspapers, TV news programs, and the Internet are good sources of current information.**

PRACTICE CHOOSING MEDIA Have students select the best form(s) of media to answer these questions:

- How do I get to the Statue of Liberty?
- Will it rain tonight?
- What is the history of Central Park?

- Selection Comprehension with Short Response
- Focus Skill
- Robust Vocabulary
- Draw Conclusions
- Grammar
- Fluency Passage *FRESH READS*
-  Podcasting: Assessing Fluency

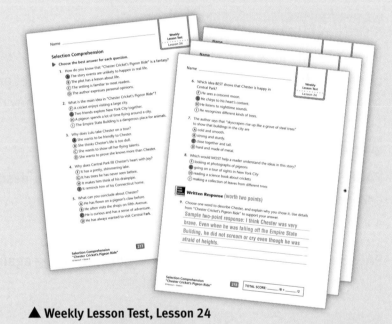

▲ Weekly Lesson Test, Lesson 24

GO online For prescriptions, see pp. A2–A6. Also available electronically on *StoryTown Online Assessment* and ExamView®.

Leveled Readers
Reinforcing Skills and Strategies

BELOW-LEVEL

Jar of Wings

SUMMARY Lewis the inchworm dreams of becoming a beautiful moth. When that day arrives, he wakes up to find himself in an interesting situation.

- **Literary Devices**
- **Answer Questions**
- **VOCABULARY:** *excursions, giddy, pinnacle, gleeful, panic, turbulent, precious*

Build Background/Set Purpose

Have students look at the book's cover and illustrations. Ask them what they can tell about the main characters. Remind students that answering questions while reading can help them better understand what they read.

Guided Reading

PAGE 5  **LITERARY DEVICES How does the author describe Jade in her cocoon?** (He uses the simile "wound tight as a mummy" to explain that she is completely encased, and her cocoon is wound tightly around her.)

PAGES 12–13 MAKE INFERENCES Why did Jade bang against Bella's screen? (She was trying to get inside to help Lewis escape.)

After Reading

Have students work in pairs to summarize the selection.

FLUENCY: PACE Have pairs of students take turns rereading a page from the book aloud. As they read, tell them to focus on their reading pace.

Think Critically *(See inside back cover for questions.)*

1. Cookie tells Lewis what happened to him and helps him escape.

2. She was interested in the cocoon and wanted to watch it open.

3. The author describes the moon as "a lone spotlight." This is effective because the moon can look like a solitary light in the sky.

4. Answers will vary.

5. Answers will vary.

LEVELED READER TEACHER GUIDE

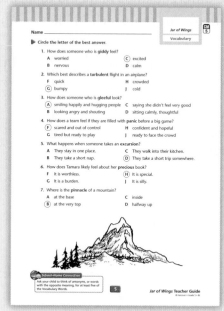

▲ Vocabulary, p. 5

▲ Comprehension, p. 6

www.harcourtschool.com/storytown

★ Leveled Readers Online Database
Searchable by Genre, Skill, Vocabulary, Level, or Title
★ Student Activities and Teacher Resources, *online*

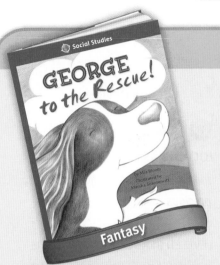

ON-LEVEL

George to the Rescue!

SUMMARY George tries to keep his friendship with Woody a secret, but when Woody has a problem, George needs the help of his friends.

- Literary Devices
- Answer Questions
- **VOCABULARY:** *excursions, giddy, pinnacle, gleeful, panic, turbulent, precious*

LEVELED READER TEACHER GUIDE

▲ Vocabulary, p. 5

Build Background/Set Purpose

Have students preview the book by reading the title and looking at the illustrations. Ask them to predict what they think the book is about. Remind them that answering questions can help clear up confusing ideas or concepts.

Guided Reading

PAGES 12–13 LITERARY DEVICES **How does the author help you picture the characters and events on pages 12–13?** (Comparing George's letdown to a deflating balloon helps you see how disappointed he is.)

PAGES 12–14 DRAW CONCLUSIONS **Do you think the raccoons will steal from the squirrels again?** (No. They're afraid of the dogs.)

After Reading

Have groups of students summarize "George to the Rescue!"

FLUENCY: PACE Have pairs of students take turns rereading a section of the book aloud. As students read, partners should give feedback on pace.

Think Critically *(See inside back cover for questions.)*

1. He thinks they will make fun of him for befriending a squirrel.

2. The other dogs admit they all have other animals as friends; they want to help George and Woody.

3. Yes; Woody seemed hungry and said food was scarce.

4. "The pinnacle of excitement" tells about his high level of excitement.

5. Answers will vary.

▲ Comprehension, p. 6

Leveled Readers
Reinforcing Skills and Strategies

Best Bugs

SUMMARY Dan and his dragonfly friends search for food one morning when Dan has an accident. He makes some unexpected friends during his recovery.

- 🔄 **Literary Devices**
- 🔄 **Answer Questions**
- **VOCABULARY:** *excursions*, *giddy*, *pinnacle*, *gleeful*, *panic*, *turbulent*, *precious*

Build Background/Set Purpose

Ask students to describe what they know about a pond's ecosystem. Have them describe different insects and animals that live there and how they usually interact with each other. Then have students preview the book. Point out that the creatures in this story do not behave like real birds and insects do. Ask students to predict what might happen. Remind them to answer questions as they read if they encounter confusing text.

During Reading

COMPLETE A STORY MAP Distribute the story map on *Teacher Resource Book* page 81 to pairs of students. Have students complete it as they read.

After Reading

Have students work in pairs to summarize the story. Then have them point out parts of the story where asking and answering questions cleared up confusion.

FLUENCY: PACE Have partners take turns rereading parts of the book aloud. Tell them to give each other feedback on pace.

Think Critically *(See inside back cover for questions.)*

1. Hue is too busy showing off, and then he is chased by swallows.

2. Dan is creative, resourceful, and cares about his friends.

3. The author mentions Enid "busily" weaving; Enid is able to bandage Dan; Enid has enclosed an entire area of trees in her web.

4. She describes the pond as a "shiny silver coin in the sun." Answers will vary.

5. Answers will vary.

LEVELED READER TEACHER GUIDE

▲ Vocabulary, p. 5

▲ Comprehension, p. 6

E L L

Calling All Crickets

SUMMARY This book is all about crickets. It describes their physical features and explains how humans have used crickets.

- **Build Background**
- **Concept Vocabulary**
- **Scaffolded Language Development**

Build Background/Set Purpose

Explain that the insect in the pictures is a *cricket*. Point out and name its *hind legs*, and explain that it makes a *chirping* sound. Remind students that answering questions can help clear up confusion.

Guided Reading

As students read, tell them to look for words that signal connections, such as *as a result* and *because*. Clarify the idiom *they kept on*.

PAGE 6 **LITERARY DEVICES** **How does the author help you understand how a cricket chirps?** (The author compares the way a cricket produces sound to the way a violin is played, and she calls the cricket a musician.)

PAGES 9–13 MAIN IDEA AND DETAILS **List three ways crickets have been important to people in China.** (The words *summer* and *autumn* are taken from the cricket's shape; people carried crickets with them so they could hear their songs; crickets are a symbol of good luck.)

After Reading

FLUENCY: PACE Reread the book aloud at an appropriate pace. Then have partners reread a page, slowing their pace when they encounter unfamiliar words.

Encourage students to use the concept words *cricket, cages, tubes,* and *chirp* while discussing the book.

Scaffolded Language Development

See inside back cover for teacher-led activity.

Provide additional examples and explanation as needed.

LEVELED READER TEACHER GUIDE

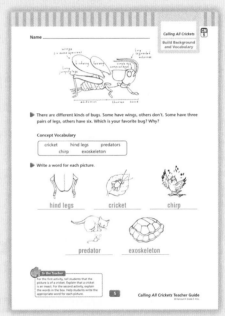

▲ **Build Background, p. 5**

▲ **Scaffolded Language Development, p. 6**

Lesson 25
Theme Review and Vocabulary Builder

WEEK AT A GLANCE

 Vocabulary

INTRODUCE *loathe, bland, mentor, dilapidated, coordination, altruism, sensibility, advocacy, mistreated, compassionate*

REVIEW Lessons 21–24 Vocabulary

Comprehension REVIEW

 Author's Purpose and Perspective

 Literary Devices

 Summarize

 Answer Questions

Reading

READERS' THEATER

"The Compassion Campaign"
NEWS REPORT

COMPREHENSION STRATEGIES

"How Beaver Stole Fire" by Nancy Van Laan
FOLKTALE

Fluency REVIEW
• Expression
• Pace

Decoding/Word Attack

REVIEW
• Structural Analysis: Word Parts *in-, out-, down-, up-*
• Structural Analysis: Word Parts *-ation, -ition, -sion, -ion*
• Silent Letters
• Structural Analysis: Unusual Plurals

Spelling REVIEW
• Words with Word Parts *in-, out-, down-, up-*
• Words with Word Parts *-ation, -ition, -sion, -ion*
• Words with Silent Letters
• Words with Unusual Plurals

Writing: Revise and Publish REVIEW
• Writing Trait: Sentence Fluency
• Writing Trait: Organization

Grammar REVIEW
• Action and Linking Verbs
• Present Tense; Subject-Verb Agreement
• Past and Future Tenses
• Perfect Tenses

 = Focus Skill   = Focus Strategy   = Tested Skill

One stop *for all* *your* **Digital** *needs*

Digital
CLASSROOM

 www.harcourtschool.com/storytown
To go along with your print program

FOR THE TEACHER

Prepare Professional Development
in the Online TE

 Videos for Podcasting

Plan & Organize Online TE & Planning Resources*

Teach/ Review  Transparencies
access from the Online TE

Assess Online Assessment*
with Student Tracking System and Prescriptions

FOR THE STUDENT

Read  Student eBook*

 Strategic Intervention Interactive Reader

 Leveled Readers

Practice & Apply Comprehension Expedition CD-ROM

 Also available on CD-ROM

eBook
STUDENT EDITION

STUDENT EDITION

The Compassion Campaign

Genre: News Report

HOW BEAVER STOLE FIRE

Genre: Folktale

◀ **Audiotext** *Student Edition selections are available on Audiotext Grade 5, CD8.*

Accelerated Reader™

◀ *Practice Quizzes for the Selection*

THEME CONNECTION: MAKING A DIFFERENCE
Comparing Readers' Theater and Folktale

Paired Selections

READERS' THEATER REVIEW

 SOCIAL STUDIES **The Compassion Campaign, pp. 640–649**
SUMMARY A television program profiles five children who participate in community service activities.

COMPREHENSION STRATEGIES REVIEW

SOCIAL STUDIES **How Beaver Stole Fire, pp. 650–655**
SUMMARY In this North American folktale, a courageous beaver steals the secret of fire from pine trees.

Support for Differentiated Instruction

 GO online **LEVELED READERS**

● **BELOW-LEVEL**　　● **ON-LEVEL**　　● **ADVANCED**　　**ELL**

LEVELED PRACTICE

◀ **Strategic Intervention Resource Kit, Lesson 25**

◀ **Strategic Intervention Interactive Reader, Lesson 25**
Strategic Intervention Interactive Reader Online

◀ **ELL Extra Support Kit, Lesson 25**

◀ **Challenge Resource Kit, Lesson 25**

● **BELOW-LEVEL**
Extra Support Copying Masters, pp. 145–149

● **ON-LEVEL**
Practice Book, pp. 145–152

● **ADVANCED**
Challenge Copying Masters, pp. 145–149

ADDITIONAL RESOURCES

◀ **Picture Card Collection**
◀ **Fluency Builders**
◀ **Literacy Center Kit, Lesson 25**
• Test Prep System
• Writer's Companion, Lesson 25
• Grammar Practice Book, pp. 89–90
• Spelling Practice Book, pp. 99–102
• Reading Transparencies R105–R107
• Language Arts Transparencies LA159–LA160

ASSESSMENT

✔ **Weekly Lesson Tests, Lesson 25**
• Comprehension
• Robust Vocabulary

✔ **Rubrics, pp. R5, R7, R8**

 GO online
www.harcourtschool.com/storytown
• Online Assessment
Also available on CD-ROM—ExamView®

Suggested Lesson Planner

90+ Minutes

GO online Online TE & Planning Resources

Step 1 Whole Group
45·60+ Minutes

Oral Language
- Question of the Day
- Listening Comprehension

Comprehension
- Skills and Strategies

Vocabulary

Reading
- Fluency
- Cross-Curricular Connections
- Decoding/Word Attack

Step 2 Small Groups
45·60+ Minutes

Step 3 Whole Group
45+ Minutes

Language Arts
- Spelling
- Writing
- Grammar

Review Spelling Words
1. indecisive	11. autumn
2. outpatient	12. knowledge
3. downgrade	13. rhyme
4. uptight	14. scenery
5. acceleration	15. wrestled
6. demolition	16. armies
7. pension	17. shelves
8. champion	18. radios
9. authorization	19. tomatoes
10. cancellation	20. videos

Day 1

QUESTION OF THE DAY *Have you ever planted a garden? If so, what did you plant?*

READ ALOUD, pp. T284–T285

 **COMPREHENSION:**
Author's Purpose and Perspective, p. T308

 VOCABULARY:
Introduce Vocabulary, p. T287

READ:  **READERS' THEATER**
"The Compassion Campaign," pp. T290–T299: Model Fluent Reading

 ▲Student Edition

FLUENCY: EXPRESSION, PACE:
Model Oral Fluency, pp. T290–T299

DECODING/WORD ATTACK:
Structural Analysis: Word Parts *in-, out-, down-, up-,* p. T312

Day 2

QUESTION OF THE DAY *How did T. J. Mark know his band was a hit with the senior citizens?*

READ ALOUD, p. T285

 **COMPREHENSION:**
Literary Devices, p. T309

 VOCABULARY: Develop Deeper Meaning, p. T288

READ:
READERS' THEATER
"The Compassion Campaign," pp. T290–T299: Monitor Comprehension

▲Student Edition

FLUENCY: EXPRESSION, PACE:
Reading for Fluency, pp. T290–T299

DECODING/WORD ATTACK:
Structural Analysis: Word Parts *-ation, -ition, -sion, -ion,* p. T312

Suggestions for Differentiated Instruction. *(See pp. T278–T279)*

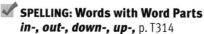 **SPELLING: Words with Word Parts**
in-, out-, down-, up-, p. T314

 WRITING: Review Assignments, p. T316

Writing Prompt *Many people who volunteer in their community are inspired to do so. Think of something that would inspire you to volunteer. Now, write a paragraph describing what you can do to better your community.*

 GRAMMAR: Action and Linking Verbs, p. T318

Daily Proofreading
1. He are uncompetent. (He is incompetent.)
2. Gloria and Janelle wants permision to go on the hike. (want; permission)

 SPELLING: Words with Word Parts
-ation, -ition, -sion, -ion, p. T314

 WRITING: Revise, p. T316

Writing Prompt *Many people's lives have been affected by hurricanes. Think of a time you and your family were affected by weather conditions. Now, describe what the weather conditions were, and how they altered your daily activities.*

 GRAMMAR: Present Tense; Subject-Verb Agreement, p. T318

Daily Proofreading
3. Last autunm Wes is the student council leader. (autumn; Wes was)
4. Now the council made safety videoes for kids. (makes; videos)

 = Focus Skill    = Focus Strategy    = Tested Skill

REVIEW

Focus Skills

Focus Strategies

- Vocabulary
- Fluency
- Spelling
- Writing
- Grammar

VOCABULARY

loathe	altruism
bland	sensibility
mentor	advocacy
dilapidated	mistreated
coordination	compassionate

Day 3

QUESTION OF THE DAY *Would you be able to detect a compassionate person? How?*

READ ALOUD, p. T285

 **COMPREHENSION:**

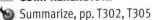 Summarize, pp. T302, T305

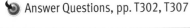 Answer Questions, pp. T302, T307

 **VOCABULARY:** Reinforce Word Meanings, p. T301

FLUENCY:

READERS' THEATER

"The Compassion Campaign," pp. T290–T299: Assign Roles

▲Student Edition

READ: "How Beaver Stole Fire," pp. T302–T307

DECODING/WORD ATTACK:
Silent Letters, p. T313

Day 4

QUESTION OF THE DAY *How might Felix have convinced his friends to help at the animal shelter?*

READ ALOUD, p. T285

 **COMPREHENSION:**
Literary Patterns and Symbols, p. T310
Draw Conclusions, p. T311

 VOCABULARY:
Extend Word Meanings, p. T301

FLUENCY:

READERS' THEATER

"The Compassion Campaign," pp. T290–T299: Rehearse

▲Student Edition

DECODING/WORD ATTACK:
Structural Analysis: Unusual Plurals, p. T313

Day 5

QUESTION OF THE DAY *Why are the rain forests endangered? What are some things students in your school could do to help protect the environment?*

READ ALOUD, p. T285

 VOCABULARY:
Cumulative Review, p. T301

FLUENCY:

READERS' THEATER

"The Compassion Campaign," pp. T290–T299, T300: Perform

 ▲Student Edition

● BELOW-LEVEL   ● ON-LEVEL   ● ADVANCED   E L L

 SPELLING: Words with Silent Letters, p. T315

 WRITING: Proofread, p. T317

Writing Prompt *Everyone has a cause he or she would like to support. Think about a charitable cause that you would like to advocate. Now, write a persuasive essay encouraging people to aid or help in your campaign.*

GRAMMAR: Past and Future Tenses, p. T319

Daily Proofreading

5. Volunteers often dusts off shelfs for elderly residents. (dust; shelves)

6. Last year volunteers show great dedicasion during the storm. (showed; dedication)

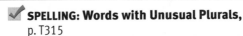 **SPELLING: Words with Unusual Plurals,** p. T315

 WRITING: Publish, p. T317

Writing Prompt *People show compassion in different ways. Think about someone you know who has acted compassionately toward you. Now, write a paragraph describing what that person did.*

 GRAMMAR: Perfect Tenses, p. T319

Daily Proofreading

7. The tomatos be ripe next month. (tomatoes; will be)

8. The gardeners has cleared the derbis from the shed. (have cleared; debris)

 SPELLING: Posttest, p. T315

 WRITING: Present, p. T317

Writing Prompt *Everyone has been inspired by someone. Think about which young leader from "The Compassion Campaign" inspired you. Imagine you could interview that person. Now, write several questions you would ask that person.*

 GRAMMAR: Cumulative Review, p. T319

Daily Proofreading

9. My sister have volunteered at the clinic (has; clinic.)

10. By Friday she will have became someone's companyon. (will have become; companion.)

Suggested Small-Group Planner

45-60+ Minutes

	Day 1	Day 2
BELOW-LEVEL 15-20+ Minutes	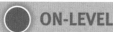 **Teacher–Directed** Leveled Readers: Before Reading, p. T320 **Independent** ⭐ Word Study Center, p. T282 Extra Support Copying Masters, p. 146 ▲ Leveled Reader	**Teacher–Directed** Reread the Selection, pp. T290–T299 **Independent** ⭐ Writing Center, p. T283 *Audiotext Grade 5*, CD8 Extra Support Copying Masters, pp. 145, 147 ▲ Student Edition
ON-LEVEL 15-20+ Minutes	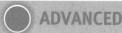 **Teacher–Directed** Leveled Readers: Before Reading, p. T321 **Independent** ⭐ Reading Center, p. T282 Practice Book, p. 146 ▲ Leveled Reader	**Teacher–Directed** Monitor Comprehension of the Selection, pp. T290–T299 **Independent** ⭐ Word Study Center, p. T282 Practice Book, pp. 145, 147 ▲ Student Edition
ADVANCED 15-20+ Minutes	**Teacher–Directed** Leveled Readers: Before Reading, p. T322 **Independent** ⭐ Writing Center, p. T283 Challenge Copying Masters, p. 146 ▲ Leveled Reader	**Independent** ⭐ Fluency Center, p. T283 Leveled Readers: Partner Reading, p. T322 Challenge Copying Masters, pp. 145, 147 ▲ Leveled Reader

ELL

English-Language Learners

In addition to the small-group suggestions above, use the ELL Extra Support Kit to promote language development.

LANGUAGE DEVELOPMENT SUPPORT	**LANGUAGE DEVELOPMENT SUPPORT**
Teacher–Directed Leveled Readers: Build Background, p. T323 ELL Teacher Guide, Lesson 25 **Independent** ELL Copying Masters, Lesson 25 ▲ Leveled Reader	**Teacher–Directed** Scaffold Core Skills ELL Teacher Guide, Lesson 25 **Independent** *Audiotext Grade 5*, CD8 ▲ ELL Student Handbook

Intervention

▲ Strategic Intervention Resource Kit   ▲ Strategic Intervention Interactive Reader

| Strategic Intervention Teacher Guide, Lesson 25 Strategic Intervention Practice Book, Lesson 25 | Catch a Wave, Lesson 25 Strategic Intervention Teacher Guide, Lesson 25 Strategic Intervention Interactive Reader ▲ |

     = Literacy Center Cards

Teacher–Directed
Leveled Readers:
During Reading, p. T320

Independent
 Reading Center, p. T282

 ▲ Leveled Reader

Teacher–Directed
Leveled Readers:
Guided Fluency, p. T320

Independent
 Technology Center, p. T283
Extra Support Copying Masters,
pp. 148–149

 ▲ Leveled Reader

Teacher–Directed
Leveled Readers:
Responding, p. T320

Independent
 Fluency Center, p. T283
Leveled Readers:
Rereading for Fluency, p. T320

 ▲ Leveled Reader

Teacher–Directed
Leveled Readers:
During Reading, p. T321

Independent
 Technology Center, p. T283

 ▲ Leveled Reader

Teacher–Directed
Leveled Readers:
Guided Fluency, p. T321

Independent
 Fluency Center, p. T283
Practice Book, pp. 148–149

 ▲ Leveled Reader

Teacher–Directed
Leveled Readers:
Responding, p. T321

Independent
 Writing Center, p. T283
Leveled Readers:
Rereading for Fluency, p. T321

 ▲ Leveled Reader

Teacher–Directed
Leveled Readers:
During Reading, p. T322

Independent
 Word Study Center, p. T282

 ▲ Leveled Reader

Independent
 Reading Center, p. T282
Challenge Copying
Masters, pp. 148–149
Classroom Library:
Self-Selected Reading

 ▲ Leveled Reader

Teacher–Directed
Leveled Readers:
Responding, p. T322

Independent
 Technology Center, p. T283
Leveled Readers:
Rereading for Fluency, p. T322
Classroom Library:
Self-Selected Reading

 ▲ Leveled Reader

LANGUAGE DEVELOPMENT SUPPORT

Teacher–Directed
Leveled Readers:
During Reading, p. T323
ELL Teacher Guide, Lesson 25

Independent
ELL Copying Masters, Lesson 25

 ▲ Leveled Reader

LANGUAGE DEVELOPMENT SUPPORT

Teacher–Directed
Leveled Readers:
Guided Fluency, p. T323
ELL Teacher Guide, Lesson 25

Independent
ELL Copying Masters, Lesson 25

 ▲ Leveled Reader

LANGUAGE DEVELOPMENT SUPPORT

Teacher–Directed
Leveled Readers:
Responding, p. T323
ELL Teacher Guide, Lesson 25

Independent
Leveled Readers:
Rereading for Fluency, p. T323

 ▲ Leveled Reader

Catch a Wave,
Lesson 25
Strategic Intervention Teacher
Guide, Lesson 25
Strategic Intervention
Practice Book, Lesson 25

 Strategic Intervention
Interactive Reader ▲

Catch a Wave,
Lesson 25
Strategic Intervention Teacher
Guide,
Lesson 25

 Strategic Intervention
Interactive Reader ▲

Catch a Wave,
Lesson 25
Strategic Intervention Teacher
Guide,
Lesson 25

 Strategic Intervention
Interactive Reader ▲

Leveled Readers & Leveled Practice
Reinforcing Skills and Strategies

LEVELED READERS SYSTEM

- **Leveled Readers**
- **Leveled Readers CD**
- **Leveled Reader Teacher Guides**
  - *Vocabulary*
  - *Comprehension*
  - *Oral Reading Fluency Assessment*
- **Response Activities**
- **Leveled Readers Assessment**

See pages T320–T323 for lesson plans.

For extended lesson plans, see *Leveled Reader Teacher Guides.*

BELOW-LEVEL

- **Robust Vocabulary**
- **Comprehension**

LEVELED READER TEACHER GUIDE

▲ **Vocabulary, p. 5**

▲ **Comprehension, p. 6**

ON-LEVEL

- **Robust Vocabulary**
- **Comprehension**

LEVELED READER TEACHER GUIDE

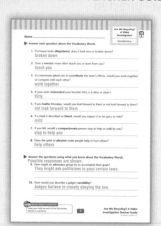

▲ **Vocabulary, p. 5**

▲ **Comprehension, p. 6**

www.harcourtschool.com/storytown

★ **Leveled Readers Online Database**
Searchable by Genre, Skill, Vocabulary, Level, or Title
★ **Student Activities and Teacher Resources,** *online*

ADVANCED

- **Robust Vocabulary**
- **Comprehension**

LEVELED READER TEACHER GUIDE

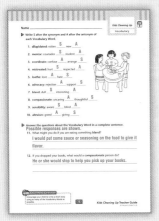

▲ **Vocabulary, p. 5**

▲ **Comprehension, p. 6**

ELL

- **Build Background**
- **Concept Vocabulary**
- **Scaffolded Language Development**

LEVELED READER TEACHER GUIDE

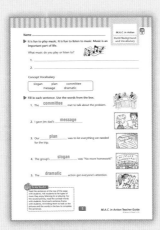

▲ **Build Background, p. 5**

▲ **Scaffolded Language Development, p. 6**

CLASSROOM LIBRARY
for Self-Selected Reading

EASY

▲ *Doña Flor* by Pat Mora.
TALL TALE

AVERAGE

▲ *Eleanor* by Barbara Cooney.
BIOGRAPHY

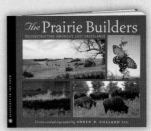

CHALLENGE

▲ *The Prairie Builders: Reconstructing America's Lost Grasslands*
by Sneed B. Collard III.
EXPOSITORY NONFICTION

▲ **Classroom Library Books Teacher Guide**

Literacy Centers

15+ Min. each

Management Support

While you provide direct instruction to individuals or small groups, other students can work on these activities.

▲ Literacy Centers Pocket Chart

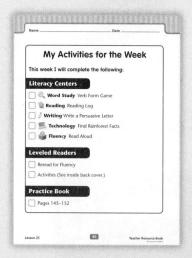

▲ Teacher Resource Book, p. 60

 ## Homework for the Week

Teacher Resource Book, page 28

The *Homework Copying Master* provides activities to complete for each day of the week.

GO online www.harcourtschool.com/storytown

 WORD STUDY

Verb Form Game

Objective
To identify and correctly use forms of irregular verbs

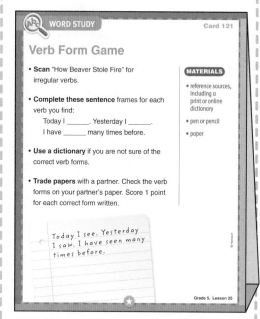

WORD STUDY   Card 121

Verb Form Game

- **Scan** "How Beaver Stole Fire" for irregular verbs.

- **Complete these sentence** frames for each verb you find:
  Today I _____. Yesterday I _____.
  I have _____ many times before.

- **Use a dictionary** if you are not sure of the correct verb forms.

- **Trade papers** with a partner. Check the verb forms on your partner's paper. Score 1 point for each correct form written.

MATERIALS
- reference sources, including a print or online dictionary
- pen or pencil
- paper

Today I see. Yesterday I saw. I have seen many times before.

Grade 5, Lesson 25

⭐ **Literacy Center Kit,** Card 121

Today I see. Yesterday I saw. I have seen many times before.

Today I run. Yesterday I ran. I have run many times before.

Today I fall. Yesterday I fell. I have fallen many times before.

Today I keep. Yesterday I kept. I have kept many times before.

 READING

Reading Log

Objective
To select and read books independently

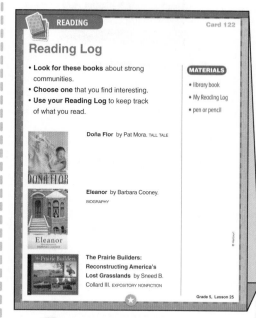

READING   Card 122

Reading Log

- **Look for these books** about strong communities.
- **Choose one** that you find interesting.
- **Use your Reading Log** to keep track of what you read.

MATERIALS
- library book
- My Reading Log
- pen or pencil

Doña Flor by Pat Mora. TALL TALE

Eleanor by Barbara Cooney. BIOGRAPHY

The Prairie Builders: Reconstructing America's Lost Grasslands by Sneed B. Collard III. EXPOSITORY NONFICTION

Grade 5, Lesson 25

⭐ **Literacy Center Kit,** Card 122

www.harcourtschool.com/storytown

Go online

★ Additional Literacy Center Activities
★ Resources for Parents and Teachers

● BELOW-LEVEL   ● ADVANCED   ● ON-LEVEL

Differentiated *for Your Needs*

WRITING

Write a Persuasive Letter

Objective
To write a persuasive letter

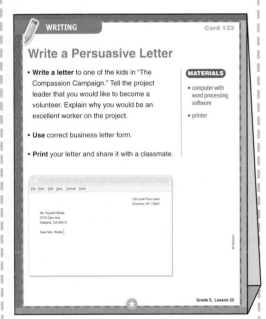

WRITING   Card 123

Write a Persuasive Letter

- **Write a letter** to one of the kids in "The Compassion Campaign." Tell the project leader that you would like to become a volunteer. Explain why you would be an excellent worker on the project.

- **Use** correct business letter form.

- **Print** your letter and share it with a classmate.

MATERIALS
- computer with word processing software
- printer

135 Lone Pine Lane
Oneonta, NY 13820

Ms. Kiyoshi Wada
3775 Glen Ave.
Oakland, CA 94610

Dear Mrs. Wada |

Grade 5, Lesson 25

⭐ **Literacy Center Kit,** Card 123

File Print Edit Save Format Tools

135 Lone Pine Lane
Oneonta, NY 13820

Ms. Kiyoshi Wada
3775 Glen Ave.
Oakland, CA 94610

Dear Mrs. Wada: |

TECHNOLOGY

Find Rainforest Facts

Objective
To gather, evaluate, and select data to support a position

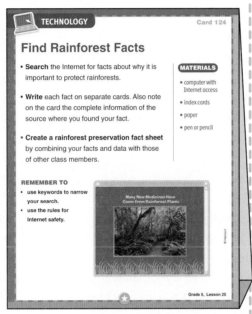

TECHNOLOGY   Card 124

Find Rainforest Facts

- **Search** the Internet for facts about why it is important to protect rainforests.

- **Write** each fact on separate cards. Also note on the card the complete information of the source where you found your fact.

- **Create a rainforest preservation fact sheet** by combining your facts and data with those of other class members.

MATERIALS
- computer with Internet access
- index cards
- paper
- pen or pencil

REMEMBER TO
- use keywords to narrow your search.
- use the rules for Internet safety.

Many New Medicines Have Come from Rainforest Plants

Grade 5, Lesson 25

⭐ **Literacy Center Kit,** Card 124

Rainforest Preservation Fact Sheet

- Onse modolendre faccum nulputpat nibh et, vullumm olorer ilis dolore ming enibh et nonsequi tin elit at. Utem dipit incing eugueri.
- Obor si. Gait niamcore min henim et dolorer il erat, susto endiatisi.
- Am quis at.
- Xeros eugait inim qui exeros dion ullam quipsustrud et iriliquam vulla conulpute vel doloreros alit dip
- Am quis at.

FLUENCY

Read Aloud

Objective
To read aloud with appropriate expression and pace

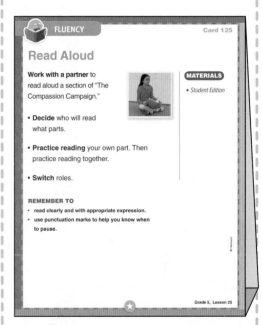

FLUENCY   Card 125

Read Aloud

Work with a partner to read aloud a section of "The Compassion Campaign."

- **Decide** who will read what parts.

- **Practice reading** your own part. Then practice reading together.

- **Switch** roles.

MATERIALS
- *Student Edition*

REMEMBER TO
- read clearly and with appropriate expression.
- use punctuation marks to help you know when to pause.

Grade 5, Lesson 25

⭐ **Literacy Center Kit,** Card 125

Lesson 25 • **T283**

Listening Comprehension *Read-Aloud*

He Even Kissed a Pig
by Ann Volk

Eleven-year-old Cullinan Williams has done some amazing things. He's spoken with members of Congress and former President Bill Clinton. He's raised more than $40,000 going door-to-door. He's even kissed a pig! ❶

It hasn't always been easy. "Let's just say the pig's nose wasn't too dry," recalls Cullinan.

So why does he do it? Since he was six, Cullinan Williams has had a disease called *Type 1 diabetes*. His goal is to help find a cure. ❷

Living with Diabetes

In people with Type 1 diabetes, the body does not make enough of an important chemical called *insulin*.

Cullinan's Mission

Cullinan had to learn the skills he would need to keep himself healthy. At age eight, he went to a camp sponsored by the American Diabetes Association. What he learned there changed his life.

At camp, Cullinan learned how to check his own blood sugar and how to give himself shots of insulin. He also learned to be an advocate—someone who speaks out and works to support a cause.

Cullinan decided to raise money to support scientists who are trying to cure diabetes. When he came home from the camp, Cullinan and his dad went door-to-door to collect money for diabetes research.

The first year, he raised $3,800. A year later he raised $12,000. The next year, $25,000. He has been the top fund-raiser in New York State.

Because of his abilities as a speaker and fund-raiser, Cullinan was named National Youth Advocate by the American Diabetes Association. He has met with members of Congress to talk about diabetes and the need for a cure.

Cullinan has also worked to pass laws in New York State that increase money for research and help people with diabetes to get needed medical supplies. For his work, Cullinan was given the Central New York Citizen of the Year award. He was the first young person to receive this honor.

Searching for a Cure

There is no cure for diabetes . . . yet! But there is hope. Scientists have succeeded in putting cells from a healthy pancreas into people with diabetes. Many people who received these cells did not need insulin shots for more than a year.

Researchers are also working to create a device that will work almost as well as a healthy pancreas. The machine is being designed to give insulin and to check the person's blood glucose. Then it should be able to deliver insulin whenever the body needs it. ❸

While the research continues, people with diabetes have to find a way to overcome the daily challenges posed by this disease.

"What gets me through every day is knowing that this is about more than me," says Cullinan. "No one should have to fight this disease alone." Cullinan encourages kids at diabetes camps to become advocates and to begin their own search for a cure.

People with diabetes and their families look forward to a day when the disease can be cured. Because of the work of Cullinan and his fellow youth advocates, their dream may become a reality.

— Cullinan Willams kissed a pig at Camp Discovery in Kansas. The American Diabetes Association holds Kiss-a-Pig events for people who raise the most money to fight the disease. The winner greets a pig with a kiss.

Begin the Read-Aloud

MODEL ORAL FLUENCY: EXPRESSION AND PACE Tell students that good readers

- show expression through volume and tone of voice.
- do not read too quickly or too slowly for listeners to understand.

  Display **Transparency R105.** Have students follow along as you read the passage aloud with appropriate expression and at an appropriate rate.

Interact with the Text

Routine Card 1 Continue reading aloud "He Even Kissed a Pig." Pause to point out or ask students the following items.

❶ Going door-to-door is the process of knocking on the door of every home in an area, usually to try to persuade residents to buy or do something. **UNDERSTANDING VOCABULARY**

❷ Why do you think Cullinan Williams chose the goal of helping to find a cure for Type 1 diabetes? (Possible response: If he can find a cure, he will become healthier and so will many others.) **CAUSE AND EFFECT**

❸ What cures for Type 1 diabetes are scientists working on now? (putting healthy pancreas cells into people with diabetes; creating a device that will do the job of the pancreas) **MAIN IDEA AND DETAILS**

When you have finished reading the article, ask:

- **What is Cullinan doing to help find a cure for diabetes? Explain why he is doing this.** (He is working to raise money to help find a cure and speaking to people to educate them about the disease. He works for a cure to help others with diabetes.) **RETURN TO PURPOSE**

- **What reasons do you think Cullinan gives when he tells kids at diabetes camps to become advocates?** (Possible response: If a cure is found, they and many others will live better lives.) **DRAW CONCLUSIONS**

Connect to Reading

Tell students that next they will read a fictional news report about some other young people who are doing important things.

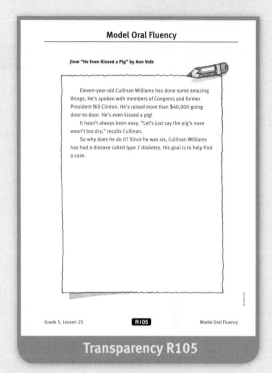

Transparency R105

Model Oral Fluency

from **"He Even Kissed a Pig" by Ann Volk**

Eleven-year-old Cullinan Williams has done some amazing things. He's spoken with members of Congress and former President Bill Clinton. He's raised more than $40,000 going door-to-door. He's even kissed a pig!

It hasn't always been easy. "Let's just say the pig's nose wasn't too dry," recalls Cullinan.

So why does he do it? Since he was six, Cullinan Williams has had a disease called *type 1 diabetes.* His goal is to help find a cure.

Grade 5, Lesson 25   **R105**   Model Oral Fluency

Suggested Daily Read-Aloud

To model fluency and promote listening comprehension, read aloud from one of these books throughout the week:

- *Sea Turtles* by Lorraine A. Jay. NorthWord, 2000.
- *The Kids' Volunteering Book* by Arlene Erlbach. Lerner, 1998.
- *Neighborhood Odes* by Gary Soto. Harcourt, 2005.
- *Chester Cricket's New Home* by George Selden. Random House, 1984.
- *My Backyard Garden* by Carol Lerner. Morrow, 1998.

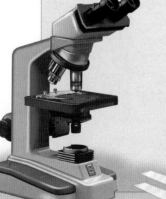

 # Build **Background**
for "The Compassion Campaign"

Access Prior Knowledge

DRAW A WEB Tell students that in the next selection they will read about a television news report describing children who do things to help their communities. Ask students to brainstorm projects children could do to make their community a better place to live. Have volunteers add concepts to a web like the one below.

clean up
trash

plant
trees

Making the
Community a Better
Place

start a
garden

help prepare
food for needy
people

Develop Concepts

DISCUSS COMPASSION Use the ideas in the web to develop selection concepts. Discuss the following points:

• Many people want to help others in their community who are having difficulties in their lives.

• A person who wants to help people in need feels compassion toward those people.

• People can help their community in many other ways. Often there is a way for people to help by doing something they are good at and like to do.

ELL

Content-Area Background Use *Picture Card 58* along with simple explanations to scaffold background and vocabulary as needed:

• A **garden** can make a **community** a nicer place. (show photo)

• Kids can help grow fruits and vegetables in a **garden**. (show photo)

Discuss with students what they know about gardening.

Picture Card 58 ▶

shovel

watering can

hose

seeds

garden

See *ELL Teacher Guide* Lesson 25 for support in scaffolding instruction.

Build Robust Vocabulary

5-DAY **VOCABULARY**
DAY 1 Vocabulary, pp. T287–T288
DAY 2 Vocabulary Review, p. T291
DAY 3 Reinforce Word Meanings, p. T301
DAY 4 Extend Word Meanings, p. T301
DAY 5 Cumulative Review, p. T301

Introduce Vocabulary

BUILD WORD MEANING Display **Transparency R106**. Have a volunteer read aloud the first Vocabulary Word and its explanation. Then ask students the first question below. Continue in this way until students have answered a question about each of the Vocabulary Words.

1. What kind of weather do you **loathe**? Why?

2. What makes food less **bland**?

3. What makes a person a good **mentor**?

4. What might a **dilapidated** car look like?

5. Why does cooking and serving a holiday meal for many people take a lot of **coordination**?

6. How might someone show **altruism** after a natural disaster?

7. What activities might a person with an artistic **sensibility** choose?

8. What do **advocacy** groups do?

9. How might a **mistreated** animal behave?

10. What is a good job for a **compassionate** person?

Vocabulary: Lesson 25

loathe	altruism
bland	sensibility
mentor	advocacy
dilapidated	mistreated
coordination	compassionate

▼ **Student-Friendly Explanations**

Robust Vocabulary

1. **loathe** If you loathe something, you hate it.

2. **bland** Something that is bland is dull and unexciting.

3. **mentor** A mentor is a trusted person who gives a person helpful advice.

4. **dilapidated** A dilapidated building looks worn out and run down.

5. **coordination** Coordination involves organizing the different parts of something so that they work well together.

6. **altruism** Altruism is being concerned about others before worrying about oneself.

7. **sensibility** A sensibility is a special awareness in a certain area; for example, a person can have an artistic sensibility or a musical sensibility.

8. **advocacy** Advocacy is giving support to a person, idea, or cause.

9. **mistreated** If something is mistreated, it is used in a way that harms or hurts it.

10. **compassionate** A compassionate person is kindhearted and understanding.

Grade 5, Lesson 25   **R106**   Robust Vocabulary

Transparency R106

Build **Robust Vocabulary**

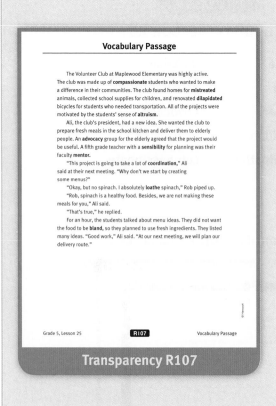

Vocabulary Passage

The Volunteer Club at Maplewood Elementary was highly active. The club was made up of **compassionate** students who wanted to make a difference in their communities. The club found homes for **mistreated** animals, collected school supplies for children, and renovated **dilapidated** bicycles for students who needed transportation. All of the projects were motivated by the students' sense of **altruism.**

Ali, the club's president, had a new idea. She wanted the club to prepare fresh meals in the school kitchen and deliver them to elderly people. An **advocacy** group for the elderly agreed that the project would be useful. A fifth grade teacher with a **sensibility** for planning was their faculty **mentor.**

"This project is going to take a lot of **coordination**," Ali said at their next meeting. "Why don't we start by creating some menus?"

"Okay, but no spinach. I absolutely **loathe** spinach," Rob piped up.

"Rob, spinach is a healthy food. Besides, we are not making these meals for you," Ali said.

"That's true," he replied.

For an hour, the students talked about menu ideas. They did not want the food to be **bland,** so they planned to use fresh ingredients. They listed many ideas. "Good work," Ali said. "At our next meeting, we will plan our delivery route."

Grade 5, Lesson 25 | **R107** | Vocabulary Passage

Transparency R107

Develop Deeper Meaning

ASK QUESTIONS Read the passage on **Transparency R107** aloud. Pause after the first paragraph. Ask questions 1–4 about the highlighted words. Read the rest of the selection, and have students answer questions 5–10. If students are unable to give reasonable responses, review the Student-Friendly Explanations (See Transparency R106).

1. Why might a **compassionate** person join the Volunteer Club?

2. Why do **mistreated** animals need help?

3. What would a **dilapidated** bicycle look like?

4. How do members of the Volunteer Club show their **altruism**?

5. Why was it a good idea for Ali to talk with an **advocacy** group for the elderly?

6. How could a **sensibility** for planning help someone plan a project effectively?

7. Did the Volunteer Club have a good **mentor**? Explain.

8. Why would a meal project require a lot of **coordination**?

9. Do you think Ali should have asked other club members to say which foods they **loathe**? Why or why not?

10. Why do you think the students did not want to serve **bland** food?

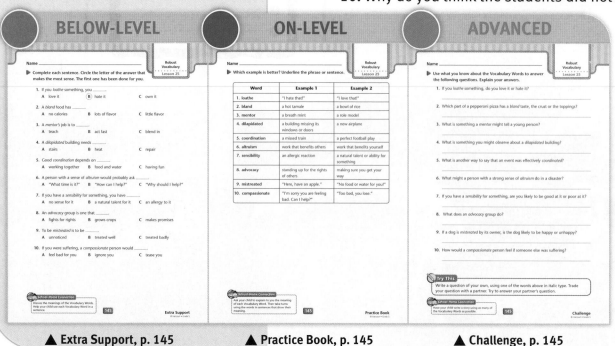

▲ **Extra Support, p. 145**   ▲ **Practice Book, p. 145**   ▲ **Challenge, p. 145**

E L L

• Group students according to academic levels, and assign one of the pages on the left.

• Clarify any unfamiliar concepts as necessary. See *ELL Teacher Guide* Lesson 25 for support in scaffolding instruction.

Managing Readers' Theater
"The Compassion Campaign"

Set the Stage

OVERVIEW Use the following suggestions to help students prepare a Readers' Theater presentation of "The Compassion Campaign." See page T300 for additional performance ideas.

MODEL FLUENT READING Model fluent reading by reading aloud the script on *Student Edition* pages 640–649 (pp. T290–T299) as students follow along. Tell students that the reporters' lines should be read expressively to match the way real-life television reporters speak. Also, point out where the pace of the reading should change to show excitement. Then have students choral-read pp. 641–642.

MONITOR COMPREHENSION Read the script with students. Use the Monitor Comprehension questions to help students grasp the story line. Guide students to read at an appropriate pace and with proper expression. Then have students summarize what they read.

ASSIGN ROLES/REHEARSE Assign students to small groups, and give each student a role in the script. Distribute copies of the script (*Teacher Resource Book*, pp. 115–119), and have students highlight their lines. Allow time for students to rehearse their parts in their groups. Have groups read aloud the complete script.

REHEARSE Have students work in their groups from Day 3, reading through the script as many times as possible. Informally observe the groups and discuss with students their choices for using punctuation cues to guide pace and expression. You may want to have students rehearse while using the backdrop for "The Compassion Campaign." See *Teacher Resource Book*, p. 94.

PERFORM Assign each group a section to perform. Have students stand in a row at the front of the class and read the script aloud. Groups that are not speaking become the audience. Encourage the audience to give feedback about each group's overall performance.

Professional Development

 Podcasting: Readers' Theater

▲ **Teacher Resource Book**
pp. 115–119

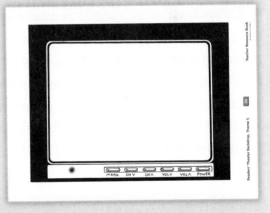

▲ **Teacher Resource Book,**
p. 94

TECHNOLOGY

 Audiotext This Readers' Theater selection is available on *Audiotext Grade 5*, CD8.

SOCIAL STUDIES

Read the Selection

Objectives
- *To identify the distinguishing character-istics of a television news report*
- *To read aloud a television news report as a Readers' Theater*

Genre Study

DISCUSS NEWS REPORTS Tell students that the selection they will read is a television news report. Point out that

- Most of the characters are television news reporters.

- The reporters give factual information about a real-life topic.

Revisit Selection Vocabulary

DISCUSS VOCABULARY: PAGE 640 Ask a volunteer to read aloud the list of words on page 640. Remind students that these words were introduced earlier. If necessary, review with students the Student-Friendly Explanations on **Transparency R106**. (See page T287.)

Review Fluency

DISCUSS FLUENCY: PAGE 640 Have students read the fluency information on page 640. Discuss with them what they have learned about pace and expression.

READERS' THEATER

- loathe
- bland
- mentor
- dilapidated
- coordination
- altruism
- sensibility
- advocacy
- mistreated
- compassionate

Reading for Fluency
When reading a script aloud,

- Read with expression to match your character's emotions.

- Adjust your pace to match the action in the text.

640

ELL

Assign Roles Initially, students with lower levels of reading fluency may take on simpler roles, such as Friends or Family. Ensure that the modeling of other roles by more fluent readers during rehearsals helps students gain confidence in any role.

The Compassion Campaign

illustrated by Sally Wern Comport

Characters

Penny Baldwin	Brent	Sheila
Eva Soto	Jacob Stein	Randy Vasquez
Kiyoshi	Kavi	Felix
Friends	Family	
T. J. Mark	Addison Base	

Penny Baldwin: Good afternoon, I'm Penny Baldwin, and you've tuned in to television's most inspiring program, "The Compassion Campaign." Each month, we profile five kids who make their communities better places to live. Reporter Eva Soto joins us now from California.

641

TECHNOLOGY

eBook "The Compassion Campaign" is available in an eBook.

Audiotext "The Compassion Campaign" is available on *Audiotext Grade 5*, CD8 for subsequent readings.

REVIEW VOCABULARY

Theme Vocabulary In addition to the Vocabulary Words introduced on page 640, students will encounter the following Vocabulary Words that were introduced in this theme: *excursion, basking, detect, fervor, vital, damaged, bustled, giddiest, precious,* and *enterprising.*

Preview/Set Purpose

Routine Card 3

PREVIEW AND PREDICT Tell students that they will read a television news report about children who are working for important causes in their communities. Have students preview the selection and predict what different activities the children are involved in. Ask

- **What kinds of projects do you think these news reporters will tell about?** (Possible response: projects that help people in need)

- **What might you learn from the report?** (Possible response: some ways in which kids are making their communities better)

MODEL SETTING A PURPOSE Remind students that good readers set a purpose for reading based on their preview of the selection and what they know about the genre. You may want to use this model:

Think Aloud In this selection, a group of reporters interviews the young leaders of five successful community improvement projects. One purpose for reading could be to find out what the goal of each project is.

Monitor Comprehension

1 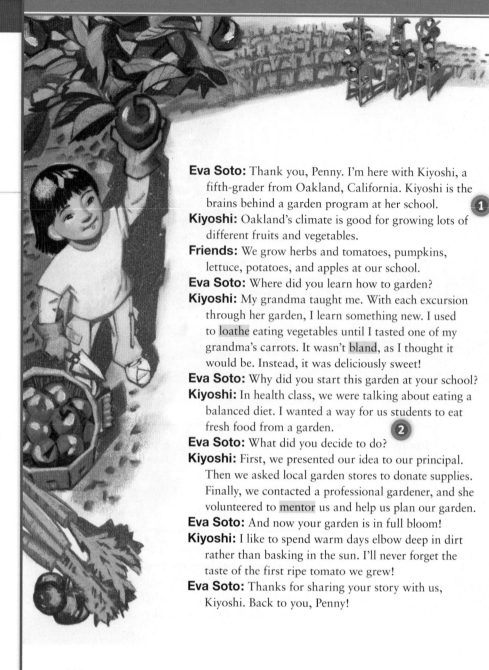 **LITERARY DEVICES**
What is the meaning of the phrase *the brains behind a garden program*? (Possible response: "the person who planned and organized the program")

2 **MAIN IDEA AND DETAILS**
What did Kiyoshi do to make her community a better place? (Possible response: She started a garden program at her school that gives students a chance to eat fresh fruits and vegetables.)

3 **CAUSE AND EFFECT**
How did Brent and his friends learn about an opportunity to help others in their community? (A nurse at a senior citizens home suggested that their band come and play music for the residents.)

Eva Soto: Thank you, Penny. I'm here with Kiyoshi, a fifth-grader from Oakland, California. Kiyoshi is the brains behind a garden program at her school. **1**

Kiyoshi: Oakland's climate is good for growing lots of different fruits and vegetables.

Friends: We grow herbs and tomatoes, pumpkins, lettuce, potatoes, and apples at our school.

Eva Soto: Where did you learn how to garden?

Kiyoshi: My grandma taught me. With each excursion through her garden, I learn something new. I used to loathe eating vegetables until I tasted one of my grandma's carrots. It wasn't bland, as I thought it would be. Instead, it was deliciously sweet!

Eva Soto: Why did you start this garden at your school?

Kiyoshi: In health class, we were talking about eating a balanced diet. I wanted a way for us students to eat fresh food from a garden.

Eva Soto: What did you decide to do? **2**

Kiyoshi: First, we presented our idea to our principal. Then we asked local garden stores to donate supplies. Finally, we contacted a professional gardener, and she volunteered to mentor us and help us plan our garden.

Eva Soto: And now your garden is in full bloom!

Kiyoshi: I like to spend warm days elbow deep in dirt rather than basking in the sun. I'll never forget the taste of the first ripe tomato we grew!

Eva Soto: Thanks for sharing your story with us, Kiyoshi. Back to you, Penny!

642

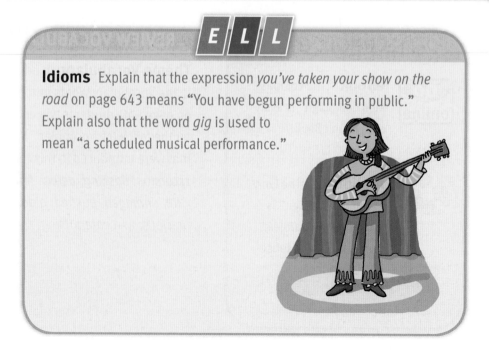

E L L

Idioms Explain that the expression *you've taken your show on the road* on page 643 means "You have begun performing in public." Explain also that the word *gig* is used to mean "a scheduled musical performance."

Theme Review

Fluency Tip

Think about how a reporter tells the news. Match your expression to that of a reporter's.

Penny Baldwin: Thank you, Eva. Now we turn our attention to Houston, Texas, and reporter T. J. Mark.

T. J. Mark: Many music legends began their careers by playing in the family garage. Let's meet one young man who started the same way. Brent, how did you form your band?

Brent: I've always enjoyed playing the guitar. A couple of my friends play other instruments. One day we started practicing in my parents' garage.

T. J. Mark: I hear you've taken your show on the road.

Brent: Yes. My grandfather lives in Larson Manor, a place for senior citizens. The residents miss going out for entertainment. A nurse suggested our band bring some entertainment to the residents. **3**

Friends: We loved the idea!

Brent: I was afraid they might not like our music. But their enjoyment wasn't hard to detect. They cheered!

Friends: One man even asked if he could join in on the drums!

Brent: You should come with us the next time we play. We have a gig there next week.

T. J. Mark: I'll be there! Back to you, Penny.

643

Reading for Fluency

Fluency Tip **EXPRESSION** Have a volunteer read aloud the fluency tip on page 643. Point out that a television news reporter would emphasize important words and pause between phrases.

Then point out the exclamation marks at the end of the Friends' lines on page 643. Remind students that sentences ending with exclamation marks should be read a bit louder and faster than other sentences. Model for students how you would read the Friends' first line:

Think Aloud **This sentence should be read a bit louder and faster than other sentences to show excitement. The most important word in the sentence is *loved*. This word should be read louder and at a higher pitch than the other words.**

Have students locate other sentences on pages 642–643 that end with exclamation marks. Have them identify the most important word or words in each sentence and then practice reading the sentence with appropriate expression.

HEALTH

SUPPORTING STANDARDS

Fruits and Vegetables Remind students that Kiyoshi and her friends grow fruits and vegetables in their garden program. Discuss with students the nutritional value of fruits and vegetables as compared to grains or fats. Then discuss ways they can influence others to make positive nutritional choices.

Monitor Comprehension

4 **NOTE DETAILS**

What did Kavi have to do to achieve her plan? (ask city officials for permission to fix up the houses; ask tradespeople to do the work for free)

5 **MAKE JUDGMENTS**

Do you think what Kavi did was important? Explain. (Responses will vary.)

6 **Focus Skill** **AUTHOR'S PURPOSE AND PERSPECTIVE**

Judging by Jacob Stein's last line on page 645, what do you think is the author's purpose in this text? How do you know? (Possible response: To persuade; the author uses the word *altruism*, which means "to selflessly help someone," suggesting that what Kavi did was a good thing and others should do the same.)

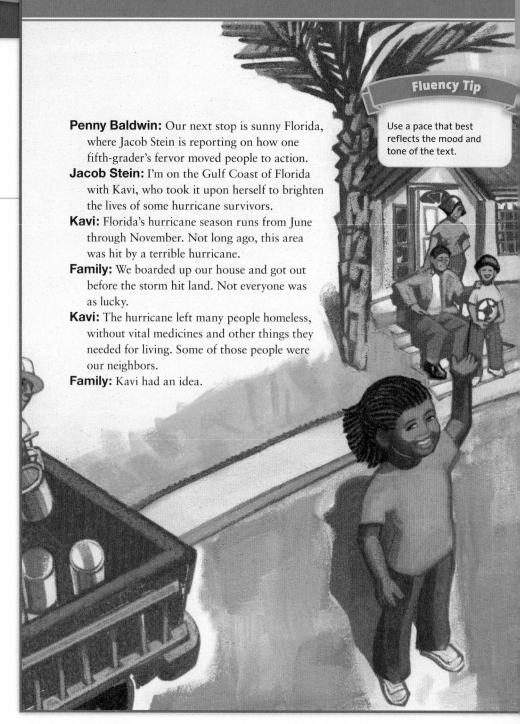

Penny Baldwin: Our next stop is sunny Florida, where Jacob Stein is reporting on how one fifth-grader's fervor moved people to action.

Jacob Stein: I'm on the Gulf Coast of Florida with Kavi, who took it upon herself to brighten the lives of some hurricane survivors.

Kavi: Florida's hurricane season runs from June through November. Not long ago, this area was hit by a terrible hurricane.

Family: We boarded up our house and got out before the storm hit land. Not everyone was as lucky.

Kavi: The hurricane left many people homeless, without vital medicines and other things they needed for living. Some of those people were our neighbors.

Family: Kavi had an idea.

Fluency Tip

Use a pace that best reflects the mood and tone of the text.

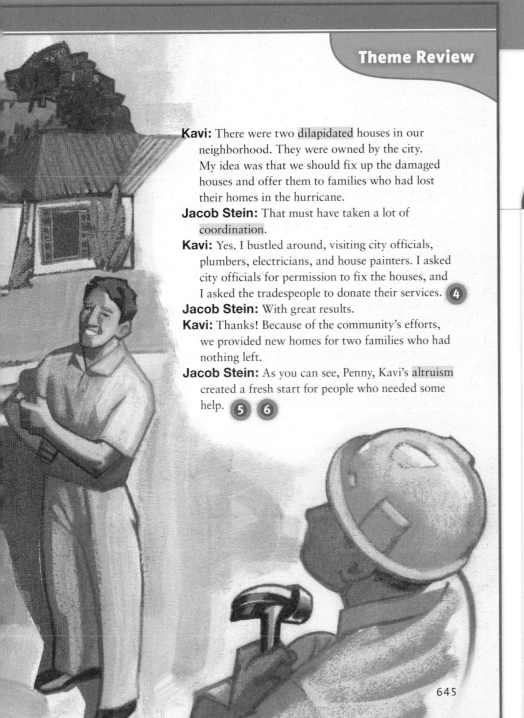

Kavi: There were two dilapidated houses in our neighborhood. They were owned by the city. My idea was that we should fix up the damaged houses and offer them to families who had lost their homes in the hurricane.

Jacob Stein: That must have taken a lot of coordination.

Kavi: Yes. I bustled around, visiting city officials, plumbers, electricians, and house painters. I asked city officials for permission to fix the houses, and I asked the tradespeople to donate their services. ④

Jacob Stein: With great results.

Kavi: Thanks! Because of the community's efforts, we provided new homes for two families who had nothing left.

Jacob Stein: As you can see, Penny, Kavi's altruism created a fresh start for people who needed some help. ⑤ ⑥

645

ANALYZE WRITER'S CRAFT

Word Choice Point out the word *fervor* in the third line on page 644. Ask students what other words the author might have used that mean the same as *fervor*. (Possible responses: *enthusiasm, passion, intense feeling*) Then have students identify each word's shade of meaning, or how strong each word is. Discuss with them if the author's use of *fervor* was the best word choice, or if there was a better choice, and have students explain their reasoning.

Reading for Fluency

Fluency Tip **PACE** Have students read the Fluency Tip on page 644. Remind students that pace is how fast or slow a person reads. Ask

- **When a character is talking about a situation that caused harm to people, should you read the words faster or slower than normal? Why?** (Possible response: slower; because it is a serious topic)

- **When a character feels hopeful that he or she can help people in difficulty, should you read the words faster or slower than normal? Why?** (Possible response: faster; because it is a happy topic)

Have students look at each line of dialogue listed below, identify each character's emotion, and tell whether the dialogue should be read faster or slower than normal.

- **page 644, Kavi's second set of lines** (Possible response: sad, serious; slower)

- **page 645, Kavi's first set of lines** (Possible response: excited; faster)

- **page 645, Kavi's third set of lines** (Possible response: excited, hopeful; faster)

Monitor Comprehension

7 **CONTEXT CLUES**

What does Penny Baldwin mean when she says that the report on Kavi's project is a *moving* story? (Possible response: It is a story that causes the audience to feel strong emotions.)

8 **AUTHOR'S PURPOSE AND PERSPECTIVE**

Focus Skill

What do you think is the author's perspective about rain forests? (Possible response: That they should be preserved.) **How does the author's perspective influence the text?** (Possible response: The author tells about the positive efforts Sheila and her friends made toward helping preserve rain forests.)

9 **COMPARE AND CONTRAST**

What is one difference between Sheila's project and the projects described earlier in the article? (Possible response: Sheila's project involves helping plants and animals. The other projects focus on helping people.)

Penny Baldwin: What a moving story. Next, let's go to Ohio **7** and Addison Base, our reporter who's talking with Sheila.

Addison Base: Sheila used her artistic sensibility and her passion for the environment to connect people from Columbus, Ohio, with people around the world. Sheila, please tell us about it.

Sheila: Last summer, I was the giddiest girl in all of Ohio! My uncle invited me to go with him on an ecological research trip to Costa Rica.

Addison Base: How was the trip?

Sheila: It was a great adventure! The rain forest is an amazing place that everyone *should* be able to enjoy. But soon people may not be able to, because the rain forests there are in big trouble.

Addison Base: So you decided to take action.

Sheila: I thought people might be more interested in preserving these precious forests if they could see how beautiful they are. I asked twelve of my friends to each draw a rain forest scene based on the photographs my uncle had taken. We put our illustrations together to make calendars.

Addison Base: That must have been fun.

Sheila: It was! We sold copies of the calendars at a craft fair and donated all the money to an advocacy group that works to protect rain forests.

Addison Base: Sheila's enterprising effort really paid off! Back to you, Penny. **8** **9**

646

ADVANCED

Rain Forests in Costa Rica Use a world map or a globe to show students Costa Rica's location. Explain that more than 25% of Costa Rica's territory is protected forests and reserves. Tell students that one of the better-known rain forests in Costa Rica is the Monteverde Cloud Forest Reserve, which is home to more than 100 species of mammals, 400 species of birds, and 2,500 species of plants. Have students discuss if they think protecting such land area is important, and why or why not.

Theme Review

Reading for Fluency

Fluency Tip **PACE** Have students read the Fluency Tip on page 646. Review reasons to read at a slower or faster pace. Then ask

- **Which character on page 646 communicates excitement through dialogue?** (Sheila)

- **Would you read this dialogue faster or slower than normal?** (faster)

- **Which character speaks thoughtfully and carefully?** (Addison Base)

- **Would you read that dialogue faster or slower than normal?** (slower)

"RESEARCH SAYS"

"The main conclusion of this study was that repeated reading worked."
—Dowhower
(1987)

ANALYZE WRITER'S CRAFT

Varying Dialogue Length Point out to students the length of reporter Addison Base's introduction of Sheila, and the brevity of her questions and comments during the interview. Tell students that television reporters introduce the people they are interviewing and then let those people do most of the talking during the interview. Point out that the writer of the script has the reporters follow this procedure.

Monitor Comprehension

10 **CHARACTER'S MOTIVES**

Why does Felix come to the animal shelter every Saturday? (Possible responses: He wants to help the animals feel less lonely; he enjoys playing with animals.)

11 **AUTHOR'S PURPOSE AND PERSPECTIVE**

What do you think was the author's purpose for writing "The Compassion Campaign"? (Possible response: to persuade readers to want to participate in helpful projects in their communities)

12 **THEME**

What is the theme of this selection? (Possible responses: People should take the time to help others; even small things can make big differences.)

Fluency Tip

How does Felix feel about his accomplishments? Read with expression to show his emotions.

Penny Baldwin: For our last story, we go to Atlanta, Georgia, where Randy Vasquez talks to Felix and his furry friends.
Randy Vasquez: Felix, you have a greyhound, a golden retriever, and a poodle—all wanting to be petted.
Felix: These dogs can't get enough attention. That's the main reason I spend so much time at the animal shelter. Animals get lonely, too. **10**

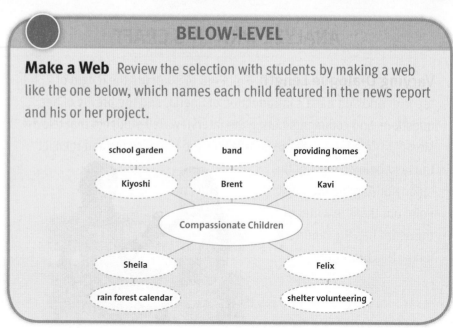

BELOW-LEVEL

Make a Web Review the selection with students by making a web like the one below, which names each child featured in the news report and his or her project.

- school garden
- band
- providing homes
- Kiyoshi
- Brent
- Kavi
- Compassionate Children
- Sheila
- Felix
- rain forest calendar
- shelter volunteering

Randy Vasquez: The shelter director told me that you come here every Saturday with a group of friends.

Felix: For my birthday, my dad took me to the shelter to pick out a puppy. I ended up getting a clumsy mutt named Rascal. He's my pal, and he goes with me everywhere. Visiting the shelter made me feel bad for all of the other animals, though.

Randy Vasquez: So you organized a program?

Felix: Right. We take the dogs on walks. They love to stretch their legs and enjoy the fresh air. We use old socks and string to make toy mice for the cats. They love to chase them around.

Randy Vasquez: What is the most unusual animal you've seen in the shelter?

Felix: Once, a pig was brought to the shelter. We named him Mr. Oink. Mr. Oink had been mistreated. We helped build his trust again by being gentle and patient with him.

Randy Vasquez: What other kinds of animals are in the shelter?

Felix: Sometimes birds are brought in. When birds are under stress, they can lose their feathers. You know they're feeling safe again when their feathers grow back.

Randy Vasquez: Maybe you'll grow up to be a veterinarian one day or have a shelter of your own! Keep up the good work, Felix. Penny, back to you.

Penny Baldwin: All five stories today show that good things happen when kids turn compassionate feelings into compassionate actions. Tune in next month, when we travel to New York to check out murals in the making. Good-bye for now!

649

Reading for Fluency

 EXPRESSION Have students read the Fluency Tip on page 648. Then ask

- **How could you use intonation, volume, and pace to express happiness?** (Possible responses: Use a higher pitch than normal; speak a bit louder and more quickly than normal.)

- **How would you use them to show sadness?** (Possible responses: Use a lower pitch; speak more softly and more slowly than normal.)

You might want to use this model to show students how to read Felix's third set of lines on page 649:

Think Aloud The first two sentences give information. They can be read with normal expression. The third sentence tells about a sad situation. It should be read slowly, using a lower pitch. The fourth sentence tells how the volunteers helped the animal feel better. This sentence should be read more quickly and a bit louder, using a higher pitch.

Then have volunteers read the lines using appropriate expression.

SOCIAL STUDIES   SUPPORTING STANDARDS

Community Service Tell students that in a democracy, it is important for people to participate through community service, civic involvement, and political activities. Invite students to discuss ideas for participation in community service that they have read about in "The Compassion Campaign" and ideas for participation that they have thought of themselves.

Performing **Readers' Theater**

Objectives

- *To read aloud with appropriate expression and pace*
- *To listen carefully to text that is read aloud*

▲ **Teacher Resource Book**
pp. 94, 115–119

Fluency Support Materials

Fluency Builders, Grade 5, Lesson 25

Audiotext "The Compassion Campaign" is available on *Audiotext Grade 5,* CD8 for subsequent readings.

PRESENTATION STRATEGIES

SHARE STRATEGIES Share with students these strategies for participating in a Readers' Theater:

SPEAKING STRATEGIES

- Practice reading your part until you can read it naturally, with appropriate **expression** and **pace**.
- Use appropriate facial expressions and gestures.
- Read loudly and clearly.

LISTENING STRATEGIES

- Listen carefully for cues that signal your turn to read.
- Listen carefully to each reader's expression and pace.

RUBRIC See rubric for Presentations on page R5.

PERFORMANCE IDEAS

SHARE IDEAS Choose from among the following ideas.

PREPARE Have students use their highlighted scripts. (See *Teacher Resource Book,* pp. 115–119.)

- Project the backdrop as the setting for the Readers' Theater. (See *Teacher Resource Book,* page 94.)
- Brainstorm with students props and costumes to use in their performance and work with them to gather the items.

REHEARSE Have students practice their parts individually and in groups.

- Give students feedback on their expression and pace.
- Have students rehearse the script, using the backdrop, props, and costumes.

PERFORM Have students design, create, and distribute invitations.

- The invitations should include the date, time, place, and title of the performance.
- Have students create posters advertising the performance.

15 Min. each

Enriching Robust Vocabulary

5-DAY VOCABULARY
DAY 1 Vocabulary, pp. T287–T288
DAY 2 Vocabulary Review, p. T291
DAY 3 Reinforce Word Meanings, p. T301
DAY 4 Extend Word Meanings, p. T301
DAY 5 Cumulative Review, p. T301

REINFORCE WORD MEANINGS

Objective
- *To demonstrate knowledge of word meanings*

REVISIT SELECTION VOCABULARY
Use these questions to discuss "The Compassion Campaign."

1. What did Kiyoshi **loathe**?
2. Would you expect people to choose **bland** foods? Explain.
3. What did Kiyoshi's **mentor** agree to do?
4. What might the **dilapidated** houses look like now?
5. What required **coordination**?
6. Who showed the most **altruism**? Explain.
7. How did Sheila use her artistic **sensibilities** on her project?
8. Why do you think Sheila gave money to an **advocacy** group?
9. How did being **mistreated** affect Mr. Oink?
10. Which student do you think was most **compassionate**? Why?

EXTEND WORD MEANINGS

Objective
- *To extend meanings of words in context*

CRITICAL THINKING Have students discuss the following questions.

1. Why don't people pay high prices for **dilapidated** homes?
2. What do **advocacy** groups do?
3. Are veterinarians usually **compassionate**? Explain.
4. How can **sensibilities** help someone do something well?
5. What was one event at your school that required **coordination**?
6. In what way could you be a good **mentor** for younger students?
7. Why should **mistreated** pets be given new homes?
8. What is a **bland** food you dislike?
9. What type of shoes would you **loathe** wearing?
10. Whom do you admire for his or her **altruism**?

CUMULATIVE REVIEW

Objective
- *To use word relationships to determine meaning*

REVIEW VOCABULARY Discuss students' answers to these questions.

1. What kind of person might **loathe basking** in the sun?
2. Is a **bland** diet **vital** for health? Explain.
3. Why might you want an **enterprising** person as a **mentor**?
4. Why might a **damaged** car be called **dilapidated**?
5. What type of **excursion** requires **coordination**?
6. How can you **detect altruism** in a person's actions?
7. What might be **precious** to a person with an artistic **sensibility**?
8. Why might an **advocacy** group display **fervor**?
9. Do people act **giddiest** when they are **mistreated**? Explain.
10. Why might someone who **bustled** about an animal shelter be thought of as **compassionate**?

Tested ✔

Vocabulary

Lessons 21–24 Review		Lesson 25	
basking	detect	loathe	altruism
vital	precious	bland	sensibility
enterprising	fervor	mentor	advocacy
damaged	giddiest	dilapidated	mistreated
excursion	bustled	coordination	compassionate

READ AND RESPOND

 SOCIAL STUDIES

Comprehension Strategies *Review*

Objectives
- *To recognize the distinguishing character-istics of a folktale*
- *To use comprehension strategies effectively*

Reading Folktales

DISCUSS GENRE: PAGE 650 Have students read the information about folktales on page 650. Discuss with them the characteristics of folktales.

Review the Focus Strategies

DISCUSS COMPREHENSION STRATEGIES: PAGE 650 Have students read the Compre-hension Strategy information on page 650.

REVIEW SUMMARIZE Remind students that as they read, they should pause now and then to summarize what they have read.

REVIEW ANSWER QUESTIONS Remind stu-dents that as they read, they should stop pe-riodically to ask themselves questions about what they are reading and then look back to find the answers.

Lesson 25

COMPREHENSION STRATEGIES
Review

Reading Fiction

Bridge to Reading for Meaning Folktales reflect the values and customs of the culture from which they come. They are passed down from one generation to the next and often teach a lesson. The notes on page 651 point out characteristics of folktales, including story elements and explanations for things in nature. Understanding these characteristics can help you better understand the lesson the folktale is teaching.

Review the Focus Strategies

You can use the strategies you learned about in this theme to help you better understand the literature you read.

Summarize
Stop now and then to summarize the most important events. That will help you understand and remember what you have read.

Answer Questions
Use your prior knowledge and the information in the text to answer questions about what you are reading.

As you read "How Beaver Stole Fire" on pages 652–655, think about where and how to use comprehension strategies.

650

BELOW-LEVEL

Beavers, Cedars, and Pines Read aloud the title of the selection on page 651. Preview the selection with students, pointing out pictures of the beaver, the pines, and the cedar. Ask students to share what they know about beavers. Then tell students that pines and cedars are evergreen trees—trees that do not drop leaves—and that these trees can grow very tall.

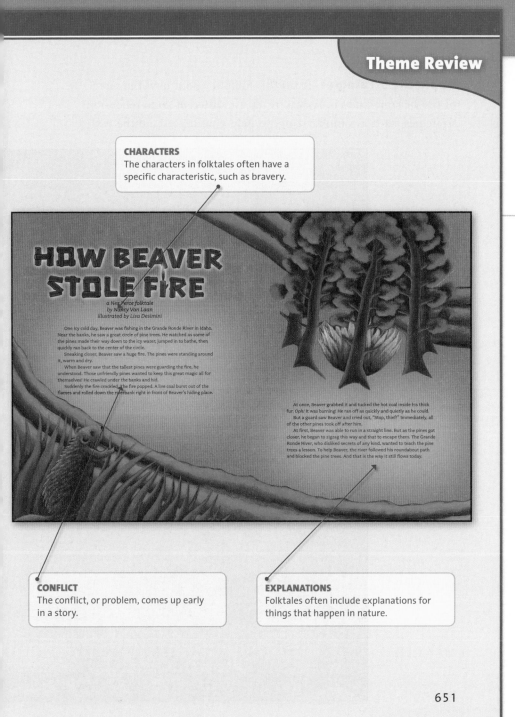

Theme Review

CHARACTERS
The characters in folktales often have a specific characteristic, such as bravery.

HOW BEAVER STOLE FIRE

a Nez Perce folktale
by Nancy Van Laan
illustrated by Lisa Desimini

One icy cold day, Beaver was fishing in the Grande Ronde River in Idaho. Near the banks, he saw a great circle of pine trees. He watched as some of the pines made their way down to the icy water, jumped in to bathe, then quickly ran back to the center of the circle.

Sneaking closer, Beaver saw a huge fire. The pines were standing around it, warm and dry.

When Beaver saw that the tallest pines were guarding the fire, he understood. Those unfriendly pines wanted to keep this great magic all for themselves! He crawled under the banks and hid.

Suddenly the fire crackled. The fire popped. A live coal burst out of the flames and rolled down the riverbank right in front of Beaver's hiding place.

At once, Beaver grabbed it and tucked the hot coal inside his thick fur. *Oph!* It was burning! He ran off as quickly and quietly as he could.

But a guard saw Beaver and cried out, "Stop, thief!" Immediately, all of the other pines took off after him.

At first, Beaver was able to run in a straight line. But as the pines got closer, he began to zigzag this way and that to escape them. The Grande Ronde River, who disliked secrets of any kind, wanted to teach the pine trees a lesson. To help Beaver, the river followed his roundabout path and blocked the pine trees. And that is the way it still flows today.

651

CONFLICT
The conflict, or problem, comes up early in a story.

EXPLANATIONS
Folktales often include explanations for things that happen in nature.

Preview/Set Purpose

PREVIEW AND PREDICT Have students page through the story. Ask them to discuss what they notice in the pictures. Then have them predict how Beaver stole the fire.

MODEL SETTING A PURPOSE Have students set their own purpose for reading, based on their preview of the selection and what they know about folktales. You may want to use this model:

> Think Aloud The pictures show a beaver, and many tall trees surrounding a fire. One purpose for reading would be to find out how Beaver stole fire and what role the trees play in the story.

Discuss Text Features

Point out the distinguishing features of folktales noted on *Student Edition* page 651.

CHARACTERS Many folktales have animal characters that represent human qualities.

CONFLICT In many folktales, the conflict is introduced at the beginning of the story.

EXPLANATIONS Some folktales explain how things in the world came to be.

TECHNOLOGY

 eBook "How Beaver Stole Fire" is available in an eBook.

Monitor Comprehension

1 **LITERARY DEVICES**
Focus Skill
What is an example of personification the author uses? (Possible response: The trees jump into the river to bathe.)

2 **NOTE DETAILS**
How did Beaver discover that the trees had fire? (He saw them jump into the icy river and then hurry back to stand in a circle. When he went to see what was going on inside the circle, he saw a fire that was warming the trees.)

3 **DRAW CONCLUSIONS**
Why do you think Beaver decided to run away with the live coal? (Possible response: He had seen that fire was very useful, and he wanted to share it with others.)

4 **MAKE JUDGMENTS**
Did Beaver really steal fire from the trees? Explain. (Possible responses: Yes; he took something that belonged to the trees. No; the burning coal rolled away from the fire and toward Beaver, so it was his to take.)

Apply the Strategies Read this folktale about how the secret of fire became known. As you read, use different comprehension strategies, such as summarizing, to help you understand the text.

HOW BEAVER STOLE FIRE

a Nez Perce folktale
by Nancy Van Laan
illustrated by Lisa Desimini

One icy cold day, Beaver was fishing in the Grande Ronde River in Idaho. Near the banks, he saw a great circle of pine trees. He watched as some of the pines made their way down to the icy water, jumped in to bathe, then quickly ran back to the center of the circle.
1
Sneaking closer, Beaver saw a huge fire. The pines were standing around it, warm and dry.
2
When Beaver saw that the tallest pines were guarding the fire, he understood. Those unfriendly pines wanted to keep this great magic all for themselves! He crawled under the banks and hid.
Suddenly the fire crackled. The fire popped. A live coal burst out of the flames and rolled down the riverbank right in front of Beaver's hiding place.

652

E L L

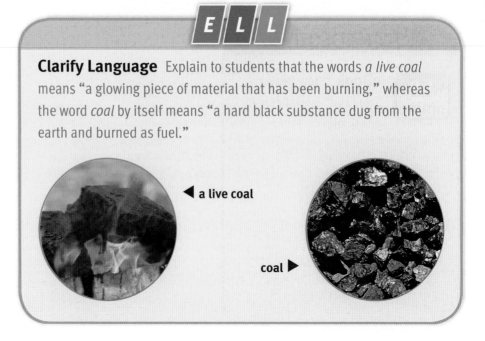

Clarify Language Explain to students that the words *a live coal* means "a glowing piece of material that has been burning," whereas the word *coal* by itself means "a hard black substance dug from the earth and burned as fuel."

◀ a live coal

coal ▶

Stop and Think

Theme Review

As you read, summarize the steps Beaver takes to steal fire. **SUMMARIZE**

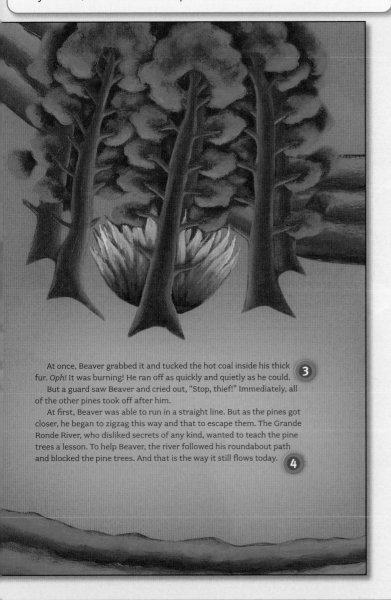

At once, Beaver grabbed it and tucked the hot coal inside his thick fur. *Oph!* It was burning! He ran off as quickly and quietly as he could. **3**

But a guard saw Beaver and cried out, "Stop, thief!" Immediately, all of the other pines took off after him.

At first, Beaver was able to run in a straight line. But as the pines got closer, he began to zigzag this way and that to escape them. The Grande Ronde River, who disliked secrets of any kind, wanted to teach the pine trees a lesson. To help Beaver, the river followed his roundabout path and blocked the pine trees. And that is the way it still flows today. **4**

653

Stop and Think

Apply Comprehension Strategies

Summarize

APPLY THE STRATEGY Have students read the information in the Stop and Think box at the top of page 653. Remind them to apply the strategy as they read the text. Model using the strategy:

Think Aloud Beaver discovers that the pine trees have a powerful new element, fire, which they are keeping for themselves. When a live coal rolls toward Beaver, he picks it up and tries to sneak away, but the trees discover what he is doing and chase him.

Then have volunteers summarize what they have read so far.

SOCIAL STUDIES SUPPORTING STANDARDS

The Nez Perce Tell students that the setting of this folktale is the traditional homeland of the Nez Perce native peoples. Explain that the Nez Perce helped the United States Corps of Discovery, headed by Meriwether Lewis and William Clark, travel through this region late in the year 1805. The region was then called the Louisiana Purchase, and it stretched from the Mississippi River westward to the Rocky Mountains. The land added by the Louisiana Purchase makes up almost 25% of the United States today.

Monitor Comprehension

5 **NOTE DETAILS**

Why weren't the trees able to catch Beaver? (Possible responses: Beaver could run because he had legs, but the trees only had trunks and they kept falling.)

6 **AUTHOR'S PURPOSE AND PERSPECTIVE**

Focus Skill

What do you think the author's purpose was for retelling this folktale? (Possible responses: She wanted to entertain people with a tale about how some things in nature came to be the way they are. She wanted to tell people not to be selfish.)

7 **MAIN IDEA AND DETAILS**

What unusual occurrences in nature in the Grande Ronde-Snake River area does this folktale explain? (Possible responses: why the Grande Ronde follows a zigzag course; why pine trees grow very near the Grande Ronde's waters; why a single cedar tree grows in a place so far away from other cedars)

The pines soon grew tired, for they had only fat trunks, not legs to run with like Beaver. One by one, they tripped and fell, tripped and fell, as their roots caught on the scraggly brush. All but the tallest finally gave up. They stopped, up, down, and around the riverbanks. And that is exactly where they stand today. **5**

But the great cedar kept running. He did not want the other trees and animals to learn about fire. He alone understood its tremendous power. He knew that fire could be used unwisely. Cedar, of course, was right, for today fire is one of the greatest enemies of all trees.

So Cedar called out to the others, "I will go to the top of the hill and see how far ahead Beaver is."

He reached the top just in time to see Beaver dive into the Big Snake River, right where the Grande Ronde now enters it. He saw Beaver swim across and give fire to the willows, then cross back again to give fire to the birches, then far, far down the river, to give fire to some of the other trees. And he saw these trees become the givers of fire by rubbing the sticks of their branches just so, to create new fire.

654

BELOW-LEVEL

Scaffolding a Response If students have difficulty responding to item 6, suggest that they look on pages 653–655 to find out what happened as the result of

- the Grande Ronde River's efforts to slow the trees down.
- the trees' fatigue, which caused them to trip and fall.
- the great cedar's pursuit of Beaver.

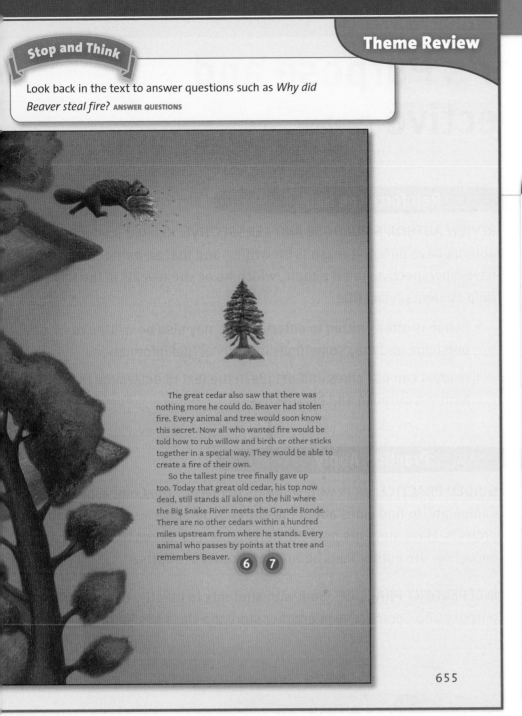

Stop and Think

Look back in the text to answer questions such as *Why did Beaver steal fire?* ANSWER QUESTIONS

The great cedar also saw that there was nothing more he could do. Beaver had stolen fire. Every animal and tree would soon know this secret. Now all who wanted fire would be told how to rub willow and birch or other sticks together in a special way. They would be able to create a fire of their own.

So the tallest pine tree finally gave up too. Today that great old cedar, his top now dead, still stands all alone on the hill where the Big Snake River meets the Grande Ronde. There are no other cedars within a hundred miles upstream from where he stands. Every animal who passes by points at that tree and remembers Beaver. **6** **7**

655

Stop and Think

Apply Comprehension Strategies

Answer Questions

APPLY THE STRATEGY Have students read the information in the Stop and Think box at the top of page 655. Remind them to apply the strategy as they read the text. You may want to use this model:

Think Aloud The question asks why Beaver stole fire. By rereading page 652, you will recall that Beaver saw how useful fire is when he looked into the tree circle, and you will also recall that Beaver realized that the trees were trying to keep this for themselves. With this information you can answer the question: Beaver stole fire because he knew it was useful, and he realized that if he didn't steal it, only the trees would ever have fire.

Then have students share questions they had while reading.

 WRITING CONNECTION

Retell a Folktale Have students each recall a folktale they have read or heard. Tell them to retell this folktale in writing. Explain that they should tell the main events as they remember them but not worry about including precise details, and that they should include at least a few lines of dialogue. You may want to have students read aloud their completed retellings.

Author's Purpose and Perspective *Review*

Objectives

- *To understand that authors have different purposes for writing*
- *To identify and discuss an author's perspective*

Skill Trace

 Tested **Author's Purpose and Perspective**

Introduce	pp. T30–T31
Reteach	pp. S2–S3, S10–S11
Review	pp. T56–T57, T106–T107, T132–T133, T308
Test	Theme 5
Maintain	p. T274, Theme 6

Reinforce the Skill

REVIEW AUTHOR'S PURPOSE AND PERSPECTIVE Remind students that authors have different reasons for writing and that an author may also have a perspective about a topic, which he or she reveals in the text. Help students recall that

- fiction is often written to entertain but may also be written to persuade and may sometimes include factual information.
- readers can use clues and details in the text to determine the author's purpose and perspective.

Practice/Apply

GUIDED PRACTICE Work with students to revisit "The Compassion Campaign" to find clues about the author's perspective on community projects. Have students note the news reporters' words that let a reader know how the author feels about these kinds of efforts.

INDEPENDENT PRACTICE Work with students to identify the author's purpose and perspective in another story the class has read.

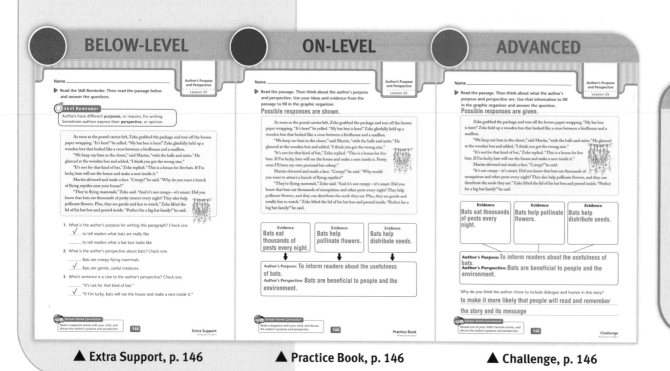

▲ **Extra Support, p. 146**   ▲ **Practice Book, p. 146**   ▲ **Challenge, p. 146**

ELL

- Group students according to academic levels, and assign one of the pages on the left.

- Clarify any unfamiliar concepts as necessary. See *ELL Teacher Guide* Lesson 25 for support in scaffolding instruction.

Literary Devices
Review

Reinforce the Skill

REVIEW LITERARY DEVICES Remind students that authors use literary devices to help readers clearly picture ideas in a text and to enhance a text. Help students recall that

- imagery uses vivid language to describe people, places, things, and ideas.
- figurative language uses words that have meanings other than their literal meanings.

Practice/Apply

GUIDED PRACTICE Have pairs of students look back at the final paragraph on *Student Edition* page 652 and identify the literary devices the author uses to describe the sound and appearance of the fire and the movements of the live coal.

INDEPENDENT PRACTICE Have students each choose a short fiction story and read the first few pages silently looking for examples of literary devices. Then have students explain how the examples they found are used to describe people, feelings, or objects.

Objectives

- *To recognize and understand literary devices*
- *To identify and use sensory language*

Skill Trace

 Tested Literary Devices

Introduce	pp. T166–T167
Reteach	pp. S20–S21, S28–S29
Review	**pp. T192–T193, T226–T227, T254–T255, T309**
Test	Theme 5
Maintain	p. T144, Theme 6

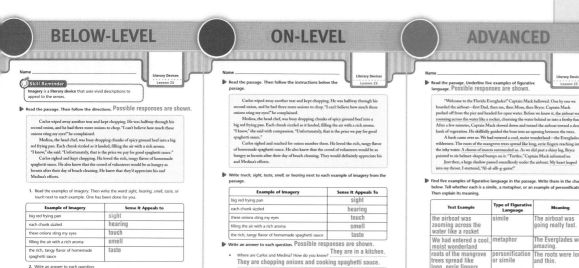

▲ Extra Support, p. 147   ▲ Practice Book, p. 147   ▲ Challenge, p. 147

E L L

- Group students according to academic levels, and assign one of the pages on the left.

- Clarify any unfamiliar concepts as necessary. See *ELL Teacher Guide* Lesson 25 for support in scaffolding instruction.

Literary Patterns and Symbols
Review

Objective

- *To identify and evaluate archetypal patterns and symbols in literary texts*

Skill Trace

 Tested **Literary Patterns and Symbols**

Introduce	pp. T68–T69, Theme 4
Reteach	pp. S8–S9, Theme 4
Review	**pp. T194, T310**
Test	Theme 4
Maintain	p. T210, Theme 6

Reinforce the Skill

REVIEW LITERARY PATTERNS AND SYMBOLS Remind students that many folktales and fables have familiar patterns and symbols. Review the following:

- Characters in folktales are often animals or other things in nature that act like humans and represent certain human qualities.

- Often, the characters in a folktale or fable represent values, beliefs, and ideas that are important to many people.

Practice/Apply

GUIDED PRACTICE Ask students what things in nature the characters represent in "How Beaver Stole Fire." (an animal, some trees, a river) Then have students review the selection and identify the values the folktale wants to share. (Possible response: It is important to share something that can benefit others.)

INDEPENDENT PRACTICE Have pairs of students look at another folktale. Tell them to identify and note what things in nature the characters represent, and what values, beliefs, or ideas are expressed in the folktale.

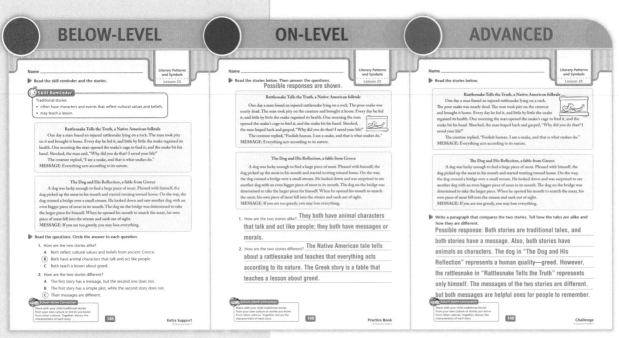

▲ Extra Support, p. 148 ▲ Practice Book, p. 148 ▲ Challenge, p. 148

E L L

- Group students according to academic levels, and assign one of the pages on the left.

- Clarify any unfamiliar concepts as necessary. See *ELL Teacher Guide* Lesson 25 for support in scaffolding instruction.

Draw Conclusions
Review

Reinforce the Skill

REVIEW DRAWING CONCLUSIONS Remind students that because authors do not explain everything in stories, readers must draw conclusions to figure out things the author does not directly state. Use the information below to review:

- Use information given in the story along with your knowledge and experience.
- For a conclusion to be valid, it must be supported by text evidence.

Practice/Apply

GUIDED PRACTICE Have students reread *Student Edition* page 645. Point out that the author does not explain why the tradespeople volunteered to donate their time. Help students to recall story information and what they know from real life to conclude why the tradespeople did this. (Possible response: Because they wanted to help people who had lost their homes.)

INDEPENDENT PRACTICE Have students choose a piece of fiction they have read recently and draw a conclusion about a character's motives in a section of the story.

Objectives

- *To draw conclusions about text information*
- *To support conclusions with text evidence and personal experience*

Skill Trace

Tested **Draw Conclusions**

Introduce	pp. T134–T135
Reteach	pp. S16–S17
Review	**pp. T256, T311**
Test	Theme 5
Maintain	p. T209, Theme 6

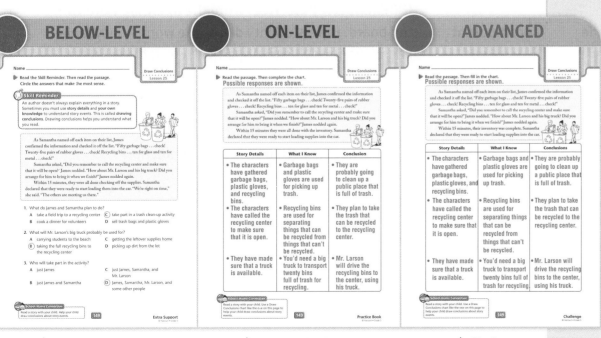

▲ Extra Support, p. 149   ▲ Practice Book, p. 149   ▲ Challenge, p. 149

ELL

- Group students according to academic levels, and assign one of the pages on the left.

- Clarify any unfamiliar concepts as necessary. See *ELL Teacher Guide* Lesson 25 for support in scaffolding instruction.

Decoding/Word Attack
Review

Lesson 21

Structural Analysis: Word Parts
in-, out-, down-, up-

Objective
- *To use structural analysis to decode longer words*

Reinforce the Skill

DECODE LONGER WORDS Write the words *income, outpatient, downstairs,* and *upright* on the board and read them aloud. Guide students to divide the words into syllables and then blend the syllables to read the words. (in/come; out/patient; down/stairs; up/right)

Practice/Apply

INDEPENDENT PRACTICE Write the following words on the board. Have students identify the prefix in each word, divide the word into syllables, and blend the syllables together to read the word.

outspoken	**downgrade**	**incompetent**
out/spo/ken	down/grade	in/com/pe/tent

outgoing	**downbeat**	**inorganic**
out/go/ing	down/beat	in/or/gan/ic

Lesson 22

Structural Analysis: Word Parts
-ation, -ition, -sion, -ion

Objectives
- *To review word parts -ation, -ition, -sion, -ion*
- *To use knowledge of word parts to decode longer words*

Reinforce the Skill

DECODE LONGER WORDS Write the word *alteration* on the board and read it aloud. Then guide students to divide the word into syllables. (al/ter/a/tion) Model blending the syllables to say the whole word.

Next, write the word *invention* on the board. Then guide students to divide the word into syllables. (in/ven/tion) Then help students blend the syllables together to read the whole word.

Practice/Apply

INDEPENDENT PRACTICE Write the following words on the board. Have students divide the word into syllables, and blend the syllables together to read the word.

resignation	**digestion**
res/ig/na/tion	di/ges/tion

authorization	**prediction**
au/tho/ri/za/tion	pre/dic/tion

Silent Letters

Objectives
- *To correctly pronounce words with silent letters*
- *To apply knowledge of letter-sound correspondences to recognize words*

Reinforce the Skill

DECODE LONGER WORDS Write the word *wreath* on the board and read it aloud. Circle the *w* and remind students that a consonant in a word may be silent, as *w* is in *wreath*.

Next, remind students that silent letters can appear at the beginning, in the middle, or at the end of words. Write the words *autumn*, *knead*, and *glisten* on the board. Have students read each aloud. Then guide them to identify the silent letter in each word. (*n, k, t*)

Practice/Apply

INDEPENDENT PRACTICE Write the following words on the board: *crumb, solemn, hasten, castle*. Have students work in pairs and circle the silent letter in each word. Then have them read aloud each word.

crum(b)
solem(n)
has(t)en
cas(t)le

Structural Analysis: Unusual Plurals

Objective
- *To decode unusual plurals*

Reinforce the Skill

DECODE LONGER WORDS Write the following word pairs on the board and read them aloud: *stitch/stitches, army/armies, shelf/shelves, echo/echoes, radio/radios*. Review with students the rule that applies to each plural.

- The ending *-es* is added to words that end in *sh*, *ch*, *ss*, *s*, *x*, or *z*, such as in *stitch*. It forms its own syllable when it follows a consonant.

- In words that end in consonant plus *y*, such as in *army*, the *y* changes to *i* when *-es* is added. Although the spelling changes, the vowel sound stays the same.

- In many words that end in *f*, such as *shelf*, the *f* changes to *v* when *-es* is added. The *f* sound becomes /v/ and the *-es* ending is pronounced /z/.

- In some words that end in *o*, such as *echo*, the ending *-es* is added. The *oe* makes the long *o* sound.

- In some words that end in *o*, such as *radio*, only *-s* is added. The *o* retains the long *o* sound.

Practice/Apply

INDEPENDENT PRACTICE Write these words on the board: *leaf, tomato, address, country, studio*. Have students make word pairs by writing the plural for each word. Tell them to explain how they formed each plural. Then have them read aloud the word pairs.

Spelling
Review

15 Min. each

Objectives

- *To spell correctly words with word parts in-, out-, up-, and down-*
- *To spell correctly words with word parts -ation, -ition, -sion, and -ion*
- *To spell correctly words with silent letters and unusual plurals*

Review Spelling Words

1. **indecisive**	11. **autumn**
2. **outpatient**	12. **knowledge**
3. **downgrade**	13. **rhyme**
4. **uptight**	14. **scenery**
5. **acceleration**	15. **wrestled**
6. **demolition**	16. **armies**
7. **pension**	17. **shelves**
8. **champion**	18. **radios**
9. **authorization**	19. **tomatoes**
10. **cancellation**	20. **videos**

Day 1 — Lesson 21

Words with Word Parts *in-, out-, up-, down-*

ADMINISTER THE PRETEST Use the Dictation Sentences under Day 5. Help students self-check their pretests, using *Practice Book* page 150.

Routine Card 10 **LESSON REVIEW** Write the words *indecisive*, *outpatient*, *downgrade*, and *uptight* on the board. Point out the word part in each. Remind students that when these word parts are added to a base word, the spelling of the base word does not change.

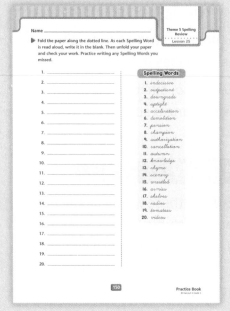

▲ Practice Book, p. 150

▲ Spelling Practice Book, p. 99

Day 2 — Lesson 22

Words with Word Parts *-ation, -ition, -sion, -ion*

LESSON REVIEW Write the words *acceleration*, *demolition*, *pension*, and *champion* on the board. Point out the word part in each. Remind students that the word part *-ation* and *-ition* are each spelled with a *t*.

ADD-A-WORD PART Write the following on the board. Have students write the correct word part, *-ation*, *-ition*, *-sion*, or *-ion*, in each blank.

demol<u>ition</u>
pen<u>sion</u>
acceler<u>ation</u>
authoriz<u>ation</u>
champ<u>ion</u>
cancell<u>ation</u>

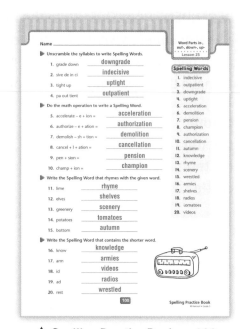

▲ Spelling Practice Book, p. 100

Words with Silent Letters

LESSON REVIEW Write the words *autumn*, *knowledge*, *rhyme*, and *wrestled* on the board and have students copy them. Read each word aloud and have students circle the silent letter or letters. Point out that a silent letter can come at the beginning, middle, or end of a word.

ADD A LITTLE SILENCE Write each incomplete word on the board. Have students copy these, replacing each blank with the silent letter that should appear there.

rhym<u>e</u>   <u>w</u>res<u>t</u>led
autum<u>n</u>   kno<u>w</u>led<u>g</u>e

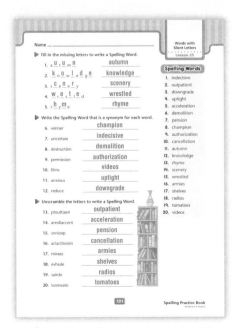

▲ Spelling Practice Book, p. 101

Words with Unusual Plurals

LESSON REVIEW Review the following:

• The ending *-es* is added to words ending in *sh*, *ch*, *ss*, *s*, *x*, or *z*.

• In words ending in consonant plus *y*, the *y* changes to *i* when *-es* is added.

• In many words ending in *f*, the *f* changes to *v* when *-es* is added.

• In some words ending in *o*, the ending *-es* is added. In others, the ending *-s* is added.

COMPLETE THE PATTERN Have students copy and complete these patterns.

one radio, two <u>radios</u>
one shelf, two <u>shelves</u>
one army, two <u>armies</u>
one tomato, two <u>tomatoes</u>

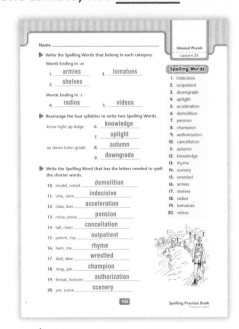

▲ Spelling Practice Book, p. 102

DICTATION SENTENCES

1. Cal was **indecisive** in the store.

2. An **outpatient** goes home after treatment.

3. The doctor may **downgrade** the patient's condition.

4. When you feel **uptight**, you should take a deep breath.

5. This car has great **acceleration**.

6. The **demolition** of the old fence begins today.

7. My grandmother receives checks from her **pension**.

8. We cheered the **champion**.

9. You cannot enter without **authorization**.

10. The **cancellation** of the show disappointed everyone.

11. Is **autumn** your favorite season?

12. A quiz tests your **knowledge**.

13. Pam likes poems that **rhyme**.

14. Utah is known for its **scenery**.

15. Two kittens **wrestled** playfully.

16. The **armies** marched swiftly.

17. I cannot reach those **shelves**.

18. Some **radios** are portable.

19. Ripe **tomatoes** smell wonderful.

20. We stayed indoors and watched **videos**.

Writing: Revise and Publish
Portfolio Selections

15 Min. each

Objectives

- *To revise writing for sentence fluency and organization*
- *To refine a selected piece to publish*

Editor's Marks

✗ delete text
∧ insert text
◌ move text
¶ new paragraph
≡ capitalize
/ lowercase
○ correct spelling
○ close up letters
∿ transpose letters

120   Teacher Resource Book

▲ **Teacher Resource Book, p. 120**

Writer's Companion Grade 5

▲ **Writer's Companion, Lesson 25**

Day 1   REVIEW

REVIEW PREVIOUS ASSIGNMENTS

Tell students that they can choose to revise their persuasive compositions or one of the four writing assignments they completed in Theme 5. Explain that when they choose a piece of writing to revise and publish, their choice should demonstrate their ability to write persuasively.

DISTRIBUTE RUBRIC Distribute to students a copy of the scoring rubric on page R7. Point out to students the characteristics of an excellent paper with a score of 6. Tell students to reread the writing assignment they chose to see how they could improve it.

Day 2   REVISE

REVISE FOR SENTENCE FLUENCY

Remind students that good writers use sentence variety to keep readers engaged. They include questions and exclamations as well as statements. They vary the length of sentences.

Then have students review their writing to find places where they can improve their writing. For example, they can rewrite one or more statements as questions or exclamations, or they can combine short sentences to achieve variety in sentence length.

Note: A 4-point rubric appears on page R8.

SCORING RUBRIC

	6	**5**	**4**	**3**	**2**	**1**
FOCUS	Completely focused, purposeful.	Focused on topic and purpose.	Generally focused on topic and purpose.	Somewhat focused on topic and purpose.	Related to topic but does not maintain focus.	Lacks focus and purpose.
ORGANIZATION	Ideas progress logically; paper conveys sense of completeness.	Organization mostly clear; paper gives sense of completeness.	Organization mostly clear, but some lapses occur; may seem unfinished.	Some sense of organization; seems unfinished.	Little sense of organization.	Little or no sense of organization.
SUPPORT	Strong, specific details; clear, exact language; freshness of expression.	Strong, specific details; clear, exact language.	Adequate support and word choice.	Limited supporting details; limited word choice.	Few supporting details; limited word choice.	Little development; limited or unclear word choice.
CONVENTIONS	Varied sentences; few, if any, errors.	Varied sentences; few errors.	Some sentence variety; few errors.	Simple sentence structures; some errors.	Simple sentence structures; many errors.	Unclear sentence structures; many errors.

REPRODUCIBLE RUBRIC appears on page R7.

THEME 5 WRITING		
Reading-Writing Connection	Persuasive Composition	Sentence Fluency
LESSON	**FORM**	**TRAIT**
21	Persuasive Letter	Sentence Fluency
22	Persuasive Paragraph	Sentence Fluency
23	Poem	Organization
24	Narrative	Organization
25 REVIEW	**Revise and Publish**	**Sentence Fluency/Organization**

Day 3 — PROOFREAD

REVISE FOR ORGANIZATION Remind students that good writers organize their compositions in a way that makes sense. Tell students to

- make sure persuasive letters, paragraphs, and composition include reasons and details that support each persuasive point.

- make sure creative writing includes specific details that appeals to the senses.

Day 4 — PUBLISH

FINAL COPIES Tell students to create final copies from their drafts. If students use a word processing program, provide these tips:

- choose a style of type that is easy to read.

- use the grammar-check feature to make sure your sentences are written correctly.

- always use a dictionary when you are unsure of a spelling.

HANDWRITING Remind students to use their best handwriting on any parts of their final copies that are not created electronically.

Day 5 — PRESENT

PRESENTATION Students may present their writing by posting it on a bulletin board or by reading it aloud.

LISTENING AND SPEAKING STRATEGIES Share the following information with students who are presenting their writing orally. Speakers should

- practice reading before reading aloud to the class.

- make eye contact with the audience.

- speak clearly and loudly.

Share the following information with students who are listening:

- pay attention to the speaker.

- show interest by nodding at appropriate times.

Lesson 25 — WEEKLY LESSON TEST

- Selection Comprehension with Short Response

- Robust Vocabulary

 Podcasting: Assessing Fluency

 For prescriptions, see pp. A2–A6. Also available electronically on *StoryTown Online Assessment* and ExamView®.

▲ Weekly Lesson Test, Lesson 25

Grammar
Review

15 Min. each

Day 1 Lessons 21 & 22

Daily Proofreading

1. He are uncompetent. (He is incompetent.)

2. Gloria and Janelle wants permission to go on the hike. (want; permission)

REVIEW VERBS Display **Transparency LA159** and review the concepts with students.

APPLY THE CONCEPTS Tell students to decide whether each underlined verb in sentences 1–4 is an action verb (*A*) or a linking verb (*L*).

Have students identify the correct present-tense verb forms in items 5–8.

Day 2 Lessons 21 & 22

Daily Proofreading

3. Last autunm Wes is the student council leader. (autumn; Wes was)

4. Now the council made safety videoes for kids. (makes; videos)

PROOFREAD VERBS Remind students that when they proofread, they should make sure that all verbs agree with their subjects.

PROOFREAD Have students rewrite each sentence correctly.

1. Spring are the best time to plant a garden. (Spring is)

2. Each spring the mentor show volunteers proper methods of planting. (shows OR showed)

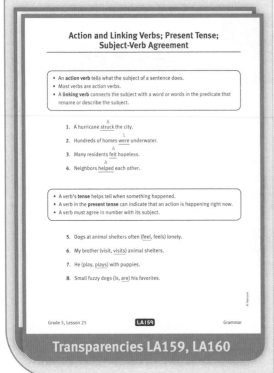

Action and Linking Verbs; Present Tense; Subject-Verb Agreement

- An **action verb** tells what the subject of a sentence does.
- Most verbs are action verbs.
- A **linking verb** connects the subject with a word or words in the predicate that rename or describe the subject.

      A
1. A hurricane <u>struck</u> the city.
      L
2. Hundreds of homes <u>were</u> underwater.
      A
3. Many residents <u>felt</u> hopeless.
      A
4. Neighbors <u>helped</u> each other.

- A verb's **tense** helps tell when something happened.
- A verb in the **present tense** can indicate that an action is happening right now.
- A verb must agree in number with its subject.

5. Dogs at animal shelters often (<u>feel</u>, feels) lonely.
6. My brother (visit, <u>visits</u>) animal shelters.
7. He (play, <u>plays</u>) with puppies.
8. Small fuzzy dogs (is, <u>are</u>) his favorites.

Grade 5, Lesson 25   **LA159**   Grammar

Transparencies LA159, LA160

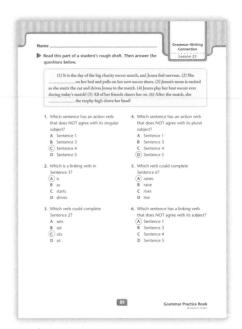

▲ Grammar Practice Book, p. 89

Objectives
- *To use correctly verbs and verb tenses in speaking and writing*
- *To use correct subject-verb agreement*

Day 3 | **Lessons 23 & 24**

Daily Proofreading

5. Volunteers often dusts off shelfs for elderly residents. (dust; shelves)

6. Last year volunteers show great dedicasion during the storm. (showed; dedication)

REVIEW VERBS Display **Transparency LA160** and review the concepts with students.

APPLY THE CONCEPTS Have students complete sentences 1–4 by writing the correct past- or future-tense form of the verb in parentheses.

Have students read sentences 5–8. Tell them to decide whether each underlined verb is in the present-perfect tense, the past-perfect tense, or the future-perfect tense.

Day 4 | **Lessons 23 & 24**

Daily Proofreading

7. The tomatos be ripe next month. (tomatoes; will be)

8. The gardeners has cleared the derbis from the shed. (have cleared; debris)

PROOFREAD FOR VERBS Remind students that when they proofread, they should make sure that all verbs are in the correct tense.

PROOFREAD Have students proofread each sentence and rewrite it correctly.

1. Meg's band will performs at the senior center tomorrow. (will perform)

2. Last week they play at the school picnic. (played)

3. Her band have become my favorite. (has become)

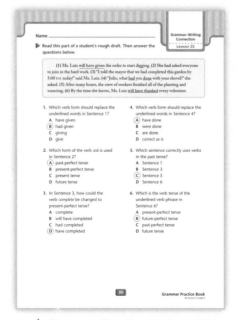

▲ Grammar Practice Book, p. 90

Cumulative Review

Day 5 | **Lesson 25**

Daily Proofreading

9. My sister have volunteered at the clinic (has; clinic.)

10. By Friday she will have became someone's companyon. (will have become; companion.)

ACTION AND LINKING VERBS Have students identify each action verb and linking verb.

1. Darius is Tom's assisstant. (L)

2. Some win awards for their work. (A)

SUBJECT-VERB AGREEMENT Have students identify the correct present-tense verb form.

3. Valerie and Jody (hope, hopes) for an award this year.

4. Each (spend, spends) five hours a week as a volunteer.

PAST AND FUTURE TENSES Have students write the correct verb form.

5. Next week Valerie will decorate recycling containers. (decorate)

6. The old ones looked ugly, as these photos show. (look)

PERFECT TENSES Have students identify the tense of each verb form.

7. By tomorrow night I will have finished painting. (future perfect)

8. I had expected to finish it yesterday. (past perfect)

Leveled Readers
Reinforcing Skills and Strategies

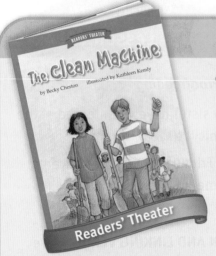

BELOW-LEVEL

The Clean Machine

SUMMARY Two students have formed a group called *The Clean Machine* to clean up their school and community.

- Author's Purpose and Perspective; Literary Devices
- Summarize; Answer Questions
- **VOCABULARY:** *loathe, bland, mentor, dilapidated, coordination, altruism, sensibility, advocacy, mistreated, compassionate*

Build Background/Set Purpose

Have students read the title and look at the illustrations. Ask them what they think *The Clean Machine* might be. Tell students that summarizing and answering questions can help them better understand main events.

Guided Reading

PAGES 3–14 AUTHOR'S PURPOSE AND PERSPECTIVE **Why do you think the author wrote this Readers' Theater?** (to entertain and inspire students to take an active role in community projects)

PAGE 10 LITERARY DEVICES **How does the author make the commercial for "Liquid Cool" more interesting?** (She makes it rhyme and uses interesting and colorful language.)

After Reading

Have students work in pairs to write a short summary of the Readers' Theater.

FLUENCY: EXPRESSION AND PACE Have student pairs take turns rereading a section aloud. Remind them to focus on expression and pace.

Think Critically *(See inside back cover for questions.)*

1. to clean up and add new plants to their school grounds

2. A few students form a group to clean up their school grounds. Two group members speak about their work and ideas on a radio program.

3. They will reach a larger audience and get more support for their group.

4. Yes, they are working together to improve their community.

5. Answers will vary.

LEVELED READER TEACHER GUIDE

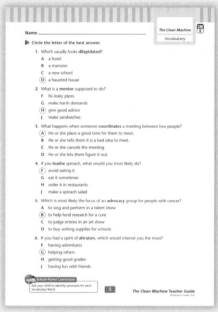

▲ Vocabulary, p. 5

▲ Comprehension, p. 6

www.harcourtschool.com/storytown

★ Leveled Readers Online Database
Searchable by Genre, Skill, Vocabulary, Level, or Title
★ Student Activities and Teacher Resources, *online*

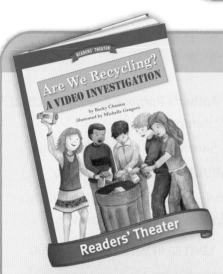

Readers' Theater

ON-LEVEL

Are We Recycling? A Video Investigation

SUMMARY In this play a group of students investigates how well their school's recycling program is working.

- ● Author's Purpose and Perspective; Literary Devices
- ● Summarize; Answer Questions
- **VOCABULARY:** *loathe, bland, mentor, dilapidated, coordination, altruism, sensibility, advocacy, mistreated, compassionate*

Build Background/Set Purpose

Have students read the title and page through the play. Ask them to predict what they think this play will be about. Remind them that summarizing and answering questions can help clear up confusion.

Guided Reading

PAGES 3–14 ● **AUTHOR'S PURPOSE AND PERSPECTIVE How do you think the author feels about recycling?** (The author thinks it is important to do.)

PAGES 9–10 ● **LITERARY DEVICES How does the author use humor when describing the students filming the teachers' lounge trash can?** (Will says they will *get the inside scoop,* meaning "story," but Mr. Travis thinks they will actually *scoop* trash out of the trash can.)

After Reading

Have students work in pairs to write a short summary of the Readers' Theater.

FLUENCY: EXPRESSION AND PACE Have pairs of students reread two pages aloud. Tell them to focus on their expression and pace.

Think Critically *(See inside back cover for questions.)*

1. to see if the school's recycling program is being followed

2. He is the director of the video. He organizes the shots and chooses the location.

3. Answers will vary.

4. For a class project, students film a video about their school's recycling program.

5. to entertain and to inform readers about recycling

LEVELED READER TEACHER GUIDE

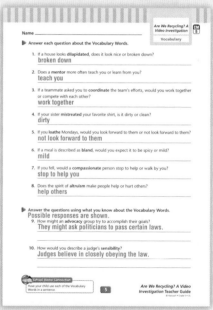

▲ Vocabulary, p. 5

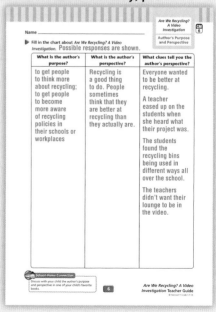

▲ Comprehension, p. 6

Leveled Readers
Reinforcing Skills and Strategies

Readers' Theater

ADVANCED

Kids Cleaning Up

SUMMARY Some students appear on a television show to explain how they are helping their school reduce, reuse, and recycle.

- **Author's Purpose and Perspective; Literary Devices**
- **Summarize; Answer Questions**
- **VOCABULARY:** *loathe, bland, mentor, dilapidated, coordination, altruism, sensibility, advocacy, mistreated, compassionate*

Build Background/Set Purpose

Write the words *reduce, reuse*, and *recycle* on the board. Ask students what these words mean in the context of recycling. Then have them preview the story and predict what it will be about. Remind them that summarizing and answering questions can help them understand events as they happen.

During Reading

CREATE A CHART Distribute the three-column chart on *Teacher Resource Book* page 87 to pairs of students. Have students write the words *Reduce, Reuse,* and *Recycle* as column heads and then record what the students in the play are doing to help their school with each task.

After Reading

Have partners write a paragraph summarizing the Readers' Theater.

FLUENCY: EXPRESSION AND PACE Have students adopt roles and reread the story aloud. Tell them to give each other feedback on expression and pace.

Think Critically *(See inside back cover for questions.)*

1. Members of the student advocacy group Kids Cleaning Up fight pollution in different ways for their school. They are discussing their work on a TV show.

2. Marcus means that he is excited to share his news.

3. They are excited about their projects and are encouraging of one another's ideas. They speak with enthusiasm and are well informed.

4. Answers will vary.

5. to entertain and to raise readers' environmental awareness

LEVELED READER TEACHER GUIDE

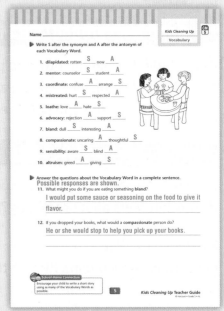

▲ Vocabulary, p. 5

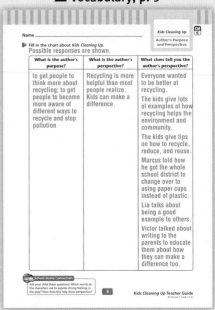

▲ Comprehension, p. 6

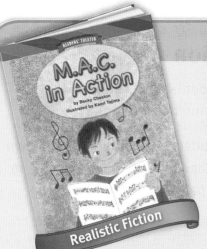

M.A.C. in Action

SUMMARY When Manny's school cuts the music programs, he and his friends decide to take action.

- **Build Background**
- **Concept Vocabulary**
- **Scaffolded Language Development**

Build Background/Set Purpose

Discuss with students different things that can be done to get a message across. Discuss the use of *committees, slogans, flyers,* and *plans*. Then preview the Readers' Theater with students, reminding them to summarize and ask questions when they encounter confusing or unfamiliar text.

Guided Reading

As students read, tell them to look for words that signal transitions, such as *when* and *finally*. Also clarify the idioms *poured his thoughts, public hearing,* and *budget cuts*.

PAGE 3 LITERARY DEVICES **How does the author make the description of the flutes more interesting?** (The author says that the flutes "sang.")

PAGES 3–14 AUTHOR'S PURPOSE AND PERSPECTIVE **What do you think the author's purpose was in writing this play?** (to entertain and to inform readers about things people can do to raise awareness for a cause)

After Reading

FLUENCY: EXPRESSION AND PACE Reread the story aloud. Then have partners take turns rereading a page aloud with appropriate expression and pace.

Encourage students to use the concept words *message, dramatic, slogan,* and *flyers* while discussing the story.

Scaffolded Language Development

See inside back cover for teacher-led activity.

Provide additional examples and explanation as needed.

LEVELED READER TEACHER GUIDE

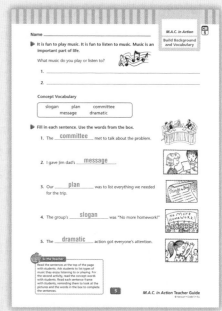

▲ **Build Background, p. 5**

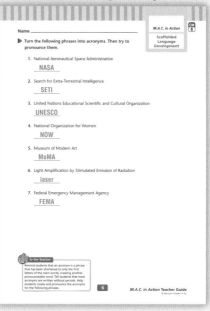

▲ **Scaffolded Language Development, p. 6**

Theme Wrap-Up and Review

Discuss the Literature

Use the questions below to guide students in making connections across the texts in this theme.

- **In what way do the selections in this theme tell about communities?** (Possible response: The selections show different types of communities and ways that people can work to make a community better.)

- **Why do you think "Chester Cricket's Pigeon Ride" was included in this theme?** (Possible response: The selection shows us that it can be exciting to explore a new community, even though at first it might seem a little scary to do so.)

- **Imagine that you could join one of the community projects you read about in this theme. Which project would you choose and why?** (Responses will vary.)

Return to the Theme Connections

Have students review and revise their graphic organizers to include information about all the selections they have read about and listened to.

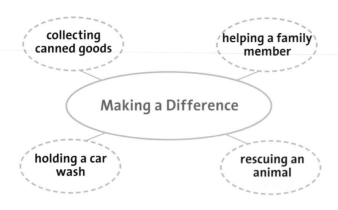

Response Option

 REFLECT Have students reflect on what they've learned about communities.

SELF-ASSESSMENT Students can reflect on their own progress using the My Reading Log copying master on *Teacher Resource Book*, page 34.

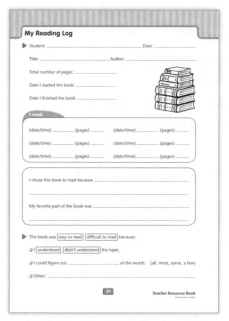

▲ Teacher Resource Book, p. 34

LITERATURE CRITIQUE CIRCLES Have students meet in small groups to discuss and reflect on the literature in this theme. Encourage students to share their likes and dislikes about the following:

- genres

- subjects or topics

- author's craft

- illustrations or photographs

Remind students to support their options with text-based reasons and details.

 Routine Card 12 Students may also use this time to recommend to classmates any books they read and enjoyed during independent reading. Have them list promising titles for future reading.

A Community Service Project

PRESENT PLANS   Each group that has completed a plan should select a spokesperson to present it to the class. Encourage students to demonstrate what they have learned in creative ways.

PRESENTATION IDEA   You may want to suggest that students create a display that identifies the community problem and lays out the plan for class participation in the solution.

- **Have each group's spokesperson present** their plan to convince classmates to take it on.

- **After each group has presented, conduct a vote** to determine which plan or plans students would most like to do. Then provide them with appropriate class time to participate.

- **To evaluate students' work,** you may wish to use the Rubric for Presentations on page R5.

School-Home Connection

Theme Project Presentations

You may want to invite students' parents and family members to watch the Theme Project Presentations. Have students collaborate to write an invitation for the event. Tell them to include the date, time, and location of the presentation. Students may also want to create a program that lists the title of the presentation, the order of presenters, and the community service project each presenter will discuss.

Monitor Progress
at the end of Theme 5

THEME 5 TEST After instruction for Theme 5, assess student progress in the following areas:

- Comprehension of grade-level text
- Comprehension Skills
- Robust Vocabulary
- Spelling
- Writing to a prompt
- Grammar
- Fluency*

(*Note on Fluency: Assessment can be staggered to make sure all students can be individually assessed.)

 Podcasting: Assessing Fluency

 ONLINE ASSESSMENT

✓ Theme 5 Test

✓ Weekly Lesson Tests

✓ Student Profile System to track student growth

✓ Prescriptions for Reteaching

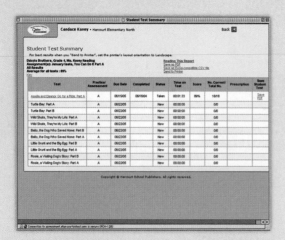

 www.harcourtschool.com/storytown

MONITOR PROGRESS

Use Data to Inform Instruction for Theme 6

IF performance is	THEN, in addition to core instruction, use these resources:
BELOW-LEVEL: Reteach	• Below-Level Leveled Readers • Leveled Readers System • Extra Support Copying Masters • Strategic Intervention Resource Kit • Intervention Station, Intermediate
ON-LEVEL: Reinforce	• On-Level Leveled Readers • Leveled Readers System • Practice Book
ADVANCED: Extend	• Advanced Leveled Readers • Leveled Readers System • Challenge Copying Masters • Challenge Resource Kit

Read-Aloud
(continuation)

"Dog Gone"
(continued from page T164)

Chip in Their Shoulders

For some pet owners, though, a tattoo isn't the answer to keeping their lost animals findable. They want something more high-tech.

That's where the pet microchip comes in. Vets can insert a chip about the size of a grain of rice under the skin of dogs or cats. The chip holds an identification number read by a special scanner.

Although the microchip is the high-tech way of finding a lost pet, it still has problems. Few people can tell if an animal has a chip. And not all scanners read the special chips.

So what's the best way to find a missing animal? Despite all the supersleuthing and complex technology, the answer may be simple: Make sure your dog is wearing proper tags.

"Keeping Cool With Crickets"
(continued from page T224)

Each song has a meaning. Some serve as calling songs to attract females, others as courting songs to encourage mating or as fighting songs to repel other males. In Japan it is said that they sing, "Kata sase suso sase samusa ga kuruzo," or "Sew your sleeves, sew your skirts, the cold weather is coming."

Charlie Cricket was quiet as I put down a thin layer of dirt in his home, stocked his pantry with lettuce and potatoes, and added the antique water dish. Now, how was I going to get that bundle of energy from carton to house? I lifted the cardboard flap, and Charlie eyed me, ready to do battle. Using all ten fingers, a soothing voice, and lots of encouragement, I soon had him safely in his house.

Drugged by the summer heat, I hung Charlie from the eaves on the balcony. Nearby, wind chimes tinkled melodiously with each gentle breeze.

"Cool me off," I pleaded. "Chirp, Charlie, chirp." The heat hung suspended around me. And Charlie chirped! The garden bells tinkled in accompaniment. It was as if the enchanting sounds and the whirring of cricket wings awakened the air and stirred it about me ever so gently.

"Sing, Charlie!" His song sounded like the clinking of ice cubes in chilled crystal goblets. The heat seemed to waft away. I had learned the Japanese art of keeping cool with crickets.

Teacher's Notes

Small-Group Instruction

SMALL-GROUP INSTRUCTION

Author's Purpose and Perspective

Objectives

- *To understand that authors have different purposes for writing*
- *To identify and discuss an author's perspective*

Author's Purpose and Perspective

REVIEW THE SKILL Remind students that the **author's purpose** is the author's reason for writing. The author's **perspective** is his or her opinion—how he or she feels—about the topic of the text.

USE GENRE Point out that identifying the genre of the selection can help readers determine the author's purpose. Nonfiction is often written to inform or persuade. Fiction is often written to entertain.

USE WORD CHOICE The words an author chooses can reveal his or her perspective. Words such as *good*, *bad*, and *important* can show the author's feelings about the topic.

GUIDED PRACTICE Write on the board these examples and work with students to identify the author's purpose.

- a letter requesting a donation to help save sea turtles (to persuade)

- an article explaining sea turtle migration (to inform)

- a story about a sea turtle who joins a dolphin on an adventure (to entertain)

MONITOR PROGRESS

Author's Purpose and Perspective After reteaching the skill, are students able to identify and discuss an author's purpose and perspective? If not, additional resources are available in the *Strategic Intervention Resource Kit*.

Strategic ▶ Intervention Resource Kit

Author's Purpose and Perspective

USE A GRAPHIC ORGANIZER Review with students *Student Edition* pages 538–539. Remind them that every author has a **purpose**, or reason, for writing. Explain that the author's **perspective** is his or her opinion about the topic. Have students revisit a selection they have read recently and identify the author's purpose and perspective. Ask them to explain how they used the genre and the author's word choice to determine the author's purpose and perspective.

Determine Purpose and Perspective

EXTEND THE SKILL Have students write about an animal they are interested in. Tell them to establish a purpose for writing and to choose a genre that suits their purpose. Remind them to include words and details that reveal their perspective. Then have them exchange papers with a partner and determine the purpose and perspective of their partner's paper.

ELL

Author's Purpose and Perspective List these purposes on the board and read them aloud: **to entertain, to inform, to persuade.** For each purpose, display and briefly summarize a text written with that purpose, explaining whether it is fiction or nonfiction. For example, you might display and describe an encyclopedia article as an example of a nonfiction text meant to inform. Then provide students with additional examples and ask them to name the genre and the purpose for each.

Robust Vocabulary

Objective

- *To develop and demonstrate knowledge of word meanings*

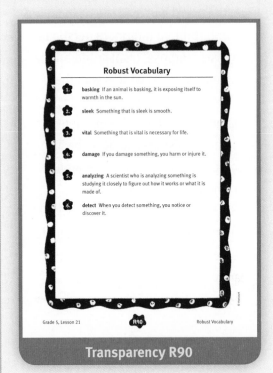

Transparency R90

MONITOR PROGRESS

Robust Vocabulary After reteaching the Vocabulary Words, are students able to use them successfully in speaking and writing? If not, additional resources are available in the *Strategic Intervention Resource Kit*.

**Strategic ▶
Intervention
Resource Kit**

BELOW-LEVEL **RETEACH**

Robust Vocabulary

REVIEW VOCABULARY Display **Transparency R90**. Read aloud the first Vocabulary Word and have students repeat after you.

Then read the accompanying Student-Friendly Explanation. Pause to answer any questions about the explanation. Repeat for the rest of the words.

WORDS IN CONTEXT Read aloud each sentence below, and pause to clarify meaning, if necessary. Then ask the question in parentheses and have students respond, using the Vocabulary Word in their answers.

- The seal on the beach is **basking** in the sun. (What kind of day is ideal for **basking**?)

- The cat cleaned its **sleek** fur every day. (What does the cat's **sleek** fur look like?)

- Drinking milk is **vital** for strong, healthy bones. (What else is **vital** for your health?)

- Huge waves can **damage** a boat. (How could you accidentally **damage** a glass vase?)

- By **analyzing** the rock carefully, the scientist was able to figure out that it was not gold. (What is something you have been **analyzing** at school?)

- A sound of dripping water helped me **detect** a leaky pipe. (How might you **detect** a fire?)

GUIDED PRACTICE Have each student choose a Vocabulary Word and write a sentence using it. Then ask students to read their sentences aloud to the group.

Robust Vocabulary

REVIEW WORD MEANING Display **Transparency R90**. Have students take turns reading aloud each Vocabulary Word and its Student-Friendly Explanation. Answer any questions students have about pronunciation or meaning.

WORDS IN CONTEXT Read the sentence on *Student Edition* page 540 that contains the Vocabulary Word *vital*.

Then model for students restating the sentence by replacing the Vocabulary Word with its meaning. For example, you might say: *Long ago, the panther was a **very important** resident of Florida and parts of Louisiana and Tennessee.*

Guide students to repeat the process for the remaining Vocabulary Words.

Extend Robust Vocabulary

USE VOCABULARY IN WRITING Display **Transparency R90** and have students read the Vocabulary Words and Student-Friendly Explanations silently. Then have them work in pairs to complete the following activity.

1. One student chooses and says one of the Vocabulary Words.

2. The other student uses the word in a sentence that shows its meaning.

3. Partners switch roles and repeat the process until all the words have been used at least once.

ELL

Robust Vocabulary Display **Transparency R90**. Read aloud the Vocabulary Words. Have students repeat each word after you. Monitor their pronunciation. Then reread each word along with its Student-Friendly Explanation and have students echo-read. Clarify the explanations for students, using illustrations, photographs, gestures, or examples.

Selection Comprehension
"Interrupted Journey: Saving Endangered Sea Turtles"

Objective
• *To demonstrate comprehension of a text*

Selection Comprehension
Use the completed *Practice Book* page 124 to review the selection with students, pointing out important ideas and details as you go. Lead students to use this information to develop an oral summary of each section.

MONITOR PROGRESS

Selection Comprehension After reteaching, are students able to summarize the selection concisely and accurately? If not, additional resources are available in the *Strategic Intervention Resource Kit.*

**Strategic ▶
Intervention
Resource Kit**

BELOW-LEVEL RETEACH

Support Comprehension

REVIEW THE SELECTION Remind students that a summary of an expository nonfiction selection includes only the most important ideas and details. Display the completed *Practice Book* page 124. Tell students that the graphic organizer on this page can help them identify the most important ideas and details. Help students restate the most important information from each section in one or two sentences. Guide them to include these sentences in their summaries.

ON-LEVEL REINFORCE

Reinforce Comprehension

WRITE A SUMMARY Display the completed *Practice Book* page 124. Remind students that the graphic organizer on this page can help them identify the most important ideas and details in the text and help them organize their summaries. Guide students to use the information in the boxes to refine their summaries.

ADVANCED EXTEND

Extend Comprehension

COMPARE IDEAS Have students conduct research to learn about other volunteer efforts to protect a different endangered species. Ask them to take notes on what they learn about the efforts. Then have students write a paragraph comparing the efforts to those described in "Interrupted Journey: Saving Endangered Sea Turtles."

Fluency
Focus: Expression

Objectives
- *To demonstrate the characteristics of fluent, effective reading*
- *To read aloud with prosody, using appropriate expression*

BELOW-LEVEL RETEACH

Fluency: Expression

REVIEW EXPRESSION Explain to students that they read with expression when they emphasize certain words or change the volume of their voice when they read aloud.

MODEL FLUENT READING Have students turn to *Student Edition* page 547. Have them track the print as you read the page. Use expression to show the uncertainty the scientists feel about whether the turtle is still alive.

GUIDED PRACTICE Reread the passage as students read along. Monitor their expression. If necessary, pause to have them echo-read a sentence or sentences, matching your expression.

ON-LEVEL REINFORCE

Fluency: Expression

PRACTICE EXPRESSION Remind students that reading aloud with expression means reading in a way that helps the listener feel the mood of the text or the emotions of the characters. Have students turn to page 547 and read the page quietly. Then have them read the page aloud to a partner. Have them explain how they used expression to reflect the scientists' uncertainty.

ADVANCED EXTEND

Fluency: Expression

EXTEND THE SKILL Ask students to reread pages 547 and 553 from "Interrupted Journey: Saving Endangered Sea Turtles." Then have students work in pairs to rewrite the pages as dialogue. Students should convey the tone and emotions of the scenes through their writing. When partners have finished, have them read aloud the dialogue they wrote, focusing on using the appropriate expression.

Expression Have students turn to page 547. Model reading aloud the passage as students follow along. Use expression to convey the scientists' uncertainty about whether the turtle is alive. Then reread the page, sentence by sentence, as students echo-read with you, matching your expression.

Expression After reteaching the skill, are students able to read aloud with appropriate expression? If not, additional resources are available in the *Strategic Intervention Resource Kit.*

Strategic ▶ Intervention Resource Kit

Grammar and Writing
Action and Linking Verbs

Objective
- *To use action and linking verbs correctly in writing and speaking*

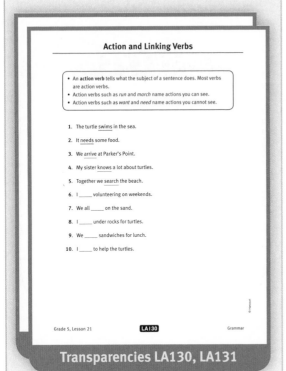

Action and Linking Verbs

- An **action verb** tells what the subject of a sentence does. Most verbs are action verbs.
- Action verbs such as *run* and *march* name actions you can see.
- Action verbs such as *want* and *need* name actions you cannot see.

1. The turtle <u>swims</u> in the sea.
2. It <u>needs</u> some food.
3. We <u>arrive</u> at Parker's Point.
4. My sister <u>knows</u> a lot about turtles.
5. Together we <u>search</u> the beach.
6. I _____ volunteering on weekends.
7. We all _____ on the sand.
8. I _____ under rocks for turtles.
9. We _____ sandwiches for lunch.
10. I _____ to help the turtles.

Grade 5, Lesson 21   **LA130**   Grammar

Transparencies LA130, LA131

 BELOW-LEVEL **RETEACH**

Action and Linking Verbs

REVIEW THE SKILL Display **Transparency LA130** and **Transparency LA131**. Review the information about each type of verb, using the examples to clarify as needed.

GUIDED PRACTICE Write the following sentences on the board. Read each sentence aloud. Then guide students to identify the verb in each sentence and tell whether it is an action verb or a linking verb.

- He <u>examined</u> the turtle. (action)
- The turtle <u>was</u> sick. (linking)
- She <u>splashed</u> in the water. (action)

- They <u>thought</u> about the problem. (action)
- That cake <u>looks</u> delicious! (linking)
- He <u>became</u> tired. (linking)

APPLY TO WRITING Ask students to write four sentences about a time they helped someone. Tell them to use action verbs in two sentences and linking verbs in two sentences.

✔ MONITOR PROGRESS

Grammar and Writing After reteaching the skills, are students able to use action verbs and linking verbs in speaking and writing? If not, additional resources are available in the *Strategic Intervention Resource Kit*.

Strategic ▶ Intervention Resource Kit

Action and Linking Verbs

APPLY TO WRITING Display **Transparencies LA130** and **LA131**. Have volunteers read aloud the information about **action verbs** and **linking verbs**.

Then ask students to write a paragraph describing important classroom events from the past week. Tell them to use action verbs in some sentences and linking verbs in others. Remind students to use a variety of sentence types in their paragraph.

ADVANCED EXTEND

Write to Persuade

EXTEND THE SKILL Ask students to imagine that they are on vacation and they want their best friend to come and join them. Have students write a paragraph to their friend to persuade him or her to come. Tell them to include both action verbs and linking verbs in the paragraph. Remind them to use a variety of sentence types.

E L L

Action Verbs and Linking Verbs Write on the board these verbs: *swim, is, are.* Point out that the action verb can be acted out while the linking verbs cannot. Guide students to use the verbs to complete these sentence frames:

• I _____ in the water.

• She _____ happy.

• You _____ my classmate.

Author's Purpose and Perspective

Objectives
- *To understand that authors have different purposes for writing*
- *To identify and discuss an author's perspective*

MONITOR PROGRESS

Author's Purpose and Perspective After reteaching the skill, are students able to identify and discuss an author's purpose and perspective? If not, additional resources are available in the *Strategic Intervention Resource Kit.*

Strategic ▶ Intervention Resource Kit

BELOW-LEVEL RETEACH

Author's Purpose and Perspective

REVIEW THE SKILL Remind students that an author's **purpose** is his or her reason for writing. An author's **perspective** is his or her opinion about the text's subject.

MULTIPLE PURPOSES Point out that an author may have more than one purpose, or reason, for writing. For example, while the main purpose for writing a play may be to entertain, the author may also want to inform people about a particular topic or persuade people to think or act in a particular way.

CHARACTER'S WORDS AND ACTIONS Tell students that in a work of fiction, a character's words and actions may reveal the author's perspective about the topic.

GUIDED PRACTICE Read aloud the paragraph below. Guide students to determine the author's purpose and perspective.

> **Tara remembered that Mr. Johnson liked sports, so she chose some newspaper articles about his favorite team. Then she headed next door to read to him. She loved seeing his face light up when she walked in the door, and she enjoyed hearing his stories about what life was like when he was younger.**

Ask the following:

- Is the author's purpose to entertain or to inform? (entertain)

- What is the author's perspective? (Spending time with an older person can be enjoyable.)

Author's Purpose and Perspective

DETERMINE PERSPECTIVE Remind students that an author's **purpose** is his or her reason for writing. An author's **perspective** is how he or she feels about a topic. Point out that in a work of fiction, the character's words and actions can reveal the author's perspective. Read aloud these examples and have students determine the author's perspective.

- Jenna frowned when she saw the trash in the park.
  (Parks should be kept clean.)

- Carlos cheerfully volunteered to help Mrs. Ruiz rake her leaves.
  (Helping others can be rewarding.)

- Cho regularly walks her dog and plays with him.
  (Responsible pet owners spend time with their pets.)

ADVANCED **EXTEND**

Determine Purposes and Perspectives

EXTEND THE SKILL Have students read a travel article or restaurant review from a newspaper. Ask them to determine the author's purpose and perspective. Then have students discuss with a partner how the author's perspective might influence readers.

Robust Vocabulary

Objective

- *To develop and demonstrate knowledge of word meanings*

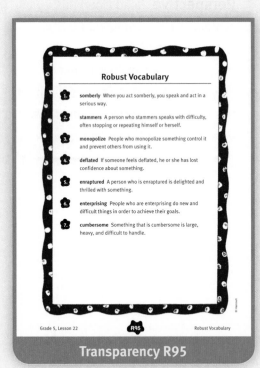

Robust Vocabulary

1. **somberly** When you act somberly, you speak and act in a serious way.
2. **stammers** A person who stammers speaks with difficulty, often stopping or repeating himself or herself.
3. **monopolize** People who monopolize something control it and prevent others from using it.
4. **deflated** If someone feels deflated, he or she has lost confidence about something.
5. **enraptured** A person who is enraptured is delighted and thrilled with something.
6. **enterprising** People who are enterprising do new and difficult things in order to achieve their goals.
7. **cumbersome** Something that is cumbersome is large, heavy, and difficult to handle.

Grade 5, Lesson 22   R95   Robust Vocabulary

Transparency R95

MONITOR PROGRESS

Robust Vocabulary After reteaching the Vocabulary Words, are students able to use them successfully in speaking and writing? If not, additional resources are available in the *Strategic Intervention Resource Kit*.

Strategic ▶ Intervention Resource Kit

BELOW-LEVEL RETEACH

Robust Vocabulary

Routine Card 2

REVIEW VOCABULARY Display **Transparency R95**. Read aloud the first Vocabulary Word and have students repeat after you. Then read the accompanying Student-Friendly Explanation. Repeat the process with each Vocabulary Word.

WORDS IN CONTEXT Read aloud each sentence below, and pause to clarify meaning, if necessary. Then ask the question in parentheses and have students respond, using the Vocabulary Word in their answers.

- We reacted **somberly** when we heard the bad news. (Would you behave **somberly** at a party?)

- When I get nervous, I **stammer**. (When you **stammer**, is it easy to speak?)

- The players **monopolized** the court for hours. (How would you feel if your brother **monopolized** the television?)

- She felt **deflated** after losing the spelling bee. (What might make a coach feel **deflated**?)

- **Enraptured** by Eleni's beautiful singing, we cheered and applauded. (If a book **enraptured** you, was it hard to put down or hard to finish?)

- Pat is so **enterprising** that he started two businesses at once. (Why would it help a salesperson to be **enterprising**?)

- When my backpack is stuffed with books, it becomes **cumbersome** to carry. (Would you want to carry a **cumbersome** box a long distance?)

GUIDED PRACTICE Have each student choose a Vocabulary Word and write a sentence using it. Then ask students to read their sentences aloud to the group.

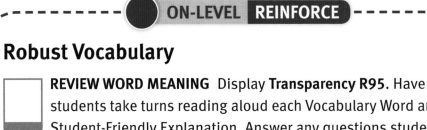

Robust Vocabulary

REVIEW WORD MEANING Display **Transparency R95**. Have students take turns reading aloud each Vocabulary Word and its Student-Friendly Explanation. Answer any questions students have about pronunciation or meaning. Then have students choose three Vocabulary Words and create a word web for each.

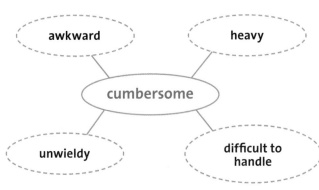

Robust Vocabulary Display **Transparency R95**. Point out and read aloud the Vocabulary Words. Have students repeat each word after you. Monitor their pronunciation. Then reread each word along with its Student-Friendly Explanation. Clarify the explanation for students, using illustrations, photographs, gestures, or examples.

Extend Robust Vocabulary

WRITE A COLLABORATIVE STORY Display **Transparency R95**. Have students work in a small group to compose a collective story using all of the Vocabulary Words. The first student should start the story with a sentence that uses one of the words. The next student continues the story by adding a sentence that uses another Vocabulary Word. Group members should continue until all the words have been used and the story is complete.

Selection Comprehension
"The Power of W.O.W.!"

Objective
- *To demonstrate comprehension of a text*

Selection Comprehension

Explain that when you summarize a play, you tell **who** is in it, **where and when** it takes place, and **what happens**. Use the completed *Practice Book* page 130 to review the play with students. Demonstrate how to use this page to develop an oral summary.

Selection Comprehension
After reteaching, are students able to give a complete summary of the play? If not, additional resources are available in the *Strategic Intervention Resource Kit*.

Strategic ▸ Intervention Resource Kit

Support Comprehension

REVIEW THE SELECTION Model writing a statement that introduces the characters and setting. Then guide students to briefly restate the conflict, plot events, and resolution and add these statements to their summaries.

Reinforce Comprehension

REVISE A SUMMARY Display the completed *Practice Book* page 130. Remind students that the story map on this page can help them identify the main narrative elements in a story or play. Guide students to use the information in the story map to write sentences to add to or revise their summaries.

Extend Comprehension

WRITE A SUMMARY Have students find out about mobile library services in your community. Then have them write a summary of what they have learned, comparing the services offered to those they learned about while reading "The Power of W.O.W.!"

Fluency
Focus: Expression

Objectives
- *To demonstrate the characteristics of fluent, effective reading*
- *To read aloud with prosody, using appropriate expression*

 BELOW-LEVEL RETEACH

Fluency: Expression

REVIEW THE SKILL Remind students that readers emphasize words or change the volume of their voice to express the mood and tone of the text.

MODEL FLUENT READING Have students turn to *Student Edition* page 573. Have them track the print as you read aloud. Use expression to show that Ileana is sad and shocked by the news that W.O.W. will be shut down.

GUIDED PRACTICE Reread the passage. This time have students read aloud with you. Monitor their expression and give feedback as necessary.

 ON-LEVEL REINFORCE

Fluency: Expression

PRACTICE EXPRESSION Remind students that reading aloud with expression helps the listener feel the mood of the story or the emotions of the characters. Discuss ways to use emphasis, volume, and pace to express Ileana's feelings on *Student Edition* page 573 about the news that W.O.W. will be shut down. Then have students work in pairs to take turns reading the passage aloud, giving feedback on each other's use of expression as necessary.

 ADVANCED EXTEND

Fluency: Expression

EXTEND THE SKILL Provide pairs of students with a small number of self-stick notes. Ask partners to revisit "The Power of W.O.W.!" and decide what kind of expression the various parts of the play should be read aloud with. Have students write stage directions for reading with expression on the self-stick notes and place the notes on the pages where they belong. You might suggest these words to help students get started: **louder, softer, sadly, more lively.**

 **E L L**

Expression Have students turn to page 573 in "The Power of W.O.W.!" Model reading aloud the page as students follow along. Use expression to convey how Ileana feels when she learns that W.O.W. will be shut down. Then reread the passage, sentence by sentence, as students echo-read with you.

 MONITOR PROGRESS

Expression After reteaching the skill, are students able to read aloud with appropriate expression? If not, additional resources are available in the *Strategic Intervention Resource Kit.*

Strategic ▶ Intervention Resource Kit

Draw Conclusions

Objectives

- *To draw conclusions about text information*
- *To support conclusions with text evidence and personal experience*

Draw Conclusions

Sometimes readers must **draw conclusions** by using **story details** and **their own knowledge** to understand story events.

Even though the sun had yet to rise, Hindatu was already brushing her teeth. She was so anxious that she could barely tie her shoes. When she went downstairs, her mom was waiting for her in the kitchen.

"You have to eat before you go," her mom said.

"I don't have time, Mom. May I just take some toast to go?"

Hindatu's mom understood. Today was the day bulldozers were supposed to tear up Happy Meadows Park. In the last few weeks, her daughter had spent all her free time talking about the park. Her mother handed Hindatu a slice of toast and gave her a goodbye hug.

As Hindatu rode her bike to the park, the morning air relaxed her. From two blocks away, she saw a crowd of familiar faces gathered around the park entrance. She saw her teacher and her best friend holding signs saying *People Need Parks, Not Parking Lots*. Hindatu smiled. There were a lot of people hoping to save the park, and more would be coming.

Story Details	What I Know	Conclusions
• Hindatu is up early. • She's anxious. • She wants to skip breakfast and get to the park.	People who are anxious are eager to find out what is going to happen. They are in a hurry because they are expecting something big to happen.	Hindatu wants to find out what is going to happen at the park.
• Bulldozers are supposed to tear up the park. • People have gathered with signs at the entrance.	People who want to save a place may gather together and express their opinions peacefully.	Hindatu and her friends are hoping to save the park.

Grade 5, Lesson 22   **R96**   Draw Conclusions

Transparency R96

MONITOR PROGRESS

Draw Conclusions After reteaching the skill, are students able to draw conclusions about story information and support them with personal knowledge and details from the text? If not, additional resources are available in the *Strategic Intervention Resource Kit*.

Strategic ▶ Intervention Resource Kit

BELOW-LEVEL **RETEACH**

Draw Conclusions

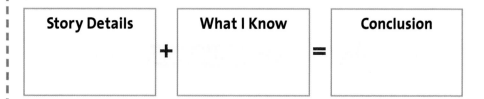

REVIEW THE SKILL Display **Transparency R96** and review the information in the box at the top. Tell students that readers must use story details and their own knowledge to **draw conclusions** about story events and characters.

USE GRAPHIC ORGANIZERS Tell students that a graphic organizer like the one below is a useful way to keep track of conclusions they draw as they read.

Story Details		What I Know		Conclusion
	+		**=**	

GUIDED PRACTICE Read aloud the passage below. Ask students to draw a conclusion about the outcome of Norma's soccer game.

Tami knew that her sister, Norma, was nervous about her big soccer game. Her team had to win to go to the championships. When Norma walked in, Tami asked, "How did the game go?" Norma just grinned and pumped her fist in the air.

Draw Conclusions

USE DETAILS AND EXPERIENCE Remind students that an author does not explain everything in a story; readers must put together **story details** and **what they already know** to **draw conclusions** about story characters and events. Have students reread *Student Edition* pages 572–573. Ask: **Does Mrs. Nguyen think it is likely that W.O.W. can be saved?** Have students record their conclusion in a chart like the one below.

Story Details	What I Know	Conclusion

Extend the Ending

EXTEND THE SKILL Have students write an extension of the play in which they include clues that can lead readers to draw conclusions. Then have partners exchange stories and write conclusions. Each original writer should review the partner's conclusion to decide whether his or her intended conclusion was understood.

Draw Conclusions Tell students that asking themselves questions such as "How would I feel?" and "What would I do?" can help them draw conclusions about a character's feelings and actions. Guide students to draw a conclusion about a character from "The Power of W.O.W.!"

Grammar and Writing
Present Tense; Subject-Verb Agreement

Objectives
- *To use correct subject-verb agreement*
- *To identify forms of the verb* be

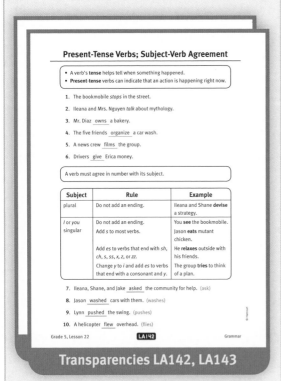

Present-Tense Verbs; Subject-Verb Agreement

- A verb's **tense** helps tell when something happened.
- **Present-tense** verbs can indicate that an action is happening right now.

1. The bookmobile *stops* in the street.
2. Ileana and Mrs. Nguyen *talk* about mythology.
3. Mr. Diaz *owns* a bakery.
4. The five friends *organize* a car wash.
5. A news crew *films* the group.
6. Drivers *give* Erica money.

A verb must agree in number with its subject.

Subject	Rule	Example
plural	Do not add an ending.	Ileana and Shane **devise** a strategy.
I or you singular	Do not add an ending. Add *s* to most verbs. Add *es* to verbs that end with *sh, ch, s, ss, x, z,* or *zz.* Change *y* to *i* and add *es* to verbs that end with a consonant and *y.*	You **see** the bookmobile. Jason **eats** mutant chicken. He **relaxes** outside with his friends. The group **tries** to think of a plan.

7. Ileana, Shane, and Jake _asked_ the community for help. (ask)
8. Jason _washed_ cars with them. (washes)
9. Lynn _pushed_ the swing. (pushes)
10. A helicopter _flew_ overhead. (flies)

Grade 5, Lesson 22   LA142   Grammar

Transparencies LA142, LA143

 MONITOR PROGRESS

Grammar and Writing After reteaching the skills, are students able to correctly use present-tense verbs and subject-verb agreement in speaking and writing? If not, additional resources are available in the *Strategic Intervention Resource Kit.*

Strategic ▶ Intervention Resource Kit

 BELOW-LEVEL **RETEACH**

Present Tense and Subject-Verb Agreement

REVIEW THE SKILL Display **Transparency LA142**. Read aloud the information in the top box. Then remind students that a verb must agree in number with its subject. Review the chart on the transparency, pointing out and reading aloud the rules for forming present-tense verbs. Display **Transparency LA143** and use it to discuss easily confused verbs.

GUIDED PRACTICE Write the following sentences on the board.

- Ileana (choose/chooses) a book.
- Jake (sits/sets) down in the chair.
- You (lie/lay) on the bed.
- The babies (cries/cry) at night.

Guide volunteers to choose the correct verb to complete each sentence.

APPLY TO WRITING Have students write four sentences in the present tense about the car wash in "The Power of W.O.W.!" Tell them to use a different verb in each sentence and a variety of singular and plural subjects.

ON-LEVEL REINFORCE

Present Tense and Subject-Verb Agreement

APPLY TO WRITING Display **Transparency LA142**. Have a volunteer read aloud the information in the box at the top. Then use a chart to review subject-verb agreement. Display **Transparency LA143**. Read aloud the information in the box about easily confused verbs.

Then ask students to write a brief paragraph that describes one scene in "The Power of W.O.W.!" Tell them to use present-tense verbs throughout the paragraph. Remind them to make sure that the verb agrees with the subject in each sentence. When students finish, have them proofread their own work for the correct use of present-tense verbs and subject-verb agreement.

ADVANCED EXTEND

Write a Persuasive Paragraph

EXTEND THE SKILL Have students imagine that Ileana and her friends want to raise enough money to get a second W.O.W. bookmobile for their city. Tell students that they will write a short newspaper article that discusses the importance of a second bookmobile. Have students use present-tense verbs in their article. Remind them to proofread their writing.

E L L

Present Tense and Subject-Verb Agreement Use these sentences to show how a verb changes to agree with its subject.

• I *wash* the car.

• Julie *washes* the car.

• Julie and Sal *wash* the car.

Point out that when the subject is *I* or *you* or the subject is plural, an ending is **not** added to the verb.

Literary Devices

Objectives

- *To recognize and understand literary devices*
- *To identify and use sensory language*

 MONITOR PROGRESS

Literary Devices After reteaching the skill, are students able to recognize and understand imagery and sensory language as literary devices? If not, additional resources are available in the *Strategic Intervention Resource Kit*.

Strategic ▶ Intervention Resource Kit

 BELOW-LEVEL **RETEACH**

Literary Devices

REVIEW THE SKILL Remind students that authors use many kinds of **literary devices** to make their writing lively and interesting.

Review with students that **imagery** is a literary device that uses vivid language to describe people, places, things, and ideas.

SENSORY LANGUAGE Point out that language that appeals to one of the five senses—sight, hearing, smell, taste, or touch—is called sensory language.

GUIDED PRACTICE Write the sentences below on the board and read them aloud. Work with students to identify the sensory language in each sentence and underline it. Then help them figure out which sense(s) the language appeals to. Have students describe the images the language creates in their mind.

- Their <u>faces were apple-red</u> from the cold. (sight)
- The kitchen was filled with the <u>rich aroma of vegetable soup</u>. (smell)
- Becca gently rubbed the sleeve of her <u>feather-soft sweater</u>. (touch)
- The chili was <u>zesty and delicious</u>. (taste)
- June, Hector, and Ezra came <u>thundering up the steps</u>. (hearing)

Literary Devices

IDENTIFY IMAGERY/SENSORY LANGUAGE Use the information and examples on *Student Edition* pages 590–591 to review with students the concepts of literary devices, imagery, and sensory language. Then write the sentences below on the board and read them aloud. Have students identify the sensory language in each sentence and tell which sense(s) the language appeals to. Afterwards, have students write five sentences of their own using imagery and sensory language.

- Their <u>faces were apple-red</u> from the cold. (sight)

- The kitchen was filled with the <u>rich aroma of vegetable soup</u>. (smell)

- Becca gently rubbed the sleeve of her <u>feather-soft sweater</u>. (touch)

- The chili was <u>zesty and delicious</u>. (taste)

- June, Hector, and Ezra came <u>thundering up the steps</u>. (hearing)

Write a Description

EXTEND THE SKILL Have students write a short paragraph describing their favorite animal. Tell them to use vivid, precise sensory language to help readers picture the animal in their minds. Remind students to use sensory language that appeals to various senses, not just sight.

Imagery and Sensory Language
Write on the board these descriptions:

- apple red

- flowery aroma

- soft and fuzzy

- sugary sweet

- booming

Guide students to categorize each description in a chart like the one below. Then work with students to compose an oral sentence for each description.

sight	smell	touch	taste	sound
apple red	flowery aroma	soft and fuzzy	sugary sweet	booming

Robust Vocabulary

Objective

- *To develop and demonstrate knowledge of word meanings*

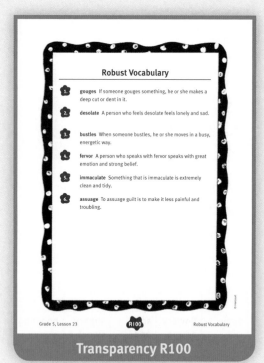

Robust Vocabulary

1. **gouges** If someone gouges something, he or she makes a deep cut or dent in it.

2. **desolate** A person who feels desolate feels lonely and sad.

3. **bustles** When someone bustles, he or she moves in a busy, energetic way.

4. **fervor** A person who speaks with fervor speaks with great emotion and strong belief.

5. **immaculate** Something that is immaculate is extremely clean and tidy.

6. **assuage** To assuage guilt is to make it less painful and troubling.

Grade 5, Lesson 23   R100   Robust Vocabulary

Transparency R100

✓ MONITOR PROGRESS

Robust Vocabulary After reteaching the Vocabulary Words, are students able to use them correctly in speaking and writing? If not, additional resources are available in the *Strategic Intervention Resource Kit.*

**Strategic ▶
Intervention
Resource Kit**

BELOW-LEVEL RETEACH

Robust Vocabulary

 REVIEW VOCABULARY Display **Transparency R100**. Read aloud the first Vocabulary Word and have students repeat after you. Then read the accompanying Student-Friendly Explanation. Pause to answer any questions. Repeat for the rest of the words.

WORDS IN CONTEXT Read aloud each sentence below, and pause to clarify meaning, if necessary. Then ask the question in parentheses and have students respond, using the Vocabulary Word in their answers.

- The grizzly bear **gouges** the tree trunk with its giant claws. (If you **gouge** something, do you make a dent or a small scratch?)

- I felt **desolate** when my best friend moved to another state. (What might make you feel **desolate**?)

- Mom **bustles** around the kitchen when she makes dinner. (How do you feel when you **bustle** around?)

- He spoke with **fervor** about his work. (What is something you would speak with **fervor** about?)

- After an hour of mopping, dusting, and vacuuming, our house was **immaculate**. (Which is **immaculate**, a clean white shirt or a torn, stained one?)

- Myra's words helped **assuage** my sadness. (What might a coach say to **assuage** his team's disappointment over losing a game?)

GUIDED PRACTICE Have students write each Vocabulary Word in a sentence that shows its meaning.

Robust Vocabulary

REVIEW WORD MEANING Display **Transparency R100**. Have students take turns reading aloud each Vocabulary Word and its Student-Friendly Explanation. Answer any questions students have about pronunciation or meaning.

WORDS IN CONTEXT Have students turn to *Student Edition*, page 592. Read aloud the sentence that contains the word *bustles*.

*Delilah the cat normally **bustles** around her Wisconsin home and neighborhood each day.*

Then model for students restating the sentence by replacing the Vocabulary Word with its meaning. For the example, you might say:

*Delilah the cat normally **moves busily** around her Wisconsin home and neighborhood each day.*

Guide students to repeat the process for the remaining Vocabulary Words.

Robust Vocabulary Display **Transparency R100**. Point out and read aloud the Vocabulary Words. Have students repeat each word after you. Monitor their pronunciation. Then reread each word along with its Student-Friendly Explanation. Clarify the explanation for students, using illustrations, photographs, gestures, or examples.

ADVANCED **EXTEND**

Extend Robust Vocabulary

USE VOCABULARY IN WRITING Display **Transparency R100** and have students read the Vocabulary Words and Student-Friendly Explanations silently. Then have students identify a synonym for each Vocabulary Word. Tell them to use each Vocabulary Word and its synonym in a sentence.

The mouse *bustles* into the hole and then *scurries* back out.

Selection Comprehension
"Any Small Goodness"

Objective
- *To demonstrate comprehension of a text*

Selection Comprehension

Use the completed *Practice Book* page 136 to review the story with students, pointing out the setting and important events. Lead students to use this information to develop an oral summary of each section.

Selection Comprehension
After reteaching, are students able to give a complete summary of the selection? If not, additional resources are available in the *Strategic Intervention Resource Kit*.

Strategic ▶ Intervention Resource Kit

BELOW-LEVEL **RETEACH**

Support Comprehension

REVIEW THE SELECTION Remind students that a summary of a realistic fiction story includes only the main story elements. Display the completed *Practice Book* page 136. Tell students that the graphic organizer on this page can help them identify the most important story elements. Help students restate the most important information from each section in one or two sentences. Guide them to include these sentences in their summaries.

ON-LEVEL **REINFORCE**

Reinforce Comprehension

REVIEW STORY ELEMENTS Display the completed *Practice Book* page 136. Remind students that the graphic organizer can help them identify the main story elements. Model writing a sentence that states the conflict. Then guide students to use the information in the other boxes to write sentences to add to or refine their summaries.

ADVANCED **EXTEND**

Extend Comprehension

WRITE A SPEECH Have students write a speech honoring Leo Love as a local hero. The speech should describe Huitla's escape and Leo Love's role in her rescue and safe return.

Fluency
Focus: Pace

 BELOW-LEVEL RETEACH

Fluency: Pace

REVIEW PACE Remind students that good readers read aloud at a steady, conversational pace that is not too slow or too fast.

MODEL FLUENT READING Have students turn to *Student Edition* page 600. Model reading aloud the page at an appropriate pace as students follow along.

GUIDED PRACTICE Reread the passage. This time have students read aloud chorally, matching your pace. If students' pace slows or quickens inappropriately, pause and guide them to adjust their speed.

ON-LEVEL REINFORCE

Fluency: Pace

PRACTICE PACE Remind students that good readers read aloud at a steady pace—not too slow or too fast. Have students turn to *Student Edition* page 600. Have students echo-read as you read the passage, matching your pace. Then have students form pairs and read the passage again, giving each other feedback about their pace.

 ADVANCED EXTEND

Fluency: Pace

EXTEND THE SKILL Tell students that skillful use of pace can make an exciting moment in a story even more gripping for listeners. Have students read aloud the passage on page 600 in "Any Small Goodness" when Leo Love calls to tell the Rodriguez family that he has their cat. Encourage students to experiment with pace, speeding it up, slowing it down, and adding dramatic pauses, to make this scene in the story as exciting as possible.

Objectives
- *To demonstrate the characteristics of fluent, effective reading*
- *To read aloud with prosody, using appropriate pace*

 **E L L**

Pace Have students turn to *Student Edition* page 600 in "Any Small Goodness." Model reading aloud the passage at an appropriate pace as students follow along. Then reread the passage, sentence by sentence, as students echo-read with you. Next, have them choral-read the page, focusing on reading at a steady pace.

 MONITOR PROGRESS

Pace After reteaching the skill, are students able to read aloud at an appropriate pace? If not, additional resources are available in the *Strategic Intervention Resource Kit*.

Strategic ▶ Intervention Resource Kit

Grammar and Writing
Past and Future Tenses

Objective

- *To use past-, present-, and future-tense verbs correctly in speaking and writing*

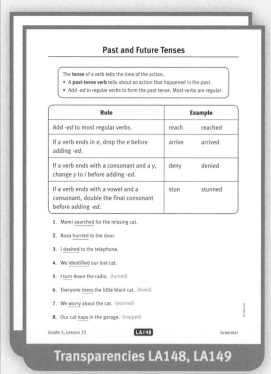

Past and Future Tenses

The **tense** of a verb tells the time of the action.
- A **past-tense verb** tells about an action that happened in the past.
- Add *-ed* to regular verbs to form the past tense. Most verbs are regular.

Rule	Example	
Add *-ed* to most regular verbs.	reach	reached
If a verb ends in *e*, drop the *e* before adding *-ed*.	arrive	arrived
If a verb ends with a consonant and a *y*, change *y* to *i* before adding *-ed*.	deny	denied
If a verb ends with a vowel and a consonant, double the final consonant before adding *-ed*.	stun	stunned

1. Mami searched for the missing cat.
2. Rosa hurried to the door.
3. I dashed to the telephone.
4. We identified our lost cat.
5. I turn down the radio. (turned)
6. Everyone loves the little black cat. (loved)
7. We worry about the cat. (worried)
8. Our cat naps in the garage. (napped)

Grade 5, Lesson 23   **LA148**   Grammar

Transparencies LA148, LA149

MONITOR PROGRESS

Grammar and Writing After reteaching the skills, are students able to use past- and future-tense verbs correctly in speaking and writing? If not, additional resources are available in the *Strategic Intervention Resource Kit*.

Strategic ▶ Intervention Resource Kit

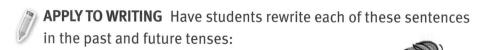

BELOW-LEVEL RETEACH

Past and Future Tenses

REVIEW THE SKILL Display **Transparency LA148**. Read aloud the information about the past tense, including the rules for forming regular past-tense verbs. Then display **Transparency LA149** and read aloud the information about future-tense verbs.

GUIDED PRACTICE Write the following sentence frames and verbs on the board.

- Luis _____ the phone. (answer)
- They _____ each other joyfully. (hug)
- The mice _____ across the floor. (scurry)
- She _____ up in the air. (jump)

Guide students to use the verb in parentheses to complete each sentence in the simple-present tense. Then have students use the same verb to complete the sentence in the simple-past tense and the simple-future tense.

APPLY TO WRITING Have students rewrite each of these sentences in the past and future tenses:

- Huitla escapes.
- Papi worries about the cat.
- Huitla climbs the tree.
- Leo Love rescues the cat.

ON-LEVEL REINFORCE

Past- and Future-Tense Verbs

APPLY TO WRITING Display **Transparencies LA148** and **LA149**. Review the information about past and future tenses. Then guide students to write sentences using the following verbs in both their past-tense and future-tense forms:

- hug
- jump
- scurry
- drop
- answer
- pause

I **hugged** my cat after she was rescued.

I **will hug** my cat after she is rescued.

Past and Future Tenses Use these sentences to model forming the simple tenses. Then have students complete each sentence by replacing the verb *call about* with the verb *rescue*.

Today Leo Love *calls* about the cat.

Yesterday, Leo Love *called* about the cat.

Tomorrow, Leo Love *will call* about the cat.

ADVANCED EXTEND

Write an Explanation

EXTEND THE SKILL Have students write a paragraph from Arturo's point of view describing how Huitla got out and what he will do to prevent it from happening again. Tell students to use the past tense to describe how Huitla got out and the future tense to explain how Arturo will prevent it from happening again.

Literary Devices

Objectives

- *To recognize and understand literary devices*
- *To identify and use sensory language*

Literary Devices

REVIEW THE SKILL Remind students that **figurative language** is a literary device. Review that figurative language has a meaning other than its literal one.

GUIDED PRACTICE Write the sentences below on the board and read them aloud. Guide students to name the type of figurative language in each sentence. Discuss their responses.

- The flames jumped and danced in the fireplace. (personification)

- That idea is pure gold! (metaphor)

- His smile was as sweet as honey. (simile)

- The full moon hid its face behind the clouds. (personification)

Then read aloud to students selections from a poetry anthology, and ask them to identify examples of figurative language in the poetry. Discuss with students the type and meaning of each example.

MONITOR PROGRESS

Literary Devices After reteaching the skill, are students able to identify and understand different types of figurative language? If not, additional resources are available in the *Strategic Intervention Resource Kit*.

Strategic ▶
Intervention
Resource Kit

ON-LEVEL REINFORCE

Literary Devices

REINFORCE UNDERSTANDING Review *Student Edition* page 614 with students. Remind them that **figurative language** is a literary device that authors use to help readers visualize story characters and events. Then write on the board the sentences below. Guide students to identify the type of figurative language in each sentence.

The car was a rocket. (metaphor)

The wind blew on my face. (personification)

It was as hot as an oven outside. (simile)

The moon peeked out from behind the clouds. (personification)

ADVANCED EXTEND

Write Animal Riddles

EXTEND THE SKILL Have students use each type of figurative language in a riddle describing an animal without naming it. Have students exchange riddles with a partner and interpret the figurative language to identify the animal their partner described.

I am like a summer symphony.

I am a living violin.

I am conducting my own orchestra.

What am I? (a cricket)

Robust Vocabulary

Objective

• *To develop and demonstrate knowledge of word meanings*

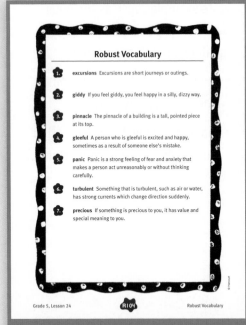

Robust Vocabulary

1. **excursions** Excursions are short journeys or outings.
2. **giddy** If you feel giddy, you feel happy in a silly, dizzy way.
3. **pinnacle** The pinnacle of a building is a tall, pointed piece at its top.
4. **gleeful** A person who is gleeful is excited and happy, sometimes as a result of someone else's mistake.
5. **panic** Panic is a strong feeling of fear and anxiety that makes a person act unreasonably or without thinking carefully.
6. **turbulent** Something that is turbulent, such as air or water, has strong currents which change direction suddenly.
7. **precious** If something is precious to you, it has value and special meaning to you.

Grade 5, Lesson 24   R104   Robust Vocabulary

Transparency R104

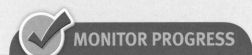

MONITOR PROGRESS

Robust Vocabulary After reteaching the Vocabulary Words, are students able to use them correctly in speaking and writing? If not, additional resources are available in the *Strategic Intervention Resource Kit*.

Strategic ▶ Intervention Resource Kit

BELOW-LEVEL   RETEACH

Robust Vocabulary

 REVIEW VOCABULARY Display **Transparency R104**. Read aloud the first Vocabulary Word and have students repeat after you. Then read the accompanying Student-Friendly Explanation. Pause to answer any questions. Repeat for the rest of the words.

WORDS IN CONTEXT Write these sentences on the board, and have students replace the underlined word or words with a Vocabulary Word.

• They enjoy weekly <u>trips</u> to the park. (excursions)
• She felt <u>dizzy and silly</u> after riding the roller coaster. (giddy)
• They stood at the <u>top</u> of the mountain. (pinnacle)
• Pat was <u>happy</u> when he heard the news. (gleeful)
• Teresa felt <u>sudden fear</u> when she couldn't find her homework. (panic)
• The storm made the ocean <u>rough</u>. (turbulent)
• The photograph of my grandmother is <u>valuable</u> to me. (precious)

GUIDED PRACTICE Have students use each Vocabulary Word in a sentence that shows its meaning.

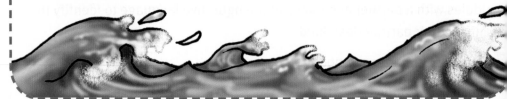

ON-LEVEL REINFORCE

Robust Vocabulary

REVIEW WORD MEANING Display **Transparency R104**. Have students take turns reading aloud each Vocabulary Word and its Student-Friendly Explanation. Answer any questions students have about pronunciation or meaning. Then have students use each Vocabulary Word in a sentence that shows its meaning.

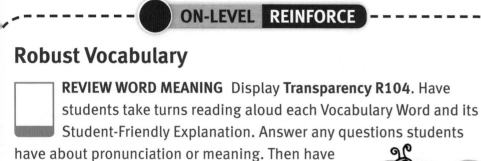

ADVANCED EXTEND

Extend Robust Vocabulary

USE VOCABULARY IN WRITING Display **Transparency R104**. Have students write a short story about an exciting trip they have taken or would like to take. Tell them to use all seven Vocabulary Words in their story. When students have finished writing, have them share their stories with the group.

ELL

Robust Vocabulary Display **Transparency R104**. Point out and read aloud the Vocabulary Words. Have students repeat each word after you. Monitor their pronunciation. Then reread each word and its Student-Friendly Explanation. Clarify the explanation for students, using illustrations, photographs, gestures, or examples.

Selection Comprehension
"Chester Cricket's Pigeon Ride"

Objective
- *To demonstrate comprehension of a text*

Selection Comprehension

Use the *Practice Book* page 141 to review the story. Lead students to use this information to develop an oral summary of each section.

MONITOR PROGRESS

Selection Comprehension After reteaching, are students able to write a complete summary of the selection? If not, additional resources are available in the *Strategic Intervention Resource Kit*.

**Strategic ►
Intervention
Resource Kit**

BELOW-LEVEL **RETEACH**

Support Comprehension

REVIEW THE SELECTION Remind students that a summary of a story includes the characters, setting, conflict, plot events, and resolution. Discuss with students these narrative elements in "Chester Cricket's Pigeon Ride."

GUIDED PRACTICE Work with students to complete *Practice Book* page 141. Then help them identify the ideas that should be included in a complete summary of the story.

ON-LEVEL **REINFORCE**

Reinforce Comprehension

REVIEW STORY ELEMENTS Display the completed *Practice Book* page 141. Remind students that the story map on this page can help them identify the most important parts of the story. Discuss with students the information in the boxes. Then help them identify areas in their summaries that could be refined.

ADVANCED **EXTEND**

Extend Comprehension

COMPARE AND CONTRAST Have students write a paragraph that compares and contrasts Chester Cricket and Lulu. Tell students to explain how these characters are similar and different. Remind them to use details from the story to support their ideas about each character.

Fluency
ocus: Pace

 BELOW-LEVEL RETEACH

Fluency: Pace

REVIEW PACE Remind students that *pace* is the speed at which they read. Remind them that their pace should be steady and even, similar to a spoken conversation.

MODEL FLUENT READING Have students turn to *Student Edition* page 620 in "Chester Cricket's Pigeon Ride." Model reading aloud the page at a conversational pace as students follow along silently. Note punctuation marks such as commas or dashes that signal the need to pause during Chester's and Lulu's conversation.

GUIDED PRACTICE Reread the page. This time have students read aloud with you, matching your pace. For additional practice, have small groups reread the page one more time chorally.

 ON-LEVEL REINFORCE

Fluency: Pace

PRACTICE PACE Remind students that good readers read aloud at a steady, conversational pace. Have students turn to *Student Edition* page 620. Model reading aloud the page at an appropriate pace. Then have students reread the page chorally focusing on reading at a conversational pace.

 ADVANCED EXTEND

Fluency: Pace

EXTEND THE SKILL Remind students that they should change their pace to match the action in the story. Have students read the passage on *Student Edition* page 624. Encourage students to experiment with speeding up the pace, slowing it down, or adding dramatic pauses to make this scene in the story as exciting as possible. Then have partners take turns reading the page aloud.

Objectives
- *To demonstrate the characteristics of fluent, effective reading*
- *To read aloud with prosody, using appropriate pace*

Pace Have students turn to *Student Edition* page 620. Model reading aloud the page at an appropriate pace as students follow along silently in their books. Note punctuation marks such as commas or dashes that signal a pause during Chester's and Lulu's conversation. Then reread the page sentence by sentence, as students echo-read. Tell students to match your pace.

 MONITOR PROGRESS

Pace After reteaching the skill, are students able to read aloud at an appropriate pace? If not, additional resources are available in the *Strategic Intervention Resource Kit.*

Strategic ▶ Intervention Resource Kit

Grammar and Writing
Perfect Tenses

Objectives

- *To use perfect-tense verbs correctly in speaking and writing*
- *To conjugate verbs correctly*

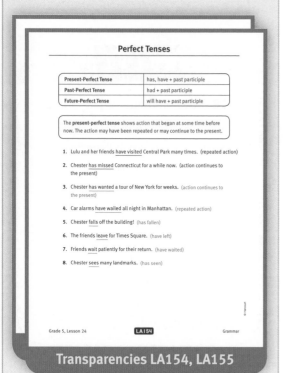

Perfect Tenses

Present-Perfect Tense	has, have + past participle
Past-Perfect Tense	had + past participle
Future-Perfect Tense	will have + past participle

The **present-perfect tense** shows action that began at some time before now. The action may have been repeated or may continue to the present.

1. Lulu and her friends <u>have visited</u> Central Park many times. (repeated action)
2. Chester <u>has missed</u> Connecticut for a while now. (action continues to the present)
3. Chester <u>has wanted</u> a tour of New York for weeks. (action continues to the present)
4. Car alarms <u>have wailed</u> all night in Manhattan. (repeated action)
5. Chester <u>falls</u> off the building! (has fallen)
6. The friends <u>leave</u> for Times Square. (have left)
7. Friends <u>wait</u> patiently for their return. (have waited)
8. Chester <u>sees</u> many landmarks. (has seen)

Grade 5, Lesson 24   LA154   Grammar

Transparencies LA154, LA155

MONITOR PROGRESS

Grammar and Writing After reteaching the skills, are students able to use perfect-tense verbs correctly in speaking and writing? If not, additional resources are available in the *Strategic Intervention Resource Kit*.

Strategic ▶ Intervention Resource Kit

BELOW-LEVEL RETEACH

Perfect Tenses

REVIEW THE SKILL Display **Transparency LA154**. Review the information about the **present-perfect tense**. Then display **Transparency LA155** and read aloud the boxed information about verbs in the **past-perfect tense**. Use sentences 1 and 2 as examples. Then read aloud the boxed information about the **future-perfect tense**, using sentence 5 as an example.

GUIDED PRACTICE Write the following sentences on the board and guide students to identify whether each sentence is in the present-perfect tense, the past-perfect tense, or the future-perfect tense. Have them circle the helping verb and underline the past participle in each sentence.

- He (has) <u>practiced</u> each day. (present perfect)
- She (had) <u>explored</u> the city. (past perfect)
- The snow (will have) <u>melted</u> in March. (future perfect)
- The cricket (had) <u>chirped</u> all day. (past perfect)

Have students rewrite each sentence in the tense indicated in parentheses.

- By afternoon, the parade will end. **(future perfect)**
  (By afternoon, the parade will have ended.)
- We met him last year. **(past perfect)**
  (We had met him last year.)
- Chester chirped each day. **(present perfect)**
  (Chester has chirped each day.)

ON-LEVEL REINFORCE

Perfect Tenses

APPLY TO WRITING Display **Transparencies LA154** and **LA155**. Review the information about perfect tenses. Then have students write five sentences about Chester Cricket's adventure. Tell them to use each perfect tense at least once.

Perfect Tenses Use the examples below to show students that when they form perfect tenses, the helping verbs change but the main verb is always the past participle.

• Chester *has* chirped. (present perfect)

• Chester *had* chirped. (past perfect)

• Chester *will have* chirped. (future perfect)

ADVANCED EXTEND

Write About Activities

EXTEND THE SKILL Have students write two sentences in the present-perfect tense describing activities they have done recently. Then have them write sentences in the past-perfect tense describing activities they did last month. Finally, have students write sentences in the future-perfect tense describing activities they plan to do in the future.

Teacher's Notes

Assessment

Assessment

Good assessments tell you what your students need to learn to meet grade-level standards.

It's not just about scoring the students—or the teacher, for that matter. It's about helping teachers **know what to teach and how much.**

Reading education is a **growing science.** We know more about how children learn to read than we did in the past. This **knowledge gives us the power** to use assessment to inform instruction. Assessment exposes the missing skills so that teachers can fill in the gaps.

Good assessment is part of instruction.

Think about it: if you are testing what you are teaching, then the test is another **practice and application** opportunity for children. In addition, when tests focus on the skills that are essential to better reading, testing informs teachers about which students need more instruction in those essential skills.

What is the best kind of assessment to use?

Using more than one kind of assessment will give you the clearest picture of your students' progress. **Multiple measures** are the key to a well-rounded view.

First, consider the assessments that are already **mandated** for you: your school, your district, and your state will, of course, tell you which tests you must use, and when. In addition to these, you should use **curriculum-based assessments** to monitor your students' progress in *StoryTown.*

The following curriculum-based assessments are built into *StoryTown.*

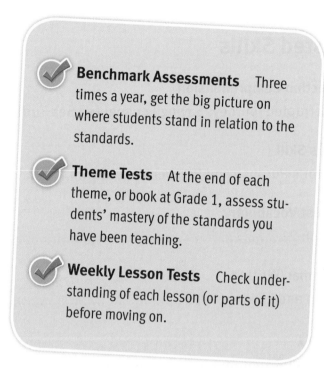

Benchmark Assessments Three times a year, get the big picture on where students stand in relation to the standards.

Theme Tests At the end of each theme, or book at Grade 1, assess students' mastery of the standards you have been teaching.

Weekly Lesson Tests Check understanding of each lesson (or parts of it) before moving on.

On a daily basis, point-of-use **Monitor Progress** notes help you check understanding and reteach or extend instruction. Additional checklists and rubrics are provided to help you monitor students' comprehension, writing, listening, and speaking.

The *Benchmark Assessments,* the *Theme Tests,* and the *Weekly Lesson Tests* are all available online. Students can take the tests on the computer, or you can use pencil-and-paper and enter the scores into the database later. Either way, *StoryTown Online Assessment* will help you track students' progress and share their growth with administrators and families.

 StoryTown Online Assessment

Using Assessment to Inform Instruction
Specific prescriptions based on Harcourt Reading Assessments.

Tested Skills   Prescriptions

Selection Comprehension

"Interrupted Journey: Saving Endangered Sea Turtles" .... Reteach, p. S6

Focus Skill

Author's Purpose and Perspective.................................. Reteach, pp. S2–S3

Robust Vocabulary

Lesson 21.. Reteach, pp. S4–S5

Grammar/Writing

Action and Linking Verbs .... Reteach, pp. S8–S9

Fluency

Expression .... Reteach, p. S7

Weekly Test

Tested Skills

Prescriptions

Selection Comprehension

"The Power of W.O.W.!" .... Reteach, p. S14

Focus Skill

Author's Purpose and Perspective.................................. Reteach, pp. S10–S11

Robust Vocabulary

Lesson 22 .... Reteach, pp. S12–S13

Comprehension

Draw Conclusions.. Reteach, pp. S16–S17

Grammar/Writing

Present Tense; Subject-Verb Agreement.......................... Reteach, pp. S18–S19

Fluency

Expression .... Reteach, p. S15

Tested Skills   Prescriptions

Selection Comprehension

"Any Small Goodness: A Novel of the Barrio"................... Reteach, p. S24

Focus Skill

Literary Devices.. Reteach, pp. S20–S21

Robust Vocabulary

Lesson 23 .... Reteach, pp. S22–S23

Comprehension

Literary Symbols and Patterns .... Reteach, pp. S8–S9, Theme 4

Grammar/Writing

Past and Future Tenses... Reteach, pp. S26–S27

Fluency

Pace .... Reteach, p. S25

Weekly Tests

Lesson 24 Tested Skills

Prescriptions

Selection Comprehension

"Chester Cricket's Pigeon Ride" .... Reteach, p. S32

Focus Skill

Literary Devices... Reteach, pp. S28–S29

Robust Vocabulary

Lesson 24 .... Reteach, pp. S30–S31

Comprehension

Draw Conclusions... Reteach, pp. S16–S17

Grammar/Writing

Perfect Tenses... Reteach, pp. S34–S35

Fluency

Pace .... Reteach, p. S33

Lesson 25 Tested Skills

Selection Comprehension

"The Compassion Campaign" .... Monitor Comprehension, pp. T290–T299

Robust Vocabulary

Lesson 25 .... *Extra Support Copying Master,* p. 145

Theme 5 Test

Tested Skills

Prescriptions

Selection Comprehension .... Reteach, pp. S6, S14, S24, S32

Robust Vocabulary .... Reteach, pp. S4–S5, S12–S13,
S22–S23, S30–S31

Grammar.. Reteach, pp. S8–S9, S18–S19,
S26–S27, S34–S35

Spelling .... *Spelling Practice Book,* pp. 99–102

Writing.. Reteach, pp. S8–S9, S18–S19,
S26–S27, S34–S35

Fluency .... Reteach, pp. S7, S15, S25, S33

BELOW-LEVEL **RETEACH**

- Below-Level Leveled Readers
- Leveled Readers System
- Extra Support Copying Masters
- Strategic Intervention Resource Kit
- Intervention Station, Intermediate

ON-LEVEL **REINFORCE**

- On-Level Leveled Readers
- Leveled Readers System
- Practice Book

ADVANCED **EXTEND**

- Advanced Leveled Readers
- Leveled Readers System
- Challenge Copying Masters
- Challenge Resource Kit

To determine whether students need even more support, use your district-approved diagnostic and screening assessments.

Resources

ADDITIONAL RESOURCES

Using Rubrics

*A **rubric** is a tool a teacher can use to score a student's work.*

*A **rubric** lists the criteria for evaluating the work, and it describes different levels of success in meeting those criteria.*

***Rubrics** are useful assessment tools for teachers, but they can be just as useful for students. In fact, rubrics can be powerful teaching tools.*

RUBRIC Rubrics for Retelling and Summarizing

- There are separate rubrics for narrative and for nonfiction. Before students begin their retellings or summaries, ask them which rubric should be used. Then point out the criteria and discuss each one.

- Have students focus on the criteria for excellence listed on the rubric so that they have specific goals to aim for.

RUBRIC Rubrics for Presentations

- Before students make a presentation, discuss the criteria listed on the rubric. Have students focus on the criteria for excellence listed on the rubric so that they can aim for specific goals.

- Discuss the criteria for listening with students who will be in the audience. Point out the criteria for excellence listed on the rubric so that they target specific goals.

RUBRIC Rubrics for Short and Extended Responses

- Before students begin a short or an extended response, discuss the criteria for excellence listed on the rubrics to give students specific goals.

- Tell students that the short-response task should take about five to ten minutes to complete, and the extended-response task should take about ten to fifteen minutes to complete.

RUBRIC Rubrics for Writing

- When you introduce students to a new kind of writing through a writing model, discuss the criteria listed on the rubric, and ask students to decide how well the model meets each criterion.

- Before students attempt a new kind of writing, have them focus on the criteria for excellence listed on the rubric so that they have specific goals to aim for.

- During both the drafting and revising stages, remind students to check their writing against the rubric to keep their focus and to determine if there are any aspects of their writing they can improve.

- Students can use the rubrics to score their own writing. They can keep the marked rubric in their portfolios with the corresponding piece of writing. The marked rubrics will help students see their progress through the school year. In conferences with students and family members, you can refer to the rubrics to point out both strengths and weaknesses in students' writing.

Score of 4

The student:

- names and describes the main and supporting characters and tells how they change or learn.
- tells about the setting.
- retells the plot in detail.
- describes the problems and resolutions in the story.
- uses phrases, language, vocabulary, sentence structure, or literary devices from the story.
- accurately describes the theme or meaning of the story.
- provides extensions of the story, such as making connections to other texts, relating relevant experiences, and/or making generalizations.
- requires little or no prompting.

Score of 3

The student:

- names and describes the main characters.
- tells about the setting.
- retells most of the plot accurately.
- describes some of the problems and resolutions in the story.
- uses some phrases, language, vocabulary, or literary devices from the story.
- relates some aspects of the theme or meaning of the story.
- provides some extensions of the story, such as making connections to other texts or relating relevant experiences.
- may require some prompting.

Score of 2

The student:

- tells some details about the story elements, including characters, setting, and plot, with some omissions or errors.
- uses little language and vocabulary from the story.
- shows minimal understanding of the theme or meaning of the story.
- provides minimal extensions of the story.
- requires some prompting to retell the story.

Score of 1

The student:

- tells few if any details about the story elements, with errors.
- has little or no awareness of the theme of the story.
- provides no extensions of the story.
- is unable to retell the story without prompting.

Score of **4**	Score of **3**	Score of **2**	Score of **1**
The student: • provides a summarizing statement. • relates the main idea and important supporting details. • creates a focused, coherent, logical, and organized structure; stays on topic; and relates important points to the text. • understands relationships in the text such as cause-and-effect, chronological order, or classifying, grouping, comparing, or contrasting information. • discriminates between reality and fantasy, fact and fiction. • uses phrases, language, vocabulary, or sentence structure from the text. • clearly tells the conclusion or point of the text with details. • identifies the author's purpose for creating the text. • provides extensions of the text, such as making connections to other texts, relating relevant experiences, and/or making generalizations. • requires little or no prompting.	The student: • tells the topic of the text. • relates the main idea and relevant details. • creates a coherent structure and stays on topic. • mostly understands relationships in the text, such as cause-and-effect, chronological order, or classifying, grouping, or comparing information. • discriminates between reality and fantasy. • uses some phrases, language, or vocabulary from the text. • tells the conclusion or point of the text. • identifies the author's purpose. • provides some extensions of the text, such as making connections to other texts or relating relevant experiences. • may require some prompting.	The student: • minimally relates the topic of the text. • shows minimal understanding of main idea, and omits many important details. • provides some structure; might stray from topic. • understands few, if any, relationships in the text, such as chronological order, classifying, or grouping. • uses little or no language and vocabulary from the text. • does not fully understand the conclusion or point of the text. • shows some awareness of the author's purpose. • provides few, if any, extensions of the text. • requires some prompting.	The student: • shows little or no understanding of main idea, and omits important details. • provides a poorly organized or unclear structure. • does not understand relationships in the text. • does not understand the conclusion of the text. • provides no extensions of the text. • is unable to summarize the text without prompting.

Scoring RUBRIC for Presentations: Speaking and Listening

	SPEAKING	VISUALS	MARKERS	WORD PROCESSING	HANDWRITING
Score of 6	The speaker uses very effective pace, volume, intonation, and expression.	The writer uses visuals such as illustrations, charts, graphs, maps, and tables very well. The text and visuals clearly relate to each other.	The title, subheads, page numbers, and bullets are used very well. They make it easy for the reader to find information in the text. These markers clearly show organized information.	Fonts and sizes are used very well, which helps the reader enjoy reading the text.	The slant of the letters is the same throughout the whole paper. The letters are clearly formed and the spacing between words is equal, which makes the text very easy to read.
Score of 5	The speaker uses effective pace, volume, intonation, and expression consistently.	The writer uses visuals well. The text and visuals relate to each other.	The title, subheads, page numbers, and bullets are used very well. They help the reader find information.	Fonts and sizes are used well.	The slant of the letters is almost the same through most of the paper. The letters are clearly formed. The spacing between words is usually equal.
Score of 4	The speaker uses effective pace, volume, intonation, and expression fairly consistently.	The writer uses visuals fairly well.	The title, subheads, page numbers, and bullets are used fairly well. They usually help the reader find information.	Fonts and sizes are used fairly well, but could be improved upon.	The slant of the letters is usually the same. The letters are clearly formed most of the time. The spacing between words is usually equal.
Score of 3	The speaker uses somewhat effective pace, volume, intonation, and expression, but not consistently.	The writer uses visuals with the text, but the reader may not understand how they are related.	The writer uses some markers such as a title, page numbers, or bullets. However, the use of markers could be improved upon to help the reader get more meaning from the text.	Fonts and sizes are used well in some places, but make the paper look cluttered in others.	The slant of the letters is readable. There are some differences in letter shape and form, slant, and spacing that make some words easier to read than others.
Score of 2	The speaker uses somewhat effective pace, volume, intonation, and expression.	The writer tries to use visuals with the text, but the reader is confused by them.	The writer uses very few markers. This makes it hard for the reader to find and understand the information in the text.	Fonts and sizes are not used well. The paper looks cluttered.	The handwriting is somewhat readable. There are many differences in letter shape and form, slant, and spacing that make some words hard to read.
Score of 1	The speaker's techniques are unclear or distracting to the listener.	The visuals do not make sense with the text.	There are no markers such as title, page numbers, bullets, or subheads.	There are too many different fonts and sizes. It is very distracting to the reader.	The letters are not formed correctly. The slant and spacing are not the same throughout the paper, or there is no regular space between words. The paper is very difficult to read.

Scoring RUBRIC for Short and Extended Responses

	EXTENDED RESPONSE	SHORT RESPONSE
Score of 4	The response indicates that the student has a thorough understanding of the reading concept embodied in the task. The student has provided a response that is accurate, complete, and fulfills all the requirements of the task. Necessary support and/or examples are included, and the information is clearly text-based.	
Score of 3	The response indicates that the student has an understanding of the reading concept embodied in the task. The student has provided a response that is accurate and fulfills all the requirements of the task, but the required support and/or details are not complete or clearly text-based.	
Score of 2	The response indicates that the student has a partial understanding of the reading concept embodied in the task. The student has provided a response that is essentially correct and text-based, but the information is too general or too simplistic. Some of the support and/or examples and requirements of the task may be incomplete or omitted.	The response indicates that the student has a complete understanding of the reading concept embodied in the task. The student has provided a response that is accurate, complete, and fulfills all the requirements of the task. Necessary support and/or examples are included, and the information given is clearly text-based.
Score of 1	The response indicates that the student has very limited understanding of the reading concept embodied in the task. The response is incomplete, may exhibit many flaws, and may not address all requirements of the task.	The response indicates that the student has a partial understanding of the reading concept embodied in the task. The student has provided a response that is essentially correct and text-based, but the information is too general or too simplistic. Some of the support and/or examples may be incomplete or omitted.
Score of 0	The response indicates that the student does not demonstrate an understanding of the reading concept embodied in the task. The student has provided a response that is inaccurate; the response has an insufficient amount of information to determine the student's understanding of the task; or the student has failed to respond to the task.	The response indicates that the student does not demonstrate an understanding of the reading concept embodied in the task. The student has provided a response that is inaccurate; the response has an insufficient amount of information to determine the student's understanding of the task; or the student has failed to respond to the task.

Scoring RUBRIC for Writing

	Score of 6	Score of 5	Score of 4	Score of 3	Score of 2	Score of 1
FOCUS	The writing is completely focused on the topic and has a clear purpose.	The writing is focused on the topic and purpose.	The writing is generally focused on the topic and purpose.	The writing is somewhat focused on the topic and purpose.	The writing is related to the topic but does not have a clear focus.	The writing is not focused on the topic and purpose.
ORGANIZATION	The ideas in the paper are well-organized and presented in logical order. The paper seems complete to the reader.	The organization of the paper is mostly clear. The paper seems complete.	The organization is mostly clear, but the paper may seem unfinished.	The paper is somewhat organized, but seems unfinished.	There is little organization to the paper.	There is no organization to the paper.
SUPPORT	The writing has strong, specific details. The word choices are clear and fresh.	The writing has strong, specific details and clear word choices.	The writing has supporting details and some variety in word choice.	The writing has few supporting details. It needs more variety in word choice.	The writing has few supporting details and very little variety in word choice.	There are few or no supporting details. The word choices are unclear.
CONVENTIONS	The writer uses a variety of sentences. There are few or no errors in grammar, spelling, punctuation, and capitalization.	The writer uses a variety of sentences. There are few errors in grammar, spelling, punctuation, and capitalization.	The writer uses some variety in sentences. There are few errors in grammar, spelling, punctuation, and capitalization.	The writer uses simple sentences. There are some errors in grammar, spelling, punctuation, and capitalization.	The writer uses simple sentences. There are many errors in grammar, spelling, punctuation, and capitalization.	The writer uses unclear sentences. There are many errors in grammar, spelling, punctuation, and capitalization.

Scoring RUBRIC for Writing

	IDEAS	ORGANIZATION	VOICE	WORD CHOICE	SENTENCE FLUENCY	CONVENTIONS
Score of 4	The paper is clear and focused. It is engaging and includes enriching details.	The ideas are well-organized and in a logical order.	The writer consistently uses creative ideas and expressions.	The writer uses vivid verbs, specific nouns, and colorful adjectives well. The writing is very detailed.	The writing flows smoothly. The writer uses a good variety of sentences.	The writer uses standard writing conventions well, with few or no errors.
Score of 3	The paper is generally clear and includes good supporting details, with minor focusing problems.	The ideas are generally well-organized and in a logical order.	The writer's ideas and expressions are generally creative.	The writer uses some vivid verbs, specific nouns, and colorful adjectives. The writing is detailed.	The writing flows generally well. The writer uses some variety in sentences.	The writer uses most standard writing conventions well, but makes some errors.
Score of 2	The paper is somewhat clear but the writer does not effectively use supporting details.	The ideas are somewhat organized.	The writer's ideas and expressions are somewhat creative.	The writer uses few interesting words. The writing is somewhat detailed.	The writing flows smoothly in places. The writer does not use much sentence variety.	The writer uses some writing conventions well, but makes distracting errors.
Score of 1	The paper has no clear central idea. The details are either missing or unclear.	The ideas are not well-organized and not in a logical order.	The writer lacks creativity in ideas and expressions.	The writer lacks interesting word choice and detail.	The writing does not flow smoothly. The writer uses little or no sentence variety, and some sentences are unclear.	The writer makes continuous errors with most writing conventions, making text difficult to read.

Additional Reading

GRADE 5 This list is a compilation of the additional theme- and topic-related books cited in the lesson plans. You may wish to use this list to provide students with opportunities to read **at least thirty minutes a day** outside of class.

Theme 5 ▸ MAKING A DIFFERENCE

Curlee, Lynn.
Liberty. Aladdin, 2003. Discusses all the planning and efforts that went into the construction of one of the most famous symbols of the United States—the Statue of Liberty. *ALA Notable Book.* **AVERAGE**

Dahl, Roald.
Esio Trot. Puffin, 1999. Mr. Hoppy is smitten with Mrs. Silver, whose main concern is her tortoise. He devises a plan to win her heart by teaching her a spell to make her tortoise grow bigger. Mr. Hoppy keeps substituting ever-larger tortoises for Mrs. Silver's pet Alfie, in hopes of convincing her to marry him. *Award-Winning Author.* **AVERAGE**

Ditchfield, Christin.
Serving Your Community. Children's Press, 2004. Focuses on the different ways that people can help out in their community, from volunteering to saving the planet. **EASY**

Erlbach, Arlene.
The Kids' Volunteering Book. Lerner, 1998. Presents some opportunities for young people to perform volunteer service, and briefly profiles some children who are volunteers. *Award-Winning Author.* **CHALLENGE**

George, Jean Craighead.
How to Talk to Your Cat. HarperTrophy, 2003. Describes how cats communicate with people through their behavior and sounds, and explains how to talk back to them using sounds, behavior, and body language. *Children's Choice.* **AVERAGE**

Glaser, Jason.
Sea Turtles. Bridgestone, 2006. Explores sea turtles including where they live, what they eat, how they produce young, and the dangers they face. **EASY**

Jay, Lorraine A.
Sea Turtles. NorthWord, 2000. Describes the habitat, physical characteristics, behaviors, and life cycle of the seven species of sea turtles, and discusses their endangered status. **CHALLENGE**

Kalman, Bobbie.
What Is a Community?: From A to Z. Crabtree, 2000. Discusses the different aspects that define communities, including buildings, family, and teamwork. **AVERAGE**

Lerner, Carol.
My Backyard Garden. Morrow, 1998. Explains how to start your own vegetable garden and how to cope with common problems, describing the round of activities from month to month throughout the year. *Award-Winning Author.* **CHALLENGE**

Mann, Elizabeth.
The Brooklyn Bridge: The Story of the World's Most Famous Bridge and the Remarkable Family That Built It. Mikaya, 2006. Describes about the design and construction of this magnificent bridge through historical photographs, informative diagrams, and powerful illustrations. *Award-Winning Author.* **EASY**

Pyers, Greg.
Rain Forest Explorer. Raintree, 2005. Presents information about the different plants and animals that inhabit the Amazon rain forest. **EASY**

Schaefer, A. R.
Forming a Band. Capstone, 2004. Describes the steps musicians take to form a band, including selecting band members, a name, music style, and appearance. **AVERAGE**

Selden, George.
Chester Cricket's New Home. Random House, 1984. Chester Cricket's stump that he calls home collapses, forcing him to find another place to live. Will he ever find another place to call his own? *Award-Winning Author.* **CHALLENGE**

Soto, Gary.
Neighborhood Odes. Harcourt, 2005. Twenty-one poems about growing up in an Hispanic neighborhood, highlighting the delights in such everyday items as sprinklers, the park, the library, and pomegranates. *Notable Social Studies Trade Book.* **CHALLENGE**

White, Nancy.
Why Do Cats Do That?: Facts About Real Cats and Why They Act the Way They Do! Scholastic, 1997. Offers an array of fun facts about this popular pet and answers questions such as, "Why do cats rub up against your leg?" **EASY**

Lesson Vocabulary

Theme 5

The following words are introduced in Grade 5, Lessons 21–25.

Lesson 21	Lesson 22	Lesson 23	Lesson 24	Lesson 25
basking	somberly	gouges	excursions	loathe
sleek	stammers	desolate	giddy	bland
vital	monopolize	bustles	pinnacle	mentor
damage	deflated	fervor	gleeful	dilapidated
analyzing	enraptured	immaculate	panic	coordination
detect	enterprising	assuage	turbulent	altruism
	cumbersome		precious	sensibility
				advocacy
				mistreated
				compassionate

Cumulative Vocabulary

The following words appear in the *Student Edition* selections in Grade 5.

absentminded
acclimate
accumulate
accustomed
achievement
adjust
advocacy
aghast
altruism
amends
analyzing
appalled
appealed
appropriate
asset
assuage
assured
baffled
basking
bellowing
betrayed
bickering
bland
boisterous
brimming
broached
bustles
charity
circulate
coaxed
compartments
compassionate
conceited
concoction
conducted
coordination
cramped
crisis
crucial
crusaded
cumbersome
customary
damage
debris
deduction
deflated
designated

desolate
desperately
destiny
detect
device
dignified
dilapidated
disgruntled
disheartened
dismal
dismayed
dramatically
dwell
earnestly
eccentric
elastic
elongates
embarked
eminent
encountered
endeavor
enraptured
enterprising
envisioned
equivalent
escapades
essence
essential
esteem
exceptional
excursions
exhilarated
expectations
extravagant
faze
feat
fervor
feverishly
fickle
flop
floundered
fret
fringes
genial
gesture
giddy
gleeful

gouges
gourmet
grateful
grim
grudgingly
grueling
hesitating
hiatus
humiliation
ignited
immaculate
impassable
inadequate
indication
indignantly
industry
inflammable
infuriated
insights
instinct
insufficient
intently
internal
intricate
invasion
invest
irrepressible
irresistible
isolated
jettisoned
laden
loathe
maneuvered
maven
measly
mentor
mistreated
modest
monopolize
monotonous
mortified
nudged
ordeal
outcast
outlandish
overcome
panic

parched
peril
perseverance
persuading
pesky
phobia
pinnacle
poised
portable
potentially
practical
precarious
precious
prestigious
pried
proclaimed
profusely
prognostication
proportion
proposed
protest
protrude
provoke
raspy
recoil
recount
regal
reigned
relented
remote
replenishing
reputation
residents
resisted
restrain
revelers
rigid
rowdy
ruckus
scholars
scours
secure
seldom
sensibility
shatter
sincere
sleek

smirk
sneered
somberly
sorrowful
specialized
specimens
spectacular
squinting
stammers
streamlined
stricken
summit
sustain
swarmed
swayed
teeming
tempted
tendency
terrain
throng
tranquility
turbulent
underlying
unfathomable
unimaginable
uninhabitable
urgently
vanish
vetoed
vital
wispy
wistful
withered
yearning

Handwriting

Individual students have various levels of handwriting skills, but they all have the desire to communicate effectively. To write correctly, they must be familiar with concepts of

- size (tall, short)
- open and closed
- capital and lowercase letters
- manuscript vs. cursive letters
- letter and word spacing
- punctuation

To assess students' handwriting skills, review samples of their written work. Note whether they use correct letter formation and appropriate size and spacing. Note whether students follow the conventions of print, such as correct capitalization and punctuation. Encourage students to edit and proofread their work and to use editing marks. When writing messages, notes, and letters, or when publishing their writing, students should leave adequate margins and indent new paragraphs to help make their work more readable for their audience.

Stroke and Letter Formation

Most manuscript letters are formed with a continuous stroke, so students do not often pick up their pencils when writing a single letter. When students begin to use cursive handwriting, they will have to lift their pencils from the paper less frequently and will be able to write more fluently. Models for Harcourt and D'Nealian handwriting are provided on pages R14–R17.

Position for Writing

Establishing the correct posture, pen or pencil grip, and paper position for writing will help prevent handwriting problems.

Posture Students should sit with both feet on the floor and with hips to the back of the chair. They can lean forward slightly but should not slouch. The writing surface should be smooth and flat and at a height that allows the upper arms to be perpendicular to the surface and the elbows to be under the shoulders.

Writing Instrument An adult-sized number-two lead pencil is a satisfactory writing tool for most students. As students become proficient in the use of cursive handwriting, have them use pens for writing final drafts. Use your judgment in determining what type of instrument is most suitable.

Paper Position and Pencil Grip The paper is slanted along the line of the student's writing arm, and the student uses his or her nonwriting hand to hold the paper in place. The student holds the pencil or pen slightly above the paint line—about one inch from the lead tip.

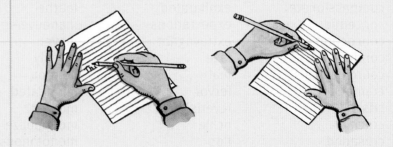

Meeting the Needs of All Learners

The best instruction builds on what students already know and can do. Given the wide range in students' handwriting abilities, a variety of approaches may be needed.

Extra Support For students who need more practice keeping their handwriting legible, one of the most important understandings is that legible writing is important for clear communication. Provide as many opportunities for classroom writing as possible. For example, students can

- **Make a class directory listing the names of their classmates.**
- **Draw and label graphic organizers, pictures, and maps.**
- **Contribute entries weekly to their vocabulary journals.**
- **Write and post messages about class assignments or group activities.**
- **Record observations during activities.**

ELL English-Language Learners can participate in meaningful print experiences. They can

- **Write signs, labels for centers, and other messages.**
- **Label graphic organizers and drawings.**
- **Contribute in group writing activities.**
- **Write independently in journals.**

You may also want to have students practice handwriting skills in their first language.

Challenge To ensure continued rapid advancement of students who come to fifth grade writing fluently, provide

- **A wide range of writing assignments.**
- **Opportunities for independent writing on self-selected and assigned topics.**

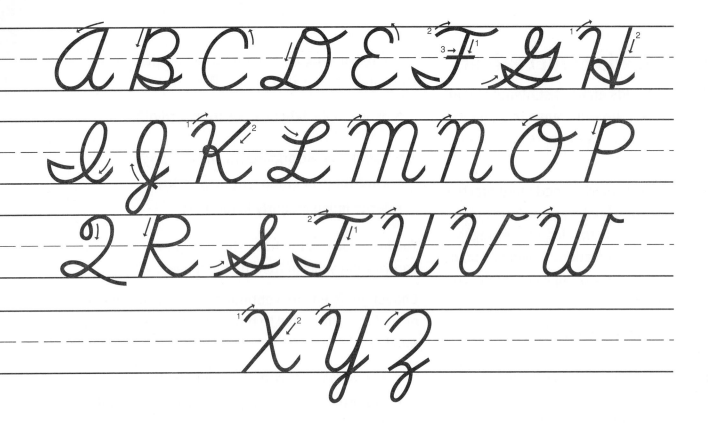

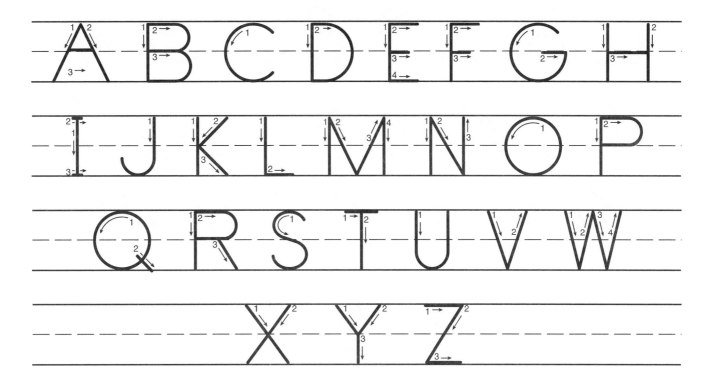

D'Nealian Handwriting Cursive Alphabet

A B C D E F G H

I J K L M N O P

Q R S T U V W

X Y Z

a b c d e f g h

i j k l m n o p

q r s t u v w

x y z

D'Nealian Handwriting — Manuscript Alphabet

A B C D E F G H

I J K L M N O P

Q R S T U V W

X Y Z

a b c d e f g h

i j k l m n o p

q r s t u v w

x y z

Introducing the Glossary

MODEL USING THE GLOSSARY Explain to students that a glossary often is included in a book so that readers can find the meanings of words used in the book.

- Read aloud the introductory pages.

- Model looking up one or more words.

- Point out how you rely on **alphabetical order** and the **guide words** at the top of the Glossary pages to locate the **entry word**.

- Demonstrate how to use the **pronunciation key** to confirm the correct pronunciation.

As students look over the Glossary, point out that illustrations accompany some of the Student-Friendly Explanations. Have students read a Word Origins or Academic Language note and discuss the type of information in each.

Encourage students to look up several words in the Glossary, identifying the correct page and the guide words. Then have them explain how using alphabetical order and the guide words at the top of each page helped them locate the words.

Tell students to use the Glossary to confirm the pronunciation of Vocabulary Words during reading and to help them better understand the meanings of unfamiliar words.

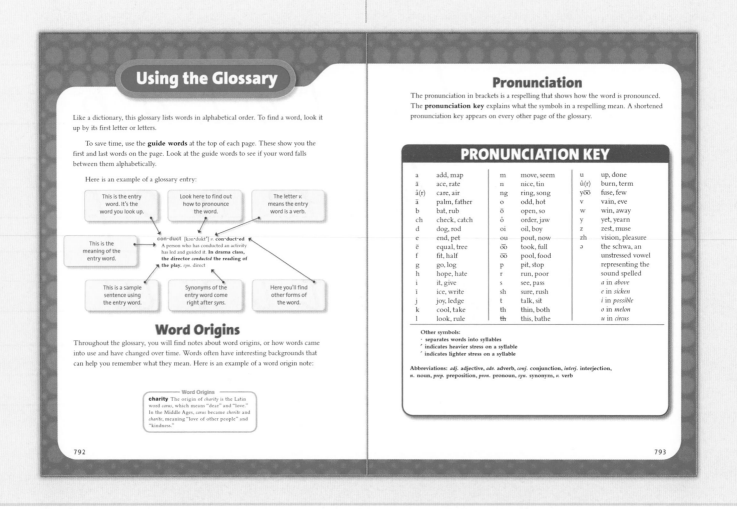

A

ab·sent·mind·ed [ab′sənt·mīn′did] *adj.* Someone who is absentminded forgets things easily. **Naomi thought Pedro was *absentminded* because he forgot to order food for the party.** *syn.* forgetful

ac·cli·mate [ak′lə·māt] *v.* If you acclimate to something, you adjust to a new condition or environment. **The goldfish had to *acclimate* to the larger tank.** *syns.* adapt, adjust

acclimate

ac·cu·mu·late [ə·kyo͞om′yə·lāt] *v.* When things accumulate, they collect over time. **When I noticed the newspapers *accumulate* in front of Mr. Smith's house, I realized he was probably out of town again.** *syn.* pile up

> **FACT FILE**
> **accumulate** Literally, *accumulate* means "to heap up." This meaning is reflected in the name *cumulus* clouds for the big, fluffy clouds that heap up in the sky.

> **ACADEMIC LANGUAGE**
> **accuracy** When you read with *accuracy*, you read without making mistakes.

ac·cus·tomed [ə·kus′təmd] *adj.* If you are accustomed to something, you are used to it because it has been a regular part of your life. **Charlie became *accustomed* to eating cereal for a snack.** *syn.* acclimated

a·chieve·ment [ə·chēv′mənt] *n.* An achievement is the result of a successful effort. **Janice was proud of her *achievement* as winner of the spelling bee.** *syns.* accomplishment, success

ad·just [ə·just′] *v.* When you adjust, you change your behavior to fit a new situation. **When the cat moved from the shelter to a home with three small children, it had to *adjust* to its new environment.** *syn.* modify

ad·vo·ca·cy [ad′və·kə·sē] *n.* Advocacy is giving support to a person, idea, or cause. **Amar showed his *advocacy* for stray animals by asking his parents if he could adopt a dog from the Humane Society.** *syns.* support, backing

a·ghast [ə·gast′] *adj.* If you are aghast, you feel shocked and disgusted about something. **Keisha was *aghast* at her friend's rude behavior.** *syn.* appalled

al·tru·ism [al′tro͞o·iz·əm] *n.* Altruism is being concerned about others before worrying about oneself. **David showed that *altruism* was part of his nature when he volunteered to read to children at the day-care center.** *syn.* kindness

a·mend [ə·mend′] *v.* **a·mends** When you amend something, you make positive changes, such as amending a shopping list or a recipe. **After forgetting to invite Xenia to her party, Aylana *amends* her mistake by inviting Xenia to a sleepover.** *syn.* correct

an·a·lyze [an′ə·līz] *v.* **an·a·lyz·ing** A scientist who is analyzing something is studying it closely to figure out how it works or what it is made of. **The scientist in the laboratory is *analyzing* the water to make sure it is safe to drink.** *syn.* examine

ap·pall [ə·pôl′] *v.* **ap·palled** Someone who is appalled is shocked and horrified at something. **After the storm, Mercedes was *appalled* to find that a tree had fallen on the roof of her house.** *syn.* dismay

> **Word Origins**
> **appall** The word *appall* traces its roots back to the French word *apallir,* which means "to become or make pale." It was not used to mean "shock and dismay" until the nineteenth century.

ap·peal [ə·pēl′] *v.* **ap·pealed** If you have appealed to someone, you have made a request with a lot of feeling. **Alejandro *appealed* to Ramona's good nature when he begged her to help him study for the math test.** *syn.* plead

ap·pro·pri·ate [ə·prō′prē·it] *adj.* If you wear appropriate clothing, you choose an outfit that is right for the situation. **Dwayne felt that a suit and tie would be the *appropriate* attire for the award ceremony.** *syn.* suitable

as·set [as′et] *n.* An asset is a resource, person, or object that is valuable to have. **My mother says her most valuable *asset* is her family.** *syn.* resource

as·suage [ə·swāj′] *v.* To assuage guilt is to make it less painful and troubling. **To *assuage* his bad feelings about spilling ketchup on his father's best shirt, Dan mowed the lawn.** *syn.* pacify

as·sure [ə·sho͝or′] *v.* **as·sured** If someone has assured you of something, he or she has said words to make you feel positive that things will be all right. **My older brother *assured* me that he had changed the flat tire and that it was safe to continue our trip.** *syn.* guarantee

> **ACADEMIC LANGUAGE**
> **autobiography** An *autobiography* is the story of a real person's life written by that person.

B

baf·fled [baf′əld] *adj.* Someone who is baffled by something cannot understand or explain it. **Emiko was *baffled* when she saw that her mother had sent cookies and candy, instead of the usual sandwich, for lunch.** *syn.* puzzled

bask [bask] *v.* **bask·ing** If an animal is basking, it is exposing itself to warmth in the sun. **Miguel was *basking* in the backyard on the lawn chair.** *syn.* sunbathe

bel·low·ing [bel′ō·ing] *adj.* A bellowing sound is a loud, low-pitched sound, usually made to show distress. **My dog makes *bellowing* sounds when he goes to the veterinarian.** *syn.* crying

be·tray [bi·trā′] *v.* **be·trayed** If you betrayed someone who trusted you, you gave away his or her plans, ideas, or secrets to others. **Megan said I had *betrayed* her when I told Stephanie her secret.** *syn.* double-cross

bick·er [bik′ər] *v.* **bick·er·ing** People who are bickering are arguing about something unimportant. **Jeff and Hilda are *bickering* about who gets the window seat on the plane ride.** *syn.* argue

> **ACADEMIC LANGUAGE**
> **biography** A *biography* is the story of a real person's life written by another person.

bland [bland] *adj.* Something that is bland is dull and unexciting. **Aunt Elena's chicken casserole was *bland* because she had forgotten to add salt and pepper.** *syn.* flavorless

bois·ter·ous [bois′tər·əs *or* bois′trəs] *adj.* A boisterous person or animal is noisy and has lots of energy. **The *boisterous* new puppy was constantly jumping on the furniture.** *syn.* rowdy

brim [brim] *v.* **brim·ming** Something that is brimming is filled to the very top. **Liang was thirsty, so he filled his cup until it was *brimming* with juice.** *syn.* full

brimming

broach [brōch] *v.* **broached** A ship that has broached is in danger of sinking because it has veered so that the waves strike its side. **I saw a movie in which a ship *broached* and objects were falling overboard.** *syn.* capsize

bus·tle [bus′əl] *v.* **bus·tles** When someone bustles, he or she moves in a busy, energetic way. **When my mother has guests for dinner, she *bustles* about the kitchen making sure the food is correctly prepared.** *syn.* dart

C

char·i·ty [char′ə·tē] *n.* Charity is showing kindness by giving money or gifts to organizations that need them. **She shows *charity* by giving some of her allowance to the Animal Rescue League.** *syn.* goodwill

> **Word Origins**
> **charity** The origin of *charity* is the Latin word *carus*, which means "dear" and "love." In the Middle Ages, *carus* became *cherité* and *charite*, meaning "love of other people" and "kindness."

a	add	e	end	o	odd	o͞o	pool	oi	oil	th	this	ə = *a* in *above*
ā	ace	ē	equal	ō	open	u	up	ou	pout	zh	vision	*e* in *sicken*
â	care	i	it	ô	order	û	burn	ng	ring			*i* in *possible*
ä	palm	ī	ice	o͝o	took	yo͞o	fuse	th	thin			*o* in *melon*
												u in *circus*

cir·cu·late [sûr′kyə·lāt] *v.* When you circulate, you move freely around an area. **When the doorbell rang, Susan had just begun to *circulate* among the guests at her party.** *syn.* wander

coax [kōks] *v.* **coaxed** If you are coaxed into doing something, you are gently talked into it by someone else. **Akedo *coaxed* Aretha into jogging with him, even though she doesn't like outdoor exercise.** *syn.* persuade

com·part·ment [kəm·pärt′mənt] *n.* **com·part·ments** An item that has compartments has separate sections for keeping things. **My craft box has many *compartments,* in which I store items such as crayons, markers, and brushes.** *syn.* section

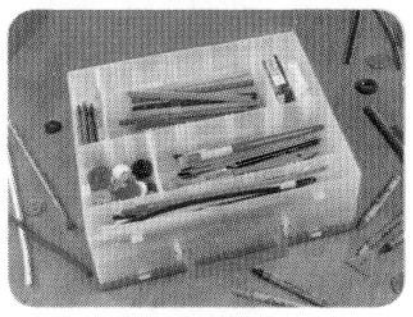

compartment

com·pas·sion·ate [kəm·pash′ən·it] *adj.* A compassionate person is kindhearted and understanding. **Isabel showed that she was *compassionate* by inviting the new girl to eat lunch with her.** *syn.* kind

con·ceit·ed [kən·sē′tid] *adj.* A conceited person thinks too highly of herself or himself. **Michael's announcement that he is the most well-liked student in the school shows how *conceited* he is.** *syn.* arrogant

con·coc·tion [kən·kok′shən] *n.* A concoction is a mix of different things, often one put together without much planning. **In science class, we put together a *concoction* of white glue, food coloring, and rock salt to make objects that represented precious stones.** *syn.* mixture

con·duct [kən·dukt′] *v.* **con·duct·ed** A person who has conducted an activity has led and guided it. **In drama class, the director *conducted* the reading of the play.** *syn.* direct

> **ACADEMIC LANGUAGE**
> **conventions** A *convention* is an agreement about what is correct in usage or custom. Conventions of the English language include the rules of grammar, spelling, punctuation, and capitalization.

co·or·di·na·tion [kō·ôr′də·nā′shən] *n.* Coordination involves organizing the different parts of something so that they work well together. **The sports award assembly was successful thanks to the *coordination* by Marshall.** *syn.* management

cramped [krampt] *adj.* A place that is cramped is uncomfortable because there is very little free space. **Sitting around the dinner table gets especially *cramped* when Aunt Sylvia and Uncle Harry bring their children to visit.** *syn.* crowded

cri·sis [krī′səs] *n.* A crisis is a situation that suddenly becomes very dangerous or difficult. **Chita smelled smoke and immediately knew a *crisis* existed in her apartment building.** *syn.* emergency

cru·cial [kro͞o′shəl] *adj.* If something is crucial, it is extremely important. **Manuel's mother and father made a *crucial* decision to move to another state.** *syn.* important

cru·sade [kro͞o·sād′] *v.* **cru·sad·ed** A person who has crusaded has worked hard to make a change based on his or her beliefs. **Pam's parents *crusaded* for her school to include an art program and a music program as part of the curriculum.** *syn.* campaign

cum·ber·some [kum′bər·səm] *adj.* Something that is cumbersome is large, heavy, and difficult to handle. **My suitcase was too *cumbersome* to lift into the overhead compartment, so I put it under my seat.** *syn.* unwieldy

cus·tom·ar·y [kus′tə·mâr′ē] *adj.* Something that is customary is what is usual or normal. **In the spring, it is *customary* for Sergio and his friends to play baseball in the park.** *syn.* usual

D

dam·age [dam′ij] *v.* If you damage something, you harm or injure it. **A hurricane can *damage* the electrical system of an entire region.** *syn.* harm

de·bris [də·brē′] *n.* Debris is scattered pieces of something that has been destroyed. **The tornado turned our storage shed into a trail of *debris.*** *syn.* rubble

> **FACT FILE**
> **debris** The word *debris* comes from the French word *débriser,* which means "to break down or crush." Nearly thirty percent of the words in the English language have a French origin.

de·duc·tion [di·duk′shən] *n.* A deduction is a conclusion you reach, based on the information you have been given. **Tomás read the buyer's guide and made the *deduction* that the more expensive bicycle was the better choice.** *syn.* conclusion

de·flate [di·flāt′] *v.* **de·flat·ed** If someone feels deflated, he or she has lost confidence about something. **Janice felt *deflated* and unsure of her baking abilities after she lost the cookie-baking contest.** *syn.* drain

des·ig·nat·ed [dez′ig·nāt·ed] *adj.* If a place is designated, it is chosen for a special purpose. **The bookstore was the *designated* meeting place for Guillermo and George.** *syn.* assigned

des·o·late [des′ə·lit] *adj.* A person who feels desolate feels lonely and sad. **Jenny felt *desolate* after all her friends went out of town for the summer.** *syn.* lonely

des·per·ate·ly [des′pər·it·lē] *adv.* Wanting something desperately means wanting it so much that you'll do almost anything to get it. **Darnel *desperately* wants to become a famous writer and the author of best-selling books.** *syn.* greatly

des·ti·ny [des′tə·nē] *n.* To believe in destiny is to feel that certain things will happen because they were meant to be. **When Toshi found a violin in the attic, he felt it was his *destiny* to enter music school.** *syn.* fate

de·tect [di·tekt′] *v.* When you detect something, you notice or discover it. **She would be a good computer technician because she can *detect* and repair problems in computer hardware.** *syns.* discover, notice

de·vice [di·vīs′] *n.* A device is an object that has been made for a special purpose. **Tony's aunt wears a hearing aid, a *device* that helps people with hearing loss.** *syn.* tool

dig·ni·fied [dig′nə·fīd] *adj.* To act in a dignified way means to behave in a calm, serious, and respectful manner. **Everyone behaved in a *dignified* manner during the meeting.** *syn.* respectful

dignified

di·lap·i·dat·ed [di·lap′ə·dā·təd] *adj.* A dilapidated building looks worn out and run down. **After the neighbors complained that the *dilapidated* house was dangerous, the owner made repairs to make the place safe.** *syns.* run down, decayed

dis·grun·tled [dis·grun′təld] *adj.* If you are disgruntled, you are unhappy because things have not turned out the way you wanted. **The worker was *disgruntled* and wanted a better job.** *syn.* unhappy

dis·heart·ened [dis·här′tənd] *adj.* If you are disheartened, you feel disappointed and less hopeful. **Lisa wants to be an actor, so she was *disheartened* that she didn't get a part in the movie.** *syn.* disappointed

dis·mal [diz′məl] *adj.* Something that is dismal is bleak and depressing. **The constant rain made April a *dismal* month.** *syn.* gloomy

> **Word Origins**
> **dismal** In medieval times, certain days were thought to be unlucky. These days were said to be *dies mali,* which in Latin means "bad days." Over the years, *dies mali* came into English as *dismal* and means "gloomy."

a	add	e	end	o	odd	o͞o	pool	oi	oil	th	this	ə = *a* in *above*
ā	ace	ē	equal	ō	open	u	up	ou	pout	zh	vision	*e* in *sicken*
â	care	i	it	ô	order	û	burn	ng	ring			*i* in *possible*
ä	palm	ī	ice	o͝o	took	yo͞o	fuse	th	thin			*o* in *melon*
												u in *circus*

dis·may [dis·mā′] *v.* **dis·mayed** When you are dismayed, you are upset about something and unsure of how to deal with it. **Eduardo's sisters were *dismayed* when he refused to let them ride on his new bike.** *syn.* upset

dra·mat·i·cal·ly [drə·mat′i·klē] *adv.* If something is done dramatically, it is done in a striking or impressive way. **Connie *dramatically* and excitedly told about seeing a bear while camping with her family in a national park.** *syns.* vividly, spectacularly

dwell [dwel] *v.* The place where you dwell is where you live. **I think it might be hard to *dwell* in an igloo for a long time.** *syns.* reside, inhabit

E

ear·nest·ly [ûr′nist·lē] *adv.* Someone who speaks earnestly says things in an especially serious and honest way. **In his report about the environment, Terrel *earnestly* expressed his views.** *syn.* candidly

ec·cen·tric [ik·sen′trik] *adj.* An eccentric person has habits or opinions that seem odd to other people. **Everyone thinks Akemi is *eccentric* because she walks backward up flights of stairs.** *syns.* odd, unusual

Word Origins

eccentric The word *eccentric* comes from the Greek word *ékkentros*, which means "out of the center." It wasn't until the early 1800s that the term *eccentric* was used to describe a person who seemed odd or unusual.

e·las·tic [i·las′tik] *adj.* Something that is elastic stretches easily. **These shorts have an *elastic* waistband.** *syn.* flexible

FACT FILE

elastic If something is *elastic*, it might be made of rubber. Natural rubber comes from the juice of fig-like trees that grow in areas near the equator.

e·lon·gate [i·lông′gāt] *v.* **e·lon·gates** Something that elongates stretches to a longer length. **Mark *elongates* the clay pieces he uses for the hair of his sculpture.** *syns.* lengthen, extend

em·bark [im·bärk′] *v.* **em·barked** If you have embarked on a journey, you have begun a new adventure. **After Lana packed her gear, she *embarked* on her trip to the mountains.** *syn.* start

em·i·nent [em′ə·nənt] *adj.* An eminent person is well known and important. **The *eminent* doctor developed a number of procedures for saving lives.** *syns.* renowned, famous

en·coun·ter [in·koun′tər] *v.* **en·coun·tered** If you encountered someone, you met that person unexpectedly. **Shuko was very surprised when he *encountered* his father in the fast-food restaurant.** *syn.* meet

en·deav·or [in·dev′ər] *n.* An endeavor is an activity or task you take on in an effort to accomplish it. **In her *endeavor* to raise money for band uniforms, Rosario organized a car wash.** *syn.* effort

en·rap·ture [in·rap′chər] *v.* **en·rap·tured** A person who is enraptured is delighted and thrilled with something. **The students planted a garden and were *enraptured* when they saw the flowers bloom.** *syn.* enchant

en·ter·pris·ing [en′tər·prīz·ing] *adj.* People who are enterprising do new and difficult things in order to achieve their goals. **Andrew took the *enterprising* step of opening an art gallery at the school.** *syn.* adventurous

en·vi·sion [in·vizh′ən] *v.* **en·vi·sioned** If you have pictured something in your mind, you have envisioned it. **Reneé *envisioned* herself arriving at a castle on a winged horse.** *syn.* visualize

e·quiv·a·lent [i·kwiv′ə·lənt] *adj.* Things that are equivalent are equal. **My twin sister and I received *equivalent* gifts at our birthday party.** *syn.* alike

es·ca·pade [es′kə·pād] *n.* **es·ca·pades** Escapades are carefree, mischievous, or reckless adventures. **Carmen and Gabriella play board games for fun and never go on *escapades*.** *syn.* adventure

es·sence [es′əns] *n.* The essence of something is its most basic, important quality. **The *essence* of being a mathematician is being able to work well with numbers.** *syn.* core

es·sen·tial [i·sen′shəl] *adj.* Something that is essential is absolutely necessary. **Jerome knew that it was *essential* to study in order to pass the test.** *syns.* necessary, crucial

es·teem [i·stēm′] *v.* To esteem something means to judge it to be of value. **I *esteem* it an honor to be elected to student council.** *syns.* regard, value

ex·cep·tion·al [ik·sep′shən·əl] *adj.* Something that is exceptional is special, and it stands above others like it. **Ramón's *exceptional* character showed when he decided to volunteer at the senior citizen center.** *syn.* extraordinary

ex·cur·sion [ik·skûr′zhən] *n.* **ex·cur·sions** An excursion is a short journey or outing. **Melanie's family went on an *excursion* down the river.** *syn.* outing

excursion

ex·hil·a·rate [ig·zil′ə·rāt′e] *v.* **ex·hil·a·rat·ed** If you feel exhilarated, you feel very excited and energetic. **Ryan was *exhilarated* to learn that he placed first in the swimming competition.** *syns.* excite, thrill

ex·pec·ta·tion [ek·spek·tā′shən] *n.* **ex·pec·ta·tions** Expectations are hopes about how well others will do or about how they should behave. **Wilma's parents have *expectations* that she will be on her best behavior at summer camp.** *syns.* hope, belief

ACADEMIC LANGUAGE

expository nonfiction *Expository nonfiction* presents and explains facts about a topic. Photographs, captions, and headings are commonly found in these texts.

expression Reading aloud with *expression* means using your voice to match the action of the story and the characters' feelings.

ex·trav·a·gant [ik·strav′ə·gənt] *adj.* Something extravagant is much more costly or elaborate than what is really needed. **Nina thought the *extravagant* ring was beautiful.** *syn.* excessive

extravagant

F

ACADEMIC LANGUAGE

fable A *fable* is a short story that teaches a lesson or moral about life. Fables often include animals as characters.

fantasy A *fantasy* is an imaginative story that may have unrealistic characters and events.

faze [fāz] *v.* If things faze you, they bother or confuse you. **Even though Steve wanted to make the chess team, it didn't *faze* him that the tryouts were cancelled.** *syn.* daunt

feat [fēt] *n.* A feat is a difficult act that impresses people. **Climbing the highest mountain in the world is a *feat* not many people in the world can claim.** *syn.* accomplishment

fer·vor [fûr′vər] *n.* A person who speaks with fervor speaks with great emotion and strong belief. **Frances spoke to the students with *fervor* in her speech at the graduation ceremony.** *syn.* enthusiasm

fe·ver·ish·ly [fē′vər·ish·lē] *adv.* If you are working feverishly, you are working quickly and excitedly. **As the thunderstorm became more threatening, Gibran worked *feverishly* to bring the lawn furniture inside.** *syn.* busily

fick·le [fik′əl] *adj.* Fickle people keep changing their minds about what they like or want. **Shantell is *fickle* about her clothes because she wears her outfits a couple of times but then wants to give them away and get new ones.** *syn.* indecisive

flop [flop] *n.* A flop is a failure. **Jorge's ant farm was a *flop* at the science fair because all the ants died.** *syn.* failure

a add	e end	o	odd	o͞o	pool	oi	oil	th	this	ə =	*a* in *above*
ā ace	ē equal	ō	open	u	up	ou	pout	zh	vision		*e* in *sicken*
â care	i it	ô	order	û	burn	ng	ring				*i* in *possible*
ä palm	ī ice	o͝o	took	yo͞o	fuse	th	thin				*o* in *melon*
											u in *circus*

floun·der [floun′dər] *v.* **floun·dered** People or animals that have floundered have made wild movements trying to get something done. **Otis *floundered* about on the dance floor as he tried to learn the new dance step.** *syn.* blunder

ACADEMIC LANGUAGE

focus Writers *focus* on a topic by connecting every idea and detail to the topic. Fiction writers use focus to concentrate the reader's attention on a theme or story element.

folktale A *folktale* is a story that reflects the customs and beliefs of a culture. Folktales were first told orally and have been passed down through generations in a region or culture.

fret [fret] *v.* When you fret about something, you keep thinking and worrying about it. **Brad tried not to *fret* about giving his book report in front of the class.** *syn.* worry

fringe [frinj] *n.* **fring·es** The fringes of a place are areas along its edges, far away from the center of action. **In the cattle drives of the late 1800s, cattle were herded to the railroads from the *fringes* of the territory.** *syns.* border, outskirts

ACADEMIC LANGUAGE

functional text *Functional text* is writing used in everyday life, such as e-mail messages, manuals, and directions.

G

gen·ial [jēn′yəl] *adj.* A genial person is warm and friendly. **Nora welcomed her cousins in a *genial* way and invited them to stay for dinner.** *syns.* friendly, hospitable

ges·ture [jes′chər] *n.* A gesture is something you say or do in order to express a feeling to someone. **Elliot gave Sierra a new set of drumsticks as a *gesture* of welcoming her to the band.** *syn.* token

gid·dy [gid′ē] *adj.* If you feel giddy, you feel happy in a silly, dizzy way. **Tamika felt *giddy* when she got on her new bike for the first time.** *syn.* excited

glee·ful [glē′fəl] *adj.* A person who is gleeful is excited and happy, sometimes as a result of someone else's mistake. **When Abby spelled her third word correctly, she had the *gleeful* feeling that she could win the spelling bee.** *syn.* joyful

gouge [gouj] *v.* **goug·es** If someone gouges something, he or she makes a deep cut or dent in it. **Using a sharp tool, Tito's dad *gouges* a design in the wood frame.** *syn.* cut

gour·met [go͝or·mā′] *adj.* Gourmet food is food that is expensive, rare, or carefully prepared. **My father always makes a *gourmet* meal to celebrate my birthday.**

FACT FILE

gourmet The word *gourmet* came from the Old French word *groumet*, which meant "a person who grooms horses." In time, the word came to be spelled *gourmet* and referred to any servant in a house. Over time, the name applied to servants who tasted people's food and drink for them.

grate·ful [grāt′fəl] *adj.* To be grateful is to feel thankful for someone or something. **Peggie is *grateful* that his grandparents let him spend every summer on their farm because he wants to be a farmer, too.** *syn.* appreciative

grim [grim] *adj.* If something looks grim, it appears serious and forbidding. **With their frowns and crossed arms, Joann and Debbie looked *grim*.** *syn.* dour

grim

grudg·ing·ly [gruj′ing·lē] *adv.* If you say something grudgingly, you say it without really wanting to. **Bob *grudgingly* told Frank that he could use his computer.** *syn.* reluctantly

gru·el·ing [gro͞o′əl·ing] *adj.* A grueling experience is extremely difficult and exhausting. **The jogger chose to run in the morning because working out in the afternoon heat was too *grueling*.** *syns.* demanding, exhausting

H

hes·i·tate [hez′ə·tāt] *v.* **hes·i·tat·ing** If you are hesitating, you are pausing before doing something because you are feeling unsure. **Hector is *hesitating* before entering the music contest because he is not sure he will have enough time to practice.** *syn.* vacillate

hi·a·tus [hī·ā′təs] *n.* A hiatus is a break for a period of time between events. **Miya had an unexpected *hiatus* from the basketball team when she sprained her ankle.** *syns.* break, pause

ACADEMIC LANGUAGE

historical documents *Historical documents* are papers written in the past.

historical fiction *Historical fiction* stories are set in the past and portray people, places, and events that did happen or could have happened.

hu·mil·i·a·tion [hyo͞o·mil′ē·ā′shən] *n.* Humiliation is a feeling of shame or embarrassment. **Julio guided the new student to the right classroom to spare her the *humiliation* of arriving in class late.** *syn.* embarrassment

I

ig·nite [ig·nīt′] *v.* **ig·nit·ed** When something is ignited, it is lit or made to burn. **The workers who *ignited* the Fourth of July fireworks were trained in a special safety course.** *syn.* inflame

im·mac·u·late [i·mak′yə·lət] *adj.* Something that is immaculate is extremely clean and tidy. **Liana's house is ready for guests at any moment because she keeps it in *immaculate* shape.** *syn.* clean

im·pass·a·ble [im·pas′ə·bəl] *adj.* A road or path that is impassable is impossible to travel on. **In the winter, certain roads through the Sierra Nevada are *impassable* because of heavy snows.** *syn.* blocked

in·ad·e·quate [in·ad′ə·kwit] *adj.* Something that is inadequate is not as good or as large as it needs to be. **The number of pancakes the chef had prepared was *inadequate* for the huge breakfast crowd.** *syn.* insufficient

Word Origins

inadequate The word *inadequate* is made up of the Latin prefix *in*, which means "not" and the Latin word *adaequātus*, which means "equalized."

in·di·ca·tion [in·də·kā′shən] *n.* An indication is a sign that something exists or might happen. **The baby's crying all night was an *indication* that he was sick.** *syn.* sign

in·dig·nant·ly [in·dig′nənt·lē] *adv.* When you say something indignantly, you show irritation because you feel you have been insulted or treated unfairly. **Ira declared *indignantly* that if he couldn't sit in the front seat, he didn't want to go on the trip.** *syn.* resentfully

in·dus·try [in′dəs·trē] *n.* An industry is all the people and companies that make a certain type of product or provide a certain type of service. **The automobile *industry* puts on shows every year to introduce the new models.** *syn.* business

Word Origins

industry The origin of the word *industry* can be traced back to the Latin word *indostruus*, whose root, *struere*, means "to build." The Latin word part *indu* means "in." The word came to have its present usage in the mid-sixteenth century.

in·flam·ma·ble [in·flam′ə·bəl] *adj.* Something that is inflammable can catch fire easily and burn rapidly. **Parents should be careful not to dress their babies in pajamas that are *inflammable*.** *syn.* combustible

ACADEMIC LANGUAGE

informational narrative An *informational narrative* is a story that presents information and facts.

informational text *Informational text* presents information and facts.

a add	e end	o	odd	o͞o	pool	oi	oil	th	this	ə =	*a* in *above*
ā ace	ē equal	ō	open	u	up	ou	pout	zh	vision		*e* in *sicken*
â care	i it	ô	order	û	burn	ng	ring				*i* in *possible*
ä palm	ī ice	o͝o	took	yo͞o	fuse	th	thin				*o* in *melon*
											u in *circus*

infuriate — laden

in·fu·ri·ate [in·fyŏŏr′ē·āte] *v.* **in·fu·ri·at·ed** Something that infuriated you made you feel extremely angry. **Jay was *infuriated* when his brother ate the last piece of Jay's birthday cake.** *syn.* enrage

in·sight [in′sīt] *n.* **in·sights** If you have insights, you notice or understand important things that other people may not see. **The teacher seemed to have special *insights* about which of her students would make good leaders.** *syn.* perception

in·stinct [in′stingkt] *n.* An instinct is a natural, almost automatic way that people or animals react to things. **The mother bear's *instinct* was to protect her cub from other animals.** *syn.* intuition

in·suf·fi·cient [in·sə·fi′shənt] *adj.* If something is insufficient, there is not enough of it or it is not good enough to meet the need. **The two cans of paint Pat bought were an *insufficient* amount to paint the entire house.** *syn.* inadequate

in·tent·ly [in·tent′lē] *adv.* When you do something intently, you do it with great concentration. **I enjoy learning about the oceans, so I watched and listened *intently* to the documentary about global currents.** *syn.* attentively

in·ter·nal [in·tûr′nəl] *adj.* Something that is internal is inside a person, an object, or a place. **Sharing with others and caring for people are some of Zena's *internal* qualities.** *syn.* inner

ACADEMIC LANGUAGE

interview An *interview* is a series of questions and answers that give information about a topic or about the person being interviewed.

intonation *Intonation* is the rise and fall of your voice as you read aloud.

in·tri·cate [in′tri·kit] *adj.* If something is intricate, it is complicated or involved and has many small parts or details. **Psychologists try to understand the *intricate* reasons for certain behavior.** *syn.* complicated

in·va·sion [in·vā′zhən] *n.* An invasion happens when someone interrupts or disturbs you in an unwelcome way. **Elizabeth felt it was an *invasion* when her little brother eavesdropped on her phone conversation.** *syn.* intrusion

in·vest [in·vest′] *v.* To invest money in a project means that you put your funds into it, with the hope that in the future, it will earn more money. **Lester decided to *invest* in his uncle's successful business so that he, too, could earn a profit.** *syn.* finance

ir·re·pres·si·ble [ir·i·pres′ə·bəl] *adj.* A feeling or action that is irrepressible cannot be controlled or held back. **The scientist's *irrepressible* desire to explore nature led to his discovering a new species of ant.** *syns.* unmanageable, uncontainable

ir·re·sis·ti·ble [ir·i·zis′tə·bəl] *adj.* Something that is irresistible is difficult to turn away from. **Mother found the sparkling bracelet *irresistible*, so she bought it right away.** *syns.* appealing, desirable

i·so·lat·ed [ī′sə·lāt′əd] *adj.* A place that is isolated is a long way from large towns and is difficult to reach. **Sofia lives out in the countryside on an *isolated* farm.** *syn.* secluded

isolated

J

jet·ti·son [jet′ə·sən] *v.* **jet·ti·soned** Something that is jettisoned is deliberately cast away from a moving object, sometimes to make the object lighter. **Before the boat sank, we *jettisoned* the extra cargo and paddled to shore.** *syn.* discard

Word Origins

jettison The word *jettison* can be traced to the Latin word *jectáre*, meaning "to toss about." Later, the French changed *jectáre* to *getaison* and used it to mean "the act of throwing (goods overboard)."

L

lad·en [lād′ən] *v.* If something is laden, it is weighed down with a heavy load. **Sandra was *laden* with stacks of books to use for her research report.** *syn.* overloaded

802

legend — myth

ACADEMIC LANGUAGE

legend A *legend* is a story passed down through time and often reflects the beliefs or values of a culture. It may be based on real people or places.

loathe [lōth] *v.* If you loathe something, you hate it. **My friends *loathe* being asked to wear formal clothing to parties.** *syns.* dislike, detest

M

ACADEMIC LANGUAGE

magazine article A *magazine article* gives information on a topic and usually includes photographs with captions.

ma·neu·ver [mə·n(y)ōō′vər] *v.* **ma·neu·vered** To have maneuvered something is to have moved it or guided it very carefully. **The captain *maneuvered* the boat into its slip near the dock.** *syns.* manipulate, manage

ma·ven [mā′vən] *n.* A maven is someone with special knowledge about a particular subject. **My science teacher is a *maven* on the subject of migrating birds.** *syn.* expert

meas·ly [mēz′lē] *adj.* A measly amount of something is a very small amount. **Sherwin got a *measly* half-cup of soup with his sandwich.** *syns.* scanty, insufficient

men·tor [men′tər] *n.* A mentor is a trusted person who gives a person helpful advice. **Trina's volleyball *mentor* teaches excellent playing strategies that she learned while playing on a professional team.** *syn.* teacher

FACT FILE

mentor In Greek mythology, Mentor was a friend of Odysseus, the hero of Homer's epic poem *The Odyssey*. Mentor was the helper and teacher of Odysseus' son, Telemachus. After Odysseus went away to battle, Mentor often helped Telemachus choose the right course of action.

mis·treat [mis·trēt′] *v.* **mis·treat·ed** If something is mistreated, it is used in a way that harms or hurts it. **Sam thought his younger sister *mistreated* her bicycle by leaving it outside on the wet grass every evening.** *syn.* harm

mod·est [mod′əst] *adj.* A modest person does not brag or show off. **Hardly anyone knew that Sally had shown her paintings in several art galleries because she was *modest* about her talent.** *syn.* humble

mo·nop·o·lize [mə·nop′ə·līz] *v.* People who monopolize something control it and prevent others from using it. **Marcos tries not to *monopolize* the remote control when he watches TV with his friends.** *syn.* dominate

FACT FILE

monopolize *Monopolize* can be traced back to the Greek word *monopolion*. The word part *mono* means "single," and *polein* means "to sell." The popular board game *Monopoly*, in which players buy and sell property, appeared in 1935.

mo·not·o·nous [mə·not′ə·nəs] *adj.* If something is monotonous, it is repetitive and boring. **Juanita says that practicing the musical scales over and over on the piano is *monotonous*.** *syns.* boring, tedious

mor·ti·fy [môr′tə·fī] *v.* **mor·ti·fied** If you feel mortified, you feel extremely embarrassed or ashamed. **Shawna was *mortified* during the play when she couldn't remember her most important lines.** *syns.* humiliate, embarrass

ACADEMIC LANGUAGE

myth A *myth* is an imaginative story that explains how people and places came to be. Myths are often based on what a group of people in the past believed.

a	add	e	end	o	odd	ōō	pool	oi	oil	th	this	ə =	a in *above*
ā	ace	ē	equal	ō	open	u	up	ou	pout	zh	vision		e in *sicken*
â	care	i	it	ô	order	û	burn	ng	ring				i in *possible*
ä	palm	ī	ice	ŏŏ	took	yōō	fuse	th	thin				o in *melon*
													u in *circus*

803

narrative nonfiction — personal narrative

N

ACADEMIC LANGUAGE

narrative nonfiction *Narrative nonfiction* is a story that tells about people, things, events, or places that are real.

nudge [nuj] *v.* **nudged** If you nudged a person or thing, you pushed it or poked it gently. **I forgot to set my alarm clock last night, so it's a good thing my dog *nudged* me when it was time to get up.** *syn.* push

O

or·deal [ôr·dēl′ *or* ôr·dē′əl] *n.* An ordeal is a very difficult experience that is unpleasant to go through. **Living through the flood was an *ordeal*, but rebuilding our community was just as difficult.** *syn.* challenge

ACADEMIC LANGUAGE

organization Writers create *organization* by ordering ideas in ways that make sense, such as in a time-order sequence. Stories, poems, essays, and other genres are organized according to rules and patterns specific to each writing form.

out·cast [out′kast] *n.* An outcast is someone who has been rejected or driven out by others. **After Hannah became a theater star, she was an *outcast* among her old friends because she went for weeks without calling them.** *syn.* outsider

out·land·ish [out·lan′dish] *adj.* If something is outlandish, it is bizarre, strange, and unusual. **The clowns wore *outlandish* outfits, making everyone smile.** *syn.* peculiar

outlandish

o·ver·come [ō·vər·kum′] *v.* When you are overcome by something, you are overpowered by it. **Derek was *overcome* by a sudden fear of speaking in front of the group.** *syn.* overwhelm

P

ACADEMIC LANGUAGE

pace Reading aloud at an appropriate *pace* means reading with smoothness and consistency, not too fast or too slow.

pan·ic [pan′ik] *n.* Panic is a strong feeling of fear and anxiety that makes a person act unreasonably or without thinking carefully. **When the burglar alarm sounded, Jocelyn went into a state of *panic* and started to scream.** *syn.* fear

FACT FILE

panic The word *panic* comes from *Pānikós*, the Greek word that means "of Pan." In Greek mythology, Pan is the god of the woods. The Greek people believed that Pan startled animals in the woods and caused them to run or fly away.

parched [pärcht] *adj.* Something that is parched is dried out from lack of water. **The farmer hoped the rain clouds in the distance would bring much-needed water to his *parched* fields of corn.** *syn.* dehydrated

per·il [per′əl] *n.* Peril is great danger. **Claire visited the library during the day because walking alone at night would put her in *peril*.** *syns.* danger, risk

per·se·ver·ance [pûr·sə·vir′əns] *n.* If you try hard and don't give up, you are showing perseverance. **Margaret's many hours of practicing her gymnastics routine showed her *perseverance*.** *syn.* determination

ACADEMIC LANGUAGE

personal narrative In *personal narratives*, authors reveal thoughts and feelings about their experiences. Personal narratives are told in first-person point of view.

804

persuade — precious

per·suade [pər·swād′] *v.* **per·suad·ing** Persuading someone means trying to get him or her to agree with your plan or opinion. **Richard was intent on *persuading* Fernando to play tennis with him.** *syn.* convince

ACADEMIC LANGUAGE

persuasive text *Persuasive text* is written to persuade readers to take action or to convince them of the author's viewpoint on a topic. Editorials, reviews, and advertisements are examples of persuasive text.

pes·ky [pes′kē] *adj.* Something that is pesky is annoying but not important. **Picnics are a lot of fun until those *pesky* ants show up!** *syns.* annoying, irritating

pho·bi·a [fō′bē·ə] *n.* To have a phobia is to be terrified of something without having a good reason for the fear. **Tyrell's *phobia* of flying kept him from traveling to faraway places.** *syn.* fear

ACADEMIC LANGUAGE

photo essay A *photo essay* gives information through photographs and captions.

phrasing *Phrasing* is grouping words into meaningful "chunks," or phrases, when you read aloud.

pin·na·cle [pin′ə·kəl] *n.* The pinnacle of a building is a tall, pointed piece at its top. **The *pinnacle* of the Empire State Building lights up at night.** *syns.* peak, top

pinnacle

ACADEMIC LANGUAGE

play A *play* is a story that is meant to be performed for an audience. Plays often include stage directions that tell the characters how to act and may be divided into acts and scenes.

poetry *Poetry* is a form of expressive writing that uses verse.

poised [poizd] *adj.* When you are poised, you are calm and ready to get started. **The ballerina stood *poised* in the wings, waiting for her cue.** *syn.* composed

port·a·ble [pôr′tə·bəl] *adj.* Something that is portable can be moved or carried by hand. **We laughed because Dad brought a *portable* TV and his cell phone on the camping trip.** *syn.* movable

po·ten·tial·ly [pə·ten′chə·lē] *adv.* Something that could potentially happen could possibly happen. **If Ken studies more, he *potentially* could get all *A*'s.** *syn.* probably

prac·ti·cal [prak′ti·kəl] *adj.* Something that is practical is useful. **Even though the winter coat was on sale, Erin didn't think it would be *practical* for her summer vacation in Arizona.** *syns.* useful, realistic

Word Origins

practical The word *practical* came from the Greek word *praktikos*, which means "fit for action." It was used later in Middle English as *practicale*.

pre·car·i·ous [pri·kâr′ē·əs] *adj.* In a precarious situation, things are uncertain and can suddenly become dangerous. **Cheng didn't hear the lifeguard's warning and found himself in the *precarious* state of swimming in rough water.** *syns.* risky, uncertain

pre·cious [presh′əs] *adj.* If something is precious to you, it has value and special meaning to you. **Martha never misses appointments for her dog's check-ups because he is *precious* to her.** *syn.* valued

a	add	e	end	o	odd	ōō	pool	oi	oil	th	this	ə =	a in *above*
ā	ace	ē	equal	ō	open	u	up	ou	pout	zh	vision		e in *sicken*
â	care	i	it	ô	order	û	burn	ng	ring				i in *possible*
ä	palm	ī	ice	ŏŏ	took	yōō	fuse	th	thin				o in *melon*
													u in *circus*

805

pres·ti·gious [pres·tē′jəs] *adj.* Something that is prestigious is highly respected and admired. **The principal of a school has a *prestigious* job.** *syns.* impressive, noteworthy

pro·claim [prō·klām′] *v.* **pro·claimed** If you have announced something to a group of people, you have proclaimed it. **The referee *proclaimed* to the crowd that the hometown team was the district winner.** *syns.* announce, declare

pro·fuse·ly [prō·fyo͞os′lē] *adv.* Something done profusely is done in great quantity. **Clifton apologized *profusely* after insulting his good friend.** *syns.* lavishly, exuberantly

prog·nos·ti·ca·tion [prog·nos′tə·kā′shən] *n.* A prognostication is a forecast or prediction. **After watching the football team of every school, the sports writer made a *prognostication* about which team would be the best that year.** *syn.* prediction

pro·por·tion [prə·pôr′shən] *n.* If something is in proportion, none of its parts are too large or too small. **The class's diorama of New York City showed the figures and automobiles in the correct *proportion* to the tall buildings.** *syns.* ratio, size

pro·pose [prə·pōz′] *v.* **pro·posed** A person who proposed something put forth the ideas to do it. **The best ideas for the fund-raiser were *proposed* by the new girl because she had ideas we had never thought of.** *syns.* suggest, recommend

pro·test [prō′test] *n.* A protest is a way of demonstrating that you are against something. **The parents held a *protest* about having too many soda machines and not enough water fountains in the school building.** *syn.* objection

pro·trude [prō·tro͞od′] *v.* To protrude is to stick out. **If the lumber will *protrude* from the back of the truck, you should tie a red cloth to the end of it so that other drivers can see it.** *syns.* jut, obtrude

pro·voke [prə·vōk′] *v.* When you provoke someone, you do something to make him or her feel angry. **Kathryn didn't mean to *provoke* Sol when she didn't return the CD she had borrowed.** *syns.* aggravate, irritate

pry [prī] *v.* **pried** If you have pried something off, you have forced it away from a surface. **A nail can usually be *pried* from a board by using the right tool.** *syn.* extract

pry

R

rasp·y [ras′pē] *adj.* A raspy noise sounds rough and harsh, like sandpaper scraping wood. **Leon's voice sounded *raspy* because he had a chest cold.** *syns.* gruff, harsh

> **ACADEMIC LANGUAGE**
>
> **reading rate** Your *reading rate* is how quickly you can read a text correctly and still understand what you are reading.
>
> **realistic fiction** *Realistic fiction* stories have characters, settings, and plot events that are like people, places, and events in real life. The characters face problems that could really happen.

re·coil [ri·koil′] *v.* To recoil means to jerk back suddenly. **The dog's loud barking made the cat *recoil* and run away.** *syn.* withdraw

re·count [ri·kount′] *v.* If you recount a story, you tell what happened. **Glendina's reading assignment was to *recount* the story in a summary.** *syn.* tell

re·gal [rē′gəl] *adj.* If something is regal, it is fit for a king or queen. **The German hotel looked *regal*, and we found out later that it had once been a real palace.** *syn.* majestic

reign [rān] *v.* **reigned** If someone has reigned, he or she has been very important in a particular place. **Principal Jones *reigned* over Southeast Middle School until he retired last June.** *syn.* preside

re·lent [ri·lent′] *v.* **re·lent·ed** Someone who has relented has agreed to something he or she once refused. **The students cheered when the school principal *relented* and allowed them to have a "bring-your-pet-to-school" day.** *syn.* yield

re·mote [ri·mōt′] *adj.* A remote place is far away from cities and towns. **Kyle's grandparents live in such a *remote* area that the only things they hear outside are the wind, the birds, and the insects.** *syns.* faraway, secluded

re·plen·ish [ri·plen′ish] *v.* **re·plen·ish·ing** Replenishing something means refilling it or making it complete again. **Next weekend, my parents will be going to the market and *replenishing* our refrigerator with food.** *syns.* refill, restock

rep·u·ta·tion [rep′yə·tā′shən] *n.* A person's reputation is what he or she is known for. **The senator has a *reputation* for being honest and fair, so many people in the government trust him.**

res·i·dent [rez′ə·dənt] *n.* **res·i·dents** Residents are the people or animals that live in a place. **Alligators and snakes are *residents* of many swamps.** *syns.* inhabitant, dweller

re·sist [ri·zist′] *v.* **re·sist·ed** If a person or an object has resisted, that person or object was very difficult or impossible to change. **The painting *resisted* all of Barry's attempts to restore it to its original condition.** *syn.* oppose

re·strain [ri·strān′] *v.* If you restrain something, you hold it back or limit it. **To *restrain* the sheep from wandering too far, the rancher put up a fence.** *syn.* control

rev·el·er [rev′əl·ər] *n.* **rev·el·ers** Revelers are people who are having fun at a lively party or celebration. **Cinco de Mayo is a Mexican holiday in which *revelers* enjoy parades and parties.** *syn.* partygoer

rig·id [rij′id] *adj.* An object that is rigid is stiff and does not change shape easily. **When the clay hardens, the sculpture becomes *rigid*.** *syn.* firm

> **Word Origins**
>
> **rigid** The word *rigid* is based on the Latin word *rigere*, which means "to be stiff."

row·dy [rou′dē] *adj.* People who are rowdy are noisy, rough, and out of control. **Guards monitored the crowd of *rowdy* fans as they exited the rugby stadium.** *syn.* disorderly

ruck·us [ruk′əs] *n.* To raise a ruckus is to make a lot of noise and fuss about something. **The dog alerted its sleeping owner of danger by making a *ruckus*.** *syn.* disturbance

S

schol·ar [skol′ər] *n.* **schol·ars** Scholars are people who have studied certain topics and know a lot about them. **Many English professors are *scholars* in the literature of a particular time period.** *syn.* intellectual

scour [skour] *v.* **scours** If someone scours a place for something, he or she searches thoroughly for it. **Penelope *scours* the yard in hopes of finding her necklace.** *syn.* search

se·cure [si·kyo͝or′] *adj.* Something that is secure is safe and not likely to give way. **Evelyn uses a *secure* lock on her door to keep out intruders.** *syns.* safe, protected

secure

> **Word Origins**
>
> **secure** The word *secure* came from the Latin phrase *se cura*, which means "free from care." The word was first used in English with its current meaning in about 1533.

sel·dom [sel′dəm] *adv.* If something seldom happens, it hardly ever happens. **Rainbows are *seldom* seen in desert areas.** *syns.* rarely, infrequently

a add	e end	o odd	o͞o pool	oi oil	th this	ə = a in *above*
ā ace	ē equal	ō open	u up	ou pout	zh vision	e in *sicken*
â care	i it	ô order	û burn	ng ring		i in *possible*
ä palm	ī ice	o͝o took	yo͞o fuse	th thin		o in *melon*
						u in *circus*

sen·si·bil·i·ty [sen′sə·bil′ə·tē] *n.* A sensibility is a special awareness in a certain area; for example, a person can have an artistic sensibility or a musical sensibility. **The interior designer has a *sensibility* for creating a mood through the use of color.** *syn.* feeling

> **ACADEMIC LANGUAGE**
>
> **sentence fluency** Writers use a variety of *sentence* types and lengths to add interest to their writing. Simple, compound, and complex sentences are a few of the sentence types writers use.

shat·ter [shat′ər] *v.* When things shatter, they break suddenly and violently into small pieces. **If the puppies knock over the vase, it will *shatter* into a hundred pieces.** *syns.* break, destroy

sin·cere [sin·sir′] *adj.* If you are being sincere, you are being honest, and you mean what you say. **Joyce was *sincere* when she told the teacher she liked doing science experiments.** *syns.* honest, genuine

> **FACT FILE**
>
> **sincere** Most experts trace the word *sincere* to the Latin word *sincerus*, meaning "clean, pure, or sound." However, other experts say the word has its roots in the marble quarries of the sixteenth century, in which workers would rub wax on marble blocks to hide flaws. In time, the government declared that all marble had to be *sine cera*, or "without wax."

sleek [slēk] *adj.* Something that is sleek is smooth. **A seal's wet fur looks *sleek*.** *syns.* shiny, glossy

sleek

smirk [smûrk] *n.* A smirk is an unkind smile. **The producer had a *smirk* on his face as he talked about the famous actor having trouble finding work.** *syn.* simper

sneer [snir] *v.* **sneered** If you sneered at someone, you showed with your words and expression that you had little respect for that person. **The arrogant hotel guest *sneered* at the desk clerk when he couldn't find her reservation.** *syn.* scoff

som·ber·ly [som′bər·lē] *adv.* When you act somberly, you speak and act in a serious way. **The news anchor *somberly* reported the details of the train accident.** *syns.* seriously, sadly

sor·row·ful [sor′ə·fəl] *adj.* If you feel sorrowful, you are sad. **The listeners were *sorrowful* as they heard about the victims of the fire.** *syns.* distressed, unhappy

spe·cial·ize [spesh′əl·īz] *v.* **spe·cial·ized** Someone who has specialized in something has given it most of his or her time and attention. **The doctor *specialized* in heart surgery.** *syns.* concentrate, focus

spec·i·men [spes′ə·mən] *n.* **spec·i·mens** Specimens are examples of things scientists collect in order to study. **Entomologists collect *specimens* of insects.** *syn.* sample

spec·tac·u·lar [spek·tak′yə·lər] *adj.* Something that is spectacular is very impressive and draws a lot of attention. **Lei's room faces west, giving her views of the region's *spectacular* sunsets.** *syn.* amazing

squint [skwint] *v.* **squint·ing** Someone who is squinting is squeezing his or her eyes partly shut in order to see. **It's hard to have a picture taken on a bright, sunny day without *squinting*.** *syn.* peer

stam·mer [stam′ər] *v.* **stam·mers** A person who stammers speaks with difficulty, often stopping or repeating himself or herself. **Because she is nervous, Ines *stammers* as she gives her speech.** *syn.* stutter

stream·lined [strēm′līnd] *adj.* A streamlined design is efficient and has no unneeded parts. **The car salesperson boasted about the *streamlined* design of the new, faster sports model.** *syn.* sleek

strick·en [strik′ən] *v.* If you are stricken, you are suddenly and badly affected by something, such as illness or fear. **When Stanley heard that the tornado had demolished all of the houses in his community, he was *stricken* with grief.** *syn.* afflict

sum·mit [sum′it] *n.* A mountain's summit is its very top. **While touring Africa, Janeka climbed to the *summit* of Mt. Kilimanjaro.** *syns.* top, peak

> **Word Origins**
>
> **summit** The word *summit* has its origins in the Latin word *summus*, meaning "highest." When the French adopted the word *summus*, they changed it to *sommette*, meaning "the highest part or top of a hill."

sus·tain [sə·stān′] *v.* When you sustain something, you keep it going by giving it what it needs. **In order to *sustain* the school library, the parents donated money and books.** *syns.* maintain, continue

swarm [swôrm] *v.* **swarmed** If animals have swarmed, they have moved quickly and gathered in large numbers. **In the spring, honeybees *swarmed* around the nest to protect the queen bee.** *syns.* group, cluster

sway [swā] *v.* **swayed** Something that swayed was moving back and forth. **The audience *swayed* to the music of the orchestra.** *syn.* rock

T

> **ACADEMIC LANGUAGE**
>
> **tall tale** A *tall tale* is a humorous story about impossible or exaggerated happenings.

teem [tēm] *v.* **teem·ing** Something that is teeming is overflowing with life or energy. **The stadium was *teeming* with fans for the championship soccer game.** *syn.* abound

tempt [tempt] *v.* **tempt·ed** If you are tempted to do something, you really want to do it, even though you know you shouldn't. **Natalia is *tempted* to listen to her new CD instead of writing her book report.** *syn.* entice

ten·den·cy [ten′dən·sē] *n.* To have a tendency is to have a habit of doing something in a certain way. **Because Arup has a *tendency* to wait until the last minute to do his assignments, he often turns in his work late.** *syn.* inclination

ter·rain [tə·rān′] *n.* Terrain is the kind of land that is found in a place; for example, terrain might be rocky, hilly, or swampy. **Laticia enjoys hiking the rocky *terrain* in the state park.** *syns.* land, territory

terrain

> **Word Origins**
>
> **terrain** The word *terrain* can be traced back to the Latin word *terra*, meaning "earth." The word was later used by the French as *terrain*.

> **ACADEMIC LANGUAGE**
>
> **textbook** *Textbooks* are organized by chapter titles and headings within chapters. Textbooks provide information without giving the authors' opinions.

throng [throng] *n.* A throng is a crowd of people. **The shouts became louder as the *throng* waited for the doors to open.** *syns.* crowd, mass

> **ACADEMIC LANGUAGE**
>
> **time line** A *time line* shows information about events in the order in which they happened.

tran·quil·i·ty [trang·kwil′ə·tē] *n.* A feeling of tranquility is a feeling of calm and peace. **Jessica finds *tranquility* in sitting beside the pond and observing nature.** *syn.* serenity

tur·bu·lent [tûr′byə·lənt] *adj.* Something that is turbulent, such as air or water, has strong currents which change direction suddenly. **The captain of the airplane turned on the seat-belt sign and announced that the weather had become *turbulent*.** *syn.* unsettled

a add	e end	o odd	o͞o pool	oi oil	th this	ə = a in *above*
ā ace	ē equal	ō open	u up	ou pout	zh vision	e in *sicken*
â care	i it	ô order	û burn	ng ring		i in *possible*
ä palm	ī ice	o͝o took	yo͞o fuse	th thin		o in *melon*
						u in *circus*

un·der·ly·ing [un′dər-lī′ing] *adj.* Something that is underlying is located below or beneath something. **An ant mound's underlying soil has a network of tunnels made and used by thousands of ants.**

un·fath·om·a·ble [un-fath′əm-ə-bəl] *adj.* If something is unfathomable, it cannot be understood or known. **Without an understanding of basic arithmetic, college algebra would be *unfathomable.*** *syn.* incomprehensible

un·im·ag·i·na·ble [un-i-maj′ə-nə-bəl] *adj.* If something is unimaginable, it is impossible to think that it might happen or exist. **A summer without sunshine is *unimaginable.*** *syns.* unthinkable, inconceivable

un·in·hab·it·a·ble [un-in-hab′it-ə-bəl] *adj.* A place that is uninhabitable cannot be lived in. **This place will be *uninhabitable* until the water can be made clean and safe to drink.** *syn.* inhospitable

ur·gent·ly [ûr′jənt-lē] *adv.* If you urgently tell someone to do something, it is important that it be done right away. **Phillip's father *urgently* needs him to help make all the deliveries before dark.** *syn.* immediately

van·ish [van′ish] *v.* To vanish is to disappear suddenly. **The magician made the tiger seem to *vanish* and then appear again.** *syn.* disappear

veto [vē′tō] *v.* **ve·toed** If someone has vetoed something, he or she has rejected it. **Congress passed the bill, but the President *vetoed* it.** *syn.* reject

FACT FILE

veto During government sessions in ancient Rome, elected members, called tribunes, yelled *"Veto!"* if they did not want a law to pass. *Veto* is Latin for "I forbid."

vi·tal [vīt′əl] *adj.* Something that is vital is necessary for life. **Food, air, and water are *vital* for survival.** *syn.* essential

ACADEMIC LANGUAGE

voice The term *voice* is used to describe a writer's tone, attitude, or personality. A reader might perceive a writer's voice as formal, confident, or mischievous.

wisp·y [wisp′ē] *adj.* Something that is wispy is thin, lightweight, and easily broken. **Rosa's china doll was so fragile and *wispy* that she was afraid to play with it.** *syn.* delicate

wist·ful [wist′fəl] *adj.* You are wistful if you feel as though your wishes probably won't come true. **Sheila felt *wistful* knowing she wouldn't be going to music camp this summer.** *syn.* melancholy

with·ered [with′ərd] *adj.* Something that is withered is dried up and faded. **The fallen leaves were brown and *withered.*** *syn.* wilted

withered

ACADEMIC LANGUAGE

word choice A writer may choose sensory, vivid, and precise words to help the reader imagine people, places, and events. *Word choice* helps writers express a personal voice, or personality, in their writing.

yearn·ing [yûr′ning] *n.* A yearning is a great desire to have something that you may never be able to get. **Gracie has a *yearning* to travel to the Amazon rain forest to see the many flowers that she has only read about.** *syns.* desire, longing

Index of Titles and Authors

Page numbers in green refer to biographical information.

Professional Bibliography

Armbruster, B.B., Anderson, T.H., & Ostertag, J.
(1987). Does text structure/summarization instruction facilitate learning from expository text? *Reading Research Quarterly,* 22 (3), 331–346.

Ball, E. & Blachman, B.
(1991). Does phoneme awareness training in kindergarten make a difference in early word recognition and developmental spelling? *Reading Research Quarterly,* 26 (1), 49–66.

Baumann, J.F. & Bergeron, B.S.
(1993). Story map instruction using children's literature: effects on first graders' comprehension of central narrative elements. *Journal of Reading Behavior,* 25 (4), 407–437.

Baumann, J.F., Seifert-Kessell, N., & Jones, L.A.
(1992). Effect of think-aloud instruction on elementary students' comprehension monitoring abilities. *Journal of Reading Behavior,* 24 (2), 143–172.

Beck, I.L., Perfetti, C.A., & McKeown, M.G.
(1982). Effects of long-term vocabulary instruction on lexical access and reading comprehension. *Journal of Educational Psychology,* 74 (4), 506–521.

Bereiter, C. & Bird, M.
(1985). Use of thinking aloud in identification and teaching of reading comprehension strategies. *Cognition and Instruction,* 2, 131–156.

Blachman, B.
(2000). Phonological awareness. In M. Kamil, P. Mosenthal, P.D. Pearson, & R. Barr (Eds.), *Handbook of Reading Research,* (Vol. 3). Mahwah, NJ: Erlbaum.

Blachman, B., Ball, E.W., Black, R.S., & Tangel, D.M.
(1994). Kindergarten teachers develop phoneme awareness in low-income, inner-city classrooms: Does it make a difference? *Reading and Writing: An Interdisciplinary Journal,* 6 (1), 1–18.

Brown, I.S. & Felton, R.H.
(1990). Effects of instruction on beginning reading skills in children at risk for reading disability. *Reading and Writing: An Interdisciplinary Journal,* 2 (3), 223–241.

Chall, J.
(1996). *Learning to read: The great debate (revised, with a new foreword).* New York: McGraw-Hill.

Dowhower, S.L.
(1987). Effects of repeated reading on second-grade transitional readers' fluency and comprehension. *Reading Research Quarterly,* 22 (4), 389–406.

Ehri, L. & Wilce, L.
(1987). Does learning to spell help beginners learn to read words? *Reading Research Quarterly,* 22 (1), 48–65.

Fletcher, J.M. & Lyon, G.R.
(1998) Reading: A research-based approach. In Evers, W.M. (Ed.), *What's Gone Wrong in America's Classroom,* Palo Alto, CA: Hoover Institution Press, Stanford University.

Foorman, B., Francis, D., Fletcher, J., Schatschneider, C., & Mehta, P.
(1998). The role of instruction in learning to read: Preventing reading failure in at-risk children. *Journal of Educational Psychology,* 90 (1), 37–55.

Fukkink, R.G. & de Glopper, K.
(1998). Effects of instruction in deriving word meaning from context: A meta-analysis. *Review of Educational Research,* 68 (4), 450–469.

Gipe, J.P. & Arnold, R.D.
(1979). Teaching vocabulary through familiar associations and contexts. *Journal of Reading Behavior,* 11 (3), 281–285.

Griffith, P.L., Klesius, J.P., & Kromrey, J.D.
(1992). The effect of phonemic awareness on the literacy development of first grade children in a traditional or a whole language classroom. *Journal of Research in Childhood Education,* 6 (2), 85–92.

Juel, C.
(1988). Learning to read and write: A longitudinal study of fifty-four children from first through fourth grades. *Journal of Educational Psychology,* 80, 437–447.

Lundberg, I., Frost, J., & Petersen, O.
(1988). Effects of an extensive program for stimulating phonological awareness in preschool children. *Reading Research Quarterly,* 23 (3), 263–284.

McKeown, M.G., Beck, I.L., Omanson, R.C., & Pople, M.T.
(1985). Some effects of the nature and frequency of vocabulary instruction on the knowledge and use of words. *Reading Research Quarterly,* 20 (5), 522–535.

Nagy, W.E. & Scott, J.A.
(2000). Vocabulary processes. In M. Kamil, P. Mosenthal, P.D. Pearson, & R. Barr (Eds.), *Handbook of Reading Research,* (Vol. 3). Mahwah, NJ: Erlbaum.

National Reading Panel
(2000). *Teaching Children to Read.* National Institute of Child Health and Human Development, National Institutes of Health, Washington, D.C.

O'Connor, R., Jenkins, J.R., & Slocum, T.A.
(1995). Transfer among phonological tasks in kindergarten: Essential instructional content. *Journal of Educational Psychology,* 87 (2), 202–217.

O'Shea, L.J., Sindelar, P.T., & O'Shea, D.J.
(1985). The effects of repeated readings and attentional cues on reading fluency and comprehension. *Journal of Reading Behavior,* 17 (2), 129–142.

Paris, S.G., Cross, D.R., & Lipson, M.Y.
(1984). Informed strategies for learning: A program to improve children's reading awareness and comprehension. *Journal of Educational Psychology,* 76 (6), 1239–1252.

Payne, B.D. & Manning, B.H.
(1992). Basal reader instruction: Effects of comprehension monitoring training on reading comprehension, strategy use and attitude. *Reading Research and Instruction,* 32 (1), 29–38.

Rasinski, T.V., Padak, N., Linek, W., & Sturtevant, E.
(1994). Effects of fluency development on urban second-grade readers. *Journal of Educational Research,* 87 (3), 158–165.

Rinehart, S.D., Stahl, S.A., & Erickson, L.G.
(1986). Some effects of summarization training on reading and studying. *Reading Research Quarterly,* 21 (4), 422–438.

Robbins, C. & Ehri, L.C.
(1994). Reading storybooks to kindergartners helps them learn new vocabulary words. *Journal of Educational Psychology,* 86 (1), 54–64.

Rosenshine, B. & Meister, C.
(1994). Reciprocal teaching: A review of research. *Review of Educational Research,* 64 (4), 479–530.

Rosenshine, B., Meister, C., & Chapman, S.
(1996). Teaching students to generate questions: A review of the intervention studies. *Review of Educational Research,* 66 (2), 181–221.

Sénéchal, M.
(1997). The differential effect of storybook reading on preschoolers' acquisition of expressive and receptive vocabulary. *Journal of Child Language,* 24 (1), 123–138.

Shany, M.T. & Biemiller, A.
(1995) Assisted reading practice: Effects on performance for poor readers in grades 3 and 4. *Reading Research Quarterly,* 30 (3), 382–395.

Sindelar, P.T., Monda, L.E., & O'Shea, L.J.
(1990). Effects of repeated readings on instructional- and mastery-level readers. *Journal of Educational Research,* 83 (4), 220–226.

Snow, C.E., Burns, S.M., & Griffin, P.
(1998). *Preventing Reading Difficulties in Young Children.* Washington, D.C.: National Academy Press.

Stahl, S.A. & Fairbanks, M.M.
(1986). The effects of vocabulary instruction: A model-based meta-analysis. *Review of Educational Research,* 56 (1), 72–110.

Stanovich, K.E.
(1986) Matthew effects in reading: Some consequences of individual differences in the acquisition of literacy. *Reading Research Quarterly,* 21 (4), 360–406.

Torgesen, J., Morgan, S., & Davis, C.
(1992). Effects of two types of phonological awareness training on word learning in kindergarten children. *Journal of Educational Psychology,* 84 (3), 364–370.

Torgesen, J., Wagner, R., Rashotte, C., Rose, E., Lindamood, P., Conway, T., & Garvan, C.
(1999). Preventing reading failure in young children with phonological processing disabilities: Group and individual responses to instruction. *Journal of Educational Psychology,* 91(4), 579–593.

Vellutino, F.R. & Scanlon, D.M.
(1987). Phonological coding, phonological awareness, and reading ability: Evidence from a longitudinal and experimental study. *Merrill-Palmer Quarterly,* 33 (3), 321–363.

White, T.G., Graves, M.F., & Slater, W.H.
(1990). Growth of reading vocabulary in diverse elementary schools: Decoding and word meaning. *Journal of Educational Psychology,* 82 (2), 281–290.

Wixson, K.K.
(1986). Vocabulary instruction and children's comprehension of basal stories. *Reading Research Quarterly,* 21 (3), 317–329.

Program Reviewers & Advisors

Elizabeth A. Adkins,
Teacher
Ford Middle School
Brook Park, Ohio

Jean Bell,
Principal
Littleton Elementary School
Avondale, Arizona

Emily Brown,
Teacher
Orange Center Elementary School
Orlando, Florida

Stephen Bundy,
Teacher
Ventura Elementary School
Kissimmee, Florida

Helen Comba,
Language Arts Supervisor K-5
Southern Boulevard School
Chatham, New Jersey

Marsha Creese,
Reading/Language Arts Consultant
Marlborough Elementary School
Marlborough, Connecticut

Wyndy M. Crozier,
Teacher
Mary Bryant Elementary School
Tampa, Florida

Shirley Eyler,
Principal
Martin Luther King School
Piscataway, New Jersey

Sandy Hoffman,
Teacher
Heights Elementary School
Fort Myers, Florida

Amy Martin,
Reading Coach
Kingswood Elementary School
Wickenburg, Arizona

Rachel A. Musser,
Reading Coach
Chumuckla Elementary School
Jay, Florida

Dr. Carol Newton,
Director of Elementary Curriculum
Millard Public Schools
Omaha, Nebraska

Alda P. Pill,
Teacher
Mandarin Oaks Elementary School
Jacksonville, Florida

Dr. Elizabeth V. Primas,
Director
Office of Curriculum and Instruction
Washington, District of Columbia

Candice Ross,
Staff Development Teacher
A. Mario Loiderman Middle School
Silver Spring, Maryland

Sharon Sailor,
Teacher
Conrad Fischer Elementary School
Elmhurst, Illinois

Lucia Schneck,
Supervisor/Language Arts, Literacy
Irvington Board of Education
Irvington, New Jersey

RuthAnn Shauf,
District Resource Teacher
Hillsborough County Public Schools
Tampa, Florida

Jolene Topping,
Teacher
Palmetto Ridge High School
Bonita Springs, Florida

Betty Tubon,
Bilingual Teacher
New Field Primary School
Chicago, Illinois

Janet White,
Assistant Principal
MacFarlane Park Elementary School
Tampa, Florida

KINDERGARTEN REVIEWERS

Denise Bir,
Teacher
Destin Elementary School
Destin, Florida

Linda H. Butler,
Reading First State Director
Office of Academic Services
Washington, District of Columbia

Julie Elvers,
Teacher
Aldrich Elementary School
Omaha, Nebraska

Rosalyn Glavin,
Principal
Walter White Elementary School
River Rouge, Michigan

Jo Anne M. Kershaw,
*Language Arts Program Leader,
K-5*
Longhill Administration Building
Trumbull, Connecticut

Beverly Kibbe,
Teacher
Cherry Brook Elementary School
Canton, Connecticut

Bonnie B. Macintosh,
Teacher
Glenallan Elementary School
Silver Spring, Maryland

Laurin MacLeish,
Teacher
Orange Center Elementary School
Orlando, Florida

Mindy Steighner,
Teacher
Randall Elementary School
Waukesha, Wisconsin

Paula Stutzman,
Teacher
Seven Springs Elementary School
New Port Richey, Florida

Martha Tully,
Teacher
Fleming Island Elementary School
Orange Park, Florida

EDITORIAL ADVISORS

Sharon J. Coburn
National Reading Consultant

Hector J. Ramirez
National Reading Consultant

Dr. Nancy I. Updegraff
National Reading Consultant

Scope and Sequence

	Gr K	Gr 1	Gr 2	Gr 3	Gr 4	Gr 5	Gr 6
Reading							
Concepts About Print							
Understand that print provides information	▨						
Understand how print is organized and read	▨						
Know left-to-right and top-to-bottom directionality	▨						
Distinguish letters from words	▨						
Recognize name	▨						
Name and match all uppercase and lowercase letter forms	▨						
Understand the concept of word and construct meaning from shared text, illustrations, graphics, and charts	▨						
Identify letters, words, and sentences	▨						
Recognize that sentences in print are made up of words	▨						
Identify the front cover, back cover, title page, title, and author of a book	▨	▨					
Match oral words to printed words	▨	▨	▨				
Phonemic Awareness							
Understand that spoken words and syllables are made up of sequences of sounds	▨						
Count and track sounds in a syllable, syllables in words, and words in sentences	•						
Know the sounds of letters	•						
Track and represent the number, sameness, difference, and order of two or more isolated phonemes	•						
Match, identify, distinguish, and segment sounds in initial, final, and medial position in single-syllable spoken words	•						
Blend sounds (onset-rimes/phonemes) to make words or syllables	•						
Track and represent changes in syllables and words as target sound is added, substituted, omitted, shifted, or repeated	•						
Distinguish long- and short-vowel sounds in orally stated words	▨						
Identify and produce rhyming words	•						
Decoding: Phonic Analysis							
Understand and apply the alphabetic principle	▨						
Consonants; single, blends, digraphs in initial, final, medial positions	•	•	•	•			
Vowels: short, long, digraphs, r-controlled, variant, schwa	•	•	•	•			
Match all consonant and short-vowel sounds to appropriate letters	•	•					
Understand that as letters in words change, so do the sounds	•	•					
Blend vowel-consonant sounds orally to make words or syllables	•	•					
Blend sounds from letters and letter patterns into recognizable words	•						
Decoding: Structural Analysis							
Inflectional endings, with and without spelling changes: plurals, verb tenses, possessives, comparatives-superlatives		•	•	•			
Contractions, abbreviations, and compound words		•	•	•			
Prefixes, suffixes, derivations, and root words			•	•	•	•	•
Greek and Latin roots					•	•	•
Letter, spelling, and syllable patterns							
Phonograms/word families/onset-rimes							
Syllable rules and patterns							
Decoding: Strategies							
Visual cues: sound/symbol relationships, letter patterns, and spelling patterns		•					
Structural cues: compound words, contractions, inflectional endings, prefixes, suffixes, Greek and Latin roots, root words, spelling patterns, and word families		•					
Cross check visual and structural cues to confirm meaning							

Key:
Shaded area - Explicit Instruction/Modeling/Practice and Application
- *Tested—Assessment Resources: Weekly Lesson Tests, Theme Tests, Benchmark Assessments*

	Gr K	Gr 1	Gr 2	Gr 3	Gr 4	Gr 5	Gr 6
Word Recognition							
One-syllable and high-frequency words	•	•	•				
Common, irregular sight words	•	•	•				
Common abbreviations			•				
Lesson vocabulary		•	•	•	•	•	•
Fluency							
Read aloud in a manner that sounds like natural speech							
Read aloud accurately and with appropriate intonation and expression		•	•	•	•	•	•
Read aloud narrative and expository text with appropriate pacing, intonation, and expression			•	•	•	•	•
Read aloud prose and poetry with rhythm and pace, appropriate intonation, and vocal patterns			•	•	•	•	•
Vocabulary and Concept Development							
Academic language							
Classify-categorize		•					
Antonyms			•	•	•	•	
Synonyms			•	•	•	•	
Homographs				•			
Homophones				•			
Multiple-meaning words				•	•	•	•
Figurative and idiomatic language					•		•
Context/context clues				•	•	•	•
Content-area words							
Dictionary, glossary, thesaurus				•	•	•	
Foreign words							•
Connotation-denotation							
Word origins (acronyms, clipped and coined words, regional variations, etymologies, jargon, slang)							
Analogies							
Word structure clues to determine meaning				•	•	•	•
Inflected nouns and verbs, comparatives-superlatives, possessives, compound words, prefixes, suffixes, root words			•	•	•	•	•
Greek and Latin roots, prefixes, suffixes, derivations, and root words					•	•	•
Develop vocabulary							
Listen to and discuss text read aloud							
Read independently							
Use reference books							
Comprehension and Analysis of Text							
Ask/answer questions							
Author's purpose		•	•	•	•	•	
Author's perspective					•	•	
Propaganda/bias							
Background knowledge: prior knowledge and experiences							
Cause-effect		•	•	•	•	•	
Compare-contrast		•	•	•	•	•	•
Details		•	•	•	•	•	•
Directions: one-, two-, multi-step			•	•	•		•
Draw conclusions		•			•	•	•
Fact-fiction					•	•	•

Key:

Shaded area - Explicit Instruction/Modeling/Practice and Application

   • *Tested—Assessment Resources: Weekly Lesson Tests, Theme Tests, Benchmark Assessments*

	Gr K	Gr 1	Gr 2	Gr 3	Gr 4	Gr 5	Gr 6
Fact-opinion					•	•	
Higher order thinking							
Analyze, critique and evaluate, synthesize, and visualize text and information							
Interpret information from graphic aids			•	•		•	
Locate information			•		•		
Book parts				•	•		
Text features				•	•		
Alphabetical order		•		•			
Main idea: stated/unstated		•			•	•	•
Main idea and supporting details	•	•	•	•	•	•	•
Make generalizations						•	
Make inferences		•	•	•		•	
Make judgments						•	•
Make predictions/predict outcomes	•	•	•	•	•		
Monitor comprehension							
Adjust reading rate, create mental images, reread, read ahead, set/adjust purpose, self-question, summarize/paraphrase, use graphic aids, text features, and text adjuncts					•		
Organize information							
Alphabetical order							
Numerical systems/outlines							
Graphic organizers							
Paraphrase/restate facts and details					•	•	
Preview							
Purpose for reading							
Referents							
Retell stories and ideas			•	•			
Sequence		•		•	•	•	•
Summarize			•	•	•	•	•
Text structure							
Narrative text			•	•	•	•	
Informational text (compare and contrast, cause and effect, sequence/chronological order, proposition and support, problem and solution)			•	•	•	•	•
Study Skills							
Follow and give directions			•	•	•		•
Apply plans and strategies: KWL, question-answer relationships, skim and scan, note taking, outline, questioning the author, reciprocal teaching							•
Practice test-taking strategies							
Research and Information							
Use resources and references			•		•	•	•
Understand the purpose, structure, and organization of various reference materials							
Title page, table of contents, chapter titles, chapter headings, index, glossary, guide words, citations, end notes, bibliography			•	•	•		
Picture dictionary, software, dictionary, thesaurus, atlas, globe, encyclopedia, telephone directory, on-line information, card catalog, electronic search engines and data bases, almanac, newspaper, journals, periodicals			•	•	•	•	•
Charts, maps, diagrams, time lines, schedules, calendar, graphs, photos			•		•	•	•
Choose reference materials appropriate to research purpose					•	•	•
Viewing/Media							
Interpret information from visuals (graphics, media, including illustrations, tables, maps, charts, graphs, diagrams, time lines)			•	•			•

Key:

Shaded area - Explicit Instruction/Modeling/Practice and Application

   • *Tested—Assessment Resources: Weekly Lesson Tests, Theme Tests, Benchmark Assessments*

	Gr K	Gr 1	Gr 2	Gr 3	Gr 4	Gr 5	Gr 6
Analyze the ways visuals, graphics, and media represent, contribute to, and support meaning of text							•
Select, organize, and produce visuals to complement and extend meaning							
Use technology or appropriate media to communicate information and ideas							
Use technology or appropriate media to compare ideas, information, and viewpoints							
Compare, contrast, and evaluate print and broadcast media							
Distinguish between fact and opinion							
Evaluate the role of media							
Analyze media as sources for information, entertainment, persuasion, interpretation of events, and transmission of culture							
Identify persuasive and propaganda techniques used in television and identify false and misleading information							
Summarize main concept and list supporting details and identify biases, stereotypes, and persuasive techniques in a nonprint message							
Support opinions with detailed evidence and with visual or media displays that use appropriate technology							

Literary Response and Analysis

Genre Characteristics

	Gr K	Gr 1	Gr 2	Gr 3	Gr 4	Gr 5	Gr 6
Know a variety of literary genres and their basic characteristics			•	•			
Distinguish between fantasy and realistic text							
Distinguish between informational and persuasive texts							
Understand the distinguishing features of literary and nonfiction texts: everyday print materials, poetry, drama, fantasies, fables, myths, legends, and fairy tales			•	•			
Explain the appropriateness of the literary forms chosen by an author for a specific purpose							

Literary Elements

Plot/Plot Development

	Gr K	Gr 1	Gr 2	Gr 3	Gr 4	Gr 5	Gr 6
Important events		•	•	•			
Beginning, middle, ending of story	•	•	•	•			
Problem/solution		•	•	•			•
Conflict					•	•	•
Conflict and resolution/causes and effects					•	•	•
Compare and contrast			•	•	•	•	

Character

	Gr K	Gr 1	Gr 2	Gr 3	Gr 4	Gr 5	Gr 6
Identify	•	•	•				
Identify, describe, compare and contrast			•	•	•		
Relate characters and events							•
Traits, actions, motives					•	•	•
Cause for character's actions					•	•	
Character's qualities and effect on plot					•	•	•

Setting

	Gr K	Gr 1	Gr 2	Gr 3	Gr 4	Gr 5	Gr 6
Identify and describe	•	•	•	•			
Compare and contrast			•	•			•
Relate to problem/resolution							•

Theme

	Gr K	Gr 1	Gr 2	Gr 3	Gr 4	Gr 5	Gr 6
Theme/essential message					•	•	•
Universal themes							•

Mood/Tone

	Gr K	Gr 1	Gr 2	Gr 3	Gr 4	Gr 5	Gr 6
Identify							•
Compare and contrast							

Key:

Shaded area - Explicit Instruction/Modeling/Practice and Application

    • *Tested— Assessment Resources: Weekly Lesson Tests, Theme Tests, Benchmark Assessments*

Literary Devices/Author's Craft	Gr K	Gr 1	Gr 2	Gr 3	Gr 4	Gr 5	Gr 6
Rhythm, rhyme, pattern, and repetition							•
Alliteration, onomatopoeia, assonance, imagery						•	•
Figurative language (similes, metaphors, idioms, personification, hyperbole)				•	•	•	•
Characterization/character development				•	•	•	•
Dialogue							
Narrator/narration							
Point of view (first-person, third-person, omniscient)						•	•
Informal language (idioms, slang, jargon, dialect)							
Response to Text							
Relate characters and events to own life							
Read to perform a task or learn a new task							
Recollect, talk, and write about books read							
Describe the roles and contributions of authors and illustrators							
Generate alternative endings and identify the reason and impact of the alternatives							
Compare and contrast versions of the same stories that reflect different cultures							
Make connections between information in texts and stories and historical events							
Form ideas about what has been read and use specific information from the text to support these ideas							
Know that the attitudes and values that exist in a time period or culture affect stories and informational articles written during that time period							
Self-Selected Reading							
Select material to read for pleasure							
Read a variety of self-selected and assigned literary and informational texts							
Use knowledge of authors' styles, themes, and genres to choose own reading							
Read literature by authors from various cultural and historical backgrounds							
Cultural Awareness							
Connect information and events in texts to life and life to text experiences							
Compare language, oral traditions, and literature that reflect customs, regions, and cultures							
Identify how language reflects regions and cultures							
View concepts and issues from diverse perspectives							
Recognize the universality of literary themes across cultures and language							

Writing

Writing Strategies	Gr K	Gr 1	Gr 2	Gr 3	Gr 4	Gr 5	Gr 6
Writing process: prewriting, drafting, revising, proofreading, publishing							
Collaborative, shared, timed writing, writing to prompts		•	•	•	•	•	•
Evaluate own and others' writing							
Proofread writing to correct convention errors in mechanics, usage, and punctuation, using handbooks and references as appropriate				•	•	•	•
Organization and Focus							
Use models and traditional structures for writing							
Select a focus, structure, and viewpoint							
Address purpose, audience, length, and format requirements							
Write single- and multiple-paragraph compositions			•	•	•	•	•
Revision Skills							
Correct sentence fragments and run-ons							
Vary sentence structure, word order, and sentence length							
Combine sentences							

Key:

Shaded area - Explicit Instruction/Modeling/Practice and Application

• *Tested—Assessment Resources: Weekly Lesson Tests, Theme Tests, Benchmark Assessments*

	Gr K	Gr 1	Gr 2	Gr 3	Gr 4	Gr 5	Gr 6
Improve coherence, unity, consistency, and progression of ideas		░	░	░	░	░	░
Add, delete, consolidate, clarify, rearrange text	░	░	░	░	░	░	░
Choose appropriate and effective words: exact/precise words, vivid words, trite/overused words	░	░	░	░	░	░	░
Elaborate: details, examples, dialogue, quotations	░	░	░	░	░	░	░
Revise using a rubric		░	░	░	░	░	░

Penmanship/Handwriting

	Gr K	Gr 1	Gr 2	Gr 3	Gr 4	Gr 5	Gr 6
Write uppercase and lowercase letters	░	░	░	░			
Write legibly, using appropriate word and letter spacing	░	░	░	░			
Write legibly, using spacing, margins, and indention		░	░	░	░	░	░

Writing Applications

	Gr K	Gr 1	Gr 2	Gr 3	Gr 4	Gr 5	Gr 6
Narrative writing (stories, paragraphs, personal narratives, journals, plays, poetry)	░	•	•	•	•	•	•
Descriptive writing (titles, captions, ads, posters, paragraphs, stories, poems)	░	•	•	░	░	░	░
Expository writing (comparison-contrast, explanation, directions, speech, how-to article, friendly/business letter, news story, essay, report, invitation)	░	░	░	░	•	•	•
Persuasive writing (paragraph, essay, letter, ad, poster)					•	•	•
Cross-curricular writing (paragraph, report, poster, list, chart)	░	░	░	░	░	░	░
Everyday writing (journal, message, forms, notes, summary, label, caption)	░	░	░	░	░	░	░

Written and Oral English Language Conventions

Sentence Structure

	Gr K	Gr 1	Gr 2	Gr 3	Gr 4	Gr 5	Gr 6
Types (declarative, interrogative, exclamatory, imperative, interjection)		•	•	•	•	•	•
Structure (simple, compound, complex, compound-complex)		•	•	•	•	•	•
Parts (subjects/predicates: complete, simple, compound; clauses: independent, dependent, subordinate; phrase)		•	•	•	•	•	•
Direct/indirect object						•	•
Word order		•					

Grammar

	Gr K	Gr 1	Gr 2	Gr 3	Gr 4	Gr 5	Gr 6
Nouns (singular, plural, common, proper, possessive, collective, abstract, concrete, abbreviations, appositives)	░	•	•	•	•	•	•
Verbs (action, helping, linking, transitive, intransitive, regular, irregular; subject-verb agreement)	░	•	•	•	•	•	•
Verb tenses (present, past, future; present, past, and future perfect)		•	•	•	•	•	•
Participles; infinitives						•	•
Adjectives (common, proper; articles; comparative, superlative)		•	•	•	•	•	•
Adverbs (place, time, manner, degree)				•	•	•	•
Pronouns (subject, object, possessive, reflexive, demonstrative, antecedents)	░	•	•	•	•	•	•
Prepositions; prepositional phrases					•	•	•
Conjunctions					•	•	•
Abbreviations, contractions			•	•	•	•	•

Punctuation

	Gr K	Gr 1	Gr 2	Gr 3	Gr 4	Gr 5	Gr 6
Period, exclamation point, or question mark at end of sentences	░	•	•	•	•	•	•
Comma							
Greeting and closure of a letter						•	•
Dates, locations, and addresses						•	•
For items in a series					•	•	•
Direct quotations						•	•
Link two clauses with a conjunction in compound sentences					•	•	•
Quotation Marks							
Dialogue, exact words of a speaker					•	•	•
Titles of books, stories, poems, magazines					•	•	•

Key:

Shaded area - Explicit Instruction/Modeling/Practice and Application

• *Tested—Assessment Resources: Weekly Lesson Tests, Theme Tests, Benchmark Assessments*

	Gr K	Gr 1	Gr 2	Gr 3	Gr 4	Gr 5	Gr 6
Parentheses/dash/hyphen						•	•
Apostrophes in possessive case of nouns and in contractions		•	•	•	•	•	•
Underlining or italics to identify title of documents					•	•	•
Colon							
Separate hours and minutes						•	•
Introduce a list						•	•
After the salutation in business letters						•	•
Semicolons to connect dependent clauses							•

Capitalization

	Gr K	Gr 1	Gr 2	Gr 3	Gr 4	Gr 5	Gr 6
First word of a sentence, names of people, and the pronoun *I*		•	•	•	•	•	•
Proper nouns, words at the beginning of sentences and greetings, months and days of the week, and titles and initials of people		•	•	•	•	•	•
Geographical names, holidays, historical periods, and special events			•	•			•
Names of magazines, newspapers, works of art, musical compositions, organizations, and the first word in quotations when appropriate						•	•
Use conventions of punctuation and capitalization			•	•	•	•	•

Spelling

	Gr K	Gr 1	Gr 2	Gr 3	Gr 4	Gr 5	Gr 6
Spell independently by using pre-phonetic knowledge, sounds of the alphabet, and knowledge of letter names							
Use spelling approximations and some conventional spelling							
Common, phonetically regular words		•	•	•	•	•	•
Frequently used, irregular words		•	•	•	•	•	•
One-syllable words with consonant blends			•	•	•	•	•
Contractions, compounds, orthographic patterns, and common homophones				•	•	•	•
Greek and Latin roots, inflections, suffixes, prefixes, and syllable constructions				•	•	•	•
Use a variety of strategies and resources to spell words							

Listening and Speaking

Listening Skills and Strategies

	Gr K	Gr 1	Gr 2	Gr 3	Gr 4	Gr 5	Gr 6
Listen to a variety of oral presentations such as stories, poems, skits, songs, personal accounts, or informational speeches							
Listen attentively to the speaker (make eye contact and demonstrate appropriate body language)							
Listen for a purpose							
Follow oral directions (one-, two-, three-, and multi-step)							
For specific information							
For enjoyment							
To distinguish between the speaker's opinions and verifiable facts							
To actively participate in class discussions							
To expand and enhance personal interest and personal preferences							
To identify, analyze, and critique persuasive techniques							
To identify logical fallacies used in oral presentations and media messages							
To make inferences or draw conclusions							
To interpret a speaker's verbal and nonverbal messages, purposes, and perspectives							
To identify the tone, mood, and emotion							
To analyze the use of rhetorical devices for intent and effect							
To evaluate classroom presentations							
To respond to a variety of media and speakers							
To paraphrase/summarize directions and information							
For language reflecting regions and cultures							

Key:

Shaded area - Explicit Instruction/Modeling/Practice and Application

   • *Tested—Assessment Resources: Weekly Lesson Tests, Theme Tests, Benchmark Assessments*

	Gr K	Gr 1	Gr 2	Gr 3	Gr 4	Gr 5	Gr 6
To recognize emotional and logical arguments						▓	
To identify the musical elements of language			▓	▓		▓ •	▓
Listen critically to relate the speaker's verbal communication to the nonverbal message					▓		

Speaking Skills and Strategies

	Gr K	Gr 1	Gr 2	Gr 3	Gr 4	Gr 5	Gr 6
Speak clearly and audibly and use appropriate volume and pace in different settings	▓	▓	▓	▓	▓	▓	▓
Use formal and informal English appropriately	▓	▓	▓	▓	▓	▓	▓
Follow rules of conversation	▓	▓	▓	▓	▓	▓	▓
Stay on the topic when speaking		▓	▓	▓	▓	▓	▓
Use descriptive words		▓	▓	▓	▓	▓	▓
Recount experiences in a logical sequence		▓	▓	▓	▓	▓	▓
Clarify and support spoken ideas with evidence and examples			▓	▓	▓		▓
Use eye contact, appropriate gestures, and props to enhance oral presentations and engage the audience			▓	▓	▓	▓	▓
Give and follow two-, three-, and four-step directions		▓	▓	▓	▓	▓	▓
Recite poems, rhymes, songs, stories, soliloquies, or dramatic dialogues	▓	▓	▓	▓	▓	▓	▓
Plan and present dramatic interpretations with clear diction, pitch, tempo, and tone		▓	▓	▓	▓	▓	▓
Organize presentations to maintain a clear focus			▓	▓	▓	▓	▓
Use language appropriate to situation, purpose, and audience		▓	▓	▓	▓	▓	▓

Make/deliver

	Gr K	Gr 1	Gr 2	Gr 3	Gr 4	Gr 5	Gr 6
Oral narrative, descriptive, informational, and persuasive presentations			▓	▓	▓	▓	▓
Oral summaries of articles and books			▓	▓	▓	▓	▓
Oral responses to literature			▓	▓	▓	▓	▓
Presentations on problems and solutions			▓	▓	▓	▓	▓
Presentation or speech for specific occasions, audiences, and purposes			▓	▓		▓	▓
Vary language according to situation, audience, and purpose			▓	▓	▓	▓	▓
Select a focus, organizational structure, and point of view for an oral presentation			▓	▓		▓	▓
Participate in classroom activities and discussions	▓	▓	▓	▓	▓	▓	▓

Key:

Shaded area - Explicit Instruction/Modeling/Practice and Application

- *Tested— Assessment Resources: Weekly Lesson Tests, Theme Tests, Benchmark Assessments*

Index

Echo-Read, **5-1:** T64, T138, T202, T258; **5-2:** T62, T140, T202, T262; **5-3:** T62, T142, T208, T268; **5-4:** T72, T150, T212, T276; **5-5:** T62, T138, T198, T258; **5-6:** T64, T146, T212, T276

Expression, **5-2:** T29, T55, T62, T105, T133, T140, T289, T293, T294, T297, T301, T304, S7, S17; **5-5:** T29, T62, T105, T131, T138, T285, T289, T290, T293, T299, T300, S7, S15

Intonation, **5-3:** T29, T55, T62, T105, T135, T142, T295, T299, T300, T303, T309, T310, S7, S17; **5-4:** T29, T65, T72, T115, T143, T150, T303, T307, T308, T311, T315, T318, S7, S17

Literacy Center Activities, **5-1:** T27, T105, T163, T227, T283; **5-2:** T27, T103, T165, T227, T287; **5-3:** T27, T103, T167, T233, T293; **5-4:** T27, T113, T175, T237, T301; **5-5:** T27, T103, T163, T223, T283; **5-6:** T27, T109, T171, T237, T301

Pace, **5-3:** T169, T199, T208, T235, T261, T268, T295, T299, T300, T305, T307, T310, S27, S37; **5-5:** T165, T191, T198, T225, T253, T258, T285, T289, T290, T295, T297, T300, S25, S33

Partner Reading, **5-1:** T57, T64, T133, T138, T202, T258; **5-2:** T55, T62, T140, T195, T202, T262; **5-3:** T55, T62, T142, T199, T208, T268; **5-4:** T72, T143, T150, T205, T212, T276; **5-5:** T62, T131, T138, T191, T198, T258; **5-6:** T64, T146, T212, T269, T276

Phrasing, **5-2:** T167, T195, T202, T229, T257, T262, T289, T293, T294, T299, T303, T304, S25, S35; **5-6:** T173, T203, T212, T239, T269, T276, T303, T307, T308, T311, T315, T318, S23, S33

Readers' Theater, **5-1:** T290–T299; **5-2:** T294–T303; **5-3:** T300–T309; **5-4:** T308–T317; **5-5:** T290–T299; **5-6:** T308–T317

Reading Rate, **5-1:** T165, T195, T202, T229, T253, T258, T285, T289, T290, T295, T297, T299, T300, S25, S35; **5-4:** T177, T205, T212, T239, T242, T253, T257, T269, T276, T303, T307, T308, T313, T317, T318, S27, S37

Recorded Reading, **5-2:** T257; **5-4:** T65; **5-5:** T55; **5-6:** T141

Repeated Reading, **5-1:** T195; **5-2:** T133; **5-3:** T135, T261; **5-5:** T253; **5-6:** T57, T203

Timed Reading, **5-1:** T253; **5-4:** T269

Fluency Builders, 5-1: T64, T138, T202, T258, T300; **5-2:** T62, T140, T202, T262, T304; **5-3:** T62, T142, T208, T268, T310; **5-4:** T72, T150, T212, T276, T318; **5-5:** T62, T138, T198, T258, T300; **5-6:** T64, T146, T212, T276, T318

Focus
See **Writing,** traits

Focus Skills
Author's Purpose and Perspective, **5-5:** T30–T31, T40, T42, T48, T50, T56–T57, T106–T107, T118, T122, T124, T126, T132–T133, T294, T296, T298, T306, T308, S2–S3, S10–S11

Cause and Effect, **5-3:** T170–T171, T180, T182, T186, T188, T194, T200–T201, T256, T302, T306, T316, T319, S22–S23, S32–S33

Character's Motives, **5-1:** T166–T167, T176, T180, T182, T184, T186, T196–T197, T230–T231, T240, T244, T246, T248, T254–T255, T292, T304, S20–S21, S30–S31

Compare and Contrast, **5-3:** T29, T30–T31, T40, T42, T44, T48, T50, T56–T57, T169, T180, T186, T188, T306, T314, T318, S2–S3, S12–S13

Fact and Opinion, **5-6:** T173, T174–T175, T188, T192, T196, T198, T204–T205, T240–T241, T250, T252, T254, T258, T262, T270–T271, T310, T314, T316, T324, T327

Literary Devices, **5-5:** T166–T167, T178, T180, T182, T186, T192–T193, T226–T227, T236, T238, T240, T244, T246, T250, T254–T255, T292, T309, S20–S21, S28–S29

Main Idea and Details, **5-4:** T178–T179, T188, T194, T198, T206–T207, T240–T241, T250, T256, T258, T260, T262, T270–T271, T312, T316, T322, T327, S22–S23, S32–S33

Make Inferences, **5-4:** T30–T31, T42, T44, T46, T50, T52, T54, T66–T67, T116–T117, T128, T132, T134, T136, T138, T144–T145, T310, T314, T322, T326, S2–S3, S12–S13

Plot: Conflict and Resolution, **5-1:** T30–T31, T40, T44, T50, T52, T58–T59, T108–T109, T120, T122, T124, T126, T128, T131, T134–T135, T176, T184, T294, T298, T304, T306, S2–S3, S12–S13

Summarize and Paraphrase, **5-6:** T30–T31, T40, T44, T48, T50, T58–T59, T112–T113, T122, T124, T126, T128, T130, T134, T136, T139, T142–T143, T312, T314, T324, T326

S26, S28, S30, S32, S34, S35, S36;
5-2: T22, T98, T160, T222, T282,
S2, S4, S6, S7, S8, S10, S12, S14,
S16, S17, S18, S20, S22, S24, S25,
S26, S28, S30, S32, S34, S35, S36;
5-3: T22, T98, T162, T228, T288,
S2, S4, S6, S7, S8, S10, S12, S14,
S16, S17, S18, S20, S22, S24, S26,
S27, S28, S30, S32, S34, S36, S37,
S38; **5-4:** T22, T108, T170, T232,
T296, S2, S4, S6, S7, S8, S10, S12,
S14, S16, S17, S18, S20, S22, S24,
S26, S27, S28, S32, S34, S36, S37,
S38; **5-5:** T22, T98, T158, T218,
T278, S2, S4, S6, S7, S8, S10, S12,
S14, S15, S16, S18, S20, S22, S24,
S25, S26, S28, S30, S32, S33, S34;
5-6: T22, T104, T166, T232, T296,
S2, S4, S6, S7, S8, S10, S12, S14,
S15, S16, S18, S20, S22, S23, S24,
S26, S28, S30, S32, S33, S34

Strategic Intervention Teacher Guide,
5-1: T22–T23, T64, T100–T101,
T138, T158–T159, T202, T222–
T223, T258, T278–T279; **5-2:**
T22–T23, T62, T98–T99, T140,
T160–T161, T202, T222–T223,
T262, T282–T283; **5-3:** T22–T23,
T62, T98–T99, T142, T162–T163,
T208, T228–T229, T268, T288–
T289; **5-4:** T22–T23, T72, T108–
T109, T150, T170–T171, T212,
T232–T233, T276, T296–T297;
5-5: T22–T23, T62, T98–T99,
T138, T158–T159, T198, T218–
T219, T258, T278–T279; **5-6:**
T22–T23, T64, T104–T105, T146,
T166–T167, T212, T232–T233,
T276, T296–T297

See also **Small-Group Planner**

Intervention Reader
See **Intervention,** strategic
intervention interactive reader

Interview
See **Writing,** forms

Intonation
See **Fluency**

Irregular Verbs
See **Grammar**

Journal
See **Vocabulary**

Journal Entry
See **Writing,** forms

Judgments
See **Comprehension Skills,** make
judgments

K-W-L Charts
See **Graphic Organizers,** charts

Language Arts
See **Grammar; Reading-Writing
Connection; Spelling;
Vocabulary,** content-area
vocabulary; **Writing**

Language Arts Checkpoints
See **Assessment,** prescriptions,
grammar and writing

Language Development
See **Classroom Management,** small-
group planner; **English-Language
Learners**

Language Structures
See **Grammar**

Latin Word Parts
See **Decoding/Word Attack,** structural
analysis: Latin word parts;
Spelling

Learning Centers
See **Literacy Centers**

Learning Stations
See **Literacy Centers**

Lesson Overview, xii–xv; **5-1:** T16–
T25, T94–T103, T152–T161,
T216–T225, T272–T281; **5-2:**
T16–T25, T92–T101, T154–T163,
T216–T225, T276–T285; **5-3:**
T16–T25, T92–T101, T156–T165,
T222–T231, T282–T291; **5-4:**
T16–T25, T92–T101, T154–T163,
T216–T225, T276–T285; **5-5:** T16–
T25, T92–T101, T152–T161, T212–
T221, T272–T281; **5-6:** T16–T25,
T98–T107, T160–T169, T226–T235,
T290–T299

Lesson Planners

Small-Group Planners, **5-1:** T22–
T23, T100–T101, T158–T159,
T222–T223, T278–T279; **5-2:**
T22–T23, T98–T99, T160–T161,
T222–T223, T282–T283; **5-3:**
T22–T23, T98–T99, T162–T163,
T228–T229, T288–T289; **5-4:**
T22–T23, T108–T109, T170–
T171, T232–T233, T296–T297;
5-5: T22–T23, T98–T99, T158–
T159, T218–T219, T278–T279;
5-6: T22–T23, T104–T105, T166–
T167, T232–T233, T296–T297

Whole-Group Planners, **5-1:** T20–
T21, T98–T99, T156–T157,
T220–T221, T276–T277; **5-2:**
T20–T21, T96–T97, T158–T159,
T220–T221, T280–T281; **5-3:**
T20–T21, T96–T97, T160–T161,
T226–T227, T286–T287; **5-4:**
T20–T21, T106–T107, T168–
T169, T230–T231, T294–T295;

T175, T235, T291, T303; **5-6:** T39, T121, T183, T249, T309, T321

Read-Aloud Comprehension, **5-1:** T29, T107, T165, T229, T285; **5-2:** T29, T105, T167, T229, T289; **5-3:** T29, T105, T169, T235, T295, **5-4:** T29, T115, T177, T239, T303; **5-5:** T29, T105, T165, T225, T285; **5-6:** T29, T111, T173, T239, T303

Spelling, **5-1:** T66, T140, T204, T260, T314; **5-2:** T64, T142, T204, T264, T318; **5-3:** T64, T144, T210, T270, T324, **5-4:** T74, T152, T214, T278, T332; **5-5:** T64, T140, T200, T260, T314; **5-6:** T66, T148, T214, T278, T332

Vocabulary, **5-1:** T35, T113, T171, T235, T287; **5-2:** T35, T111, T173, T235, T291; **5-3:** T35, T111, T175, T241, T297; **5-4:** T35, T121, T183, T245, T305; **5-5:** T35, T111, T171, T231, T287; **5-6:** T35, T117, T179, T245, T305

Write a Summary, **5-1:** T53, T129, T187, T249; **5-2:** T51, T129, T191, T253; **5-3:** T51, T131, T195, T257; **5-4:** T59, T139, T199, T265; **5-5:** T51, T127, T187, T247; **5-6:** T51, T137, T199, T263

Routines
  See **Question of the Day; Read Aloud; Routine Cards**

Rubrics
  4-Point Rubric, **5-1:** R8; **5-2:** R8; **5-3:** R8; **5-4:** R8; **5-5:** R8; **5-6:** R8
  Presentation: Speaking and Listening, **5-1:** T72, T146, T210, T266, T300, R5; **5-2:** T70, T148, T210, T270, T304, R5; **5-3:** T70, T150, T216, T276, T310, R5; **5-4:** T80, T158, T220, T284, T318, R5; **5-5:** T70, T146, T206, T266, T300, R5; **5-6:** T72, T154, T220, T284, T318, R5

Retell and Summarize Fiction, **5-1:** T53, T187, R3; **5-2:** T51, T129, R3; **5-3:** T51, T195, R3; **5-4:** T59, T139, T199, R3; **5-5:** T127, T187, T247, R3; **5-6:** R3

Summarize Nonfiction, **5-1:** T129, T249, R4; **5-2:** T191, T253, R4; **5-3:** T131, T257, R4; **5-4:** T265, R4; **5-5:** T51, R4; **5-6:** T51, T137, T199, T263, R4

Using, **5-1:** R2; **5-2:** R2; **5-3:** R2; **5-4:** R2; **5-5:** R2; **5-6:** R2;

Writing: Extended Response, **5-1:** T186, R6; **5-2:** T128, R6; **5-3:** T50, R6; **5-4:** T58, R6; **5-5:** T246, R6; **5-6:** T262, R6

Writing: Scoring, **5-1:** R7; **5-2:** R7; **5-3:** R7; **5-4:** R7; **5-5:** R7; **5-6:** R7

Writing: Short Response, **5-1:** T52, T128, T248, R6–R7; **5-2:** T50, T128, T190, T252, R6; **5-3:** T130, T194, T256, R6; **5-4:** T138, T198, T264, R6; **5-5:** T50, T126, T168, R6; **5-6:** T50, T136, T198, R6

See also **Writing,** rubrics

School-Home Connection
  See **Teacher Resource Book**
Schwa
  See **Decoding/Word Attack,** unaccented syllables: schwa + *n*, schwa + *l*, schwa + *r*; **Spelling,** endings: /ən/, /əl/, /ər/
Science
  See **Content-Area Reading; Vocabulary,** content-area vocabulary
Science Textbook
  See **Genre**

Scope and Sequence, 5-1: R28–R35; **5-2:** R28–R35; **5-3:** R28–R35; **5-4:** R28–R35; **5-5:** R28–R35; **5-6:** R28–R35

Second-Language Support
  See **English-Language Learners**
Self-Correct
  See **Comprehension Strategies,** monitor comprehension: self-correct; **Focus Strategies,** monitor comprehension: self-correct
Self-Selected Reading
  See **Classroom Library Collection**
Sentence Fluency
  See **Writing, traits**
Sentence Structure
  See **Grammar,** clauses and phrases: complex sentences, declarative and interrogative sentences, imperative and exclamatory sentences: interjections, simple and compound sentences; **Writing,** forms; **Writing,** analyze writer's craft: sentences
Sentence Variety
  See **Writing,** sentence fluency
Sentences
  See **Grammar,** clauses and phrases: complex sentences, simple and compound sentences
Sequence
  See **Comprehension Skills,** sequence: story events, text structure: sequence; **Focus Skills,** text structure: sequence
Set a Purpose for Listening
  See **Purpose Setting,** purposes for listening
Set a Purpose for Reading
  See **Purpose Setting,** purposes for reading
Setting
  See **Comprehension Skills**

Acknowledgments

For permission to reprint copyrighted material, grateful acknowledgment is made to the following sources:

Beyond Words Publishing, Hillsboro, Oregon: From "Babe Didrikson" in *Girls Who Rocked the World* by Amelie Welden (Retitled: "Babe Didrikson: A Biography") by Amelie Welden. Text copyright © 1998 by Amelie Welden.

Bluffton News Publishing Company: From "Language and the Circus" by Evie Reece in *Hopscotch* Magazine, June/July 2002. Text copyright © 1991 by the Bluffton News Publishing and Printing Co.

Carus Publishing Company, 30 Grove Street, Suite C, Peterborough, NH 03458: From "The Golden Age of Invention and Innovation" by Roberta Baxter in *COBBLESTONE: The Gilded Age,* April 2000. Text copyright 2000 by Cobblestone Publishing Company. "From the Notebooks of Leonardo" by Nick D'Alto from *ODYSSEY: Looking at Leonardo's Science* November 2001. Text copyright © 2001 by Cobblestone Publishing Company. From "The Western Country" by Barbara Kubik in *COBBLESTONE: Lewis and Clark,* April 2004. Text copyright © 2004 by Carus Publishing Company. From "Mangia!" by Ira Rosofsky in *FACES: Italy,* October 2005. "Snowshoe Thompson: California's Historic Mail Carrier" by Ginger Wadsworth from *CALIFORNIA CHRONICLES: High Sierra,* January 2000. Text copyright 2000 by Cobblestone Publishing Company.

Laura Cecil Literary Agency, on behalf of the James Reeves Estate: "The Sea" from *Collected Poems for Children* by James Reeves. Text © by James Reeves. Published by Heinemann.

The Cricket Magazine Group, a division of Carus Publishing Company: "Dava's Talent" by Lee Ebler from *Spider* Magazine, April 1994. Text © 1994 by Lee Ebler. "Truman's Last Chance" by Andrew W. Hamilton from *Spider* Magazine, June 2005. Text © 2005 by Carus Publishing Company. "The Danderfield Twins: The Hostess Gift" by Polly Horvath from *Spider* Magazine, November 2004. Text © 2004 by Carus Publishing Company. "Sea of Grass" by Kathleen Weidner Zoehfeld from *Click* Magazine, September 2005. Text © 2005 by Kathleen Weidner Zoehfeld. "Pack Horse Librarians" from *Click* Magazine, February 2005. Text © 2005 by Carus Publishing Company.

Charles Downey: "Dog Gone" by Charles Downey from *Boys' Life* Magazine, February 1997. Published by the Boy Scouts of America.

Harcourt, Inc.: From "The Deaf Musicians" in *Pete Seeger's Storytelling Book* by Pete Seeger and Paul DuBois Jacobs. Text copyright © 2000 by Pete Seeger and Paul DuBois Jacobs.

Health Communications, Inc., www.hcibooks. com: "A Little Coaching" by Noah Edelson from *Chicken Soup for the Preteen Soul,* edited by Jack Canfield, Mark Victor Hansen, Patty Hansen, and Irene Dunlap. Text copyright © 1997 by Noah Edelson.

Highlights for Children, Inc., Columbus, Ohio: From "He Even Kissed a Pig" by Ann Volk in *Highlights for Children* Magazine, February 2005. Text copyright © 2005 by Highlights for Children, Inc. "Lost in the Everglades" by Tricia Workman from *Highlights for Children* Magazine, August 1998. Text copyright © 1998 by Highlights for Children, Inc.

Holiday House, Inc.: From *George Washington: An Illustrated Biography* by David A. Adler. Text copyright © 2004 by David A. Adler.

Houghton Mifflin Company: From "Land of Ancient Waters" in *Minn of the Mississippi* by Holling Clancy Holling. Text copyright 1951 by Holling Clancy Holling.

Lois Jacobson: "Keeping Cool with Crickets" by Lois Jacobson from *Cricket* Magazine, August 1992.

Lerner Publications Company: From "Dial-a-Fish" in *The Kids' Invention Book* by Arlene Erlbach. Text copyright © 1997 by Arlene Erlbach.

Moo-Cow Fan Club Magazine, P. O. Box 165, Peterborough, NH 03458: "Such Great Heights" by Becky Ances from *Moo-Cow Fan Club* Magazine, Issue No. 27, Summer 2005.

Penguin Books Ltd.: From author information in *Around the World in Eighty Days* (Titled: "Jules Verne"). Originally published 1874; reissued by Puffin Books 1994, 2004.

Pleasant Company Publications: "Lending a Paw" from *American Girl* Magazine, March/April 2000. Text copyright © 2000 by American Girl, LLC.

Random House Children's Books, a division of Random House, Inc.: From *Caught by the Sea: My Life on Boats* by Gary Paulsen. Text copyright © 2001 by Gary Paulsen.

Weekly Reader Corporation, Stamford, CT, www.weeklyreader.com: From "Letters to Young Writers" by Ralph Fletcher, Amy Krouse Rosenthal, and Caryn Mirriam-Goldberg in *Writing* Magazine, Sept. 2005. Text published and copyrighted by Weekly Reader Corporation. From "Weaving Real Life into Your Writing" by Dallas Nicole Woodburn in *Writing* Magazine, Nov/Dec 2005. Text published and copyrighted by Weekly Reader Corporation.

Photo Credits:

Placement key: (r) right, (l) left, (c) center, (b) bottom

S18 (inset) © Michael Newman/PhotoEdit; S21 (inset) © MICHAEL NEWMAN\PHOTOEDIT; S26 (inset) SuperStock, Inc.; S31 (inset) © Stefano Bianchetti/Corbis; T15 (inset) © Ed Kashi/ CORBIS; T64 (cr) © Steve Mason/ GettyImages; T72 (cr) © David Young-Wolff / PhotoEdit; T85 (br) © RICHARD HUTCHINGS/PHOTOEDIT INC; T104 (inset) © Ken Karp/Harcourt School; T110 (bl) © Cindy Charles / PhotoEdit; T111 (b) © Livia Corona / Taxi / GettyImages; T112 (b) © James Shaffer / PhotoEdit; T12 (tr) © Bettmann/ CORBIS; T124 (inset) © Dennis MacDonald / PhotoEdit; T125 (inset) © Michael Newman / PhotoEdit; T130 (inset) © Dirk Anschutz/Stone Collection/GettyImages; T138 (cr) © Tony Freeman / PhotoEdit; T146 (cr) © BILL ARON / PHOTOEDIT; T162 (inset) Ken Karp/Harcourt School; T163 (bc) © image100/Corbis; T168 (b) © Burstein Collection/CORBIS; T169 (b) C Squared Studios/GettyImages; T170 (b) © Cindy Charles/PhotoEdit; Inc.; T172 (inset) © Royalty-Free/Corbis; T179 (inset) © James Strachan/ GettyImages; T202 (cr) © Christina Kennedy / PhotoEdit; T203 (bl) S Mader/U Schmid / GettyImages; T210 (inset) © image100/Corbis; T226 (inset) Ken Karp/Harcourt School; T227 (cl) CORBIS; T227 (inset) Ken Karp/Harcourt School; T233 (b) © Ben Lê/Corbis; T234 (b) © Chris Duskin/Nonstock/Jupiter Images; T251 (inset) © Bettmann/CORBIS; T266 (inset) Ken Karp/ Harcourt School; T272 (b) © Rich-Heape Films, Inc. www.richheape.com; T282 (inset) Ken Karp/Harcourt School; T283 (b) Andres Stapff/ Reuters/Corbis; T283 (inset) Ken Karp/Harcourt School; T302 (br) image100/Corbis; T325 (r) Ken Karp/Harcourt School.

All other photos property of Harcourt School Publishers

Acknowledgments

For permission to reprint copyrighted material, grateful acknowledgment is made to the following sources:

Atheneum Books for Young Readers, an imprint of Simon & Schuster Children's Publishing Division: From *Ultimate Field Trip 3: Wading into Marine Biology* by Susan E. Goodman, photographs by Michael J. Doolittle. Text copyright © 1999 by Susan E. Goodman; photographs copyright © 1999 by Michael J. Doolittle.

Curtis Brown, Ltd.: "Summer Hummers" by Linda Sue Park. Text copyright © 2001 by Linda Sue Park. Originally published in *Cricket* Magazine, November 2001 by Carus Publishing Company.

Candlewick Press, Inc., Cambridge, MA: From *Interrupted Journey* by Kathryn Lasky, photographs by Christopher G. Knight. Text copyright © 2001 by Kathryn Lasky; photographs copyright © 2001 by Christopher G. Knight.

Carus Publishing Company, 30 Grove St., Suite C, Peterborough, NH 03458: "Got a Problem? Get a Plan!" by Karen Bledsoe from *APPLESEEDS: Kids Can Change the World,* September 2005. Text © 2005 by Carus Publishing Company. "Central Park" by John J. Bonk from *COBBLESTONE: New York City,* June 1995. Text © 1995 by Cobblestone Publishing. "Voyage into the Past" by Ann Collins from *APPLESEEDS: American Places, San Diego,* May 2000. Text © 2000 by Cobblestone Publishing. "Journey on the Silk Road" by Luann Hankom from *APPLESEEDS: Children of China Long Ago,* October 2002. Text © 2002 by Carus Publishing Company. "Sourdough" by Jane Scherer from *COBBLESTONE: The California Gold Rush,* December 1997. Text © 1997 by Cobblestone Publishing.

Children's Press, an imprint of Scholastic Library Publishing, Inc.: From *Lewis and Clark* by R. Conrad Stein. Text © 1997 by Children's Press®, a division of Grolier Publishing Co., Inc.

Chronicle Books LLC, San Francisco, ChronicleBooks.com: From *The Man Who Went to the Far Side of the Moon: The Story of Apollo 11 Astronaut Michael Collins* by Bea Uusma Schyffert. Text and illustrations copyright © 1999 by Bea Uusma Schyffert; translation © 2003 by Chronicle Books LLC.

Clarion Books, a Houghton Mifflin Company imprint: From *Project Mulberry* by Linda Sue Park, cover illustration by Debora Smith. Text copyright © 2005 by Linda Sue Park; cover illustration copyright © 2005 by Debora Smith.

The Cricket Magazine Group, a division of Carus Publishing Company: "Ninth Inning" by Anna Levine from *Cricket* Magazine, June 2004. Text © 2004 by Anna Levine. "Take a Bow!" by Anna Levine from *Cricket* Magazine, January 2005. Text © 2004 by Anna Levine.

Darby Creek Publishing, a division of Oxford Resources, Inc.: "Line Drive" by Tanya West Dean from *Sport Shorts: An Anthology of Short Stories.* Text © 2005 by Tanya West.

Dial Books for Young Readers, a Division of Penguin Young Readers Group, A Member of Penguin Group (USA) Inc., 345 Hudson Street, New York, NY 10014: "On Top of the World" from *A World of Wonders: Geographic Travels in Verse and Rhyme* by J. Patrick Lewis, illustrated by Alison Jay. Text copyright © 2002 by J. Patrick Lewis; illustration copyright © 2002 by Alison Jay.

Farrar, Straus and Giroux, LLC: From *Chang and the Bamboo Flute* by Elizabeth Starr Hill, cover illustration by Lesley Liu. Text copyright © 2002 by Elizabeth Starr Hill; cover illustration copyright © 2002 by Lesley Liu. From *Chester Cricket's Pigeon Ride* by George Selden, illustrated by Garth Williams. Text copyright © 1981 by George Selden Thompson; illustrations copyright © 1981 by Garth Williams.

HarperCollins Publishers: From *When the Circus Came to Town* by Laurence Yep, cover illustration by Suling Wang. Text copyright © 2002 by Laurence Yep; cover illustration copyright © 2002 by Suling Wang.

Highlights for Children, Inc., Columbus, OH: "When Our Family Bands Together" by Teresa Bateman from *Highlights for Children* Magazine, August 2003. Text copyright © 2003 by Highlights for Children, Inc. "The Alligator Race" by Karen Dowicz Haas from *Highlights for Children* Magazine, August 2004. Text copyright © 2004 by Highlights for Children, Inc. From "The Artist's Eye" by Joan T. Zeier in *Highlights for Children* Magazine, March 2004. Text copyright © 2004 by Highlights for Children, Inc.

Houghton Mifflin Company: "Steam" from *Splish Splash* by Joan Bransfield Graham. Text copyright © 1994 by Joan Bransfield Graham. From *The Top of the World: Climbing Mount Everest* by Steve Jenkins. Copyright © 1999 by Steve Jenkins.

Alfred A. Knopf, an imprint of Random House Children's Books, a division of Random House, Inc.: From *The Daring Nellie Bly: America's Star Reporter* by Bonnie Christensen. Copyright © 2003 by Bonnie Christensen. "Stormalong" from *American Tall Tales* by Mary Pope Osborne. Text copyright © 1991 by Mary Pope Osborne. From "How Beaver Stole Fire" in *In a Circle Long Ago* by Nancy Van Laan, illustrated by Lisa Desimini. Text copyright © 1995 by Nancy Van Laan; illustrations copyright © 1995 by Lisa Desimini.

Lerner Publications Company: From *Nellie Bly's Book: Around the World in 72 Days* (Retitled: "A Proposal to Girdle the Earth"), edited by Ira Peck. Text copyright © 1998 by Ira Peck.

Little, Brown and Co., Inc.: From *Into a New Country: Eight Remarkable Women of the West* (Retitled: "Klondike Kate") by Liza Ketchum. Text copyright © 2000 by Liza Ketchum.

Mary Anne Lloyd: Illustrations by Mary Anne Lloyd from "Kids in Action" by Elizabeth Schleichert in *Ranger Rick®* Magazine, September 2005.

Gina Maccoby Literary Agency: "Ice Cycle" by Mary Ann Hoberman from *Once Upon Ice,* selected by Jane Yolen. Text copyright © 1997 by Mary Ann Hoberman. Published by Boyds Mills Press, Inc.

National Geographic Society: From "The Zoo Crew" by Laura Daily in *National Geographic WORLD* Magazine, February 2000. Text copyright © 2000 by National Geographic Society. From *Inventing the Future* by Marfé Ferguson Delano. Text copyright © 2002 by National Geographic Society.

National Wildlife Federation®: From "Kids In Action" by Elizabeth Schleichert in *Ranger Rick®* Magazine, September 2005. Text copyright 2005 by the National Wildlife Federation®.

North-South Books Inc., New York: Sailing Home: A Story of a Childhood at Sea by Gloria Rand, illustrated by Ted Rand. Text copyright © 2001 by Gloria Rand; illustrations copyright © 2001 by Ted Rand.

G. P. Putnam's Sons, A Division of Penguin Young Readers Group, A Member of Penguin Group USA (Inc.), 345 Hudson Street, New York, NY 10014: From *Leonardo's Horse* by Jean Fritz, illustrated by Hudson Talbott. Text copyright © 2001 by Jean Fritz; illustrations copyright © 2001 by Hudson Talbott.

Marian Reiner, on behalf of August House Publishers, Inc.: "Paul Bunyan Makes Progress" from *Sweet Land of Story: Thirty-Six American Tales to Tell* by Pleasant deSpain. Text © 2000 by Pleasant deSpain. Published by August House Publishers, Inc.

Scholastic Inc.: "The Night of San Juan" and cover illustration from *Salsa Stories* by Lulu Delacre. Text and cover illustration copyright © 2000 by Lulu Delacre. From *Any Small Goodness: A Novel of the Barrio* by Tony Johnston, cover illustration by Raúl Colón. Text copyright © 2001 by Roger D. Johnston and Susan T. Johnston as Trustees of the Johnston Family Trust; cover illustration copyright © 2001 by Raúl Colón. Published by The Blue Sky Press. "Rain, Dance!" from *Splash! Poems of Our Watery World* by Constance Levy. Text copyright © 2002 by Constance Kling Levy. Published by Orchard Books. From *In 1776* by Jean Marzollo. Text copyright © 1994 by Jean Marzollo. "The Ant and the Dove," "The Lion and the Mouse," and cover illustration from *Aesop's Fables,* retold by Ann McGovern. Text and cover illustration copyright © 1963 by Scholastic Inc. Published by Apple Classics. *Nothing Ever Happens on 90th Street* by Roni Schotter, illustrated by Kyrsten Brooker. Text copyright © 1997 by Roni Schotter; illustrations copyright © 1997 by Kyrsten Brooker. Published by Orchard Books. From *A Drop of Water* by Walter Wick. Text and photographs copyright © 1997 by Walter Wick. Published by Scholastic Press.

Brian Selznick: Cover illustration by Brian Selznick from *The School Story* by Andrew Clements. Illustration copyright © 2001 by Brian Selznick.

Simon & Schuster Books for Young Readers, an Imprint of Simon & Schuster Children's Publishing Division: When Washington Crossed the Delaware by Lynne Cheney, illustrated by Peter M. Fiore. Text copyright © 2004 by Lynne Cheney; illustrations copyright © 2004 by Peter M. Fiore. From *The School Story* by Andrew Clements. Text copyright © 2001 by Andrew Clements.

TIME For Kids: "Tree Houses for Everyone" by Tiffany Sommers from *TIME For Kids* Magazine, September 24, 2004. From "Evren Ozan, Musician" by Harsha Viswanathan in *TIME For Kids* Magazine, October 27, 2003.

Albert Whitman & Company: From *Rope Burn* by Jan Siebold, cover illustration by Layne Johnson. Text copyright © 1998 by Jan Siebold; cover illustration © 1998 by Layne Johnson.

Photo Credits

Placement Key(t) top; (b) bottom; (l) left; (r) right; (c) center; (bg) background; (fg) foreground; (i) inset.

17 (b) Peter Bennett/Ambient Images; 17 (tr) Scala/Art Resource; 18 Images.com/Corbis; 22 (b) Joe Atlas/PictureQuest; 23 (tr) VStock LLC/Index Stock; 24 (b) Zoran Milich/Getty; 44 (l) Peter McBride Photography; 45 (tr) Peter McBride Photography; 53 (b) Brandon D. Cole/Corbis; 56 (b) Brandon D. Cole/Corbis; 57 (tr) Larry West/Bruce Coleman, Inc.; 77 (tr) Jon Shireman/Getty; 79 (bl) Lester Lefkowitz/Corbis; 80 (br) James Marshall/Corbis; 81 (tr) Siede Preis/Getty; 83 (tr) Tim Hawkins/Corbis; 85 (b) Wright State University; 86 (bl) Wright State University; 86 (br) Wright State University; 87 (bl) Henry Ford Museum & Greenfield Village; 87 (br) Wright State University; 88 (br) National Air and Space Museum; 89 (tr) Bettman/Corbis/Magma; 91 (b) LIbrary of Congress; 92 (b) LIbrary of Congress; 93 (t) Library of Congress; 93 (br) Smithsonian Institution; 94 (bl) Library of Congress; 95 (c) Library of Congress; 95 (bl) Library of Congress; 97 (b) Wright State University; 98 (br) Library of Congress; 98 (bl) Wright State University; 99 (b) Wright State University; 102 Corbis; 109 (b) Jerry Cooke/Corbis; 112 (bl) Bettmann/Corbis; 113 (tr) Tony Duffy/Allsport/Getty; 128 (t) Stephen Dalton/Photo Researchers Inc.; 129 (c) OSF/Howard Hall/Animals Animals; 131 (tr) Jim Vecchi/Corbis; 150 Anna Pugh/Lucy Campbell Gallery; 157 (tr) Stockdisc/Superstock; 179 (b) David Stoecklein/Corbis; 180 (b) Michael Wells/Getty; 181 (tr) Bigshots/Getty; 182 (b) Michael Cogliantry/Getty; 201 (br) Comstock/Superstock; 201 (bcr) Thinkstock/Superstock; 205 (bl) Robert Dowling/Corbis; 206 (bl) Ludovic Maisant/Corbis; 207 (tr) Tom Nebbia/Corbis; 208 (bl) Bettmann/Corbis; 208 (br) Hulton-Deutsch Collection/Corbis; 209 (tr) Bettmann/Corbis; 224 (bl) Standard Insurance Company; 225 (l) Paul A. Souders/Corbis; 225 Standard Insurance Company; 228 (b) Kevin R. Morris/Corbis; 230 (b) Gordon Whitten/Corbis; 231 (tr) Ed Kashl/Corbis; 234 Ben Klaffke/Millbrook Press/Lerner Publishing Group; 236 (t) Ben Klaffke/Millbrook Press/Lerner Publishing Group; 237 (r) Ben Klaffke/Millbrook Press/Lerner Publishing Group; 238 (tl) Ben Klaffke/Millbrook Press/Lerner Publishing Group; 238 (b) Ben Klaffke/Millbrook Press/Lerner Publishing Group; 239 (tr) Ben Klaffke/Millbrook Press/Lerner Publishing Group; 239 (br) Ben Klaffke/Millbrook Press/Lerner Publishing Group; 240 Ben Klaffke/Millbrook Press/Lerner Publishing Group; 241 (r) Ben Klaffke/Millbrook Press/Lerner Publishing Group; 242 (l) Ben Klaffke/Millbrook Press/Lerner Publishing Group; 243 (tl) Ben Klaffke/Millbrook Press/Lerner Publishing Group; 243 Ben Klaffke/Millbrook Press/Lerner Publishing Group; 244 (t) Ben Klaffke/Millbrook Press/Lerner Publishing Group; 245 (b) Ben Klaffke/Millbrook Press/Lerner Publishing Group; 248 (l) Setboun/Corbis; 249 Ed Kashi/Corbis; 250 (l) Justin Sullivan/Getty; 251 (r) Barry Smith/Scholastic; 253 (tr) Dan Lamont/Corbis; 267 James L. Amos/Corbis; 268 James L. Amos/Corbis; 271 (l) Tom Bean/Corbis; 272 Christie's Images/Corbis; 275 (b) Paul A. Souders/Corbis; 276 (b) Royalty-free/Getty; 277 (tr) MedioImages Inc./Index Stock; 278 (b) Norbert Wu/Minden Pictures; 279 (tr) Bill Curtsinger/National Geographic Image Collection; 281 (t) Bill Curtsinger/Tilbury House; 282 (tl) Bill Curtsinger/Tilbury House Publishers; 282 (bl) Bill Curtsinger/Tilbury House Publishers; 282 (c) Bill Curtsinger/Tilbury House Publishers; 283 (tr) Bill Curtsinger/Tilbury House Publishers; 284 (tl) Bill Curtsinger/Tilbury House Publishers; 284 (cr) Bill Curtsinger/Tilbury House Publishers; 286 (tl) Bill Curtsinger/Tilbury House Publishers; 286 (bl) Bill Curtsinger/Tilbury House Publishers; 286 (br) Bill Curtsinger/Tilbury House Publishers; 287 (br) Bill Curtsinger/Tilbury House Publishers; 289 Bill Curtsinger/Tilbury House Publishers; 290 (t) Bill Curtsinger/Tilbury House Publishers; 290 (b) Bill Curtsinger/Tilbury House Publishers; 291 (c) Bill Curtsinger/Tilbury House Publishers; 292 (tr) Bill Curtsinger/Tilbury House Publishers; 292 (br) Bill Curtsinger/Tilbury House Publishers; 292 (tl) Bill Curtsinger/Tilbury House Publishers; 293 (b) Bill Curtsinger/Tilbury House Publishers; 294 (b) Bill Curtsinger/Tilbury House Publishers; 296 (br) Lester V. Bergman/Corbis; 296 (t) Tom Brakefield/Getty; 297 (tr) Lester V. Bergman/Corbis; 299 (tr) Steve Terrill/Corbis; 300 (b) Ludovic Maisant/Corbis; 301 (br) National Geographic/Zuma/Corbis; 301 (b) Wolfgang Kaehler/Corbis; 303 (b) Peter Adams/Zefa/Corbis; 305 (tr) Theo Allofs/Corbis; 306 (b) Darrell Gulin/Corbis; 307 (tr) Veer; 308 (cr) Galen Rowell/Corbis; 308 (bl) Galen Rowell/Corbis; 309 (r) Galen Rowell/Corbis; 324 Tilbury House Publishers; 325 (t) Jason Stemple/Boyds Mills Press; 325 (b) Jason Stemple/Boyds Mills Press; 327 (tr) Kennan Ward/Corbis; 329 (b) P. Wilson/Zefa/Corbis; 332 (b) Hulton Archives/Getty; 333 (tr) Bettmann/Corbis; 364 (b) Royalty-free/Corbis; 365 (tr) Lew Robertson; 367 (r) Royalty free/Corbis; 404 Bettmann/Corbis; 406 (bl) Royalty-free/Corbis; 406 (cr) Royalty-free/Corbis; 406 (t) Royalty-free/Corbis; 407 (bl) Royalty-free/Corbis; 407 (cl) Royalty-free/Corbis; 407 (cr) Royalty-free/Corbis; 408 (b) Royalty-free/Corbis; 409 (r) age fotostock/Superstock; 410 (b) HIP/Art Resource; 411 (r) Fine Art Photographic Library, London/Art Resource; 428 Calder Foundation/ARS; 429 (br) Art Resource; 429 (cl) Calder Foundation/ARS; 430 Art Resource; 430 Art Resource; 430 Art Resource; 430 Art Resource; 430 (bl) Calder Foundation/ARS; 431 (b) Calder Foundation/ARS; 431 (t) Calder Foundation/ARS; 433 (tr) Royalty-free/Corbis; 434 (br) Ingo Boddenberg/Zefa/Corbis; 440 (b) Royalty-free/Corbis; 441 (cr) Comstock/Superstock; 441 (tr) Royalty-free/Corbis; 442 (b) Image Source Photography/Veer; 461 (b) Royalty-free/Corbis; 463 Images.com/Corbis; 464 (b) Denis Scott/Corbis; 465 (r) Royalty-free/Corbis; 467 (tr) James Noble/Corbis; 483 (br) Jose Fuste Raga/Corbis; 484 (c) Kelly-Mooney Photography/Corbis; 487 (r) Macduff Everton/Corbis; 488 (b) Jeff Chiu/San Francisco Chronicle; 489 (r) John Kalucki; 490 Joan Marie Arbogast/Boyds Mills Press; 491 (tl) Joan Marie Arbogast/Boyds Mills Press; 491 (c) Stan Shoneman/Omni Photo Communications, Inc.; 492 (bl) The Save Lucy Committee, Inc.; 492 (r) The Save Lucy Committee, Inc.; 493 (br) The Save Lucy Committee, Inc.; 493 (cr) The Save Lucy Committee, Inc.; 494 (bl) The Save Lucy Committee, Inc.; 494 (br) The Save Lucy Committee, Inc.; 495 (br) Joan Marie Arbogast/Boyds Mills Press; 495 (tr) The Save Lucy Committee, Inc.; 495 (tc) The Save Lucy Committee, Inc.; 496 (l) Stan Shoneman/Omni Photo Communications, Inc.; 497 Boyds Mills Press; 498 (b) South Dakota Department of Tourism, Corn Palace Convention and Visitors Bureau; 499 (t) South Dakota Department of Tourism, Corn Palace Convention and Visitors Bureau; 500 (b) "DUTCH WONDERLAND® Family Amusement Park, Lancaster, PA; (C) 2006 Wonderland Amusement Management LLC. DUTCH WONDERLAND is a registered trademark used under license."; 500 (tl) Enchanted Forest, Turner, Oregon; 501 (tr) Joan Marie Arbogast/Boyds Mills Press; 501 (b) Joan Marie Arbogast/Boyds Mills Press; 502 (tl) Boyds Mills Press; 502 (b) Peter Bennett/Ambient Images; 503 (t) Lincoln Highway Heritage Corridor, Pennsylvania; 505 (c) Dog Bark Park Inn B&B; 509 (t) Royalty-free/Corbis; 528 Stapleton Collection/Corbis; 531 (tr) Erich Lessing/Art Resource; 531 (bl) Erich Lessing/Art Resource, NY; 532 (bl) Karl Weatherly/Corbis; 533 (tr) S. Carmona/Corbis; 533 (cr) Yiorgos Karahalis/Reuters/Corbis; 534 (b) Charles O'Rear/Corbis; 535 (r) Ludovic Maisant/Corbis; 537 (l) Corbis/Christie's images; 537 (t) Stock Montage; 538 Art Resource/Erich Lessing; 540 Wolfgang Kaehler; 541 (c) Art Resource/Scala; 541 (t) Corel; 541 (r) Wolfgang Kaehler; 542 Art Resource/Erich Lessing; 543 (t) Corbis/Bettman; 544 (br) Art Resource/Scala; 544 (bl) Getty Images/Hulton Archives; 545 (t) Unicorn Stock Photos/Patti McConville; 546 (c) DigitalGlobe Inc.; 547 (c) Gary Hershorn; 548 (l) Ruggero Vanni; 553 (tr) Erich Lessing/Art Resource; 554 (b) Charles O'Rear/Corbis; 556 (b) Le Segretain P./Corbis Sygma; 557 (b) Lester Lefkowitz/Corbis; 560 Keren Su/Getty; 562 (b) Helen Norman/Botanica/PictureQuest; 563 (tr) M. Timothy O'Keefe/Bruce Coleman, Inc.; 564 (b) Mimmo Jodice/Corbis; 565 (tr) Mimmo Jodice/Corbis; 567 Zhang Zongkun/Imaginechina; 568 (t) O. Louis Mazzatenta/National Geographic Society Image Collection; 569 (tr) Private Collection/Bonhams, London, UK/Bridgeman Art Library; 569 (br) Zhou Kang/Imaginechina.com; 570 (bl) Giraudon/Art Resource; 571 (tr) O. Louis Mazzatenta/National Geographic Society Image Collection; 572 (tr) Private Collection/Bonhams, London, UK/Bridgeman Art Library; 573 (br) O. Louis Mazzatenta/National Geographic Society image Collection; 574 (bl) O. Louis Mazzatenta/National Geographic Society Image Collection; 575 (cr) Imaginechina.com; 575 (b) Zhou Kang/Imaginechina.com; 576 (tl) Patrick Aventurier/Gamma; 576 (tr) Patrick Aventurier/Gamma; 576 (br) Patrick Aventurier/Gamma; 576 (bl) Tomb of Qin shi Huang Di, Xianyang, China/Bridgeman Art Library; 577 (br) O. Louis Mazzatenta/National Geographic Society Image Collection; 577 (t) Tomb of Qin shi Huang Di, Xianyang, China/Bridgeman Art Library; 578 (t) O. Louis Mazzatenta/National Geographic Society Image Collection; 579 (r) Doug Stern/National Geographic Society Image Collection; 579 (r) Doug Stern/National Geographic Society Image Collection; 579 (l) O. Louis Mazzatenta/National Geographic Society Image Collection; 580 (t) Giraudon/Art Resource; 581 (bl) Dagli Orti/The Art Archive; 582 Royalty-free/Corbis; 583 (bc) National Geographic Society/Image Collection; 583 (bl) Pablo Corral Vega/Corbis; 585 (tr) Wilfried Krecichwost/Image Bank/Getty; 587 (b) ImageState-Pictor/PictureQuest; 609 (tr) Joe Atlas/PictureQuest; 611 (b) Jacob Halaska/Index Stock; 612 (br) Scala/Art Resource; 613 (r) Sandro Vannini/Corbis; 614 (br) Giraudon/Art Resource; 615 (tr) Michele Burgess/Visuals Unlimited; 637 (tr) Paul Hardy/Corbis; 656 The Andy Warhol foundation, Inc./Art Resource; 659 (bl) NASA/JPL-Caltech; 662 (br) NASA/JPL-Caltech/UMD; 663 (tr) NASA/JPL-Caltech/UMD; 680 (tr) NASA; 681 (b) NASA; 681 (cl) NASA; 684 (b) Denis Scott/Corbis; 690 (b) The Mariners' Museum/Corbis; 691 (cr) Montague B. Black/Corbis; 691 (cl) Ralph White/Corbis; 692 (b) Stephen Frink/Getty; 696 John Batchelor/www.publishingsolutions.co.uk; 699 John Batchelor/www.publishingsolutions.co.uk; 701 (t) John Batchelor/www.printsolutions.co.uk; 702 (tl) Artville, LLC/Getty Images; 703 (b) Woods Hole Oceanographic Institution/Rod Catanach; 705 National Geographic Society Image Collection/Emory Kristof; 707 (b) Ralph White/Corbis; 709 (b) Larry Anderson; 713 (l) Brian Payne Photography; 713 (r) Brian Payne Photography; 714 (br) Brian Payne Photography; 715 (bl) Brian Payne Photography; 715 (br) Brian Payne Photography; 717 (tr) Ralph White/Corbis; 720 (bl) Royalty-free/Corbis; 772 Erich Lessing/Art Resource, NY.

All other photos © Harcourt School Publishers. Harcourt photos provided by Harcourt Index, Harcourt IPR, and Harcourt Photographers: Weronica Ankarorn, Eric Camden, Doug DuKane, Ken Kinsie, April Riehm and Steve Williams

Illustration Credits

Cover Art: James Shepherd, Background art by: Laura and Eric Ovresat, Artlab, Inc.

Teacher's Notes

Teacher's Notes

Teacher's Notes